THE ROUGH GUIDE TO
ROMANIA

ROUGH GUIDES

Contents

Introduction to
Romania

Travel in Romania is as rewarding as it is challenging. The country's mountain scenery, its great diversity of wildlife and cultures, and a way of life that at times seems little changed since the Middle Ages, leave few who visit unaffected. Try to accept whatever happens as an adventure – encounters with Gypsies, wild bears and tricky officials are likely to be far more interesting than anything touted by the tourist board.

Romanians trace their **ancestry** back to the Romans, and have a noticeable Latin character – warm, spontaneous and appreciative of style. In Transylvania, in addition to ethnic Romanians, one and a half million Magyars and around the same number of Rroma (Gypsies) follow their own path, while dwindling numbers of Transylvanian Germans (Saxons) reside around the fortified towns and churches built by their ancestors. Along the coast, in the Delta and in the Banat, there's a rich mixture of Russians, Ukrainians, Serbs, Slovaks, Bulgars, Gypsies, Turks and Tatars.

Two decades of dictatorial rule by Nicolae Ceauşescu brought Romania to the brink of ruin, with economic collapse and repression by the feared Securitate bringing about a stark deterioration in living standards. Although it's almost thirty years since Ceauşescu's overthrow in what was Europe's bloodiest revolution of 1989, the country is, in many ways, only just emerging from his shadow – though Romania's admission into NATO in 2004 and then, somewhat more controversially, the **European Union** in 2007, has at least cemented its place in the wider international community.

As fascinating as the urban centres are – such as the capital, Bucharest, Braşov, Sighişoara, Timişoara and, most enchantingly, Sibiu – Romania's true charm lies in the remoter regions. Any exploration of rural **villages** will be rewarding, with sights as diverse as the log houses in Oltenia, Delta villages built of reeds, and the magnificent wooden churches, with their sky-scraping Gothic steeples, of Maramureş, not to mention the country's more traditional churches, which reflect a history of competing communities and faiths. Romania also offers some of the most unspoiled wilderness on the continent, from the majestic peaks of the Carpathian mountains and the verdant, rolling hills of Bucovina to the extraordinary wetlands of the Danube Delta.

FACT FILE

- Occupying an **area** of 237,000 square kilometres, and with a **population** of around twenty million, Romania is one of East-Central Europe's largest nations. Its capital, Bucharest, lies in the far south of the country on the plains of Wallachia, located between the Danube and the mountainous region of Transylvania to the north. The highest peak is Moldoveanu (2544m), in the Carpathian mountains.
- The constitution set in place a **parliamentary system of government**, elected every four years, with the prime minister at its head – the president is head of state.
- **Tourism** is one of the fastest-growing sectors of the Romanian economy, with mountain, coastal and health spa resorts absorbing the bulk of the country's tourist traffic. Romania's most important **exports** are textiles and footwear, metal products, and machinery and equipment, and its main trading partners are Italy and Germany.
- Romania's most famous **historical figure** is Vlad Ţepeş (c.1431–76), also known as Vlad the Impaler and, more familiarly, as Dracula.

SCHEIA, EASTERN ROMANIA

Where to go

The first point of arrival for many visitors is the capital, **Bucharest**. While not an easy city to love – its wide nineteenth-century Parisian-style boulevards are choked with traffic, once-grand *fin de siècle* buildings crumbling and the suburbs dominated by grim apartment blocks – its cultural institutions, abundant greenery and lively Old Town nightlife reward patience. In recent years, the gastronomic scene has improved beyond recognition, while a wave of artisan coffee joints has revitalized the city's café culture.

From the capital, most visitors make a beeline for the province of **Transylvania** to the north, setting for the country's most thrilling scenery and home to its finest cities: the gateway is **Braşov**, whose medieval Old Town is a good introduction to the Saxon architecture of the region, which reaches its peak in the fortified town of **Sibiu** and the jagged skyline of **Sighişoara**, Romania's most atmospherically sited town and the birthplace of Vlad the Impaler (Dracula).

North and west of here, the great Magyar cities of **Târgu Mureş, Cluj** and **Oradea** have retained a wealth of medieval architecture, as well as impressive Baroque and Secession buildings. In the southwest, near the Serbian border, is hugely enjoyable **Timişoara**, source of the 1989 revolution.

SPAS

Romania boasts one third of all Europe's mineral springs, and around 160 **spa resorts** (*băile*), many of which were made fashionable by the Habsburgs during the nineteenth century.

Spa holidays are tremendously popular, the theory being that you stay in a resort for about eighteen days, following a prescribed course of treatment, and ideally return regularly over the next few years. However, if you can get cheap accommodation, a spa can also make a good base for a one-off holiday. In any case, it's worth bearing in mind that even the smallest spas have campsites and restaurants.

The basic treatment naturally involves drinking the **waters**, which come in an amazing variety: alkaline, chlorinated, carbogaseous, and sodium-, iodine-, magnesium-, sulphate- or iron-bearing. In addition, you can bathe in hot springs or sapropelic muds, breathe in foul fumes at mofettes, or indulge in a new generation of complementary **therapies** such as ultrasound and aerosol treatment, ultraviolet light baths, acupuncture and electrotherapy.

The spas all have their own areas of **specialization**: Sovata is the best place for gynaecological problems; Covasna, Vatra Dornei and Buziaş deal with cardiovascular complaints; Călimăneşti-Căciulata, Slănic Moldova, Sângeorz-Băi and Băile Olăneşti with digestion; and others (notably Băile Herculane and Băile Felix) with a range of locomotive and rheumatic ailments. **Mountain resorts** such as Sinaia, Băile Tuşnad and Moneasa treat nervous complaints with fresh air, which has an ideal balance of ozone and ions.

The best of Romania, though, is its countryside, and in particular the wonderful mountains. The wild **Carpathians**, forming the frontier between Transylvania and, to the east and south, Moldavia and Wallachia, shelter bears, stags, chamois and eagles. The Bucegi, Făgăraş and Retezat ranges and the Padiş plateau, meanwhile, offer some of the most spectacular hiking opportunities in Europe. The **Black Sea coast** is full of brash resorts, notably Mamaia, but it does have its charms, not least the old port of Constanţa.

Just north of here, the **Danube Delta** is set apart from the rest of the country; here life has hardly changed for centuries and boats are the only way to reach many settlements. During spring and autumn, hundreds of species of birds migrate through this area or come to breed. While not quite as remote, the villages of **Maramureş**, bordering Ukraine in the north, retain a medieval feel with their fabulous wooden churches. Close by, sprinkled amid the soft, rolling hills of **Bucovina**, are the wonderful painted monasteries, whose religious frescoes are among the most outstanding in Europe.

When to go

The **climate** is pretty crucial in planning a trip to Romania. **Winters** can be brutal – snow blankets much of the country, temperatures of -15°C to -20°C are not uncommon, and a strong, icy wind (the *crivaţ*) sweeps down from Russia. Conditions improve with **spring**, bringing rain and wild flowers to the mountains and the softest of blue skies over Bucharest, and prompting a great migration of birds through the Delta. By May, the lowlands are warming up and you might well find strong sunshine on the coast before the season starts in July. Although by far the hottest time of the year, **summer or early autumn** is the perfect time to investigate Transylvania's festivals and

BEAR LAKE, TRANSYLVANIA

AVERAGE DAILY TEMPERATURES

	Jan	Feb	Mar	Apr	May	Jun	Jul	Aug	Sep	Oct	Nov	Dec
BRAȘOV (THE MOUNTAINS)												
(°C)	1	1	6	11	16	19	21	21	18	13	7	2
(°F)	34	34	42	52	61	66	69	69	65	55	45	36
BUCHAREST												
(°C)	-3	-1	4	11	17	21	23	22	18	12	5	1
(°F)	26	31	40	52	62	69	71	70	65	53	41	34
CONSTANȚA (THE COAST)												
(°C)	-1	1	3	13	19	24	26	26	22	17	11	6
(°F)	31	34	39	55	66	75	79	79	70	62	52	43
TIMIȘOARA (THE BANAT)												
(°C)	-2	1	5	11	16	19	21	21	18	12	6	1
(°F)	28	34	41	52	61	66	70	70	65	53	43	34

hiking trails (though brief but violent thunderstorms are common in the Carpathians during this period), and to see the painted monasteries of Bucovina, while flocks of birds again pass through the Delta in **late autumn**.

PIATRA CRAIULUI, THE CARPATHIAN MOUNTAINS

Author picks

Our authors have wined and dined, tramped and traipsed, driven and danced their way around Romania for this eighth edition of the Guide. What follows is a selection of their personal highlights.

Spectacular drive Snaking its way for some 90km across the southern section of the Carpathians, the spectacular Transfăgărașan Highway is the ultimate Romanian road trip (see page 143).

Wildlife encounters Romania is a wildlife haven, from bear-watching and wolf-tracking in the Carpathians (see page 140) to birdwatching and fishing in the Danube Delta (see page 350).

Stay with a count Spend some time with real-life nobility at Count Kálnoky's beautiful guesthouses in the remote village of Micloșoara, in deepest, darkest Transylvania (see page 144).

Fantastic fortified churches Southern Transylvania is replete with ancient Saxon churches, though none is more impressive than Prejmer's commanding citadel (see page 141).

Awesome castle An immense Gothic masterpiece, Corvin Castle in Hunedoara is Romania's most theatrical fortress (see page 175).

Gypsy grooves From the extraordinary polyphonic sounds of the Taraf de Haidouks, to the booming brass beats of Fanfare Ciocărlia, these outrageously talented musicians provide an experience not to be missed (see page 397).

Magnificent monasteries The rolling hills of Bucovina provide the setting for a succession of richly painted monasteries, notably Moldovița (see page 262), Sucevița (see page 263) and Voroneț (see page 259).

Tough treks Romania's classic trek is the five-day Făgăraș ridge (see page 142); there's also the knife-edge of the Piatra Craiului (see page 139), and the stunning peaks and lakes of the Retezat massif (see page 179).

VIDRARU DAM, TRANSYLVANIA

CORVIN CASTLE, HUNEDOARA

> Our author recommendations don't end here. We've flagged up our favourite places – a perfectly sited hotel, an atmospheric café, a special restaurant – throughout the Guide, highlighted with the ★ symbol.

20

things not to miss

It's not possible to see everything Romania has to offer in one trip – and we don't suggest you try. What follows, in no particular order, is a selective and subjective taste of the country's highlights: outstanding architecture, natural wonders, spectacular hikes and unforgettable festivals. All entries are colour-coded by chapter and have a page reference to take you straight into the Guide, where you can find out more.

1

1 BEAR- AND WOLF-TRACKING
See page 140

Spend a day trailing Romania's largest carnivores – if you're lucky, you may see one of these magnificent creatures up close.

2 MERRY CEMETERY, SĂPÂNŢA
See page 293

True to its name, the Merry Cemetery is a riot of beautifully carved and coloured wooden headstones.

3 WOODEN CHURCHES OF MARAMUREŞ
See page 283

The beguiling landscape of this isolated region is dominated by marvellous wooden churches, such as those at Budeşti.

4 TIMIŞOARA
See page 326

The crucible of the 1989 revolution, this most cosmopolitan of Romanian cities promises handsome architecture, fine parks and a vibrant arts scene.

5 PELEŞ CASTLE, SINAIA
See page 122

Once a refuge for Ceauşescu and visiting dignitaries, Peleş remains the country's most opulent palace.

6 BUCHAREST

See page 40

Romania's noisy, chaotic capital boasts a number of terrific museums, remarkable architecture and some of the best nightlife in the Balkans.

7 BLACK SEA

See page 359

Strewn with lively resorts and sandy beaches, the Black Sea coast offers everything from wakeboarding to kayaking, while Constanţa is the seaboard's cultural hub.

8 DANUBE DELTA

See page 342

This remote and beautiful landscape is teeming with fabulous wildlife, and promises some of the finest birdwatching in Europe.

9 FORTIFIED CHURCHES

See page 156

Scattered among the lush hills of southern Transylvania are dozens of marvellous fortified Saxon churches; those at Biertan and Prejmer are among the most impressive.

10 CONSTANTIN BRÂNCUŞI

See page 106

Romania's greatest sculptor has bequeathed an impressive legacy of striking works of art, such as the *Endless Column* in Târgu Jiu.

11 SIBIU
See page 156
Beautiful architecture, terrific museums and fabulous festivals make the once great Saxon town of Sibiu an alluring destination.

12 BUCOVINA HILLS
See page 256
Cloaked in beech, fir and pine, the gorgeous rolling Bucovina hills are a walker's paradise.

13 BRAŞOV
See page 128
Shadowed by mountains and boasting a fine Baroque centre, this erstwhile Saxon settlement is one of Transylvania's most appealing cities.

14 VIŞEU DE SUS TRAIN RIDE
See page 302
Jump aboard the early-morning logging train for a meandering ride up the picturesque Vaser valley.

15 SIGHIŞOARA
See page 147
Atmospheric medieval town with a brooding skyline of ramparts, towers and spires.

11

12

13

14

15

16

17

16 FĂGĂRAŞ MOUNTAIN HIKING

See page 142

The spectacular peaks of the Făgăraş provide access to some rewarding hikes.

17 DRACULA

See pages 101 and 398

The Princely Court at Târgovişte and Poienari Castle are just two of the many sites linked to the Dracula legend.

18 PAINTED MONASTERIES

See page 259

The monasteries of southern Bucovina and Moldavia are renowned for their magnificent exterior frescoes.

19 FOLK AND GYPSY MUSIC

See page 397

Don't miss the wild, irrepressible sounds of Romanian folk and Gypsy music.

20 THE CARPATHIAN RANGE

See page 32

One of Europe's least spoiled mountain ranges, full of wildlife and first-class hiking trails.

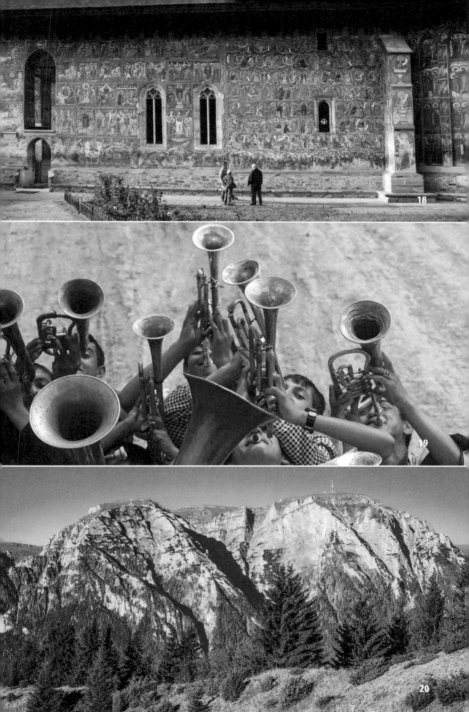

Itineraries

Romania rewards exploration – the major towns and cities have countless unmissable sights, but it's by getting off the beaten track that you'll discover the country's most bewitching charms. These itineraries encourage you to do just that: breathe mountain air in the Carpathians, visit timeless rural villages in Maramureş or enjoy the unparalleled birdlife of the Danube Delta.

THE GRAND TOUR

This itinerary leads you around the country's must-see sights, taking in everything from Dracula and the Danube Delta to Bucharest and the Black Sea Coast.

❶ **Bucharest** By turns chaotic and compelling, the Romanian capital features Stalinist architecture, ancient churches, intriguing museums, and a fast-improving gastronomic scene. See page 40

❷ **Braşov** This vibrant city, a former Saxon stronghold, retains one of the country's most picturesque Old Town squares, dominated by the magnificent Black Church. See page 128

❸ **Sighişoara** This place of medieval towers and needle spires is a suitably spooky setting for the birthplace of Vlad Ţepeş, aka Dracula. See page 147

❹ **Timişoara** The most appealing of the Banat cities, Timişoara offers plentiful reminders of the 1989 revolution, which began here. See page 326

❺ **Maramureş** Romania's remote, northernmost region is also its most enchanting, with villages seemingly lost in time and ancient customs still thriving. See page 274

❻ **Bucovina** Lush valleys and forested hills aside, Bucovina is famed for its painted monasteries, whose startling exterior wall paintings remain supreme works of art. See page 256

❼ **Danube Delta** One of Europe's most evocative landscapes, the Delta offers an array of birdlife unmatched anywhere else on the continent – stunning during migration season. See page 342

❽ **Black Sea coast** Bountiful sun, sea and sand combine to make the Romanian coastline the perfect spot to rest up for a day or two. See page 359

THE GREAT OUTDOORS

Underground, overground or on the water, Romania offers countless opportunities to embrace activities ranging from the sedate to the fast-paced and action-packed.

❶ **Caving in the Apuseni** The karst zone of the Apuseni offers fabulous possibilities to explore subterranean wonders such as Meziad and the even more spectacular "Bears' Cave" at Chişcău. See page 317

❷ **Hiking the Făgăraş** Cutting across the country are the sinuous Carpathian mountains, whose best-known range is the awesome Făgăraş, harbouring Romania's loftiest peaks, the highest of which is Moldoveanu (2544m). See page 142

❸ **Wildlife-watching in the Carpathians** Explore forests looking for markings made by large carnivores – there's a good chance of spotting bears from purpose-made hideouts, though wolves are more elusive. See page 140

④ Skiing The superior slopes and facilities of Poiana Braşov exert the greatest pull, though there's also terrific skiing at Buşteni, Predeal and Sinaia. See page 136

⑤ Birdwatching in the Delta Europe's most extensive wetland, with the continent's largest pelican colonies, the Delta is heaven for birdwatchers, especially during the spring and autumn migrations. See page 389

⑥ Coastal activities The coast provides all manner of possibilities for fun-filled diversions, such as wakeboarding, waterskiing and kayaking. See page 366

AWESOME ARCHITECTURE

Romania has some of the most distinctive structures in Europe, from the UNESCO-listed wooden churches of rural Maramureş to the bold architectural statements of Bucharest.

① Bucharest From the monochrome concrete jungle of the Centru Civic and its compellingly monstrous Palace of Parliament, to French-inspired buildings like the magnificent Atheneum, the Romanian capital is endlessly fascinating. See page 40

② Horezu monastery The finest example in Romania of the Brâncovenesc school, an architectural style conceived by the seventeenth-century Wallachian ruler, Constantin Brâncoveanu, Horezu is an elegant fusion of Baroque, Renaissance and Ottoman elements. See page 107

③ Saxon churches, Transylvania Transylvania's Saxon villages are defined by their fortified churches, such as the one at Biertan, a commanding structure set in rings of walls, and the delightful example at Mălâncrav. See page 156

④ Secession masterpieces, Oradea Oradea showcases the country's most impressive range of Art Nouveau architecture; fine examples include the Moskovits Palace and the legendary Vultural Negru building. See page 308

⑤ Wooden churches, Maramureş Scattered all over Maramureş, these wonderful eighteenth-century wooden churches are distinguished by steeply sloping shingled roofs, slender bell towers and fine porches – those at Surdeşti and Ieud are unmissable. See page 283

⑥ Painted monasteries, Bucovina The so-called Moldavian style – integrating Gothic and Byzantine – is showcased to spectacular effect in these ancient monuments, typically featuring a large enclosure with thickset walls and an imposing entrance gate. See page 259

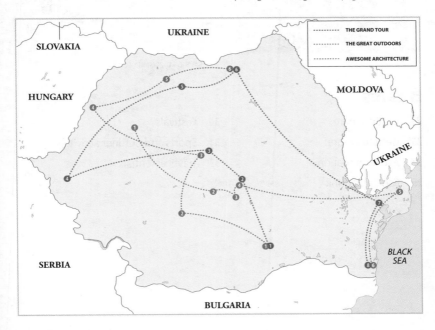

TRADITIONAL ROMANIAN CHEESE

Basics

Getting there

Flying is the easiest way to reach Romania, with several airlines now operating direct from the UK. Flying from North America, Australasia or South Africa will entail one or more changes. Travelling to Romania from the UK by train is a long haul, though with a rail pass you can take in the country as part of a wider trip.

If **flying**, you can often cut costs by going through a specialist flight agent, who in addition to dealing with discounted flights may also offer student and youth fares and travel insurance, rail passes, car rental, tours and the like.

Flights from the UK and Ireland

Flying from the UK to Romania takes between three and three and a half hours. British Airways and TAROM, the Romanian national carrier, both have **daily direct scheduled flights** from London Heathrow to Bucharest. A number of budget carriers – including Wizz Air, easyJet, Ryanair and the Romanian carrier Blue Air – now serve a host of Romanian cities, including Bacău, Bucharest, Cluj, Constanţa, Iaşi, Satu Mare, Sibiu, Târgu Mureş and Timişoara, though many of these are seasonal. Both Blue Air and Ryanair fly from Dublin to Romania.

Prices depend on how far in advance you book, although **season** is also a factor: unless you book very well in advance, a ticket to anywhere between June and September will generally cost more than at other times (excluding Christmas and New Year). Book far enough in advance with one of the low-cost airlines and you can pick up a ticket for around £60–70 return, even in summer; book anything less than three or four weeks in advance and this could triple in price. Search engines such as Ⓦskyscanner.net, Ⓦkayak.co.uk or Ⓦmomondo.com are invaluable for researching the best connections and prices.

Flights from the US and Canada

There are **no direct flights** from North America to Romania, though most major airlines offer one- or two-stop flights via the bigger European cities, often in conjunction with TAROM, the national carrier. From the east coast of the US, expect to pay around US$700 low season and US$1000 high season; and from the west coast around US$1100 low season and US$1400 high season. From Canada, expect to pay around Can$1300 low season from Toronto (Can$1700 high season) and Can$1900 low season from Vancouver (Can$2300 high season).

Flights from Australia, New Zealand and South Africa

There are **no direct flights** from Australia or New Zealand to Romania, so you'll have to change airlines, either in Asia or Europe, although the best option is to fly to a Western European gateway for a connecting flight. A return fare from eastern **Australia** is around Aus$2200 low season and Aus$2700 high season. From **New Zealand**, a return fare costs from around NZ$2400 low season and NZ$3000 high season.

There are **no direct flights** from South Africa to Romania, but plenty of airlines offer one-stop flights via European hubs such as London, Frankfurt or Paris. Flying with an airline such as Lufthansa from **Johannesburg** via Frankfurt costs around ZAR9000 in low season, ZAR11,000 in high season.

By train

Travelling **by train** is likely to be considerably more expensive than flying. The shortest journey takes about 36 hours, with a standard second-class **return ticket**, incorporating Eurostar, costing around £350. From London St Pancras International, take the Eurostar to Paris Gare du Nord, and then walk to the Gare de l'Est for a train to either Munich or Vienna, where you change for Budapest. In Budapest, change again for the last leg to Romania.

Deutsche Bahn is the best option for making seat reservations on continental trains and its website

---

A BETTER KIND OF TRAVEL

At Rough Guides we are passionately committed to travel. We believe it helps us understand the world we live in and the people we share it with – and of course tourism is vital to many developing economies. But the scale of modern tourism has also damaged some places irreparably, and climate change is accelerated by most forms of transport, especially flying. We encourage our authors to consider the carbon footprint of the journeys they make in the course of researching our guides.

(W bahn.de) is an excellent resource for checking railway timetables, while The Man in Seat Sixty-One (W seat61.com) is invaluable on most aspects of rail travel in Europe.

Rail passes

If you're planning to visit Romania as part of a more extensive trip around Europe, it may be worth buying a rail pass. InterRail passes (W interrail.eu) are only available to those who have been resident in Europe for six months or more. They come in first- and second-class for those aged 28 and over and (cheaper) under-28 versions. The passes are available to a combination of countries for five days within a fifteen-day period (£245 second class, £190 under-28), seven days within one month (£292 second class, £233 under-28) and ten days within one month (£347 second class, £278 under-28); there's also travel for fifteen consecutive days (£384 second class, £307 under-28), 22 consecutive days (£449 second class, £359 under-28) or one month unlimited (£580 second class, £465 under-28). Pass holders also receive a discounted rate on the Eurostar service.

The other InterRail scheme is the **one-country pass**, which allows you to travel a certain number of days during a one-month period. For Romania, three says within one month costs £84 for 28 and over/£73 under-28s; four days within one month £104/£91 under-28s; six days in one month £141/£122; eight days in one month £173/£150; however, this doesn't represent particularly great value given how cheap it is to travel by train in Romania.

Non-European residents qualify for the **Eurail pass** (W eurail.com), which must be bought before arrival in Europe, or from RailEurope in the UK. The pass allows unlimited first-class travel in 28 European countries, including Romania, and is available in various increments; for example, a fifteen-day continuous pass costs US$705 for those aged 28 and over/US$567 under-28s, 22 days ($907/$727), and one month ($1112/$893). There are also a number of other passes available, including a One-Country Pass and a Select Pass, which allows you to travel in two-, three- or four neighbouring countries.

By car from the UK

Driving to Romania, a distance of some 2000km from London, is really only worth considering if you are planning to travel around Romania extensively or want to make various stopovers en route.

Once across the channel (Eurotunnel UK ☎ +44(0) 844 335 3535, international ☎ +33(0)321 002 061, W eurotunnel.com), the best **route** (around 30hr

at a leisurely pace with plenty of stops) is through Belgium, Germany, Austria and Hungary, passing Brussels, Frankfurt, Nuremberg, Regensburg, Linz, Vienna and Budapest, and then taking the E60 down to the Borş border crossing near Oradea or the E75/ E68 to Nădlac near Arad. Route plans can be obtained from the websites of Michelin (W viamichelin.com), the AA (W theaa.com) or the RAC (W rac.co.uk). See page 26 for details of driving within Romania.

Airlines, agents and operators

AGENTS AND OPERATORS

North South Travel UK ☎ 01245 608 291, W northsouthtravel. co.uk. Friendly, competitive travel agency, offering discounted fares worldwide. Profits are used to support projects in the developing world, especially the promotion of sustainable tourism.

STA Travel UK ☎ 0333 321 0099, W statravel.co.uk, US ☎ 1800 781 4040, Australia ☎ 134 782, New Zealand ☎ 0800 474 400, South Africa ☎ 0861 781 781. Worldwide specialists in independent travel; also student IDs, travel insurance, car rental, rail passes and more. Good discounts for students and under-26s.

Trailfinders UK ☎ 0207 084 6500, W trailfinders.com. One of the best-informed and most efficient agents for independent travellers.

Travel CUTS Canada ☎ 1800 667 2887, W travelcuts.com. Canadian youth and student travel firm.

USIT Ireland ☎ 01 602 1906, W usit.ie. Ireland's main student and youth travel specialists.

SPECIALIST OPERATORS

Balkan Holidays ☎ 020 7543 5555, W balkanholidays.co.uk. Southeastern Europe specialists offering summer and winter package deals, mainly to Poiana Braşov.

Beyond the Forest ☎ 01900 824 329, W beyondtheforest.com. Comprehensive Romania specialists offering package and special interest tours (wilderness, wine and culture, riding, spas, Dracula), flights, accommodation, car rental and rail tickets.

Birdfinders ☎ 01258 839 066, W birdfinders.co.uk. Ten-day birdwatching tour of Transylvania, the Danube Delta and the Black Sea coast in April.

Eastern Eurotours Australia ☎ 1800 242 353, W easterneurotours.com.au. Classical tour throughout Romania, including Transylvania, the painted monasteries and Dracula, and a Danube Delta hike and bike tour.

Exodus ☎ 020 8131 0395, W exodus.co.uk. Guided walking tours and bear-watching in the Carpathians, cycle trips, and winter walking and snowshoeing tours.

Explore Worldwide ☎ 01252 888 543, W explore.co.uk. Trekking in Transylvania, village folklore in Maramureş and the Danube Delta, and a family winter adventure tour.

Go Barefoot ☎ 020 3290 9591, W gobarefoot.travel. Nine-day walking tours through Maramureş, visiting the wooden churches, and Bucovina, visiting the painted monasteries.

Hooked on Cycling ☎ 01506 635 399, ⓦ hookedoncycling.co.uk.
Eight-day self-guided cycling tour (easy to moderate) through the
Carpathians, staying in local guesthouses.

Limosa Holidays ☎ 01692 580 623, ⓦ limosaholidays.co.uk.
Week-long spring and autumn birding tours in the Danube Delta
and along the Black Sea Coast, plus one tour which combines birds
and bear-watching.

Naturetrek ☎ 01962 733 051, ⓦ naturetrek.co.uk. Offers a
Wildlife of Transylvania tour alongside a Danube Delta and
Carpathian mountains trip.

Quest Tours and Adventures US ☎ 1800 621 8687, ⓦ romtour.
com. Wide range of tours and fully customized packages, including
monastery and Dracula tours, as well as combined tours with
Bulgaria.

Rediscover ☎ 01989 730 552, ⓦ rediscover.co.uk. Tailor-made
holidays and small group tours covering just about every region
of the country.

Ride World Wide ☎ 01837 82544, ⓦ rideworldwide.com. Seven-
day riding holidays in the Carpathians between April and Oct; four
to six hours' riding daily and accommodation in local guesthouses.

Romania Travel Centre ☎ 01892 779 718,
ⓦ romaniatravelcentre.com. Romania specialists offering a
comprehensive programme including Bucharest city breaks,
coastal, ski and spa holidays, ecotours and biking trips. Flights and
tailor-made accommodation deals too.

The Slow Cyclist ☎ 020 7060 4487, ⓦ theslowcyclist.co.uk.
Excellent cycling and walking tours through forests and meadows
in Transylvania, staying in traditional cottages and guesthouses.

Travelling Naturalist ☎ 01305 267 994, ⓦ naturalist.co.uk.
Spring and autumn birdwatching tours to the Danube Delta, and a
summer Birds and Bears in Transylvania trip.

Wilderness Travel US ☎ 1800 368 2794, ⓦ wildernesstravel.com.
Fifteen-day hiking and sightseeing expedition starting in Bulgaria
before crossing into Romania and the Carpathians. There's also a
fifteen-day Great Carpathian Traverse, taking in five countries.

RAIL CONTACTS

Trainline ⓦ trainline.eu.
Eurostar UK ☎ 08432 186 186, ⓦ eurostar.com.
Rail Europe ⓦ raileurope.com.

Getting around

**Most Romanian towns are easily reached
by bus or maxitaxi (minibus), both
long-distance services and local connections, though the driving often leaves
much to be desired. The rail system
is in poor health, and there's barely a
skeleton service on major routes, taking
much longer than they did a decade ago
– however, both forms of transport are
still remarkably cheap. Driving can be**

**an attractive, if frustrating, proposition,
allowing you to visit anywhere you please.**

By rail

Despite severe cutbacks, interminable delays and
aged carriages, the **SNCFR** (*Societatea Naţională a
Căilor Ferate Române*, generally known as the **CFR**,
or ChéFéRé) network has many wonderfully scenic
routes, particularly in Transylvania, and it remains an
incredibly cheap way of getting around.

There are two types of train: **Regio** (R) services,
which stop everywhere, and **InterRegio** (IR), calling
only at major towns, which are more comfortable and
more expensive. **EuroCity** (EC) and **EuroNight** (EN)
trains are international services.

Train **timetables** (*orar trenurilor*) are displayed in
stations and CFR offices; arrivals are on a white board,
departures on a yellow one. Watch out for services
that run only during certain seasons (*circulă numai*, eg
Intre 9.V și 8.IX – between May 9 and Sept 8), or only on
particular days (1 represents Mon, 2 represents Tues
and so on; *nu circula Sâmbăta și Duminica* means the
service doesn't run on Sat or Sun). You can find details
online at ⓦ cfrcalatori.ro, and you should always check
at the station. Details of main **routes** are given in the
Guide chapters.

Left luggage offices (*bagaje de mănă*) exist in
many train stations, where you'll usually have to pay
around €1.

Tickets

Fares (calculated by distance travelled) are similar
to bus fares; for example, a journey of 100km on an
InterRegio service will cost around €7 second class,
and around €10 first class (around €3/€5 on a Regio),
which makes first-class travel a bargain. InterRegio
tickets include a seat allocation. Ticketing is now
computerized, with all information on one piece of
paper, while return tickets (*bilet dus-întors*) can now
be issued too.

Some long-distance overnight trains have **sleeping
cars** (*vagon de dormit*) and couchettes (*cușete*), for
which a surcharge of around €13–35 and €7.60–11
respectively (depending upon how many berths
there are) is levied.

By bus or maxitaxi

Romania's **bus network** consists of a confusing and
uncoordinated array of private companies, but is
often unavoidable. Many towns have several bus/
maxitaxi stations and calling points, which means that
locating the right bus in the right place can be a tricky

DRIVING RULES AND REGULATIONS

Traffic drives on the right and **speed limits** for vehicles are 50km/h in built-up areas, 90km/h on the open road (100km/h on European roads, denoted by E) and 130km/h on the motorway. Otherwise, the most important rules are the wearing of seat belts and the use of **dipped headlights** outside towns and cities. It is forbidden to use a hand-held phone while driving, and **drinking** and driving is severely punished. **Police** (*poliția*) are empowered to levy on-the-spot **fines** for road traffic offences, but they cannot collect them; instead you'll be issued with a ticket (typically €40–80); if you settle up within 48 hours – at a town hall or one of the CEC savings banks – then you'll only have to pay half the fine. If you have an **accident**, you're legally obliged to await the arrival of the police. You can get **technical assistance** and information from **ACR** (Romanian Automobile Club; **ⓦ** acr.ro), whose main Bucharest office is at Str. Tache Ionescu 27 (**ⓣ** 021 315 5510). In the event of a breakdown, call ACR's 24-hour **breakdown service** on **ⓣ** 021 222 2222, whereupon an English-speaking operator will direct you to the nearest point of assistance.

proposition; indeed, in the countryside knowing when and where to wait for the bus is a local art form; on Sundays many regions have no local buses at all.

Complementing the buses are maxitaxis (essentially minibuses), which serve a wider number of destinations, and more frequently. As efficient as they can be, they are often overloaded (with little room for luggage) and there's scant regard for safety – don't expect an entirely comfortable, or relaxing, ride. Timetables for both buses and maxitaxis can be found on **ⓦ** autogari.ro and **ⓦ** cdy.ro. Expect to pay around €5 from Bucharest to Pitești (100km), or €10 from Bucharest to Brașov (250km). Maxitaxis often begin and end their journeys from the local bus or train station. Details of main routes are given in the Guide chapters.

All towns have **local bus services**, and in the main cities you'll also find **trams** (*tramvai*) and **trolley buses** (*troleibuz*). Tickets are normally sold in pairs (around €0.30) from street kiosks or machines. Validate them yourself aboard the vehicle; stiff fines apply if you don't.

By car

Outside the major towns and cities, you'll find the roads **relatively traffic-free**, and many routes, particularly through Transylvania, are wonderfully scenic. That said, the overall state of the roads varies enormously, while Romanian driving habits often leave much to be desired; indeed, Romania has one of the highest traffic accident fatality rates in the EU.

Owing to a combination of corruption and incompetence, construction of Romania's motorways (*autostrada*) continues at snail's pace, At present, the only fully complete motorway is the A2 between Bucharest and Constanța, while a few sections of the A1 – which will eventually link Bucharest with Nadlac on the Hungarian border – are now complete, namely the sections between Bucharest and Pitești, Sibiu and Deva, and Lugoj and Nadlac. The **main roads** (*drum național* or DN) are, generally speaking, in good condition. The quality of the **county roads** (*drum județean*), however, is variable, while many of the local roads are disintegrating – potholes are a particularly nasty hazard. Being such a big country, long distances are best covered at a steady pace, especially if driving in the more mountainous regions where greater powers of concentration are required.

Aside from the very Balkan habit of overtaking at absurdly risky moments, other potential hazards include horses and carts, which are commonplace even on main roads, and stray dogs – squashed canines lying on the side of the road are an all too common sight. For these reasons, **avoid driving after dark** wherever possible.

If bringing your own car into the country you must purchase a sticker which acts as a road toll, known as a vignette (*rovigneta*; **ⓦ** roviniete.ro), which cost €3 for a week, €7 for a month or €13 for three months; these are available online or from border entry points, most petrol stations or post offices.

Petrol stations (*benzinarie*) can be found almost everywhere, even in the most rural backwaters – the most common are those run by ROMPETROL, OMV-PETROM, LUKOIL (Russian) and MOL (Hungarian), many of which have good refreshment and toilet facilities, as well as wi-fi. Unleaded fuel (*fără plomb*) currently costs around €1.20 per litre. Credit cards are accepted at most stations. While most service stations operate from around 7am to 8 or 9pm, quite a few are open around the clock, usually those on the outskirts of larger towns and cities as well as the main roads.

ACCOMMODATION PRICES

We give a room price for all establishments reviewed in this guide. Unless otherwise stated, this represents the price for **the cheapest available double or twin room in high season**. Consequently, at other times of the year, or during special promotions, you'll often find a room for a lower price than that suggested. Though you will generally pay for your room in lei, the codes are expressed in euros as many hotels are priced this way. For **youth hostels**, where relevant, we give the price of a double room and of a dormitory bed. At **campsites**, the price listed is for two people, a pitch and a vehicle, unless otherwise stated.

Car rental

Renting a car is simple enough, provided you are 21 or older and hold a valid national driving licence. The **cheapest prices** are almost always online; expect to pay around €35–45 for a day's rental, though the price drops the longer the rental period. Most of the major companies have branches in Bucharest (and Henri Coandă airport) and all the other major cities, and airports. However, you may find that **local companies**, such as Pan Travel (see page 203), offer better deals. Note that you may be able to take the car into neighbouring countries, although most companies charge extra for this.

By bicycle

Given the mountainous terrain and the poor state of many of the country roads, you'll need to be fit and self-reliant to **cycle** around Romania. Cycle shops are few and far between, although most village mechanics can manage basic repairs. Carry a spare tyre and a few spokes, and check carrier nuts regularly, as the potholes and corrugations will rapidly shake them loose. A touring bike is better than a mountain bike unless you want to go off-road; with the immense network of forestry roads (*drum forestiere*) and free access to the hills, genuine mountain biking is wonderful here. If you do bring your own bike, avoid cycling in **Bucharest**. Carrying your bike by train is easiest on Regio services, where you can simply put it in the carriage; on InterRegio, it can be stored in the baggage van (this should be indicated on the timetable).

By plane

Romania has a reasonably comprehensive network of **domestic flights**, serving most of the larger cities, which can be a useful alternative to the increasingly decrepit railway system. **TAROM**'s (ⓦtarom.ro) domestic services depart most days from Bucharest's Henri Coandă airport to Baia Mare, Cluj, Constanţa, Iaşi, Oradea, Satu Mare, Sibiu, Suceava Târgu Mureş and Timişoara. In addition, **Blue Air** (ⓦblueairweb.

com) flies from Bucharest to Bacău, Cluj and Iaşi. Singles start from around €30–40.

Hitchhiking

Hitchhiking (*autostop* or *occasie*) is an integral part of the Romanian transport system to supplement patchy or nonexistent services on back roads – it's even common (although illegal) on the *autostrada*. It's accepted practice to pay (equivalent to a bus fare) for lifts; although this is often waived, make sure you've got some small change to hand. As anywhere, exercise caution.

Accommodation

You should have little trouble finding a bed in Romania, whatever the season. Hotels run the full gamut from bland, basic dives to plush establishments – there are now a few design hotels popping up, too. You can also choose from a good number of youth hostels, in addition to a spread of private rooms and village homestays, the last of which typically offer wonderfully peaceful retreats.

In summer, it's safer (though only really essential on the coast) to make advance hotel **reservations**. If you're keen to save money on accommodation and you're travelling around a lot, you can use the **trains** to your advantage. On the long overnight journeys by train, it only costs a little more to book a comfortable sleeping car or couchette.

Hotels and pensions

Hotels use the traditional five-star **grading system** for classification, although in many cases this often gives only the vaguest idea of **prices**, which can fluctuate wildly according to the locality and season. For example, in Bucharest you can get some excellent deals at many high-end hotels in summer when the traditional business market is slack, while along the

TOP FIVE HOTELS

Athénée Palace Hilton Bucharest. See page 48

Casa Raţiu Turda. See page 211

Christina Bucharest. See page 72

Count Kálnoky's Guesthouses Micloşoara. See page 144

Valea Verde Cund. See page 154

coast prices can drop by as much as a third outside July and August.

Outside Bucharest and the coast, the average three-star hotel can charge anything between €30 and €60 for a double room. But note that ratings are not always indicative of the quality of a place; what might be considered a four-star hotel in Romania is often the equivalent of a three-star in Western Europe. That said, the plushest four- and five-star hotels offer all the luxuries one would expect, while three-star hotels can be unpredictable in terms of both quality and cost; you should, however, expect a reasonable standard of comfort, as well as private bathroom, TV, air conditioning and minibar, in most. Whatever the rating, just about every hotel now has wi-fi, and it's usually excellent.

There is now a high number of **pensions** throughout the country; these are often smaller and more personable than hotels, as well as offering much better value for money.

Village homestays and private rooms

Village homestays (*agroturism*) – rural farmhouse-style accommodation – offer visitors the opportunity to spend some time with a Romanian family (most of whom won't speak English) in often lovely surrounds. The downside is that many places are in fairly remote locations, and are therefore difficult to reach without your own transport. Homestays are **graded** according to a **daisy classification system**; four or five daisies (of which there are few) denotes a house with large, well-furnished rooms with private bathroom or shower/toilet, while one or two daisies represents a more basic place offering shared shower and toilet facilities. Expect to pay €10–15 per person per night depending upon the category; many places also offer breakfast (around €3) and dinner (€5–7) upon request. The excellent website Ⓦ ruralturism.ro lists a number of homestays throughout the country. The official nationwide body for homestays is **ANTREC** (the National Association of Rural, Ecological and Cultural Tourism; Ⓦ antrec.ro).

You'll also come across many places advertising **private rooms** (*cazare* or *camere de inchiriat*), particularly in the more touristed areas of Transylvania and along the coast. Indeed, in places like Braşov, Sighişoara and in some of the coastal resorts, you're likely to be greeted by people at the train station offering a room. Expect to pay between €10–15 for a bed, though breakfast is unlikely to be provided. In the countryside, where there is a strong custom of hospitality, people may take you in and refuse payment, but you should offer something anyway, or come armed with a few packets of coffee, which make welcome presents.

Hostels

Romania has a reasonable network of **HI youth hostels** (Ⓦ hostelling.ro), plus many which are independently run. There are around a dozen or so in Bucharest, as well as good options in Braşov, Cluj, Sibiu, Sighişoara and Timişoara, while you'll find the odd one in towns and resorts like Deva, Miercurea Ciuc, Suceava and Vama Veche. Expect to pay around €10–12 for a dorm bed, €15–20 for a bed in a double room, and €25 for a single-bed room – breakfast is usually extra.

While **student accommodation** is largely in short supply, you may find the odd student residence willing to let out a bed, though these are largely available only in July and August – however, these are unlikely to be advertised, so ask for details at the local tourist office or town agency.

Cabanas

In the countryside, particularly in the mountainous areas favoured by hikers, there are well over a hundred **cabanas** or hikers' huts, ranging from chic alpine villas with dozens of bedrooms to fairly primitive chalets with bunk beds and cold running water. The hikers' cabanas are generally friendly and serve as useful places to pick up information about trails and the weather. Some (mainly in the Bucegi range) can be easily reached by cable car, while others are situated on roads just a few kilometres from towns; however, the majority are fairly isolated and accessible only by mountain tracks or footpaths. The location of the cabanas is shown precisely on hiking maps. Cabanas are supposed not to turn hikers away, but in the Făgăraş mountains, in particular, it might be wise to **book in advance**, by phone or through a local agency. Beds in remoter areas cost about €3–4, a little more for a private room or in one of the more comfortable cabanas.

Camping

Romania has a reasonable spread of **campsites** throughout the country, which vary in quality from very rudimentary places with minimal facilities to first-class sites with **cabins** or bungalows (*căsuțe*) for rent, hot showers and even a restaurant. You'll generally pay about €3 per person per night, plus €5 for a car.

In the mountains, certain areas may be designated as a camping area (*loc de campare*), but these are few and far between. However, providing you don't light fires in forests, leave litter or damage nature reserves, officialdom turns a blind eye to tourists **camping wild**, or, at the worst, may simply tell you to move along.

Food and drink

Romanian cuisine tends to be filling and wholesome rather than particularly tasty or imaginative, with menus dominated by meat, in common with the rest of the Balkans. Similarly, the range and quality of restaurants remains fairly average, the one exception being Bucharest, where there is now a genuinely exciting gastronomic scene. That said, the likes of Cluj, Brașov and Sibiu are also experiencing a mini culinary renaissance. For a glossary of food and drink terms, see page 408.

Breakfast and snacks

Unless you're staying in a four- or five-star hotel, where a full buffet is the norm, **breakfast** (*micul dejun*) is usually a fairly dull – sometimes even depressing – affair, typically consisting of bread rolls with butter and jam, the ubiquitous omelette, and perhaps some salty cheese or a long, unappealing skinless sausage – the coffee, meanwhile, is invariably lamentable.

For **snacks**, known as *gustări* (also the Romanian word for hors d'oeuvres), head to a bakery (*brutărie*), which you can find everywhere. Just about all of these dispense *covrigi*, plain or seeded bread rings straight from the oven, sold as a bunch and tied to a piece of string. Bakeries are also good for *pateuri*, flaky pastries stuffed with cheese, meat or fruit fillings, and brioche (*cozonac*), a Moldavian speciality. Street vendors and beer gardens dispense a variety of grilled meats, the most popular of which are *mititei* (more commonly known as *mici*), succulent grilled beef rissoles served with a dollop of mustard.

TOP FIVE RESTAURANTS
The Artist, Bucharest. See page 77
Beca's Kitchen, Bucharest. See page 76
Bistro de L'Arte, Brașov. See page 135
Old Lisbon, Sibiu. See page 162
D.O.R., Bran. See page 138

Restaurants

Given the affordability of eating out in Romania, it's best to go **upmarket** if you can, since the choice of dishes in cheaper **restaurants** is invariably very predictable. Generally speaking, in better restaurants you should be able to get a decent two-course meal, with a glass of wine or beer, for a bargain €12–15.

It's always worth enquiring *Care feluri le serviți astazi, vă rog?* ("What do you have today?") or *Ce Óhmi recomandați?* ("What do you recommend?") before studying the menu too seriously. An increasing number of restaurants, including some of the better establishments, now offer daily set menus, typically a two- or three-course meal, with a drink, for around €6, which is usually offered Monday to Friday between noon and 5 or 6pm. While not exactly haute cuisine, these meals are cracking value.

Self-service *autoservire* **canteens** are not as commonplace as they once were, but you'll still find plenty of them in the coastal resorts. A far cry from the grisly canteens that Ceaușescu intended to make the mainstay of Romanian catering, these uncomplicated venues offer simple, cheap meals.

Inevitably, standards of **service** vary depending upon the type of establishment, but generally speaking don't expect anything but the most perfunctory of service, while in some places you'll be greeted (and served) with total indifference. Outside Bucharest and some of the larger cities, you'll find few staff speak English.

One thing that has changed for the better is the ban on smoking, which includes all restaurants.

Romanian cuisine

Perhaps the most authentic Romanian dish is *sarmale* – cabbage leaves stuffed with rice, meat and herbs, usually served (or sometimes baked) with sour cream or horseradish; they are sometimes also made with vine leaves (*sărmălute in foi de viță*) or, in Maramureș, with corn (*sarmale cu pasat*). *Mămăligă*, maize mush or polenta, often served with sour cream, is authentic country fare. Stews (*tocane*) and other dishes often feature a combination of meat and dairy products. *Mușchi ciobanesc* (shepherd's sirloin) is pork stuffed with ham, covered in cheese and served with mayonnaise, cucumber and herbs, while *mușchi poiana* (meadow sirloin) is beef stuffed with mushrooms, bacon, pepper and paprika, served in a vegetable purée and tomato sauce.

Keep an eye out for **regional specialities** (*specialitățile regiunii*). Moldavian cooking is reputedly the best in Romania, featuring rissoles (*pârjoale*), and more elaborate dishes such as *rasol moldovenesc cu hrean* (boiled pork, chicken or beef, with a sour cream and horseradish sauce), *tochitură moldovenească* (a pork stew, with cheese, *mămăligă*, and a fried egg on top), *rulade de pui* (chicken roulade) and *pui câmpulungean* (chicken stuffed with smoked bacon, sausage, garlic and vegetables). Because of Romania's Turkish past, you may come across moussaka and varieties of pilaf, while the German and Hungarian minorities have contributed such dishes as smoked pork with sauerkraut and Transylvanian hotpot.

Cakes and desserts are sticky and very sweet. Romanians enjoy pancakes and pies with various fillings, as well as Turkish-influenced baclava and *savarină* (crisp pastry soaked in syrup and filled with whipped cream).

Romanian **cheese** (*brânză*) is mainly handmade from sheep's milk by shepherds who spend the summers in the hills with their flocks. The standard hard cheese is known as *cașcaval*, while *caș* is a less salty version of feta, and *telemea* is a soft and creamy white cheese matured in brine.

Vegetarian food

The situation for vegetarians remains predictably dull. You can try requesting something *fără carne, vă rog* ("without meat, please"), or checking *este cu carne?* ("does it contain meat?"), but you're unlikely to get very far. It's worth asking for *ghiveci* (mixed stewed veg); *ardei umpluți* (stuffed peppers); *ouă umpluțe picante* or *ouă umpluțe cu ciuperci* (eggs with a spicy filling or mushroom stuffing); *ouă românești* (poached eggs); or vegetables and salads. However, in practice you're likely to end up with omelette, *mămăligă* or *cașcaval pané* (cheese fried in breadcrumbs).

Drinks

Most **cafés** (*cafenea* or *cofetărie)* serve the full range of beverages, from coffee (and occasionally tea) to soft drinks and beer, while many also offer cakes, pastries and ice cream. Romanians usually take their coffee black and sweet in the Turkish fashion; ask for *cafea cu lapte* if you prefer it with milk, or *fără zahăr* without sugar. Other types of coffee, such as cappuccino, are invariably hit-or-miss affairs, ranging from good quality to insipid cups with a dollop of cream on top. The good news, though, is that the third-wave coffee movement has hit Romania big-time, and there are now some superb, and superbly designed, artisan coffee houses staffed by knowledgeable, enthusiastic baristas; whilst Bucharest, inevitably, is at the forefront of this, other cities, notably Cluj, Constanța, Brașov and Iași, as well as an increasing number of smaller towns, now boast some terrific coffee houses. **Bars and pubs** run the full gamut, from dark rough-and-ready dives to flash, modern concerns. A *crama* is a wine cellar, while a *gradina de vară* or *terasa* is a terrace or garden, usually offering *mititei* as well as beer.

The **national drink** is *țuică*, a tasty, powerful brandy usually made of plums, taken neat. In rural areas, home-made spirits can be fearsome stuff, often twice distilled (to over fifty percent strength, even when diluted) to yield *palincă*, much rougher than grape brandy (*rachiu* or *coniac*).

Most **beer** (*bere*) is European-style lager (*bere blondă*). You'll see Silva (from Reghin), Ciucaș (from Brașov), Ciuc (from Miercurea Ciuc), Timișoreana (from Timișoara) and Ursus (from Cluj – which, to all intents and purposes, is the national beer), while Bergenbier and Eggenburger are acceptable mass-produced brands; you will also occasionally find brown ale (*bere neagră* or *brună*). More excitingly, and as with the craft coffee movement, there is now an increasing number of craft beers on the market, with in excess of thirty micro-breweries around the country; ones to look out for include Zăganu and Sikaru from Bucharest, Hophead from Cluj, and Cazino from Constanța. Beer is usually sold by the bottle, so a request for *o sticlă* will normally get you one of whatever's available; draught beer is known as *halbă*.

Romania's best **wines** – and they are pretty good – are the white Grasa from Cotnari, near Iași; Tămâioasă, a luscious, late-harvested Moldavian dessert wine; blackberryish red Fetească Neagră from Dealu Mare, in Buzău county; and the sweet dessert wines from Murfatlar (notably Merlot and Cabernet Sauvignon, and white Muscat Ottonel). They can be obtained in most restaurants, while some places may just offer you a choice of red or white. Sparkling (*spumos*) wines from Alba Iulia and Panciu (north of Focșani) are very acceptable. Wine is rarely sold by the glass, but it does no harm to ask – *Serviți vin la pahar?*

Festivals

While Romania is not particularly known for its range of festivals, there are a

number of increasingly diverse events taking place throughout the country, especially in music and film. Inevitably, the cities – in particular Bucharest, Cluj and Sibiu – boast the most impressive roster of events, though there remains an excellent spread of local festivals based around strongly rooted seasonal traditions.

Aside from the main festivals listed below, there are dozens of other, more local, events taking place across the country, some of which are also described in the Guide. However, obtaining information on dates and locations for most festivals is notoriously difficult, so contact a tourist office or local agency wherever possible.

APRIL

Pageant of the Juni Braşov, first Sunday after Easter. Colourful parade in which the town's youth don elaborate costumes and ride through town on horseback, accompanied by brass bands.

MAY

Measurement of the Milk Festival Ciucea, first or second Sunday of May. Hugely entertaining gathering in which shepherds compete to see who has the most productive flock.

Europafest Bucharest, mid-May. A dynamic ten days of pop, rock, jazz and blues constitutes the capital's foremost contemporary music festival.

Transylvanian International Film Festival Cluj, end May/beginning June Ⓦ tiff.ro. Romania's premier film festival puts on ten days of top-quality domestic and international movies shown at the city's many picture houses.

JUNE

Bucharest International Film Festival mid-June Ⓦ biff.ro. Now one of the Balkans' most important film gatherings, with a terrific selection of both domestic and foreign screenings.
International Theatre Festival Sibiu, mid-June Ⓦ sibfest. ro. Wonderful open-air jamboree serving up classical, rock and world music, alongside contemporary dance, film, theatre and art.

JULY

Girl Fair of Muntele Găina Avram Iancu, the closest Sunday to July 20. The match-making origins of this boisterous event, taking place atop Mount Găina, have largely given way to a feast of music and dance, though it remains a hugely enjoyable spectacle.
Medieval Arts Festival Sighişoara, last weekend of July Ⓦ sighisoaramedievala.ro. Medieval Transylvania comes to life in the town's atmospheric citadel, with street performers, open-air concerts and handicraft displays.

AUGUST

Untold Festival Cluj, beginning August. Ⓦ untold.com. Romania's largest dance and electronic music festival is a riotous affair taking place over four days in the massive Cluj Arena Stadium as well as other more intimate venues around the city.
Songs of the Olt Călimăneşti, first week of August. Superb gathering of musicians and folklore ensembles from Oltenia performing in the streets of this small spa town.
Anonimul Film Festival Sfântu Gheorghe, mid-August Ⓦ festival-anonimul.ro. International independent film fest with an eclectic mix of long and short films, competitions and open-air screenings, all in a delightful Delta setting.
Transylvanian International Guitar Festival Cluj Ⓦ transilvaniaguitar.ro. Brings together some of the world's foremost guitarists, and stages competitions, lectures and workshops.
Rowmania Tulcea, last weekend of August Ⓦ rowmania. ro. Danube river races in specially designed canoes (*canotca*), set against a backdrop of live music, food and drink along the promenade.

SEPTEMBER

Plai Festival Timişoara, second week of September Ⓦ plai.ro. The "Field Festival" is three days of top-class world and jazz music, plus theatre, art, photography and literature.
George Enescu Festival Bucharest, every odd-numbered year Ⓦ festivalenescu.ro. Romania's most prestigious festival, of any description; three weeks of world-class classical music staged in the stunning surrounds of the Romanian Atheneum.
Sachsentreffen Biertan, or another Saxon village, second or third Saturday of September. Annual gathering of Saxons, both from the region and those returning from Germany.

OCTOBER

Astra Sibiu, mid-October Ⓦ astrafilm.ro. Well-established international festival of documentary film, with presentations and screenings from around the world.
Plum Brandy Festival Vălenii de Munte, end of October. Plum brandy producers from all over Romania gather and compete to see who has the country's finest brew.

DECEMBER

Winter Customs Festival Sighet, end of December. Ancient pagan and Christian beliefs are celebrated in this vibrant coming together of costume, street theatre and music.

Sports and outdoor activities

Romania's sporting pedigree is reasonably strong, thanks largely to the exploits of the tennis player Ilie Nastase and the legendary gymnast **Nadia Comaneci, albeit their success came during the 1970s. Sporting triumph in the 1980s and 1990s came on the football field, with notable achievements by both the country's leading club side, Steaua Bucharest, and the national team, led by the country's best ever player, Gheorghe Hagi. These days, Romania's one major sporting superstar is tennis player Simona Halep.**

Football

In 1986 **Steaua Bucharest** became the first team from behind the Iron Curtain to lift the **European Cup** (the Champions' League), defeating Barcelona on penalties; they reached the final again in 1989, this time losing to AC Milan. Romanian players were only able to move freely to West European clubs after 1990, and by 1992, nine of the national team were playing abroad; this included the mercurial Hagi, dubbed the "Maradona of the Carpathians" – as much for his temperament as for his magical left foot – who went to Real Madrid.

Internationally, Romania's finest hour came at the **1994 World Cup**, where they progressed to the quarter-finals, a tournament at which **Hagi** was arguably the best player. Since Romania's last World Cup appearance in 1998, the only bright spots have been occasional qualifications for the European Championships, the latest in 2016.

For decades the **domestic game** was dominated by the three big Bucharest clubs: **Steaua** (traditionally the army team), **Dinamo** (the police and Securitate) and **Rapid** (rail workers), who regularly carved up the championship between them. In recent years, however, several other, much smaller, clubs – notably CFR Cluj – have muscled in (thanks largely to huge financial investment), winning the national title on the odd occasion. Every town has its stadium (*stadion*), and you should have no problem catching a game. **Matches** are usually played on Saturdays from August to May, with a break from November to February, and **tickets** for league games cost roughly €4–10.

Outdoor activities

The Romanian countryside lends itself perfectly to a multitude of **outdoor activities**, from hiking the dramatic peaks of the country's many mountain ranges and hitting the pistes in Poiana Braşov to tracking an astonishing range of birds in the Danube Delta or wildlife in the Carpathians.

Although two-thirds of Romania is either plains or hills and plateaux, the country's geography is dominated by **mountains**, which almost enclose the "Carpathian redoubt" of Transylvania, and merge with lesser ranges bordering Moldavia and Maramureş. Throughout these areas, there are opportunities to pursue several outdoor activities – hiking, skiing, caving and even shooting rapids. The **Danube Delta** is a totally different environment – of which only one-tenth is dry land – which attracts some three hundred species of bird during the spring and autumn migrations. A wide number of tours and trips are offered by a host of agencies (see page 24) in the UK, and, to a lesser degree, in North America and Australasia.

Hiking

Crisscrossed by an intricate nexus of forestry tracks and waymarked paths, the beautiful and unspoiled Romanian countryside offers some of the most enjoyable **hiking** anywhere in Europe, with trails to suit all abilities. Cutting across the country are the sinuous Carpathian mountains – a continuation of the Alps – whose best-known range is the Făgăraş (see page 142), between Braşov and Sibiu in the south of Transylvania, harbouring more than seventy lakes and Romania's most elevated peaks, the highest of which is Moldoveanu (2544m). However, it's the Retezat and Piatra Craiului mountains (see pages 120 and 138) which present Romania's most challenging and scenically rewarding hikes, the former spotted with dozens of glacial lakes, and the latter a small but stunning limestone ridge. Nearby, just south of Braşov, the Bucegi massif (see page 120) offers shorter and easier walks among dramatic crags, caves and waterfalls.

Less well known options include the remote and lovely Rodna mountains (see page 304), near the Ukrainian border in Maramureş; the more modest Bucovina hills (see page 256) – studded with glorious painted monasteries – immediately east; and, closing off the western end of the Transylvanian plateau, the Apuseni mountains (see page 206), which offer comparatively undemanding hikes and great karstic phenomena such as limestone caves, potholes and gorges. Scattered around all these ranges are **cabanas**, convivial places offering basic accommodation and sometimes meals.

Skiing

Although the **skiing** is nowhere near as advanced as in many other European countries, Romania's ten or so small, rapidly developing ski resorts are well equipped, efficient, safe and inexpensive. The most popular ski centre is Poiana Braşov (see page 136), thanks to its superior slopes and facilities; it also has the longest season (Nov–March/April). Elsewhere, there's good skiing at Predeal, Buşteni and Sinaia, a chain of resorts along the lovely Prahova valley (see page 120); Borşa in Maramureş (for beginners); Păltiniş south of Sibiu; Semenic in southwestern Transylvania; and Durău/Ceahlău on the edge of Moldavia. Most of Romania's pistes are rated "medium" (red) or "easy" (blue), but the major resorts have at least one "difficult" (black) run each.

Wildlife-watching

As Europe's most extensive wetland, and the world's largest continuous reedbed, the Danube Delta (see page 342) is heaven for **birdwatchers**. Millions of birds winter here, or stop over during the spring (March–May) and autumn (Aug–Oct) migrations – a unique and colourful concentration of different species, including heron, little egrets, red-breasted geese, the endangered pygmy cormorant and Europe's largest pelican colonies. The best times for viewing are April to early June and August to early October, but you'll be rewarded with a fantastic birding experience at any time of year. Agencies arrange **boat tours** down the main Delta channels, and their Tulcea offices may sometimes rent small boats, which are the only means of penetrating the backwaters where most of the birds nest. Canoes, kayaks or rowing boats are best for exploration, and it's also fun to negotiate with a local fisherman for a boat (*Pot sînchiriez o barcă?*) – he'll probably act as rower and guide.

No less exhilarating is wildlife-tracking in the Carpathian mountains, which typically entails exploration of the forests looking for markings and tracks made by large carnivores. Specially designed forest hideouts are used for **bear-watching**, and there's a reasonable chance of catching sight of these captivating animals, though you're unlikely to have the same degree of success with the magnificent **grey wolf**.

Travel essentials

Addresses

Addresses are written as Str. Eroilor 24, III/36 in the case of apartment buildings, ie Street (Strada) of Heroes, number 24, third floor, apartment 36. Some blocks have several entrances, in which case this is also given, eg scara B. Each district of Bucharest has a *sector* number, while in some towns each

---

TOP FIVE HIKES

Bucegi: Babele Cabana to Bran. See page 126

Bucovina: Putna monastery to Humor monastery. See page 266

Făgăraş: Bâlea Lac to Sâmbata monastery. See page 142

Piatra Craiului ridge See page 138

Retezat: Pietrele to Cheile Butii. See page 178

---

district (*cartier*) is named. In small villages, houses simply have a number and no street name. Streets, boulevards (*bulevardul*), avenues (*calea* or *şoseaua*) and squares (*piaţa*) are commonly named after national heroes like Stephen the Great – Ştefan cel Mare – or Michael the Brave – Mihai Viteazul – or the date of an important event, such as December 1, 1918, when Transylvania was united with the Old Kingdom.

Costs

Generally, costs are still reasonably **low** in Romania, particularly when it comes to dining and public transport. If you're on a tight budget, you could get by on around £25/€28/US$32 a day, staying in a hostel or private accommodation, eating in cheap diners and using public transport. Those on a moderate to mid-range budget (cheap to mid-range hotels, better restaurants and car rental) can expect to spend around £70/€78/US$90 a day. If you want to splash out on the best hotels, restaurants and car rental, count on spending upwards of £110/€125/US$140. In Bucharest, and, to a lesser degree, the coast, costs are appreciably higher than elsewhere.

Museum **admission** charges are extremely low, the typical fee being €1–2, though some of the major attractions (such as the Palace of Parliament and Peleş Castle) will charge several times that amount – moreover, these attractions often levy a fee (usually more than the cost of the entrance itself) for the use of cameras/camcorders. The more expensive hotels, flights, car rental and excursions are sometimes priced in **euros**, but must usually be paid for in **lei**.

Crime and personal safety

Romania remains generally **safe**, and it's unlikely that you'll have any problems; violent crime against tourists is almost nonexistent and petty crime rare.

EMERGENCY NUMBERS
For all **emergency services** dial ☎112.

The major thing to watch out for is **pickpockets**, in particular on public transport in Bucharest, where thieves are adept at relieving tourists of their belongings; wearing a (hidden) moneybelt is advisable. Take care on overnight trains, shutting the door of your sleeper compartment as securely as you can (there are no locks) and keeping valuable possessions close at hand.

If your **passport** goes missing while in Bucharest, telephone your consulate immediately; anywhere else, contact the police. Thefts and other losses can be reported to the police who will issue the paperwork required for insurance claims back home, though only slowly and with painstaking bureaucratic thoroughness.

One of the legacies of Ceaușescu's systematization policy of the 1980s, when people were forced to move into concrete apartment blocks, was that thousands of dogs were abandoned and left to roam the streets. The problem is not nearly as bad as it once was, but stray dogs remain a common nuisance, particularly in the cities, and you'll see plenty of them wandering the roadsides; should you feel threatened, just walk on slowly.

Culture and etiquette

Although **tipping** is not obligatory, it is polite to round the bill up to a convenient figure in restaurants and when taking a taxi. In common with much of the Balkans, **smoking** is commonplace, but is now officially banned in any indoor public space, including all restaurants, cafés and bars.

Most public **toilets** are acceptable enough, and usually charge a small fee, particularly in the larger train stations. In any case, you should carry a supply of paper. "*Barbați*" means men and "*Femei*" means women.

It's rare for Romanian men to subject **female tourists** to **sexual harassment**. Romanians (both male and female) are highly tactile, so you may find yourself being prodded more than you care for. Most trouble is alcohol-fuelled, so it's best to avoid going alone to any but the classiest bars. Within earshot of other people, you should be able to scare away any local pest by shouting *Lasați-ma in pace!* ("Leave me alone!") or calling for the *poliția*.

Electricity

220 volts; a standard continental adaptor enables the use of 13-amp, square-pin plugs.

Entry requirements

Citizens of the EU, US, Canada, Australia and New Zealand can enter Romania with just a passport and may stay in the country for up to ninety days. Similarly, most other European citizens can enter the country without a visa, though can only stay for thirty days. However, **visa requirements** do change, so it's always advisable to check the current situation before leaving home.

Health

No **vaccinations** are required for Romania, although having hepatitis A, polio and typhoid boosters would be wise if you're planning to stay in remote areas where hygiene can sometimes be an issue. There's a **reciprocal health agreement** between Romania and Western countries (including the UK, US, Canada, Australia and New Zealand), so emergency treatment (excluding drugs) is free.

Summers can be blisteringly hot, particularly along the coast, so make sure you take a high-factor **sun cream**, and strong **insect repellent** if visiting the Danube Delta. Conversely, conditions in the **mountainous regions**, particularly at higher altitudes, can present potential dangers – take appropriate clothing, sufficient provisions and equipment, and keep an eye on the weather. **Tap water** is safe to drink practically everywhere, though bottled water (*apă minerala*) is widely available. Avoid any contact with **stray dogs**, as there's a very slight risk of **rabies**.

All towns and most villages have a **pharmacy** (*farmacie*), where the staff – in the big towns at least – may understand English, French or German. Pharmacies are typically open Monday to Saturday from 9am to 6pm, though all cities and most towns should have at least one that's open 24 hours – failing that, dial the emergency number displayed in the pharmacy window.

In Bucharest, the British and American embassies can supply the address of an English-speaking **doctor or dentist**, and there's a special clinic for treating foreigners. In **emergencies**, dial ☎112 or ask someone to contact the local casualty (*stația de salvare*) or first-aid (*prim ajutor*) station, which should have ambulances. Each county capital has a fairly well-equipped county **hospital** (*spital judeţean*), but **hospitals** and health centres (*policlinics*) in smaller towns can be poor.

ROUGH GUIDES TRAVEL INSURANCE

Rough Guides has teamed up with WorldNomads.com to offer great travel insurance deals. Policies are available to residents of over 150 countries, with cover for a wide range of adventure sports, 24hr emergency assistance, high levels of medical and evacuation cover and a stream of travel safety information. Roughguides.com users can take advantage of their policies online 24/7, from anywhere in the world – even if you're already travelling. And since plans often change when you're on the road, you can extend your policy and even claim online. Roughguides.com users who buy travel insurance with WorldNomads.com can also leave a positive footprint and donate to a community development project. For more information, go to ⓦ roughguides.com/travel-insurance.

Insurance

Even though EU health-care privileges apply in Romania, you'd do well to take out an **insurance policy** before travelling to cover against theft, loss, and illness or injury. A typical travel insurance policy usually provides cover for the loss of baggage, tickets and – up to a certain limit – cash or cheques, as well as cancellation or curtailment of your journey. Most of them exclude dangerous sports unless an extra premium is paid.

Internet

Wi-fi is widespread and invariably excellent. Nearly all **hotels** – of any description – offer free wi-fi for their guests, as do hostels. Similarly, most restaurants and cafés, even in the smaller towns, also have wi-fi, and it's also becoming increasingly available in public spaces, especially in cities. With wi-fi so ubiquitous, **internet cafés** are now the exception rather than the rule, and even then most of these places are full of kids playing games, while connections can be slow; expect to pay around €1 per hour.

Laundry

There are several **laundries** in Bucharest, but elsewhere they can be almost impossible to find; some hostels have laundry facilities, but otherwise it's usually a choice between washing clothes yourself or paying a hotel to do it.

LGBTQ travellers

The communist regime was relentlessly **homophobic**, and sexual relations between consenting adults of the same sex were illegal. The law against homosexuality was repealed in 2000, but the majority of the population remains largely **unsympathetic** towards the gay and lesbian community, and there are very few manifestations of gay life, even in Bucharest. That said, the first **Gay Pride** was held in Bucharest in 2004 and is now an annual event (now called Bucharest Pride) usually taking place in late May or early June. Elsewhere, **Gay Film Nights** is a gay and lesbian film festival held in Cluj, though it's not an annual event and the date does change. **Accept** (ⓣ 021 252 5620, ⓦ acceptromania.ro) is a Bucharest-based organization involved in the promotion of gay and lesbian activities in Romania, and they also offer counselling and HIV testing services.

Mail

Post offices (*poştă*) are usually open Monday to Friday from 7am to 8pm, and on Saturdays from 8am to noon. **Stamps** (*timbru*) and prepaid envelopes (*pliicuri*) can be bought here. Sending mail home from Romania costs around €0.70 to overseas destinations – and takes about a week to Britain, and two weeks to North America and Australasia.

Maps

Nearly all the best **maps** of Romania are published outside the country, but they are available through most good map outlets, including a few shops in Romania itself. The country map published by the ADAC (the German motorists' association) is very detailed (at 1:500,000), as is the Szarvas/Kárpátia/ Top-O-Gráf atlas (including city plans), which can be bought at Shell fuel stations in Romania (and through Stanfords bookstore in the UK). Other quality maps are produced by Falk (1:1,000,000), Cartographia (1:750,000) and Szarvas/Kárpátia/Dimap (1:700,000), along with a Kümmerley & Frey map of Romania and Bulgaria (1:1,000,000), and the GeoCenter Euromap (1:800,000), which includes Moldova. Cartographia and Falk also publish good **maps of Bucharest**, while Top-O-Gráf/Freytag & Berndt produce maps of Transylvanian cities such as Cluj. DIMAP also publishes maps of most tourist areas.

The maps produced by the **national tourist offices** are fairly poor, though just about adequate for **motoring**, but the campsite and cabana maps are useful for hikers. There are also good **hiking maps** of the major mountain massifs, by Editura Pentru Turism and Abeona in Bucharest and Editura Focul Viu in Cluj (available from bookstores as well as tourist offices). Hikers should also look out for the booklet *Invitaţie în Carpaţi*; the text is Romanian, but it contains detailed maps of the region's 24 main hiking areas, showing trail markings, huts, peaks and so on. It's reproduced in *The Mountains of Romania* (see page 404).

Media

Western newspapers are almost impossible to track down in Romania, though the more upmarket hotels may have same-day editions. Of the **listings magazines**, *Bucharest In Your Pocket* (Ⓦ inyourpocket. com/bucharest) is by far the most informative and up to date, and often features spin-off guides to other parts of the country.

Romanian **television** offers the standard diet of news, soaps and gameshows. Once restricted to two hours a day, with half of that devoted to Ceauşescu's feats (ironically, it was TV that played a crucial role in his overthrow), these days there is no shortage of programming. Any decent hotel will have satellite TV, with CNN and BBC World most likely to feature. More annoyingly, many restaurants deem it necessary to feature huge plasma screens. Like many of the foreign-language programmes on Romanian TV, films at the **cinema** are shown in their original language with Romanian subtitles.

Money

Romania's unit of **currency** is the leu (abbreviation RON) – meaning "lion" (plural **lei**). Coins (*bani*) come in denominations of 1, 5, 10 and 50; and there are notes of 1, 5, 10, 50, 100, 200 and 500 lei. The **exchange rate** is currently around L5.30 to £1, L4.60 to €1 and L4.10 to US$1 – for current rates, check Ⓦ xe.com.

If you need to **change money**, you're best doing so at a bank (*banca*); these are generally open Monday to Friday between 9am and 4 or 5pm. Alternatively, private exchange offices (*casa de schimb valuta*) can be found in just about every town and city; in the bigger cities they are everywhere, and some may even be open 24 hours. You may well be asked to show your passport, so it's always worth taking. As a rule, neither exchange offices nor banks charge commission. If taking **cash**, a modest denomination of euros, pound sterling or US dollar bills is advisable. Make sure that you get rid of any unwanted lei before

you leave the country, as it's unlikely you'll be able to change them once outside Romania.

Cash machines (*Bancomats*) are ubiquitous, even in the smallest towns, including many railway stations. **Credit cards** are accepted in most of the better hotels, restaurants and shops.

Opening hours and public holidays

With the exception of shopping malls, which are usually open 9am to 10pm, **shops** are generally open from 9 or 10am to 6 or 8pm on weekdays, with department stores and some food stores opening from 8am to 8pm Monday to Saturday and from 8.30am to 1pm on Sunday. If you're trying to sort out flights, visas or car rental, be aware that many **offices** are closed by 4pm.

Museums (*muzeu*) are generally open Tuesday to Sunday from 9 or 10am to 5 or 6pm, though some do also close on Tuesdays. For the opening hours of **post offices**, **banks**, **pharmacies and restaurants**, see the relevant sections in town accounts of the Guide.

Public holidays in Romania are on **January 1 and 2** (New Year); Easter Monday; **May 1** (Labour Day); **December 1** (National Day) and **December 25 and 26** (Christmas).

Phones

Public payphones are still to be found in most places, but the near-ubiquity of mobile phones means they are seldom used. Following the abolition of roaming charges within the EU in 2017, UK and Irish travellers can use their home mobile data and call allowance while in Romania at no extra cost. However, monthly data allowances when abroad may vary from those at home, so check with your provider. It is not yet known whether free roaming will still be in place if and when the UK leaves the EU. Travellers from other countries should check with their own network providers about the cheapest way to make mobile phone calls while abroad; roaming charges are likely to be high. If staying for any length of time you might as well buy a local SIM card from one of the main Romanian mobile phone providers (Orange, Telekom, Vodafone), which typically cost around €5 and which you can then top up by voucher, available from phone shops or street kiosks. All mobile numbers are designated by a phone code beginning with ❶ 07. Calling a mobile from within Romania, you must dial all the numbers; calling from abroad, you need to drop the "0".

Time

Romania is two hours ahead of **GMT**, seven hours ahead of **Eastern Standard Time** and ten hours ahead of **Western Standard Time**: clocks go forward one hour for the summer at the same time as in other European countries.

Tourist information

Ensure that you pick up as much **information** as possible before you leave your own country, as getting hold of it in Romania is nigh on impossible; even where you do, there's very little available in English. The **Romanian tourist board** has a site at ⓦ romaniatourism.com, with a UK branch at 12 Harley St, London W1G 9PG (☎ 020 7224 3692), and another at 600 Third Avenue, Suite 224, New York, NY 10016 (☎ 212 545 8484). Frustratingly, tourist offices in Romania remain few and far between, though most, but by no means all, cities will have one; you may also chance upon the odd one in smaller towns – opening hours tend to be Monday to Friday 9am to 4pm, though in the bigger cities and along the coast, some keep longer hours and also open at weekends. Elsewhere, most places should have an agency (usually more concerned with selling package trips) where you might be able to extract some basic advice, and possibly a map.

Travellers with disabilities

Very little attention has been paid to the needs of people with disabilities in Romania, and there's no sign of any change in attitude. Getting around is a major problem, as **public transport** is often inaccessible and cars with hand controls are not available from rental companies. The only place where facilities for disabled people are likely to be anything like comprehensive are in some of the classier hotels. Perhaps the best solution is to book a stay in a spa, where there should be a degree of level access and some awareness of the needs of wheelchair users. Make sure you carry a **prescription** for any drugs you need, including the generic name in case of emergency, and spares of any special clothing or equipment, as it's unlikely you'll find them in Romania.

Travelling with children

Most of the better-quality hotels cater for **children**, while most restaurants (at least those of a decent standard) should be able to provide highchairs for

CALLING HOME FROM ABROAD

To make an international call, dial the international access code (in Romania it's 00) then the destination's country code, before the rest of the number. Note that the initial zero is omitted from the area code when dialling the UK, Ireland, Australia and New Zealand from abroad.
Australia international access code + 61
New Zealand international access code + 64
UK international access code + 44
US and Canada international access code + 1
Ireland international access code + 353
South Africa international access code + 27

younger children and babies. Most car rental firms provide child or baby seats for a small extra charge. Most supermarkets, and many smaller shops, are well stocked with the requisite nappies (diapers), baby food and so on.

In big coastal resorts and at Poiana Braşov there are **kindergartens** for the benefit of holidaymakers. The most obvious child-friendly destinations are the beaches along the coast, which, on the whole, are clean and safe, while there are enough water parks and fairgrounds in most resorts for further stimulation. You'll also find that most large towns have a good puppet theatre (*Teatrul de Păpuşi*). Rail transport is free for under-5s, and half-price for under-10s.

Work in Romania

Opportunities for working in Romania are relatively few. The most traditional form of work abroad, **teaching English**, is one option. The British Council (ⓦ jobs.britishcouncil.org) recruits TEFL teachers and provides information about study opportunities and teacher development programmes in Romania. **International House** (ⓦ ihworld.com) also offers **TEFL** training and recruits for teaching positions. They have branches in Bucharest, at Str. Lanariei 93–95 (☎ 0723 900 204, ⓦ ih.ro), and in Timişoara, at B-dul C.D. Loga 11 (☎ 0256 490 593, ⓦ ihtm.ro). The **TEFL** website (ⓦ tefl.com) is also worth a look. A few organizations offer work in Romanian **orphanages**: these include Volunteer Romania (ⓦ volunteerromania. co.uk) and Projects Abroad (ⓦ projects-abroad.org).

Bucharest

THE ROMANIAN ATHENAEUM

1 Bucharest

For many people, initial impressions of Bucharest (București), a sprawling, dusty city of some two million people, are less than favourable. It's Romania's centre of government and commerce, and site of its main airport, so most visitors to the country will find themselves passing through the city at some point, but its chaotic jumble of traffic-choked streets, ugly concrete apartment blocks and monumental but mostly unfinished communist developments is often enough to send most travellers scurrying off to the more obvious attractions further north. Yet it's a city that rewards patience, with a raft of terrific museums, first-rate restaurants and bars, and, behind the congested main arteries, some superb architecture and abundant greenery.

The architecture of the old city, with its cosmopolitan air, was notoriously scarred by Ceaușescu's redevelopment project in the 1980s, which demolished an immense swathe of the historic centre – including many religious buildings and thousands of homes – and replaced it with a concrete jungle, the compellingly monstrous **Centru Civic**. The centrepiece of this development was an enormous new palace for the communist leader, now known as the **Palace of Parliament**, which is Bucharest's premier tourist attraction.

The heart of the city is the **Piața Revoluției**, the scene of Ceaușescu's downfall and site of the old Royal Palace – now home to the superb **National Art Museum**, housing a fine collection of Romanian medieval art. It lies halfway along Bucharest's historic north–south axis, the **Calea Victoriei**, which is still the main artery of city life; the city's main junction, however, is the **Piața Universității**, scene of major events immediately after the 1989 revolution. To the south of here lies the scruffy but atmospheric **historic centre**, which these days owes its popularity to the welter of bars and restaurants crammed into its agreeably tatty streets.

North from Piața Victoriei, along the broad sweep of Șoseaua Kiseleff, lie Bucharest's two best museums – the **Museum of the Romanian Peasant**, with its marvellous exhibits on peasant life and superbly reconstructed buildings, and the **Village Museum**, an assemblage of vernacular buildings garnered from Romania's multifarious regions There's plenty of greenery to explore, too – most obviously the tranquil **Cișmigiu Gardens** in the heart of the city, and the more expansive **Herăstrău Park**, on the shores of the lake of the same name.

From Bucharest, there are excellent rail and road connections to the rest of the country, but local bus and train services to the towns and villages in the immediate vicinity are often limited or tortuous. There are, however, some enjoyable visits to be had just outside the capital, most notably the lake and monastery at **Snagov**, the palace at **Mogoșoaia** and the village of **Clejani**, known for its outstanding Gypsy music.

Brief history

According to legend, Bucharest was founded by a shepherd called **Bucur**, who built a settlement in the Vlăsia forest. It was recorded as a nameless "citadel on the Dâmbovița" in 1368, and named as Bucharest in an edict from the time of Vlad the Impaler (ruled 1456–76). Over the centuries, both Târgoviște and Bucharest have served as the **Wallachian capital**, but the latter finally secured its claim in 1659, its position at the convergence of the trading routes to Istanbul outweighing the defensive advantages of Târgoviște's location in the Carpathian foothills.

Highlights

① National Art Museum The country's biggest and best collection, the highlight of which is the spectacular Gallery of Romanian Medieval Art. See page 46

② Concert at the Romanian Atheneum The city's most beautiful building is also the venue for regular top-class classical concerts, including the biannual George Enescu Festival. See pages 48 and 78

③ Museum of the Romanian Peasant A superb display of traditional textiles, ceramics, carvings and replica buildings. See page 54

④ Palace of Parliament Take a tour around the colossal centrepiece of Ceauşescu's Centru Civic. See page 55

⑤ The Old Town Escape the downtown concrete jungle with a ramble around the crumbling streets of Bucharest's old quarter, replete with cafés and bars. See page 59

⑥ Herăstrău Park Combine a leisurely stroll through Bucharest's largest and greenest park with a cruise on the adjoining lake. See page 66

⑦ Village Museum A wonderful assemblage of dwellings, churches, windmills and other structures from all over Romania. See page 68

⑧ Artisan coffee Grab your caffeine kicks at *Origo* or *Steam*, just two of the new breed of craft coffee shops to have hit Bucharest. See page 76

HIGHLIGHTS ARE MARKED ON THE MAPS ON PAGES 44 AND 50

1

As the boyars (nobles) moved into the city they built **palaces** and **churches** on the main streets radiating from the centre; these streets were surfaced with timber baulks and known as "bridges" (*poduri*). Despite earthquakes and periodic attacks by Turks, Tatars, Austrians and Russians over the course of its early history, the city continued to grow and to modernize.

From the nineteenth century to communism

New **boulevards** were driven through the existing street pattern in the 1890s, after the style of Haussmann's Paris, and they still form a ring road and the main north–south and east–west axes of the city today. Most of the major buildings, such as the **Romanian Atheneum** and the **Cercul Militar**, were designed by French or French-trained architects and built in the years immediately before World War I. It was around this time that the city was dubbed the "Paris of the East", as much for its hectic and cosmopolitan social scene as for its architecture. The Romanian aristocracy was among the richest and

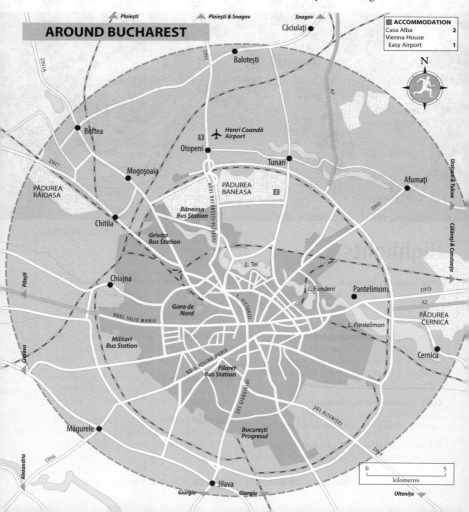

AROUND BUCHAREST

■ ACCOMMODATION	
Casa Alba	2
Vienna House	
Easy Airport	1

most extravagant in Europe, but this lifestyle depended on the exploitation of the poor, and in Bucharest the two coexisted in what Ferdinand Lasalle described as "a savage hotchpotch", with beggars waiting outside the best restaurants, and appalling slums within a few steps of the elegant boulevards.

By 1918, the city's population had grown to 380,000 and roads such as Podul Mogoşoaiei, Podul de Pământ and Podul Calacilor were widened, paved and renamed as the Calea Victoriei, Calea Plevnei and Calea Rahovei respectively, in honour of the battles of the 1877–78 War of Independence from Turkey. After **World War II**, the city was ringed with ugly apartment buildings, first in areas such as "Red Griviţa", which the Allies had bombed flat (aiming for the rail yards), then expanding into the surrounding countryside.

A massive **earthquake** in 1977 reduced large parts of the city to rubble and left over 1500 people dead. While this prompted the construction of several major city projects, including a new metro system and an airport, it also provided Ceauşescu with the perfect excuse to implement his megalomaniac vision for the city. In 1984, and in order to create a new **Centru Civic**, Ceauşescu had most of the area south of the centre levelled, which entailed the demolition of thousands of homes, as well as churches, a monastery and a hospital.

The revolution and the post-communist era

In December 1989, the city found itself at the centre of the most violent of the popular **revolutions** sweeping across Eastern Europe that year; nearly three hundred people were killed in the uprising. Ceauşescu's execution did not, however, mark a complete end to the violence, and the following summer similar scenes erupted when miners from the Jiu valley were brought in to stamp out student protests against the government, which resulted in a further seven deaths. While there are still tangible reminders of Ceauşescu's legacy, most obviously in the form of the many lumbering, half-abandoned buildings scattered around the city, the post-communist era has brought back conspicuous consumption to the city, evidenced by the proliferation of luxury hotels, a raft of new shopping centres and a stream of new restaurants, bars and clubs; indeed, the recent emergence of a genuinely dynamic culinary – and coffee – culture is one of the most exciting things to hit the city in years.

Piaţa Revoluţiei and Piaţa Enescu

Piaţa Revoluţiei (Square of Revolution), a large, irregularly shaped square sliced down the middle by Calea Victoriei, was created in the 1930s to ensure a protective field of fire around the Royal Palace in the event of revolution. While Romania's monarchy was overthrown by other means, the square fulfilled its destiny in 1989, when the Ceauşescus were forced to flee by crowds besieging Communist Party headquarters; two days of fighting left the buildings around the square burnt out or pockmarked with bullet holes – with the conspicuous exception of the Central Committee building, which was at the centre of the storm.

Across the road from the Royal Palace, you can't fail to notice the 13m-high **statue of King Carol I** on horseback, erected as recently as 2010, though not without controversy. The original statue, by renowned Croatian sculptor Ivan Meštrović, was melted down by the communists in 1948 following the abolition of the monarchy (conveniently, the bronze was reused to make a statue of Lenin), though this current edition is widely regarded as far inferior to Meštrovíc's, in part because the authorities failed to reach agreement with the Meštrovíc family over the use of the sculptor's original sketches. Behind the statue is the **University Library**, totally gutted in December 1989 – with the loss of some half a million books – but now rebuilt and housing offices. **Piaţa Enescu**

1

BUCHAREST

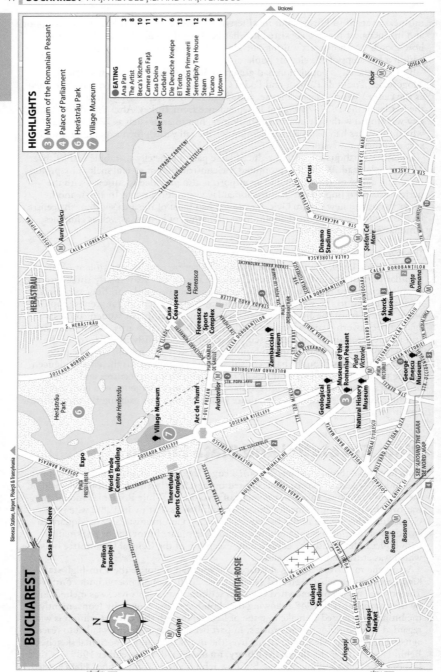

HIGHLIGHTS

3 Museum of the Romanian Peasant
4 Palace of Parliament
6 Herăstrău Park
7 Village Museum

● EATING

Ana Pan	3
The Artist	8
Beca's Kitchen	10
Camera din Față	11
Casa Doina	4
Ciorbărie	7
Die Deutsche Kneipe	6
El Torito	13
Mesgios Primaverii	1
Serendipity Tea House	12
Steam	2
Tucano	9
Uptown	5

N

Urziceni

Lake Tei

Lake Floreasca

Lake Herăstrău

HERĂSTRĂU

Herăstrău Park 6

Obor

Circus

Dinamo Stadium

Ştefan Cel Mare

Piaţa Romană

Piaţa Dorobanţilor

Storck Museum

Casa Ceauşescu

Floreasca Sports Complex

Zambaccian Museum

Museum of the Romanian Peasant 3

Piaţa Victoriei

Natural History Museum

Geological Museum

Aviatorilor

Piaţa Presei Libere

Arc de Triumf

Village Museum 7

Expo

World Trade Centre Building

Tineretului Sports Complex

Casa Presei Libere

Pavilion Expoziţiei

George Enescu Museum

SEE "AROUND THE GARA DE NORD" MAP

Gara Basarab

Basarab

GRIVIŢA-ROŞIE

Giuleşti Stadium

Crîngaşi Market

Crîngaşi

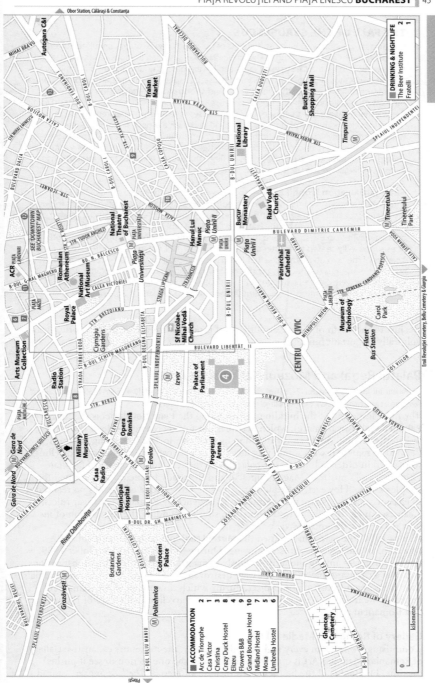

Obor Station, Călăraşi & Constanţa

DRINKING & NIGHTLIFE	
The Beer Institute	2
Fratelli	1

ACCOMMODATION	
Arc de Triomphe	2
Casa Victor	1
Christina	3
Crazy Duck Hostel	8
Elizeu	4
Flowers B&B	9
Grand Boutique Hotel	10
Midland Hostel	7
Moxa	5
Umbrella Hostel	6

Autogara C&I

MIHAI BRAVU

Traian Market

National Library

Bucharest Shopping Mall

Timpuri Noi

Tineretului Park

Bucur Monastery

Radu Vodă Church

National Theatre of Bucharest

Hanul Lui Manuc

Piaţa Unirii I

Piaţa Unirii II

SEE DOWNTOWN BUCHAREST MAP

Romanian Atheneum

National Art Museum

Piaţa Universităţii

ACR

Piaţa Unirii

Patriarchal Cathedral

Piaţa Libertăţii

Museum of Technology

Royal Palace

Cişmigiu Gardens

Sf Nicolae-Mihai Vodă Church

Carol Park

Filaret Bus Station

Arts Museum Collection

Radio Station

CENTRU CIVIC

Izvor

Palace of Parliament

BULEVARD LIBERTĂŢII

Military Museum

Opera Română

Progresul Arena

Gara de Nord

Casa Radio

Municipal Hospital

Botanical Gardens

Cotroceni Palace

Grozăveşti

Politehnica

Ghencea Cemetery

River Dâmboviţa

Eroii Revoluţiei Cemetery, Bellu Cemetery & Giurgiu

kilometres

1

THE FALL OF THE CEAUŞESCUS

Romania's revolution was the most dramatic of the popular revolts that convulsed Eastern Europe in 1989. On the morning of December 21, 1989, a staged demonstration – organized to show support for the **Ceauşescu** regime following days of rioting against it in Timişoara – backfired spectacularly. Eight minutes into Ceauşescu's speech from the balcony of the Central Committee building, part of the eighty-thousand-strong crowd began chanting "Ti-mi-şoa-ra"; the leader's shock and fear were televised across Romania before transmissions ceased. From that moment, it was clear that the end of the Ceauşescu regime was inevitable. Though the square was cleared by nightfall, larger crowds poured back the next day, emboldened by news that the army was siding with the people in Timişoara and Bucharest. Strangely, the Ceauşescus remained inside the Central Committee building until noon, when they scrambled aboard a helicopter on the roof, beginning a flight that would end with their **execution** in a barracks in Târgovişte, on Christmas Day.

The revolution was tainted by the suspicion of having been stage-managed by the **National Salvation Front (FSN)** that took power in the name of the people. The FSN consisted of veteran communists, one of whom later let slip to a journalist that plans to oust the Ceauşescus had been laid months before. Among the oddities of the "official" version of events were Iliescu's speech on the Piaţa Revoluţiei at a time when "terrorist" snipers were causing mayhem in the square, and the battle for the Interior Ministry, during which both sides supposedly ceased firing after a mysterious phone call. Given the hundreds of genuine "martyrs of the revolution", the idea that it had been simply a ploy by Party bureaucrats to oust the Ceauşescus was shocking and potentially damaging to the new regime – so the secret police were ordered to mount an investigation, which duly concluded that while manipulation had occurred, the Russians, Americans and Hungarians were to blame.

sits just to the north of Piaţa Revoluţiei, and is notable for a couple of historically and culturally important buildings.

Palatul Regal and Muzeul Naţional de Artă

Muzeul Naţional de Artă: Calea Victoriei 49–53 • Wed–Sun: May–Sept 11am–7pm, Oct–March 10am–6pm • €3.50 each for Gallery of Romanian Art and European Gallery, €5.50 for both galleries • ☎ 021 313 3030, ⓦ mnar.arts.ro

The most imposing of the buildings surrounding the Piaţa Revoluţiei is the former **Palatul Regal** (Royal Palace), which occupies most of the western side of the square. When the original single-storey dwelling burnt down in 1927, the king, Carol II, decided to replace it with something far more impressive. The surrounding dwellings were razed in order to build a new palace, with discreet side entrances to facilitate visits by Carol's mistress, Magda Lupescu, and the shady financiers who formed the couple's clique. However, the resultant sprawling brownstone edifice has no real claim to elegance and the palace was spurned as a residence by Romania's postwar rulers, Ceauşescu preferring a villa in the northern suburbs pending the completion of his own palace in the Centru Civic.

Since 1950, the palace has housed the **Muzeul Naţional de Artă** (National Art Museum) in the Kretzulescu (south) wing. During the fighting in December 1989, this building was among the most seriously damaged of the city's cultural institutions, and over a thousand pieces of work were destroyed or damaged by gunfire and vandals. After a massive reconstruction project, during which time many of the items were repaired, the museum reopened and now holds a marvellous collection of European and Romanian art.

Gallery of Romanian Medieval Art

Comprising works from every region of the country, the museum's exhaustive **Gallery of Romanian Medieval Art** is quite spectacular, and the one section to see if pushed for time. Highlights of the first few halls include a fresco of *The Last Supper* – a mid fourteenth-century composition retrieved from St Nicholas's Church in Curtea de Argeș – and a carved oak door from 1453 with shallow figurative reliefs from the chapel of Snagov monastery (which no longer exists). The Monastery Church in Curtea de Argeș (see page 100) is represented by some remarkably well-preserved icons and fresco fragments, while there are also some quite beautiful Epitaphios, liturgical veils embroidered on silk or velvet which were usually used for religious processions. Among the most memorable pieces is a sumptuous gilded Kivotos (a vessel used for holding gifts) in the shape of an Orthodox church, which was presented to Horezu monastery by Constantin Brâncoveanu, and some exquisite miniature wood-carved processional crosses from Moldavia, chiefly remarkable for the astonishing detail contained within – typically, scenes from the life of Christ. The standout items from the latter halls are the church door and iconostasis retrieved from Cotroceni Palace (see page 63), fresco fragments from Enei Church (see page 61), and a wood-carved iconostasis by Brâncoveanu from Arnota monastery. Trumping both of these, however, is a 6m-high, nineteenth-century carved walnut iconostasis taken from the Prince Șerban Church in Bucharest, albeit without the icons. The workmanship is extraordinary, featuring, in the finest detail, angels and cherubs, double-headed eagles and warriors on horseback.

Gallery of Romanian Modern Art

Up on the second floor, the **Gallery of Romanian Modern Art** features the best of the country's nineteenth- and twentieth-century painters, not least Romania's greatest artist, Nicolae Grigorescu (see page 90). Look out for his brilliant character paintings, *The Turk, Jew with a Goose, Gypsy Girl from Ghergani* and the dramatic *The Spy*. There are no less sizeable contributions from Aman and Andreescu, both of whom were heavily influenced by the Barbizon School. Pallady, meanwhile, is represented by a clutch of typically suggestive nudes.

There's a terrific assemblage of sculpture, too, by the likes of Storck (*Mystery*) and Paciurea, whose grisly *God of War* is just one of several Chimeras. Most visitors, though, come to see the work of Constantin Brâncuși, Romania's one truly world-renowned artist (see page 105). Using various media, Brâncuși displayed his versatility in a sublime body of work, including the beautiful white marble head of a sleeping woman (*Sleep*), a bronze, weeping nude (*The Prayer*) and the limestone-carved *Wisdom of the Earth*.

European Art Gallery

Though not nearly as exciting as the Romanian galleries, the **European Art Gallery** (entrance A1) nevertheless contains an impressive array of work spanning the fourteenth to the twentieth centuries. Divided by schools, it has particularly fine paintings from Italian and Spanish artists, including Tintoretto's *The Annunciation* and Cano's beautifully mournful *Christ at the Column*. Among the line-up of predominantly lesser-known artists is a sprinkling of superstar names, including El Greco (three paintings, the pick of which is a colourful *Adoration of the Shepherds*), Rubens (*Portrait of a Lady*), Monet (*Camille* and *Boats at Honfleur*) and a painting apiece by Renoir (*Landscape with House*) and Sisley (*The Church at Moret in Winter*). Look out, too, for Pieter Bruegel's spectacularly detailed and gruesome *Massacre of the Innocents*. The most prominent piece of sculpture is Meštrovíc's (see opposite) superb bronze bust of King Carol I. No less impressive is the decorative art section, which contains one of the museum's oldest items, the Reichsadlerhumpen Goblet from Bavaria, dating from 1596.

Communist Party Headquarters

The southeastern corner of Piața Revoluției is dominated by the former **Communist Party Headquarters**, a Stalinist monolith that now houses government offices. The

1

balcony where Ceaușescu delivered his last speech is surprisingly near ground level, and quite unmarked by bullet holes. Ironically, it was from the same spot, two decades earlier, that Ceaușescu had drawn cheers of approval for his denunciation of the Soviet invasion of Czechoslovakia, and made his vow that Romania would defend its own independence, casting himself as a "maverick communist" whom Western leaders could embrace. It was a delusion that persisted almost until the end; as Romanians point out, the honorary knighthood bestowed on Ceaușescu by Buckingham Palace in 1978 was only revoked after the revolution began.

There are now two very contrasting memorials dedicated to those who died in the revolution: directly in front of the headquarters is a marble **memorial** with the inscription *Glorie Martirilor Nostri* ("Glory to our Martyrs"). Close by, and more controversially (both for its lack of symbolism and style) is the oddly named **Monument of Rebirth**, a 25m-high marble column with what looks like a bird's nest sprouting from its upper reaches (it's known locally as the "Olive on a Stick"). Below, the semicircular wall is inscribed with the names of those who perished.

Diagonally across the street from the memorial is one of the city's more startling buildings; the glass-and-steel tower emerging from within a brick shell was the **former headquarters of the Securitate**, until it was mostly destroyed during the fighting in 1989; it's now the headquarters of the Union of Romanian Architects. Glance upwards at the surrounding residential buildings and you'll see that many of these are still quite heavily pockmarked with bullet holes.

Biserica Crețulescu

A short walk down from the Royal Palace stands Bucharest's most celebrated church, the **Biserica Crețulescu** (Crețulescu Church), founded in 1722 by the boyar Iordache Crețulescu and his wife Safta, the daughter of Wallachia's great seventeenth-century ruler, Constantin Brâncoveanu. High and narrow with mock arches, bricks laid in saw-toothed patterns around the towers and elaborate carvings over the entrance, the church is built in the style created by Brâncoveanu, who set out to forge a distinctive national genre of architecture (see page 106). Heavily damaged during both the 1940 earthquake and the fighting in 1989, the frescoes have largely remained intact; the interior ones – including those of the church founders – were completed by Tattarescu in 1859, while the one on the porch, which features scenes from the Apocalypse, was painted by an unknown artist.

Athénée Palace Hilton

The northern side of Piața Enescu is filled by the **Athénée Palace Hilton**, which has been one of the most prestigious hotels in Bucharest since it was built in 1912. For decades the hotel was also a notorious hotbed of espionage, beginning in the 1930s when the liveried staff and almost all the characters who populated the lobby spied for the king's police chief, for the Gestapo or for British Intelligence. Symbolic of that fevered, corrupt era, Bucharest's elite would sometimes party here through the night while police were shooting strikers in the "Red" Grivița district only a kilometre or so away. During the early 1950s the hotel was extensively refurbished as an "intelligence factory", with bugged rooms and tapped phones, to reinforce the reports of its informers and prostitutes.

Ateneul Român

Laying fair claim to being Bucharest's finest building, the **Ateneul Român** (Romanian Atheneum) is a magnificent Neoclassical structure built in 1888 by French architect Albert Galleron. It's fronted by six elegant columns, behind which, in the peristyle, are five circular mosaics, each one depicting a Romanian ruler, including King Carol I. Funded almost entirely by Bucharest's citizens, after the original patrons ran out of money, this is one of the few remaining circular auditoriums in Europe, the magnificent interior featuring a rampantly *fin-de-siècle* dome decorated with lyres. If at all possible, you should try and catch a **concert** by the resident George Enescu Philharmonic Orchestra (see page 78), named after Romania's beloved national composer. Piaţa Enescu, the tidy little **park** in front, features a statue of Enescu, who first performed at the Atheneum in 1898.

Muzeul Theodor Aman

Str. Rosetti 8 • Wed–Sun 10am–6pm • €1.50 • ☎ 021 314 5812, ⓦ muzeulbucurestiului.ro

One of many memorial houses of notable artists dotted around the city, the charming **Muzeul Theodor Aman**, in between Piaţa Enescu and Piaţa Revoluţiei, celebrates the life and work of the eponymous Romanian painter and sculptor who trained in Paris before returning to be the first director of the Bucharest Art College. A somewhat academic painter, Aman (1831–91) was a leading member of the group of Francophile intellectuals (with fellow Romanians the painter Gheorghe Tattarescu and the sculptor Karl Storck) that dominated Bucharest's cultural life in the late nineteenth century. Built in 1868 to Aman's own designs and decorated by himself and Storck, the Neoclassical house contains a wealth of genre and landscape paintings as well as family portraits, plus some finely sculpted wooden furniture, including chests and tables.

Calea Victoriei

Originally laid out in the late seventeenth century as a wood-paved avenue named Podul Mogoşoaiei, **Calea Victoriei** (Avenue of Victory) has been Bucharest's most fashionable street since wealthy boyars first built their residences along it. The arrival of the boyars encouraged Bucharest's most prestigious shops to open along the avenue and, after it was repaved and took its present name in 1918, strolling along the avenue became *de rigueur*, causing the writer Hector Bolitho to remark that "to drive down the Calea Victoriei between twelve and one o'clock will prove you a provincial or a stranger". Along the street were "huddles of low, open-fronted shops where Lyons silk and Shiraz carpets were piled in the half-darkness beside Siberian furs, English guns and Meissen porcelain", while lurking in the side streets were starving groups of unemployed, lupus-disfigured beggars and dispossessed peasants seeking justice in the capital's courts. An avenue of marked contrasts, the quieter northern end still seems verdant and sleepy with touches of Old-World elegance, while to the south it becomes an eclectic jumble of old apartment buildings, upmarket hotels, shops and banks. The entire length of Calea Victoriei is run through with one of the city's best cycle lanes (itself a rarity in Bucharest), which, encouragingly, the locals seem to have taken to with relish.

Muzeul Naţional George Enescu

Calea Victoriei 141 • Tues–Sun 10am–5pm • €1.50 • ☎ 021 318 1450, ⓦ georgeenescu.ro

Fronted by a superb clamshell-shaped porte-cochere from the early twentieth century, topped with fluttering cherubs, the fabulous Cantacuzino Palace – built in 1905 for the erstwhile mayor of Bucharest and two-time prime minister, Gheorge Cantacuzino – now houses the **George Enescu Museum**, in honour of Romania's greatest composer (see page 394). Just two rooms are packed with memorabilia and personal effects – his childhood violin, coat and tails, batons, manuscripts, concert programmes and some excellent photographs, including one of him with his protégé, Yehudi Menuhin; here,

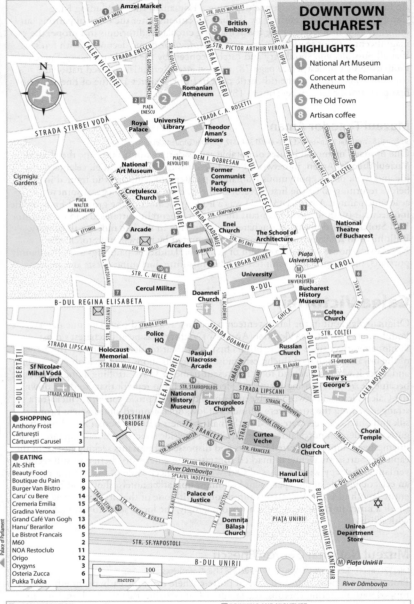

DOWNTOWN BUCHAREST

HIGHLIGHTS

1. National Art Museum
2. Concert at the Romanian Atheneum
5. The Old Town
8. Artisan coffee

SHOPPING

Anthony Frost	2
Cărturești	1
Cărturești Carusel	3

EATING

Alt-Shift	10
Beauty Food	7
Boutique du Pain	8
Burger Van Bistro	9
Caru' cu Bere	14
Cremeria Emilia	15
Gradina Verona	4
Grand Café Van Gogh	13
Hanu' Berarilor	16
Le Bistrot Francais	5
M60	2
NOA Restoclub	11
Origo	12
Orygyns	3
Osteria Zucca	6
Pukka Tukka	1

ACCOMMODATION

Ambasador	1	Little Bucharest		
Athénée Palace Hilton	2	Old Town Hostel	10	
Cişmigiu	7	Novotel	5	
Grand Hotel Continental	4	Rembrandt	9	
Intercontinental	3	Tania-Frankfurt	11	
K&K Hotel Elisabeta	6	Z Boutique	8	

DRINKING AND NIGHTLIFE

Abel's Wine Bar	10	Fabrica de Bere Bună	1	
Bordello	9	Green Hours 22 Club	2	
Control	6	Mojo	8	
Corks	7	Tribute	3	
Dianei 4	5			
English Bar	4			

too, is his death mask and moulds of his hands. There's also a lengthy audiovisual presentation, which is as informative about Romanian folk music as it is about Enescu's work.

1

Enescu (1881–1955) didn't live in the palace itself, but, for a brief period in 1945–46, did live in the **pavilion** to the rear, which has been left *in situ*, hence its rather tatty state. It's surprisingly modest, featuring a music room with piano, a bathroom and just two bedrooms, one of which contains Enescu's desk, briefcase and glasses.

Muzeul Colecţiilor de Arta

Calea Victoriei 111 • Sat–Wed: May–Sept 11am–7pm; Oct–March 10am–6pm • €3.50 • ☎ 021 212 9642, ⊚ mnar.arts.ro

Occupying the early nineteenth-century Romanit Palace is the **Muzeul Colecţiilor de Arta**, (The Arts Collection Museum), second only to the National Gallery in terms of importance. Each of the thirty or so rooms is named after the collector (typically intellectuals and professors) who passed on the works to the museum. As with the National Gallery, the majority of Romania's foremost artists are represented here, for example an entire room is given over to Grigorescu – keep an eye out for the sublime *Shepherd at Sunset* and a rare self-portrait. Similarly, Aman, Tonitza and Pallady (*White Tulips, Nude in a Chaise Longue*) feature heavily. No less enjoyable are some of the country's lesser known painters, such as Iosif Iser whose landscapes, particularly of Dobrogea and the interiors of Spain, are a delight, and expressionist Corneliu Baba, whose bold, often intense, portraits (*The Mad King*) comprise the bulk of his work here. Elsewhere, though much less exciting, there are Japanese prints and drawings, Oriental art and French furnishings.

Cercul Militar

Dominating the intersection of Calea Victoriei and Bulevardul Regina Elisabeta is the Neoclassical **Cercul Militar** (Army House), which replaced the previous monastery church of Sărindar in 1912; this is remembered in the name of the fountain directly in front. It was originally built to cater to the social, cultural and educational needs of the Romanian army, and remains an important centre for military activity, including the army's offices and library, as well as being used for banquets, so it's not usually possible to see the interior.

Biserica Doamnei

Calea Victoriei 28

Diagonally across from the Cercul Militar, an alleyway just beyond *Pizza Hut* slips off to the courtyard of the picturesque **Biserica Doamnei** (Church of the Lady), built in 1683 under the orders of Princess Maria, wife of Prince Şerban Cantacuzino. Architecturally, the most impressive aspect is the porch, featuring a thick-set stone portal and octagonal stone pillars, the first of their kind in Bucharest – albeit now set behind an ugly wood-and-glass frame. The interior is gloomy, but it's just about possible to make out some of the frescoes, by Greek painter Constantin Mina, most interestingly a painting of the Crucifixion on the western wall, which was only recently revealed following a lengthy restoration project.

Pasajul Macca-Vilacrosse

A few paces down from the Doamnei Church, an inconspicuous portal leads into the **Pasajul Macca-Vilacrosse** (Macca-Vilacrosse Passage), a covered arcade built in 1891 and named after Xavier Villacrosse, Bucharest's chief architect at that time, and

Mihalache Macca, the son-in-law of the building's architect Felix Xenopol. Its glass roof and gracefully curved arcade give an idea of why Bucharest once claimed to be the "Paris of the East", although its grandeur has faded badly over the years. The passage retains a high number of cafés and bars – most offering hookah pipes – though none particularly stand out. Walking through the passage brings you out into Strada Eugeniu Carada and the Old Town.

Muzeul Naţional de Istorie

Calea Victoriei 12 • Wed–Sun 10am–6pm • €2.50 • ☎ 021 315 8207, ⓦ mnir.ro

Housed in the former Post Office building is the **Muzeul Naţional de Istorie** (National History Museum), though really it's nothing of the sort, owing to the fact that a much-vaunted overhaul seems destined never to happen and the majority of exhibits are not on display.

If you do decide to visit, the one worthwhile section is the basement vault, which exhibits Romania's **national treasures**, a dazzling display of gold and jewellery, from prehistoric finds (see particularly the elaborate Coţofeneşti helmet) to Queen Marie's crown and the casket said to hold her heart; also look out for the sceptres of Ferdinand I and Carol II. More spectacular, however, is a glittering, gold-bound tetraevangel (ancient manuscript), printed in 1693 by Sibiu goldsmith Sebastian Hann, which was ordered and paid for by Constantin Brâncoveanu for his monastery at Horezu (see page 107). Elsewhere, the modern **lapidarium** in the courtyard features a rather haphazard assemblage of Greek, Roman and medieval tombstones and carvings, as well as plaster casts from Trajan's Column covered with depictions of his Dacian campaigns. Otherwise, there's invariably a good temporary exhibition in the capacious foyer, albeit usually only with Romanian captions.

Casa de Economii şi Consemnaţiuni and Râul Dâmboviţa

Worth more than a passing glance is the **Casa de Economii si Consemnaţiuni** (National Savings Bank, known as the CEC), directly opposite the National History Museum. Designed by French architect Paul Gottereau in the 1890s, its grimy Neoclassical facade features an impressive high arch linked together by two solid Corinthian pillars; if anything, the interior is even more impressive, starring a wonderful glass-domed ceiling.

From here, it's a short walk to the **Râul Dâmboviţa** (River Dâmboviţa). An old saying has it that whoever drinks the "sweet waters" of the Dâmboviţa will never wish to be parted from Bucharest, to which one nineteenth-century traveller retorted that anyone who ever did "would be incapable of leaving the city for ever afterwards". Always prone to flooding, the Dâmboviţa was canalized in the 1880s and now passes underground at Piaţa Unirii. The river marks the abrupt transition from the fabric of the old city to the arbitrarily imposed pattern of the Centru Civic.

Piaţa Victoriei

The northern end of Calea Victoriei culminates in **Piaţa Victoriei**, a vast circular space around which drivers maniacally jockey for position. The buildings surrounding the square are your archetypal Socialist monstrosities, not least the main government building, the hulking **Palaţul Victoria**, completed in 1944 but even then already showing a chilly Stalinist influence in its design. The main reason you're likely to wind up here is for the clutch of fine museums nearby.

1

Muzeul de Istorie Naturală Grigore Antipa

Șos Kiseleff 1 • April–Oct Tues–Sun 10am–8pm; Nov–March Tues–Fri 10am–6pm, Sat & Sun 10am–7pm • €4.50 • ☎ 021 312 8826, ⓦ antipa.ro

One squarely for the kids, the **Muzeul de Istorie Naturală Grigore Antipa** (Natural History Museum) is named after the noted conservationist and founder of Romanian ichthyology; indeed, Antipa (1867–1944) was the museum's director for more than half a century. The museum's centrepiece is *Deinotherium gigantissimus*, a 4.5m-high fossil elephant from the late Miocene period unearthed in Vaslui County, Moldavia, in 1890 and believed to be the largest of its kind in the world. The basement covers Romania's wonderfully diverse geographical regions, from the Delta and Black Sea Coast to the Carpathians, while the ground floor is devoted to world fauna; among the obligatory selection of stuffed animals, keep your eyes peeled for some rather gruesome-looking reptilia, like the hellbender salamander and the saw-scaled viper. Meanwhile, the geology section on the top floor plays a distant second fiddle to a beautiful collection of butterflies and insects.

Muzeul Țăranului Român

Șos Kiseleff 3 • Tues–Sun 10am–6pm • €2 • ☎ 021 317 9661, ⓦ muzeultaranuluiroman.ro

Housed in an imposing, neo-Brâncovenesc redbrick building, the **Muzeul Țăranului Român** (Museum of the Romanian Peasant) ranks a very close second to the Village Museum (see page 68) as the top museum in the city. On show is a wonderful display of traditional peasant artefacts from all regions of Romania, including colourfully woven linen and textiles, carvings, ceramics and a fabulous hoard of icons painted on wood and glass. Nothing, though, beats the exquisite collection of two thousand **miniature clay toys**, many shaped into zoomorphic forms, such as cuckoos, horses and lions, as well as bird- and dog-shaped pipes. Of the several impressively reconstructed **buildings** dotted around the museum, the most eye-catching is an eighteenth-century windmill from Hațeg county, an enormous contraption that took three years to piece back together. Similarly, a thick-set peasant dwelling from Gorj county, comprising three rooms, a loft for storage and a superb porch/balcony, took around a year to reconstruct. There is also an incomplete timber church from Hunedoara, around which lie some of its furnishings – altar doors, a holy table, church bells and so on. A wooden church, typical of those found in Maramureș, stands on a neat patch of grass at the rear of the museum. One of the best places in the city for souvenirs, the museum **shop** sells a beautiful assortment of rugs, costumes and other folksy objects, while, to the rear, there's a pleasant café. Look out, too, for the monthly **craft fairs** held in the courtyard.

The entire premises were actually occupied by the Museum of Communist Party History until 1990, and there are still remnants from this time in the small **basement**, which contains a curious collection of paintings and busts of former communist leaders. Notably, there's nothing pertaining to Ceaușescu – most images of the dictator were destroyed following his execution.

Muzeul Storck

Str. Vasile Alecsandri 16 • Wed–Sun 10am–6pm • €1.50 • ☎ 021 317 3889, ⓦ muzeulbucurestiului.ro.

One of Bucharest's lesser-known delights, the **Muzeul Storck** keeps a superb collection of sculptures by Frederic Storck (1872–1942), whose father, Karl, was the first Romanian teacher of the discipline. Highlights include the dramatic and sensuous *Lubire* (Love), as well as numerous family portraits, such as a self-portrait in stone and a lovely white marble bust of his wife, Cecilia-Cuțescu Storck (1879–1969), whose work was no less admired than her husband's. Indeed, Cecilia's pieces dominate the collection, from a series of expressive nudes to the vast wall compositions, though many of these are now sadly effaced. There are also one or two pieces on display by Karl Storck. The house itself, built to an English-Flemish design in 1911, but now badly in need of renovating, was originally used as a workshop; the Storcks actually lived in the house next door.

The Centru Civic

In 1971, Ceauşescu visited North Korea and returned full of admiration for the grandiose avenues of Kim II Sung's capital, Pyongyang. Thirteen years later, inspired by what he had seen, Ceauşescu set out to remodel Bucharest as "the first socialist capital for the new socialist man", and to create a new administrative centre which was to be "a symbolic representation of the two decades of enlightenment we have just lived through". In truth, of course, this **Centru Civic** was meant to embody the state's authority and that of Ceauşescu himself. Implementing this megalomaniac vision entailed the demolition of a quarter of Bucharest's historic centre (about five square kilometres), said to be slums damaged by the 1977 earthquake, but in fact containing nine thousand largely untouched nineteenth-century houses, whose forty thousand inhabitants were relocated in new developments on the outskirts of the city. There was worldwide condemnation of this vandalism, particularly since many old churches were to be swept away. Though some of the churches were in the end reprieved, they are now surrounded by huge modern apartment blocks and are separated from the urban context that gave them meaning. The core of the complex was largely completed by 1989, just in time for the dictator's overthrow.

Uniting the two halves of the Centru Civic is **Bulevardul Unirii** which, at 4km long and 120m wide, is slightly larger – intentionally so – than the Champs-Élysées, after which it was modelled. Midway along is **Piaţa Unirii** (Square of Union), an oversized expanse of concrete dominated by traffic, and notable only as a key metro interchange, as the site of the city's main department store (the Unirea) and as the best place to view the extraordinary Palace of Parliament.

Palatul Parlamentului

Calea 13 Septembrie 1 • Daily: March–Oct 9am–5pm (last tour 4.30pm); Nov–Feb 10am–4pm (last tour 3.30pm) • Standard tour €8.50, standard tour plus underground €9.50; use of cameras €7 • ☎ 021 311 3611, ⓦ cic.cdep.ro • passport required; entrance is from gate A3, right-hand side as you face it; Metro Izvor

Dominating the entire project from the western end of Bulevardul Unirii is the colossal **Palatul Parlamentului** (Palace of Parliament), claimed to be the second-largest administrative building in the world – after the Pentagon – measuring 270m by 240m, and 86m high. It epitomizes the megalomania that overtook Ceauşescu in the 1980s; here he intended to house ministries, Communist Party offices and the apartments of high functionaries. Built on the site of the former Spirei Hill, which was razed for this project, the sheer size of the building can only be grasped by comparison with the toy-like cars scuttling past below. It has twelve storeys, four underground levels (including a nuclear bunker), a 100m-long lobby and 1100 rooms, around half of which are used as offices while the remainder are redundant. The interiors are lavishly decorated with marble and gold leaf, and there are 4500 chandeliers (11,000 were planned), the largest of which weighs 1.5 tonnes, but the decoration was never finished due to the Ceauşescus' ever-changing whims. They were demanding patrons, allowing little more than a technical role to the architects, of which there were around seven hundred – one staircase was rebuilt three times before they were satisfied.

This huge white elephant was officially known as the Casa Republicii, then as the Casa Poporului, but more popularly as the Casa Nebunului (Madman's

1

House), before taking on its present name. The new government spent a long time agonizing about an acceptable use for it, and in 1994 it was finally decided to house the Senate and Parliament here; it is now also used for international conferences.

Two main **tours** are available. The standard one is a 45-minute trek through ten of the most dazzling, most representative or simply the largest of the halls, such as the extraordinary, glass-ceilinged **Sala Unirii** (Unification Hall), where legendary Romanian gymnast Nadia Comaneci was married in 1996. One of the last chambers you're led to is the Alexandru Ioan Cuza room, whose **balcony** offers defining views of the city. The second tour covers the above but also takes in the basement. The palace is so popular (particularly with tour groups) that you'd do well to time your visit for the start or the end of the day.

Muzeul Naţional de Artă Contemporană

Calea 13 Septembrie 1 • Wed–Sun: May–Sept noon–8pm; Oct–April 10am–6pm • €3.50 • ☎ 021 318 9137, ⓦ mnac.ro • Entrance is from gate E4, left-hand side as you face the palace and it's the third entrance on your right; bus #136 stops just outside

Located in the building's west wing (to the rear of the palace) is the **Muzeul Naţional de Artă Contemporană** (National Museum of Contemporary Art). Accessed via a specially constructed glass annexe and external elevators (which, as they take you up, give you some idea of the breathtaking scale of this building), it's a superbly designed space covering four floors. All the works on display are temporary (typically two- or three-month rotating programmes), featuring both Romanian and international artists, and mostly take the form of multimedia installations (including large-screen projections), sculptures, collages, montages and photographic displays.

Templul Coral

Str. Sf Vineri 9–11 • Mon–Thurs 9am–3pm, Fri & Sun 9am–1pm • Free • ☎ 021 312 2196

A short walk uphill from Piaţa Unirii stands the **Templul Coral** (Jewish Choral Temple), a striking redbrick structure of 1857 that, today, is the city's main working synagogue, serving a Jewish community that has shrunk to around three thousand from its pre-World War II figure of some seventy thousand. Serious damage was inflicted upon the temple during both the 1940 earthquake and the 1941 pogrom, while (just for good measure) the ceiling collapsed during the 1977 earthquake. Now magnificently restored, the lavish interior is a riot of colour and also holds the original 1860 chandeliers.

Sinagoga Mare

Str. Vasile Adamache 11 • Mon–Thurs 8.30am–3pm, Fri & Sun 8.30am–1pm • Free

Deliberately hidden away behind a jumble of grey apartment blocks, the **Mara Sinagoga** (Great Synagogue) is also known as the Polish Synagogue on account of its construction by the Ashkenazi-Polish community in 1846. While the exterior is bland in the extreme, the interior manifests an appealing mix of Baroque and Rococo, its walls lined with panels illustrating the Bucharest pogrom of January 21–23 1941, which left 125 dead.

Muzeul de Istorie Evreilor

Str. Mămulari 3 • Currently closed; hours normally Mon–Thurs 9am–2pm, Fri & Sun 9am–1pm • Free

The **Templul Unirea Sfântă** (Holy Union Temple), built in 1836 houses the **Museum of Jewish History**, a comprehensive collection of objects, most of which were accumulated by Moses Rosen, Romania's Chief Rabbi between 1964 and 1994. These include books, paintings and photos, as well as a handful of Jewish ritual objects, though the most impressive exhibit is an elegant sculpture commemorating the lives of some 350,000 Jews deported in 1944. At the time of writing, the temple was undergoing an extensive renovation programme, with no indication as to when it might reopen.

Biserica Mihai Vodă

Str. Sapienţei 2

Hidden away among the rows of new buildings that make up the Centru Civic are numerous tiny Orthodox churches thankfully reprieved from demolition. In Bucharest, you'll frequently find churches in inappropriate places – such as the courtyards of apartment buildings – where the city planners have built around them, but here the churches seem even more disregarded and incongruous than elsewhere.

The most striking example of this is the **Biserica Mihai Vodă** (Mihai Vodă Church), built by Michael the Brave in 1591, though its present appearance dates from 1838. In 1985, to make way for the Centru Civic development, the church was moved some 280m east on rails to its present location, an undertaking which entailed the demolition of the church's medieval cloisters and ancillary buildings. Not dissimilar to the Old Court Church (see page 60) in appearance, the Biserica Mihai Vodă manifests alternate bands of red brick and plaster, with rounded mouldings, while the interior stars a superb wood-carved iconostasis.

Biserica Sfinţii Apostoli

Str. Sf Apostoli 33A

Another of the Centru Civic's well-concealed churches is the bright, white-painted **Biserica Sfinţii Apostoli** (Holy Apostles Church), founded by Matei Basarab in 1636 and embellished in 1715 with a fine little steeple by Ştefan Cantacuzino, a portrait of whom is just about visible (to the left as you enter) among the many otherwise well-preserved interior paintings. Here too is a portrait of Basarab, as well as a richly adorned iconostasis.

Biserica Domniţa Bălaşa

Str. Sf Apostoli 60

Located just behind the Palace of Justice – in slightly more civilized surrounds – is the late nineteenth-century **Biserica Domniţa Bălaşa** (Lady Bălaşa Church), one of the most popular churches in the city. Named after Constantin Brâncoveanu's sixth daughter, Bălaşa – a statue of whom stands in the garden in front of the church – this orange-brick edifice is actually the third church on this site, the previous two having burnt down in the eighteenth century. The interior, one of the most complete in the city, features a beautiful wooden cross-shaped chandelier.

Mânăstirea Antim

Str. Antim 29

On the southern side of Bulevardul Unirii is the **Mânăstirea Antim** (Antim monastery), a large walled complex built in 1715 upon the orders of polymath Antim Ivireanul, erstwhile patriarch of the Orthodox Church in Wallachia. The centrepiece of this tranquil space is a beautifully proportioned redbrick church, featuring a superb stone portal and sculpted wooden doors, the latter crafted by Antim himself. Inside, the icons are well worth admiring, as is the unusual stone-sculpted iconostasis. Today, the monastery is home to barely a handful of monks.

1

Patriarhia

Str. Dealul Mitropoliei

The seat of the Romanian Orthodox Church, the **Patriarhia** (Patriarchal Cathedral) was built from 1655 to 1668 by Constantin Şerban and is, broadly speaking, based on designs for the cathedral in Curtea de Argeş (see page 100). The interior contains the most dazzling of the city's iconostases, as well as a couple of exquisitely carved side altars. Completing the set of buildings here is the Brâncoveanu-commissioned **campanile** – it was here that Barbu Catargiu, Romania's first prime minister, was assassinated in 1862 – the **Patriarchal Palace** (built in 1875) and the former **Palace of the Chamber of Deputies** (1907).

Biserica Bucur

Str. Radu Voda 33

It is generally acknowledged that **Biserica Bucur** (Bucur Church) was built around 1720 by monks from the Radu Voda monastery opposite, though some contend that it was first built in 1416 on the foundations of an even earlier church, possibly fifth-century – which would make it the city's oldest. Named after Bucur the Shepherd, the city's founder, this sweet yet little-known church is positioned atop a pronounced rise and squeezed, incongruously but inevitably, in between a couple of apartment blocks. A gorgeous, stone-carved portal and wooden door leads though to a spare, all-white interior which retains just a few slim wooden columns.

Parcul Tineretului and Oraselul Copiilor

Oraselul Copiilor Daily 10am–10pm • Metro to Constantin Brâncoveanu • **Bike rental** €1/hr, €3.50/day

From Piaţa Unirii, Bulevardul Dimitrie Cantemir runs south about 1km to the much older Calea Şerban Vodă, the route taken by merchants and Turkish officials heading for the Sublime Porte of Constantinople, the Sultan's Court. The two roads cover the site of Podul Şerban Vodă, destroyed by a fire in 1825, and meet at the north end of **Parcul Tineretului** (Youth Park), which is easily the best place in the city to take kids. Here you'll find several playgrounds, a lake, a go-kart track and the **Oraselul Copiilor** funfair, containing assorted rides, a miniature train and a big wheel, as well as more hair-raising rides for adults only (all rides are paid for separately). You can also **rent bikes** at the entrance to the park.

Parcul Carol

Rowing boats daily 10am–8pm • €3/hr

Inaugurated in 1906 on the occasion of the fortieth anniversary of King Carol's coronation, and venue for that year's Bucharest Fair, **Parcul Carol** is a more formal public space than Tineretului. Its tatty southern end is the site of a brutalist monument, which once held the remains of Gheorghiu-Dej, Petru Groza and other communist leaders; these were removed following the revolution and replaced by soldiers felled during World War I. This gives way to a lovely green space bisected by a long promenade and a smaller lake where, during the summer, you can rent rowing boats.

Muzeul Tehnic

Wed–Sun 10.30am–6pm • €2 • ☎ 021 336 9390

A short walk north of the lake, housed inside the last remaining pavilion from the Bucharest Fair, is the **Muzeul Tehnic** (Museum of Technology), an oddball place intended to assert Romania's technological fecundity, particularly several "firsts", such as the metal-bodied aeroplane (1912) and the streamlined motor car (1923). Ironically, it's the names of British, French and German firms that dominate the collection.

Cimitirul Eroii Revoluţiei and Cimitrul Bellu

Calea Şerban Vodă • Metro to Eroii Revoluţiei

Ten minutes' walk south of Parcul Carol along Calea Şerban Vodă, at the junction of the highways to Olteniţa and Giurgiu, is the **Cimitirul Eroii Revoluţiei** (Heroes of the Revolution Cemetery); buried here, in neat rows of identical white marble graves, are more than 280 "Heroes of the Revolution", gunned down by "terrorists" in 1989. Despite the traffic roaring by, it's an affecting place, and even more poignant given that some of the victims were as young as 13. To the left of the cemetery stands the Church of the Martyr Heroes.

Neighbouring **Cimitrul Bellu** (Bellu Cemetery) is the resting place of some of Romania's greatest writers, artists and academics, most importantly Mihai Eminescu (see page 245), who is buried in plot 9 next to another leading Romanian writer, Mihail Sadoveanu. Look out, too, for the graves of the painter Aman (plot 33) – a simple white marble tomb with his signature across the top – and the much-loved comic actor Toma Caragiu (plot 4), who was killed in the 1977 earthquake; his caricature-like bust is guaranteed to raise a smile.

Cimitirul Ghencea

B-dul Ghencea • Daily 8am–6pm • Bus #173 from Eroii Revoluţiei metro station or bus #385 from Piaţa Unirii (nearest stop is at the junction of Drumul Sării and Calea 13 Septembrie)

Nicolae Ceauşescu and his wife Elena are buried in **Cimitirul Ghencea** (Ghencea Cemetery), some 5km southwest of the city. Though the couple were originally buried under pseudonyms, their graves – little more than grubby mud plots – were subsequently marked with their own names. However, doubts existed for years as to whether the Ceauşescus were actually buried here, and in 2010 both were exhumed (Nicolae in the black coat he was wearing when executed), primarily to satisfy the remaining family members. They were subsequently reburied together in an altogether more dignified tomb, with an inscription that simply reads "Preşedintele Republicii Socialiste România". The grave is located on the left side of the central alley before the chapel, but in any case, the guards are well used to people seeking out the plot and will happily show you where it is. The grave of Ceauşescu's son, Nicu (who is buried with his sister, Zoia), is close by, just opposite the church on the left-hand side. Next door is a **military cemetery**, a surreal forest of propeller blades marking the graves of airmen.

The Old Town

Bound by Piaţa Unirii to the south, Calea Victoriei to the west and Bulevardul I.C. Brătianu to the east, the **Old Town** – an area more commonly known as Lipscani – was mercifully spared Ceauşescu's bulldozers, and it now offers a welcome respite from the concrete monotony of the Centru Civic. The main thoroughfare is Strada Lipscani itself, a lively street named after the merchants from Leipzig who traded here in the eighteenth century. An otherwise picturesque and agreeably ramshackle maze of streets and decrepit houses, Bucharest's oldest neighbourhood has been undergoing painfully slow regeneration for years, and while many parts of it remain desperately run-down, the sheer volume of restaurants, cafés and bars in the area makes it *the* place to party in town.

1

Palatul Curtea Veche

Str. Franceză · ☎ 021 314 0375, ⊕ muzeulbucurestiului.ro

Looking at the **Palatul Curtea Veche** (Old Court Palace) today, it's hard to believe that this is the oldest feudal monument in Bucharest. It was here that Prince Vlad Țepeș – "Vlad the Impaler", otherwise known as Dracula (see page 398) – built a citadel in the fifteenth century, though the building was severely damaged during Țepeș's attempt to regain the throne in 1476 (in which he succeeded, only to be murdered a few months later). In the centuries that followed, the palace functioned as the residence for numerous Wallachian rulers, including Basarab, Cantacuzino and Brâncoveanu, but it also endured numerous earthquakes and fires; it was subsequently auctioned off as wasteland. Thus, little remains of the ancient citadel – just some of the walls, arches and shattered columns, most of which was uncovered during excavations in the late 1960s. The Palace has been under wraps for some time now, pending extensive restoration, with no official timescale as to when it might reopen.

Biserica Curtea Veche

Str. Franceză

Adjoining the Palatul Curtea Veche is the handsome **Biserica Curtea Veche** (Old Court Church), established by Mircea Ciobanul ("Mircea the Shepherd") from 1546 to 1558, which makes it one of the oldest churches in Bucharest – though it was significantly enlarged in 1715 by Cantacuzino. It is a typical example of sixteenth-century Wallachian church architecture, with horizontal bands of brick facing and rows of small niches beneath the cornice. Inside, a dazzling iconostasis brightens up an otherwise gloomy interior.

Hanul lui Manuc

Str. Franceză 62

Opposite the Old Court Church stands Bucharest's most famous hostelry, **Hanul lui Manuc** (Manuc's Inn). Built as a *caravanserai* (inn) in 1808 by a wealthy Armenian, Manuc-bey Mirzaian, it was the site of talks for the Treaty of Bucharest, which put an end to the Russo-Turkish War of 1806–12. The wooden galleries and stairways within the interior courtyard are certainly worth a look, while the restaurant that now consumes this vast space is not too bad at all, even if it is slightly overpriced; indeed, the setting, if nothing else, certainly pulls in the punters.

Biserica Stavropoleos

Str. Stavropoleos 4

The Old Town's most arresting site is the diminutive **Biserica Stavropoleos** (Stavropoleos Church). Built between 1724 and 1730 for the first Phanariot ruler, Nicolae Mavrocordat, the church has a gorgeous, almost arabesque, facade, including a columned portico carved with delicate tracery – stalks, leaves and stylized flowers. The interior has a splendid iconostasis, featuring, in the upper part, medallions of the prophets and, in the middle and lower portions, scenes from the life of Christ. Have a look up at the beautiful dark-blue, star-flecked cupola. Afterwards, take a wander through the stone-built cloister, with its Neo-Roman columns and arches dating from 1904; the cloister was built on the site of the former Stavropoleos inn, which itself was demolished in the late nineteenth century. A few paces down from the church, you'll find the *Caru' cu Bere* ("The Beer Cart"), an ornately decorated tavern dating from 1875 that has long been one of the city's most popular restaurants (see page 76).

Piața Universității

Piața Universității is the focus of city life and traffic, and was one of the key sites of the 1989 revolution, as evinced by the numerous memorials (note the ten stone crosses in the road island) to those killed at Christmas 1989 and in June 1990. The latter marks the date on which miners, under Iliescu's orders, drove out students who had been on hunger strike since April 30, causing the square to be nicknamed Piața Tiananmen. The most poignant of the memorials is the black cross and wall plaque at B-dul Bălcescu 18, some 200m north of the *InterContinental* hotel – this marks the spot where the first victim, Mihai Gătlan, aged 19, fell at 5.30pm on December 21.

Teatrul Național

B-dul Nicolae Bălcescu 2 • See page 79

The *InterContinental* aside, the most imposing building on Piața Universității is the **Teațrul National** (National Theatre), which has been subject to several reworkings since its inauguration in 1973 (it had been in a previous location prior to this). In the 1980s, it became the pet project of Elena Ceaușescu, who had the facade rebuilt twice, and the roof once, before she was satisfied, the result being an undistinguished pile that resembled an Islamicized reworking of the Colosseum. The current, infinitely more appealing, edition was completed in 2014 and, with its seven halls, now ranks as one of the largest theatre venues in Europe.

The oversized, slightly odd **sculpture** in front of the theatre – featuring a dozen or so actors frolicking about on a wagon – was erected in tribute to Romania's greatest playwright, Ion Luca Caragiale, the bronze sculptures based on characters from his plays.

Bucharest University and around

Occupying the first block on Bulevardul Regina Elisabeta is **Bucharest University**, whose frontage is lined with statues of illustrious pedagogues and statesmen, as well as a regular crop of bookstalls. Established in 1859 after the union of Wallachia and Moldavia, the university equipped the sons of bourgeois families to become lawyers and men of letters until the communists took over in 1949. Technical skills and education for women were subsequently given top priority, but since the revolution, business studies and foreign languages have overtaken them in popularity.

Just behind here, on Strada Edgar Quinet, is the **School of Architecture**, built between 1912 and 1927 in the neo-Brâncovenesc style – ornate pillars, prominent, richly carved eaves and a multitude of arches. A few paces north of the School of Architecture stands the smoke-blackened **Biserica Enei** (Enei Church); built in 1702, the church is also known as the Dintr-o zi or "(Made) in One Day" church, as that's precisely how long it took to erect.

Muzeul Municipiului București

B-dul I.C. Brătianu 2 • Tues–Sun 10am–6pm • €2.50 • ☎ 021 315 6858, ⓦ muzeulbucurestiului.ro

The fine Neo-Gothic building on the southwest corner of Piața Universității was built as the Suțu Palace in 1834 for Costache Suțu, a wealthy local merchant; its superb porte-cochère was added later in the century. The interior, meanwhile, was largely designed by Karl Storck, including the grand double staircase. The palace now houses the very worthwhile **Muzeul Municipiului București** (Bucharest History Museum), with a permanent exhibition called "Timpul Orașului" (Time of the City), which traces the city's evolution from the present day to back in time – presumably in homage to the reverse-running clock that adorns the first-floor landing area. It begins with a video montage of the city and its people over the years, not least the events from December 1989, including Ceauşescu's final speech from the balcony of the Communist Party Headquarters. Indeed, the communist years are given due prominence, with some superb photos revealing the extent of the destruction wrought by Ceauşescu; there are some moving photos of the 1977 earthquake too. The timelines continue in reverse chronological order, taking in both World Wars, the *belle époque* and the nineteenth century (starring some fine old Bucharest street signs and gas lamps), before heading further back in time to the medieval period and an enlightening collection of old documents – including the first plan of Bucharest from 1778 – plus photographs, prints and coins.

Biserica Colţea

B-dul I.C. Brătianu

Standing in front of the hospital of the same name and period is the **Biserica Colţea** (Colţea Church), dating from the beginning of the eighteenth century. An elaborately carved porch gives way to a diminutive, richly ornamented interior painted by the prolific Tattarescu. The present-day hospital dates from 1888, after the original, built in 1704, was destroyed in an earthquake. A statue of its founder, Cantacuzino (he also founded the church), stands in front of the hospital, which still functions as a local health centre.

Biserica Sf Gheorghe Nou

B-dul I.C. Brătianu

Some 200m south of the Biserica Colţea stands the late sixteenth-century **Biserica Sf Gheorghe Nou** (New St George's Church), the largest church to be built in the city during the reign of Constantin Brâncoveanu, who was reburied under the church in 1720 after his wife brought him back from Istanbul. In 2014, Brâncoveanu's remains were exhumed and are now on display inside the church. The grey-brick interior is enlivened by paintings, murals and sculptures by Mutu, Popp and Caragea, while a suitably grand bronze statue of Brâncoveanu, completed by Karl Storck, stands in front of the church.

West of Piaţa Universităţii

Generally speaking, Bulevardul Regina Elisabeta – Bucharest's main east–west axis heading west from Piaţa Universităţii – merits little attention, but there are a handful of sights worth exploring the further along you go, not least the tranquil **Cişmigiu Gardens** and, beyond here, the stately **Cotroceni Palace**.

Gradina Cişmigiu

Boat and pedalo rental: May–Sept daily 10am–10pm • €3.50/hr

Midway along Bulevardul Regina Elisabeta, the lovely **Gradina Cişmigiu** (Cişmigiu Gardens) were laid out as a park on land bequeathed to the city in 1845. Originally belonging to a Turkish water inspector, the gardens now fittingly contain a serpentine lake upon which small rowing boats and pedalos glide, rented by couples seeking solitude among the swans and weeping willows. Otherwise, the gardens simply provide a tranquil space, with workers snoozing beneath the trees at lunch times and pensioners meeting for games of chess. At the park's northern end, a Roman garden contains busts of some of Romania's literary greats while, for kids, there's an attractive little playground next to the lake.

Opera Română and Casa Radio

1

Heading along Bulevardul Kogălniceanu, you'll come to the mint-green **Opera Română**, a drab 1950s building containing a collection of operatic costumes, scores, photographs and posters. Although these are not particularly interesting, do try and catch one of the highly regarded performances here if you get the chance (see page 79). Looming over the Opera building is the monstrous **Casa Radio** (Radio House), another of Ceauşescu's unfinished projects. Initially intended to house the National History, Army and Communist Party museums, as well as Ceauşescu's tomb, it was then slated to become, as the name implies, a radio centre. However, it is now due to become a shopping mall-cum-hotel complex, though, as ever in Romania, it's anyone's guess as to when – or even if – this might happen.

Memorialul Holocaustului

Str. Ion Brezoianu/Str. Ilfov

Located in a quiet, rather nondescript part of town just a short walk up from the Dâmboviţa River, the **Memorialul Holocaustului** (Holocaust Memorial) is an uncompromisingly stark, five-piece ensemble arranged around an austere, mausoleum-like building, the walls of which are lined with orange panels bearing the names of those that were killed. The most striking of the other sculptures is the Column of Memory – so-called because the letters going up the column spell out the Hebrew word for "Remember"– and the Via Dolorosa, a row of inlaid granite slabs laid out in the form of a railway track, symbolizing the death trains that left Iaşi for Transnistria. In truth, it's all a little too abstract and incoherent to be particularly moving, but that does not diminish its importance.

Palatul Cotroceni

B-dul Geniului 1, though note that the entrance is on Şos Cotroceni • Tues–Sun 9.30am–5.30pm; it's only possible to visit the palace on a guided tour (last tour 4.30pm), which must be booked in advance; passport required • €9.50, plus an additional €5 for use of cameras • ☎ 021 317 3107, ⊕ muzeulcotroceni.ro • Bus #336 from Universităţii

The **Palatul Cotroceni** (Cotroceni Palace) was built as a monastery by Şerban Cantacuzino between 1679 and 1682 and served as a base for the Austrian army in 1737, the Russian army in 1806 and Tudor Vladimirescu's rebels in 1821. Damaged by numerous fires and earthquakes over the course of its history, the original building was demolished in 1863 and the palace rebuilt from 1893 to 1895 to provide a home for the newly wed Prince Ferdinand and Princess Marie – it remained a residence for the royal family until 1939. Under communism, it served as the Palace of the Pioneers – the "Pioneers" being the Soviet-bloc equivalent of the Boy Scouts. A new south wing was added during restoration following the 1977 earthquake and this is now used for presidential functions. In 1984, Ceauşescu had the church demolished, apparently because it spoilt the view; this has since been replaced by a replica, completed in 2009. The church's original bell tower, from 1679, still stands.

Tours pass first through the remains of the monastery, where the Cantacuzino family gravestones are kept, then through the new rooms from the 1893–95 rebuild, decorated throughout by French architect, Paul Gottereau. The style is eclectic, to say the least, taking in a variety of Western styles, though there's a notably strong German influence, inevitable given Ferdinand's stock. The most eye-catching rooms are the Flowers Room, a beautifully light and airy space with richly stuccoed walls and ceilings, and Ferdinand's small, French-style library furnished in maple and sycamore wood.

1

Grădina Botanică

Şos. Cotroceni 32 • Gardens daily: mid-March to mid-Oct 8am–8pm; mid-Oct to mid-March 9am–5pm; museum and glasshouses Tues, Thurs & Fri 10am–3pm, Sat & Sun 9am–1pm • Gardens €1.50; museum €0.50; glasshouses €1 • ☎ 021 410 9139 • Bus #336 from Universităţii

A short walk down from Cotroceni Place lie the university's extensive and well-tended **Grădina Botanică** (Botanical Gardens), founded in 1860, though at that time they were located across the road in the grounds of what was then the Cotroceni monastery. A lovely, cooling retreat away from the hustle and bustle of the city centre, the gardens contain a wonderful array of exotic plants and flowers, micro-forests and lily ponds. Best of all, though, are the **glasshouses** (note the limited opening hours for these), which originally date from 1891. These include the stiflingly hot cactus house; the tropical house, centred on a large pond; the Mediterranean house, with 20m-high palms and colourful citrus trees; and a richly fragrant orchid house. By way of contrast, the dusty little botanic **museum** is eminently missable.

Muzeul Militar Naţional

Str. Mircea Vulcănescu 125 • Tues–Sun 9am–5pm • €2 • ☎ 021 319 5904

The **Muzeul Militar Naţional** (National Military Museum) occupies a former army barracks dating from the late nineteenth century. The first part of the museum is an intermittently interesting trawl through Romania's military history, featuring an impressive array of weapons, banners and uniforms. The one section of the museum that really merits a visit, however, is the exhibition on the **1989 revolution**. It's a deeply

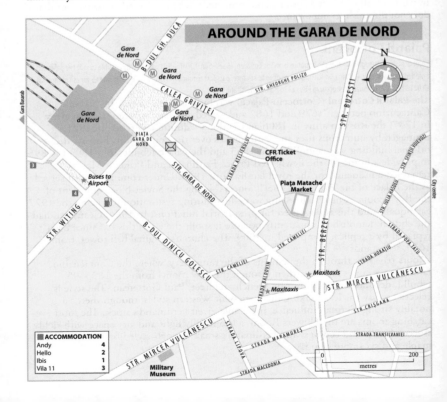

AROUND THE GARA DE NORD

ACCOMMODATION	
Andy	4
Hello	2
Ibis	1
Vila 11	3

moving presentation, comprised mainly of personal belongings donated by families of soldiers and civilians killed during the fighting – from glasses, watches and medals to more sobering items, such as bullet casings and blood-stained clothing. The main exhibit is the pistol, walkie-talkie and blood-soaked uniform of General Vasile Milea, Minister of Defence at the time of the revolution. The cause of Milea's death has long been a mystery, and an autopsy following his exhumation in 2005 was unable to determine whether he was killed (as most suspect) or committed suicide. There are also some rare English-language newspaper editions from that time, including many graphic images of the dead and those mourning the dead.

Despite the voluminous display of memorabilia on view in the remainder of the museum, Romania has rarely gone in for martial exploits; from 1958, it was the only Warsaw Pact country without Soviet troops on its soil, while Ceauşescu called vociferously for disarmament, announcing peace proposals and cuts in the defence budget. Post-communist Romania has become more involved in international concerns, contributing peace-keepers to the former Yugoslavia, as well as deploying troops in both Iraq and Afghanistan.

The northern suburbs

The **Şoseaua Kiseleff**, a long, elegant avenue lined with lime trees, extends north from Piaţa Victoriei towards the **Herăstrău Park** and the **Village Museum**, one of Romania's best open-air museums, before heading out towards the airports and the main road to Transylvania. Modelled on the Parisian *chaussées* (typically, long straight avenues made from gravel or crushed stone), though named after a Russian general, Şoseaua Kiseleff is a product of the Francophilia that swept Romania's educated classes during the nineteenth century; it even has its own version of the Arc de Triomphe.

Arc de Triumf

About 1km north along Şoseaua Kiseleff you'll come to the **Arc de Triumf**, built in 1878 for an independence parade, and patched together in 1922 for another procession to celebrate Romania's participation on the winning side in World War I and the gains achieved at the Versailles peace conference. Originally made of wood, it was more fittingly rebuilt in stone from 1935 to 1936, in the style of the Arc de Triomphe in Paris. Unless you want to risk life and limb trying to get across one of the city's busiest roundabouts, you'll have to make do with viewing it from a relative distance.

Muzeul Zambaccian

Str. Muzeul Zambaccian 21 • Wed–Sun: May–Sept 11am–7pm; Oct–April 10am–6pm • €2 • ☎ 021 230 1920, Ⓦ mnar.arts.ro

---

THE SKOPŢI COACHMEN

The **Skopţi coachmen**, who worked along the Şoseaua Kiseleff until the 1940s, made up one of the curiosities of Bucharest. Members of a dissident religious sect founded in Russia during the seventeenth century – and related to the Lipovani of the Danube Delta – the Skopţi ritually castrated themselves in the belief that the "generative organs are the seat of all iniquities", interpreting literally Christ's words on eunuchs in the Gospel of St Matthew. This was done after two years of normal married life – a period necessary to ensure the conception of future Skopţi. Driving *droshkys* pulled by black Orloff horses, the coachmen wore caftans sprouting two cords, which passengers tugged to indicate that the driver should turn left or right.

1

Another lesser-known gem to rank alongside the Storck Museum (see page 54), the **Muzeul Zambaccian** (Zambaccian Museum) houses an astonishing collection of art accumulated by wealthy Armenian businessman Krikor H. Zambaccian (1889–1962). All the Romanian big-hitters are here, including Pallady, Andreescu, Lucian and Baba, though, inevitably, Grigorescu steals the show with a fine selection of paintings – look out for the lovely *Boy with the Accordion* – and sketches, one of which is a self-portrait. Better still, there's an outstanding line-up of French artists, including paintings by Pissarro, Renoir, Matisse and Picasso (*The Bullfight*), plus what is believed to be the only painting in the country by Cézanne (*Portrait of a Little Girl*). To top it all off, there's some wonderful sculpture, with a contribution apiece by Frederic Storck (*Head of a Gypsy Woman*) and Brâncuşi (*Portrait of a Child*).

Parcul Herăstrău

May–Sept daily 10am–8pm • Rowing boats €1.50/hr; 30min lake cruise €1.50; tickets for both must be bought from the kiosk opposite the departure point • Take the metro to the Aviatorilor stop near the park's southeastern corner

Laid out in 1936, **Parcul Herăstrău** (Herăstrău Park) provides welcome respite from the city's sweltering heat. Beyond the entrance, paths run past formal flowerbeds to the shore of **Lake Herăstrău**, one of the largest of a dozen lakes strung along the River Colentina. Created by Carol II to drain the unhealthy marshes that surrounded Bucharest, these lakes form a continuous line across the northern suburbs. Arched bridges lead to the small and fragrant **Island of Roses**, where the alleyways are lined with the busts of Romanian and foreign luminaries – Brâncuşi, Eminescu, Shakespeare and the like (some are more convincing than others). Beyond here, paths wend their way round to numerous lakeside snack bars and restaurants, as well as a landing stage from where you can rent **rowing boats** (maximum three people) or take a thirty-minute lake cruise. Located near the park's other entrance, which is at the northern end of Şoseaua Kiseleff, near Piaţa Presei Libere, is the **Expo** – an enormous pavilion now hosting what must surely be one of the biggest beer halls anywhere in Europe.

The **residential area** east of the park is one of Bucharest's most exclusive neighbourhoods. It is where the communist elite, including Ceauşescu, once lived, cordoned off from the masses they governed; the area is still inhabited by technocrats, artists and members of the elite.

Casa Ceauşescu

Bulevardul Primăverii 50 • Tues–Sun 10am–5pm • €11, advance booking required • ☎ 021 318 0989, ⓦ casaceausescu.ro

For a quarter of a century the private residence of Nicolae Ceauşescu and his family, **Casa Ceausescu** (Ceauşescu's House) – also known as the Spring Palace – was originally designed by Aron Grimberg-Solari in the early 1960s, though substantially enlarged in 1971. From the outside it's a fairly unassuming, two-storey building, but once inside, it's a quite different story. Led by a suitably droll guide, you are shown some thirty or so of the palace's eighty rooms, among them the drawing room, study, sitting room, the suites of his three equally despised children (Nicu, Zoia and Valentin), a winery and cinema.

Furnished throughout in Canadian cherry wood, Carrera marble, walnut and buffalo leather, and with rooms laden with souvenirs of dubious provenance – Persian rugs from Mohammad Reza Shah, an elephant tusk from Zairean dictator Mobutu Sese Seko, and so on – it came as quite a shock to ordinary Romanians to learn that the Ceauşescu's had lived such a gilded existence; indeed, attempts to loot the palace after their downfall were largely thwarted by the army. Further highlights, for want of a better word, include the gold-domed bathroom, and bedroom with adjoining dressing room, the latter a tardis-like space with cabinets and draws packed with the pair's

ORIGO COFFEE SHOP

1

THE BATTLE OF BĂNEASA BRIDGE

The bridge immediately north of Băneasa Station, where the DN1 crosses the River Colentina, was the scene of a **crucial battle** in August 1944. The success of the August 23 coup against Marshal Antonescu (see page 76) meant that Hitler's oil supplies were more than halved, which is reckoned to have shortened the war in Europe by at least six months. At the time, however, just 2800 Romanian troops faced between twenty and thirty thousand Germans, mostly at Băneasa and Otopeni. King Mihai offered the Germans safe passage out of Romania, but they responded by bombing Bucharest. The bridge was held by a Romanian lieutenant and a handful of men until August 25, when Romanian reinforcements began to arrive from Craiova. Allied help finally came the following day when four hundred American planes bombed the German positions, and by August 27 Bucharest had been cleared of German forces (only to be occupied by the Red Army four days later).

---

clothes and accessories. Lastly there's the swimming pool, long since drained of water but still replete with dazzling wall-to-wall mosaics.

Except for a visit by the US president Richard Nixon in 1969, Ceauşescu rarely, if ever, entertained anybody here (even his closest political allies), such was his paranoia. Indeed, their every meal was prepared in a secure facility and delivered to the palace, which is why there's no kitchen. If you want to go the whole hog, 90-minute long private tours (€42) also take in the bunker, trophy room, underground tunnel and portrait gallery.

Muzeul Satului

Şos. Kiseleff 28–30 • Daily 9am–7pm • €3.50 • ☎ 021 317 9110, ⓦ muzeul-satului.ro

Bucharest's most outstanding sight is the **Muzeul Satului** (Village Museum) on the shores of Lake Herăstrău – the entrance is on Şoseaua Kiseleff, just up from the Arc de Triumf. Established in 1936, this wonderful ensemble of over three hundred dwellings, workshops, churches, windmills, presses and other structures from every region in the country illustrates the extreme diversity of Romania's folk architecture; a good cross-section of these dwellings can be entered.

Most interesting are the **oak houses** from Maramureş with their rope-motif carvings and shingled roofing, and beamed gateways carved with animals and hunting scenes, Adam and Eve and the Tree of Life, and suns and moons. The most outstanding structures are the early eighteenth-century wooden churches from the villages of Dragomireşti in Maramureş and Turea in Cluj, both of which sport vertiginous belfry towers. Other highlights are the heavily thatched dwellings from Sălciua de Jos in Alba county; dug-out homes, or "pit" houses (with straw covered roofs almost touching the ground) from Drăghiceni and Castranova in Oltenia; colourfully furnished homesteads from Moldavia; and the brightly painted dwellings from Tulcea county in the Delta – you can't miss the Jurilovca homestead with its distinctive cobalt blue and dark green painted doors and shutters. Mud-brick dwellings from the fertile plains ironically appear poorer than the homes of peasants in the less fertile highlands where timber and stone abound, while the importance of livestock to the Székely people of Harghita county can be seen by their barns, which are taller than their houses. Hidden away in one corner of the park is a delightful wooden carousel, complete with painted wooden horses and carts, dating from 1960 and which would have travelled to fairs throughout Moldavia; it was last used in 2003. Midway round, you'd do well to take a break from proceedings and grab a drink, and perhaps a bite to eat, in the rather lovely nineteenth-century *La Barieră* inn, transferred here from Valenii de Munte in the Prahova Valley. The terrific souvenir **shop** here is the best place in the city to buy folk art objects, including textiles and costumes, ceramics and woodenware.

Casa Presei Libere

Şoseaua Kiseleff ends at **Piaţa Presei Libere** (Free Press Square), in front of **Casa Presei Libere** (Free Press House), a vast white Stalinist edifice completed in 1956, and whose design was based on the main building of the Moscow State University. Once the centre of the state propaganda industry, it remains the centre of the publishing industry, with several national dailies still based here. Until 1989, the pedestal in front of the building accommodated a huge statue of Lenin, before he was carted off to Mogoşoaia Palace (see page 80) and unceremoniously dumped there – though his current whereabouts is unknown.

1

ARRIVAL AND DEPARTURE   BUCHAREST

BY PLANE

Henri Coandă airport (often still referred to as Otopeni; ☎ 021 204 1000, 🌐 bucharestairports.ro) is on the DN1 road, 16km north of the centre.

GETTING INTO TOWN

By bus The cheapest way to get from the airport to the city is by express bus #783 (24hr; every 15–20min during the day, every 40min through the night; 45min; €2, return ticket only), which departs for Piaţa Unirii, stopping at Piaţa Presei Libere, Arc de Triumf, Piaţa Victoriei, Piaţa Romană and Piaţa Universităţii along the way. Buses leave from outside the domestic arrivals hall, one floor below international arrivals; buy your ticket from the booth by the stop and punch it in the machine on board the bus. Express bus #780 (daily every 30min 5.30am–11pm; same journey time and price) heads directly to the Gara de Nord – useful if you're staying in the area or need to make a train connection.

BUCHAREST METRO

1

KEY BUS AND TROLLEY BUS ROUTES IN BUCHAREST

NORTH–SOUTH
Along B-duls Magheru and Bălcescu: #783 (express).
Along Calea Dorobanților: #131 and #301.

EAST–WEST (NORTH OF THE CENTRE)
From Gara de Nord along B-dul Dacia (via Piața Romană): #79 and #86.
Along B-dul Dacia: #133.
Along B-duls Regina Elisabeta and Carol I (via the university): #66 (Metro Obor) and #69 (Gara Obor).
From Gara de Nord to Str. Baicului (Gara Obor): #85.

EAST–WEST (SOUTH OF THE CENTRE)
Along Splaiul Independenței and B-dul Unirii: #104 (Opera–National Stadium) and #123 (Gara de Nord–Vitan).

EAST
From Piața Rosetti: #63 (to Metro Obor).

By train A train operates between the airport and the Gara de Nord (roughly every 1–2hr 5am–9.18pm; from Gara de Nord every 1–2hr 5.50am–7.45pm; 30min), although this does involve a 15min minibus transfer between arrivals and the airport train station. Tickets (€1.50 single) can be purchased from the main arrivals hall.

By taxi To order a taxi, go to one of the touch screens in the main arrivals hall on the first floor (note that there are two arrivals levels; if you arrive on the ground floor, go up to the first floor). Once you've selected a company (all fares are similar; around €12 to the city centre), you will be given a ticket with the name of the company, ID number and pick-up time; head to the exit and hand this to the driver when he arrives. Under no circumstance accept any offers from anyone within the terminal; you will almost certainly be ripped off. Avoid, too, the overpriced "Rapid Taxis" which hang about outside the arrivals hall.

BY TRAIN
Virtually all international and domestic services terminate at the Gara de Nord, to the northwest of the centre. While hardly inspiring, it's a much less intimidating place than it used to be and its facilities – which include ATMs and free wi-fi – are good. Luggage can be stored at the *bagaje de mână* (€2; 24hr) on the concourse opposite platforms 4 and 5. You can also purchase tickets from CFR's booking office, a few paces along from the *Hello* hotel at Calea Griviței 139 (Mon–Fri 8am–6pm; ☎ 021 313 2642).

Getting into town It's a 30min walk from the Gara de Nord to the city centre; head right along Calea Griviței to reach Calea Victoriei, the city's main north–south axis. Alternatively, there's the metro (line M1) to Piața Victoriei, where you can change onto line M2 to reach Piața Universității – the nearest stop to the heart of the city – and

Piața Unirii, in the Centru Civic. You can also take bus #123 to Piața Unirii.

Domestic destinations Baia Mare (2 daily; 13hr); Brașov (every 60–90min; 2hr 30min–3hr 45min); Cluj (5 daily; 9hr 30min–12hr); Constanța (7–14 daily; 2hr–3hr 30min); Craiova (hourly; 3hr–4hr 30min); Giurgiu Nord (2 daily; 2–3hr); Iași (5 daily; 6hr 30min–7hr 30min); Pitești (14 daily; 2hr); Ploiești (every 40–60min; 45min–1hr 45min); Satu Mare (1 daily; 14hr 50min); Sibiu (3 daily; 5hr 10min–6hr 10min); Sighișoara (4 daily; 5hr 15min–5hr 45min); Suceava (6 daily; 6hr 50min); Târgoviște (10 daily; 1hr 40min–2hr 10min); Timișoara (4 daily; 9hr 45min).

International destinations Budapest, Hungary (3 daily; 14hr–17hr); Chișinău, Moldova (1 daily; 13hr 50min); Istanbul, Turkey (1 daily; 19hr); Sofia, Bulgaria (1 daily; 10hr); Vienna, Austria (1 daily; 18hr).

BY BUS AND MAXITAXI
Bucharest doesn't have a central bus station, which makes locating buses and maxitaxis for specific destinations almost impossibly difficult; your best bet, initially, is to try one of the several maxitaxi stations in the environs of the Gara de Nord, such as the GSM Trans bus station on the corner of Str. Baldovin and Str. Vulcănescu, which is the best place to catch maxitaxis to Constanța and the coast, and Ploiești. If any station could be said to be the main one, then it's Filaret (in Bucharest's first railway station built in 1869), on Piața Filaret to the south of the city; a number of destinations listed below depart from here, including most international bus services. Otherwise, there's Autogară C&I on Str. Ritmului (near Obor to the east of the city), and Militari, on B-dul Păcii (Metro Păcii or bus #785).

Domestic destinations Brașov (every 30–45min; 2hr 45min); Constanța (every 45min; 3hr 15min); Pitești (every 30–45min; 1hr 45min); Ploiești (every 30min; 1hr 20min);

Sibiu (hourly; 4hr 30min); Sighişoara (8 daily; 5hr 30min); Sinaia (every 30–45min; 2hr); Târgovişte (every 30min; 1hr 40min); Târgu Mureş (8 daily; 6hr 30min).

International destinations Athens, Greece (1 daily; 15hr); Chişinău, Moldova (8 daily; 8hr); Istanbul, Turkey (4 daily; 11hr); Sofia, Bulgaria (1 daily; 6hr).

BY CAR

Driving in Bucharest is not recommended for those of a nervous disposition; endless congestion, poor roads and manic drivers all make for a somewhat nerve-shredding experience. Approaching from Transylvania on the DN1 you'll pass both airports before reaching Şos. Kiseleff, which leads directly to the centre. The approach from Giurgiu (the point of entry from Bulgaria) on the DN5 leads through high-rise suburbs until B-dul Dimitrie Cantemir finally reaches Piaţa Unirii. Likewise, the A1 motorway from Piteşti and the west brings you in through serried ranks of apartment blocks before reaching the Cotroceni Palace. From the coast, the A2 motorway leads to the DN3 through the modern suburb of Pantemelimon before reaching the older districts along B-dul Carol I.

GETTING AROUND

Public transport is a little chaotic, and often very overcrowded, but the network is extensive and it remains incredibly cheap. Apart from some express buses on the main axes, most bus and tram routes avoid the central zone, though this is covered by the metro system. Beyond the downtown thoroughfares, many roads are still so poor that buses and trams seem set to rattle themselves to pieces. As anywhere, beware pickpockets on all forms of public transport.

BY BUS, TRAM AND TROLLEY BUS

To use buses (*autobuz*), trams (*tramvai*) and trolley buses (*troleibuz*) – all of which run daily from around 5am until 11.30pm – you will first need to purchase an Activ Card (€0.75), which can be bought from kiosks (roughly Mon–Fri 6am–8pm, Sat 7am–7pm, Sun 7am–2.30pm) located next to all the major stops. Credit is added to the card and then debited each time you validate it at one of the orange machines on board; a flat fare costs around €0.30, a day pass around €1.75, and a weekly pass around €4.50. If you wish to purchase a weekly pass, you will need your passport. It costs about double the standard fare to travel on the city's express buses, using tickets with a magnetic strip, also bought in advance from the kiosks (day and weekly passes not valid). Children under the age of 7 travel free. There's an extensive network of night buses (11pm–4.30am), all of which leave from Piaţa Unirii; the most useful lines for visitors are #113, which heads up B-dul Brătianu and B-dul Magheru towards Herăstrău, and #118, which goes to the Gara de Nord. Ticket inspectors are ubiquitous, and travelling without a valid ticket will result in a fine of around €12.

BY METRO

Opened in 1979 in order to serve the working-class suburbs, the Bucharest metro is not the most user-friendly system in the world – signposting is confusing, lighting is poor and announcements are barely audible, but it is clean, safe and absurdly cheap. Trains run from around 5am until 11pm, with magnetic tickets costing around €1.20 for two rides and €4.50 for ten; a day pass costs €2 and a weekly pass €5.50. Note that Activ Cards (see above) are not valid on the metro. The M1 line (shown in yellow on maps) runs from Pantelimon in the east of the city to Dristor, before looping around the city centre; the M2 (blue), runs north–south straight through the centre; the third, M3 (red), runs east–west sharing the M1 tunnel for some of the way; the M4 (green) links Gara de Nord with Străuleşti in the northwest, although you'll have little reason to use this line. A new M5 line is currently under construction, with the first phase (Eroilor to Raul Doamnei) due to open in 2019, though this is likely to be of little use to visitors.

BY TAXI

Bucharest's taxi drivers have a deserved reputation for harassing and ripping off foreigners, and although the situation is not nearly as bad as it was, you should still be wary. As a rule, trustworthy companies have their name and phone number plastered across the top or side of the taxi, while the fare (*Pornire* – starting price, and *Pret km* – price/km) should be displayed on the driver and passenger doors. Your safest bet is to call one of the following recommended taxi companies: Cobalescu (☎021 9451), Cristaxi (☎021 9461), Meridian (☎021 9444) and Speedtaxi (☎021 9477), each of which should have an operator who speaks English. The same can't be said for the majority of drivers in the city, so make sure you have the address written down just in case. Prices are very cheap, and you should expect to pay around €0.30–0.50/kilometre.

BY BIKE

Bucharest has been very slow on the uptake when it comes to cycling, though the situation is improving. There are now a number of dedicated cycle lanes around the city, the most impressive of which is the one running the length of Calea Victoriei. Bike rental is available too; the best options include La Pedale, with outlets in Herăstrău Park and Kiseleff Park (at the junction of Str. Ion Mincu and Şos Kiseleff), which offers free rental for two hours; and i'Velo (🌐 ivelo.ro), which has bike rental at Herăstrău Park and Tineretului parks (€2.50/2hr; €6.50/day).

1

INFORMATION AND TOURS

Tourist information In the absence of a competent city tourist office, head to the privately-run Mr Tripp at Calea Victoriei 68–70 (Mon–Sat 10am–8pm, Sun till 5pm; ☎ 021 211 3366, ⊕ mrtripp.tours), which, although more concerned with selling tours, are more than happy to answer any questions you may have. Similarly, there's Romania Visitor Centre at Lipscani 47 (April–Oct daily 10am–7pm, Sat till 6pm, Sun till 5pm; Nov–March Mon–Fri 10am–6pm; ☎ 021 232 7683, ⊕ visitorcenter.ro) whose friendly staff have some basic materials to hand out; they also run two-hour (tips-based) guided walking tours of the city every day at 10.30am & 6pm. For all-round information, including up-to-date events listings, your best bet is the highly informative and on-the-ball

Bucharest In Your Pocket, published bimonthly and available free from tourist offices, hotels and bookshops.
Tours Bucharest City Tour (June to mid-Oct; ⊕ bucharestcitytour.stbsa.ro) is a hop-on, hop-off bus tour taking in fourteen of the city's main sights on a north–south route between Casa Presei Libere and Piața Unirii; tickets can be bought on board or at STB kiosks, cost €5.50 and are valid for 24hr; you must validate your ticket each time you board. Mr Tripp offers the city's most interesting and wide-ranging tours, including a 2hr Bucharest City Tour (€19) and a half-day trip to Snagov and Mogoșoaia (€49), as well as many others further afield, such as Brașov and Sighișoara, and the Danube Delta.

ACCOMMODATION

The range and quality of accommodation in Bucharest has improved markedly in recent years, though the tendency is firmly towards high-end hotels aimed at the business market, hence prices are often absurdly high – that said, it is possible to get excellent online rates, as well as some big discounts during the summer when the traditional business market is slack. While there generally remains a paucity of more affordable places, there is, inevitably, a clutch of cheap accommodation around the Gara de Nord, which remains a rather seedy (though perfectly safe) area. Most of the higher-end hotels offer airport pick-ups and transfers.

HOTELS

AROUND THE GARA DE NORD

Andy Str. Witing 2 ☎ 021 300 3050, ⊕ andyhotels.ro; map p.64. Just across from the station, this place is not exactly brimming with character, and its rooms (including triples and family) are a little boxy, but it's more than adequate if arriving late at night or leaving early; it's also the cheapest place going. Breakfast €5. **€40**

Elizeu Str. Elizeu 11–13 ☎ 021 319 1735, ⊕ hotelelizeu.ro; map p.44. In a similar vein to *Andy*, this station hotel is definitely in the no-frills category, though its rooms are slightly brighter, and some come with comfy leather sofas and a/c. Located just off B-dul Golescu, midway between Gara de Nord and Gara Basarab. **€39**

Hello Calea Griviței 143 ☎ 0372 121 800, ⊕ hellohotels.ro; map p.64. Easily the pick of the station hotels, this hospitable place offers good-sized rooms with lots of pine furnishings and wall-mounted TVs, although the rooms are only separated from the bathroom by a transparent glass door. Lots of triples, as well as three rooms for disabled guests. It's worth paying the extra €5 for a "Comfort" room. Breakfast €6. **€40**

Ibis Calea Griviței 143 ☎ 021 300 9100, ⊕ ibis. accorhotels.com; map p.64. Immediately next door to *Hello*, this enormous hotel is much like any other *Ibis* in the world, though its neat, clean and functional rooms are a cut above most places hereabouts. Breakfast €8. **€42**

AROUND PIAȚA ROMANĂ AND PIAȚA REVOLUȚIEI

★ **Athénée Palace Hilton** Str. Episcopiei 1–3 ☎ 021 303 3777, ⊕ 3.hilton.com; map p.50. With its long history of intrigue and espionage, this is Romania's most famous hotel, and, despite some stiff competition, remains Bucharest's most opulent and best-serviced establishment. Expect sumptuous rooms and first-rate facilities, including a sauna, gym and gorgeous basement pool, plus fabulous on-site dining and drinking (see page 48). **€150**

★ **Christina** Str. Ion Slatineanu 13 ☎ 021 210 7303, ⊕ hotelchristina.ro; map p.44. A superbly conceived, eco-driven hotel just a short walk from Piața Romană – though, secreted away among residential buildings, it's easy to miss. Each room is painted in one of four warm tones (grape-green, pink, lilac and yellow) and furnished with ergonomically designed beds, LED strip lighting and hanging artwork; the four slightly larger loft rooms are a lot of fun. Cheerfully staffed, this is originality and comfort at its best. **€79**

Cișmigiu B-dul Regina Elisabeta 38 ☎ 031 403 0500, ⊕ hotelcismigiu.ro; map p.50. Originally dating from 1912, but spectacularly revived just a few years ago, this is one of Bucharest's most venerable hotels. The rooms – actually mini-suites – are impeccably designed, featuring dark brown hardwood flooring, slate-grey tiled bathrooms and splashes of wall-mounted artwork, while some have a small kitchen area. **€135**

Grand Hotel Continental Calea Victoriei 56 ☎ 0372 010 300, ⊕ continentalhotels.ro; map p.50. This wonderfully renovated late nineteenth-century building just south of Piața Revoluției lays fair claim to being the city's most stylish hotel. Its big, high-ceilinged rooms are furnished in classic French style, with luxurious beds, glass-partitioned bathrooms and a stack of other nice little touches, including cool, state-of-the-art audiovisual systems. **€120**

Moxa Str. Mihail Moxa 4 ☎021 650 5555, ⓦhotelmoxa.ro; map p44. High-end boutique hotel just off Calea Victoriei with two linked buildings: contemporary-styled rooms in the glass-fronted main building, and an adjoining villa. Rooms in the latter come complete with purple and black fixtures and fittings, wood-panelled flooring and Nespresso machines. There's a terrific buffet breakfast to boot. **€150**

Novotel Calea Victoriei 37B ☎021 308 8500, ⓦnovotel.accorhotels.com; map p.50. This glass behemoth is distinguished by a faux Neoclassical facade, a replica of the Old National Theatre's, which stood on this site before being bombed during World War II. A cut above your average *Novotel*, the rooms here are as plush as anything else in the city, and there's a mezzanine-level swimming pool, gym and sauna. **€150**

AROUND PIAȚA UNIVERSITĂȚII AND THE OLD TOWN

Ambasador B-dul Magheru 8–10 ☎021 315 9080, ⓦambasador.ro; map p.50. In existence since 1937, this is a towering Art Deco pile prominently sited on one of the city's busiest thoroughfares; rooms are smart without being fancy, with those higher up offering spectacular views – especially at night – of the Palace of Parliament. **€69**

Flowers B&B Str. Plantelor 2 ☎021 311 9848, ⓦflowersbb.ro; map p.44. With a handy location close to Piața Universității, this sweet little bed and breakfast is a welcome alternative to the city's hotels, and it's realistically priced too. There are thirteen cosy a/c rooms painted in comforting pastel colours and a summery terrace on which to take breakfast. Take bus #69 or #85 to B-dul Carol I from where it's a 5min walk south. **€45**

Grand Boutique Hotel Str. Negustori 18 ☎031 425 6230, ⓦgrandboutiquehotel.ro; map p.44. This former residence of Romania's first banker is a suitably lavish affair, a graceful villa offering nineteen grandly named rooms (Ambassador, Senator, Treasury and so on) with exquisitely carved wooden bedsteads, mahogany chests and richly coloured textiles. **€99**

InterContinental B-dul N. Bălcescu 4 ☎021 310 2020, ⓦihg.com; map p.50. This towering city landmark remains the hotel of choice for businessmen and journalists – it was from here that many of the latter watched the revolution unfold – and has all the class you'd expect of a five-star establishment. Immaculate

rooms, marble-tiled bathrooms and top-notch facilities, including a spa and small rooftop pool. The citywide views are unbeatable. **€200**

K&K Hotel Elisabeta Str. Slănic 26 ☎021 311 8631, ⓦkkhotels.com; map p.50. Part of the hip Austrian-run chain of luxury boutique hotels, this is as cool as it gets. The rooms are elegantly designed – slate grey tones, lots of smooth wood and soft armchairs – with state-of-the-art amenities and service of the highest order. **€90**

★ **Rembrandt** Str. Smârdan 11 ☎021 313 9315, ⓦrembrandt.ro; map p.50. Pick of the Old Town hotels, this tall, narrow building conceals sixteen beautifully conceived rooms, each in one of three different sizes. Alluring wood furnishings – including the floor and panelling behind the bed – set the tone, along with sumptuous beds, etched glass windows and Tiffany-style lamps; larger rooms have tea/coffee-making facilities. **€90**

Tania-Frankfurt Str. Șelari 5 ☎021 319 2758, ⓦtaniahotel.ro; map p.50. If you can put up with a bit of noise, this small pleasant hotel in the Old Town is a worthwhile option, offering reasonably sized, sunny and thoroughly modern rooms, all with tea/coffee-making facilities. Good value. **€69**

★ **Z Boutique** Str. Ion Nistor 4 ☎0373 403 777, ⓦzhotels.ro; map p.50. In a pleasingly discreet location on the margins of the Old Town, *Z* is something refreshingly different in Bucharest. The super-stylish rooms offer lots of natural light to complement their eye-catching decor (bold blacks, mauves and greys), sumptuous beds and mattresses, plus welcome touches like Nespresso machines. Breakfast is taken up on the eleventh floor, with sensational citywide views. **€90**

NORTH OF THE CENTRE

Arc de Triomphe Str. Clucerului 19 ☎0372 150 700, ⓦresidencehotels.com.ro; map p.44. One of Bucharest's best small hotels where elegantly furnished rooms come with plush red carpets, wrought-iron beds, desks and chairs, carved wooden cupboards, wall pictures and pot plants. Small basement spa (hot tub and sauna) too. **€120.**

Casa Victor Str. Emanoil Porumbaru 44 ☎021 222 5723, ⓦhotelcasavictor.ro; map p.44. Located down a quiet residential street just 5min walk from the Aviatorilor metro, this privately run hotel is not particularly exciting – or tasteful – but it makes up for that with its pleasantly restful air, affordability and (somewhat surprisingly) a swimming pool. **€55**

Vienna House Easy Airport Calea Bucurestilor 283 ☎021 203 6500, ⓦviennahouse.com; map p.42. Airport hotels are pretty soulless places, but this one, just two minutes from Otopeni, certainly bucks that trend. The rooms are well turned out with striking colour schemes,

1

and the service is impeccable. A superb buffet breakfast is served from 5am for early departees, and all guests receive a complimentary transfer to the airport. And if you don't fancy traipsing into town, the restaurant isn't half bad either – the beef fillet is stunning. €80

HOSTELS

Bucharest now has a varied selection of hostels, nearly all of which are in or within striking distance of the city centre, including a handful within the Old Town area. All the hostels listed here are open year-round, though booking ahead is advisable in the summer months. Free wi-fi is standard in all these places, while laundry facilities are usually available for a small charge. Unless otherwise stated, breakfast is not included.

Crazy Duck Hostel Str. Stirbei Voda 130 ☎031 432 7128, ⍵crazyduckhostel.com; map p.44. Well-run, low-key hostel with two- and four-bed en-suite rooms as well as two dedicated family rooms (each sleeping four), which also come with a TV. A small lounge-cum-recreational area leads through to a similarly small – but well-equipped – kitchen. Dorms €14, doubles €36

Little Bucharest Old Town Hostel Str. Smârdan 15 ☎0786 055 287, ⍵littlebucharest.ro; map p.50. A short stumble from the city's greatest concentration of bars, this busy, cheerful hostel is the place to stay if you fancy a night or two on the tiles. It offers modern and colourful dorms (smallest four-bed, largest fourteen-bed), alongside a range of doubles, both with and without bathrooms. There's a good-sized kitchen too. Dorms €10, doubles €40

Midland Hostel Str. Biserica Amzei 22 ☎021 314 5323, ⍵themidlandhostel.com; map p.44. Quiet, centrally located hostel, just off Piaţa Romană, with three well-turned out dorms (sleeping four, eight and twelve) set off

a central reception/lounge area. Bathroom facilities are shared, and there's a fully equipped kitchen. Dorms €9

★ **Umbrella Hostel** Str. General Christian Tell 21 ☎021 212 5051, ⍵umbrellahostel.com; map p.44. Occupying an impressive early twentieth-century house, this very pleasant hostel offers a range of rooms – from doubles up to eight-bed dorms – complete with handcrafted wooden beds and small coffee tables; some feature the house's original ceramic stoves. With the exception of one smart en-suite double, bathroom facilities are shared. The cool, shaded yard rounds things off nicely. Breakfast included. Dorms €10.50, doubles €30

Vila 11 Str. Institutul Medico Militar 11 ☎072 249 5900, ⍵vila11.com; map p.64. Welcoming, family-run place in a peaceful backstreet just 5min walk from the station, offering a mix of four- and six-bed dorms, triples and doubles, either with shared or private bathroom, and singles (€18). Price includes a pancake breakfast. Note that there is no lift here and the stairs are steep. Exit Gara de Nord by platform one, turn right along B-dul Golescu for 200m, then left up Str. Vespasian, and first left again. Dorms €10, doubles €28

CAMPING

Casa Alba Aleea Privghetorilor 1–3 ☎021 361 7730, ⍵casaalba.ro; map p.42. Better known for its capacious restaurant, Bucharest's one campsite is situated out towards Henri Coandă airport in the Pădurea Băneasa woods. It's a large, well-guarded site with excellent facilities, including a wide range of cabins, some with showers and cooking amenities. Take bus #301 from Piaţa Romană (or #783 if coming from Henri Coandă) and get off at the "restaurant Băneasa" stop. Open year-round. Camping €18, cabins €35

EATING

Between the World Wars, Bucharest was famed for its bacchanals, gourmet cuisine and Gypsy music – but all this ended with the puritanical postwar regime of communism. The immediate post-communist era was little better – a veritable culinary wasteland – but in recent years the restaurant scene has improved beyond all recognition. There's been a welcome diversification in both the range of cuisines available and the types of establishments entering the fray, such as *The Artist*, currently performing gastronomic wonders, and *Beca's Kitchen*, where fresh, inventive cooking is the order of the day. Moreover, eating out, even at the more upmarket places, remains remarkably affordable.

Coffee, cake and snacks The most exciting recent development in Bucharest has been the emergence of the so-called third-wave coffee scene, manifest in slickly designed coffee shops staffed by young, dedicated baristas serving truly excellent craft coffee; the likes of *Origo* and

Steam are leading the way here. Otherwise, there are plenty of enjoyable cafés and patisseries dispensing freshly baked sweet and savoury pastries, cakes and confectionery. Look out, too, for the kiosks doling out *gogoş*: large, elongated doughnuts that come with a choice of fillings. Bucharest is well served with 24hr supermarkets, the most convenient of which are Mega Image on Piaţa Amzei and in the basement of the Unirea department store (see page 55) and Nic, also on Piaţa Amzei.

Where to eat The city's restaurants are widely dispersed, and it's generally the case that the best places do require a little effort to track down. With one or two exceptions, the majority of restaurants in the Old Town are best avoided, though, in any case, the sight of glamorous-looking young ladies attempting to entice punters in should be quite enough to put you off.

AROUND PIAȚA ROMANĂ AND PIAȚA REVOLUȚIEI

CAFÉS AND PATISSERIES

Boutique du Pain Str. Academiei 28 ☎0728 443 300, Ⓦboutiquedupain.ro; map p.50. Diner-style establishment rustling up food with a strong French slant (croissants, tarts, cheeses and salads) alongside great coffee (including takeaway) and cooling summer drinks (frappes and smoothies). Cracking omelette breakfasts too (€3). Mon–Fri 8am–10pm, Sat 9am–10pm, Sun 9am–9pm.

Camera din Față Str. Mendeleev 22 ☎021 311 1512, Ⓦcameradinfata.ro; map p.44. Gorgeous coffee shop – the name translates as "Front Room" – with striking, black-painted walls adorned with Turkish coffee pots (*cezve*) and black-and-white prints of old Bucharest. Coffee is served in beautifully painted little cups, though where this place differs from other coffee houses is in its range of drinks, with teas, chocolates, wines and cocktails among its lengthy repertoire. Mon–Fri 8am–10pm, Sat & Sun 9am–10pm.

M60 Str. Mendeleev 2 ☎031 410 0010; map p.50. This stylish coffee house is a big hit with the Mac crowd, owing to its laidback loungey feel, manifest in big bay windows, squidgy sofas and mix-and-match tables and chairs. The owners produce their own blend of coffee, but there are also craft beers and wines available – all in all, this is the kind of place you could happily laze around in all afternoon. Mon–Fri 8am–midnight, Sat & Sun 10am–midnight.

RESTAURANTS

Alt-Shift Str. Constantin Mille 4 ☎0727 316 245, Ⓦaltshift.ro; map p.50. The distinctively youthful vibe at this modern restaurant, with its understatedly cool, industrial-chic design, owes much to its location directly above the equally brilliant *Control* club (see page 78). Pasta freshly made on the premises is the pick of the menu (green tagliatelle with beef tenderloin, sun-dried tomatoes and truffle oil €7). Mon–Thurs & Sun noon–3am, Fri & Sat noon–6am.

Burger Van Bistro Str. George Vraca 4 ☎0720 287 437; map p.50. It isn't a van at all, rather a cracking little burger joint doling out the juiciest patties in the city, for example lamb burger with goat's cheese and caramelized orange (€5), and beef burger with pesto and mozzarella; you can either take your morcel away or park yourself in their quiet seating area across the road. Daily noon–10pm.

Le Bistrot Francais Str. Nicolae Golescu 18 ☎0756 018 393, Ⓦlebistrotfrancais.ro; map p.50. In a handsome villa just behind the Atheneum concert hall, this high class Relais & Chateaux restaurant offers a stunning French menu, featuring the likes of brie cheese with truffles (€15), foie gras marinated in Armagnac (€13) and brioche *perdue* with orange flowers and mascarpone ice cream, the last of these pairing perfectly with a glass of sumptuous Hungarian *Tokaji* wine. Although one of the city's most expensive places to eat, it's worth every penny. Daily noon–3pm & 6–11pm.

★ **Pukka Tukka** Piața Amzei 13 ☎0733 145 034, Ⓦpukkatukka.ro; map p.50. A welcome addition to the city's culinary landscape, this well-conceived organic food bar offers a limited, but very appetizing, range of dishes, including a handful each of salads, soups, mains (baked flounder with zucchini and spinach €11) and desserts (raspberry panna cotta €5). All the drinks (juices, wine, beer and coffee) are organically produced too. Tues–Sat 11.30am–midnight.

EAST OF BULEVARDUL G. MAGHERU AND BULEVARDUL N. BĂLCESCU

CAFÉS AND PATISSERIES

Gradina Verona Str. Pictor Arthur Verona 13 ☎0732 003 060; map p.50. Located to the rear of the fine Cărturești bookshop (see page 79), this large, vine-shaded garden terrace is the ideal spot to kick back with a book and a glass of wine, though on wetter days the adjacent timber-framed barn is no less atmospheric. Daily 9am–midnight.

Orygyns Str. Jules Michelet 12 ☎021 313 0094; map p.50. The location might not be the most enticing, but the welcoming vibe, cheery crew and outstanding coffee (especially their espresso and cold brew tonics) make this terrific venue a worthy addition to the roster of speciality coffee shops flooding the city. Mon–Fri 8am–7pm, Sat & Sun 9am–7pm.

Serendipity Tea House Str. Dumbrava Roșie 12 ☎0743 283 342; map p.44. Enchanting little tea house serving up a wide range of hot and chilled teas, though the house variety – a fruity blend of roses and strawberries – is particularly delicious. Concerts (usually jazz) are occasionally staged in the courtyard. Mon–Fri 2pm–midnight, Sat & Sun noon–midnight.

RESTAURANTS

Beauty Food Str. Jean Louis Calderon 34 ☎0759 030 609, Ⓦbeauty-food.ro; map p.50. A cheerful, low-key affair offering home-cooked food at its very best. The dishes look and taste great without being overcomplicated: for example, homemade pasta with walnut sauce and toasted coconut flakes, and pork in a pineapple and balsamic marinade (€9). An even better reason to visit is for breakfast – perhaps for eggs benedict or omelette with goat's cheese and sage and pepper chutney (€5). You'll also find a decent selection of craft beers to wash it all down with, though not with breakfast, obviously. Mon–Fri 9am–10pm, Sat 10am–10pm, Sun noon–6pm.

1

★ **Beca's Kitchen** Str. Mihai Eminescu 80 ☎0722 308 960, ⓦbecaskitchen.ro; map p.44. Prize contender for Bucharest's friendliest and prettiest restaurant, and the food's not half bad either. Dishes are chalked up on a board, which Beca herself is likely to bring to your table, and might include turkey fillet with red onion chutney and crispy veg (€8) or home-made ice cream with fresh mint and caramelized almonds (€4). Jams and chutneys for sale too. Mon–Fri 5.30–10.30pm.

El Torito Str. Iancu Capitanu 30 ☎021 252 6688, ⓦeltorito.ro; map p.44. By some distance the capital's best Mexican restaurant, a funky and friendly venue whose specialities – tacos, burritos, enchiladas, quesadillas and the like – are made from the freshest, most authentic ingredients. Factor in a terrific drinks menu and great music, and you've got a cracking evening in store. Tram #21 along Calea Moșilor. Daily noon–midnight.

Osteria Zucca Str. Jean Louis Calderon 41 ☎031 420 6814, ⓦosteriazucca.ro; map p.50. Housed in a delightful-looking villa, this quiet and friendly *trattoria* offers a highly creditable, affordably priced Italian menu, with the emphasis on steaming plates of fresh pasta (tagliatelle with Tuscan sausage and wild mushrooms €8.50). The discreet little side terrace is a lovely spot to dine in warmer weather. Daily noon–11pm.

THE OLD TOWN AND PIAȚA UNIRII

CAFÉS AND PATISSERIES

★ **Cremeria Emilia** Str. Franceza 38–42 ☎0727 126 996; map p.50. If you owe yourself a little treat after pounding the streets, then try this place, a long, all-white Italian-style counter doling out the city's best ice cream, plus wickedly enticing bowls of semifreddo and panna cotta, all of which is freshly made on the premises. There are plenty of other goodies on offer, and you can also grab a decent *ristretto* or *lungo* here. Mon–Thurs & Sun 11am–11pm, Fri & Sat until midnight.

Grand Café Van Gogh Str. Smârdan 9 ☎031 107 6371; map p.50. This most enjoyable of Old Town cafés features a coolly lit, orange-tinted interior furnished with high, window-facing tables, and also has one of the best terraces going. Dutch finger food is the order of the day, perhaps *Frikendal* (minced meat hot dog) or *Bitterballen* (deep-fried meatballs; €6), best washed down with a draught beer. The gut-busting weekend brunches bring in a loyal crowd. Mon–Fri 8.30am–midnight, Sat & Sun 10am–midnight.

★ **Origo** Str. Lipscani 9 ☎0757 086 688, ⓦorigocoffee. ro; map p.50. Despite increasingly fierce competition, *Origo* still lays fair claim to being the city's best coffee shop. Not only is the coffee fantastic (it's brought to you on little wooden trays), the neat decor and furnishings – jet black walls, pinewood tables and benches, miniature coffee cups strung upside down from the ceiling – add to the sense

of finesse. At sundown, the shop magically morphs into a rather funky cocktail bar. Don't bother opening your laptop either – they're banned. Well, inside at least. Mon–Thurs & Sun 7.30am–1am, Fri & Sat 9am–3am.

RESTAURANTS

Caru' cu Bere Str. Stavropoleos 5 ☎0726 282 373, ⓦcarucubere.ro; map p.50. Thanks to the fabulous surrounds, featuring splendid decor and Gothic vaulted ceilings, this is often the first stop for tourists but – always a good sign – it's also heavily frequented by locals. The food is very good – typically *mititei* (grilled spicy sausages), Moldavian *tochitură* (pork stew; €9) and *sărmăluțe* (cabbage leaves stuffed with minced meat; €6) – and the atmosphere terrific; expect impromptu audience participation when the house band strikes up. The daily set menus are great value (Mon–Fri noon–6pm; €5.50), and they brew their own beer. Mon–Thurs & Sun 8am–midnight, Fri & Sat until 2am

Hanu' Berarilor Str. Poenaru Bordea 2 ☎021 336 8009, ⓦhanuberarilor.ro; map p.50. Occupying the historic Casa Oprea Soare, dating from 1914, with a sprawling terrace that is packed to the rafters most days (and nights) of the week with punters chomping away on hearty, calorific fare such as vine leaves stuffed with minced goose (€10), grilled lamb pastrami with polenta (€9) and the ubiquitous *mititei*. Wash it all down with a big jug of the eminently drinkable house brew. Good fun. Mon–Thurs & Sun 8am–midnight, Fri & Sat until 2am.

NOA Restoclub Calea Victoriei 26 ☎0799 747 557, ⓦnoarestoclub.ro; map p.50. Slickly designed, vaguely Art Deco themed restaurant-cum-bar/club located on the fringes of the Old Town. The prodigious menu combines Asian, French and Italian influences, hence exciting dishes such as goat's cheese mousse with avocado (€6), and tagliatelle with boletus, honey mushrooms and prosciutto (€8.50); the action hots up on Wednesdays and Fridays courtesy of live music sessions, and then it's club night on Saturdays. Daily noon–midnight.

NORTH OF THE CENTRE

CAFÉS AND PATISSERIES

Ana Pan Str. Radu Beller 8 ☎021 230 6700; map p.44. Clean and modern sit-down or takeaway patisserie with more than a dozen outlets around the city, serving croissants, sweet and savoury pastries, tarts and yoghurts. Mon–Fri 7.30am–8pm, Sat 7.30am–6pm, Sun 9am–1.30pm.

★ **Steam** Str. Uruguay 22 ☎0743 049 080; map p.44. You'll do well to find this tiny bolthole just off Piața Charles de Gaulle, but when you do, you're likely to hang around for a while; the white-painted brick interior, with its chrome bar and wooden bench seating looks great, the staff really do know their beans, and the beautifully crafted, freshly roasted coffee is contender for best in town. Mon–Fri 7.30am–7pm, Sat & Sun 9am–6pm.

Tucano Calea Dorobanților 18 ☎0769 271 552, ⓦtucanocoffee.com; map p.44. This striking villa, extravagantly furnished with a marble staircase and stucco reliefs, is now home to one of the city's most enjoyable cafés; slink back into a squishy sofa and admire the African-themed artwork with a mug of freshly roasted coffee and a generous slice of home-made cheesecake, which some say is the city's best. Mon–Fri 7.30am–10pm, Sat & Sun 9am–midnight.

RESTAURANTS

★ **The Artist** Calea Victoriei 147 ☎0728 318 871, ⓦtheartist.ro; map p.44. This sublime restaurant's Dutch chef, Paul Oppenkamp, is currently producing a level of cuisine above and beyond anything else in the city. A playful, beautifully crafted menu (which changes with the seasons) might include dishes such as plum wood smoked salmon with poppy seed crackers and trout caviar (€14), and striploin steak with green peppercorn and king oysters (€22) – but if you really can't decide, consider tackling one of the tasting menus, served on spoons, whereby you get to sample a little bit of everything (€17 for tasting of six mains). Tues–Sun noon–4pm & 5–11pm.

Casa Doina Şos. Kiseleff 4 ☎021 222 6717, ⓦcasadoina. ro; map p.44. Occupying a prime location on the edge of a wooded park, this superb late nineteenth-century building – built to a design by Ion Mincu – accommodates an elegant and formal restaurant serving an upscale expensive take on Romanian dishes (grilled duck liver with caramelized apples €21; pork knuckle on braised sauerkraut €12), though the

real joy is the sprawling leafy terrace, the most elegant in the city. Daily 11am–1pm.

Ciorbărie Calea Dorobanților 73 ☎0772 039 002, ⓦciorbaria.ro; map p.44. For lunch (well, soup) on the run, you can't beat this ace little place, which typically has five soups (€4) on the go at any one time, the most popular of which is the mildly fiery goulash; throw in a hunk of granary and you've got yourself a cheap and filling meal. Mon–Fri 10am–10pm Sat & Sun 11am–9pm.

Die Deutsche Kneipe Str. Stockholm 9 ☎0722 284 560; map p.44. Terrific, family-run Bavarian restaurant in a quiet residential street, offering gut-busting portions of succulent German sausages served with lashings of sauerkraut and washed down with German Pils or keg beer. Tricky to find; take a left off Calea Dorobanților down Str. Madrid, then left again. Mon–Sat 3–11.30pm.

Mesogios Primaverii Str. Helesteului 30 49 ☎0722 200 232, ⓦmesogios.ro; map p.44. Close to Ceaușescu's palace in the exclusive Primaverii neighbourhood, *Mesogios* is *the* place to come for seafood, though it is at the higher end of the price scale with mains at around €14. There are all manner of treats to feast on, including cuttlefish, monkfish, octopus, red snapper and lobster served various ways. Daily noon–midnight.

Uptown Str. Rabat 2 ☎021 231 4077, ⓦuptown. ro; map p.44. A pleasantly secluded place just off B-dul Aviatorilor (or a 10min walk from Piața Dorobanților) that's been quietly going about its business for years. The fairly pricey menu is French-Asian oriented, for example foie gras with red wine and fig jam, and tuna with wasabi mayonnaise and avocado (€14), though the beefsteak dishes aren't half bad – try and grab a table in the elegant horseshoe-shaped conservatory. Closed first two weeks Aug. Mon–Sat 10am–10pm, Sun 10am–5pm.

DRINKING AND NIGHTLIFE

Bucharest does not immediately strike visitors as a place bursting with nightlife, but this is partly because, like the best of the city's restaurants, many places are discreetly tucked away or concentrated in unlikely areas of the city. That said, the **Old Town** quarter has undergone a remarkable resurgence, and on any given night you'll find the tightly packed ranks of cafés and bars full to the gills. It's here, too, that you'll find a growing number of **wine bars**, something that it was hitherto impossible to find in Bucharest. The city's **club scene** is among the best in the Balkans, and there are now some choice venues scattered around town, increasingly catering to a more discerning range of musical tastes. Bucharestians, however, have long been starved of decent **live music**, a situation reflected in the dearth of quality venues.

Abel's Wine Bar Str. Nicolae Tonitza 10 ☎0371 033 643, ⓦabelswinebar.ro; map p.50. Cosy, good-looking bar on the less frenetic margins of the Old Town offering an

extensive range of both Romanian and international wines which you can sample either by the glass or bottle, though the wine flight is fun (five samples plus cheese for €20). Mon–Thurs & Sun noon–midnight, Fri & Sat until 2am.

Bordello Str. Selari 9–11 ☎0748 881 085, ⓦbordellos. ro; map p.50. Try not to be put off by the skimpily dressed girls beckoning punters into this most vibrant of Old Town bars, which stages a diverse array of happenings, including live music, quiz nights and burlesque on Sat; meanwhile, the upstairs *Mulanruj* dining theatre puts on cabaret, comedy and theatre Thurs to Sat. Excellent choice of draught beers and a tasty selection of tapas too. Daily noon–3am.

The Beer Institute Calea Dorobanților 31–33 ☎0765 346 715; map p.44. Tucked away just inside the Carrefour supermarket, this is actually more shop than bar (though there are a few tables for tasting to the rear), and with in excess of 130 craft beers from around thirty Romanian

1

micro-breweries (among them Hop Hooligan, 3 Happy Brewers, and Ground Zero), you'll be left scratching your head at the myriad choices. Daily 9am–9pm.

★ **Control** Str. Constantin Mille 4 ☎ 0733 927 861, ⓦ control-club.ro; map p.50. A firm favourite with locals and visitors alike, thanks to its humming, vine-covered terrace and equally chilled-out indoor room. When there isn't a live act on – and *Control* has a better roster of acts than most other places in the city – DJs pump out house and electronica, usually out on the terrace. Daily noon–6am.

Corks Str. Bacani 1 ☎ 021 311 2265, ⓦ corks.ro; map p.50. Whether you're a dedicated oenophile, or just have little more than a passing interest in wine, this fabulous, brick-lined bar, with recessed window seats and candle-topped tables, is *the* place to come for a tipple, with in excess of 150 wines from all over the world. Staff are extremely friendly and knowledgeable, too. Twenty percent off during Cozy Hour (daily 3–7pm). Mon–Thurs 3pm–2am, Fri & Sat until 4am, Sun until midnight.

★ **Dianei 4** Str. Dianei 4 ☎ 0745 208 186, ⓦ dianei4. translucid.ro; map p.50. Contender for the city's most atmospheric drinking spot, this nineteenth-century house is in a delightfully decrepit state, its walled stripped of any ornamentation save for a few patches of the original painting, while the original parquet flooring and elegant ceramic stove remain *in situ*. That aside, this is one of the best places in the city to sample craft beers, wine and gin; the food is exceptional too, especially the daily brunch (10am–3pm; €6), which is something of an institution. Daily 10am–1am.

English Bar Str. Episcopiei 1–3 ☎ 021 303 3777; map p.50. Located inside the *Athénée Palace Hilton*, this is one of Bucharest's more sophisticated venues, a charmingly old-fashioned bar with thick-beamed ceilings, lush patterned carpets, leather armchairs and soft lighting. The perfect place to kick back with a glass of champagne, a mojito or perhaps a late-night whisky. Daily 11am–2am.

Fabrica de Bere Bună Calea Victoriei 91–93 ☎ 0770 550 234; map p.50. Great-looking bar run by the folk of *Zăganu* brewery, though that's not to say they don't feature other craft beers; in fact, you'll typically find a dozen or so ales on tap at any one time as well as loads more bottled varieties. Daily noon–midnight.

Fratelli Str. Glodeni 1–3 ☎ 0722 115 115, ⓦ fratelli. ro; map p.44. Superbly located on the shores of Lake Herăstrău, *Fratelli* is one swanky club, its predominantly all-white/silver decor adding to the air of sophistication. DJs pump out house, soul and electronica from a bank of Macs up on the stage, though there's no dance floor as such. Although the venue itself is not too pretentious, if you want a table, you'll have to pay for it. Note that things don't really get going until well after midnight. Fri & Sat 11am–4pm.

Green Hours 22 Club Calea Victoriei 120 ☎ 0788 452 485, ⓦ greenhours.ro; map p.50. *Green Hours* remains Bucharest's jazz club of choice; an intimate cellar bar with live turns two or three times a week and, in summer, gigs taking place in the leafy courtyard, itself a lovely place to kick back. Look out, too, for performances by the "Monday Theatre" company, which, despite the name, can actually take place any night of the week. Daily 9am–1am.

Mojo Str. Gabroveni 14 ☎ 0737 220 220, ⓦ mojomusic. ro; map p.50. A good-time atmosphere is guaranteed in this rollicking Old Town hangout split over three levels. The basement Brit Room plays host to weekend gigs (both by the entertaining house band and visiting groups), the ground floor operates as a sports bar and karaoke is belted out in the top-floor acoustic lounge. Daily 1pm–5am.

Tribute Calea Victoriei 118 ☎ 0728 742 883; map p.50. Along with *Mojo*, this is Bucharest's most dynamic live music venue; aside from the resident house band, the club provides a consistently exciting programme of rock gigs most nights, and the acoustics are first-rate. Thurs–Sat 10am–5am.

ENTERTAINMENT

Bucharest's cultural forte is undoubtedly **classical music**, thanks largely to the work of the internationally renowned George Enescu Philharmonic Orchestra. **Opera**, **ballet** and **theatre** performances, too, are invariably excellent, with ostentatious sets and huge casts. Prices for performances are incredibly cheap, typically costing between €5 and €15. It's still the case that few genuinely major rock or pop stars play Bucharest, and – with a few exceptions – those that do tend to be past their sell-by date. Note that most theatres and concert halls close during the summer.

in the city centre. The major multiplexes are IMAX/Cinema City in the Palace Cotroceni complex (see page 63) and the Hollywood Multiplex in the Bucureşti Mall, at Calea Vitan 55–59. The best of the few remaining city-centre cinemas (where films are much cheaper) are Cinema Pro, a one-screen cinema near Universitate at Str. Ion Ghica 3, and the Elvira Popescu Hall, in the French Institute at B-dul Dacia 77, which is usually a good place to catch arthouse and world films. Films are shown in their original language with Romanian subtitles. Prices are cheap at around €3–6.

CINEMAS

Cinemas are plentiful, and while the majority are, inevitably, suburban multiplexes, there are still a few places clinging on

CONCERT VENUES AND THEATRES

Atheneum Str. Franklin 1 ☎ 021 315 2567, ⓦ fge.org. ro. Home to the renowned George Enescu Philharmonic

Orchestra, the architecturally and acoustically superb Atheneum is the city's premier musical venue. Box office Tues–Fri noon–7pm, Sat & Sun 4–7pm.

Circul Metropolitan Aleea Circului 1 ☎021 210 4998, ⊕ circulmetropolitan.ro Permanent big-top circus that also hosts a range of variety shows, with performances more often than not at weekends, though it's closed through the summer months. Box office Wed–Sun 10am–6pm.

National Theatre B-dul Bălcescu 2 ☎021 314 7171, ⊕ tnb.ro. This huge theatre (with seven auditoriums) is the premier venue for domestic and foreign theatre productions (unfortunately, none in English). Box office Mon 10am–4pm, Tues–Sun 10am–7pm.

Romanian National Opera (Opera Română) B-dul Kogălniceanu 70–72 ☎021 314 6980, ⊕ operanb.ro. The principal venue for operatic and ballet performances; both forms are highly regarded and tickets are cheap. Box office daily 10am–1pm & 2–6pm.

Sala Palatului Str. Ion Câmpineanu 28 ☎021 315 7372, ⊕ salapalatului.ro. Hulking communist-era edifice behind the Royal Palace hosting all manner of concerts, including the few mainstream – and invariably old-time – artists that visit the city. Box office Mon–Fri 10am–6pm.

Sala Radio Str. Berthelot 62 ☎021 314 6800, ⊕ salaradio.ro. Although the National Radio Building plays a distant second fiddle to the Atheneum, that's certainly no bad thing; high-quality classical music concerts are performed here by the resident, and extremely popular, National Radio Orchestra. Box office Mon–Fri 1–7pm.

Tăndărică Puppet Theatre Str. E. Grigorescu 24 ☎021 315 2377, ⊕ teatrultandarica.ro. With the emphasis very much on the visual, this lovely little puppet theatre puts on productions that might just surmount the linguistic barrier; intriguingly, they have shows for adults too. Box office Mon–Sat 9am–5pm, Sun 9am–1pm.

SHOPPING

The biggest and best of the city's many shopping malls (all 10am–10pm) is Băneasa Shopping City out near the defunct Băneasa airport (bus #131 or #301), followed by the AFI Cotroceni, just beyond the Cotroceni Palace on B-dul Vasile Milea (Metro Politehnica). The most central is the Unirea department store (see page 55) on Piaţa Unirii.

Anthony Frost Str. Edgar Quinet 9 ☎0732 003 004, ⊕ anthonyfrost.ro; map p.50. Beautiful little bookshop devoted exclusively to English-language titles, including an excellent selection of Romanian writers in translation, plus books on Romania; friendly and knowledgeable staff too. Daily 10am–8pm.

Cărtureşti Str. Pictor Arthur Verona 13–15 ☎021 317 3459, ⊕ carturesti.ro; map p.50. Somewhat out of kilter with its unedifying concrete surrounds, this lovely nineteenth-century Bucharest house is now home to a beautifully laid-out bookshop, stocking an extensive selection of English-language books including Romanian history and politics, fiction and nonfiction, and some excellent children's books; it's also the best place to find Romanian music. The café out the back is a great spot to indulge in your new favourite read (see page 75). Daily 10am–10pm.

Cărtureşti Carusel Str. Lipscani 55 ☎0728 828 922, ⊕ carturesticarusel.ro; map p.50. Following a superb renovation, this late nineteenth-century building – and erstwhile communist department store – is now Lipscani's most conspicuous building, and is worth a look even if you aren't contemplating buying anything. With six balconied floors set around a central atrium, it is first and foremost a bookshop, though you can also purchase music, gifts and other knick-knacks. There's a gallery, exhibition space and top-floor bistro to boot. Mon–Wed 10am–10pm, Thurs & Sun 10am–10.30pm, Fri & Sat 10am–midnight.

Museum of the Romanian Peasant and Village Museum (see pages 54 and 68). If you're looking to pick up traditional souvenirs, avoid any of the so-called souvenir shops in the centre and head to either of these excellent museums, whose gift shops sell a beautiful assortment of authentic peasant handiwork, including ceramics, textiles and clothing, painted glass icons and so on. Tues–Sun 10am–6pm; Village Museum Tues–Sun 9am–7pm.

DIRECTORY

Embassies and consulates Bulgaria, Str. Rabat 5 (☎021 230 2150, ⊕ bgembassy-romania.org); Canada, Str. Tuberozelor 1–3 (☎021 307 5000, ⊕ canadainternational. gc.ca/romania-roumanie); Hungary, Str. Jean Luis Calderon 63–65 (☎031 620 4300, ⊕ bukarest.mfa.gov.hu); Ireland, Str. Buzeşti 50–52 (☎021 310 2131, ⊕ embassyofireland. ro); Moldova, Aleea Alexandru 40 (☎021 230 0474, ⊕ romania.mfa.md); Serbia, Calea Dorobanţilor 34 (☎021 211 9871, ✉ mail@ambserbia.ro); UK, Str Michelet 24 (☎021 201 7200, ⊕ ukinromania.fco.gov.uk); Ukraine, B-dul Aviatorilor 24 (☎021 230 3660); US, B-dul Liviu Librescu 4–5 (☎021 200 3300, ⊕ ro.usembassy.gov).

Health For emergency treatment, you should go to the Emergency Clinic Hospital (Spitalul Clinic de Urgenţa) at Calea Floreasca 8 (Metro Ştefan cel Mare; ☎021 599 2300), or the private Bio-Medica International Centre, Calea Floreasca 111–113 (☎021 311 7793, for emergencies ☎0722 338 383). Your embassy can recommend doctors speaking your language. There's excellent dental treatment available at the German-run B.B. Clinic, Calea Dorobanţilor

1

208 (☎021 231 8856) and Str. Ionescu Gion 4 (☎021 320 0151).

Internet Wi-fi is available in just about every bar and café (you will, of course, be obliged to buy a drink), as well as all the usual fast-food outlets. If you do need a PC, try the British Council, Calea Dorobanţilor 14 (Tues–Fri 9am–7.30pm, Sat 9am–1.30pm; ☎021 307 9600) or Cyber Espace, inside the French Institute at B-dul Dacia 77 (Tues, Wed & Fri 10am–6pm, Thurs 11am–9pm, Sat 10am–3pm; ☎0374 125200).

Pharmacies Sensiblu Pharmacy has dozens of outlets throughout the city, including a 24hr pharmacy at Str. Radu Beller 6 (☎021 233 8961). Help Net pharmacy has 24hr outlets at B-dul Unirii 27 (☎0746 123 814) and B-dul Ion Mihalache 92 (☎0746 123 815). Usefully, there's also a pharmacy inside the Gara de Nord (6.30am–10pm).

Police Each sector has its own police station, but the most central is at B-dul Lascăr Catargiu 22 (☎021 212 5684). Traffic accidents (with damage) should be dealt with at Str. Logofăt Udrişte (☎021 323 3030).

Post offices Str. Matei Millo 12 (Mon–Fri 8am–7.30pm, Sat 9am–1pm); Calea Victoriei 91–93 (Mon–Fri 8am–9.30pm, Sat 9am–1pm); Piaţa Gării de Nord (Mon–Fri 8am–9.30pm); inside the Gara de Nord (Mon–Fri 8am–9.30pm, Sat & Sun 8am–1pm).

Mogoşoaia Palace

Tues–Sun: May–Sept 9am–7pm; Oct–April 9am–5pm • €2 • ☎021 350 6616, Ⓦ palatebrancovenesti.ro • The easiest way to get to Mogoşoaia is to make your way up to the Laromet tram terminus (trolley bus #97), and take a maxitaxi from there

The lovely palace at **MOGOŞOAIA**, 10km northwest of Bucharest along the DN1, is perhaps Wallachia's most important non-religious monument. Designed by Constantin Brâncoveanu between 1698 and 1702 as a summer residence for his family, it's a two-storey building of red brick with a fine Venetian-style loggia overlooking a lake. After Brâncoveanu's execution, the palace became an inn then, after a fire destroyed the interior, a warehouse. Towards the end of the nineteenth century, the palace was passed to the Bibescu family (descendants of Brâncoveanu), before finally being handed over to the state in 1956, following the arrest of Martha Bibescu (1886–1973); one of Romania's great literary heroines, Bibescu spent the remainder of her life in Paris.

At the end of the long drive, which extends from the main road up to the palace, you pass the small **St George's Chapel** (built in 1688) before entering the complex proper through the entry tower: to the left is the L-shaped great house; to the right, the old kitchen; and straight in front, the main palace building, fronted by a splendid columned porch decorated with fresco remains. Its **interior** is largely the result of extensive renovation work carried out by Martha Bibescu between the wars; Venetian gold mosaics and elaborate marble flooring set the scene for some beautifully furnished rooms complete with richly woven tapestries, vestments and glass- and wood-painted icons. There's a fine loggia, too, overlooking the Colentina River.

The fine vaulted **cellar**, meanwhile, houses numerous frescoes retrieved from some of the monasteries in and around Bucharest that Ceauşescu was in the process of destroying, as well as other bits of statuary. Otherwise, the lush **gardens** and the neighbouring woodlands make for some lovely rambling.

Snagov

SNAGOV, a sprawling village 40km north of Bucharest, is the most popular weekend destination for Bucharestians. Its beautiful 19km-long **lake** has watersports facilities and a reserve for water plants, such as Indian waterlily, arrowhead and oriental beech. In the centre of the lake is an island occupied by a **monastery** built in 1519. King Mihai and later Ceauşescu and other high functionaries had their weekend villas around the shore, and the lake was also the scene of the summit which saw Yugoslavia's expulsion from the Warsaw Pact in 1948. Bălcescu and other revolutionaries of 1848 were held in the monastery's prison, as was the Hungarian leader Imre Nagy following the Soviet invasion of 1956.

Visitors now come here principally to seek the **tomb of Dracula**, sited in front of the monastery's church altar. Though lacking identifying inscriptions, it's likely that this is indeed the burial place of Vlad the Impaler: the richly dressed corpse exhumed in 1935 had been decapitated, as had Vlad, whose head was supposedly dispatched, wrapped and perfumed, as a gift to the Sultan. Vlad's murder is believed to have occurred in the forests nearby, and the monks would have been predisposed to take the body, since both Vlad and his father had given money to the monastery. Indeed, Vlad is thought to have had quite a hand in its development, insisting that several features be added, including, appropriately enough, a prison and torture chamber. To get across to the island, you can rent a **rowing boat** (€4/hr) from the jetty on the southern shore of the lake, just past the Complex Astoria; follow the reeds round to the left until the monastery comes into view. Give yourself a good couple of hours to make the trip over and back. Note that you must be appropriately dressed to gain admittance to the monastery. A good way to visit Snagov is to take an **organized tour** (see page 72), which is usually combined with a trip to Mogoşoaia.

ARRIVAL AND DEPARTURE   SNAGOV

By bus Maxitaxis #444 and #446 depart regularly from in front of the Free Press House on Piaţa Presei Libere (see page 69); note that buses drop off in Snagov village itself, from where it's around 1km to the Complex Astoria, a large leisure park on the lake's southern shore.

Clejani

Some 40km southwest of Bucharest is the small village of **CLEJANI**, renowned throughout the region as a centre for **Gypsy music**, spawning members of the world-famous bands Taraf de Haidouks and Mahala Rai Banda (see page 397), as well as a number of other wonderfully talented musicians. If you're a fan of such music, or if you're just interested in experiencing Gypsy culture close up, then take half a day to visit the village – if you're lucky, you may get to hear some of the spellbinding music first-hand.

The village itself is unremarkable, but the Gypsy settlement – little more than a dusty, mud-dried street lined with crumbling, one-roomed homes – is easily found. While you're here, there's a good chance that you'll find a group happy to put on an impromptu **performance**. It's expected that you'll offer some money in return for the band's efforts (€10–15 would be appropriate), and a few bottles of beer wouldn't go amiss either. While at the settlement, have a wander around; it's likely you'll get invited into someone's house, which will give you the opportunity to witness first-hand the poverty of Gypsy life.

ARRIVAL AND DEPARTURE   CLEJANI

By train To get to Clejani from Bucharest, take one of the eight daily trains from the Gara Basarab to Vadu Lat. From the station, it's a 3km walk: turn right and continue along the tracks for 100m until you come to some steps set into an embankment; from here, walk along the path across the field until you come to the main road, then turn left and carry on walking for 2km – there's also a good chance you'll be able to hitch a ride. Upon arriving at the village, take the first left, continue walking for 400m and you'll find the settlement on your right.

Wallachia

THE DANUBE GORGE

Wallachia

2

Centuries before the name "Romania" appeared on maps of Europe, foreign merchants and rulers had heard of Wallachia, the land of the Vlachs or Wallachs, known in Romanian as Ţara Românească ("Land of the Romanians"). A distant outpost of Christendom, it succumbed to the Turks in 1417 and was then largely forgotten about until 1859 when it united with Moldavia – the first step in the creation of modern Romania. The region is mainly comprised of flat and featureless agricultural land, interspersed with grimy industrial centres, though as it is home to the nation's capital, Bucharest, people will invariably find themselves passing through en route to Transylvania, the coast or Bulgaria.

The most rewarding part of Wallachia is its western half, known (after its chief river) as Oltenia, which stretches from Bucharest to the Iron Gates on the Danube. Here, the foothills of the Carpathians are largely scenic and unspoiled, and possessed of the region's most attractive and historically interesting towns, such as **Curtea de Argeş**, north of which is **Poienari Castle**, the latter with its connections to Vlad Ţepeş – better known as **Dracula** – who once ruled Wallachia, even though modern myth links him with Transylvania. In addition, a string of fine monasteries, such as the one at **Horezu,** runs along the foothills; most were razed at the behest of "progressive" despots (who otherwise spent their time fighting the Turks and repressing their own peasantry), but were rebuilt in the late seventeenth century in the distinctively Romanian style developed by Constantin Brâncoveanu.

The remainder of the region is dominated by large industrialized centres, such as **Ploieşti**, **Piteşti**, **Craiova** and **Târgu Jiu**, the last of which does at least have the work of Romania's world-renowned sculptor Constantin Brâncuşi as an incentive to visit. The most worthwhile of the three major towns north and northwest of Bucharest is **Târgovişte**, the old capital of Wallachia, boasting several ancient churches, the ruins of Vlad Ţepeş's court and the barracks where the Ceauşescus were executed. Otherwise, there's a fine excursion to be had up along the **Kazan gorge**, where the Danube marks the border with Serbia.

Note that **tourist information** is pretty much nonexistent throughout the region.

GETTING AROUND   WALLACHIA

By train and maxitaxi Getting around the region is easy enough: trains fan out from Bucharest in all directions, serving most places listed here, while regular maxitaxis shuttle between towns and link Bucharest to destinations as far afield as Craiova and Târgu Jiu.

Ploieşti

An oily smell and the eerie night-time flare of vented gases proclaim **PLOIEŞTI** as Romania's biggest oil town. In 1857, the world's first oil wells were sunk both here and in Petrolia, Canada; the first ever refinery was built in Ploieşti, and in 1858 Bucharest became the first city in the world to be lit by oil lamps. By the outbreak of World War I, there were ten refineries in the town, all owned by foreign oil companies; these were wrecked in 1916 by British agents to deny them to the Germans, and patched together again only to be destroyed once more, this time by the retreating German forces in 1918. However, it was the townsfolk who really paid the price,

FRESCO PAINTINGS, HOREZU MONASTERY

Highlights

❶ Military Barracks, Târgovişte Revisit the place where the Ceauşescus spent their last days and met their grisly end. See page 92

❷ Curtea de Argeş Attractive small town with two of the region's most striking ecclesiastical monuments – the Princely Church and Episcopal Church. See page 100

❸ Dracula's Castle Take Vlad's trail up to the dramatically sited Poienari Castle – the real Dracula's castle. See page 101

❹ Bujoreni open-air museum, Râmnicu Vâlcea Fascinating assemblage of local

buildings and other structures from the Olt valley region. See page 103

❺ Brâncuşi's sculptures, Târgu Jiu Outdoor collection of some of the great Romanian's most famous sculptures, including the *Endless Column*. See page 105

❻ Horezu monastery Brâncoveanu's marvellous seventeenth-century complex features the Great Church, replete with Byzantine frescoes. See page 107

❼ Kazan gorge Bisected by the Danube, the sheer cliffs of the Kazan gorge offer some of Wallachia's most dramatic scenery. See page 110

HIGHLIGHTS ARE MARKED ON THE MAP ON PAGE 86

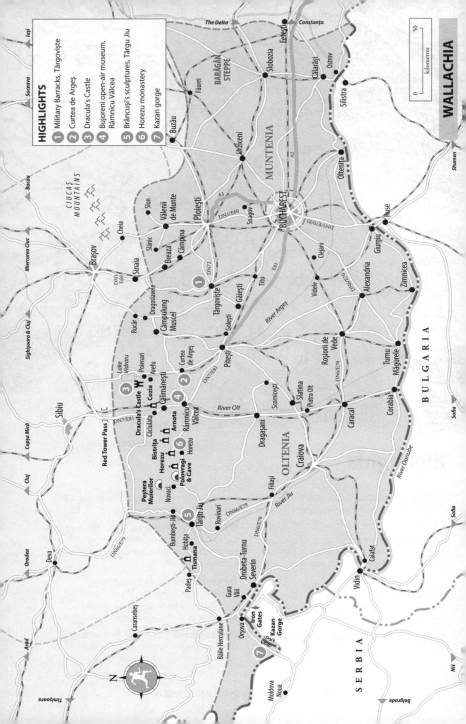

WALLACHIA

HIGHLIGHTS

1. Military Barracks, Târgovişte
2. Curtea de Argeş
3. Dracula's Castle
4. Bujoreni open-air museum, Râmnicu Vâlcea
5. Brâncuşi's sculptures, Târgu Jiu
6. Horezu monastery
7. Kazan gorge

when Allied aircraft carpet bombed Ploiești in 1944 – hence the town centre's concrete uniformity today. That said, you could spend quite some time exploring the disproportionately large number of fascinating museums.

Muzeul National al Petrolului

Str. Dr Bagdasar 8 • Tues–Sun 9am–5pm • €2 • ☎ 0244 597 585

The history of Romania's rich oil industry is comprehensively relayed in the **Muzeul National al Petrolului** (National Oil Museum), the only one of its kind in the country, and somewhat more enlightening than it sounds. Among the voluminous exhibits on display are the first documents pertaining to the extraction of oil in Ploiești, scale models, miner's lamps and the first oil lamps from Bucharest. The industry's key pioneers are given due prominence too, not least Lăzar Edeleanu, who was attributed with inventing the modern method of refining crude oil, and Virgiliu Tacit, who, in 1912, patented the first blow-out preventer. Out in the yard, meanwhile, you'll find all manner of pumps, compressors, condensers and engines.

Muzeul Ceasului

Str. Simache 1 • Tues–Sun 9am–5pm • €2 • ☎ 0244 542 861

One museum not to be missed is the fabulous little **Muzeul Ceasului** (Clock Museum), whose collection – sundials, carriage clocks, grandfather clocks, pocket watches and other timepieces – is as varied as it is entertaining. Standout items include a brace of gorgeous Viennese mantel clocks (the one dating from 1544 is the museum's oldest piece), saloon pendulum clocks from France and gyroscopic clocks from Germany. Best of all, though, is an ingenious water clock by London clockmaker Charles Rayner dating from 1654. Keep an eye out for clocks belonging to Theodor Aman and Mihail Kogălniceanu, and a more elaborate astronomical contraption owned by Prince Ioan Cuza.

Casa de Târgoveț Hagi Prodan

Str. Democrației 2 • Tues–Sun 9am–5pm • €2 • ☎ 0244 529 439

The delightful, whitewashed **Casa de Târgoveț Hagi Prodan** is a late nineteenth-century townsman's house that belonged to the eponymous local merchant. After you enter the house through a fine wooden porch, an open salon leads off to a trio of small, immaculately appointed rooms, each one furnished with beautifully carved wooden tables and trunks, and fancy Turkish ornaments – vessels, lamps, hookahs and the like. The house's decorative centrepiece is the so-called "Jerusalem icon", a brightly coloured wallpiece depicting scenes from the Old Testament, which Prodan himself is said to have bought from Jerusalem in 1819.

Muzeul de Istorie și Arheologie Prahova

Str. Toma Caragiu 10 • Tues–Sun 9am–5pm • €2 • ☎ 0244 514 437

The **Muzeul de Istorie și Arheologie Prahova** (History and Archeology Museum) offers an enlightening romp through the region's rich history. It starts with a treasure trove of relics from the Neolithic to Roman periods, featuring some beautiful specimens – buckles, bracelets, gemstones, bone tools, oil lamps and the like. The history section upstairs is no less engaging, with a stash of objects that once belonged to prominent Romanians: Elena Cuza's secretaire and prayer book, Maria Rosetti's embroidered skirt, a crown with monogram worn by Mihail Kogălniceanu, and the writer Ioan Bassarabescu's top hat and waistcoat. Look out, too, for some splendid photos of King Ferdinand, particularly the one of him standing on a Moldovan battlefield in 1917.

2

ARRIVAL AND DEPARTURE

PLOIEŞTI

By train Generally speaking, trains to and from Transylvania use Ploieşti Vest station, southwest of town at the end of Str. Mărăşeşti, while those to and from Moldavia use Ploieşti Sud, 1km south of town on Piaţa 1 Decembrie 1918; trains from Bucharest may arrive at either. The two stations are linked by bus #2, which stops near the post office in the centre of town.

Destinations Braşov (every 30min–1hr; 2hr 10min–3hr 20min); Bucharest (every 20min–1hr; 40min–1hr 35min); Iaşi (5 daily; 5hr 40min–6hr 20min); Slănic Prahova (4 daily; 1hr 20min–2hr); Vălenii de Munte (4 daily; 1hr 10min).

By bus The bus station is 200m west of the Sud train station.

Destinations Bucharest (every 30min; 1hr–1hr 30min); Câmpina (every 30min; 35min); Sinaia (every 30min; 1hr 30min); Slanic Prahova (every 45min–1hr; 1hr 10min); Târgovişte (every 45min–1hr; 1hr–1hr 20min).

ACCOMMODATION

Central B-dul Republicii 1 ☎0244 526 641, ⓦhotelcentralploiesti.ro; map p.88. Consuming an entire block, this large hotel on the main boulevard won't set the pulse racing but it's decent enough; there are two main categories of room, with the larger four-star ones more comprehensively furnished – most rooms have balconies. €69

Prahova Plaza Str. Dobrogeanu-Gherea 11 ☎0244 526 850; map p.88. This unprepossessing high-rise block has a determinedly business feel about it, but the rooms are generously sized and well furnished and don't skimp on colour. A half-decent breakfast, too. €72

Sud Str. Depoului 2 ☎0244 597 411, ⓦhotelsudploiesti. ro; map p.88. Respectable budget option despite the unpromising exterior and downbeat location, and convenient for the train and bus stations; clean, modern rooms (including triples) with low-slung wooden beds, flatscreen TVs and a/c. €30

Vigo Hotel B-dul Independenţei 28 ☎0244 514 501, ⓦvigohotel.ro; map p.88. In a lovely white *belle époque* building midway between the stations and town, this classy

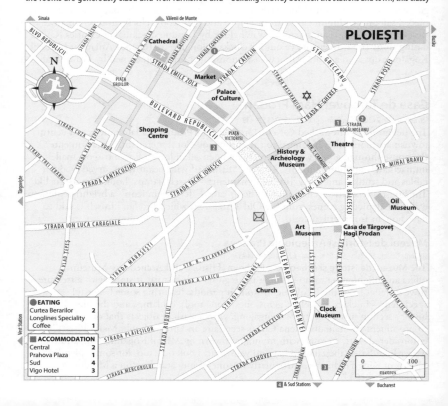

EATING
Curtea Berarilor	2
Longlines Speciality	
Coffee	1

ACCOMMODATION
Central	2
Prahova Plaza	1
Sud	4
Vigo Hotel	3

THE PLOIEŞTI PLOY

In 1940 it was feared that Germany would occupy Romania – as in World War I – to guarantee oil supplies from what was then Europe's second-largest producer (after the Soviet Union). The neutral Romanian government gave tacit support to Anglo-French plans **to sabotage the oil wells**, thus making a German invasion pointless, but technical problems and bad luck meant that these never went ahead. The backup plan, to stop the oil barges reaching Germany along the Danube by sinking barges in the Iron Gates gorge and blocking the navigable channel, was a greater fiasco: the Germans soon found out about the British barges making their way upstream from Galaţi, and forced the Romanian authorities to expel the crews (naval ratings ill-disguised as art students).

A third plan involved the RAF bombing the oil wells from its bases around Larissa in Greece. However, the 660km route would have taken the early Wellington bombers over Musala, the highest peak in southeastern Europe, at close to their maximum altitude. Following severe maintenance problems, the plan was abandoned. It wasn't long before the Allies were driven out of Greece, allowing the Axis powers access to Romania's oil wells, from which they subsequently obtained a third of their aviation fuel. On August 1, 1943, 178 new American Liberator B-24Ds took off from bases in North Africa to strike Ploieşti in the **longest-range bombing raid** yet attempted; although 440 aircrew were killed and 220 captured, a heavy blow was dealt to the Nazi war machine. By 1944, continuing raids from Italy had succeeded in halving oil production, despite terrible Allied losses.

establishment has colourful, individually fashioned rooms, each with ergonomically designed beds, hydro-massage baths and many other neat little touches, such as Nespresso machines. **€90**

EATING

Curtea Berarilor Str. Kogălniceanu 52 ☎0725 982 771; map p.88. Occupying the one-time army house and town theatre, this capacious, brick-vaulted beer hall is the most enjoyable place in town for a chow-down. Austrian spiced pork sausages with cabbage stewed in black beer (€4) and Bavarian smoked ribs are just a couple of the meaty treats on offer. The beer, mostly from the Timişoreana brewery, is delicious and includes several unfiltered varieties. Mon–Wed & Sun 1pm–1am, Thurs–Sat 1pm–4am.

Longline Speciality Coffee Str. Unirii 8; map p.88. Ploieşti has joined the ranks of towns offering speciality coffee courtesy of this superb little joint run by the affable Iulia, who knocks up a mean flat white among many other expertly prepared drinks; tempting pastries too. Mon–Fri 8am–5pm, Sat 9am–5pm, Sun 9am–2pm.

Câmpina

From Ploieşti, the main DN1 road heads north towards the Prahova valley and Transylvania. Thirty-two kilometres along the road lies **CÂMPINA**, another of Romania's key oil towns which, like Ploieşti, was heavily bombed during the war. Despite the town's lack of visual appeal and practical facilities, it has two tourist sights that merit a stopoff if you're passing by.

Muzeul Memorial Nicolae Grigorescu

B-dul Carol I 108, 1km north of the centre, across the rail tracks and up by the bend in the road • Tues–Sun 9am–5pm • €2 • ☎0244 335 598

Even those with little more than a passing interest in Romania's greatest painter won't want to miss out on a visit to the **Muzeul Memorial Nicolae Grigorescu**, where the artist spent the last years of his life (see box above). Occupied by the Germans during World War I, and then almost completely destroyed by fire, the house was restored by Grigorescu's son, Gheorghe, who then moved in himself. There's a wide-ranging selection of Grigorescu's work on display, including several pieces from his so-called white period, the last phase of his working life; apparently, Grigorescu was so fond

2

NICOLAE GRIGORESCU

Romania's most famous painter, **Nicolae Grigorescu**, was born in 1838 and came to Bucharest at the age of 10 to train as a church painter; his earliest signed works, dating from 1853, are in the church of Sf Constantine and Helena in Baicoi (near Ploieşti). Grigorescu subsequently worked in Căldăruşani (1854–55), in Zamfira (1856–58) and in Agapia (1858–60), where his work represents the high point of **Romanian classicism**. Here he met Kogălniceanu, who arranged a grant for him to study in Paris, where he became a friend of Millet, joining the Barbizon group and beginning to paint *en plein air*. In 1869 he returned to Romania, where he painted society portraits, but also toured the Prahova, Dâmboviţa and Muscel counties painting local characters in a mobile studio in an adapted coach. From 1877 to 1878 he accompanied the army in the War of Independence, producing, among others, major works of the battle of Griviţa. His first solo exhibition in 1881 was a great success, and from 1881 to 1884 he lived in Paris, developing a more Impressionist style. He kept a studio there until 1894, although from 1890 he spent increasing amounts of time with his companion Maria Danciu in Câmpina, where he died in 1907; he is also buried in the town.

of the picture in the easel, entitled *The Artist's Pencil*, that it's the only one he refused to sell. Also on show are many of his personal effects, including his palette, oils and brushes, glasses and a business card. The most remarkable exhibit, however, is the large tapestry in the living room; Grigorescu found half of this in France, before discovering the other half, nine years later, in Florence; the seam, where he had the two parts stitched back together, is quite visible. Look out, too, for the painter's fine collection of leather-bound French books in the library.

Castelul Iulia Hasdeu

B-dul Carol I 199 • Tues–Sun: March–Oct 9am–5pm; Nov–Feb 8am–4pm • €2 • ☎ 0244 335 599, ⓦ muzeulhasdeu.ro

Castelul Iulia Hasdeu (Hasdeu Castle) is an odd cruciform structure with battlements and buttresses, built between 1894 and 1896 by historian and linguist Bogdan Petriceico Hasdeu (1838–1907), one of the progenitors of the nationalist and anti-Semitic philosophy that infected Romanian politics throughout the twentieth century. He built the castle as a memorial to his daughter Julia, to plans he claimed were transmitted by her in séances. After finishing high school, Julia went to study in Paris, and would have been the first Romanian woman to receive a doctorate from the Sorbonne had she not died of tuberculosis in 1888, aged just 19. Among the many items retained within the castle is the desk she used in France, her diary and mathematics book. She also left three volumes of plays and poetry, all published after her death; she is buried in Bellu Cemetery in Bucharest (see page 59).

ARRIVAL AND DEPARTURE   CÂMPINA

By train The train station is 3km west of town but is connected to the centre by frequent maxitaxis. Destinations Braşov (every 30min–1hr; 1hr 30min); Ploieşti (16 daily; 20–30min).

By bus The bus station is south of town on Str. Bălcescu. Destinations Ploieşti (every 30min; 35min); Sinaia (hourly; 45min).

The Teleajen valley

From Ploieşti, the much quieter DN1A runs along the lovely **Teleajen valley** into the foothills of the Carpathian mountains, with a couple of attractions worth stopping off for.

Vălenii de Munte

Muzeul Memorial Nicolae Iorga Str. G. Enescu 3 • Tues–Sun 9am–5pm • €2 • ☎ 0244 280 861

Some 30km north of Ploieşti, up into the lovely **Teleajen valley** and the foothills of the Carpathian mountains, the small, rather nondescript town of **VĂLENII DE MUNTE** is chiefly of interest as the location for a fine **memorial house** dedicated to the great historian and former prime minister Nicolae Iorga, who lived here from 1910 until his murder by the Iron Guard in 1940. Ironically, Iorga founded the National Democratic Party, a predecessor of the Guard. A prolific author, Iorga wrote, or contributed to, in excess of a thousand publications, a number of which are on display here. In addition, there's a neatly preserved collection of handwritten letters, items of clothing, family photos and portraits, as well as some beautiful furniture. Among the many paintings on display is a portrait of Iorga by one of his nephews, as well as a couple of pieces by Grigorescu. There's also a good ethnographic collection in the neighbouring wing, featuring some superb icons painted on glass and wood.

ARRIVAL AND DEPARTURE   VĂLENII DE MUNTE

By train The train station is at the southern end of B-dul   Destinations Ploieşti (4 daily; 1hr 10min).
N. Iorga.

Slănic

From Vălenii, a minor road heads west for 11km to **SLĂNIC** (sometimes known as Slănic Prahova, to distinguish it from Slănic Moldova, to the north). Here, the Muntele de Sare, or Salt mountains – a product of the salt mining that has taken place in the area since at least 1532 – stand between two lakes in which you can swim in summer.

Minier Unirea and Muzeul Sării

Minier Unirea Str. Crizantemelor • Tues–Sun 9am–3pm • €4.50 • ☎ 0244 240 994 • **Muzeul Sării** Str. 23 August 9 • Tues–Sun: May–Sept 9am–7pm; Oct–Apr 9am–5pm • €1 • ☎ 0244 240 961

A ten-minute walk east across the bridge is the **Minier Unirea** (Unirea Mine Complex), which, in 1970, was, bizarrely, simultaneously converted into a sanatorium for lung disorders and a tourist attraction. Since the elevators stopped working several years ago (probably a blessing in disguise), visitors are taken by minibus 210m below the surface into the belly of the former salt mine, which comprises two levels and fourteen chambers. Carved into the salt walls are scenes from Romanian history, as well as sculptures of Roman and Dacian gods, Traian and Decebal, and historical figures such as Mihai Viteazu and Mihai Eminescu. More bizarrely, some of the chambers have been transformed into recreational areas, football pitches and the like; you can even have a game of billiards. If you wish to learn more about the town's salt-working heritage, pop into the tiny **Muzeul Sării** (Museum of Salt), housed in the Casa Cămărăşiei (the former Salt Chancellery, built in 1800), a five-minute walk away from the mine.

ARRIVAL AND DEPARTURE   SLĂNIC

By train The train station is a short walk south of the mine   Destinations Ploieşti Sud, via Ploieşti Vest (5 daily;
on Str. Vasile Alecsandri.   1hr 20min).

ACCOMMODATION

Baia Roşie resort B-dul Muncii 86 ☎ 0244 240 131, ⓦ baiarosieresort.ro. Located at the entrance to the village, this is the best place to stay in Slănic, with four villas housing modern, reasonably accomplished double rooms. Its comprehensive facilities include three outdoor pools (one for children and one containing salt water), a hot-tub, a playground and restaurant. Non-guests can use the pool complex. **€70**

2

Târgovişte

TÂRGOVIŞTE, 50km west of Ploieşti on the DN72, was the capital of Wallachia for more than two centuries, vestiges of which can be seen in the old **Princely Court** complex, the town's principal attraction. In recent times, the town has been best known as an industrial centre, producing equipment for the oil industry, but it gained notoriety when Nicolae and Elena Ceauşescu were executed in its **military barracks** on Christmas Day, 1989.

Military Barracks

B-dul Carol I • Tues–Sun 9am–5pm • €2

Located just a few paces up from the train station, the **military barracks** where the Ceauşescus met their grisly end was finally opened up to the public in 2013. The small room to the right as you enter (the Commandant's room) was where the couple underwent medical checks before the trial, which took place in another, not much bigger, room just across the way; it's arranged exactly as it was during the trial, with the very same tables and chairs, and signs indicating where the main protagonists sat. Down the corridor is the room where the couple spent their last four nights, sleeping

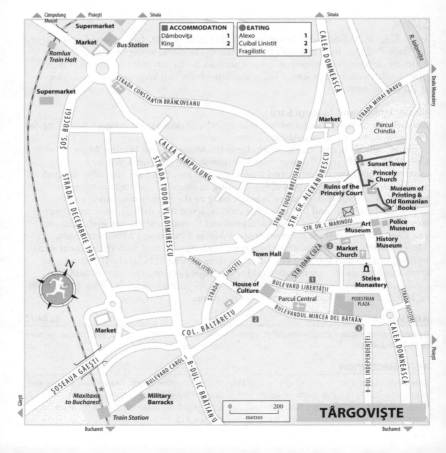

on hard, iron-framed beds and eating off metal plates, as ignominious an ending as it's possible to imagine for a couple who were used to dining off the finest silver. From here, you head out into the grubby courtyard and the execution site; two, rather comedic, white painted outlines mark the spots where they fell, and a volley of bullet holes pepper the wall – apparently, the Ceaușescus were shot too quickly for the event to be captured live on video, so many of the holes you see were actually fired after they had been executed.

Curtea Domnească

Calea Domnească 181 • Tues–Sun: April–Oct 9am–6pm; Nov–March 9am–5pm • €2.50 • ☎ 0245 613 946

Now a mass of crumbling ramparts, with a few well-preserved sections, the **Curtea Domnească** (Princely Court) was once the royal seat of Wallachia (1415–1659), from where 33 *voivodes* (princes) exercised their rule – all of whom are denoted on the inside wall of the southern gate, the entrance to the complex. The Princely Court figured large in the life of Vlad the Impaler (see page 398), who spent his early years here, until he and his brother Radu were sent by their father to Anatolia as hostages. Following the murder of his father and his eldest brother, Mircea, who was buried alive by Wallachia's boyars, Vlad returned to be enthroned here in 1456, and waited three years before taking his revenge. Invited with their families to feast at court on Easter Sunday, the boyars were half-drunk when guards suddenly grabbed them and impaled them forthwith upon stakes around town, sparing only the fittest who were marched off to labour on Vlad's castle at Poienari (see page 101).

Dominating the complex is the 27m-high **Turnul Chindiei** (Sunset Tower), built during the fifteenth century and originally used as a watchtower for Vlad's soldiers; it's an odd, cylindrical brick structure atop a truncated pyramidal base. It's worth climbing to the top for terrific views of the complex and the rest of town. Nearby stands the handsome **Princely Church**, built in 1583 and painted in 1698, with a vast iconostasis as well as dozens of frescoes of Wallachian princes, such as Basarab, Cantacuzino and Brâncoveanu. Basarab's wife, Elena, is buried in the church. Also located within the complex is the **Muzeul Tiparului și Cărții Vechi Românesti** (Museum of Printing and Old Romanian Books), which holds a superb collection of rare and ancient manuscripts, the most important of which is Dimitrie Cantemir's seminal tome, *A History of the Ottoman Empire*, first printed in London in 1734, as well as editions by Bălcescu and Kogălniceanu; sadly, though, all captions are in Romanian only.

Muzeul Poliţei Române

Calea Domnească 187 • Tues–Sun 9am–5pm • €1.50 • ☎ 0245 212 990

The **Muzeul Poliţei Române** (Museum of the Romanian Police) is, unsurprisingly, the only one of its kind in the country, and despite its rather dusty appearance, does retain a certain novelty value. As well as charting the history and evolution of the Romanian police, it exhibits costumes garnered from numerous forces from around the world – the mannequins themselves are a hoot – alongside a lethal assortment of weaponry. The most peculiar – if not macabre – exhibit is that which documents the crimes of Romania's most notorious serial killer, Ion Rimaru, aka the "Butcher of Bucharest"; convicted of multiple murders, and many more violent attacks, in the capital between 1970 and 1971, Rimaru was eventually sentenced to death. Displayed in a cabinet are photos of some of his victims, alongside a handful of his possessions, including, rather bizarrely, his death mask.

Mânăstirea Stelea

Str. Stelea 6 • Free • ☎ 0245 213 723

Enclosed within a moderately high wall, **Mânăstirea Stelea** (Stelea monastery) is a striking building in the same Moldavian Gothic style of the famous Church of the Three Hierarchs in Iași (see page 240), its exterior carved with chevrons and rosettes studded with green discs. Built in 1645 by Moldavia's Basil the Wolf as part of a peace agreement with the Wallachian ruler, Matei Basarab – busts of whom stand just inside the courtyard – it inspired the design of many Wallachian churches. The monastery was closed from 1863 to 1992 (although it served as a parish church), but is once more in use. It houses a rare seventeenth-century iconostasis and Byzantine-influenced frescoes, of which the more interesting were painted from 1705 to 1706 under Constantin Brâncoveanu.

ARRIVAL AND DEPARTURE TÂRGOVIȘTE

By train Târgoviște's train station is southwest of town on Piața Gării, from where it's a pleasant 15min walk to the centre along B-dul Carol I; alternatively, bus #5 will take you into town.

Destinations Bucharest (7 daily; 1hr 20min–1hr 40min); Titu (11 daily; 30–45min).

By bus The large and disorganized bus station is 1km west of town by the Romlux train halt and linked to the centre by buses and maxitaxis along Calea Câmpulung. Maxitaxis for Bucharest arrive and depart every 30min or so from a point 200m to the left of the station as you exit.

Destinations Bucharest (every 15–30 min; 1hr 45min); Câmpulung (1 daily; 1hr 50min); Ploiești (every 45–60min; 1hr–1hr 20min).

ACCOMMODATION

Dâmbovița B-dul Libertății 1 ☎0245 213 370, ⓦ hoteldambovita.ro; map p.92. The unprepossessing, communist-era facade does little to inspire, but it's a solid, fairly priced three-star with reasonably polished rooms, most of which overlook the leafy park. **€40**

King B-dul Carol 17 ☎0345 401 480, ⓦ hotel-king. ro; map p.92. Set back a few paces from the road and concealed within an attractive U-shaped courtyard, this commendable hotel offers fragrant, streamlined rooms with low-slung wooden beds, chocolate brown decor and sparkling bathrooms. Price includes use of the basement spa facilities, which includes a gorgeous little pool. **€50**

EATING

Alexo Calea Domnească 179 ☎0732 125 396; map p.92. Fun, if noisy, pub-like pizzeria that makes for an ideal pit stop after exhausting the neighbouring Princely Court. Set within attractive garden pavilions, it offers delicious, thin-crust pizzas (€5) straight from a log-fired oven and a decent selection of draught beers. Mon–Thurs & Sun 9am–11pm, Fri & Sat 9am–midnight.

Cuibal Linistit Str. Al. I. Cuza 19 ☎0737 058 517, ⓦ cuiballinistit.ro; map p.92. The soothing ambience of the "Quiet Hive", with its vintage-style decor (dinky wooden tables, cushioned stools and squidgy sofas, and walls framed by black-and-white pictures of old Târgoviște) is the perfect spot in which to indulge in a cuppa – perhaps champagne and blackcurrant, or honey and raspberry – along with a thick wedge of home-made cake. Mon–Thurs & Sun 9am–9pm, Fri & Sat 9am–10pm.

Fragilistic Bd Mircea del Batran 10 ☎0720 707 512; map p.92. Fabulous bookstore-cum-coffee shop doling out the town's freshest, tastiest caffeine; grab yourself an espresso or one of their delicious filter coffees prepared various ways (V60, Aeropress) then kick back with a good read. Prompt and friendly service to boot. Mon–Fri 7.45am–6.45pm, Sat & Sun 9am–5.30pm.

Pitești

Situated 100km northwest of Bucharest, **PITEȘTI** is another of Wallachia's industrial towns, and in truth it's one of the grimmest, though it does make a useful base for forays up into the Argeș valley. Much of the town's architectural charm has been lost to earthquakes and subsequent rebuilding, and these days it's dominated by the woodworking and petrochemical industries, and by the Dacia factory (now owned by Renault) – origin of most of Romania's cars – 11km north in Mioveni. If you do find yourself with a couple of hours to spare here, there are a couple of unusual museums to occupy your time.

Muzeul Județean Argeș

Str. Armand 44 • Wed–Sun 9am–5pm • €1.50 • ☎ 0248 212 561

Housed in the turn-of-the-twentieth-century prefecture building, the **Muzeul Județean Argeș** (County Museum) offers a standard review of the region's history, including various Bronze and Iron Age bits and bobs, and remnants from Poienari Castle (see page 101). Amid all this, however, are objects belonging to some notable historical figures, such as King Carol I's throne and trench coat, a few pieces owned by Elena Cuza, and a hoard of items belonging to Pitești-born politician Armand Călinescu, prime minister for six months until his assassination in 1939.

Muzeul Sport Argeșean

Str. Armand 44 • Wed–Sun 9am–5pm • €1 • ☎ 0248 212 561

The **Muzeul Sport Argeșean** (Museum of Sports) documents the exploits of the county's sporting heroes, thanks to a wealth of memorabilia. While few names will mean much to the average visitor – save perhaps for Adrian Mutu, former Chelsea and Romanian national footballer, and tennis player Victor Hănescu – there is some fascinating stuff here, including the boots and vest skins worn by triple-jumper Marian Oprea in the 2004 Olympics, where he won silver; the bike belonging to the 1960s Olympian Gabriel Moiceanu; and a signed shirt worn by Ion Barbu during the Romania versus England football match at Wembley in 1968.

Galeria de Artă Naivă and Planetariu

Str. Armand 44 (entrance on B-dul Eroilor) • Galeria de Artă Naivă Wed–Sun 9am–5pm; Planetariu shows 10am, noon, 2pm & 4pm; 20–30min • €1

The only one of its kind in Romania, the **Galeria de Artă Naivă** (Naïf Art Gallery) features a wonderfully exuberant collection of works by unschooled painters. The

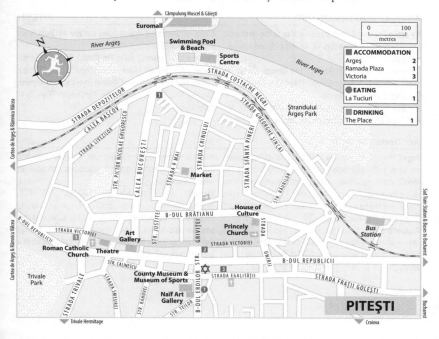

2

PITEȘTI PRISON

For older Romanians, Pitești is synonymous with its **prison**, the scene under the early Stalinist regime of some of the most brutal psychiatric abuse anywhere in the Soviet bloc. In May 1948, there were mass arrests of dissident students, and from December 1949 about a thousand of them were brought here, to the "Student Re-education Centre", for a **programme** aimed at "readjusting the students to communist life" and eliminating the possibility of any new opposition developing. In fact, it simply set out to destroy the personality of the individual: by starvation, isolation, and above all by forcing prisoners to torture each other, breaking down all distinctions between prisoner and torturer, and thus between individual and state. "United by the evil they have both perpetrated and endured, the victim and the torturer thus become a single person. In fact, there is no longer a victim, ultimately no longer a witness", as Paul Goma put it in his book *The Dogs of Death*. Sixteen students died during this atrocious "experiment".

The programme was extended to Gherla, other prisons and the Danube–Black Sea Canal labour camps, but security was looser here and the torture stopped when word got out. The experiment was abandoned in 1952, when the Stalinist leader Ana Pauker was purged; it was claimed that the authorities had not been involved, and in 1954, those running the Pitești prison were tried secretly for murder and torture. The leader of the "Organization of Prisoners with Communist Convictions", Eugen Turcanu, was executed along with several of his henchmen, while others were sentenced to forced labour for life. Nevertheless, because of the guilt of all involved – both prisoners and guards – there followed a conspiracy of silence, which only began to break in 1989.

pictures on display are consistently fresh and vibrant, occasionally kitsch and sometimes just plain bizarre, but always entertaining – typically paintings of festivals, weddings and other scenes pertaining to everyday village life. Although the art is practised throughout the country, its most popular centres are around Reșița, near Arad, and around Bacău and Iași in Moldavia. In the same building, the **Planetariu** has a rotating programme of astronomically themed shows.

ARRIVAL AND DEPARTURE   PITEȘTI

By train The town's train station is 1km to the southeast, linked to the centre by buses #2, #8 and #19, and frequent maxitaxis.

Destinations Bucharest (hourly; 1hr 40min); Curtea de Argeș (3 daily; 50min); Golești (14 daily; 10min); Titu (10 daily; 55min–1hr 20min).

By bus The large, disorganized bus station is to the northwest of the train station on Str. Târgul din Vale, though

buses for Bucharest depart from outside *McDonald's* on B-dul Republicii.

Destinations Brașov (2 daily; 3hr 30min); Bucharest (every 30min; 1hr 45min); Câmpulung (hourly; 1hr 20min); Craiova (5 daily; 2hr 20min); Gaiești (every 45min; 40min); Râmnicu Vâlcea (every 30–45min; 1hr 20min); Târgu Jiu (4 daily; 4hr).

ACCOMMODATION

Argeș Piața Muntenia 3 ☎0248 223 399, ⊛hotelarges. ro; map p.95. This rather modest-looking hotel is the town's most appealing option, with spotlessly clean, well-proportioned and attractively furnished rooms complemented by a very good breakfast. There's a pleasant little coffee shop attached too. **€50**

Ramada Plaza Calea București 31 ☎0372 480 500, ⊛ramadapitesti.ro; map p.95. Luxury hotel offering a level of comfort you'd expect from this competent chain. Although very business orientated, the amply sized rooms

retain a degree of personality, are superbly furnished throughout, and feature spacious bathrooms with fabulous walk-in showers. **€70**

Victoria Str. Egalității 21 ☎0248 220 777, ⊛victoriahotel.ro; map p.95. A large, highly conspicuous establishment, the *Victoria* has a mix of three- and four-star rooms in two separate buildings, though there's not an awful lot to choose between them. There's a spa facility as well. **€50**

EATING

La Tuciuri Str. Primăverii 11 ☎0348 415 343; map p.95. Warm and colourful peasant-themed restaurant cluttered with folksy-cum-kitschy ornamentation, which is all part of the fun. Expect the likes of peasant-style pork ribs (€7) or oven-roast shank of pork with bean stew and pickled cabbage (€6), plus plenty of musical accompaniment. Daily 10am–midnight.

DRINKING AND NIGHTLIFE

The Place Str. Victoriei 15 ☎0733 956 287, ⓦtheplacepitesti.ro; map p.95. With its fetching grey-white painted brick interior, and high wooden tables and stools, *The Place* has a somewhat cooler, less boisterous ambience than the majority of bars clustered down this end of Str. Victoriei, hence it draws a slightly more sophisticated crowd. Mon–Sat 10am–5am, Sun 10am–midnight.

Goleşti

Muzeul Viticulturii şi Pomiculturii • Tues–Sun: April–Sept 9am–6pm; Oct–March 8am–4pm • €4 • ☎0248 266 364, ⓦmuzeulgolesti.ro

The village of **GOLEŞTI**, 8km east of Piteşti just off route 7 (the road running parallel to the Bucharest–Piteşti highway), was once the fiefdom of the Golescus, one of the leading liberal families of nineteenth-century Wallachia – not only were they active members of both the 1821 and 1848 revolutions, but they also worked in favour of Romanian union in 1859 and Romanian independence in 1877.

Their home – now at the heart of a hugely enjoyable open-air **Muzeul Viticulturii şi Pomiculturii** (Museum of Fruit and Vine Growing) – is in fact a *conac* or summer residence (winters would be spent in Bucharest or Paris), and is beautifully cool, with authentic furnishings and historical displays. The museum itself is behind the house, settled among plum and pear orchards, and comprising over one hundred structures from Romania's fruit- and vine-growing communities, mainly dwellings (including the fabulous dugout homes, or "pit houses") – some of which you can enter – but also churches, wine presses and wells. The oldest structure is the wooden church of Drăguteşti, built in 1814. Over the gateway is the immaculately restored *foişor* or watchtower of Tudor Vladimirescu, leader of the 1821 peasant revolt, who was captured here and taken to Târgovişte to be executed. Beside this stands an early nineteenth-century schoolhouse, which still retains some original fixtures and fittings, including German, Greek and Latin textbooks, and a sandbox that was used for practising writing. There's also an interesting little **Ethnographic Museum** in the grounds, exhibiting various viticultural implements, peasant costumes and craftworks.

ARRIVAL AND DEPARTURE   GOLEŞTI

By bus You can get to Goleşti by one of the regular maxitaxis which depart from the Bălcescu hospital in Piteşti (on B-dul I.C. Brătianu).

By train Goleşti station is a 10min walk from the village centre.
Destinations Câmpulung (2 daily; 1hr 5min); Piteşti (13 daily; 10min).

Câmpulung Muscel

Câmpulung, or **CÂMPULUNG MUSCEL** (as it is properly known), 53km north of Piteşti, dates back to pre-Roman times and has played an important role in Wallachia's history, including a stint as the region's first capital after the *voivodate* was forged around 1300. While the town is no great shakes, it's a convenient place to break a journey to Transylvania, with a couple of diversions to keep you occupied.

Mânăstirea Negru Vodă

Str. Negru Vodă 64 • Free

About 500m north of the train station on Str. Negru Vodă, Câmpulung's main drag, is the town's major sight, the **Mânăstirea Negru Vodă** (Negru Vodă monastery), attributed to its namesake, Romania's legendary thirteenth-century Black Prince. The present building, incorporating stonework from the original, was completed in 1832; the most notable tomb is that of Nicolae Basarab, supposedly the oldest princely tombstone in the country; the infirmary chapel to its rear dates from 1718. The monastery's most striking feature is the massive seventeenth-century gate tower – at 35m the highest in Wallachia – with its heavy beech gates, and a twelfth-century stone carving of a doe high up to the left as you enter; this was brought from a nearby Dominican monastery and is remarkably Western European in style.

2

Castrul Roman Jidava

6km south of town en route to Piteşti, by the Pescăreasa rail halt • Tues–Sun 9am–5pm • €1.50 • Maxitaxis en route to Câmpulung stop on the road outside

The remains of the **Roman fort**, or *castrum*, of **Jidava**, part of the Limes Transalutanus defensive line, was built between 190 and 211 then destroyed by the Goths in 244 AD. Partially reconstructed, the site comprises the neatly aligned *praetorium* (commander's office), *principia* (officer's mess) and *horreum* (grain store), beyond which lie the barracks; at its peak, the camp held some five hundred soldiers. Of the four gates, only a section of one survives. The small museum houses some fascinating fragments excavated from the site, including ceramic vessels, helmets, jewellery and bits of weaponry, as well as a mock-up of how the camp would have looked.

ARRIVAL AND DEPARTURE   CÂMPULUNG MUSCEL

By train Trains from Goleşti (just east of Piteşti) terminate at Câmpulung Station, 2km south of town, and are met by maxitaxis.

Destinations Goleşti (2 daily; 1hr 5min).

By bus Regular maxitaxis to and from Piteşti depart from the following locations: the main bus station, located to the east of town across the river at Str. I.C. Frimu; just north of the Negru Vodă Church; and a small terminal by the bridge just south of the town centre.

Destinations Braşov (5 daily; 2hr 50min); Bucharest (9 daily; 2hr 30min); Curtea de Argeş (2 daily; 1hr 40min); Lereşti (hourly; 30min); Piteşti (every 30min; 1hr 25min); Râmnicu Vâlcea (2 daily; 2hr 30min); Târgovişte (1 daily; 1hr 55min).

ACCOMMODATION AND EATING

Pensiunea Nico Pardon Str. Negru Vodă 122 (entrance is actually located on Str. C. Brâncoveanu behind the Bărătei complex) ☎ 0248 510 858, ✉ pensiunea.nico.pardon@yahoo.com. Reasonable, if unexciting, pension possessing nine rooms, whose decor is of rather dubious distinction, but it's clean and cheap. **€30**

Select Str. Republicii 18 ☎ 0722 246 706. It comes as some surprise to find such an accomplished restaurant in Câmpulung, yet *Select* is just that, a happy, convivial establishment offering some terrific dishes, from oven baked polenta to smoked ribs. Daily 10am–10pm.

North to Transylvania

The scenery becomes increasingly dramatic on the road north from Câmpulung into Transylvania. Eight kilometres beyond Câmpulung (at the junction of a lovely road to Târgovişte, to the right), a road branches left to the village of **Nămăesti** (served by maxitaxis), site of a gorgeous little rock church complete with an ancient icon (said to miraculously cure ailments) and cells hewn from sandstone by sixteenth-century monks. Today, the small monastery complex is inhabited by a handful of nuns.

Some 3km further along the road to Braşov, the austere, lighthouse-shaped **Mateias Mausoleum** marks the spot where Romanian troops managed to repel a major German offensive over 45 days in 1916. More than two thousand Romanians lost their lives, their remains now kept in a large glass chest in the ossuary. The walls and ceiling of the mausoleum, meanwhile, are beautifully decorated with mosaics, depicting scenes of war as well as some of Romania's most prominent historical figures, including Mircea the Old, Constantin Brâncoveanu and Vlad Ţepeş.

Beyond the monument, the road continues to the villages of **Dragoslavele** and **Rucăr**, with their traditional wooden houses and verandas. Dragoslavele also has an eighteenth-century wooden church. From Rucăr, the road continues up in a series of hairpin bends towards the Bran (or Giuvala) Pass, encountering the **Bridge of the Dâmbovita**, a spectacular passage between the Dâmboviciorei and Plaiu gorges to the north and the yet narrower Dâmboviţei gorges to the south (see page 165 for the continuation of the route beyond the Bran Pass).

Curtea de Argeş

Thirty-six kilometres northwest of Piteşti, and easily reached by road and rail, the attractive little town of **CURTEA DE ARGEŞ** was another former princely capital – Wallachia's second after Câmpulung and before Târgovişte. While it's not exactly bursting with excitement, the town does boast some of the country's most important religious architecture, and is the ideal base for forays up to Dracula's Castle further north.

Court of Argeş

B-dul Basarabilor • Tues–Sun 10am–6pm • €1.50

At the beginning of the main through street, Bulevardul Basarabilor, stands the **Court of Argeş**, the oldest church in Wallachia. Enclosed by a wall of river boulders, the thirteenth-century complex was rebuilt in the fourteenth century by Radu Negru, otherwise known as Basarab I, the founder of Wallachia. Distinguished by alternate bands of grey stone and red brick, its **Biserica Sfântul Nicolae Domnesc** (Princely Church of St Nicholas) was constructed in 1352 and its interior decorated with frescoes in 1384; later restoration work has now been largely removed to reveal the original frescoes, which are fully in the Byzantine tradition but wonderfully alive and individual, reminiscent of Giotto rather than the frozen poses of the Greek masters. The early Basarab rulers are buried here.

Muzeul Municipal

Str. Negru Vodă 2 • Tues–Sun 9am–4pm • €1 • ☎ 0248 721 446

Numerous artefacts from the Princely Church are on display in the **Muzeul Municipal** (Town Museum), located just across the road in the pink-and-white painted villa. Among the more interesting items here (and there's good English captioning too) is a 600-year-old stone slab bearing the coat of arms of Vlad Ţepeş's father, Vlad Dracul, a fine collection of ceramic stove plaques, including a superb one of a Wallachian prince on horseback, and the tailcoats and other personal possessions of Armand Călinescu (prime minister for just six months in 1939).

Biserica Episcopala

B-dul Basarabilor • Daily 8am–7pm • €2.50

Resembling the creation of an inspired confectioner, the monastery, or **Biserica Episcopala** (Episcopal Church), is a boxy structure enlivened by whorls, rosettes and fancy trimmings, rising into two twisted, octagonal belfries, each festooned with little spheres and the three-armed cross of Orthodoxy.

In the park across the road, **Manole's Well** is a spring said to have been created by the death of **Manole**, the Master Builder of Curtea de Argeş. Legend has it that Manole was marooned on the rooftop of his creation, the Episcopal Church, when Prince Neagoe Basarab, who had commissioned him to build it, ordered the scaffolding to be removed, to ensure that the builder could not repeat his masterwork for anyone else. Manole tried to escape with the aid of wings made from roofing shingles – only to crash to his death, whereupon a spring gushed forth immediately. The story is perhaps that of a crude form of justice, for legend also has it that Manole had immured his wife within the walls of the monastery – at the time it was believed that *stafia* or ghosts were needed to keep buildings from collapse.

The current Episcopal Church is not Manole's original creation of 1512 to 1517 but a re-creation of 1875 to 1885 by the Frenchman Lecomte de Noüy, who grafted on all the Venetian mosaics and Parisian woodwork; he wanted to do the same to the Princely Church (see page 93), but the historian Nicolae Iorga managed to get legal backing to stop him. Inside the garish red, green and gold interior lie the ostentatiously crafted tombs of King Carol I (1866–1914) and his wife Elizabeth, and King Ferdinand (1914–27) and his wife Marie, as well as the tomb of Basarab himself.

ARRIVAL AND DEPARTURE
CURTEA DE ARGEŞ

By train The ornate but now sadly decrepit Mughal-style train station is a 5min walk from the town centre on Str. 1 Mai – turn left out of the station then right up Str. Traian and left on Str. Negru Vodă. This continues as B-dul Basarabilor; it's one-way northbound, so maxitaxis loop south on Str. 1 Mai.
Destinations Piteşti (3 daily; 50min).

By bus The bus station is adjacent to the train station. Note that maxitaxis run from outside the Princely Church (every 15min) as far as Bascov, from where you get another maxitaxi to Piteşti, 10km to the south.
Destinations Arefu (hourly; 20min); Bucharest (8 daily; 2hr 20min); Câmpulung (2 daily; 1hr 40min); Râmnicu Vâlcea (2 daily; 1hr 40min).

ACCOMMODATION AND EATING

Domnesc B-dul Basarabilor 106 ☏0727 364 716, ⓦrestaurantuldomnesc.ro. The most enjoyable spot in town for a bite to eat (pizza, pasta, grilled meats and traditional Romanian dishes) or a drink, be it a daytime caffeine hit or an evening beer; lounge-type seating, big bay windows and large TV screens add to the air of informality. Daily 7am–12.30am.
Pensiunea Montana B-dul Basarabilor 72 ☏0248 722 364, ⓦpensiunea-montana.ro. It's been around for years,

and the plain, pine-furnished rooms are nothing special, but it's a clean, friendly establishment and is as cheap as you could reasonably expect. **€32**
Posada B-dul Basarabilor 27 ☏0248 721 451, ⓦhotelposada.ro. Located 300m up from the *Montana*, this ugly, concrete low-rise has two categories of room, all with flatscreen TVs and a/c, though there's only a marginal price difference between them. **€40**

Arefu, Cetatea Poienari and Lacul Vidraru
Cetatea Poienari On a crag north of the village, 4km north on the road from Arefu • Daily 9am–5pm • €1

Twenty-five kilometres north of Curtea de Argeş is **AREFU** (or Aref), a long, ramshackle village 3km west of the valley road – if you're travelling by car, be warned that the surface from the main road to the village is very rough. It was to here, in 1457, that the survivors of Vlad the Impaler's massacre in Târgovişte (see page 398) were marched to begin work on his castle. Although the tourist industry focuses on Bran castle in Transylvania (see page 137), which has almost no connection to the Dracula myth (aside from the fact that he may have attacked it on occasion), **Cetatea Poienari** (Poienari Castle, aka Dracula's Castle) was once Vlad the Impaler's residence, and its location in the foothills of the Făgăraş mountains makes for a wonderfully dramatic setting.

The castle can only be reached by climbing 1480 steps (about a 30min walk) from the hydroelectric power station (and a kiosk selling refreshments), which proves a powerful disincentive to most visitors. There are plenty of maxitaxis from Curtea de Argeş, but only as far as Arefu, so you'll need to walk (or hitch a lift) beyond there. Struggle to the top and you'll find that the citadel is surprisingly small, one-third having collapsed down the mountainside in 1888. Entering by a narrow wooden bridge, you'll come across the crumbling remains of two towers within; the prism-shaped one was the old keep, Vlad's residential quarters, from where, according to legend, the Impaler's wife flung herself out of the window, declaring that she "would rather have her body rot and be eaten by the fish of the Argeş" than be captured by the Turks, who were then besieging the castle. Legend also has it that Vlad himself escaped over the mountains on horseback, fooling his pursuers by shoeing his mount backwards – or, according to some versions, by affixing horseshoes that left the impression of cow prints.

From Poienari, you can continue up the twisting road for 4km to **Lacul Vidraru** (Lake Vidraru), held back by a spectacular dam (165m) constructed in 1965 and some 10km long. Beyond the lake, the spectacular **Transfăgărașan Highway** continues across the **Făgăraș mountains** and into Transylvania (see page143).

ACCOMMODATION   AREFU AND AROUND

Cabana la Cetate Just below Poienari Castle ☎0728 827 769, ⊕ cabanalacetate.ro. A very convenient stopover before pushing on into Transylvania, this convivial roadside pension offers big, balconied rooms with simple dark wood furnishings; triples also available. Even if you're not staying, the restaurant is a good place for a bite to eat. Breakfast costs €4. **€28**

Cabana de Pesti Lake Vidraru, some 8km on from the dam, above the main road beside the lake ☎0248 506 047. This popular fishermen's hotel has comfortable, if fairly dull, rooms as well as an excellent range of recreational facilities and a very creditable fish restaurant. **€40**

Râmnicu Vâlcea

The **River Olt** runs south from its source in Transylvania through the Red Tower Pass below Sibiu, carving a stupendous 50km gorge through the Carpathians down into Wallachia, where it passes through **RÂMNICU VÂLCEA**, 34km west of Curtea de Argeş, and continues south to the Danube.

Sprawling across successive terraces above the River Olt, Râmnicu Vâlcea is a typically systematized town, with many communist-era apartment blocks and more modern malls, but there are half a dozen attractive old churches as well as an excellent open-air museum here. Just about everything of interest is on, or just off, the town's main street, Calea lui Traian, which runs along the western side of the main square, Piaţa Mircea cel Bătrân.

Muzeul de Istorie and Muzeul de Artă

Muzeul de Istorie Calea lui Traian 143 • Tues–Sun: April–Oct 10am–6pm; Nov–March 9am–5pm • €1 • ☎ 0350 401 898 **Muzeul de Artă** Str. Carol I 25 • Wed–Sun 10am–6pm • €1 • ☎ 0250 738 121

Archeology fans certainly won't feel short-changed by the **Muzeul de Istorie** (History Museum), thanks to its glittering hoard of local finds: pitchers, ceramic urns and grave goods (bracelets, beads, earrings and the like). The most intriguing item is a gold Dacian mask from Ocniţa, which Ceauşescu kept in his office until his overthrow in 1989.

Directly behind the County Museum, the grand Casa Simian houses the **Muzeul de Arta**. As well as a painting apiece by Grigorescu (*March of the Peasants*) and Pallady (*Woman in Armchair*), there are works by Tonitza, Petrascu and Ion Ţuculescu, the last represented here by some delightful street scenes painted in oil. The impressive sculpture collection is dominated by the prolific Storck family (see page 54), namely Karl, his son Frederic, and his wife, Cecilia Cutescu-Storck.

Muzeul Satului Vâlcea

On the E81, at the northern town limits • Tues–Sun: April–Sept 10am–6pm; Oct–March 9am–5pm • €1.50 • ☎ 0250 746 869 • Take a maxitaxi from town

A fifteen-minute walk south from the Bujoreni train station, the superb **Muzeul Satului Vâlcea** (Bujoreni open-air museum) comprises a fine ensemble of some eighty structures laid out as per a typical village from the Vâlcea region. It's possible to enter a good cross section of these units, including a splendidly preserved inn (1899), one of the village's largest buildings and its social focus, a perfectly furnished village school (1904), complete with period books and maps, and a *cula* or watchtower, dating from 1802. The two oldest buildings are wooden churches, one dating from 1785 complete with a candelabrum featuring wooden eggs hanging below wooden birds, and some original icons, and the other – a relatively new addition – dating from 1655, whose roof slopes almost all the way down to the ground.

ARRIVAL AND INFORMATION

By train The train station is east of the centre on Str. V. Popescu, from where it's a 10min walk along Str. Regina Maria (50m to the left of the station as you exit) to Piaţa Mircea cel Bătrân and Calea lui Traian.

Destinations Călimăneşti (9 daily; 15–25min); Craiova (4 daily; 2–4hr); Piatra Olt (10 daily; 1hr 10min–2hr 20min); Podu Olt (5 daily; 1hr 50min–2hr 20min); Sibiu (5 daily; 2hr 15min–2hr 50min).

RÂMNICU VÂLCEA

By bus The bus station is south of the river on Str. G. Coşbuc, from where it's a short walk to the left along Str. Dacia and right on Calea lui Traian to cross the bridge into the centre.

Destinations Bucharest (every 30min; 3hr); Câmpulung (2 daily; 2hr 45min); Cozia (every 20–30min; 50min); Craiova (6 daily; 2hr 45min); Curtea de Argeş (2 daily; 1hr 40min); Horezu (every 45min; 1hr 15min); Piteşti (every 30min; 1hr 20min); Sibiu (hourly; 2hr 15min); Târgu Jiu (8 daily; 2hr 45min).

ACCOMMODATION AND EATING

Castel Str. Praporgescu 5 ☎ 0250 730 003, ⊛ hotel-castel.ro. A 5min walk north of Piaţa Mircea cel Bătrân, this quirkily designed building offers a warm welcome and colourfully decorated rooms, which are further enlivened by bits of artwork. **€48**

Hanul Haiducilor Calea lui Traian 171 ☎ 0250 717 956. Although not especially refined, the rustically themed "Outlaws Inn" is a terrific place to tuck into a big bowl of Romanian stew (*tocana*) or plate of sausages (*mititei*) washed down with a pint of Ursus; the restaurant's long hours ensures a constant flow of hungry punters. Cheap and good fun. Daily 8am–1am.

★ **Simfonia** Str. G. Enescu 42–44 ☎ 0350 800 000, ⊛ hotelsimfonia.ro. This quiet residential street south of the river, is the last place – indeed this is the last town – you'd expect to find a hotel as chic as this. The three floors are designed according to a particular theme, namely Classic (light beige decor, dark mahogany furnishings and floral-patterned textiles), Modern (striking contemporary furnishings in bold reds and blacks) and Mediterranean (gentle blues and turquoise-marbled bathrooms). The restaurant, too, looks stunning with its beautifully laid, candle-topped tables and an immensely enticing menu of contemporary international dishes such as escalope of foie gras with miso sauce and peaches (€15), and salmon ravioli with vodka sauce. **€65**

The Olt valley

The twin settlements of Călimăneşti–Căciulata mark the entrance to the **Olt valley**, a deep twisting gorge of great beauty and the site of several monasteries, the most notable of which is **Cozia**. While the main road runs along the Olt's west bank, a lesser road (as far as Cozia) and the rail line follow the other side of the defile.

Cozia monastery

1km north of Căciulata • Open access

Beautifully pitched amid elegant pine trees and fragrant rose bushes, **Cozia monastery** is the earliest example of Byzantine architecture in Wallachia. Built by Serb architects in 1388 – thanks to the patronage of Vlad Țepeș's grandfather, Mircea the Old (who is buried within the monastery) – the church's principal architectural features include alternating bands of brick and stone, filigree latticework and fluted, false pillars. The church portico was added by Constantin Brâncoveanu in the early eighteenth century, although it's not a particularly striking example of the Brâncovenesc style. Note, too, the stained-glass windows featuring Mircea as well as notable historical figures such as Burebista and Decebal; believe it or not, in 1986 portraits of the Ceaușescus were added to two of the windows, before being unceremoniously removed just a few years later – and presumably destroyed since.

The monastery also houses a small **museum of religious art**, exhibiting a dazzling collection of church treasures – mostly seventeenth- to nineteenth-century icons.

Târgu Jiu

Forewarned about **TÂRGU JIU** and the surrounding **Jiu valley** – with its grim coal and lignite mines – visitors often decide to ignore them completely. Although Târgu Jiu has no links with coal mining itself, it still suffered the gross "modernization" imposed by Ceaușescu on Romania's coal-mining centres, with homes knocked down to make way for unattractive and impractical concrete blocks. However, this busy, dusty town does merit a visit on the strength of the monumental sculptures that **Constantin Brâncuși** (see box below) created in the late 1930s as a war memorial for the town of his boyhood. He offered a series of twelve sculptures, but completed only four before he

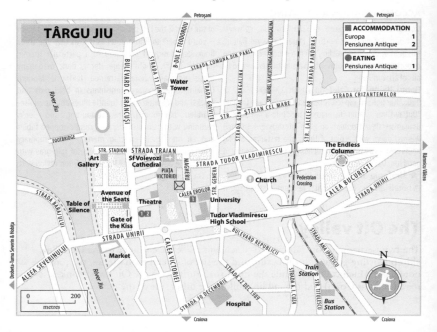

CONSTANTIN BRÂNCUȘI

One of the greatest sculptors of the twentieth century, **Constantin Brâncuși** was born in 1876 in a peasant cottage at Hobița, some 28km west of Târgu Jiu. He came to town at the age of 9 to work as an errand boy, and later learned the techniques of the local woodcarvers, who chiselled sinuous designs on rafters, verandas and wells in the region. Through the sponsorship of local boyars, he was able to attend an art college in Craiova and went on to the **National School of Fine Arts** in Bucharest, before arriving at the Ecole des Beaux Arts in Paris in 1904 with a government scholarship of 600 Lei. He stayed in France for over fifty years, helping create a revolution in sculpture with his strikingly strong and simple works. With a circle of friends that included Picasso, Gide and Pound, he was at the centre of the intellectual ferment of Paris at its height.

He worked briefly in Rodin's studio, then, in company with Amadeo Modigliani, discovered the primitive forms of African masks and sculptures, concentrating thereafter on stripping forms down to their fundamentals. In 1907, he claimed that "what is real is not the exterior form but the essence of things", a credo which he pursued for the rest of his career. In 1920, his *Prințesa X* was removed by police from the Salon des Indépendents because it was considered obscenely phallic; it was bought by Fernand Léger and Blaise Cendrars, but Brâncuși never exhibited in Paris again. A different sort of scandal followed in 1926 when Brâncuși took his *Măiastra (Magic Bird)* with him to New York. US Customs classified it as "a piece of metal" and levied import duty of $10; Brâncuși appealed against the decision, thereby starting a furore which made him a household name in America. During that same trip, the photographer Edward Steichen gave credibility to Brâncuși's work by publicly announcing that he had bought one of the sculptor's bronze *Birds in Flight* for $600 – by 1967, it was worth $175,000. Brâncuși died in 1957, with his series of sculptures for Târgu Jiu unfinished, and is buried in Montparnasse cemetery in Paris. As well as Târgu Jiu, you'll find examples of his work in Craiova and Bucharest, and also in London, New York, Philadelphia and Washington; his last studio is preserved in Paris.

died – indeed, these were the only large-scale projects by Brâncuși to come to fruition anywhere.

Coloană Infinita

Parcul Coloanei Fără Sfârșit, at the eastern end of Calea Eroilor

The most iconic of Brâncuși's works is the stunning **Coloană Infinita** (*Endless Column*), a vast 30m-high totem pole of seventeen (fifteen whole) smooth rhomboidal blocks, cast in iron and threaded onto a carbon steel post embedded into the ground; the column's rippling form is echoed in many of the verandas of the old wooden houses throughout the region. Brâncuși actually began working on variations of the column in 1918 (the original, oak, one is in the Museum of Modern Art in New York), though this structure wasn't installed until 1938, following a request from the local authorities to create a memorial for those killed during World War I. It is, without question, one of the most striking – and recognizable – pieces of architecture not just in Romania, but anywhere in Europe.

Poarta Sărutului, Aleea Scaunilor and Masa Tăcerii

Parcul Municipal Constantin Brâncuși

Brâncuși's other sculptures lie at the opposite end of Calea Eroilor, which runs 1.7km west from the *Endless Column* to the municipal park on the banks of the Jiu River: at the entrance to the park is the **Poarta Sărutului** (*Gate of the Kiss*), composed from travertine (limestone) from Banpotoc in Hunedoara county, and whose distinctive kiss motifs appear on the two chunky pillars. This opens up onto the **Aleea Scaunilor** (*Avenue of Seats*), flanked by lime trees and thirty stone chairs clustered into groups of three (these are not intended for sitting on, a rule that is surprisingly well respected), which in turn leads to the **Masa Tăcerii** (*Table of Silence*), surrounded by twelve hourglass-shaped stools representing the continuity of the months and the traditional number of seats at a funeral feast; interestingly, the seats are positioned a little distance from the table itself. Unfortunately, the vista east from the park to the *Endless Column* is blocked by a modern, ugly church.

ARRIVAL AND DEPARTURE TÂRGU JIU

By train and bus The train and bus stations are just a stone's throw apart on Str. Titulescu, a 20min walk east of town.

Destinations (Train) Filiași (12 daily; 1hr 10min–2hr 20min); Petroșani (6 daily; 1hr 10min–1hr 40min); Simeria (2 daily; 3hr 10min); Subcetate (2 daily; 2hr 20min).

Destinations (Bus) Baia de Fier (every 90min; 1hr 20min); Bucharest (6 daily; 5hr 45min); Craiova (hourly; 2hr); Drobeta-Turnu Severin (4 daily; 2hr 15min); Horezu (hourly; 1hr 20min); Petroșani (hourly; 1hr 20min); Pitești (4 daily; 4hr); Polovragi (8 daily; 1hr 20min); Râmnicu Vâlcea (6 daily; 2hr 45min); Tismana (8 daily; 1hr 20min).

ACCOMMODATION AND EATING

Europa Calea Eroilor 22 ☎ 0253 211 810, ⊛ hotelrestauranteuropa.ro; map p.104. The town's most prominent hotel won't set the pulse racing, but the rooms are generously sized and well furnished, even if the decor isn't the most tasteful. **€52**

★ **Pensiunea Antique** B-dul Constantin Brâncuși 33 ☎ 0353 415 120, ⊛ pensiuneaantique.ro; map p.104. By some distance the most agreeable place in town to stay, this classy little pension's ten rooms are furnished with smooth hardwood flooring, mahogany beds, polished brass fittings and colourfully patterned bedspreads and drapes, plus the odd bit of wall-mounted artwork. The restaurant here is really the only place in town worth considering, but that's no bad thing; a handsome, brick-vaulted cellar with a menu offering an upscale take on mainly Italian dishes. **€45**

Horezu

Set amid apple and plum orchards, sweet chestnut trees and wild lilac, 16km east of Polovragi on the main road to Râmnicu Vâlcea, is the small town of **HOREZU** – so-called after the numerous owls (*huhurezi*) that reside here (the town is also shown as Hurez on some maps). Although wooden furniture and wrought-iron objects are also

---

CONSTANTIN BRÂNCOVEANU

Constantin Brâncoveanu (1654–1714) became ruler of Wallachia in 1689 after the usual Byzantine family intrigues, and was instrumental in bringing about a cultural renaissance by establishing a printing press in Bucharest and a school of architecture and sculpture at the monastery of Horezu. He created an **architectural style** that was a fusion of Western (especially Venetian) Renaissance and Ottoman elements, characterized by a harmonious layout and fine ornamental stone carving, especially on balconies, external staircases and arcades. In the early twentieth century a neo-Brâncovenesc style was very popular, especially in Wallachia and Moldavia, as an expression of the new nation's cultural identity.

Politically, he sought to distance Wallachia from its Ottoman overlords (partly because he wanted to keep some of the massive taxes they demanded to use for his building projects). At the outbreak of a Russo-Turkish War in 1710 he sought alliances with the Russians, as well as the Habsburgs, while also being prepared to fight on the Turkish side if they seemed likelier winners. However, he was arrested, tortured and (with his four sons and grand treasurer Enache Văcărescu) executed in 1714 in Constantinople. He was succeeded by his cousin Ștefan Cantacuzino, who was soon deposed and executed by the Ottomans and replaced by Nicolai Mavrocordat, the first Phanariot ruler of Wallachia (having already been the first Phanariot ruler of Moldavia).

In 1992 Brâncoveanu, and those executed with him, were declared saints and martyrs by the Romanian Orthodox Church, honoured as protectors of the Orthodox faith against Islam. Nevertheless, to the outside world it is his artistic and cultural achievements that are his lasting legacy.

produced here, Horezu is best known for its **pottery**, especially its plates, which by tradition are given as keepsakes during funeral wakes. The Cocoşul de Horezu **pottery fair**, held on the first Sunday of June, is one of the year's biggest events in the area – though if you miss it, you can still see many wares displayed in dozens of roadside huts just east of the centre. There's also an exhibition of local pottery in a large hut by the car park leading up to Horezu monastery, where you can view and buy items.

Mânăstirea Hurezi

Near the village of Romanii de Jos, around 3km northeast of Horezu , turning off the main road 2km east of Horezu • Open access • ☎ 0250 860 071 • Taxis available via tourist office (see below)

2

Built between 1691 and 1697, and now a UNESCO World Heritage Site, **Mânăstirea Hurezi** (Horezu monastery) is the largest and finest of Wallachia's Brâncoveanu complexes, and is the site of the school which established the Brâncovenesc style. The complex is centred around the **Great Church**, built in 1693 and entered via a marvellous ten-pillared porchway, its capitals adorned with stone-carved acanthus leaves and its doors of carved pearwood framed by a beautiful marble portal; to the right of the entrance, and largely protected from the elements, is a still vibrantly colourful *Last Judgement* fresco. Inside, the late seventeenth-century **frescoes**, once tarnished by the smoke from fires lit by Turkish slaves who camped here, have been restored, and you can now make out portraits of Constantin Brâncoveanu and his family, Cantacuzino, Basarab, and the monastery's first abbot, Ioan, as well as scenes from Mount Athos and the Orthodox calendar. To the right of the church as you enter is a vacant tomb, which was Brâncoveanu's intended resting place – as it is, he is buried in St George's Church in Bucharest (see page 62).

The monastery actually held a community of monks until 1872, at which point it became a nunnery. Opposite the church is the nuns' domed refectory, which contains some more but poorly preserved frescoes and, to the left, another Brâncoveanu porch, featuring a splendid stone balustrade carved with animal motifs. In one of the upper cloisters, there's a collection of sacral art, mainly seventeenth-century icons.

ARRIVAL AND INFORMATION   HOREZU

By bus The bus station is in the centre of town on the main DN65 road.

Destinations Bucharest (6 daily; 4hr); Horezu monastery (5 daily; 15min); Râmnicu Vâlcea (hourly; 1hr 15min); Sibiu (4 daily; 3hr 30min); Târgu Jiu (8 daily; 1hr 20min).

Tourist information A surprising but welcome find, the helpful tourist office is 200m from the bus station at Str. Vladimirescu 63A (Mon–Fri 8am–7pm, Sat & Sun 10am–4pm; ☎ 0350 801 575, ⚑ horezu-infoturism.ro). If you want to visit the monastery but don't have your own wheels or don't want to rely on buses, the tourist office can order a taxi (around €10 return).

ACCOMMODATION

Pensiunea Criveanu Str. Căpitan Maldăr 5 ☎ 0768 103 205, ⚑ pensiuneacriveanu.ro. Located around 300m behind the bus station, this is easily the most enticing of the town's many guesthouses, a warm, family-run place with seven en-suite rooms plus a kitchen and garden, both of which guests are free to avail themselves of. Breakfast not included. €20

Popasul Trei Stejari 2km back out on the road to Târgu Jiu ☎ 0767 976 486. Decent, if basic, campsite, which also has tiny, bunker-like wooden huts sleeping two (twin beds only). Toilet and shower facilities available. Tent €3, huts €10

Hobiţa

Casa Memorială Brâncuşi Near the main crossroads in the centre of the village • Wed–Sun 9am–5pm • €1 • If it's closed, you can ask in the shop at the crossroads for the museum's custodian to let you in

The small scenic towns and villages to the west of Târgu Jiu are a complete contrast to the flat, grimy mining areas to the east and south. Buses run from Târgu Jiu along the DN67d, stopping close to most of the sites of interest. From Peştişani, 21km west of Târgu Jiu, it's 3km south to the small village of **HOBIȚA**, birthplace of Constantin Brâncuși (see box opposite). An attractive, traditional cottage, surrounded by plum and cherry trees, the sculptor's childhood home has been turned into a small **museum**, the **Casa Memorială Brâncuși**. Originally built by his father around 1870, the three-roomed abode was inherited by his sister, Firzina Brânza, who then had the house moved from its original location and set up here, on new foundations, some 200m away. While you'll learn relatively little about Brâncuși here, it's worth seeing the lovely, abundant ceramics and textiles displayed inside, and the intricate spiral motifs on the veranda posts.

Drobeta-Turnu Severin

DROBETA-TURNU SEVERIN (usually known simply as Severin) lies on the north side of the **River Danube**, the country's natural border with Serbia and Bulgaria. The river narrows below Moldova Veche before surging through the **Kazan gorge** towards Orșova, only to be tamed and harnessed by the dam at the mighty **Iron Gates** before reaching the town. Dubbed the "town of roses" for its beautiful parks, notably the archeological park around the Museum of the Iron Gates, with its lovely roses and walnut trees, the towns has a modern appearance that belies its origins as the Dacian settlement of Drobeta, more than two thousand years ago. As pleasant as Severin is, there's not a lot to get excited about, but it does make a decent base if you're intent on exploring the Kazan gorge.

Podul lui Traian

The town's Roman conquerors left some enduring landmarks, notably the ruins of **Podul lui Traian** (Trajan's Bridge), which Apollodorus of Damascus built to span the Danube at the order of the emperor in 103 to 105 AD. As the travel writer Patrick Leigh Fermor put it, "two great stumps of his conglomerate masonry still cumbered the Romanian side", and these can be seen from the train or from the grounds of the Museum of the Iron Gates, which, it seems, is destined never to open. Within

---

THE IRON GATES

The **Iron Gates** is a cliff-lined stretch of the River Danube which once had a formidable reputation, owing to the navigational hazards (eddies, whirlpools and rocks) that formerly restricted safe passage during the two hundred days of the year when the river was in spate. The blasting of a channel in 1896 obviated these terrors, and the building of a **hydroelectric dam** at Gura Văii, 10km upstream of Drobeta-Turnu Severin, finally tamed the river.

Conceived in 1956, the Porțile de Fier I hydroelectric project was undertaken as a joint venture; Romania and Yugoslavia (as it was then) each built a 1GW turbine plant and locks for shipping on their respective banks, linked by a slipway dam and an international road crossing. That task took from 1960 until 1972 and raised the river level by 33m. Romantics have deplored the results, which, in the words of Patrick Leigh Fermor, "has turned 130 miles of the Danube into a vast pond which has swollen and blurred the course of the river beyond recognition", turning "beetling crags into mild hills". The damming has submerged two places worthy of footnotes in history – the island of **Ada Kaleh** and old **Orșova** – and reduced the Danube's peak flow, so that the pollution of Central Europe is no longer flushed out to sea but gathers here, killing fish and flora. On the E70 (DN6) 10km west of Drobeta-Turnu Severin, the dam can be reached by bus #3 (*Baraj*) from the local *autogară* at the junction of Strada Traian and Strada Calărasi, just east of the Roman fort in Severin.

the museum precincts, or *Parc Arheologic*, are the remains of a Roman bath and the foundations of both the fort that guarded Trajan's bridge and the fourteenth-century **Metropolitan's Basilica**.

Castelul de Apă

Castelul de Apă Str. Crişan • Daily 8am–9pm

The town's most striking piece of architecture is the **Castelul de Apă** (Water Castle), a monumental, 27m-high structure dating from 1910, and which supplied the city with its water until 1980. Visitors have the option of clambering the four hundred or so steps, or taking the lift to the top, from where there are sensational views of the Danube; lit up at night, the castle looks quite spectacular.

ARRIVAL AND DEPARTURE   **DROBETA-TURNU SEVERIN**

By train From the train station it's a 15min walk east along B-dul Carol I to the centre.

Destinations Băile Herculane (3 daily; 50min); Caransebeş (3 daily; 2hr 20min); Craiova (5 daily; 2–3hr); Orşova (5 daily; 30min); Timişoara (3 daily; 3hr 50min).

By bus The main bus station is to the east of the centre on Str. Topolniţei (buses #1 and #45).

Destinations Băile Herculane (8 daily; 1hr); Craiova (10 daily; 2hr); Orşova (hourly; 30min–1hr); Tårgu Jiu (4 daily; 2hr 15min); Timişoara (9 daily; 4hr 15min).

ACCOMMODATION AND EATING

Clipa Str. Brâncoveanu 165 ☎0352 401 723; map p.109. The town's most accomplished hotel offers plush red carpeted rooms furnished in smooth pine, while the lounge-like café is pretty much the only place in Drobeta to get a decent cup of coffee. **€38**

Continental B-dul Carol I 2 ☎02523 306 730, ✆continentalhotels.ro; map p.109. The obvious

draw in what is otherwise a tremendously average hotel are the views from the river-facing rooms, though it's also a friendly and very reasonably priced establishment. **€30**

D-L-Goe Str. Adrian 113 ☎0252 331 431; map p.109. Above the café of the same name, this ordinary looking pizzeria actually rustles up terrific thin-crust pizzas, as well as a few pasta dishes and salads, and you've also got brilliant views of the Water Castle directly outside. Mon–Fri 8am–10pm, Sat 5–11pm, Sun 9am–noon.

Hostel Tineretului Str. Crişan 25 ☎ 0252 317 999; map p.109. Located within the town's Youth Hall, this simple hostel offers rooms with either two or three beds, all with bathroom. No breakfast. **€16**

The Kazan gorge

Some 40km upstream of Drobeta-Turnu Severin, on both sides of the village of **DUBOVA**, the sheer cliffs of the **Kazan gorge** (Cazanele Dunării) fall 600m into the tortuous river. Rather than attempt to cut a path through the rock, the Romans bored holes into the side of the cliff and added beams and planks to roof over the road and discourage Dacian ambushes. The first proper road was created on the northern side of the gorge on the initiative of the nineteenth-century Hungarian statesman Count Szechenyi, but had not long been finished when the 1920 Trianon Treaty transferred it to Romania, whereupon it was neglected and finally submerged in the 1970s by the rising waters. Since the building of the dam, modern roads have been built on both sides of the river, and the dramatic landscape makes this an excursion not to be missed. The authorities aren't keen on tourists canoeing down the Danube (mainly because of the industrial barges using the river and the proximity of the border with Serbia), but it's a great drive.

CROSSING INTO BULGARIA: CALAFAT AND GIURGIU

The neat, orderly town of **Calafat**, 84km southwest of Craiova, is one of the two major border crossings into Bulgaria. Linking Calafat with Vidin in Bulgaria is the rather grandly titled **New Europe Bridge**, completed in 2013; the toll is currently €6. It's less than ten minutes' walk straight ahead from the train station (just east of the port) to the centre of Calafat, marked by a war memorial; to the right is the market, and to the left is the House of Culture (Casa de Cultură), next to a couple of cafés and snack bars.

The second major crossing point into Bulgaria, and more convenient if travelling from Bucharest, is via the 3km-long **Danube Bridge** from **Giurgiu**, 64km south of the capital, to Ruse; the road toll is currently €2. Hourly maxitaxis depart from Bucharest to Giurgiu, while trains crawl from Bucharest's Gara de Nord to Giurgiu Nord Station just outside the town (2 direct daily; 8 via Videle; 1hr 45min); alternatively, you can travel from the Gara de Nord to Videle and wait for a connection to Giurgiu Station, in the town next to the bus terminal. From Bucharest, one train a day stops at Giurgiu Nord en route to Istanbul, and another stops en route to Sofia. Further east of the Danube Bridge, there's a ferry service across the Danube from Călăraşi to Silistra (6 daily).

Craiova

Almost every locomotive on the tracks of Romania originally emerged from the Electroputere workshops of **CRAIOVA**, while the city is also a centre for the Romanian automobile industry, the former Oltcit works (now Ford Romania) having produced many of the country's cars. These industries are here because of the ready availability of oil, whose presence is attested to by the derricks surrounding what is now the chief city of Oltenia and capital of Dolj county. Craiova does have a longer history than it might appear from its industrial heritage, having begun life as the Roman town of Pelendava, and **Michael the Brave** (see page 377) began his career here as deputy governor. Today, it's a sprawling and hectic place, but you may find yourself breaking a journey to or from Bulgaria, in which case there's a cluster of impressive museums to while away the time. On the southern edge of the city (down Calea Unirii) is the superb **Parcul Romanescu**, laid out by French architects in 1901–03, with a zoo and lake and the first cable suspension bridge in Europe.

Palatul Jean Mihail and Muzeul de Artă

Calea Unirii 15 • Tues–Sun 10am–5pm • €2.50 • ☎ 0251 412 342, ⓦ muzeuldeartacraiova.ro

Built from 1900 to 1907 by the renowned French architect, Paul Gottereau, for Constantin Mihail, one of Romania's richest men, the elegant neo-Baroque **Palatul Jean Mihail** has played host to some notable figures over the years, including Kings Ferdinand and Mihai, both of whom lived here for short periods. It was also from this palace that Tito (the future Yugoslav president) conducted the liberation of Belgrade in October 1944, before it served as home to Nicolae Ceauşescu in the early 1950s when he was local party secretary.

Since 1954, it has housed the fine **Muzeul de Artă** (Museum of Art), one of the most complete collections of Romanian art outside Bucharest. All the big-hitters are here; Andreescu, Pallady, Tattarescu, Tonitza and so on, but there's a particularly fine selection of paintings by Aman, including a clutch of delightful miniatures (*Cossack* and *Milkman*), while Grigorescu is represented by some two dozen paintings ranging from his traditional peasant landscapes to more dramatic works like the brilliant *Smârdan Attack*. The museum's undisputed draw, however, is the room housing half a dozen pieces by Brâncuşi, which are the only examples of the sculptor's work in Romania outside Bucharest and Târgu Jiu. Perhaps the most celebrated of these is the masterful stone composition, *The Kiss*, though no less stunning are the three bronzes: *Head of a Child*, *Pride* and, best of all, *Mademoiselle Pogany*, a model of the eponymous

Hungarian painter whom he met in Paris in 1911. More unusually, there's a wooden corner chair that he sculpted whilst a student at the Craiova School of Arts and Crafts.

Muzeul Ştiinţele Naturii

Str. Popa Şapcă 4 • Tues–Sun 9am–5pm • €1 • ☎ 0251 411 906, ⓦ muzeulolteniei.ro

The **Muzeul Ştiinţele Naturii** (Natural History Museum) offers a bit more than the usual grim assortment of stuffed animals. The main ground floor exhibition is entitled Terra Fossils, an above average collection of fossilized remains from Oltenia, though the star of the show is a magnificent pair of tusks from a Mastodon discovered in 1927 in the village of Stoina in Gorj county, and a substantial hoard of cave bear remains from the Peştera Muierilor, near Baia de Fier, 120km north of Craiova. The first floor is taken up with the requisite flora and fauna, and a mock-up of the Peştera Cave, while up on the second floor there's a somewhat random exhibition on the solar system, the most interesting exhibit being three lumps of a meteorite that fell nearby in 1927.

Muzeul de Etnografie

Str. Matei Basarab 14 • Tues–Sun 9am–5pm • €1 • ☎ 0351 444 030, ⓦ muzeulolteniei.ro

The oldest civic building in the city, the Casa Băniei (governor's residence) originally dates from the late fifteenth century (only the cellar remains) but was reconstructed by Brâncoveanu in 1699. During the eighteenth century, it functioned as the premises for the Austrian administration. These days, it's occupied by the very worthwhile **Muzeul de Etnografie** (Ethnographic Museum), with a fabulous assortment of local costumes, ceramics from Horezu, porch pillars and some exquisitely carved staffs.

ARRIVAL AND DEPARTURE
CRAIOVA

By plane Craiova's airport (☎ 0251 416 860, ⓦ aeroportcraiova.ro), currently with flights to London Luton and a handful of other European destinations, is some 5km east of the centre out on the E70 road to Piteşti; bus #9 (€0.75) runs from the stop in front of the airport into the centre.

By train and bus Craiova's train and bus stations are located side by side northeast of the centre on Str. Dacia, from where it's a 20min walk along B-dul Carol I (or minibuses #1, #5, #12 and #29) to the main through road, Calea Bucureşti.

Destinations (Train) Bucharest (10 daily; 3hr–4hr 15min); Calafat (2 daily; 3hr 20min); Drobeta-Turnu Severin (6 daily; 2–3hr); Filiaşi (12 daily; 30–50min); Piatra Olt (8 daily; 45min–1hr 20min); Piteşti (4 daily; 2hr 30min–4hr); Sibiu (3 daily; 4hr 50min); Târgu Jiu (12 daily; 1hr 40min–3hr); Timişoara (3 daily; 5hr 50min).

Destinations (Bus) Băile Herculane (5 daily; 3hr 10min); Bucharest (hourly; 3hr 30min); Calafat (4 daily; 1hr 45min); Drobeta-Turnu Severin (8 daily; 2hr); Piteşti (4 daily; 2hr 20min); Râmnicu Vâlcea (6 daily; 2hr 45min); Târgu Jiu (12 daily; 2hr); Timişoara (4 daily; 7hr).

ACCOMMODATION

Casa cu Tei Str. Amaradiei 4 ☎ 0372 981 433, ⓦ casacutei.com; map p.110. Housed in a handsome, stucco-encrusted villa just a short walk uphill from the centre, the "Linden House" is the city's most restful accommodation: fourteen large, light-filled rooms with white-wood furnishings and colourful rugs, and a pleasant garden terrace. **€45**

Golden House Str. Brestei 18 ☎ 0728 616 131, ⓦ goldenhouse.ro; map p.110. Set in the middle of extensive, fragrant gardens, this large villa is one of the most luxurious places in town; gorgeous, artfully decorated rooms with some nice touches such as Nespresso machines. Swimming pool too. **€70**

Hostel Sport Str. Brestei 25 ☎ 0251 412 022, ⓦ hotel-sport.ro; map p.110. The friendly *Sport* is the cheapest option in town, offering small a/c double rooms with ageing, rather haphazardly arranged, furniture, including 70s-style TVs and phones. Breakfast included. **€35**

Parc Str. Bibescu 12 ☎ 0251 417 257, ⓦ hotel-parc-craiova.ro; map p.110. Once the Communist Party's guesthouse, this rather austere looking building now conceals surprisingly bright, well-renovated rooms, some with balconies. **€45**

EATING

Kabina Str. A.I. Cuza 4; map p.110. Buzzy, enthusiastically run café with a distinctly Brit-themed vibe (the red telephone box is a bit of a giveaway) that also serves the freshest, tastiest coffee in town; it's no less enjoyable for an evening sup too. Mon–Fri 8.30am–midnight, Sat & Sun 9.30am–midnight.

Pizzeria Trevi Str. Kogălniceanu 3 ☎0768 650 155, ⓦpizzatrevi.ro; map p.110. Authentic, atmospheric Italian-run trattoria with just a handful of simple wooden chairs and tables covered with checked tablecloths; the pizzas (€6), served on oval wooden plates, are terrific, best enjoyed with a glass of local red wine and rounded off with a shot of Limoncello. Mon–Fri noon–3pm & 6–10pm, Sat noon–10pm.

2

Transylvania

SIBIU OLD TOWN

Transylvania

Thanks to Bram Stoker and Hollywood, Transylvania (from the Latin for "beyond the forest") is famed as the homeland of Dracula, a mountainous place where storms lash medieval hamlets, while wolves – or werewolves – howl from the surrounding woods. The fictitious image is accurate up to a point: the scenery is breathtakingly dramatic, especially in the Prahova valley, the Turda and Bicaz gorges and around the high passes; there are spooky Gothic citadels, around Braşov and at Sibiu, Sighişoara and Bran; and there was a Vlad, born in Sighişoara, who earned the grim nickname "The Impaler" and later became known as Dracula (see page 398).

But the Dracula image is just one element of Transylvania, whose near 100,000 square kilometres take in alpine meadows and peaks, caves and dense forests sheltering bears and wild boar, and lowland valleys where buffalo cool off in the rivers. The **population** is an ethnic jigsaw of Romanians, Magyars, Germans and Gypsies, among others, formed over centuries of migration and colonization. Most Hungarians view Erdély ("the forest land", their name for Transylvania) as a land first settled by them but "stolen" in 1920 by the Romanians, who continue to oppress some two million Magyars. Romanians, who call it Ardeal, assert that they appeared first in Transylvania and that for centuries it was the Magyars who oppressed them. Meanwhile, Transylvania's Gypsies (Ţigani) go their own way, largely unconcerned by prejudice against them. The result is an intoxicating brew of characters, customs and places.

The Saxon colonists, invited by the Hungarian monarchy in the thirteenth century to guard the mountain passes against the Tatars, settled in the fertile southeastern corner of Transylvania. After the 1989 revolution, many of their descendants left the villages, with their regimented layouts and **fortified churches**, for Germany – today, under ten percent of the Saxon population remains. The *Stuhls*, the former seats of Saxon power, remain very striking with their medieval streets, defensive towers and fortified churches. **Sighişoara** is the most picturesque and an ideal introduction to Transylvania, followed **Braşov** and **Sibiu**. However one of Transylvania's greatest pleasures is the exploration of quiet backwaters and the smaller Saxon settlements like **Cisnădioara**, **Hărman**, **Prejmer**, **Viscri** and **Biertan**. The other highlight is the castle at **Bran**, which looks just how a vampire count's castle should: a grim facade, perched high on a rock bluff, its turrets and ramparts rising in tiers against a dramatic mountain background.

The **Carpathian mountains** are never far away, one of Europe's most beautiful, least exploited regions for walking. **Hikes** in the stunning Făgăraş, Apuseni and Retezat ranges can last several days; briefer yet equally dramatic forays include the Piatra Craiului or Bucegi mountains (see page 120), or to one of Transylvania's many gorges. To the north and east, cities such as **Cluj**, Transylvania's largest city, with a lively cultural and social scene, and **Târgu Mureş** have a strong Hungarian influence, while **Miercurea Ciuc** and **Sfântu Gheorghe** are the cultural centres of the Székely, a closely related ethnic group. **Southwestern Transylvania** is a region of peaks and moorland peppered with the citadels of the Dacians, rulers of much of Romania before the Roman conquest. It's also an area where the legacy of Hungarian rule is apparent, but the peasantry has always been Romanian. Over the millennia, the tribes that huddled around the caves and hot springs of the Carpathian foothills developed into a cohesive society, and eventually into the Dacian kingdom, with its strongholds south of Orăştie. The Roman conquerers marched up from the Danube and founded their capital nearby in the Haţeg depression, which became one of the earliest centres of Romanian culture in Transylvania, with some of the country's oldest and most charming churches.

Highlights

❶ Braşov Wander the beautiful Baroque streets and medieval ramparts of Braşov's Old Town. See page 128

❷ Wildlife-watching in the Carpathians Take to the woods on the trail of the brown bear, lynx, chamois and wolf. See page 140

❸ Hiking in the Făgăraş and Retezat mountains The dramatic schists of the Făgăraş and the quieter beauty of the Retezat offer Romania's most exceptional trekking. See pages 142 and 179

❹ Sighişoara With its spiky skyline and quintessentially medieval Old Town, Sighişoara is a fitting birthplace for Vlad the Impaler. See page 147

❺ Saxon fortified churches Biertan's Saxon church is the most prominent of the massive and austerely fortified churches that dominate many of the region's villages. See page 152

❻ Sibiu With its gorgeous cobbled squares, outstanding museums and colourful festivals, this is the most engaging of Romanian cities. See page 156

❼ The Girl Fair at Muntele Găina Its matchmaking origins may have faded, but the annual Girl Fair is still a magnificent spectacle. See page 212

❽ Folk music Transylvania is full of great musical happenings, from organized festivals to impromptu displays, particularly the village of Sic. See page 218

HIGHLIGHTS ARE MARKED ON THE MAP ON PAGE 118

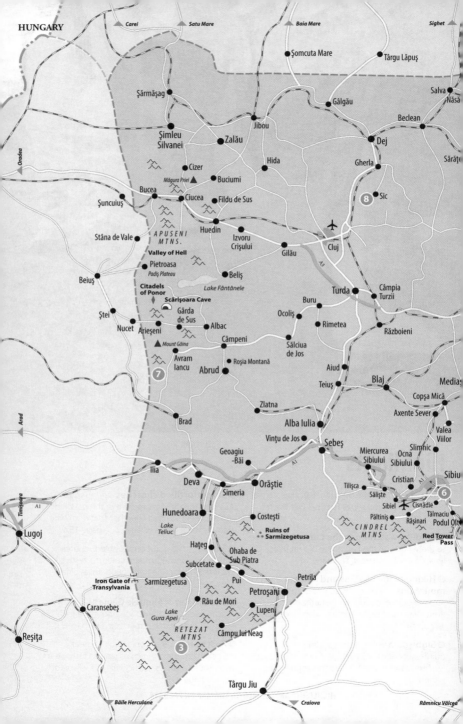

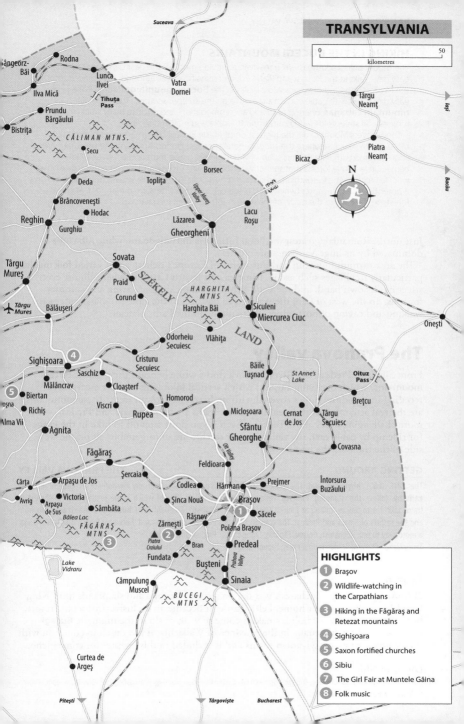

HIKING IN THE BUCEGI MOUNTAINS

The mountains of southeastern Transylvania provide much of the best hiking in Romania, with easy day-walks in the Bucegi and Piatra Craiului massifs, as well as longer expeditions through the Făgăraş and Cindrel ranges. Most walks in the **Bucegi mountains** (Munţii Bucegi) are easy day-hikes, with cable cars an alternative on the steeper sections. There are plenty of **mountain cabanas**, offering food and accommodation, and if you're really stuck, maps show refuges and sheepfolds (*refugiu* and *stână*), where you may find shelter.

Snow covers Mount Omu, the highest point of the Bucegi (2505m), for two hundred or more days a year. Elsewhere the snow generally retreats during April, and the meadows are soon covered with wild flowers such as ladies' gloves, grape-ferns and edelweiss. Golden eagles circle above forests that shelter woodcock, hazel grouse and nightingales, while other wildlife includes the Carpathian red deer and wild boar. The last, like wolves and bears, are only a potential threat in winter (when food is scarce), or if their litters are threatened. Above the forest, on the cliffs to the north of the massif, you may well see chamois.

3

Just north, Romania's greatest medieval fortress is in **Hunedoara**, while **Alba Iulia** is dominated by its huge Vaubanesque citadel.

The area surrounding Cluj harbours some of Europe's richest, most varied **folk music**, particularly in villages such as Sic, Rimetea and Izvoru Crişului, where almost every street has its own band, and there are rich musical pickings at spring and summer festivals. To the west of Cluj the wide green pastures of the Apuseni massif offer easy **walking** and **caving** opportunities, particularly on the Padiş plateau.

The Prahova valley

From Sinaia to Predeal, the River Prahova froths white beneath the gigantic **Bucegi mountains**, which overhang Buşteni with a vertical kilometre of sheer escarpment, receding in grandiose slopes covered with fir, beech and rowan trees. These mountains are the real attraction of the area: the easiest walks are above Sinaia and Predeal, with more challenging hikes above Buşteni. Even if you don't stop off to hike in the range (or ride up by cable car), the valley's upper reaches are unforgettable: sit on the west side of the train for the best views.

GETTING AROUND   **THE PRAHOVA VALLEY**

The DN1 (E60) **highway** and the Bucharest–Braşov **railway** follow the stunning Prahova valley: express trains take 3hr to Braşov, calling at Ploieşti (see page 84) and the resorts of Sinaia and Predeal. The construction of a motorway to link Bucharest, Braşov, Făgăraş, Sighişoara, Targu Mureş, Cluj and Oradea is under way, though progress is painfully slow and only a handful of sections are currently complete (one of which is the section from Bucharest to Ploieşti). Frequent local **buses** and **maxitaxis** run from Ploieşti to Sinaia and between Sinaia, Buşteni, Azuga, Predeal and Braşov.

Sinaia

SINAIA, 122km from Bucharest, was the preserve of hermits and shepherds until King Carol I built his summer home, Peleş Castle. It became an exclusive aristocratic resort, but nowadays hordes of holidaymakers come to walk or ski in the dramatic **Bucegi mountains**. Though actually in the province of Wallachia, it has much in common with the neighbouring Transylvanian towns and is included in this chapter for convenience.

Dimitrie Ghica Park

Bucegi Natural Park Museum Tues–Sun 9am–5pm • €0.60 • **Casino** Wed–Sun 10am–6pm; art gallery Tues–Sun 10am–6pm, winter to 5pm • €1 art gallery/€3 full tour

Above the train station (dating from 1913), **Dimitrie Ghica Park** is home to red squirrels and several fine neo-Brâncovenesc buildings, as well as the **Bucegi Natural Park Museum**, offering a limited overview of the mountains' flora and fauna plus temporary exhibitions. At the north end of the park is the grand **Casino**, opened in 1913; it's now a conference centre but can usually be visited, including its rather naff art gallery. Immediately west, outside the park, a World War I military cemetery also houses a poetic **memorial** to the US airmen killed over Romania in World War II.

Sinaia monastery

Str. Mănăstirii 2 • Daily 10am–4pm • €1

Sinaia monastery was founded by Prince Mihai Cantacuzino in 1690, following a pilgrimage to Mount Sinai; his **Old Church** (Biserica Veche), decorated with a fine *Last Judgement* soon after it was built, is not the one before you as you enter, but is hidden through a passageway to the left. The **Great Church** (Biserica Mare), added in 1842–6, is distinguished by a fine Brâncovenesc-style porch and an unusual green enamel belt

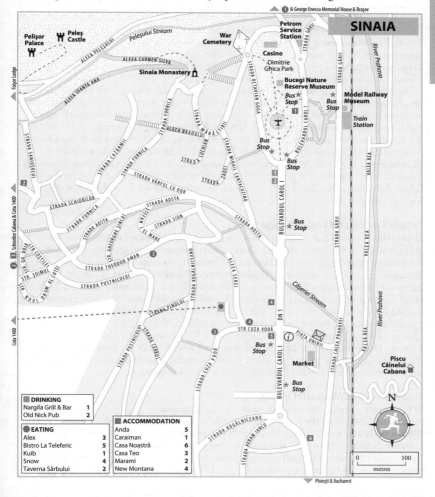

3

SINAIA

DRINKING
Nargila Grill & Bar	1
Old Nick Pub	2

EATING
Alex	3
Bistro La Teleferic	5
Kuib	1
Snow	4
Taverna Sârbului	2

ACCOMMODATION
Anda	5
Caraiman	1
Casa Noastră	6
Casa Teo	3
Marami	2
New Montana	4

with a twisted rope motif encircling the building. Four of the five fresco portraits on the inside west wall, painted by the Dane Aage Exner in 1903, are of King Carol I, Queen Elisabeta, their youngest daughter Maria and Cantacuzino himself. There are currently around a dozen monks here.

Peleş Castle

Wed 11am–4.15pm, Thurs–Sun 9.15am–4.15pm (closed Nov) • Signs lead to a ticket window and on to the separate entry for foreigners; wait in the entry hall for a guide; ground floor €6.50, with 1st floor €13 • ☎ 0244 310 918, Ⓦ peles.ro • Note that the only toilets are by the path up to the castle

Just behind the monastery, a long cobbled path lined with souvenir stalls leads to one of Romania's most popular and rewarding sights, **Peleş Castle**. Set in a large English-style park, the castle outwardly resembles a Bavarian Schloss. Built in 1875–83 for Carol I, and largely decorated by his eccentric wife Elisabeta (better known as the popular novelist Carmen Sylva), it contains 160 rooms, richly done out in ebony, mother of pearl, walnut and leather – all totally alien to traditional styles of Romanian art – and stuffed with antiques and copies of paintings housed in Bucharest's National Art Museum. How a man of such reputedly austere tastes as Carol managed to live here is something of a mystery, and indeed it hasn't been lived in since his death in 1914. Peleş was opened to the public in 1953, with one interruption when Ceauşescu appropriated it as a "state palace". In 2008 the castle was finally handed back to the king, reuniting Mihai with his birthplace and childhood home; it remains open to visitors, as does Pelişor, which is still state property.

The basic 45-minute **tour** takes in fourteen ground-floor rooms, with the option of also seeing the Imperial Suite, decorated for Kaiser Franz Josef's visit in 1896. You start with the Reception Hall, awash with fantastic walnut carvings, alabaster reliefs and French tapestries, not to mention the 16m-high glass ceiling that opens up in summer. More extravagantly decorated rooms follow, including the Florentine Hall, with kitschy Murano chandeliers; an Alhambra-style Moorish hall containing a Carrera marble fountain; and the Louis XIV room (with paintings by a young Gustav Klimt), housing Romania's first cinema. For an extra fee, you get to see a further sixteen rooms on the upper floor. Note that the castle gets incredibly busy, so you'd do well to time your visit for first thing in the day (or at the end).

Pelişor Palace and Foişor Lodge

Castelul Pelişor Wed 11am–4.15pm, Thurs–Sun 9.15am–4.15pm (closed late Oct) • €4.50 • **Foişor Park** Wed–Sun 9am–4pm

A short walk up the hill from Peleş Castle stands **Pelişor Palace**, built in 1899–1903 for Ferdinand and Marie, Carol I's heirs. Although its exterior is also in the German Renaissance style, the interior is far more restrained and mostly Art Nouveau. The exception is the dazzling Gold Room, covered in 24-carat gold leaf and with a Tiffany lamp from Chicago. Although Ceauşescu hosted dignitaries such as US presidents Gerald Ford and Richard Nixon, and Libyan leader Colonel Gaddafi here, he preferred the seclusion of the **Foişor Lodge**, just above. Finished in 1878, this was home to Queen Elisabeta from 1914, and then to Prince Carol (later King Carol II) and Princess Helen from 1921; here, Carol met the Jewish Magda Lupescu, his mistress and the power behind the throne for thirty years, outraging Romanian society. The lodge is used for government protocol, but the **park** is open to the public.

George Enescu Memorial House

Str. Yehudi Menuhin 2 • Tues–Sun 10am–5pm • €1.50 • ☎ 0244 311 753, Ⓦ georgeenescu.ro

Across the DN1 from the lower gate of the Peleş park, signs lead to the **George Enescu Memorial House**, in Cumpătu, 2km north of the town centre. Known as the **Vila Luminiş** (Sunshine House), it was built for the great composer-violinist in 1921–6 in the style of a *conac* (Turkish administrator's house); he spent his summers here until 1946, when he left the country for good. The ground floor contains Oriental,

Biedermeyer and traditional Romanian furnishings, and Enescu's Ibert piano; upstairs are his simple bedroom (as well as student Yehudi Menuhin's more conventional room) and his workroom, looking west to the Bucegi peaks. **Tours** are accompanied by Enescu's lushly romantic music, CDs of which are for sale.

ARRIVAL AND INFORMATION

SINAIA

By train All trains between Bucharest and Braşov call here, some continuing across Transylvania. Steps lead up from the station to the main street, B-dul Carol I.

Destinations Braşov (every 30min–1hr; 1hr–1hr 15min); Bucharest (every 30min–1hr; 1hr 30min–3hr); Sibiu (3 daily; 3hr 50min–4hr 30min); Sighişoara (4 daily; 3hr 45min).

By bus Buses and maxitaxis between Bucharest and Braşov run along Str. Gării, stopping immediately north of the station.

Tourist information In front of the town hall at B-dul Carol I 47 (Mon–Fri 8.30am–4.30pm; ☎0244 315 656, ✉contact@infosinaia.ro).

GETTING AROUND

Local buses run from B-dul Carol I up to the hillside areas of Platoul Izvor and Furnica: bus T1 runs hourly (6am–9am) via the station to Sinaia monastery and Piaţeta Foişor and bus T2 hourly (6.20am–10.20pm) via the monastery and Piaţeta Foişor to the *telegondola* and occasionally to the end of the road at Cota 1400, the cable car's mid-station.

ACCOMMODATION

Anda B-dul Carol I 30 ☎0244 306 020, ⊛hotelanda.ro; map p.121. Smaller than the town's other ski hotels, and while nothing like the four-star place it purports to be, it's a polished, modern and comfortable place. Pleasant wine-cellar restaurant, too. **€50**

Caraiman B-dul Carol I 4 ☎0244 311 542, ⊛palacesinaia.ro; map p.121. Sinaia's first hotel, opened in 1881, is still a pretty grand pile, even if the rooms are a little cramped and the furnishings somewhat dated. **€72**

Casa Noastră B-dul Republicii 9 ☎0244 314 556 or ☎0745 655 895, ⊛casanoastrasinaia.ro; map p.121. Odd-looking, narrow wooden high-rise, with simple wood-furnished rooms, including triples and quads. There's a decent restaurant, too. **€18**

Casa Teo Calea Codrului 40 ☎0244 311 062, ⊛casa-teo.ro; map p.121. Excellent, pleasantly tranquil location on the edge of the forest just down from the gondola, this classy hotel has nine nicely presented rooms, all with wood-fired jacuzzis; they've also got mountain bikes to rent, as well as a stylish teahouse and terrace. **€75**

Marami Str. Furnica 52 ☎0244 315 560, ⊛marami.ro; map p.121. One of Sinaia's more welcoming hotels, this has large, well-equipped rooms, each decorated in a different colour. Sauna, jacuzzi, gym and an excellent bar-pizzeria. **€42**

New Montana B-dul Carol I 24 ☎0244 312 751, ⊛newmontana.ro; map p.121. It's not the most prepossessing of buildings, but this large hotel on the main street is as slick as you'd expect from somewhere mainly catering to ski groups, with pool, sauna and gym. **€65**

EATING

Alex Str. Aman 9 ☎0244 315 497, ⊛alexturism.ro; map p.121. Enjoyable, rustic-styled Hungarian restaurant serving classic Magyar dishes such as *bograč* (a steaming goulash pot of mixed meat, onion and potatoes) and *somlói* (a gooey chocolate, vanilla and walnut sponge trifle). Daily 8am–11pm.

Bistro La Teleferic Str. Cuza Vodă 6 18 ☎0723 648 380; map p.121. There's fine home cooking to be enjoyed in this engaging family-run restaurant which has just five or so tables; popular dishes on a wide-ranging menu include onion soup, bean soup served in a half-loaf of bread, and roast duck leg or goose thigh, though it is a tad more expensive than most places in town. Reservations required. Mon & Thurs–Sun 2–4.30pm & 6–9.30pm.

Kuib Str. Str. Gârbovei 10 ☎0735 189 107, ⊛kuib.ro; map p.121. Located north of town on the other side of the DN1, this large, wood-clad restaurant is worth trekking to

for its appealing range of dishes such as pan-fried trout in an almond crust (€9), though the foundues (three cheeses, or chocolate with fruits; €12) are well worth a punt; raw vegan dishes too, as well as a cracking breakfast menu served between 8am and 10.30am. Daily 8am–10.30pm.

Snow Str. Cuza Vodă 2 ☎0722 111 666; map p.121. Buzzy restaurant with a distinctive apres-ski type feel, thanks in the main to its two large *terasas*, serving big bowls of steaming soup, homemade sausages, pork knuckle and other meaty treats. In colder weather, the interior, with its pretty, painted wood furnishings is lovely. Daily noon–10.30pm.

Taverna Sârbului Calea Codrului 39 ☎0726 353 353, ⊛sinaia.tavernasarbului.ro; map p.121. Ten minutes north by car (or hourly bus; see above) – towards Cota 1400, this hugely popular and convivial Serbian restaurant serves

ACTIVITIES AROUND SINAIA

There's easy access to the mountains above Sinaia, making them rather crowded and litter-strewn, but it's not hard to find less spoiled places. An excellent 1:35,000 hiking map of the Munţii Bucegi, produced by Schubert & Franzke (Ⓦschubert-franzke.com), is available in many shops and hotels.

From a terminal on Strada Cuza Vodă, a small **cable car** (*telecabina*; summer Tues–Fri 8.30am–4pm, Sat & Sun till 5pm; €4.50 one-way, €7.50 return; Ⓦteleferic.ro) whisks you to an altitude of 1400m (Cota 1400) at the roadhead halfway up the hill, site of a hotel, various cabanas and ski-rental shacks. From here, another cable car (same hours; €7 one-way from Sinaia, €11 return) runs to Cota 2000, and a chairlift (Mon & Wed–Sun 9am–5pm; €4.50 one-way, €7 return) to Cota 1950, both just a five-minute walk from the (now closed) Mioriţa cabana on Mount Furnica. A new **gondola** has been installed from Cota 1000, 150m above the *Taverna Sârbeasca*, to Cota 1400 (Mon & Wed–Sun 9am–5pm; spring/autumn to 6pm; summer to 7pm; Tues from noon all year; €4/€7 one-way/return); it carries mountain bikes, and is reached by an hourly bus (see page 123). Indeed, at Cota 1400, 10km of biking trails comprise the new **Bike Resort Sinaia** (same times as gondola; Ⓦsinaiago.ro), featuring four trails ranging from beginner to expert (€4.50 one ride, €25 day pass). A second stage from Cota 1400 to Cota 2000 (Vârful Furnica) opened at the end of 2015.

Below Cota 1950, to the south, is the Valea Dorului cabana (☏0244 313 531), from where there's a three-hour circular walk to the beautiful Lacuri **tarns**, marked with yellow crosses (outwards) and red stripes (returning).

There's an attractive and easy 45-minute **walk** north from Mount Furnica to Piatra Arsă cabana, from where blue triangles lead down to Buşteni (2hr) via La Scari, a spectacular "stairway" hewn into rock. Another path (marked with blue stripes) drops westwards to the Peştera hotel and cave (see page 127), in the central depression of the Bucegi. A paved track leads south from the plateau to the Dichiu cabana (☏0245 708 541 or ☏0735 506 111, Ⓦcarpatmontana-serv.ro), a thirty-minute drive from Sinaia on the Târgovişte road.

As for **skiing**, two wide and fairly easy ski areas extend from Cota 2000 east to Cota 1400 and west to Valea Dorului (1820m) and Valea Soarelui (1760m); the runs back down to Cota 1400 are among Romania's toughest. Expect to pay around €30 for a day pass.

---

huge portions of meat-heavy cuisine (most mains €7–10), typically *čorba pasulj* (bean soup with smoked meat), *čevapi* (grilled rissoles of meat) and *pljeskavica* (oversized burgers). Daily 11am–midnight.

DRINKING

Nargila Grill & Bar B-dul Carol I 8 ☏0244 302 923, Ⓦnargila.ro; map p.121. In the front of the *Sinaia* hotel, this place serves authentic kebabs and Arabic salads, plus burgers, but the loud music makes it a place for drinking rather than eating; hookah pipes are available, and there's belly dancing at weekends. Daily 8am–1am.

Old Nick Pub B-dul Carol I 8 ☏0244 312 491; map p.121. Claiming the longest bar in Romania (33m), this is a lively party pub with DJs and karaoke, plus a garden; tapas are available. Daily 9am–midnight.

Buşteni

BUŞTENI, 10km up-valley from Sinaia, is a small, bustling resort overshadowed by Europe's highest conglomerate cliffs and the sheer peaks of Caraiman (2384m) and Coştila (2490m). Caraiman is marked by a huge cross (a war memorial erected for Queen Marie in 1926–8), and Coştila by a rocket-like TV tower. Buşteni is a good base for walking, but there's nothing much in the town itself, other than a church founded by Carol I and Queen Elisabeta in 1889, and the former home of writer **Cezar Petrescu** (1892–1961), in a handsome villa north of town on Str. Petrescu (Tues–Sun 9am–5pm; €1.50).

Cantacuzino Castle

Str. Zamora 1 • Daily 10am–6pm, Sat until 7pm (tours at 5 min past the hour) • €8.50 (castle, art gallery and park), €6.50 (castle and park) • ☎ 0722 960 606, ⓦ cantacuzinocastle.ro

The **Cantacuzino Castle**, under 1km east of the station (where you can see Romania's first industrial electric locomotive), was built in 1909–11 by Prince Gheorghe Cantacuzino, known as "The Nabob" because of his fabulous wealth; restituted to his heirs and sold, it's

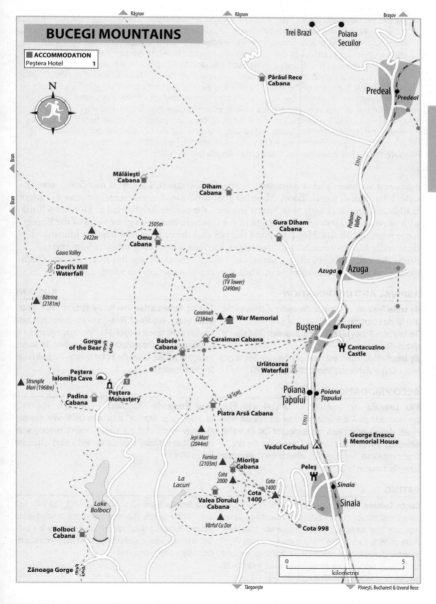

3

3

ACTIVITIES AROUND BUŞTENI

There's great **hiking** in the mountains west of Buşteni, with access by the small cable car (Mon & Wed–Sun 7.30am–5.45pm; €7.50 each way) above the *Hotel Silva* on Strada Telecabiniei (head left/south from the station and right at the country's oldest paper mill). From the *Silva* an easy path marked with red dots leads to the Urlătoarea waterfall and back to the road at Poiana Ţapului (2hr). A harder path, marked with blue crosses, takes you 1235m up the Jepi valley to the **cabanas** at Caraiman (☎0734 659 590) and Babele (☎0723 191 265). The latter offers a panoramic view, and is only five minutes' walk from an impressive skull-like rock formation, the Babele Sphinx. From here, you can walk (1hr) or ride another cable car (same hours and price) down to the *Peştera* hotel and monastery (see opposite). North of Babele, a path marked by yellow stripes leads to Mount Omu (3–4hr), also reached by a blue-striped path up the Ialomiţa valley from Peştera (3hr). There's a small **hut** here (☎0244 320 677; closed winter), without running water. Though completely cloudless days are rare around Mount Omu, there should be views west to the ridge of the Piatra Craiului and the Făgăraş range beyond. From Omu, a path marked with red stripes descends a glacial valley past eroded rock "chimneys" to the Mălăieşti **hut** (the first in the Bucegi, dating from 1882) in two to three hours; from Buşteni there's also a lower route to Malaieşti following red triangles (5–6hr). Two paths lead down from Omu to Bran in about six hours – the one indicated by yellow triangles is easier, while the one marked with red crosses drops down the superb Gaura valley past the Cascada Moara Dracului ("Devil's Mill Waterfall"), a fitting approach to "**Dracula's Castle**" in the village below.

now open for **tours**, and also houses a prestigious restaurant. Largely in neo-Brâncovenesc style, it has Italian mosaic floors, Venetian glass windows, a monumental staircase of Carrara marble and fireplaces with polychrome mosaics; the double-height Hall of Honour is lined with portraits and stained-glass images of the Cantacuzinos, with great views of the Bucegi range from its balcony. However, given the fact that the castle is now largely unfurnished, there really isn't very much to see; moreover, the tour is just thirty minutes long and in Romanian only, so all in all, not particularly useful. The castle also has an art gallery, which usually has pretty good exhibitions, while the extensive gardens are worth a stroll.

ARRIVAL AND INFORMATION   BUŞTENI

By train The train station is in the centre of town on the DN1 (B-dul Libertăţii).
Destinations Braşov (22 daily; 1hr); Bucharest (20 daily; 1hr 40min–3hr).
By bus Plentiful buses and maxitaxis between Bucharest, Sinaia, Braşov and nearby towns run along the DN1.

Tourist information The Bucegi Natural Park's visitor centre (July & Aug Mon & Wed–Sun 9am–5pm; Sept–June Fri–Sun same times; ☎0344 141 055; ⑩bucegipark.ro) is on the road up to the cable car at Str. Telecabinei 34; there's a machine outside to pay the €2 fee to enter the park (valid for three months).

ACCOMMODATION

Vila Leonida Str. Şoimului 11 ☎0244 320 913, ⑩vilaleonida.ro. A delightful boutique guesthouse with eleven elegant rooms, each one configured and decorated differently; service is first class and there's also the fine *La Cerdac* restaurant and a garden offering great mountain views. Tremendous value. **€60**

Casa Freya Str. Făgetului 31 ☎0371 302 996, ⑩casafreya.ro. Near the Cantacuzino Castle, with stunning mountain views, this is a stylish modern building with comfortable but small rooms, a spa and a good restaurant but no lift. **€65**

EATING

Canta Cuisine Cantacuzino Castle ☎0735 151 318, ⑩cantacuisine.ro. With fantastic mountain views, especially from the terrace, there's genuine fine dining here (with prices to match). The menu comprises a long list of inventive dishes such as truffle cappuccino soup, red tuna tartar with avocado and oyster sauce, and turbot with broccoli mousse and almond sauce. Daily 11am–11pm.

Casa Ancuţa B-dul Libertăţii 73 ☎0244 323 040. Just south of the centre, this lively restaurant serves a good range of Romanian standards (notably bean soup in a half-loaf of bread); service is surprisingly good but payment is by cash only. Daily 11am–10pm.

Peştera

Peştera Ialomiţa: Mon & Wed–Sun 9am–7pm May–Sept, 9am–4pm Oct–April • €2.50

The Bucegi massif forms a U-shape around the Ialomiţa valley, known for its limestone caves and wildlife; it's reached by a recently paved road from the south and by two connecting cable cars from Buşteni via Babele (see box opposite). From the lower cable car terminal (at 1600m altitude) a track leads south past some modern guesthouses to the Peştera monastery, where you can turn on to a path down into a gorge and up to the **Peştera Ialomiţa** – a 1128m-long cave with a small chapel dramatically set in its mouth. Once the haunt of Dacian priests, and then a refuge from Asiatic hordes, a hermitage was built here in the sixteenth century, burnt down in 1961 and finally rebuilt in 1993. Now equipped for visits, there's a mixture of huge chambers and narrow passages (very low at times), with water still flowing beneath the walkway in places.

An unmarked path leads northwest from the cable car terminal up the Batrâna valley past several waterfalls, the "Gorge of the Bear" and two natural bridges. Walking south, it's half an hour to the **Padina cabana** (☏0788 207 553, ⓦcabana-padina.ro), at 1509m, from where a road continues past a few more guesthouses and the artificial Lake Bolboci, eventually emerging onto the Sinaia–Târgovişte road.

3

ACCOMMODATION   PEŞTERA

Camping Zanoaga ☏0735 506 111. Just south of the Lake Bolboci dam, this has fourteen two-bed chalets and plenty of space for caravans and tents. Camping **€3**, caravan **€7**, chalet **€11**

Peştera Hotel ☏0372 733 321, ⓦhotelpestera.ro; map p.125. An incongruously large block which has a range of smart rooms – all of which are gradually being

upgraded – as well as a swimming pool and sauna, and a decent restaurant. **€60**

Pensiunea Octavian ☏0786 033 113, 0725 or ☏381 294, ⓦpensiuneaoctavian.ro. A modern three-storey block near the cable-car terminal, with fourteen en-suite rooms and a pretty standard restaurant. **€27**

Azuga

The village of **AZUGA**, between Buşteni and Predeal, is known for the country's longest ski run, served by a modern gondola (Fri–Sun 9am–4pm; €4.50 one way) 1.5km east of the main DN1. There's also good hiking and mountain biking, in the hills to the east rather than the mountains to the west.

Rhein Azuga Cellar

Str. Independenţei 24 • Mon–Sat 8.30am–4pm, Sun 8.30am–2pm; shop open summer Mon–Fri till 8pm, Sat till 4pm, Sun till 3.30pm • €5 • ☏0244 326 560, ⓦhalewood.com.ro

Founded in 1892, the **Rhein Azuga Cellar**, about 500m east of the DN1, has supplied sparkling wine to Romania's royal family since 1920. Owned by the British company Halewood, who also make wine in the Dealu Mare region just south of the Prahova valley, you can do wine-tasting sessions here, along with a tour of the cellars. There's a shop, the area's best restaurant, and the lovely *Rhein Guesthouse*.

ACCOMMODATION

Azuga Ski and Bike Resort Str. Sorica 3 ☏0244 326 811, ⓦazugaresort.ro. At the foot of the gondola (which it owns), this comfortable modern place has modest-looking rooms and apartments with balconies, a sauna, gym and sports facilities such as table tennis and bowling, as well as bike rental. **€40**

Pensiunea Rhein Str. Independenţei 24 ☏0244 326 560, ⓦhalewood.com.ro. Recently upgraded, this has sixteen restful, rustically styled rooms in a historic building set in lovely gardens, with badminton and table-tennis facilities. **€20**

Predeal

PREDEAL, right on the pass into Transylvania (and thus the highest town in Romania), is a popular winter sports centre, with three main pistes served by a modern chairlift.

CABANAS AROUND PREDEAL

There's excellent hiking both east and west of Predeal, with a good selection of huts in which to have lunch or a snack, or to stay the night (from €18). **Gârbova** (☎0734 376 808, ⓦcabanagirbova.ro) and **Susai** (☎0268 457 204, ⓦsusai.ro) are within a few kilometres of the Clăbucet-Plecare chairlift. In the foothills of the Bucegi massif, northwest of Predeal, are the hotel-like **Trei Brazi**, 5km west of Predeal at the top of Strada Trei Brazi (☎0747 027 929, ⓦcabanatreibrazi.com); the **Poiana Secuilor** (☎0768 551 162 or ☎0728 154 634), a short distance east; and the **Pârâu Rece** complex 5km down the Râșnov road (2km west of Trei Brazi), which also has camping (☎0268 456 491 or ☎0740 204 868). The **Diham** cabana (☎0726 203 262, ⓦdiham.ro) is higher up and further south, with a slalom run nearby.

There's good **walking** in these hills, not as dramatic as in the Bucegi above Sinaia and Bușteni but with fine views to the high peaks and cliffs, and plenty of **cabanas** to aim for.

ARRIVAL AND INFORMATION — PREDEAL

By train All trains between Bucharest and Brașov call here, some continuing across Transylvania.
Destinations Brașov (every 30min–1hr; 35–40min); Bucharest (every 30min–1hr; 2–3hr); Sibiu (3 daily; 3hr 50min–4hr 30min); Sighișoara (4 daily; 3hr 45min).

By bus Hourly maxitaxis between Brașov and Bucharest run along the main DN1. From the station there are local buses to Brașov (11 daily), Sinaia (every 2hr) and Pârâul Rece (9 daily).

Ski and bike rental Ski equipment and mountain bikes can be rented around the Clăbucet-Sosire chairlift terminal.

ACCOMMODATION

Bulevard B-dul Săulescu 129 ☎0741 224 770, ⓦbulevard-predeal.ro. This Art Nouveau jewel, on the main road just north of the station, has been well refurbished, though the rooms don't quite live up to the promise of the exterior; 21 double rooms and eight suites as well as a decent restaurant. €36

Carmen B-dul Săulescu 121 ☎0268 456 517, ⓦhotelcarmenpredeal.ro. Just south of the station, this prominent hotel has been immaculately refurbished, though its tidily furnished – if rather staid – rooms still remain very affordable; pool, hot-tub and sauna round things off. €62

Fulg de Nea Str. Teleferic 1 ☎0723 277 571, ⓔcabanafulgdeneapredeal@gmail.com. On the road to the Clăbucet chairlift, this large and welcoming chalet

has simple but perfectly acceptable accommodation in the shape of three- and four-bed rooms, though the concrete interior is a bit weird; it's very much a ski place but is open all year. Breakfast €4. €28

Orizont Str. Trei Brazi 6 ☎0268 455 150, ⓦhotelorizont. ro. Despite its cumbersome looking exterior, the interior of this four-star hotel is contemporary and well designed, with rooms bursting with colour; extras include pool, spa, sauna and jacuzzi and tennis courts. €62

Predeal Comfort Suites Str. Trei Brazi 33 ☎0268 455 795, ⓦpredealcomfortsuites.ro. This huge pile, 500m up the Trei Brazi road, has rooms with wrought-iron furnishings and huge corner baths – it's not as grand as it thinks it is, though. There's also a Lebanese restaurant (with some ancient Egyptian decor...). €44

EATING

Hanul Domnitorilor B-dul Săulescu 32 ☎0766 531 172. Just south of the station, the "Ruler's Inn" is a busy, vaguely medieval-themed place spread over several floors, serving all the usual Romanian suspects, as well as those other Romanian suspects, pizza and pasta; service is friendly and surprisingly fast. Daily 8am–10pm.

Vârful cu Dor Str. Libertății 1 ☎0728 303 080. Located just north of the station near the bridge across the railway, this place offers a very affordable menu of the usual Romanian dishes such as *mușchi* or *cotlet de vita* as well as pasta and pizzas. Daily 8am–11pm.

Brașov

With an eye for trade and invasion routes, the Saxons sited their largest settlements close to the Carpathian passes. One of the best placed, **BRAȘOV** (Kronstadt to the Saxons and Brassó to the Hungarians) grew prosperous as a result, the economic power of its Saxon elite long outlasting its feudal privileges. During the 1960s, the communist regime drafted thousands of Moldavian villagers to Brașov's new factories, making it Transylvania's second-largest city. Economic collapse led to **riots** in November 1987 and December 1989, since which time many factories have closed and Brașov's population has continued to decline. Hence the city's increased reliance on tourism, which comes fairly naturally owing to its central location, accessibility, and a stack of wonderful sights. Moreover, the town's proximity to a host of attractions – such as the **Piatra Craiului** mountain range, the alpine resort of **Poiana Brașov**, the fortified Saxon churches of **Hărman** and **Prejmer**, and "Dracula's Castle" at **Bran** – makes it an excellent base.

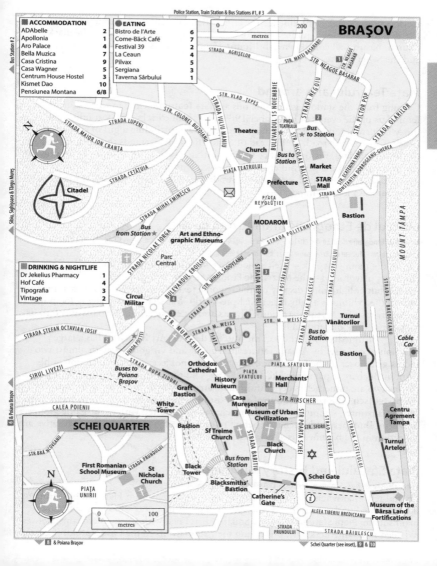

Police Station, Train Station & Bus Stations #1, # 3

■ ACCOMMODATION	
ADAbelle	2
Apollonia	1
Aro Palace	4
Bella Muzica	7
Casa Cristina	9
Casa Wagner	5
Centrum House Hostel	3
Kismet Dao	10
Pensiunea Montana	6/8

● EATING	
Bistro de l'Arte	6
Come-Bäck Café	7
Festival 39	2
La Ceaun	4
Pilvax	5
Sergiana	3
Taverna Sârbului	1

■ DRINKING & NIGHTLIFE	
Dr Jekelius Pharmacy	1
Hof Café	4
Tipografia	3
Vintage	2

BRAȘOV

0 — 200 metres

3

SCHEI QUARTER

0 — 100 metres

& Poiana Brașov

Schei Quarter (see inset), 9 & 10

THE TRANSILVANIA CARD

A bit of a misnomer, the **Transilvania Card** (ⓦ transilvania-card.ro) is basically a pass for visits to fifty Saxon churches across southern Transylvania. It costs €11 and can be obtained from the main churches in Braşov, Sighişoara and Sibiu, from the Foundation for Fortified Churches in Sibiu (Str. Gen. Magheru 4; ☎ 0269 221 010, ⓦ kirchenburgen.org), Kultours in Sibiu (Piaţa Mică 16), Wanderlust Tours in Sighişoara (Piaţa Muzeului 6; Tues–Sun 10am–6pm), and the bookshops in Biertan (in the church), Mediaş (Str. Enescu 8) and Sibiu (Piaţa Mare 7 and Str. Mitropoliei 30). The Foundation for Fortified Churches can also give information about accommodation in the churches.

Most visitors make a beeline for the largely Baroque **Old Town**, around **Piaţa Sfatului**, a strikingly handsome, quintessentially Germanic square dominated by the **Black Church**. Nearby, all coiled beneath Mount Tâmpa, are museums, medieval ramparts and the Schei quarter.

Piaţa Teatrului and around

Coming from the station, get off the bus at **Piaţa Teatrului**, close to some stark reminders of the events of December 1989; in a small park by the post office stand thirty headstones, memorials to those gunned down, including a girl of 6 caught in crossfire. Across the road, at the head of Strada Republicii, stands the pockmarked **Modarom building**, the only edifice still exhibiting any damage; cast your eyes upwards and you'll see half a dozen bullet holes preserved within a square frame. From here, it's a pleasant, if congested, stroll down **Strada Republicii** (Purzengasse), thronged with cafés, bars and ice-cream parlours.

Muzeul de Etnografie and Muzeul de Artă

Muzeul de Etnografie B-dul Eroilor 21 · Tues–Sun: April–Sept 10am–6pm; Oct–March 9am–5pm · €1.20 · ☎ 0268 476 243, ⓦ etnobrasov.ro · **Muzeul de Arta** · same times and entrance fee · ☎ 0268 477 286, ⓦ muzeulartabv.ro

Facing the main city park – itself a nice place for a stroll and with an excellent children's playground – the **Muzeul de Etnografie** (Ethnographic Museum) has a modest but enlightening display on the regional textile industry and local costume; the pick of the exhibits is a fully functional pre-World War I Jacquard weaving loom from Germany (ask for a demonstration). There's also a neat selection of craftworks for sale, together with books and CDs.

Immediately next door, the **Muzeul de Artă** (Art Museum) has a large selection of canvases by Aman, Tattarescu, Pallady and Grigorescu, with almost two rooms given over to the last of these artists; whilst not as exciting a collection as his work in Bucharest, paintings like *Oxen Resting* and the portraits *Naughty Boy* and *Lost in Thoughts* are nonetheless delightful. There are also works by Braşov-born **János Máttis-Teutsch** (1884–1960), one of the most influential of modern Romanian artists. He was a painter, sculptor, writer and teacher who exhibited with avant-garde groups in Berlin, Budapest and Bucharest before returning to figurative art. The decorative arts collection in the basement is also worth a peek.

Piaţa Sfatului and History Museum

History Museum · Tues–Sun 10am–6pm · €2 · ☎ 0268 472 350, ⓦ brasovistorie.ro

Legend tells that when the Pied Piper enticed the children from Hamelin in Germany, they vanished underground and emerged in Transylvania near what is now Braşov's main square, **Piaţa Sfatului** (Council Square). It is lined with sturdy merchants' houses, red-tiled roofs tilted rakishly, presenting their shop fronts to the **Casa Sfatului** (Council

House) in the centre of the square. This was built by 1420, rebuilt in the eighteenth century, and now houses the **Muzeul de Istorie** (History Museum), which tells the story of the Saxon guilds – locksmiths, goldsmiths, milliners and so on – who dominated Brașov and met in the Hirscher Haus or **Merchants' Hall** (Casa Negustorilor) on the eastern side of the square. Built in "Transylvanian Renaissance" style in 1544–5, this now contains shops, a wine cellar and the *Casa Hirscher* restaurant.

Casa Mureșenilor

Piața Sfatului 25 · Mon–Sat 9am–5pm · €1 · ☎ 0268 477 864, ⓦ muzeulmuresenilor.ro

Just to the west of Piața Sfatului, across Strada Mureșenilor, an upstairs apartment – now the **Casa Mureșenilor** – served as the dynastic home of the politically and culturally influential Mureșianu family, one of whose number, Andrei, composed what was to become the Romanian national anthem, *Deșteaptă-te, române!*, in 1848. Although there are some of his instruments and scores on display, most of the exhibits here are devoted to the deeds of Andrei's cousin, Iacob, founding editor of *Gazeta Transilvaniei*, the first Romanian-language newspaper to be published in Transylvania, and as such, the leading campaigner for civil rights of Romanians in the territory. Elsewhere there are letters, photos and keepsakes; look out for recitals which are held here on a regular basis.

Museum of Urban Civilization

Piața Sfatului 15 · Tues–Sun: May–Sept 10am–6pm; Oct–April 9am–5pm · €2 · ☎ 0268 475 565, ⓦ mcubrasov.ro

The Muzeu Civilizației Urbane (**Museum of Urban Civilization**) occupies a merchant's house dating from the thirteenth/fourteenth century but rebuilt in 1566 and typical of the Transylvanian Renaissance style. It's been beautifully restored, notably its sixteenth- and eighteenth-century murals. Exhibits focus on the city's trading past, with charters and other documents in the basement, re-creations of shops with painted chests, gingerbread moulds, guns and swords, and upstairs a patrician (Saxon noble) home interior and costumes, embroidery and millinery (including rabbit-fur felt), and a photographic studio with many interesting late-nineteenth century portraits. The attic houses temporary exhibitions.

Orthodox Cathedral and Sf Treime (Holy Trinity) Church

An archway off the main square leads to the **Orthodox Cathedral** (Piața Sfatului), built in Byzantine style in 1895–9; its dark, richly painted interior features an 8m-high iconostasis and marble flooring from 1963, while the brightly coloured wall paintings in the courtyard were added in 2003. Across the square, and similarly hidden away down an alley, the smaller **Sf Treime (Holy Trinity) Church** (Str. Barițiu 12), built in 1786–7, also features an elaborately decorated altar screen, painted in Vienna in 1855.

Black Church

May–Sept Tues–Sat 10am–7pm, Sun noon–7pm; Oct–April Tues–Sat 10am–4pm, Sun noon–4pm; closed on religious and public holidays; organ recitals 6pm: June & Sept Tues; July & Aug Tues, Thurs & Sat · €2 · ☎ 0268 511 824, ⓦ bisericaneagra.ro

To the southwest, the square is dominated by the pinnacles of the town's most famous landmark, the **Black Church**, stabbing upwards like a series of daggers. Allegedly the largest Gothic church between Vienna and Istanbul, it took almost a century to complete (1383–1477) and is so-called for its once soot-blackened walls, the result of a fire started by the Austrian army that occupied Brașov in 1689. It's a classic example of a three-nave hall church, though the interior is largely unornamented, apart from the mostly seventeenth-century **Turkish prayer mats** hung along the nave walls and galleries – a superb collection built up from the gifts of merchants returning from the east; there's also a fine late-fifteenth century tympanum of the *Virgin and Child with Two Saints* in the south porch. The four-thousand-pipe organ is one of the largest in southeastern Europe, and it's worth catching one of the regular **recitals**. On the fourth pillar to your left as you enter, look out for four bullet holes, left by shots fired through the nearby wooden door as people cowered inside during the fighting in 1989. To the south of the church is the **Honterus Gymnasium**, the still-prestigious Saxon school named after the apostle of Luther's Reformation in Transylvania.

Synagogue

Str. Poarta Schei 27 • Mon–Fri 9am–4pm • €1 • ☎ 0268 511 867

Not far east of Piaţa Sfatului is Braşov's beautifully restored Moorish-style **synagogue**, built in 1901; the *Shalom* kosher restaurant is also here, serving the city's 120-odd remaining Jews. Just to its east is Strada Sforii (Rope Street), allegedly the narrowest alley in Romania (although at 1.3m it's more than twice as wide as some in the City of London).

The city wall and Mount Tâmpa

Cable car summer Mon noon–6pm, Tues–Sun 9am–6pm; winter Tues–Sun 9am–4pm • €2 one-way/€3.50 return • **Bastionul Graft** Tues–Sun 10am–6pm • €1

Facing Turkish attacks in the fifteenth century, Braşov built stronger fortifications, assigning each bastion to a particular guild. The length of **wall** along Aleea Brediceanu, at the foot of Mount Tâmpa, has been refurbished, and three bastions are now open (from the east, the Bastion Postăvarilor, Turnul Vânătorilor and Turnul Artelor). These give good views of the Old Town (only for the fit and agile) but the best views are from the forested heights of **Mount Tâmpa** (967m), accessible by cable car from the terminal behind the Turnul Vânătorilor, or by various winding trails (one hour following the red triangles); from the upper terminal a fairly dodgy path leads about 200m to the viewpoint by the Hollywood-style "Braşov" sign that's visible all over town. The road ends at the **Turnul Artelor**, a former powder tower that is now closed.

To the west of the Old Town, dotted along traffic-free Strada După Ziduri, are three further fortifications: first up, at the southern end, is the fourteenth-century **Black Tower** (Turnul Negru), which is actually white but was so named after a fire in 1559; the cumbersome glass roof was added during restoration in the 1990s after one side of the tower collapsed. The tower is closed but it's worth the short, steep walk up to the deck that surrounds it for super views of the city below and Mount Tâmpa opposite. Continuing along După Ziduri, and squeezed in between the fast-flowing Cheu stream (which technically is a canal) and the walls, is the formidable, early fifteenth-century **Bastionul Graft**, which hosts temporary exhibitions. From here a vertiginous flight of stone steps lead up to the **White Tower** (Turnul Alb), a mightily impressive, semi-circular structure that preceeded Bastionul Graft by some twenty years; this too is closed, but the views from here are even better than those from the Black Tower.

Museum of the Bârsa Land Fortifications

Str. Coşbuc 9 • Tues–Sun 10am–6pm; winter 9am–5pm • €1.50 • ☎ 0268 472 350, Ⓦ brasovistorie.ro

The westernmost of Braşov's original seven bastions is that of the Weavers (Bastionul Ţesătorilor; 1421–36), with three tiers of wooden galleries and meal-rooms in which the townsfolk stocked bread, meat and other provisions in case of siege. It now houses the **Museum of the Bârsa Land Fortifications**, recalling the bad old days when the surrounding region was repeatedly raided by Tatars, Turks and, on a couple of occasions, by Vlad Ţepeş (who burnt Braşov's suburbs in 1460 and impaled hundreds of captives). There's also a large model of Braşov as it was in 1600, made in 1896, with the Schei quarter added in 1968 for a visit by Ceauşescu.

THE PAGEANT OF THE JUNI

The **Pageant of the Juni** (Sărbătoarea Junilor) is held on the Sunday after Easter, traditionally the one day of the year when Romanians could freely enter the Saxon city. Dating from the eighteenth century, it celebrates a "raid" by young Romanians who galloped into Braşov on horseback one Sunday as the Saxons were emerging from church – and invited them all to a picnic on the hills above the town. The name derives from the Latin for "young men", and on this day the town's youths dress up in costumes and, accompanied by brass bands, ride through town in seven groups such as the Juni, the Old (ie married) Juni, and the Dorobanţi and Roşiori, named after famous regiments.

The parade assembles in the morning on **Piaţa Unirii**, the historic heart of Schei. It then marches along Strada Bariţiu to Piaţa Sfatului, circles it three times, returns via Strada Poarta Schei to the Schei backstreets, then climbs a narrow valley to the **Gorges of Pietrele lui Solomon**. Here, spectators settle down to watch the Horås or Round Dances, rhythmically stepping, swaying and stamping circles which served as a sanction in village society – miscreants seeking to enter the circle (and so re-enter society) were shamed when the dancing immediately ceased, resuming only when they withdrew.

3

The Schei quarter

Romanian-language school: daily 9am–5pm (opens after the service Sun morning) • €2 • ☎ 0268 511 411, ⓦ primascoalaromaneasca.ro

During the Saxon heyday, the Romanian-speaking population was compelled to live outside the walls, in the southwestern district of **Schei**. They could only enter the centre at certain times, paying a toll at the gate for the privilege of selling their produce to their neighbours. The Poarta Schei (**Schei Gate**) was built in 1825–8 by Emperor Franz I, next to the splendid Poarta Ecaterinei (**Catherine's Gate**) of 1559, which bears the city's coat of arms.

Today, Schei is a peaceful, residential dead end whose main sight is the **Church of St Nicholas**, on Piaţa Unirii, ten minutes' walk from Poarta Schei. A fetching amalgam of Byzantine, Baroque and Gothic, it was the first Orthodox church to be built in Transylvania by the *voivodes* of Wallachia, between 1493 and 1564; it was extended and the clock tower added in 1751, with interior frescoes by Braşov-born painter Mişu Popp (1856). On the left as you enter the churchyard is the first **Romanian-language school**, established in the fourteenth century; the current seventeenth-century building houses a **museum** exhibiting the first Romanian-language textbooks, a printing press and costumes worn in the Pageant of the Juni.

ARRIVAL AND DEPARTURE
BRAŞOV

By plane Shuttles to Bucharest's Otopeni airport (12 daily) leave from the *Aro Palace* hotel in the city centre – tickets (€15) from Direct Transport at Str. Weiss 18 (Mon–Fri 10am–6pm, Sat 9am–1pm; ☎ 0727 503 503, ⓦ direct-aeroport.ro).

By train Braşov is a major rail junction, served by trains from every corner of the country. There are separate ticket windows for international trains and for Regiotrans trains to Râşnov, Zărneşti and some other local destinations. The train station is over 2km northeast of the Old Town, right in the heart of Braşov's drab concrete suburbs. Bus #4 will take you down to Parc Central (also known as Titulescu), and Livada Poştei.

Destinations Bucharest (every 30min–1hr; 2h 40min–4hr); Budapest (2 daily; 13hr 15min); Cluj (6 daily; 6hr 30min–7hr 30min); Deva (3 daily; 5hr 45min); Făgăraş (9 daily; 1hr 10min–1hr 30min); Miercurea Ciuc (9 daily; 1hr 30min–2hr 15min); Sfântu Gheorghe (12 daily; 30–40min); Sibiu (7 daily; 2hr 30min–3hr 50min); Sighişoara (9 daily; 2hr 40min–3hr 15min); Sinaia (every 30min–1hr; 1hr); Târgu Mureş (1 daily; 6hr); Vienna (1 daily in summer; 16hr 30min); Zărneşti (9 daily; 40min).

By bus The town has four bus stations. Most long-distance buses and maxitaxis use Autogară 1, by the train station (☎ 0268 427 267), while buses for Râşnov, Bran and Zărneşti use Autogară 2 at Str. Avram Iancu 114 (☎ 0268 426 332). Services for the villages just east of Braşov use Autogară 3, 1km northeast of the main train station at Str. Hărmanului 47 (☎ 0268 332 002). Finally, Autogară 4 (Bartolomei; ☎ 0368 007 122), northwest of town on Calea Făgăraşului, handles international services and a few long-distance buses. Autogară 2 is reached by buses #12 and #22 from the centre, #16 from Livada Poştei and bus #23 from the train station to Stadion Tineret (Youth Stadium), close to Autogară 2. Buses #1 and #10 from the centre and #11 from the station serve Autogară 3. Bus #23/23B runs to Bartolomei (Stadionul Municipal) from in front of the train station and bus #16 from Livada Poştei and local trains from Zărneşti and Sibiu, call at the nearby Bartolomei station.

Destinations from Autogară 1 Bucharest (hourly); Chişinău, Moldova (5 daily); Covasna (8 daily); Făgăraş (hourly); Hărman (every 30–60min); Iaşi (2 daily); Piatra Neamţ (4 daily); Prejmer (every 30min); Sibiu (7 daily); Sighişoara (8 daily); Târgu Mureş (8 daily); Târgu Neamţ (2 daily); Târgu Secuiesc (10 daily).

Destinations from Autogară 2 Bran (every 30min); Câmpulung Muscel (4 daily); Făgăraş (hourly); Piteşti (2 daily); Râsnov (every 15min); Sibiu (2 daily); Zărneşti (every 30min).

Destinations from Autogară 4 Bacău/Iaşi (1 daily); Budapest (3 daily); Cluj (3 daily).

INFORMATION AND TOURS

Tourist information The city tourist office is near the Poarta Schei at Str. Prundului 1 (Mon–Thurs 10am–5pm, Fri & Sun 10am–2pm; ☎0268 327 298), though information here is limited. The magazine kiosk in front of the station will sell you a city map (bus tickets are sold at the rear).

Tours Free guided walking tours of the city are offered by Walkabout (April & May 6pm, June–Sept 10.30am & 6pm, Oct–March 3pm; (☎0744 314 110, ⓦ brasov.walkaboutfreetours.com), departing from the fountain on Piaţa Sfatului.

GETTING AROUND

By taxi Braşov's most reliable taxi companies are Martax (☎0268 313 040, ⓦ martax.ro), Rey Taxi (☎0268 411 111, ⓦ reytaxi.ro), BraTaxi (☎0268 315 555, ⓦ bratax.ro) and Tod (☎0748 321 111, ⓦ todtaxi.ro).

By bike The Ivelo bike-sharing station is on Piaţa Sfatului (April & Oct Mon–Fri 11.30am–7.30pm, Sat & Sun 9.30am–7.30pm; May & Sept Mon–Fri 11.30am–8.30pm, Sat & Sun 9.30am–8.30pm; Jun–Aug Mon–Fri 11.30am–9pm, Sat & Sun 9.30am–9pm; €1.50/hr, €4/4hr, €6/24hr).

ACCOMMODATION

There is stacks of accommodation in Braşov, and although it's not particularly exciting, there's a good mix of hotels, pensions and hostels. There are also a number of decent places to stay outside the city, in particular on the road out towards Poiana Braşov.

ADAbelle Str. Pieţii 5 ☎0268 411 080, ⓦ adabelle.eu; map p.129. Despite its hostel-like appearance, this tidy hotel has modern, well-equipped en-suite rooms with plasma TV. Breakfast €4.50. €38

Apollonia Str. Neagoe Basarab 7 ☎0268 476 163, ⓦ hotelapollonia.ro; map p.129. Smart, unassuming little hotel in a peaceful location near the centre either with small or large-sized double rooms, hence are differently priced. Sauna, massage, gym and swimming pool cost extra. €55

Aro Palace B-dul Eroilor 27 ☎0268 478 800, ⓦ aro-palace.ro; map p.129. Optimistically styling itself as a five-star establishment, this nevertheless has Braşov's most luxurious and expensive rooms; ask for a view of Mount Tâmpa. The spa has two pools and a gym. €76

Bella Muzica Piaţa Sfatului 19 ☎0268 477 956, ⓦ bellamuzica.ro; map p.129. In a lovely 400-year-old building, this gem of a hotel has modestly sized but sumptuously furnished rooms with tasteful touches such as wood-framed mirrors, pictures and plants. Its superb restaurant is a few steps down the road. €65

Casa Cristina Str. Curcanilor 62A ☎0722 322 021, ⓦ casacristina.org; map p.129. High up above Schei on an unpaved road, this tremendously hospitable guesthouse has unfussy but comfortable rooms with great views over the city. Good value. €30

Casa Wagner Piaţa Sfatului 5 ☎0268 411 253, ⓦ casa-wagner.com; map p.129. Occupying a building dating from 1477, this understatedly elegant pension has over thirty rooms, beautifully furnished with lots of wood and brass, some overlooking the square. €60

Centrum House Hostel Str. Republicii 58 ☎0727 793 169, ⓦ hostelbrasov.eu; map p.129. Super-central hostel located above a couple of noisy bars (bring earplugs), but it has a good choice of dorms (four- to fourteen beds) and private en-suite rooms plus a cellar kitchen and bar. Breakfast included. Dorm €12, double €35

BRAŞOV FESTIVALS

Other than the **Pageant of the Juni** (see page 133), Braşov's other major festivals include the **Golden Stag** (ⓦ cerbuldeaur.ro), one of the country's largest pop music gatherings, held in late August; followed by the **Jazz and Blues Festival** (ⓦ brasovjazz.ro), the **International Chamber Music Festival**, and the **Oktoberfest Beer Festival** (ⓦ oktoberfestromania.ro), all in September.

Kismet Dao Str. Democratiei 2B ☎0268 514 296, ⓦkismetdao.com; map p.129. A ten-minute walk southwest of the centre, this well-established place has clean and cheery six-, eight and ten-bed dorms and private rooms plus a sociable lounge area, kitchen and laundry facilities. Breakfast included. Dorm €12, double €30

Pensiunea Montana Stejerişului 2A ☎0268 472 731, ⓦcrofi.com; map p.129. Excellent bed and breakfast, on the road up to Poiana Braşov, with marvellous views over the city; five doubles and a suite, all with balconies. €22

EATING

★**Bistro de L'Arte** Piaţa Enescu 11 ☎0720 535 566, ⓦbistrodelarte.ro; map p.129. Tucked away in a little courtyard, this cosy low-key place offers a limited menu of excellent French-influenced food (onion soup, snails in garlic butter), but is worth a visit just for its cracking omelette breakfasts (€5–6). There's pleasant jazz/classical music (live Wed–Sat). Mon–Sat 9am–midnight, Sun noon–midnight.

Come-Bäck Café Piaţa Sfatului 7 ☎0735 444 021; map p.129. The main square is saturated with identikit cafés but this excellent Germanic bakery stands out, serving decent coffee, sandwiches, pastries and other sweet treats. Daily 7.30am–8pm.

Festival 39 Str. Republicii 62 ☎0743 339 909, ⓦfestival39.com; map p.129. Beautiful if slightly overblown Art Nouveau bistro with a more than respectable menu (salmon fillet in a cajun crust, *tort de lămâia* or lemon tartlets) complementing a long cocktail list. There's live jazz twice a week. Daily 7am–midnight.

La Ceaun Str. Weiss 27 ☎0773 727 990, ⓦlaceaun.com; map p.129. Two branches next to each other, with *lute* ("Spicy") dishing up fiery soups (bean with smoked ham and red onion) and stews (lamb with polenta and pickled mushrooms; €8) prepared in large cauldrons (*ceaun*).

and *Tihnit* ("Mild") serving somewhat gentler fare; there's often a queue for their daily specials such as mushroom pie or roast pork and sausage with polenta (€4.50). Daily noon–10pm.

Pilvax Str. Weiss 16 ☎0268 475 829, ⓦpilvax.ro; map p.129. Classy joint offering an upscale take on Hungarian standards, for example *halászé* (a spicy fish soup) and chicken paprika with *spaetzle* (egg dumpling noodles; €6). Throw in a great choice of wines by the glass (including *Tokaji* of course), and attentive service, including offering blankets for those sitting outside, and you've got yourself a thoroughly enjoyable evening. Daily 8am–10pm.

Sergiana Str. Mureşenilor 28 ☎0268 419 775, ⓦsergianagrup.ro; map p.129. In an attractive maze of cellars with lots of hidden alcoves, this has a long menu of traditional and modern Romanian dishes, such as wild boar medallions (€15) and mangalica pork stuffed with plums (€9). Daily 11am–midnight.

Taverna Sârbului Str. Republicii 55 ☎0268 410 222, ⓦbrasov.tavernasarbului.ro; map p.129. This splendid brick cellar, with thick wooden tables and bench seating, is the place for fantastically tasty portions of meat-heavy Serbian food; there's live music Fri/Sat from 8pm. Daily 9am–midnight.

DRINKING AND NIGHTLIFE

Dr Jekelius Pharmacy Str. Weiss 13 ☎0758 624 781; map p.129. Fab-looking café that successfully seeks to recreate an early nineteenth-century pharmacy, with various original fixtures and fittings; a great selection of drinks (some served in large test tubes), including teas and coffees and, some say, the best cocktails in the city. Daily 8am–midnight.

Hof Café Piaţa Sfatului 14 ☎0722 655 511, ⓦhofcafe.ro; map p.129. Set back a little from the main square, this big, contemporary space has a great feel about it, with its painted white brick interior and long concrete bar. A big list of speciality coffee, juices and cocktails keeps a loyal band of locals happy, though it's incredibly popular with travellers too. Daily 8am–midnight.

★**Tipografia** Str. Postavarului 1 ☎0722 373 090, ⓦtipo-grafia.ro; map p.129. If it's Romanian craft beer you're after, make a beeline for this convivial hub, which typically has half a dozen ales on tap at any one time, including at least a couple from the *Zăguna* brewery and one or two from the local *Mustată* (Moustache) brewery. Staffed by the friendliest folk in the city too. Mon–Thurs 7.30am–1am, Fri 7.30am–3am, Sat 9am–3am, Sun 9am–1am.

Vintage Str. Livada Poştei 1 ☎0745 050 487; map p.129. Moderately posey place that's pretty much the best in town for a boogie thanks to regular DJ sessions, though drinks are fairly pricey. Mon–Thurs & Sun 10am–midnight, Fri & Sat till 5am.

Around Braşov

Braşov sits right at the foot of the mountains, and there are opportunities for hiking and skiing just a few kilometres away at **Poiana Braşov**. The most popular excursion is to the castle of **Bran**, and in spite of the crowds it's well worth a visit. Better, though, is the ruined fort at **Râșnov**, midway between Brașov and Bran. The Bucegi mountains to the south, and the Făgăraș range to the west, including Romania's highest peaks, can both be reached by train.

Poiana Brașov

POIANA BRAȘOV sits at an altitude of 1000m on a shoulder of the spectacular Mount Postăvaru, 12km south of Brașov. Coming by car, it's worth stopping at some great viewpoints over the city at km4.5. This is Romania's premier **ski resort**, and while it's a great place to learn, with lots of English-speaking instructors, experienced skiers may soon be bored (although some slopes are steep and often icy). It's crowded at weekends, and it's no longer cheap, but there has been considerable investment in lifts and new pistes, as well as snow-making and grooming equipment so that the season can extend into late April. Ski gear can be rented at hotels and the cable car and gondola terminals.

ARRIVAL AND DEPARTURE

POIANA BRAȘOV

By bus Take bus #20 from Livada Poștei, Brașov (every 30min; 20min; €2).

ACCOMMODATION

The hotels are usually filled by package groups, but they may have space out of season; there are also plenty of guesthouses and private rooms.

Alpin ☎ 0268 262 343, ⓦ hotelalpin.ro. For a long time the biggest and best hotel here, the *Alpin* has been modernized but is still a little post-communist around the edges; still, the rooms are comfortable, there are good quality spa facilities, and they serve a hearty buffet breakfast. €130

Cabana Postăvaru ☎ 0368 101 036, ⓦ cabanapostavaru.ro. High on the mountain of the same name, this hut was founded by the Saxon Carpathian Club in 1883 and has a range of rooms, from six-bed dorms with shared shower facilities to en-suite doubles; it also makes a great lunch-stop for hikers or skiers. Dorms €13, doubles €30

ACCOMMODATION AND EATING

Coliba Haiducilor Str. Drumul Sulinar ☎ 0268 262 137. The "Outlaws' Hut" is the best-known restaurant here, a large wooden pile decorated in touristy-folk style offering authentic, pork-heavy cuisine in a noisy, cheery atmosphere with live music. Daily noon–midnight.

The Dudes Pub ☎ 0737 778 008. At the upper terminal of the Kanzel cable car, this solid stone and wood-lined bar is a great place for a drink or a snack on the mountain. Daily 9am–4pm.

Escalade Str. Poiana Soarelui 160 ☎ 0268 262 043, ⓦ escalade.ro. An excellent choice near the cable cars, with over sixty rooms (either standard or superior, though there's marginal price difference) plus gym, sauna, massage, swimming pool, table tennis and bowling alley. €55

Râșnov

Some 12km west of Poiana Brașov by a back road – where much of 2003's blockbuster *Cold Mountain* was filmed – lies **RÂȘNOV** (Rosenau). To celebrate the various historic epics filmed here there's a free festival of history films (Festival de Film și Istorii Râșnov; ⓦ ffir.ro) at the end of July in the citadel and the Cinema Amza Pellea at the corner of Piața Unirii and Strada Mihai Viteazu.

Cetatea Râsnov

Daily: May–Sept 9am–7pm; Oct–April 9am–5pm • €2.50 • ☎ 0268 230 115, ⓦ rasnov-turism.ro

Cetatea Râsnov (Râsnov Fortress), founded around 1225 by the Teutonic Knights on the site of a Dacian fort, overlooks the town; from the mid-fourteenth century it was a "peasant citadel", used by the townspeople instead of walling the town. The fort was captured only when its water supply was cut off, so a 174m-deep well was dug by

Turkish prisoners, who took seventeen years and were then granted their freedom. It last saw action during the 1848–9 revolution, after which it was abandoned, only being restored recently. Winding up from the gate tower you'll pass souvenir stalls and the walls of tiny houses before arriving at the minute seventeenth-century Lutheran chapel on the highest point. The best reason for visiting the fort, however, is to take in the glorious mountain **views** across to the Piatra Craiului. If the steep, fifteen-minute walk is beyond you, there's a funicular (daily: April–Sept 9am–7pm; Oct–March 9am– 6pm; €2.50 return) which rises up from the main square; it's through the archway next to the *Castel* pub on Piaţa Unirii.

ARRIVAL AND DEPARTURE   RÂŞNOV

Râşnov is 30min from Braşov by **bus or train**.

ACCOMMODATION

There are plenty of very affordable guesthouses, making this a good base for visiting both Bran and Braşov.

Casa Rasnoveana Str. Teiului 50 ☎ 0268 231 708 or ☎ 0745 999 050, ⓦ casarasnoveana.ro. A simple, friendly guesthouse in a peaceful location up against the forested hills just north of the centre with six cozy, largely pine-wood furnished rooms, plus a games room and playground. **€25**

Pension Stefi Piaţa Unirii 5 ☎ 0368 592 019, ⓦ hotelstefi-ro.com. A very welcoming and terrific-value guesthouse in an old Saxon house, with a handful of rooms sleeping one- two- or three people, plus a five-bed dorm; in addition there's a bar, outdoor pool and sauna. Breakfast €6. Dorm **€11**, doubles **€27**

Bran

The small town of **BRAN** (Törzburg), 28km southwest of Braşov, commands the entrance to the pass of the same name, the main route into Wallachia from Roman times. The town is utterly dominated by its **castle**, arguably Romania's single most popular attraction and hence usually besieged by tour buses – you'd do well to visit out of season if at all possible. Aside from the castle, Bran also has the open-air **Muzeul Satului** (Village Museum; mid-April to mid-Oct daily 9am–6pm; free), right by the castle gate, comprising some fine examples of local architecture, including a sawmill, fulling mill (used in the manufacture of cloth) and, most impressively, a large house dating from 1843, including a cellar and stables.

Bran is also a good base for **hikes** into the Bucegi mountains (see page 120) and onto the narrow ridge of the Piatra Craiului, the eastern extremity of the Făgăraş mountains (see page 142). Bran holds its village **festival** on August 9 (the Feast of St Pantelimon).

Muzeului Castel Bran

April–Oct Mon noon–6pm, Tues–Sun 9am–6pm; Nov–March Mon noon–4pm, Tues–Sun 9am–4pm • €8.50 • ☎ 0268 237 700, ⓦ bran-castle.com

The Saxons of Kronstadt (Braşov) built a castle in 1377–82 to safeguard this vital trade artery (replacing a wooden fort raised by the Teutonic Knights in 1212), and although what's now billed on every tourist brochure as **Dracula's Castle** has only tenuous associations with Vlad the Impaler – he may have laid siege to it in 1460, when attacking the Burzenland – Bran does look like a vampire count's residence, perched on a rocky bluff and rising in tiers of towers and ramparts from the woods against a glorious mountain backdrop.

The castle now looks much as it would have done in the time of Queen Marie of Romania, who spent her summers here from 1922 to 1938. A granddaughter of Queen Victoria who married Prince Ferdinand in 1893, Marie soon rebelled against the confines of court life – riding unattended through the streets of Bucharest, pelting citizens with roses during the carnival and appointing herself a colonel of the Red Hussars. Her popularity soared after she organized cholera camps in the Balkan war and appeared at the Paris peace conference in 1919, announcing "Romania needs a face, and I have come to show mine".

Confiscated by the communists, the castle was returned in 2009 to Marie's grandson Dominic von Habsburg, but remains open to the public. Marie called Bran a "pugnacious little fortress", but in fact it feels welcoming, a warren of spiral stairs, ghostly nooks and surprisingly cosy rooms, with some armour and a couple of Marie's dresses on display. Not surprisingly, it gets horribly crowded: try to arrive as the castle opens – the bus parties will be arriving as you leave.

ARRIVAL AND DEPARTURE   BRAN

By bus Buses run from Braşov's Autogară 2 via Râşnov and Bran to Moeciu de Jos, 3km south of Bran (Mon–Fri every 30min, Sat & Sun hourly); the two or three buses from Braşov to Piteşti and Câmpulung Muscel also call at Bran.

By car Parking is a nightmare here, and near the castle costs about twice as anywhere else in town –that's if you can find a space.

ACCOMMODATION

★ **The Guesthouse** Str. Moşoiu 365A ☎ 0744 306 062 or ☎ 0745 179 475, ⓦ guesthouse.ro. Set back from the road, a five-minute walk away from the castle, this lovely British-run place offers six beautifully designed, fragrant-smelling rooms, some with castle views, a kitchen for guest use, and attractive gardens with a great little play area. Breakfast €5.50. **€35**

Hanul Bran Str. Moşoiu 384 ☎ 0268 236 556, ⓦ hanulbran.ro. A 5min walk north of the castle, this is relatively large, with a new wing supplementing the older rooms, but needs modernizing. **€35**

Hotel Wolf Str. Branului 36 bis ☎ 0268 419 576, ⓦ complexulwolf.ro. Almost 2km towards Braşov in

Tohanul Nou, this modern complex comprises two hotels (enterprisingly called *Wolf 1* and *Wolf 2*), the latter newer and by some distance more appealing. The gorgeous pool in *Wolf 2* is available free of charge for guests of both hotels. Wolf 1 **€52**, Wolf 2 **€72**

Vampire Camping Str. Puscariu 68 ☎ 0268 238 430, ⓦ vampirecamping.com. On the main road north of Bran, this Dutch-run site has attractive emplacements for tents and caravans, rather than the usual Romanian wooden chalets. Facilities include bar, laundry and bike hire. Closed Nov–March. Camping **€5** per person plus **€4** per tent or **€6** per camper

EATING

★ **D.O.R.** Str. Branului 55 ☎ 0746 304 099. Quite frankly, D (delicious) O (organic) R (Romanian) is the sort of place you'd expect to see in the capital, not Bran. As its name suggests, ingredients are organically sourced wherever possible and the dishes are terrific, for example, fresh trout ceviche (€6), goose liver escalope, and caramelized duck breast with poached foie gras (€12). The place itself, with its modern-rustic trappings – and with a tree smack bang in the middle – looks fantastic. Daily noon–midnight.

La Lupi Str. Branului 36 ☎ 0368 401 405, ⓦ lalupi.ro. The location, next to a supermarket car park in front of the *Hotel Wolf*, couldn't be more unenticing, but the crisp, thin-crust pizzas here are top draw – and yes, there is a Dracula one. If you don't fancy one of those, there's plenty else to choose from including salads, burgers and pasta dishes. Menus from €4 too. Daily 11am–11pm.

The Piatra Craiului and Zărneşti

Mountains dominate the skyline around Bran. To the southeast is the almost sheer wall of the **Bucegi range** – it takes about seven hours to hike from Bran to Mălăieşti or eight hours to Mount Omu, where there are cabanas. To the west, gentler slopes run up to the **Piatra Craiului**, a 20km-long narrow limestone ridge known as the Royal Rock. Now a national park, it's home to bears, lynx, chamois and over a thousand species of flowers including edelweiss and the endemic Piatra Craiului pink.

The gateway to the park, and a good starting point for hikes, is **ZĂRNEŞTI**, some 25km west of Braşov and reachable by bus and train via Râşnov. The town was notorious in communist times for its 1 Mai bicycle factory, which in fact produced heavy artillery and ammunition, largely beneath a hill just east of the centre. In truth

---

HIKING ON THE PIATRA CRAIULUI

From Zărneşti, it's 1.5km west to the Piatra Craiului National Park visitor centre (Tues–Thurs 10am–4pm, Fri & Sun 10am–2pm, Sat 10am–6pm; ☎ 0268 223 165, ✪ pcrai.ro), an overweening structure where you can pick up a few leaflets. Between May and October you should also buy a ticket (€1 for 5 days, €4.50 for the season) for entry to the park from machines here, or at *Plaiul Foii* hut or the post office in Zărneşti (Str. Spirchez 12A).
It's another 10.5km up the Bârsa Mare valley to the *Plaiul Foii* cabana (☎ 0722 357 739 or ☎ 0726 380 323, ✪ cabanaplaiulfoii.ro), the area's main base for **hiking**. It's really a hotel-restaurant, with single, double (€38) and triple-bedded rooms (some with showers) and a campsite. The best day-hike leads to the *Curmătura* cabana at 1470m (☎ 0745 454 184; ✪ cabana-curmatura.ro), with beds in a cottage and annexe, camping and good food. It begins with a stiff climb (3–4hr, following red cross markings, and using fixed cables in places) to the main ridge 1400m above, and continues north along its knife-edge (following red dots), finally descending (following yellow stripes) to the right to the cabana or to the left to Zărneşti. It's a demanding route and you should be properly equipped with boots, waterproofs and plenty of water.

3

there's not much to Zărneşti these days, but it does have an excellent tourist office as well as a good stock of accommodation – useful for forays into the mountain range.

In the hills southwest of Zărneşti, between some precipitous gorges, lurk tiny shepherding settlements where there are numerous *agroturism* pensions. The best are in **MĂGURA**, 7km away and offering stunning views of the Piatra Craiului, as well as the more distant Bucegi range. From Măgura it's possible to hike down to Bran, just 6km away but a long way around by car.

Libearty Bear Sanctuary

Visits Tues–Sun: May to mid-June & Sept–Oct 9am, 10am & 11am; mid-June to Aug 9.15am, 9.45am, 10.15am, 10.45am & 11.10am; Nov–April 11am & 12.15pm • €11–€14 depending upon the time, day of the week and season • ☎ 0268 471 202, ✪ ampbears.ro

About 8km northeast of Zărneşti, the **Libearty Bear Sanctuary** was founded in 2005 to give a relatively natural home to bears rescued from cages at zoos, restaurants and even petrol stations. There are now around 100 bears here, who have access to some 70 hectares of oak forest – although some have stopped hibernating, most do in fact display natural relaxed behaviour, and may live to 40 or older, as against 25 in the wild. Visiting is strictly by guided tour only (in Romanian and English), the proceeds of which go into maintaining the sanctuary; tours take place in the morning only, when you can see the bears being fed, before they have a snooze in the afternoon shade. There are also half a dozen or so wolves here, and given that there's little chance of seeing these elusive creatures in the wild, this is a great opportunity to see them up close. Such is the sanctuary's popularity now that it can get murderously busy, so you'd do well to get on one of the earlier tours, and avoid weekends. Note that children under five are not permitted.

ARRIVAL AND INFORMATION   ZĂRNEŞTI

By bus and train Zărneşti is well served by both trains (9 daily) and buses (Mon–Fri every 30min, Sat hourly, Sun 5) from Braşov.
Tourist information The very helpful tourist office is located by the roundabout around 1.5km west of the train station at Str. Dr Tiberiu Spârchez 12A (daily 9am–4pm; ☎ 0368 003 376; ✪ visitzarnesti.ro); they can supply you with excellent maps on the town and Piatra Craiului, as well as any other info on visiting the park.

ACCOMMODATION AND EATING

ZĂRNEŞTI
Casa Rustica Str. Metianu 61 ☎ 0371 038 838. This is the town's only real eating place, but it's a surprisingly good *restaurant-crama-pizzerie*, featuring a pleasant inner court (with fish pond). Daily 9am–11pm.

Equus Silvania Şinca Nouă ☎ 0740 185 583 or ☎ 0754 227 763, ✪ equus-silvania.com. At a horseriding centre 30km north of Zărneşti, this guesthouse offers nine handsomely furnished rooms, a snug lounge bar with fireplace, in addition to activities such as archery and

WILDLIFE-WATCHING AND OTHER ACTIVITIES

The **Piatra Craiului National Park** is ideal for all kinds of outdoor pursuits, from observing animals in the wild to guided walks and sporting activities such as climbing and caving. These are organized by various local agencies, mostly members of the **Association of Ecotourism in Romania** (🖥 eco-romania.ro), dedicated to nature conservation and sustainable tourism development.

The most popular is **bear-watching**, which is now offered by dozens of companies, as well as some accommodation providers, though the following come highly recommended: Carpathian Nature Tours (☎ 0740 022 384, 🖥 cntours.eu), Absolute Carpathian (☎ 0788 578 796, 🖥 absolute-nature.ro) or Discover Romania (☎ 0722 746 262, 🖥 discoveromania.ro). You'll typically be taken up to a forest hide at dusk, and although patience is key (which is why it's unsuitable for young children), there's about an eighty percent chance of seeing a brown bear in its natural habitat – trips cost around €25–30 per person. While you're less likely to see wolves – in fact the chances of spotting one are almost non-existent – **wolf-tracking** is also popular, with the excellent Transylvanian Wolf (☎ 0744 319 708, 🖥 transylvanianwolf.ro) your best bet; they run day trips from €45.

Equus Silvania (🖥 0268 228 601 or ☎ 0740 185 583, 🖥 equus-silvania.com), 30km north of Zărnești in the village of Șinca Nouă, offers guided day (€80) and week-long (€1020) trips on horseback as well as riding lessons (€20); it also offers bear-watching in the nearby Strâmba valley, and is one of the driving forces behind the Carpathia European Wilderness Reserve (🖥 carpathia.org). In the eastern Făgaras mountains, the densely forested and largely unvisited Iezer-Papușa mountains and the Dâmbovița valley, southwest of Zărnești, they've already bought 22,000 hectares of land (and plan to double that), planting over 1.6 million saplings; the project has developed a tourism infrastructure with several hides (including overnight stays) and guided hikes. Additional facilities, including campsites, lodges and a visitor centre are planned.

swimming in a salt-water pool, and fine-dining menus of local organic food and wine. **€36**

Pensiunea Mosorel Str. Dr. Ioan Șenchea 162 ☎ 0745 024 472, 🖥 pensiuneamosorel.ro. Beyond the rather unsightly glass and concrete block are nineteen simple, pine furnished en-suite rooms, some with terrific mountain views and wonderful hospitality. Camping (€3) is possible in the large back garden and delicious home-cooked meals are also available. **€28**

Wolf House Str. Metianu 108 ☎ 0744 319 708, 🖥 transylvanianwolf.ro. Close to the station, at the corner of Str. Eminescu, this homely guesthouse is owned by the people who run Transylvanian Wolf (see page 140). There are four en-suite rooms with wood-burning stoves and traditional furnishings and ornamentation (rugs, pottery etc), one of which can sleep five. They serve superb meals of local produce and fresh herbs, and offer cooking courses in winter. **€30**

MĂGURA

Cabana Montana no.144 ☎ 0744 801 094 or ☎ 0721 369 157. Both the old and new houses offer homely rooms and delicious meals of local produce; owner Adriana's sister-in-law also offers accommodation at *Pensiunea Pepino* next door. **€25**

Pensiunea Mosorel II no. 165A ☎ 0766 226 444, 🖥 pensiuneamosorel.ro. A modern house at the far end of the village with great views across to the Bucegi mountains or into a gorge (with occasional chamois); in addition to double rooms they also have space for camping, plus six huts each with a bunk bed and toilet/shower. **€22**

Vila Hermani no. 130 ☎ 0740 022 384, 🖥 cntours.eu. Sitting on a ridge just east of the village's central junction, this big white house is home to the German-run Carpathian Nature Tours (see page 140), and makes a great base for hiking and ecotourism. The large, bright rooms all have balconies, most with stunning views across to the Bucegi; camping (€5) is possible in the front garden. **€64**

Hărman

April–Oct Mon–Sat 9am–6pm, Sun 10am–6pm; Nov–March daily 10am–4pm • €2.50 • ☎ 0729 745 210, 🖥 harmaninfo.com

HĂRMAN (Honigberg), 12km northeast of Brașov, features a **Saxon church**, once ringed by three concentric walls (the outermost has now gone); a long narrow passageway pierces the inner wall, some 12m high, reinforced with seven towers and lined with storage rooms on two levels. The church itself is a Romanesque basilica, dating from 1293, though it was rebuilt after a fire in 1595 and still displays clear Cistercian influence; there's some delightful detail to admire, including several rows of backless pinewood pews dating from the eighteenth century and, on the choir walls, a spread of Anatolian prayer rugs. Integrated within the east tower of the ring wall is a little chapel, which is of particular importance for its superb, albeit partially effaced fifteenth-century frescoes of the *Last Judgement* and the *Crucifixion*, uncovered only in the 1920s. Meanwhile, several of the old storage rooms – variously recreated as a living area, bedroom and classroom, the latter complete with recordings of the local Saxon dialect – now comprise a fabulous little **museum**. It's also possible, and a great deal of fun, to walk along a reasonable section of the inner wall – one of the few fortifications where you can do this.

ARRIVAL AND DEPARTURE   HĂRMAN

By bus Buses run from Brașov's Autogară 3 (Mon–Fri every 30min, Sat & Sun hourly); in addition, buses to/from Târgu Secuiesc and Sfântu Gheorghe, and the Prejmer maxitaxis, will drop you near the station on the main road.

By train The station, 1.5km from the centre along Str. Gării, is served by the same nine trains a day from Brașov that go on to Prejmer and half a dozen others, operated by CFR and Regiotrans.

ACCOMMODATION AND EATING

Evangelical parish house ☎0726 601 933 or ☎0748 067 962, ✉gast@honigberger.com. Simple accommodation is available in the Lutheran parish house opposite the church, with rooms sleeping one, three and four people and shared bathroom facilities. No breakfast available. Per person €15

Pensiunea Roma Antica Str. Mihai Viteazul 399 ☎0268 367 128, ⓦroma-antica.ro. An attractive Saxon house, 300m from the central crossroads, with six rooms

(including triples and quads) set amid attractive gardens, plus a swimming pool and volleyball/badminton and table tennis facilities. €30

Pizza Althaus Str. Ștefan cel Mare 295 ☎0268 367 850. A highly regarded German-Italian restaurant just 100m across from the church serving pizza from a wood-fired oven as well as pasta and salad dishes; there's seating in a nice garden at the rear. Mon–Fri noon–11pm, Sat & Sun noon–10pm.

Prejmer

April–Oct Mon–Fri 9am–6pm, Sat 9am–5pm, Sun 11am–5pm; Nov–March Mon–Sat 9am–4pm, Sun 11–3pm • €2 • ☎0268 362 052, ⓦcetateaprejmer.ro

PREJMER (Tartlau), 7km east of Hărman (on the railway, but off the main road), has the most comprehensively fortified and perhaps the most spectacular of all the region's **churches** – now on UNESCO's World Heritage List. Access is through a 30m-long vaulted gallery with a sliding portcullis in the middle. Built by 1225, the cross-shaped church was taken over by the Cistercians in 1240 and enlarged in their Burgundian early Gothic style. The nave has late Gothic vaulting, and there's a fine *Passion* altarpiece (1450–60).

After the Turkish campaign of 1421, the church was surrounded by a five-towered wall, 12m high, lined two centuries later with four tiers of store rooms – many of these can be viewed, including one housing a mocked-up classroom. Prejmer is also the only fortified church in Romania where it's possible to walk around the inside of the defensive wall in its entirety, which amounts to some 400-metres. There is also a small **museum** (closed in winter), boasting fine examples of Saxon costume.

ARRIVAL AND DEPARTURE   PREJMER

By bus Prejmer is served by maxitaxis twice an hour from Brașov's Autogară Vest (at the north end of Str. Lungă in the Bartolomei district), also stopping across the road from the main railway station. Buses to/from Buzău and Vama Buzăului also pass through.

By train There are nine trains a day each way from/to Brașov, operated by CFR and Regiotrans; note that the Ilieni train stop is closer to the town centre than Prejmer station proper.

ACCOMMODATION AND EATING

Evangelical parish house ☎0749 800 024, ✉evkirche. tartlau@yahoo.de. Simple accommodation is available in

the Lutheran parish house at the church courtesy of four double rooms, each with a bathroom. Breakfast €5. €25

Natura Parc ☎ 0786 990 744, ⊚ naturaparc.ro. On the DN11 at Chichiş, just north of Prejmer, this lakeside water park complex (also with tennis, fishing, boating and horse riding) has chalet-like bungalows sleeping two plus space for caravans and tents; there are several dining possibilities here too. May–Sept. €22

Restaurant-Pizzerie-Terasa Select Str. Cenusti 99 ☎ 0763 963 801, ⊚ pensiuneestaurantselect.ro. About 250m south of the main road, this is a very decent restaurant serving Romanian dishes, pizza, pasta and even (on occasion) sushi. Daily 10am–10pm.

Făgăraş and around

FĂGĂRAŞ (Fogarasch), 54km west of Braşov, is scarred by communist town-planning and chemical works; however it does have some affordable hotels and is a good jumping-off point for **hikes** in the mountains to the south, and for exploring the Saxon villages just north.

The citadel

June–Sept Tues–Fri 8am–7pm, Sat & Sun 10am–6pm; Oct–May Tues–Fri 8am–5pm, Sat & Sun 9am–5pm • €3.50

The **citadel**'s present walls and moat were built after Vlad had destroyed the original, with a castle added inside which housed one of the most important courts of Transylvania; a Renaissance loggia was added in the early seventeenth century by Prince Gabriel Bethlen. After 1688 it was allowed to deteriorate until it was used to house political prisoners in 1948–60; thoroughly restored, it now houses a fine **museum** of local history. Going up the stairs from the courtyard and turning right brings you to the archeological collection. This starts with 4000-year-old Bronze Age ceramics, followed by stone and bronze axes, Roman mosaics, Byzantine coins, rusty swords, medieval ceramics and sixteenth-century stove tiles. There's plenty on the Saxon guilds, with statutes, seals, coffers, tin plates and tools on display, as well as Saxon and Hungarian costumes and painted furniture. There's also a fine collection of glassware from Porumbacu de Sus (from the seventeenth century), Bixad, Bohemia and France, and eighteenth-/nineteenth-century icons on glass.

HIKING IN THE FĂGĂRAŞ MOUNTAINS

The **Făgăraş range**, composed mainly of crystalline schists with occasional limestone outcrops, is a series of pyramidal crests, linked by narrow ridges harbouring a score of lakes at heights of 1800 to 2250m. Up to about 2000m the slopes are covered with spruce forests sheltering deer, bears, chamois and other wildlife; above this level snow may linger as late as June.

Most **hiking routes** are well marked and easy to follow with Dimap's 1:60,000 Munţii Făgăraşului map, which can be bought in Braşov, Bran, Făgăraş or Sibiu, or in the mountain cabanas. It's useful, but rarely essential, to reserve accommodation. Always carry ample food and water, waterproofs and good boots – the weather is very changeable on the ridge.

Almost invariably, the starting point is one of the settlements along the Olt valley, where marked routes lead from the train stations to the mountains. All trains stop at **Ucea**, from where every couple of hours a bus heads 7km south to **Victoria**, a town dominated by its chemical works; the *Hotel Holiday Victoria* is at Str. Libertăţii 20 (☎ 0268 242 404 or ☎ 0722 218 031) and is large, clean and surprisingly decent for a post-communist relic. From the bus station, follow the main road uphill to the works gates and then the route marked with red triangles round to the right (west). A forestry track becomes a steep trail climbing past the **Turnuri cabana** (at 1520m; ☎ 0749 791 330, ⊚ turnuri.ro) to the basic **Podragu cabana** (2136m; closed mid-Oct to May; ☎ 0745 319 766, ⊚ podragu.ro), reached in 8–10 hours. From Podragu, follow the ridge path marked with red stripes, either eastwards past Romania's highest peak, **Moldoveanu** (2544m), descending the Sâmbăta valley to the friendly **Valea Sâmbetei cabana** (☎ 0757 401 346, ⊚ simbata.ro) and the Complex Turistic Sâmbăta, which has accommodation; or west to **Bâlea Lake** (2034m), where there are several huts (see page 144).

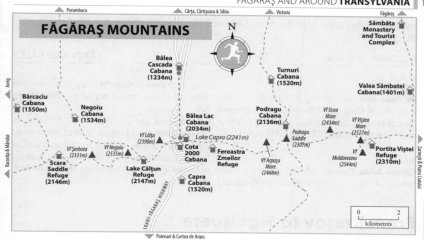

ARRIVAL AND INFORMATION

FĂGĂRAŞ

By train From the station 1km south of the centre, turn left along Str. Negoiu and pass between the market and an abandoned synagogue to reach the modern centre and the fortress. One block west is Piaţa Republicii, still the town's social hub.

Destinations Braşov (8 daily; 1hr 10min–1hr 40min); Sibiu (8 daily; 1hr 30min–2hr 30min).

By bus Local buses run from the train station to Agnita, Rupea, Ucea and Sâmbăta de Jos; buses to Braşov, Sibiu and international destinations leave from the southeastern and northwestern sides of the central roundabout.

Destinations Braşov (hourly); Sibiu (10 daily).

Tourist information The tourism office is in the Casa Municipal de Cultură at Str. Mihai Viteazul 1, across the road east of the castle (Mon–Fri 9am–4pm; ☎0268 210 000).

ACCOMMODATION AND EATING

Derby Beer House Str. Republicii 28 ☎0268 280 400, ⓦderbypub.ro. Between the main square and the citadel, this has a civilized interior with discreet sports TVs; it serves a good range of pizza, pasta and kebabs. Mon–Thurs 8am–midnight, Fri & Sat 8am–1am, Sun 10am–1am.

Merlelor Inn Str. Principală 143, Halmeag ☎0758 088 433, ⓦmerlelor.com. This excellent Dutch-owned

horseriding operation, 17km east of Făgăraş, includes a lovely guesthouse in their Saxon farmhouse, dating from 1878. **€25**

Pensiunea Bambuu Str. Eminescu 2 ☎0268 211 418 or ☎0744 126 886. Just north of the main road in a wonderful 1890s building, this is cheap but adequate, although breakfast is not available. **€25**

Cârţa and the Transfăgărăşan Highway

On the DN1 (and the railway) exactly 99km west of Braşov, the ruined Cistercian **monastery** of **Cârţa** (Kerz) is the oldest Gothic building in Transylvania, founded in 1202 and rebuilt after the Tatar attack of 1241; it was dissolved in 1474, but the choir has survived as the village church (key at Str. Principală 110; ☎0269 521 125, ⓔkerz@evang.ro). The **Transfăgărăşan Highway** starts 1km west of Cârţa and climbs fairly gently to the spectacular waterfall of Bâlea Cascada at 1234m and then (open July to late October only) winds up in spectacular switchbacks to **Bâlea Lac**, a lake stunningly set at 2034m below the main ridge of the Făgăraş mountains. This can be reached all year by a **cable car** (daily: April–Oct 8am–8pm; Nov–March 9am–5pm; min 10 people, €7/one way, baggage €2.50; ⓦbalealac.ro) from Bâlea Cascada. There are lots of souvenir stalls here, a few chalets and great hiking opportunities; from here the road passes through Romania's longest tunnel (884m) and winds down the massif's southern slopes to pass alongside the Vidraru reservoir and finish at Curtea de Argeş (see page 100). The only public transport is the Bâlea Bus (☎0269 211 344; reservation required online ⓦbaleabus.ro) from Sibiu to Bâlea Cascada (Mon, Wed & Fri at 9am & 2pm; €17).

ACCOMMODATION   **CÂRŢA AND BÂLEA**

CÂRŢA
De Oude Wilg Str. Prundului 311 ☎0269 521 347, ⓦcampingdeoudewilg.nl. Fully equipped Dutch-owned campsite where you can rent a three-person tent, caravan or chalet. April–Sept. Camping **€9.50**, caravan **€15**, chalet **€17.50**

BÂLEA
Cabana Bâlea Cascada ☎0269 211 703, ⓦbalea-turism.ro. At the bottom of the cable car, with all-year road

access, this makes a good base for hiking; it has comfortable rooms and a busy restaurant and bar. Breakfast included. **€40**
Cabana Bâlea Lac ☎0745 072 602, ⓦbalealac.ro. This wonderfully located cabana has smart ensuite rooms (sleeping two- to three people) in two chalets, in addition to a decent restaurant-bar and an attractive *terasa*, almost surrounded by water (or ice in winter). Breakfast included. **€60**

From Braşov to Sighişoara

Heading north from Braşov towards Sighişoara, the **River Olt** is lined with fish ponds (supplying roadside restaurants, and also attracting many birds in the migration seasons) and various Saxon villages with **fortified churches**; Regio trains stop at most, including Feldioara (Marienburg), where the Teutonic Knights built a citadel, refashioned into a basilica after 1241 (and now being refurbished); Rotbav (Rothbach); and Maieruş (Nussbach).

Micloşoara

In the remote village of **MICLOŞOARA** (Miklósvar), a dozen kilometres north of Maieruş, Count Kálnoky has created a number of exquisite guesthouses to fund restoration of his family's sixteenth-century **manor house**, a rare example in Romania of the Italian Renaissance style. The manor now houses the **Museum of Transylvanian Life** (Mon 2–7pm, Wed & Fri–Sun noon–7pm; €3.50), which documents Székely noble life courtesy of books, instruments, weapons and textiles; note that visits are by guided tour only, which take place every hour. The estate also offers a range of activities, including hiking, horse-riding and bear watching.

ARRIVAL AND DEPARTURE   **MICLOŞOARA**

By bus Daily buses run from Sfântu Gheorghe and Braşov via Micloşoara to Baraolt, or guests can be collected from

Augustin station (10min north), Braşov or the airports of Bucharest, Cluj or Târgu Mureş.

ACCOMMODATION

★Count Kálnoky's Guesthouses ☎0742 202 586, ⓦtransylvaniancastle.com. Small, nineteenth-century village houses are beautifully furnished in Székely and Saxon style, with colourful textiles (including gorgeous woollen bedspreads) and antiques, though the bathrooms have been modernized; you'll not find televisions here, but instead books and magazines, while wi-fi is available only in the reception building. Breakfast is taken in the

main building around a communal table (in summer, this is outside), and excellent meals are also provided (€18 for three-courses). **€49**
Stone Pub ☎0742 202 586, ⓦtransylvaniancastle.com. Just down from the main reception building is the estate's idiosyncratic pub, where guests meet for pre-dinner drinks, but is in any case a delightful spot for a beer or glass of wine at sundown in the pleasantly scruffy garden. Daily noon–8pm.

Rupea

The DN13 crosses the forested Perşani mountains, while the railway takes a slow loop along the Olt, meeting at the small Saxon town of **RUPEA** (Reps), 65km from Braşov.

From Rupea Gara, 4km before the town, it's possible to loop to the right via the station and the village of **Homorod**, where a fine Romanesque church sits within two ring walls (key at no. 29, southeast of the church).

On Rupea's main square the **Muzeu Etnografic** (Str. Republicii 191; Tues–Sun 9am–4pm; €1; ☎0268 260 790, ⊛etnobrasov.ro) has displays of cobalt-blue Saxon pottery, fishing gear, costumes and home interiors, with information in Romanian, German and English.

The fortress

Daily 9am–7pm • €2 including a good booklet in Romanian, English and German • A road loops a long way around to the fortress' rear, but turning left from the museum and left again you can fork right to climb steps through a cemetery to the rear of the ticket office

On a basalt crag above the town sits the recently restored **fortress**, with new roofs that will take a decade or so to fade to a historically authentic tone. There are three spacious courtyards, dating from the thirteenth to seventeenth centuries, leading past a four-level chapel to the lodge on the summit, in its very chapel-like eighteenth-century form. The towers have been well restored and you can climb up most, but only the **Bacon Tower** has much to see inside.

ARRIVAL AND DEPARTURE

RUPEA

By train Almost all trains between Braşov and Sighişoara call at Rupea station, 4km east.

By bus Buses between Braşov and Târgu Mureş via Sighişoara run through the town every two hours.

ACCOMMODATION AND EATING

Casa del Gusto Str. Sergent Boieru Nicolae 13 ☎0268 260 073. Neither the location, in a residential street just east of the centre, nor the exterior, promises much, but this is actually a half decent pizzeria which also serves a lengthy menu of grilled meat and seafood dishes; good-sized portions too. Daily noon–11pm.

Pensiunea Michael's House Str. Republicii 251 ☎0268 260 945 or ☎0748 359 735. A cosy and welcoming place just west of the centre, with a gateway opening onto a nice garden right below the citadel; there's an excellent breakfast and a shared kitchen. **€25**

Viscri

VISCRI (Deutsch-Weisskirch) is 80km northwest of Braşov, turning left off the main E60 at Rupea and then right before entering Dacia, on a road which is deliberately left unpaved to keep tour buses away. The village, overwhelmingly populated by Rroma and with just fifteen Saxons left, has become something of a tourist hotspot, with its church and many of its buildings having been restored in recent years. The village is also prospering thanks to a rather less likely source, namely **sock-making**. What started a few years back as a small-scale operation involving a handful of women has become a fairly substantial cottage industry. Staying in the village should present few issues as many Saxon houses have been restored as guesthouses.

Viscri Church

Daily (except for morning service on alternate Sun) 10am–1pm & 2–6pm • €1 • ☎0742 077 506, ⊛viscri-online.ro

Gleaming white, set upon a small hill and screened by trees, Viscri's Saxon **fortified church** is one of Romania's most impressive, and is on UNESCO's World Heritage List. It's largely thirteenth-century, with high walls added in 1525, and various towers from the fifteenth, seventeenth and eighteenth centuries. The interior is surprisingly small, with wooden galleries on rickety pillars, painted with seventeenth-century motifs. There's an interesting little **museum**, featuring a collection of costumes and other personal effects donated by Saxons leaving the village. Don't miss the **Lard Tower** (Speckturm), where each family would store a side of bacon, stamped with their house number, in readiness for the next siege.

Viscri 38 Str. Principală 38 ☎0748 126 616 or ☎0740 682 329, ⊚viscri38.ro. In the centre of the village, Eugen and family have three en-suite bedrooms (each containing a double and a single bed) with painted wood furnishings, woollen rugs and handmade lace, and a lovely garden with a barbecue (and rose bushes); meals available. **€30**

Str. Principală 63 & 63B ☎0724 000 351, ⊚experiencetransylvania.ro. The Mihai Eminescu Trust has done a beautiful job of restoring these two Saxon houses, each with one double room; this was once home to the village's richest family, with the largest barn. The trust also has a house at no. 129, also with one double room. Superb home-cooked meals available. **€50**

Viscri 125 Str. Principală 125 ☎0723 579 489, ⊚viscri125.ro. At the top of the main street, this is a more upmarket option, with rooms in a beautifully restored Saxon home (of course), as well as an apartment in a nearby house sleeping four; breakfast is included and meals (€18 for three courses) are also available. **€90**

Criţ and Saschiz

From Viscri it's 7km north to Buneşti, on the main E60, which bypasses **CRIŢ** (Deutschkreuz) a couple of kilometres further to the west. Founded in 1267, its Saxon **church** was rebuilt in Neoclassical style in the nineteenth century, but there are some lovely **guesthouses**, including a couple that offer cooking and similar courses.

The E60 bisects the village of **SASCHIZ** (Keisd), 7km north, where around forty Saxons still reside. Its Late Gothic hall church (Mon & Wed–Sun 10am–6pm; €1) has a magnificent free-standing bell tower that's almost identical to Sighişoara's Clock Tower, and, unusually, is not surrounded by walls; you can't fail to miss the huge crack down one side, this the result of the 1977 earthquake. In times of trouble the villagers fled instead to a **citadel** on the hill to the south, built in the fourteenth century and now in ruins; it makes a lovely half-hour walk from the church, across the small covered bridge and following the signs.

There are a couple of excellent small businesses in Saschiz promoting traditional **foodstuffs** and **crafts**: Pivniţa Bunicii ("Grandma's Cellar"; rear of Str. Principală 354; Mon–Fri 8am–5pm, daily in summer; ☎0736 637 122, ⊚pivnitabunicii.com) specializes in jams, chutneys, honey and elderflower cordial; and Casa de pe Deal (no. 199, to the right at the top of the steps north of the Orthodox church; ☎0740 286 874, ⊚casadepedeal.com) produces wonderful *zacusca*, jams and dulce de leche as well as putting on meals for groups and organizing visits to potters, beekeepers and other artisans.

By bus Buses between Braşov and Târgu Mureş via Sighişoara run through Saschiz every two hours, passing the Criţ turning.

Tourist information The tourist office is right next to the church tower in Saschiz (Wed–Sun 9am–6pm; ☎0265 711 808), though far more useful is the British-led nonprofit organization ADEPT, just a few paces away at Str. Principală 166 (May–Oct Mon–Fri 9am–6pm; ☎0265 711 635, ⊚fundatia-adept.org); their main brief is to promote sustainable rural development in the region, but they also publish excellent hiking and cycling maps and wildlife guides, and arrange excursions, for instance to a sheepfold or a beekeeper.

CRIŢ

Casa cu Zorele no. 189 ☎0744 687 557 ⊚casa-cu-zorele.ro. Also known as *Morning Glory House*, this has four authentically furnished en-suite rooms, and offers excellent organic local food with meals served in the late eighteenth-century dining room. **€57**

Convivium Transilvania no. 42 ☎0373 402 118, ⊚convivium-transilvania.ro. A patrician house, beautifully restored and furnished with local antiques, that also serves as a culinary academy, using a 200-year-old barn for cooking and teaching. Activities include foraging, truffle-hunting and visiting shepherds and blacksmiths. **€69**

Pensiunea Rozalia no. 100 ☎0374 611 766⊚cazare-crit.ro A simpler guesthouse with two double and two triple rooms; you can find out about their production of jams and syrups, and use of medicinal plants. Breakfast €5. **€25**

SASCHIZ

Hanul Cetății Str. Principală 157 ☎ 0758 040 606, ⓦ hanulcetatii.ro. The best option, with six en-suite rooms – though do request a room at the back, as the main road at the front is often busy with passing trucks – as well as a simple bar-restaurant and a kitschy courtyard. **€32**

Pensiunea Cartref Str. Principală 433 ☎ 0745 981 140. Behind a heavy traditional gate on the main road south of the church, there are seven clean and welcoming en-suite rooms; bikes are available (free) and fresh local food is served. **€24**

Sighișoara and around

A forbidding silhouette of battlements and needle spires looms over **SIGHIȘOARA** (Schässburg to Germans and Segesvár to Hungarians); as the sun descends behind the hills of the Târnava Mare valley it seems a fitting birthplace for Vlad Țepeș, "The Impaler" – the man known to so many as **Dracula** (see page 398). Now on UNESCO's World Heritage List, Sighișoara makes the perfect introduction to Transylvania, though its popularity is such that it can get uncomfortably busy during summer months.

The **Old Town** or citadel is unmissable, dominating the newer quarters from a rocky massif whose slopes support a jumble of ancient, leaning houses, overlooking the steps

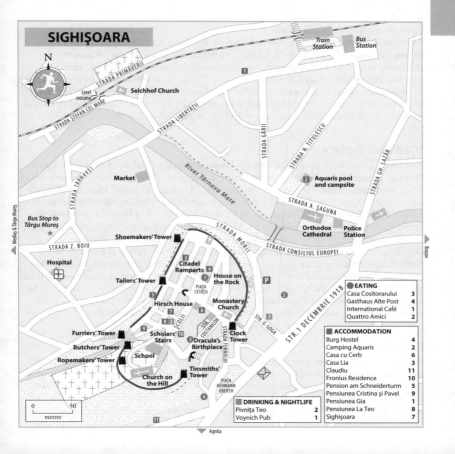

SIGHIȘOARA

EATING
Casa Cositorarului	3
Gasthaus Alte Post	4
International Café	1
Quattro Amici	2

ACCOMMODATION
Burg Hostel	4
Camping Aquaris	2
Casa cu Cerb	6
Casa Lia	3
Claudiu	11
Fronius Residence	10
Pension am Schneiderturm	5
Pensiunea Cristina și Pavel	9
Pensiunea Gia	1
Pensiunea La Teo	8
Sighișoara	7

DRINKING & NIGHTLIFE
Pivnița Teo	2
Voynich Pub	1

SIGHIŞOARA FESTIVALS

During the last weekend of July, sometimes later, a lively **Medieval Arts Festival**
(ⓦ sighisoaramedievala.ro) takes over the citadel, starring costumed musicians and street
performers. There's also an **Inter-ethnic Cultural Festival** (ⓦ proetnica.ro) in mid August,
with music from Romanian minorities such as Poles, Serbs and Tatars.

---

leading up from Piaţa Hermann Oberth to the main gateway. The lower town holds
little of note, though is useful for things of a practical nature.

Clock Tower and History Museum

History Museum 15 May–15 Sept Tues–Fri 9am–6.30pm; Sat & Sun 10am–5.30pm; 16 Sept–14 May Tues–Fri 9am–3.30pm; Sat & Sun
10am–3.30pm • €2 • ⓦ muzeusighisoara.ro

Above the gateway rises the mighty **Clock Tower** (Turnul cu Ceas), where one of seven
wooden figures emerges from the belfry at midnight to gaze over the lower town; two
figures, representing day and night, face the upper town. The tower was raised in the
fourteenth century when Sighişoara became a free town controlled by craft guilds, each
of which had to finance its eponymous bastion and defend it during wartime. The
Clock Tower, however, was different in that it belonged to the town council. The clock
was added in 1604; the tower was rebuilt after a fire in 1676; and in 1894 the roof was
covered in colourful glazed tiles.

   Originally a Saxon town known as Castrum Sex (Fort Six), Sighişoara grew rich
on the proceeds of trade with Moldavia and Wallachia, as the **History Museum** in
the tower attests. In a curious and somewhat random collection – Gothic furniture,
pharmaceutical objects and the like – the best display is on Hermann Oberth, educated
in Sighişoara, who became one of the fathers of space travel (see page 154). The main
reason to climb the tower, though, is for the marvellous views of the crooked lanes and
orange-roofed houses below, and the thickly forested hills in the distance.

Vlad's birthplace

In around 1431, in or near a three-storey house within the shadow of the Clock Tower
(at Piaţa Muzeului 6), a woman whose name is lost to posterity gave birth to a son called
Vlad, who later earned the title of "The Impaler". Abroad, he's better known as **Dracula**,
derived from Dracul or The Devil – referring to his father, **Vlad Dracul**, who was made a
knight of the Order of the Dragon in 1431. At this point, Vlad Dracul was merely the
guard commander of the mountain passes into Wallachia, but in 1436 he secured the
throne of Wallachia and moved his family to the court at Târgovişte. Vlad's privileged
childhood ended when he and his brother were sent by their father as hostages to the
Turkish Sultan; living there in daily fear of rape and the executioner's silken cord, Vlad
observed the Turks' use of terror, which he would later turn against them. Nowadays, his
birthplace contains a tacky, and not particularly good, restaurant, but you can pay (€1)
to go upstairs to see the alleged birthplace; there's nothing here save for a coffin, from
whence "Dracula" springs forth – it's worth it for the comedy value alone.

Piaţa Cetăţii

It's just a few steps from Piaţa Muzeului to **Piaţa Cetăţii** (Citadel Square), the heart of
the upper town and particularly lively in the summer when a clutch of cafés spills out
into the square. It's surrounded by fine sixteenth-century buildings, such as the **Casa
cu Cerb** (*Haus mit dem Hirschgeweih* or *Stag House*) – now a fine hotel and restaurant –
and the House on the Rock opposite it, housing a super little café (see page 151).

Scholars' Stairs and Church on the Hill

Church on the Hill Daily 10am–5pm • €2 • ☎ 0265 771 195 • **Saxon cemetery:** Daily; May–Oct 8am–8pm, Nov–April 9am–4pm

The impressive **Scholars' Stairs** lead upwards from the south end of Strada Școlii, a steep, covered wooden staircase of 178 steps and 29 landings that dates from 1642. At the top stands the Bergschule (School on the Hill), built in 1619 and still in use, its fine murals and wooden balconies now restored. Above is the main Saxon church, aptly named the **Church on the Hill** – built between 1345 and 1525 and the third largest Gothic cathedral after those in Brașov and Cluj, it has been beautifully restored, with faded murals and memorial stones in an otherwise bare interior, as well as three Gothic altars. Massively buttressed and with few windows, it is a cool and restful place. More eerie is the crypt, located beneath the choir and holding the remains of some sixty bodies buried behind cemented up niches. Beyond the church, beside the ruined citadel walls, is the atmospheric **Saxon cemetery**, a place to escape from the crowds.

Citadel towers

Of the original fourteen **citadel towers**, named after the guilds responsible for their upkeep, nine survive, the most impressive being the hexagonal Shoemakers' Tower (Turnul Cizmarilor), the Tailors' Tower (Turnul Croitorilor) and the Tinsmiths' Tower (Turnul Cositorarilor); the last of these, best viewed from the gateway of the *Pfarrhaus*, below the Church on the Hill, has a fine wooden gallery and still shows traces of its last siege in 1704. A few paces along from the church, the Ropemaker's Tower (Turnul Frânghierilor) is the only one of the nine still inhabited, currently functioning as a guard house for the cemetery. Located on the west side of the citadel are the Butcher's Tower (Turnul Măcelarilor) and, just below here, the restored Furriers' Tower (Turnul Cojocarilor).

The lower town

The **lower town** has less character than the citadel, but there's a nice ambience around **Piața Hermann Oberth**, where townsfolk gather to consume coffee, beer or pizza, conversing in Romanian, Magyar and, occasionally, antiquated German. On the far side of the river rises the Romanian **Orthodox Cathedral**, built in Byzantine style in 1937. Its gleaming white, multifaceted exterior contrasts with the dark interior. In the other direction, southwest of the centre, there's a striking **synagogue** at Str. Tache Ionescu 13. The **market**, off Strada Târnavei, sells food daily but is particularly recommended on Wednesdays and Saturdays, when craft items such as carved wooden spoons are sold for far less than in the citadel's stalls.

ARRIVAL AND INFORMATION   SIGHIȘOARA

By train and bus The train and bus stations are a 15min walk north of the centre, across the river; outside the train station you'll see an antique locomotive that once ran on the line to Agnita and Sibiu.

Destinations by train Brașov (6 daily; 2hr 30min–3hr 30min); Budapest (1 daily; 9hr 30min); Cluj (4 daily; 4hr 15min–6hr).

Destinations by bus Apold (6 daily Mon–Fri, 1 Sat & Sun); Brașov (6 daily); Bucharest (8 daily); Cluj (4 daily); Criș (3

daily Mon–Fri); Făgăraș (1 daily); Sibiu (4 daily); Sovata (3 daily); Târgu Mureș (every 30min–1hr Mon–Fri, hourly Sat & Sun).

Tours Your Guide in Transylvania (☎ 0745 501 861, ⓦ yourguideintransylvania.com) offers superb two-hour-long tours (€59 for four people) of the medieval city, which include entrances, as well as longer tours and day trips, for example a tour of the Transylvanian countryside and a visit to a gypsy home.

ACCOMMODATION

Burg Hostel Str. Bastionului 4–6 ☎ 0265 778 489, ⓦ burghostel.ro; map p.147. Right in the citadel, this has a range of rooms, from four- and five-bed dorms with shared facilities to single, double and triple rooms,

either en suite or with shared bathrooms. There's a simple menu, offering the likes of goulash and *sarmale* as well as breakfast (€3.50). Dorms €̄11, doubles €̄25

Camping Aquaris Str. Titulescu 2 ☎0265 772 110, ⓦaquariscamp.net; map p.147. Ideally located at a swimming pool between the station and the town centre, this also has space for caravans (€11) and two-person chalets (€15). Camping €4 per person, doubles €40

Casa cu Cerb Str. Școlii 1 ☎0265 774 625, ⓦcasacucerb. ro; map p.147. Named after the stag's head on its corner, this classy, warm and welcoming hotel has ten beautifully furnished rooms with wrought-iron beds. First-class restaurant, too. €52

Casa Lia Str. Tâmplarilor 6 ☎0265 771 203, ⓔmarius_adam@yahoo.com; map p.147. One of the most welcoming places imaginable, this simple guesthouse in the citadel offers clean and comfortable rooms plus a small garden; the delicious breakfast is extra. €32

Claudiu Str. Ilarie Chendi 28 ☎0265 779 882, ⓦhotelclaudiu.ro; map p.147. Lovely, restful little hotel just south of the citadel with colourfully furnished rooms and friendly staff. Secure parking. €36

Fronius Residence Str. Școlii 13 ☎0265 779 173, ⓦfronius-residence.ro; map p.147. A gem in a quiet location near the foot of the Scholars' Stairs, with eleven beautifully furnished rooms, each of which is different – some retain exposed brickwork while one even has some fresco remains; the fantastic, brick-vaulted bar is a great place to hunker down for a late night drink, and breakfast is terrific. €70

Pension am Schneiderturm Str. Zidul Cetății 4 ☎0265 771 853 or ☎0747 279 449, ⓦschneiderturm.ro; map p.147. Superbly located right next to the Tailors' Tower, this erstwhile peasant house has six small but snug en-suite rooms, one of which features a bed quite literally set atop the old city wall; there's first class hospitality and an excellent organic breakfast to send you on your way. €49

Pensiunea Cristina și Pavel Str. Cojocarilor 1 ☎0744 119 211, ⓦpensiuneafaur.ro; map p.147. Tucked away in a quieter part of the citadel, the Faur family's lovely house has a dorm room sleeping six plus en-suite doubles and triples, a kitchen and laundry facilities. Breakfast €4.50. €22

Pensiunea Gia Str. Libertății 41 ☎0265 772 486, ⓦhotelgia.ro; map p.147. Very accommodating place near the station with clean and colourful rooms for two, three or four. No breakfast, but a kitchen is available. €24

★ **Pensiunea La Teo** Str. Școlii 14 ☎0265 771 677, ⓦdelateo.ro; map p.147. Set around a flower-filled inner courtyard are three elegant neo-Baroque furnished rooms, with marble finished bathrooms; each room has a Nespresso machine and other drinks are complimentary – better still, there's the excellent *Pivnița Teo* downstairs (see below). €70

Sighișoara Str. Școlii 4 ☎0265 771 000, ⓦsighisoarahotels.ro; map p.147. The former Bishop's Palace now has four floors of big, bright rooms with solid furnishings, though the bathrooms are a little poky; there's a very pleasant *terasa* at the rear. €55

EATING

Casa Cositorarului Str. Cositorarilor 9 ☎0365 730 470; map p.147. Hidden away at the southern end of the citadel, this restful little café manifests a lovely vine-shaded terrace that's perfect for a glass of wine; alternatively cozy up inside and admire the period furnishings with a coffee and some homemade cake. Super breakfasts too. Daily 9am–midnight.

Gasthaus Alte Post Piața Oberth 38 ☎0365 430 270, ⓦgasthaus-altepost.ro; map p.147. Whilst there's not exactly a lot of competition, this hotel restaurant nevertheless offers the town's most refined food, serving authentic Transylvanian cuisine from the Saxon, Hungarian and Romanian traditions. Daily 10am–midnight.

International Café Piața Cetății 8 ☎0365 730 334, ⓦveritas.ro; map p.147. The town's best café (incorporating the best terrace), with a delicious range of home-made cookies, cakes and quiches, alongside refreshing tipples like lemonade and elderflower. Mon–Sat: June–Aug 9am–7pm; Sept–May 10am–6pm.

Quattro Amici Str. Goga 12; map p.147. Next to the scruffy car park in the lower town, this untouristy place is the best pizzeria around, with crisp oven-baked pizzas and fresh salads best enjoyed from the large terrace. Daily 9am–midnight.

DRINKING

Pivnița Teo Str. Școlii 14 ☎0265 771 677, ⓦdelateo. ro; map p.147. Prize-winning traditional *țuică* is available for tasting (€5 for three samples, €8 for five samples) and purchase in the cellar or courtyard of this friendly little pension. Daily 10am–10pm.

Voynich Pub Str. Octavian Goga 12 ☎0752 243 538, ⓦvoynichpub.ro; map p.147. Colourful and sociable café/pub down in the lower town where you can sup on a pint of draught beer at the same time as happily chatting with the locals, for whom this place is very popular. Mon–Fri 9am–midnight, Sat & Sun noon–midnight.

Mălâncrav

Church ☎0269 448 641 or ☎0744 645 473, ⓔmalmkrog@evang.ro; for access, ask at no. 86 (the *Pfarrhaus* or parish house) or no. 140, on the main street just below the church

About 11km west of Sighişoara, a side road heads south to Laslea and **MĂLÂNCRAV** (Malmkrog), a picturesque little village nestling at the head of a narrow wooded valley 13km from the DN14. More Saxons remain here, proportionally, than in any other village, and there are still church services every Sunday, as well as the Kronenfest, bringing together Saxons from the whole region on the first Sunday after June 29 (the feast of Sts Peter and Paul). The diminutive **church**, idyllically set on a low hillock, was built in the late fourteenth century and surrounded by low walls in the fifteenth century; it is noted for its Late Gothic altarpiece (c.1520) and lovely fourteenth- and fifteenth-century frescoes, especially those of *Genesis* and the *Life of Christ*, on the north wall. Facing the church is a seventeenth-century Hungarian **manor house**, an unusual presence in Saxon villages.

3

ACCOMMODATION   MĂLÂNCRAV

Mihai Eminescu Trust ☎0724 000 350, ⓦexperiencetransylvania.ro. The painstakingly renovated *conac* or manor house of the Apafi family is now a guesthouse, with five en-suite bedrooms, a library and a stately drawing room. The Trust also has guesthouses at nos. 276, 297 and 335, as well as an organic orchard with ancient varieties of apple, pear, plum and walnut, producing wonderful apple juice. All closed Nov–March. Breakfast €5. Manor house €65 per person, other guesthouses €25 per person

Biertan

Church Mon–Fri 10am–1pm & 2–7pm, Sat 10am–1pm & 2–5pm, Sun 10am–1pm (except for monthly services) & 2–7pm • €2 • ☎0269 868 262

Continuing west along the DN14, a turning by the fortified church of **Şaroş pe Târnave**, 21km from Sighişoara and 17km from Medias, leads 9km south to **BIERTAN** (Birthälm). The best known of all the Saxon **fortified churches** sits high on a hill within two-and-a-half rings of walls linked by a splendid covered staircase, not unlike that in Sighişoara. Built as late as 1493–1522 and now on UNESCO's World Heritage List, this was the seat of the Lutheran bishops from 1572 to 1867, and their fine gravestones can be seen inside the Bishops' Tower – one of seven. It's a classic Late Gothic hall church, with intricate stone-ribbed vaulting, as well as the largest triptych altar in Transylvania (1483–1512), comprising no less than 28 panels, and the extraordinary sacristy door, with no fewer than nineteen locks. A small **museum** displays winemaking tools and a replica of the room where couples wanting to divorce were supposedly shut up together for three weeks with just one bed, one plate and one knife, fork and spoon (as a result, there was only one divorce here in the three centuries up to World War II). There are also monthly **organ recitals** (usually around the second Thursday of the month).

ARRIVAL AND INFORMATION   BIERTAN

By bus and taxi Buses run from Mediaş to Biertan and Richiş (6 daily Mon–Sat, 2 Sun); from Sighişoara a taxi should cost no more than €12.

Tourist information The Punct de Informare Turistică is in the library on the northwest corner of the square (Str. 1 Decembrie 1918. 12; Mon–Fri 9am–5pm ☎0269 868 321, ⓔinfo_biertan@sibiu-turism.ro). You can also ask at the Sachsenbischof bookstall inside the church entrance (daily; May–Sept 10am–1pm & 2–7pm; April & Oct 10am–1pm & 2–5pm; closed Nov–March).

ACCOMMODATION AND EATING

Casa Dornröschen Str. Coşbuc 25 ☎0269 868 293 or ☎0736 637 121, ⓔgasthausdornroeschen@yahoo. de. The most restful place to stay is actually within the church grounds (down the path from the archway at the church entrance) – the rooms are simple, aimed at returning Saxons rather than more demanding tourists. €35

Evangelische Jugendzentrum Piaţa 1 Decembrie 1918 3 ☎0269 842 660 or ☎0745 246 485. The Lutheran church runs a youth centre in the priest's house with 21 beds in four rooms, one modern bathroom and a kitchen. €20

Mihai Eminescu Trust Str. Bălcescu 2 ☎0724 000 350, ⓦexperiencetransylvania.ro. Authentically restored cottage with furniture made by local artisans in traditional style; there are three double rooms, two bathrooms and a kitchen. **€25**

Pensiunea Oppidum Str. Coşbuc 24 ☎0740 679 119. This clean and friendly place behind the church has five rooms with shared bathrooms; a superb breakfast is included and guests are free to avail themselves of the kitchen. **€33**

Pensiunea Otto Str. Bălcescu 29 ☎0269 868 249 or ☎0740 047 300, ✉wagner.otto@ymail.com. On the

main road at the junction with Str. Avram Iancu, this has nine bedrooms, two bathrooms, two living rooms, a kitchen and space for camping (€2/tent). **€30**

Unglerus Str. 1 Decembrie 1918 1 ☎0742 024 065, ⓦunglerus.com. Just below the church, the medieval-themed *Unglerus* (Juggler) restaurant is good for a hearty meal, though rather group-oriented; all the usual meaty suspects, from roast chicken and smoked sausages to veal stew with polenta (€7). Daily 9am–10pm.

Richiş and Copşa Mare

In contrast to Biertan, which sees tourist groups dash in and dash out, **RICHIŞ** (Reichesdorf), 5km further south, attracts longer stays, largely thanks to a delightful Dutch lady who runs the village shop, bar, a fine guesthouse and campsite. Moreover, the village is home to the superb **Transylvanian Book Festival** each September, which pulls in some pretty hefty names from the literary world. The **Tourist Point** immediately south of the church (May–Oct daily 10am–4pm; ☎0269 258 585, ⓦprorichis.ro) has some good info to hand and also runs guided tours of the church.

In **COPŞA MARE**, 2km east of Biertan, the massive three-naved Gothic basilica was built by the early fourteenth century, with its choir added in 1519; the keyholder lives at the church. A village family has created a textile **museum**, with traditional looms and other equipment – ask at the *Copşamare Guesthouses* to visit.

Richiş church

For access, ask at the Tourist Point

The **church** was built over the century from 1350 and walled in about 1500, with a belltower raised in the nineteenth century over the medieval gate. There's an unusual Gothic tympanum of the Crucifixion above the main doorway; the interior has a pleasantly worn feel to it, with a couple of Anatolian carpets and an inlaid sacristy door with an intricate lock, all dating from the sixteenth century. Intriguing features include the carved heads of various Green Men, a symbol of rebirth mainly found in Western Europe, and the fingerholes outside the main door, which sinners had to hang onto while everyone else went into church.

ACCOMMODATION	**RICHIŞ AND COPŞA MARE**

Copşamare Guesthouses no. 216, Copşa Mare ☎0746 046 200, ⓦcopsamare.ro. Traditional style meets Italian flair in these four beautifully restored homes (each named a different colour), some of which have wood-panelled loft rooms. Various activities (horse riding, cycling and trekking) are offered too. **€106**

★ **La Curtea Richvini** Str. Principală 5, Richiş ☎0269 258 475, ⓦlacurtearichis.ro. The former Parish House

makes a delightful guesthouse, with spacious, well-equipped rooms; in one wing there's an apartment with four bedrooms, two bathrooms and a kitchen, while the other wing has en-suite rooms. A fine dinner (€11) is served in the cosy common room, with a wood-burning stove and plenty of interesting books. Camping is also possible here (€3/person €2/tent, €1 car). **€42**

Mediaş

The main town between Sighişoara and Sibiu is **MEDIAŞ** (Mediasch), which is ringed by tanneries and chemical works (now closed) but gets more attractive the further in you venture. Originally an Iron Age and then a Roman settlement, Mediaş was a predominantly Saxon town for many centuries, walled and with gate towers, two of which remain not far east of the bus station. After 1918, and the development of the valley's methane reserves, it developed into an industrial – and largely Romanian – town. Long overlooked by tourists, it has some decent accommodation and is a good base for visiting the surrounding area – there are still some eight hundred Saxons in Mediaş, plus twelve hundred in the nearby villages.

Turn right from the train station to reach the bus station, a few minutes' walk away opposite the **synagogue** (Sun 10am–4pm; free); from here, head left up Strada Pompierilor and then turn right down Strada Roth to the central **Piaţa Regele Ferdinand I**. This attractive triangular space is ringed by brightly painted two-storey townhouses, notably the **Schuller House** (Schullerhaus), at no. 25, built by 1588, when it hosted the Transylvanian Diet (see page 376); it's now a guesthouse and art gallery.

Evangelical Church

Str. Honterus • June–Sept daily 10am–6pm; Oct–May Mon–Fri 10am–3pm • €1.50 • ☏ 0269 841 962, ✉ kastellmediasch@yahoo.de

The fifteenth-century **Evangelical Church** overlooks the main square, its 68.5m Trumpeter's Tower slightly askew; it is a true citadel, surrounded by store rooms, high ramparts and towers, in one of which (the Tailors' Tower, now part of the German school, on the south side of the church), Vlad the Impaler was imprisoned in 1467. The interior is highly ornamented, with superbly preserved frescoes, three beautiful Gothic altars, and some forty wall-bound Anatolian rugs.

Muzeu Hermann Oberth

Şoseaua Sibiului 15 • Mon–Fri 9am–3pm, Sat & Sun 10am–noon • €1 • ☏ 0269 841 140

Just across the footbridge from the station, the **Muzeu Hermann Oberth**, in the former home of the "father of space flight", is marked by a large rocket in the front garden. Born in Sibiu in 1894, Hermann Oberth lived and taught in Medias from 1925 to 1938, writing his seminal *Wege zur Raumschiffahrt* (Ways to Space Flight); moving to Berlin, he taught Werner von Braun and worked on the Nazi ballistic missile programme during World War II and then on the NASA space programme from 1955.

ARRIVAL AND INFORMATION   MEDIAŞ

By bus The bus station is just east of the train station on Str. Unirii.
Destinations Biertan/Richiş (6 daily Mon–Fri, 2 Sat); Braşov (2 daily); Moşna (8 daily Mon–Fri); Râmnicu Vâlcea (2 daily); Sibiu (5 daily); Târgu Mureş (5 daily); Valea Viilor (5 daily Mon–Fri).
By train Almost all trains stop here, on the main line from Braşov to Cluj.

Destinations Braşov (4 daily; 3hr 20min–4hr 20min); Cluj (3 daily; 3hr 10min–4hr 10min); Sibiu (5 daily; 1hr 30min–1hr 50min).
Tourist information The Tourist Information Centre is a five-minute walk west of Piaţa Regele Ferdinand I at Str. Nicolae Iorga 2 (Mon–Fri 10am–6pm, Sat & Sun 10am–4pm; ☏ 0369 455 444, ⊚ mediasturism.ro).

ACCOMMODATION

Evangelical Church Piaţa Castelui 2 ☏ 0269 841 962, ✉ kastell@logon.ro, kastellmediasch@yahoo.de. Inside the church citadel is a simple guesthouse with seven rooms (singles and doubles), all with a bathroom, plus a kitchen for guest use. **€26**
Fabini Apartments Piaţa Regele Ferdinand I 5 ☏ 0728 714 340, ⊚ fabiniapartments.eu. Delightfully clean and comfortable studio flats (with bathroom and kitchenette), in a central but very quiet location. **€28**
Traube Piaţa Regele Ferdinand I no.16 ☏ 0269 844 898, ⊚ hoteltraube.ro. Late nineteenth century building on the main square accommodating fantastically comfortable rooms with an appealing mix of wrought-iron and handcrafted wooden furnishings; restaurant, bar and beer garden too. **€52**

★ **Valea Verde** Str. Principală 119, Cund ☏ 0265 714 399, ⊚ valea-verde.com. About 12km northeast of Mediaş, this is a superb boutique resort with accommodation in farmhouse apartments spread throughout the village and in purpose-built cottages – all wood-panelled and wonderfully equipped; other facilities include a swimming lake and there are possibilities for various activities (archery, horse riding). Owner and chef Jonas is a fantastic cook, and the meals – which can be taken in the restaurant or the courtyard – are a real treat (three-course dinner costs €25). Note that if coming from south, the road is unsurfaced, so be prepared for a interesting/bumpy ride. Breakfast €9.50. **€70**

EATING

The Bean Str. Petoefi Sandor 2 ☏0740 649 378. Craft coffee hits Mediaş courtesy of this wonderful coffee house, where the beans are roasted in the shop; grab yourself a flat white, but if it's too hot for that, perhaps try something cooler like a cold brew coffee or a mint lemonade. Mon–Fri 7.30am–9pm, Sat 9am–7pm, Sun 9am–5pm.

Cofetărie Friandise Piaţa Regele Ferdinand I 14 ☏0749 272 844. On the west side of the main square,

this classy, pink-painted pastry shop sells a mouthwatering selection of cakes as well as ice creams. Mon–Sat 9.30am–10.30pm, Sun 11am–8.30pm.

Tio Tom Bistro Express Piaţa Regele Ferdinand I 5 ☏0369 445 566, ⊚tiotom.ro. A great place for baguettes and tortilla rolls or salads, as well as coffee, teas and alcoholic drinks. Mon–Thurs 9am–10pm, Fri 9am–midnight, Sat 10am–midnight, Sun 11am–10pm.

Moşna, Alma Vii and Apoş

MOŞNA (Meschen), 10km south of Medias, is known as the first village that Prince Charles visited in Transylvania (in 1998) and is still a leader in developing sustainable farming and tourism. The beautifully restored **fortified church** (honesty box, €1) is quite unusual, with twisted columns supporting the three equally high naves, and the highest tower in any Saxon village at 53m; completed in 1385, it was converted to a hall church in 1495–8, with fine Late Gothic internal carvings. You can climb up into the roof space and the tower, and a storehouse now houses a **museum**, with a few tiles and jugs downstairs and more interesting displays upstairs, including local costumes and helmets from World War II. Not far beyond the church, a **Tourist Information** sign marks a refurbished house (no. 524; usually open in summer or ask at the very helpful village hall) that's now the base of the Eco Museum Circuit (☏0269 862 290; ⊚mosna-circuitecomuzeu.ro), a **walk** around a dozen buildings including the village mill and bakery. Moşna supposedly produces the best and biggest cabbages in Romania, a feat marked by the **Cabbage Festival** on the second Saturday of October; and there's a Saxon reunion on August 1, alternately here and in Germany.

ALMA VII (Almen), 10km south of Moşna (and now reachable by a decent road from Richiş too) was the focus of a Whole Village Project (⊚almavii.ro) in 2015, in which the Mihai Eminescu Trust worked with the community to restore buildings and infrastructure and to encourage traditional agriculture that supports the area's rich biodiversity. The **church**, rebuilt and fortified in the sixteenth century, has been refurbished and one tower now houses a **museum** of objects donated by villagers.

Around 21km southeast of Alma VII, in the pleasantly scruffy village of **APOŞ**, is the outstanding **Villa Abbatis** equestrian centre (☏0724 736 025, ⊚villaabbatis.com). Set within the grounds of the long since derelict Cistercian monastery, the owner, Mihai, chanced upon the site back in 2011 and set about building the riding school from scratch, including the stables, which have been fashioned in the style of the old Saxon hay barns. On offer are all sorts of trail rides (€110/day including lunch), carriage rides (€18/person), as well as wildlife trips on horseback; among the twenty or so horses are six Lipizzaner. The guesthouse here offers four beautiful rooms furnished with handcrafted beds and cupboards made from reclaimed materials. There's also wonderful home cooking to enjoy.

ACCOMMODATION   ALMA VII

Alma Vii no. 104 ☏0724 000 350, ⊚experience transylvania.ro. The Mihai Eminescu Trust offers accommodation in this nicely restored house, with two prettily furnished ensuite bedrooms and a living room and kitchen for guest use; meals can be arranged. **€50**

Reveria Alma Vii no. 108 ☏0269 862 559, ✉reveriacasadeoaspeti@yahoo.com, ⊚reveriacasade oaspe.wixsite.com. A delightful Bucharest family run this guesthouse, with two big rooms (each sleeping three) and fabulous home cooking such as bread, jams and *zacusca*. **€40**

Valea Viilor and Axente Sever churches

You may have to change trains for Sibiu in **Copşa Mică** (Kleinkopisch), 13km west of Mediaş, once renowned as the most polluted place in Romania, where even the snow was black. There are, however, good fortified churches in **VALEA VIILOR** (Wurmloch; 4km south of Copşa Mică), which is on UNESCO's World Heritage List (key at no. 211; ☎0269 515 266), **Axente Sever** (Frauendorf; 40km north of Sibiu) and **Agârbiciu** (Arbegen; 37km north of Sibiu). Five buses a day (Mon–Fri) run from Mediaş to Valea Viilor, while the other two are visible just east of their rail halts. It's possible to follow easy hiking trails from Agârbiciu to Valea Viilor, Moşna and Biertan.

Axente Sever's massive **church** (April–Oct Mon–Sat 10am–6pm, Sun noon–4pm; in winter by arrangement; €1; ☎0735 564 996; ⌨axentesever.com) is a Gothic hall church dating from 1305 and fortified around 1490; inside it has three separate galleries, and you can go up into the roof space and tower, for superb views. Some of the seventeenth- and eighteenth-century storage rooms inside the ring walls now house an excellent **museum** with tools and costumes, and coverage of the restoration.

3

ACCOMMODATION   VALEA VIILOR AND AXENTE SEVER

VALEA VIILOR
Evangelical Church ☎0269 515 210. The Lutheran church offers simple accommodation with four rooms for seventeen people, two bathrooms and a kitchen, plus great views of the fortified church. **€20**

AXENTE SEVER
Beim Pilger ☎0735 564 996, ⌨axentesever.com. There are four attractive guest rooms (with space for fourteen people) within the church walls, and you can also rent bikes with GPS trails. Per person **€10**

Sibiu and around

"I rubbed my eyes in amazement," wrote Walter Starkie of **SIBIU** (Hermannstadt in German and Nagyszeben in Hungarian) in 1929. "The town where I found myself did not seem to be in Transylvania, for it had no Romanian or Hungarian characteristics: the narrow streets and old gabled houses made me think of Nuremberg." Nowadays,

---

THE SAXONS

Southern Transylvania was the **Saxon heartland**, and the landscape is still marked by the vestiges of their culture. In 1143, King Géza II of Hungary invited Germans to colonize strategic regions of Transylvania, their name for which was Siebenbürgen, from their original "seven towns", of which Hermannstadt (Sibiu to the Romanians) became the most powerful.

Around them, hundreds of villages developed a distinctive culture and vernacular style of **architecture**. Although the Székely, just north, put low walls about their churches and the Moldavians raised higher ones about their monasteries, it was the Saxons who perfected this type of building; their churches were initially strengthened to give refuge from raiding Tatars, with high walls and towers then added to resist the more militarily sophisticated Turks. Some also had warrens of storerooms to hold sufficient food to survive a siege.

Alas for the Saxons, their citadels were no protection against the tide of history, which steadily eroded their influence from the eighteenth century on and put them in a difficult position during **World War II**. Although many bitterly resented Hitler's giving Northern Transylvania to Hungary in 1940, others embraced Nazism and joined the German army. As collective punishment after the war, all fit Saxon men between 17 and 45, and women between 18 and 30 (thirty thousand in all), were deported to the Soviet Union for between three and seven years of **slave labour**; many did not return, and those who did mostly found their property confiscated.

Most Saxons left the area for Germany after 1989, but most of their villages still have fortified churches and rows of houses presenting a solid wall to the street – hallmarks of their Saxon origins. They're now largely populated by Romanians and Gypsies, but church restoration and cultural projects are gathering pace.

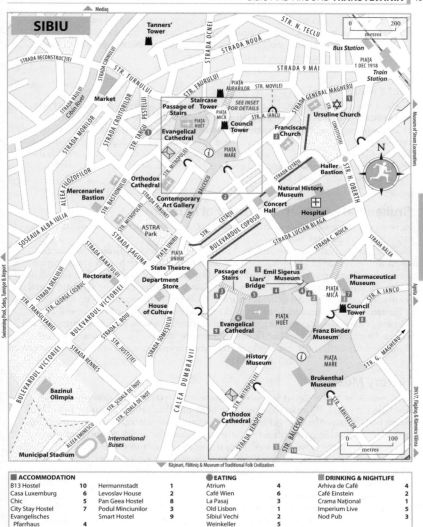

SIBIU

Mediaș

Str. N. Teclu

Tanners' Tower

STRADA OCNEI

STRADA NOUĂ

Bus Station

PIAȚA 1 DEC 1918

STRADA RECONSTRUCȚIEI

STR. TURNULUI

STR. CIBINULUI

STRADA 9 MAI

Train Station

STRADA RAIULUI Cibin River

Market

STRADA CROITORILOR

STR. TARGU PEȘTELUI

STR. FAURULUI

PIAȚA AURARILOR

STR. MOVILEI

STRADA GENERAL MAGHERU

STRADA MORILOR

Passage of Stairs

Staircase Tower

SEE INSET FOR DETAILS

STR. A. IANCU

Ursuline Church

ALEEA FILOZOFILOR

STR. BASTIONULUI

Mercenaries' Bastion

Orthodox Cathedral

Evangelical Cathedral

PIAȚA MICĂ

PIAȚA HUET

Council Tower

Franciscan Church

STR. CONSTITUȚIEI

STR. H. OBERTH

N

ȘOSEAUA ALBA IULIA

STR. MITROPOLIEI

STRADA TRIBUNEI

Contemporary Art Gallery

STR. MITROPOLIEI

STR. BĂLCESCU

PIAȚA MARE

Natural History Museum

STRADA CETĂȚII

Haller Bastion

STR. CETĂȚII

Concert Hall

Hospital

Museum of Steam Locomotives

3

STRADA ȘAGUNA

ASTRA Park

PIAȚA UNIRII

BULEVARDUL COPOSU

STRADA LUCIAN BLAGA

STRADA C. NOICA

STRADA BĂLEA

STRADA BANATULUI

STR. GEORGE COȘBUC

STRADA DEALULUI

Rectorate

State Theatre

Department Store

Passage of Stairs

Emil Sigerus Museum

Liars' Bridge

Pharmaceutical Museum

PIAȚA MICĂ

STR. A. IANCU

Agnita

BULEVARDUL VICTORIEI

STRADA TRANSILVANIEI

STR. Z. BOIU

House of Culture

Evangelical Cathedral

PIAȚA HUET

Council Tower

Franz Binder Museum

STRADA RENNES

STR. JUSTIȚIEI

SIBADA SOMEȘULUI

History Museum

PIAȚA MARE

STR. G. MAGHERU

BULEVARDUL VICTORIEI

Bazinul Olimpia

STR. ȘCOALA DE ÎNOT

STR. ȘCOALA DE ÎNOT

CALEA DUMBRĂVII

Brukenthal Museum

STR. MITROPOLIEI

STR. ARHIVELOR

DN1/7, Făgăraș & Râmnicu Vâlcea

ALEEA EMINESCU

International Buses

Municipal Stadium

Orthodox Cathedral

STR. DA. XENOPOL

STR. BĂLCESCU

Swimming Pool, Sibeș, Turnișor & Airport

Răşinari, Păltiniş & Museum of Traditional Folk Civilization

0 — 200 metres

0 — 100 metres

the illusion is harder to sustain, in a city surrounded by high-rise suburbs and virtually abandoned by the Saxons themselves, but the Old Town's brightly painted houses, with "eye" windows to ventilate their attic grain stores, are still startling. Sibiu has many fine old **churches** and some of Romania's best museums, as well as the remains of the **bastions** and fortifications.

Founded by 1191, Sibiu was the Transylvanian Saxons' chief city, dominating trade with Wallachia through the Olt gorge. In 1241 their citadel was destroyed by the Tatars, leaving only a hundred survivors; the townsfolk surrounded themselves by 1452, with four rings of walls, which repelled the Turks three times but were largely demolished in the nineteenth century. Now, the wheel has turned, and Sibiu has stronger trading links with Germany than any other Transylvanian town, and even elected a Saxon mayor, Klaus Iohannis – so successful that he was elected president in 2014. His greatest coup was Sibiu's nomination as **European Capital of Culture** for 2007, which brought a million visitors to the city.

Piaţa Mare

The old town is centred on the three conjoined squares of **Piaţa Mare** (Grosser Ring), **Piaţa Mică** (Kleiner Ring) and **Piaţa Huet** (Huetplatz). The resplendent **Piaţa Mare** (Large Square) is surrounded by the renovated premises of sixteenth- and seventeenth-century merchants, now housing cafés and hotels. Its north side is dominated by a Roman Catholic church (1726–33) and the City Hall (1900; originally a bank then the Communist Party's headquarters, where Nicu Ceauşescu notoriously dallied with the gymnast Nadia Comaneci).

Brukenthal Palace and Brukenthal Museum

Piaţa Mare 5 • Wed–Sun 9am–5pm • European Art €4.50, Romanian Art €2.50, combined ticket for Sibiu's six main museums €9.50 • ☎ 0269 217 691, ⓦ brukenthalmuseum.ro

Built in a refined late Baroque style in 1778–85 for Samuel von Brukenthal (see box opposite), governor of Transylvania, the **Brukenthal Palace** now houses Transylvania's finest art collection, partly assembled by Brukenthal himself and opened to the public in 1790, three years before the Louvre in Paris. Before entering, note the splendid portal, incorporating a gilded coat of arms (in the centre) and two large urns atop the side pillars.

The **museum**'s greatest treasures are on the second floor, most notably Antonello de Messini's *Crucifixion*, Pieter Brueghel's *Massacre of the Innocents* and, most famously, Jan van Eyck's exquisite *Man in Blue Turban*. Continuing into the building next door, the Romanian Art Gallery displays works by Transylvanian painters and other Romanian artists.

History Museum

Str. Mitropoliei 2 • Wed–Sun 9am–5pm • €4.50, treasury €1.50, combined ticket €9 • ☎ 0269 218 143, ⓦ brukenthalmuseum.ro

The Old City Hall (Primăria Veche), now housing Sibiu's **History Museum**, was built by mayor Thomas Altemberger in 1470–91 around a thirteenth-century tower. This is the largest Gothic civil edifice in Transylvania, and the arcaded **courtyard** (daily 10am–6pm; €0.25) is worth a look even if you choose not to go inside.

Entering in the dark on the first floor, you'll see dimly lit replicas of archeological scenes, with stone- and metalware and ceramics all laid out and information on TV screens. After the Roman period there's a leap to the fifteenth century, with painted furniture, ceramics and glassware, then lots of seals, chests and ballot boxes used by the Saxon guilds, and seventeenth- to nineteenth-century costumes of remarkably fine materials. On the ground floor there's a display of swords and guns, including many captured from the Turks and a monstrous sixteenth-century executioner's sword; in the basement is a **lapidarium**, based on Brukenthal's own collection of Roman votive altars and grave memorials.

The Evangelical Cathedral

Piaţa Huet • daily: May–Oct 9am–8pm; Nov–April 9am–5pm • €1, tower €1

On **Piaţa Huet**, the massive **Cathedral**, built in three phases between 1320 and 1520, dominates its neighbours, the Saxons' Gymnasium (Grammar School; 1782) and *Pfarrhaus* (Parish House; 1502). On the north wall of the choir is a fresco of the *Crucifixion* (1445) by Johannes von Rosenau, showing Italian and Flemish influences, and in the crypt is the **tomb of Mihnea the Bad**, Dracula's son; he was *voivode* of Wallachia for just three years before being exiled here and stabbed to death in 1510 on leaving the

THE ROOTS OF HOMEOPATHY

Baron **Samuel von Brukenthal**'s achievements as governor of Transylvania (from 1777 to 1787) were many, but his role in the development of **homeopathy** was the widest ranging and ultimately most important. It was Brukenthal who paid for **Samuel Hahnemann** (1755–1843) to complete his medical degree in Germany and then brought him to Sibiu as his private doctor. In recompense, Hahnemann spent the best part of two years (1777–9) cataloguing Brukenthal's immense library of 280,000 books, including a large collection of rare texts by medieval alchemists and physicians such as Paracelsus and Rumelius; his study of these authors laid the basis of his lifetime's work. Hahnemann returned to Germany, married and had children – although desperately poor, he pursued his studies, driven by dissatisfaction with the **conventional medicine** that he was obliged to practise, while gradually formulating his own theories. Although homeopathy was eventually marginalized by conventional (allopathic) medicine, by the 1870s this had itself absorbed key homeopathic principles, such as the abandonment of complex mixtures of drugs and the adoption of theories of disease based upon infectious agents.

More recently, Romania was among the first countries to legitimize homeopathy, due to the shortage of medicines and medical equipment under Ceaușescu. From 1995 only **qualified doctors** were allowed to practise homeopathy (although those already registered as homeopaths were permitted to continue).

3

cathedral. There's also the *ferula*, housing a fine array of funerary monuments, including a well-tended memorial to the dead of World War I. The cathedral is currently undergoing a major programme of restoration, and won't be open until 2020 at the earliest, though it is still possible to visit the tower, which, at a height of 73m, is worth climbing for its expansive views over the city. The cathedral also houses Romania's largest church **organ** (1914), with concerts (€2.50) on Friday lunchtimes during July and August.

Piața Mică

From Piața Huet it's a short hop into **Piața Mică** (Kleiner Ring or Small Square), where a miniature urban canyon drops below the elegant wrought-iron Iron Bridge (Podul de Fier). Built in 1859, it's nicknamed the **Liars' Bridge** (Podul Minciunilor), the story being that if someone tells a lie while standing on it the bridge will collapse. Ceaușescu managed to give a speech from it and survive, although he disliked the town and never returned.

Emil Sigerus Museum of Saxon Ethnography and Pharmaceutical Museum

Muzeul de Etnografie și Artă Populară Săsească Piața Mică 21 • Wed–Sun 9am–5pm • €1 • Ⓦ muzeulastra.ro • **Muzeul de Farmacie** Piața Mică 26 • Wed–Sun 9am–5pm • €2.50 • ☎ 0269 218 191, Ⓦ brukenthalmuseum.ro

By the Liar's Bridge, the arcaded Hall of the Butchers' Guild (Fleischerhalle, also known as the Casa Artelor or House of the Arts) was built by 1370; it houses a craft shop (Tues–Sat 10am–6pm) that's handy for souvenirs, and upstairs the **Museum of Saxon Ethnography**, a limited collection of household goods. On the eastern side of the square, the **Muzeul de Farmacie** (Pharmaceutical Museum) preserves the interior of an ancient pharmacy – beautiful carved walnut shop-fittings and a laboratory stuffed with flutes, scales and copper pans – and commemorates Samuel Hahnemann, founder of homeopathy, who lived in Sibiu in the 1770s (see box above).

Turnul Sfatului, Fingerlingsstiege and Turnul Pielarilor

Returning from Piața Mică to Piața Mare, cut through below the **Turnul Sfatului** (Council Tower; daily 10am–8pm €0.50), built in the thirteenth century as part of the city's second ring of fortifications, and rebuilt in 1588; climb the 111 steps for fine views of the city.

Alternatively, a passageway leads down through the **Fingerlingsstiege** (Staircase Tower; Piaţa Mică 24) via Piaţa Aurarilor to Strada Movilei, a street pockmarked with medieval windows, doorways and turrets. Down in the rambling lower town to the northwest are the octagonal brick **Turnul Pielarilor** (Tanners' Tower; at the junction of stradas Pulberăriei, Zidului and Rimsky-Korsakov) and a busy food **market** beside the river on Piaţa Cibin – site of the first settlement in Sibiu.

Museum of Steam Locomotives

Str. Dorobanţilor 22 • Daily 8am–8pm

Over to the east, near the train station, the enjoyable **Museum of Steam Locomotives** is an open-air collection of over thirty engines, as well as snow ploughs and steam cranes. Cross the bridge to the left/south of the station, descend the steps and go south along Strada Dorobanţilor; after 300m or so (at house no. 26), turn sharp right to the rail tracks and go left through the arch. This is the place to ask about the project to reopen the **narrow-gauge railway** from Sibiu to Agnita (Ⓦsibiuagnitarailway.com) – British enthusiasts have already rebuilt 3km of track at Cornăţel, where open days are occasionally held.

Around the ASTRA Park

Sibiu developed as an intellectual and cultural centre during the nineteenth century, and the first congress of **ASTRA** – the Association for the Propagation of Romanian Culture in Transylvania – was held in 1861 on **Strada Mitropoliei**, a street full of significance for Romanian nationalists. Avram Iancu and Mihai Eminescu both stayed here, while no. 19 was the home of poet Zaharia Boiu (1834–1903), founder of Sibiu's first Romanian-language school. Furthermore, opposite the Theological Faculty where ASTRA was founded is the **Orthodox Cathedral** (1906), based on Istanbul's Aya Sofya and embellished with all manner of neo-Byzantine flourishes and frescoes, plus mosaics from Munich. Between the cathedral and Piaţa Unirii is the **ASTRA Park**, lined with busts of Romanian worthies.

Museum of Traditional Folk Civilization

Daily: April–Sept 10am–8pm; Oct–March 9am–5pm • €4 (buildings closed Mon & Tues, & Oct–March; €3) • Ⓦ muzeulastra.ro • Bus #13 leaves the train station at 47min past the hour

To the southwest of the ASTRA park along Calea Dumbrăvii, on the edge of the Dumbrava Forest, the superb **Museum of Traditional Folk Civilization** (generally known as the Muzeul ASTRA) is Romania's best open-air museum. With grazing sheep, and eagles soaring above, it offers a fantastic insight into Romanian rural life, with almost 150 structures divided into themed areas. The ticket office, in a fine wooden house from Sârbi (Maramureş), also houses an excellent little **information office** (same times as museum); there's an excellent guiding leaflet as well as an audio guide and QR codes for those with smartphones. Highlights include neat homesteads with adjoining workshops (such as blacksmiths', wheelwrights', weavers' and potters'), several windmills and watermills (one on a pontoon) and three wooden churches.

The museum grounds (and the open-air stage in the lake) are the venue for a weekly farmers' market and **festivals** such as the Craftsmen's Fair in mid-August (usually around Aug 15) and, in September, the Festival of National Traditions, featuring folk costumes from across Romania, music, dance and much merriment.

Turnişor

Bus #10 from Bulevardul Coposu takes you to **Turnişor**, just south of the DN1/7, dropping you by the church on Strada Bielz (Kirchgasse). To Romanians, Turnişor is simply a suburb of Sibiu, but to its German populace it's a distinct village, Neppendorf. In the eighteenth century it saw an infusion of Austrian Protestants, expelled by their Catholic neighbours. Although the two groups never mixed in other villages throughout the region, here the Saxons and Landler intermarried – yet Landler and Saxon women still sit on opposite sides of the nave. Today, about two hundred Germans remain, compared to some four thousand before World War II. The **church** was never fortified – the villagers fled to Sibiu when enemies approached – but internally it's typical of Saxon village churches, with lovely paintings on the gallery; ask at the *Pfarrhaus* for the key. There's an excellent **museum** in the north transept, mapping the history of the village, with lots of old photos and plenty of text (all in German). Visible from trains to the north of Turnișor station is an amazing Gypsy palace, resembling a Japanese castle with multiple Gothic spikes.

ARRIVAL AND INFORMATION
SIBIU

By plane The airport (☏ 0269 229 161, ⊛ sibiuairport.ro), which has flights to London Luton, is just 3km west of the city centre and served by bus #11 (Mon–Fri every 20min, Sat & Sun every 40min; €0.50).

By train and bus The train and bus stations are next to each other on the northeast side of town, a ten-minute walk away.

Destinations (train) Arad (2 daily; 6hr 15min); Brașov (5 daily; 2hr 45min–4hr); Bucharest (2 daily; 5hr 50min); Budapest (2 daily; 10–11hr); Cluj (1 daily; 4hr); Deva (2 daily; 3hr); Mediaș (6 daily; 1hr 30min); Râmnicu Vâlcea (4 daily; 2hr 30min–3hr); Vienna (1 daily, summer only; 13hr 30min).

Destinations (bus) Agnita (5 daily Mon–Fri, 2 daily Sat & Sun); Bacău/Iași (2 daily); Brașov (7 daily); Bucharest (7 daily); Cisnădie (every 30min Mon–Fri, 8 daily Sat & Sun); Cisnădioara (5 Mon–Fri); Cluj (12 daily); Craiova (2 daily);

Cristian (every 1–2hr Mon–Fri, 4 daily Sat & Sun); Deva (8 daily); Gura Râului (11 Mon–Fri, 4 daily Sat & Sun); Mediaș (5 daily); Oradea (2 daily); Păltiniș (3 daily); Râmnicu Vâlcea (10 daily); Sighișoara (4 daily); Slimnic (hourly); Târgu Jiu (3 daily); Târgu Mureș (4 daily); Timișoara (6 daily); Victoria (1 daily).

Tourist information The tourist office is in the City Hall at Str. Brukenthal 2, on the north side of Piața Mare (Mon–Fri 9am–5pm, Sat & Sun 9am–1pm; ☏ 0269 208 913, ⊛ turism.sibiu.ro). The Lutheran *Pfarrhaus*, Piața Huet 1 (☏ 0269 211 203), sells a leaflet (currently in German only, with English summaries) describing the town's Kulturweg circuit of information signs, and a guide to accommodation and walks in the Saxon villages to the north. Maps and books can be bought at the Librăria Schiller (Piața Mare 7; Mon–Fri 10am–7pm, Sat 10am–6pm, Sun 11.30am–6pm) and Librăria Habitus (Piața Mică 4; Mon–Sat 10am–8pm).

GETTING AROUND

By bus City buses cost €0.40, or €1.25 for a day ticket; you can either purchase a ticket from a vending machine or use contactless cards (Maestro and Visa). Buses to Cisnădie and Păltiniș (starting from the bus station and in front of the train station, respectively) pick up at stops on B-dul Coposu.

By bike Transilvania Cycling (☏ 0770 252 673, ⊛ transilvaniacycling.ro) offers self-guided tours for €35/

bike/day (and guided tours). There are maps of cycle tracks and parking at ⊛ spadpp.sibiu.ro.

By car Autonom, Str. Bălcescu 1 (☏ 0749 151 037, ⊛ autonom.com); A-Rent, Șoseaua Alba Iulia 45 (☏ 0752 264 004, ⊛ a-rent.ro).

ACCOMMODATION

B13 Hostel Str. Bălcescu 13 ☏ 0269 701 742, ⊛ b13hostel.ro; map p.157. Set back from the main pedestrian street, in the handsome old Telephone Palace building, this is a very sleek and modern hostel with large, bright dorms, sleeping either six- or eight people; each bed has its own socket and reading light. There's also a lively social area and kitchen for guests' use too. Dorms €11

Casa Luxemburg Piața Mică 16 ☏ 0269 216 854, ⊛ casaluxemburg.ro; map p.157. This delightful, and historic, building overlooking the Liars' Bridge conceals a mix of apartments and rooms (all upstairs and no lift), some furnished in Baroque or Saxon style; there's an excellent breakfast to boot. €75

Chic Str. Moș Ion Roată 6 ☏ 0759 041 405, ⊛ pensiunea-chic.ro; map p.157. Hidden away at the bottom of the "Passage of Stairs", this simple, friendly guesthouse, in a fifteenth-century building, has ten small but clean, colourful and comfortable rooms, one of which sleeps four. Breakfast €6.50 €50

City Stay Hostel Piața Mică 26 ☏ 0269 216 445, ⊛ hostelsibiu.ro; map p.157. Fabulously located, this low-key hostel has three large, bright dorms (sleeping four, six and eight) plus a twin, and laundry facilities and a kitchen. Breakfast €2.50. Dorm €11, twin €34

Evangelisches Pfarrhaus Piața Huet 1 ☏ 0269 213 141 or ☏ 0727 819 642, ⊛ hermannstadt.evang.ro/

gaestezimmer; map p.157. The Lutheran parish house provides clean, simple, hostel-style accommodation in two twin rooms and a triple room, and there's a kitchen for use if you wish to prepare breakfast. **€20**

Hermannstadt Str. Blănarilor 13 ☏0269 212 340, Ⓦpensiuneahermannstadt-sibiu.ro; map p.157. The handiest place for the station (but also close to the centre), this breezy little guesthouse has modern, if uninspiring a/c rooms, some with bathroom across the corridor. Breakfast €4. **€30**

Levoslav House Str. Magheru 12 ☏0269 216 285, Ⓦlevoslav.ro; map p.157. Named after the eponymous composer/conductor whose house this once was, the stylish *Levoslav* has eleven large, thoughtfully designed rooms, with beds crafted from beechwood and pieces of artwork based on a musical theme; there's a cracking Swedish buffet breakfast to kickstart your day. No lift. **€75**

Pan Geea Hostel Str. Avram Iancu 4 ☏0369 801 232, Ⓦsibiuhostel.ro; map p.157. Sibiu's funkiest hostel, the "Entire Earth" has two dorms, one double room and lockers, kitchen and washing machine; also a café-bar downstairs. Dorms **€11**, double **€30**

Podul Minciunilor Str. Azilului 1 ☏0269 217 259 or ☏0747 053 457, Ⓔpodul.minciunilor@ela-hotels.ro; map p.157. The "Liars' Bridge" guesthouse, just down from the bridge and first on the left, is a friendly, old-fashioned place with six simple en-suite rooms. No breakfast, but there's a coffee machine and fridge. **€22**

Smart Hostel Pasajul Scarilor 1 ☏0731 147 049, Ⓦsmart-hostel.ro; map p.157. Just below the cathedral, this is like a stylish friend's flat, with comfy sofas and a decent guitar. There are twin and double rooms and six- and eight-person dorms, with individual sockets and reading lights. A hearty breakfast is included. Dorms **€12**, doubles **€29**

EATING

There's little to distinguish between the myriad restaurants on the three main squares, in which case you're better off heading down some of the less frequented side streets, where there are a few gems.

Atrium Piața Mică 16 ☏0723 287 486, Ⓦatriumcafe. ro; map p.157. Romantically set right by the Liars' Bridge, the sprawling terrace here is just the ticket for an evening's wining and dining: perhaps carrot and pickled ginger cream soup for starters followed by smoke-dried salt lamb with polenta (€12). Daily 10am–3am.

Café Wien Piața Huet 4 ☏0269 223 223, Ⓦcafewien. ro; map p.157. The tiny terrace on the wall overlooking the lower town makes this a great spot for *Kaffee und Kuchen* (the apple strudel is divine); the interior, meanwhile, with its crushed red velvet seating, is redolent of the grand, central European coffee houses of the early nineteenth century. Mon–Thurs & Sun 9am–midnight, Fri & Sat 9am–1am.

La Pasaj Str. Turnului 3A ☏0369 437 687, Ⓔrestaurant@lapasaj.ro; map p.157. Sprightly pizzeria with a cool brick interior, also offering a varied selection of salads and pasta, as well as chicken, beef and vegetarian options (€4.50–6.50). Friendly service, but it can be slow. Mon–Fri 11am–11pm, Sat & Sun noon–11pm.

★ **Old Lisbon** Str. Targu Pestelui 4 ☏0269 436 437, Ⓦoldlisbon.ro; map p.157. High end Portuguese cuisine is what this refined restaurant is all about, and you'll sure have a tough time deciding which of the many exciting dishes to plump for: perhaps a seafood *cataplana*, or some sautéed pork with clams and fried potato cubes in a port wine (€10). Daily noon–4pm & 5pm–midnight.

Sibiul Vechi Str. Papiu Ilarian 3 ☏0269 210 461, Ⓦsibiulvechi.ro; map p.157. Behind an obscure door just off Str. Bălcescu, this claustrophobic *crama*, its walls strewn with regional objects, offers fine, authentically Romanian food ("peasant's potatoes" with bacon, *sarmale* or *mămăligă*). Suitably attired waiters and nightly folk music rounds things off. Daily noon–midnight.

Weinkeller Str. Turnului 2 ☏0269 210 319; map p.157. At the top of the "Passage of Stairs", this is a charming little place that offers a limited range of Saxon and Romanian dishes (Saxon beef stew with mash and red cabbage; €6.50) with excellent (not cheap) wines; sit on the vine-shaded terrace or in the cellar. Daily noon–midnight.

DRINKING

There's a healthy spread of nice cafés and bars on the two main squares, Piața Mare and Piața Mică, most with convivial *terasas* in front.

★ **Arhiva de Café** Str. Arhivelor 2 ☏0740 282 437; map p.157. Blink and you really will miss this tiny bolthole, Sibiu's first class contribution to the artisan coffee scene. There's great variety here, both in terms of the beans sourced (mostly single origin) and the ways in which the coffee is prepared. Meanwhile, the small, dark wooden tables and chairs, and rows of recessed books and magazines (help

yourself) are perfectly conducive to whiling away an hour or so. Mon–Fri 9am–7pm, Sat & Sun 10am–8pm.

Café Einstein Piața Mică 13 ☏0269 242 424, Ⓦcafeeinstein.ro; map p.157. With a big terrace and a stylish interior, this is a good choice for everything from morning coffee to late-night shots with DJ tunes. Mon–Sat 9am–3am, Sun 11am–3am.

Crama Național Piața Mică 18; map p.157. A long-established and bohemian bar in a vaulted redbrick cellar; cheap drinks, and the owner may unleash his accordion. Daily 6pm–2am.

SIBIU FESTIVALS

Sibiu has one of Romania's liveliest and most varied **festival** rosters. It kicks off with the **Sibiu Jazz Festival** (ⓦsibiujazz.ro) in mid-May, one of the country's premier jazz events, followed by the superb **International Theatre Festival** (ⓦsibfest.ro), over ten days in mid-June – Romania's most important festival of performing arts features nightly performances (including music and contemporary dance) on an open-air stage on Piața Mare, plus a multitude of different events (installations, films, plays and art/photography exhibitions) elsewhere around town. There's also the **Songs of the Mountains Folklore Festival** in mid-August, the **Potters' Fair** on the first weekend of September and, in mid-October, the excellent **Astra Film Festival** (ⓦastrafilm.ro), which has non-fiction and documentaries at its heart. Finally, **CibinFest** (ⓦcibinfest.ro), on the last weekend of September, is Romania's version of Oktoberfest, a beer festival in a huge marquee on Piața Mare.

Imperium Live Str. Bălcescu 24 ☎0369 454 690; map p.157. Atmospheric old-school music pub, through the archway of a fine 1880s house and down inside a brick-vaulted cellar, with live sessions of acoustic and rock music on Friday and Saturday nights. Daily 11am–2am.

Nod Pub Piața Mică 27 ☎0754 567 250; map p.157. Whether you're after a coffee, a cocktail or a craft beer (the *Zăganu Blonda* is very decent), this cheery café-cum-pub is a great all-rounder, boasting one of the best terraces on any of the three main squares in addition to some pleasantly shaded seating under an elegant vaulted passageway. Mon–Fri 9am–midnight, Sat & Sun 10am–1am.

ENTERTAINMENT

Classical music The Filarmonica de Stat Sibiu performs in the Sala Thalia, Str. Cetății 3 (☎0735 566 486, ⓦfilarmonicasibiu.ro). The box office is open Mon–Thurs 10am–noon & 1–4pm, with tickets going for €4.50–9.

Theatre The Teatrul Național Radu Stanca is at B-dul Corneliu Coposu 2 (☎0269 210 092, ⓦtnrs.ro); tickets from the Agenție Teatrala, Str. Bălcescu 7 (Tues–Sat 11am–6pm, Sun 10am–2pm; ☎0369 101 578, ℮ticketing@sibfest.

ro), or at the theatre one hour prior to performances. There are also performances (including ballet) at the Casa de Cultură a Sindicatelor (Trades Unions' House of Culture), Str. Cioran 1A (☎0369 405 489, ⓦccsibiu.ro) and the Casa de Cultură a Studenților (Students' House of Culture) a little way out at Calea Dumbrăvii 34A (☎0269 212 883, ⓦcasastudentilorsibiu.ro) – buy tickets at the Tourist Information Centre (see page 161).

Avrig

Brukenthal Palace: Str. Lazăr 39 • Daily 10am–1pm, 2–6pm, Sun from 11am • €2 • ☎0269 523 111, ⓦpalatulbrukenthalavrig.ro

Heading south from Sibiu, the DN7 runs through the Red Tower (Turnu Roșu) Pass into Wallachia, while the DN1 turns east towards Brașov, bypassing the small town of **AVRIG**, 26km from Sibiu. The town is dominated by the **Brukenthal Palace** (Palatul Brukenthal), the one time summer residence of the eponymous baron. For years it stood neglected, and does still remain in a rather parlous state, but it is at last (very) slowly being restored to something like its former glory. Built in 1756, Brukenthal modelled the estate on the Schönbrunn in Vienna, though it remained in the family for little over a century. Thereafter it functioned as a sanatorium and continued to do so under Ceaușescu, before another short period of private ownership and then restitution to the Evangelical church (the Brukenthal Foundation) in 1999. The centrepiece of the estate is the palace itself, which, despite its current decrepit state, houses an exhibition of Saxon furnishings as well as another room of weaponry and banners. The gardens themselves, comprising French, Dutch and English sections, are laid out pretty much as they were when originally planted, while the superbly restored orangery now houses accommodation (see below) and a gloriously sunny restaurant. Brukenthal makes a suitably grand venue for the **Brukenthal Classical Music Festival** each August. Otherwise, the village attracts thousands each August for the enduringly popular **Flowers of the Olt Festival** (Florile Oltului).

By bus Braşov/Făgăraş (4 daily); Sibiu (10 daily).
By train The station is on the north side of the park, a 10min walk from the entrance.

Destinations Braşov (3 daily; 2hr 10min–3hr); Făgăraş (6 daily; 50min–1hr 20min); Sibiu (8 daily; 40min–1hr).

ACCOMMODATION

Palatul Brukenthal Str. Lazăr 39 ☎ 0269 523 111 or ☎ 0726 234 417, ⊛ palatulbrukenthalavrig.ro. One day this will be a superb château-hotel; for now, comfortable, parquet-floored rooms are available above the restaurant in the beautifully restored orangery. Particularly good breakfasts. Breakfast €6. **€38**

Cisnădie

CISNĂDIE, 12km south of Sibu, was known to the Saxons as Heltau and to the Turks as the Red Town, both for the colour of its walls and the blood that was shed attempting to breach them. A neat triangular street-cum-square surrounded by handsome two- and three-storey houses and a smattering of cafés, Piaţa Revoluţiei leads to the largely Romanesque **church**.

The church and museums
Church: Str. Cetăţii 1 • Daily 10am–1pm, 2–6pm, Sun from 11am • €1.50

A formidable bulk protected by a double wall (1460–1530) and a moat, Cisnădie's **church** is still home to an active Lutheran congregation. You can ascend the massive thirteenth-century **tower**, climbing through lofty vaults linked by creaking ladders to the belfry. The view of red rooftops and angular courtyards is superb, with the tiny Romanesque church (dating from 1223) overlooking the village of Cisnădioara just visible below the Cindrel mountains. The church grounds are the unlikely setting for a small **Museum of Communism** containing, among other things, newspaper clippings, a calendar used for bread rationing, posters and flags, some barbed wire, and objects belonging to former party members.

Outside, the church, near the tourist office, the **Museum of Textiles** (Mon–Thurs 8am–4pm, Fri 8am–2pm) is a gentle but surprisingly entertaining affair, harking back to the time when one of the largest textile factories in southern Transylvania was established here in 1919; by the onset of World War I, there were no less than 136 textile producers hereabouts – the last one closed in 1999. If the museum is closed, pop your head into the tourist office who will be only too happy to open it up.

By bus Every thirty minutes (roughly one every two hours at weekends) come from Sibiu's bus station and loop to the south of the main street, stopping on stradas Cetăţii and Târgului.

Tourist information The small but helpful tourist office is just outside the church walls on Curtea Cetăţii (Mon–Fri 9am–5pm; ☎ 0732 850 579).

ACCOMMODATION

Cerbul Carpatin ☎ 0269 562 937. This comfortable and friendly modern guesthouse, 2.5km south along Str. Cetăţii (the DJ106C) towards Sadu, has five double rooms and a triple, all en-suite, plus a kitchen. **€18**

Cisnădioara

From central Cisnădie, it's a 3km walk west along Str. Măgurii and the valley road towards the striking 70m-high rock that looms over **CISNĂDIOARA** (Michelsberg). Crowning the summit of the hill is the tiny **Romanesque church**, built in 1223, which frequently withstood Tatar attacks; the villagers defended it by hurling down rocks which had previously been carried into the citadel by aspiring husbands, the custom being that no young man could marry until he had carried a heavy rock from the riverbed up the steep track. The interior is bare save for a tiny altar – little more than a thick stone slab atop four round stones – but it still exudes a powerful sense of authority. Note the wall-bound marble tombs, inscribed with the names of those who fell during World War I. Architecturally, the most striking aspect of the church is the western portal, a splendid four-fold embrasure flanked by two pairs of bricked-up double arches. From here, the **views** over the church's 2m-high ring wall to the snow-streaked peaks of the Făgăraș mountains are superb. The stiff ten-minute climb through woods to the church begins near the bus stop in the centre of the village – there's usually someone in the small hut (daily 10am–6pm; €2) which precedes the path heading up.

ACCOMMODATION

Secret Transylvania Str. Bisericii 15 ☎0269 562 119, ⊚secrettransylvania.co.uk. A British couple offers accommodation and (if required) superb meals in two nicely refurbished Saxon houses near the Orthodox and Lutheran churches. There's a swimming pool and a great little cellar pub (honesty bar), and they also offer various tours, including bear-watching (€40–60). They also have apartments in Sibiu if you fancy a city stay. **€80**

Păltiniş

3

PĂLTINIŞ (Hohe Rinne; 1442m), 34km southwest of Sibiu, was established in 1894 as the first mountain resort in what is now Romania, and is now a decent **ski resort** that still attracts summer hikers. Three buses a day (#22) come here from Sibiu's train station, passing through the Arena Platos ski area and terminating 5km further on in the main resort, near the Muncel chairlift (summer 9am–6pm; €2.50 one way, €3.50 return; ⊚telescaunpaltinis.ro). This serves the Pârtia Oncești (Old Slope), with runs up to 1.5km long from an altitude of 1681m; the Arena Platos has five shorter slopes, but each has a drag-lift, snowmaking and floodlights. There's good tuition and equipment rental at both sites. **Hiking trails** lead across the mountains to the south and to Cisnădie (marked with red stripes; 8hr) and Rășinari (red stripes; 6hr).

ACCOMMODATION
PĂLTINIŞ

Hohe Rinne Str. Principală 1 ☎0269 215 000, ⊚hoherinne.com. The grandest and most historic hotel here, well modernized (superior front-facing rooms have balconies) and with the resort's best spa and restaurant; mountain bikes are available, as well as free shuttles to the slopes. **€54**

Perla Paltinişului ☎0374 007 722, ⊚perla-paltinisului.ro. Just below the Platos slopes, this huge modern chalet-style block has 32 rooms (with either three- or four-stars, or "daisies") with balconies, plus a big restaurant and a terrace with wide views. **€30**

The Cindrel and Lotrului mountains

Păltiniş makes a good starting point for walks into the **Cindrel and Lotrului mountains**, one of the lesser-known sections of the Transylvanian Alps, offering high open hikes on quiet trails. It's only two or three hours' walk north from Păltiniş, predominantly downhill, through the **Cibin gorges** (Cheile Cibinului), past Lake Cibin, to the *Fântânele* cabana (☎0741 251 554), following the red dots beyond the *Casa Turistilor*. From here, you can push on in a couple of hours either to **Sibiel** village following blue dots, or direct to Sibiel rail halt following blue crosses.

However, the route barely takes you above the tree line, so it's worth trying some **overnight hikes**. A two-day route, marked with red triangles, leads south via the former *Gâtu Berbecului* cabana and a forestry road along the Sadu valley and the Negovanu Mare (2135m) in the Lotrului mountains to Voineasa in the Lotru valley. If you take this route you'll need to camp, but the more popular route is to the west, into the **Parâng mountains**, east of Petroșani (see page 178), with well-spaced cabana accommodation. This route, indicated by red stripes, follows a ridge to the *Cânaia* refuge (5–6hr; ☎0746 788 218) and then crosses open moorland (poorly marked with red stripes and red crosses – be careful not to lose your way) to *Obârşia Lotrului* (another 9–10hr), at the junction of the north–south DN67C (the Transalpina) and the largely unsurfaced east–west DN7A. There's a cabana here (☎0744 700 180), as well as camping and the odd guesthouse. This is the gateway to the Parâng mountains, an alpine area with beautiful lakes; the red crosses continue up to the main ridge, from where red stripes lead you west to Petroşani.

The Mărginimea Sibiului

West of Sibiu is the **Mărginimea Sibiului** (Borders of Sibiu), an area that's fairly densely populated, mostly by Romanians rather than Saxons, with a lively folklore recorded in small village museums. There are many sheep-raising communities here, and you may see flocks on the move, with donkeys carrying the shepherds' belongings. The main DN1/7 (E68/E81) and the railway pass to the north of the villages, and Regio trains between Sibiu and Vinţu de Jos (the junction just beyond Sebeş) halt several kilometres from some villages – notably Sălişte and Tilişca – making public transport slightly problematic; however, there are good guesthouses in every village.

Cristian

In **CRISTIAN**, 10km from Sibiu, a double wall protects the largely fifteenth-century Saxon **church** of Grossau, with a Romanesque portal and massive towers. The entrance is on the riverside track at Str. X 44 (daily: April–Sept 9am–5pm; Oct–March 9am–noon; €1.50; ☎0751 146 061). After an earthquake in 1850 the tower was extended with the addition of four turrets – there are superb views from the top. In the mid-eighteenth century some 150 Austrian migrants arrived, fleeing from Catholic oppression, and there were still some three thousand Germans living here in the mid-1970s, but their number has dwindled to just forty. From April the village is home to dozens of **storks**, who construct their improbably bulky nests atop telegraph poles and chimneys.

ARRIVAL AND DEPARTURE   CRISTIAN

By train The station is on the south side of the village. Destinations Sebeş (3 daily; 1hr 30min); Sibiu (5 daily; 20min); Vinţu de Jos (3 daily; 2hr).
By bus From Sibiu a dozen or so buses a day (5 Sat & Sun) run to the south end of the village, and ten buses a day (4 on Sat & Sun) run to Gura Râului along the main road on the north side of the village.
By bike Centru închieri Biciclete (Str. X 46; ☎0723 150 815, ⊚inchirieribiciclete.eu) has a great range of bikes (from €22/day).

ACCOMMODATION

Casa Pandora Str. XXIV 12A ☎0269 579 717, ⊚casapandora.ro. Just west of the centre, this is a well-equipped modern guesthouse with eight rooms, each with split-level flooring (lounge downstairs and bedroom upstairs); there's also a fishing lake which you can boat on (and which has access to a small island) and other sports facilities, and delicious, largely home-grown food. €40
Pensiunea Kasper Str. XI 26 ☎0269 579 296, ⊚hotel-kasper.de. German-owned guesthouse west of the church with eleven rooms, secure parking and a garden with barbecue; hiking trips can be organized. €40

Sălişte, Tilişca and the Transalpina highway

From the crossroads at km330 on the DN1/7 (11km west of Cristian), it's 1km north to Sălişte station and an interchange with the A1 motorway, and 2km south to the village of **SĂLIŞTE**, famous for its peasant **choir**, which performs occasionally in the community centre, and for its cooperative, which produces carpets and embroidered costumes, the latter worn during Sălişte's Parada Junilor or **Meeting of the Village's Sons festival** (December 28). The solid village church was built by the Saxons (with frescoes dating from 1354), but is now firmly Orthodox. Just beyond it, at Piaţa Eroilor 8, is the Muzeu Valorilor Săliştene, an **ethnographic museum** displaying local costumes and artefacts; ask at the *Primăria* for entry or call a day ahead (☎0269 553 086). At Str. București 21, just southeast of the centre (☎0265 553 308 or ☎0745 980 320), Radu Ilieș – probably the last craftsman making the distinctive black felt hats worn by men in this area – lets visitors watch him as he works.

TILIȘCA, wedged between three wooded hills about 3km west, is a village that traces its origins back to Dacian times. In the heart of the village, the **church of the Archangels Michael and Gabriel** (1782) displays a belt of exterior frescoes, depicting various saints, just below the eaves on the south wall. At the bottom of Strada Școlii, by a bridge to the main road, you'll find the **Ethnographic Museum** in a restored wooden house opposite the *Primăria*, where you should ask for admission (Mon–Fri office hours; free). From Strada Hulii, west of the centre, marked paths lead up to a Dacian **citadel**, to the east, and a fourteenth-century **fort**, to the west on Dealul Cetății.

The road climbs on westwards to join the **Transalpina highway**, a recently paved forestry route through the mountains which climbs to 2145m (the highest pass in Romania) before descending into Oltenia and eventually emerging between Horezu and Târgu Jiu. It's very wild and remote, and attracts the kind of rough-stuff drivers who used to rhapsodize about the Transfăgărașan before that went mass-market.

ARRIVAL AND INFORMATION   SĂLIȘTE AND TILIȘCA

By bus There are four buses a day (2 at weekends) from Sibiu to Săliște, plus four (Mon–Fri only) to Săliște, Tilișca and Jina.

By train Regio services stop 3km north of Săliște.

Destinations Sebeș (4 daily; 1hr–1hr 30min); Sibiu (6 daily; 45min); Vințu de Jos (4 daily; 1hr 10min–1hr 45min).

Tourist information By the main bus stop on Piața Junilor in Săliște (☎0369 553 512, ✉info_saliste@sibiu-turism.ro).

ACCOMMODATION

SĂLIȘTE
Casa Rudi & Ella Str. Luncii 14 ☎0269 553 753, ⊛casa-rudi-ella.com. About 900m southeast of the centre, this is a Dutch-owned guesthouse with rooms in two modern houses and the 120-year-old wooden "Granny's House"; there's also camping space (€3/person, €2.50/tent, €4.50/car). Breakfast €5. **€27**

Pensiunea Nicoleta Str. Șaguna 35 ☎0269 553 674 or ☎0743 210 128. By a wayside cross on the Tilișca road, this is an attractive house with a first-floor terrace (and plenty of roses); they have five en-suite double rooms and a couple of triples, as well as a kitchen. **€20**

TILIȘCA
Pensiunea Irina Str. Școlii 535 ☎0269 554 009 or ☎0744 313 102. This bright-orange guesthouse has four smart doubles and two suites, and a garden with barbecue at the back; you couldn't wish for more accommodating hosts, who also offer local tours. **€27**

Alba Iulia and around

The historic tension between the Romanians of this area and their Hungarian overlords is symbolized in **ALBA IULIA**, 14km north of Sebeș, by the juxtaposition of the Roman Catholic and Orthodox cathedrals in its citadel. This hilltop was fortified by the Romans and then the Romanians before the Hungarian ruler, István I, occupied it and created the bishopric of Gyulafehérvár – the city's Magyar name – in 1009. Only after World War I did the Romanians take power here and build their own cathedral. The town is dominated by its huge **citadel**, shaped like a wonky star; in effect the **upper town**, this has been spectacularly restored in recent years. The **lower town** has been tidied up since it was partly cleared for "rationalization" in Ceaușescu's last years, and is home to a scattering of low-key Art Deco buildings, but otherwise, there's little reason to spend time here.

Many of the towns around Alba Iulia, such as **Aiud**, bear witness to the centuries of Hungarian rule; the area is easily visited on public transport, with buses more or less hourly into the Apuseni highlands and good train and bus links to Sebeș, Blaj and Aiud.

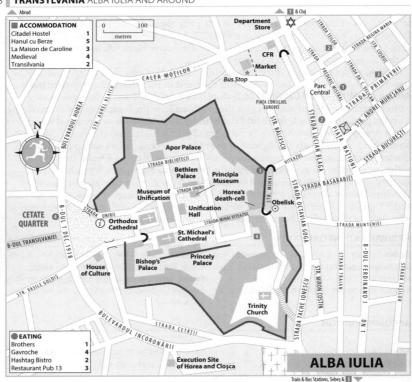

ACCOMMODATION
Citadel Hostel	1
Hanul cu Berze	5
La Maison de Caroline	3
Medieval	4
Transilvania	2

EATING
Brothers	1
Gavroche	4
Hashtag Bistro	2
Restaurant Pub 13	3

ALBA IULIA

The citadel

Route of Three Fortifications Daily 10am–5pm • €3.50 • **Muzeul Principia** Tues–Sun: May–Oct 9am–9pm, Nov–April 9am–6pm • €2.50 • **Sala Unirii** Tues–Sun 10am–5pm • Free • **Museum of Unification** Tues–Sun: May–Aug 10am–7pm, Oct–April 10am–5pm • €2.50 • ☎ 0258 813 300, ⓦ mnuai.ro

Between 1715 and 1738, twenty thousand serfs, directed by the Italian architect Giovanni Morandi Visconti, built the Vauban-style **citadel**, named Karlsburg in honour of the reigning Habsburg monarch and now tagged as Alba Carolina. Imperial levies on the countryside did much to embitter the Romanian peasants, who turned on their (mainly Hungarian) landlords in the 1784 uprising led by Horea, Cloşca and Crişan. After the uprising had been crushed, Horea and Cloşca were tortured to death, a martyrdom commemorated both at the execution site south of the citadel walls, and by a 22m-high **obelisk** on the east side of the citadel up beyond the newly restored first and second gateways. The third gateway (in fact a grand Baroque triumphal arch, raised 1715–38) incorporates Horea's tiny death-cell. Crişan cheated the executioner by committing suicide. The **Route of Three Fortifications** is a **walk** along the citadel walls that can be accessed at a couple of points on the left inside the third gate.

Within the huge citadel, there has been much excavation and beautification, including twee statues, staff in eighteenth-century costumes and a Changing of the Guard ceremony (May–Sept daily noon, plus Fri & Sat 9pm). You'll pass a short stretch of Roman wall beside the Via Principalis (now Strada Mihai Viteazul) as you enter the citadel's main plaza, where the modern glass building of the **Muzeul Principia** protects the remains of the XIII Legion Gemina's headquarters, with an open-air lapidarium in front.

The Act of Unification between Romania and Transylvania was signed on December 1, 1918 in the ornate marble **Sala Unirii** (Hall of Union), built in 1898–1900, and used as the officers' mess until 1968.; it remains, furnished with royal portraits, documents and plaques inscribed with the 1918 declaration. Facing the hall, a barracks block (1853) houses the exhaustive Muzeul al Unirii (**Museum of Unification**), embodying the credo that Romania's history has been a long search for national unity and glorifying the Wallachian prince **Michael the Brave**, who briefly united Wallachia, Transylvania and Moldavia, making Alba his capital in 1599–1600. The Magyars demolished his Coronation Church in 1713, so, unsurprisingly, the Romanians built a vast new **Orthodox Cathedral** for the coronation of King Ferdinand and Queen Marie in 1922, hence it's still referred to as the Coronation Cathedral. Entered under a 58m-high tower, the neo-Brâncovenesc cloister belies the cathedral's medieval style and its neo-Byzantine frescoes, including portraits of Michael and his wife, Stanca.

St Michael's Cathedral

Open for visits after mass (Mon–Sat 7am, Sun/holidays 9am) to 6pm

The Roman Catholic **St Michael's cathedral** to the south of Strada Mihai Viteazul testifies to the town's Hungarian connection. The foundations of the church founded by St Stephen by 1009 have been preserved, as has a superb early thirteenth-century *Maiestas* carving above a door in the south aisle. What you see now was mostly built in late Romanesque style in 1247–91, with the Gothic choir added in the fourteenth and fifteenth centuries, followed by the Renaissance Lászai and Váraday chapels in 1512 and 1524 respectively. There are also large patches of Renaissance fresco (post-1510) in the north transept. It's Romania's longest cathedral, at 89m, and has a lovely light interior. The **tomb of Hunyadi**, greatest of Transylvania's warlords, is the middle of the three tombs to the right of the west door; a century after his death, the tomb was vandalized by the Turks, still bitter about their defeats at his hands. Now it is laden with wreaths and ribbons in the colours of Hungary.

ARRIVAL AND INFORMATION
ALBA IULIA

By train Alba Iulia's train and twin bus stations are 1km south of the centre on B-dul Ferdinand I (DN1), reached by buses #103 and #104, looping via the lower town and the Cetate quarter every 5–10min, one in each direction. Strada Iaşilor, parallel to the DN1, provides a pleasant walk from the stations into town.
Destinations Cluj (3 daily; 2hr 30min–3hr); Deva (3 daily; 1hr 20min–1hr 45min); Sibiu (2 daily; 2hr 45min); Târgu Mureş (2 daily; 2hr 15min–3hr); Timişoara (2 daily; 5hr 10min).
By bus Buses for Sebeş leave every 30min from Piaţa Consiliul Europei at the top of Str. Bălcescu. Other local

services run from the Livio Dario terminal across the road from the main bus station, 1km south.
Destinations Aiud (every 30min–1hr); Bistriţa (3 daily); Blaj (9 daily); Bucharest (7 daily); Câmpeni (5 daily); Cluj (every 45min–1hr); Deva (9 daily); Haţeg (3 daily); Hunedoara (3 daily); Oradea (2 daily); Râmnicu Vâlcea (10 daily); Sibiu (every 45min–1hr); Târgu Jiu (4 daily); Târgu Mureş (3 daily); Timişoara (3 daily).
Tourist information The superb tourist office – a rarity in itself – is immediately west of the cathedrals, just below the citadel's Gate IVa at Aleea Sf Capistrano 28 (daily 9am–5pm; ☎ 0371 337 148; ⊛ visitalbaiulia.com).

ACCOMMODATION

Citadel Hostel Str. Alecsandri Vasile 64 ☎ 0740 026 205; map p.168. It's not actually in the citadel, but this cozy hostel is just a ten-minute walk north of the fort. The well-kept dorms (and en-suite doubles) have proper wooden beds with colourfully printed duvets, while the bathrooms wouldn't look out of place in a decent hotel; it's also got a nicely designed social space with tea and coffee facilities, though there is no kitchen. Dorms €12, doubles €28
Hanul cu Berze Str. Regimentul V. Vânători 83 ☎ 0258 810 129, ⊛ hanulcuberze.ro; map p.168. A friendly,

family-run place, with lively restaurants and a swimming pool, by the river 2km south of the bus and train stations (bus #113/113A). €22
La Maison de Caroline Str. Primăverii 11 ☎ 0358 101 227, ⊛ lamaisondecaroline.ro; map p.168. Immediately east of the centre, this is a very friendly guesthouse in a late nineteenth-century villa, with antique-style furniture and massage showers. The restaurant comes highly recommended. €60

3

THE UNIATE CHURCH

In 1596, the Austrian government persuaded the Orthodox Church in Galicia (now southern Poland and Ukraine) to accept the Vatican's authority and protection, hoping to detach them from Russian influence and to tie them more firmly to the Western fold. Thus was born the **Uniate Church**, also known as the Catholic Church of the Eastern Rite, or the Greco-Catholic Church, which was introduced to Transylvania in 1698, gaining its adherents civil rights that were denied to Orthodox believers.

At the end of the eighteenth century, the **Transylvanian School** (Şcoala Ardeleana), a group of Uniate clerics and teachers in Blaj, just east of Aiud, played a key role in revitalizing Romanian culture, creating a literary language and instilling a sense of nationhood into the Romanian people. The Uniate Church stood for independence of thought and self-reliance, as opposed to the more hierarchical and conformist Orthodox Church, so the communist regime called its million-plus adherents "agents of imperialism" and forcibly merged them with the Orthodox Church. Uniates remained a harassed and often imprisoned minority until the overthrow of communism. The post-communist government also supported, and was supported by, the Orthodox Church, and the Uniates have found it a long, hard struggle to reclaim even their buildings; however, in some areas, such as Maramureş, the church is seeing a strong revival.

The Uniates accept four key points of Catholic doctrine: the Filioque clause in the creed (according to which the Holy Spirit proceeds from the Father and the Son, as opposed to the Orthodox doctrine by which the Holy Spirit proceeds only from the Father); the use of wafers instead of bread in the Mass; the doctrine of Purgatory (unknown in the East); and, above all, **papal supremacy**. In other respects – the marriage of priests, a bearded clergy, the cult of icons, different vestments and rituals – they follow Orthodox practice.

Medieval Str. Militari 13 ☎0374 079 990, ⓦhotel-medieval.ro; map p.168. The only hotel in the citadel itself, in an eighteenth-century (not medieval!) building, though it doesn't really warrant its five-star rating; rooms are furnished in heavy wood with printed carpets but are otherwise a bit kitschy, as are the staff in period costume and the noon flag-raising ceremony. Guests enjoy free access to the citadel walls. **€110**

Transilvania Piaţa Iuliu Maniu 11 ☎0258 812 052, ⓦhoteltransilvania.eu; map p.168. A funky new Mondrian-inspired facade hides some perfectly agreeable and modern (if cramped) three- and four-star rooms; there's a gym and a decent restaurant, plus the *English Bar* on the foyer mezzanine. **€44**

EATING

Brothers Str. Mistral 3 ☎0747 515 885; map p.168. A lively central bistro for drinks (good lemonade) or food such as soups, salads, pizza, pasta or steak. Mon–Fri 7.30am–midnight, Sat 9am–midnight, Sun 11am–midnight.

Gavroche B-dul 1 Decembrie 1918 105 ☎0757 376 526, ⓦrestaurantgavroche.ro; map p.168. Outside the west gate of the citadel, this tries hard to be a French café-bistro, but the tasty food also (rather confusingly) includes goulash, burgers and ribs, and risottos, as well as cheesecake and carrot cake. Mon–Thurs 8am–midnight, Fri–Sun 9am–1am.

Hashtag Bistro Piaţa Natiunii 11 ☎0748 792 304; map p.168. Modern and colourful bistro whose scrummy

burgers are the best in town, though they offer much more besides including buffalo wings and a warming apple pie. Good cocktails too. Mon–Fri 7.30am–11pm, Sat 9.30am–midnight, Sun 9.30am–11pm.

Restaurant Pub 13 Aleea Sf Capistrano 1 ☎0728 444 415, ⓦpub13.ro; map p.168. A footbridge across the moat leads to this very atmospheric place inside the citadel wall; it's busy with tourists and the menu spans too ambitious a range, but the grilled meats are good as is the beer. Daily noon–11pm.

Aiud

The attractive town of **AIUD** (Nagyenyed), almost 30km north of Alba Iulia on the DN1 (E81), and 13km north of Teiuş, the junction of the rail lines from Braşov and Deva towards Cluj, has a reputation for ethnic harmony, despite the grim reputation of its prison. Having held Soviet spies during World War II, and Iron Guardists and other dissidents after the communist takeover, it remains Transylvania's largest prison, holding the country's most serious offenders. In the centre stands one of the oldest **fortresses** in Transylvania, dating back to 1302, and still boasting a full ring of walls and eight towers. It shelters two Hungarian churches, the first Lutheran (built in 1866 on a medieval ground plan), the second (dating from the early fifteenth century) which became Calvinist at a time when Aiud was that religion's main Centre in Transylvania. Across a footbridge behind the fortress, the landmark, turn-of-the-twentieth-century **Technical School** rises up like a huge Renaissance palace. Opposite the fortress are two small museums: at Strada Bethlen 1, the **Natural Sciences Museum** (Tues–Fri 8am–4pm, Sat & Sun 9am–1pm) has a display of stuffed animals, and on the corner of Strada Bethlen and Piaţa Cuza Vodă, the **History Museum** (Tues–Fri 8am–4pm, Sat & Sun 8am–noon) displays a stone slab that was part of a Dacian wine press, showing that the area's viticultural tradition dates from long before the arrival of Hungarian and Saxon settlers.

ARRIVAL AND DEPARTURE
AIUD

By train From the train station, it's a 20min walk to the centre – head up Str. Coşbuc, just to the left of the station, and after the stadium turn left on to Str. Stadionului and then right through the market to Str. Iuliu Maniu.
Destinations Alba Iulia (6 daily; 50min); Cluj (11 daily; 1hr 45min–2hr 20min); Deva (2 daily; 2hr 40min); Sighişoara (4 daily; 2–3hr); Târgu Mureş (3 daily; 1hr 30min–2hr 15min).

By bus Through-buses towards Cluj stop on Str. Cuza Vodă while those towards Blaj and Târgu Mureş stop on Str. Stadionului (Aiud–Alba local buses loop via both); local buses to villages on the fringes of the Apuseni mountains such as Rimetea run from the station.
Destinations Alba Iulia (every 30min–1hr); Cluj (every 45min–1hr 30min); Rimetea (5 daily Mon–Fri, 3 Sat, 1 Sun); Sibiu (every 30min–1hr); Târgu Jiu (4 daily).

ACCOMMODATION AND EATING

Crama Tamás Pince Str. Bethlen 2 ☏ 0744 781 709. At the rear of *La Dolce Vita*, this brick cellar is a handy place to sample local white wines; you can also visit the *Crama Papp Peter* at Str. Avram Iancu 56 (west from the fortress; ☏ 0751 088 643) or *Crama Takács* at Str. Protopop Iosif Pop 2 (on the way to the station; ☏ 0762 207 490, ⓦ takacspince.ro). Mon–Fri 10am–1pm & 3–5pm, Sat 10am–1pm.

La Dolce Vita Str. Bethlen 2 ☏ 0743 615 069. A surprisingly good *pizzerie-cafenea-restaurant* facing the fortress on the corner of Piaţa Cuza Vodă that suffices for a

quick bite if passing through. Mon–Fri 7.30am–11pm, Sat 9am–11pm, Sun 10am–11pm.

Pensiunea Melinda Str. Creangă 137 ☏ 0258 864 676 or ☏ 0740 862 873. Just east off the Blaj road, this friendly guesthouse has thirteen simple rooms (six en-suite) plus a nice garden, table tennis and billiards facilities. €22

Pensiunea Mobis Str. Transilvaniei 120 ☏ 0754 899 471, ⓦ mobis-al.ro. About 1km north of town on the Cluj road, this is a smart, fresh place with single, double and triple rooms, an indoor pool (which costs extra to use) and the town's best restaurant. €24

Orăştie

ORĂŞTIE, first recorded in 1224 as the Saxon *Stuhl* of Broos, is a quiet town 38km from Sebeş on the main road and railway west towards Deva, Timişoara and Arad. It's the jumping-off spot for various Dacian **citadels** deep in the mountains to the south, six of which are UNESCO World Heritage Sites including the most interesting, **Sarmizegetusa**, 39km south of Orăştie. The town **museum** (Tues–Sun 9am–5pm), at Piaţa Aurel Vlaicu 1, whose exhibits include ceramics, textiles, old clocks and Dacian relics, is to the right off the pedestrianized Strada Bălcescu, as is the old **citadel** (often closed) immediately east, with large Hungarian Reformed and German Evangelical churches (dating from the thirteenth century and 1823, respectively) crammed close together, along with the remains of tenth-century fortifications and a chapel.

Arsenal Park

Str. Codrului 25 • Daily 8am–5pm • €2.50 for park access; different fees apply for activities • ☏ 0799 108391, ⓦ arsenalpark.com

Turning off the DN7 at a Soviet self-propelled gun just west of town, you'll enter what used to be a secret armaments factory now reinvented as a surprisingly good military museum and adventure **park**. Dotted through the woods are Russian/Romanian tanks, helicopters and the odd jet fighter; activities include minigolf, archery, shooting, paintball, bike/horseriding, ice-skating, the longest zipline in Romania, and a vast Aquapark (adults €5.50/3hr, €10/day, children €3.50/3hr, €5.50/day). There's also a spa, a café-restaurant and accommodation.

ARRIVAL AND DEPARTURE
ORĂŞTIE

By train From the train station, 3km north of the town, trains should be met by buses for the town centre (buses to the station depart from stops along the DN7 and are less predictable – roughly every 30min – so allow some leeway).

Destinations Alba Iulia (9 daily; 1hr–1hr 30min); Cluj (3 daily; 3hr 10min–4hr); Deva (4 daily; 35–50min); Târgu Jiu (1 daily; 4hr).

By bus There's a decent little *autogară* at Str. Grădiştei 2, just southeast of the centre. Longer-distance buses stop on B-dul Eroilor (the DN7).

Destinations from the *autogară* Alba Iulia (12 daily); Cluj (10 daily); Costeşti (12 daily Mon–Fri); Deva (every 30min–1hr); Hunedoara (4 daily); Sibiu (7 daily); Timişoara (7 daily).

ACCOMMODATION AND EATING

Dacor Str. Mureşul 7 ☎ 0354 107 205, ⓦ hoteldacor.ro. On the far side of the main DN7 (and behind some blocks of flats), this is still close enough to the centre, with clean, sunny rooms (some a/c) that are terrific value. **€20**

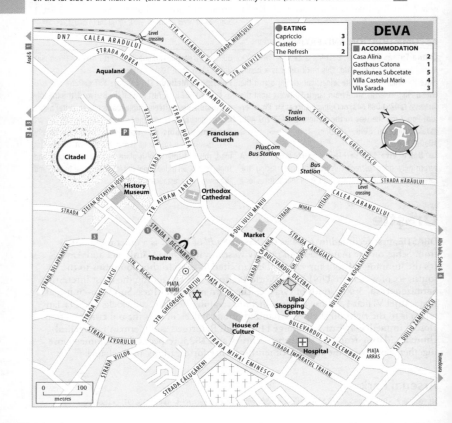

DEVA

● EATING

Capriccio	3
Castelo	1
The Refresh	2

■ ACCOMMODATION

Casa Alina	2
Gasthaus Catona	1
Pensiunea Subcetate	5
Villa Castelul Maria	4
Vila Sarada	3

Mini-Hotel Jorja Str. Bălcescu 30 ☎0731 146 212, ⓦpensiunejorja.ro. A simple but quirky little guesthouse with limited parking in the courtyard; sauna and massage available. €18

Pensiunea San Matteo Castău no. 318B ☎0767 965 837, ⓦsanmateo.ro. Just a couple of kilometres south on the road to the Dacian citadels, this modern complex offers far more spacious accommodation than anywhere in town, although there are likely to be weddings at weekends. €25

Pizzeria Rusticiana Str. Unirii 7 ☎0254 244 188, ⓦrusticiana.ro. A lively Italian place on the main DN7, with lots of pizza and pasta choices (€3–6), plus tiramisu and other desserts. Daily 8.30am–11pm.

Cetatea Costeşti and Sarmizegetusa

Cetatea Costeşti, the first of the Dacian citadels, lies south of Orăştie along the Gradiştie valley. Turn right to cross the bridge at the far end of Costeşti, 20km south, right again past the sign to the citadel, then left at a junction and sharp left at a farm (3km from the bridge; cars can be parked here) to reach the three rows of earthworks, grazed by cows and surrounded by birch and cherry trees. Steps lead to the bases of two stone towers 100m apart – the first was probably the residence of Burebista (see page 375), the second the high priest's. At the far end, go down to the sanctuary and return to the right. From the Costeşti bridge there's also a path (marked with blue stripes) leading 2km to the left to the citadel of Blidaru, where there's more stonework, including a tower and a four-sided wall to support war machines.

The largest citadel, **Sarmizegetusa**, lies deeper into the mountains. Without your own transport, you'll have to walk or hitch beyond Costeşti, continuing down the valley through the hamlet of Grădiştea de Munte and a further 8km over a newly asphalted stretch of road. This was the Dacian capital from the first century BC to 106 AD, though it requires some imagination to visualize its grandeur from the weathered walls and stumps of pillars that remain. However, Sarmizegetusa was clearly divided into two distinct parts: the citadel, used as a wartime refuge; and the sacred area, dominated by the great sanctuary, a stone circle containing a horseshoe of wooden columns where ritual sacrifices were performed. The Romans rebuilt Sarmizegetusa after its capture in 106 AD, stationing a detachment of the IV Legion here, and appropriated the shrines, shrewdly rededicating them to members of their pantheon. The Roman capital of Ulpia Traiana Sarmizegetusa, southwest of here (see page 176), took its name from Decebal's citadel, which became known as Sarmizegetusa Regia.

ACCOMMODATION   COSTEŞTI AND SARMIZEGETUSA

Casa Bunici Costeşti no 69C ☎0724 286 449. "Granny's House" is a wooden cottage in an attractive riverside garden with four rooms, each one furnished in local style; there's also table tennis, barbeque and a kitchen for guests. €18

Pensiunea Popasul Dacilor Costeşti no. 93 ☎0254 246 543 or ☎0743 089 658, ⓦpopasuldacilor.ro. This modern guesthouse, open all year with central heating, has rooms with both shared and private facilities; they also have a place in Grădiştea de Munte, 10km south of Costeşti en route to Sarmizegetusa, with six en-suite rooms (€25). €18

Deva

The capital of Hunedoara county, **DEVA**, 30km west of Orăştie (and 150km east of Arad), lies below a thirteenth-century **citadel** that was transformed into one of Transylvania's strongest fortifications by the warlord Hunyadi after 1444. It crowns a truncated volcanic cone – supposedly the result of a stupendous battle between the *djinns* (spirits) of the Retezat mountains and of the plain, hence the nickname **Hill of the Djinn**.

The citadel

Funicular Daily: May–Sept 9am–9pm; Oct–April 8am–8pm • €1.50 single, €2.50 return

Despite its builder reputedly immuring his wife in its walls to guarantee his creation's indestructability, Deva's **citadel** was destroyed in 1849, when the magazine blew up, leaving only the ramparts and barracks standing. There's also a small cavern which is a memorial to David Ferenc (1520–79), founder of the Unitarian Church (see page 202), who was martyred in the castle's prison. The expansive views over the Mureş valley are superb; if you don't fancy the stiff 184m climb to the top (following red triangle markings from the museum), you can take Romania's first **funicular** (*telecabina*) on the eastern side of the hill. Facing the lower terminal a row of busts of world-beating Romanian gymnasts, and their equally legendary coaches, stands in front of the National Sports College where they trained.

Muzeul Civilizaţiei Dacice şi Romane

Tues–Sun: May–Sept 10am–6pm; Oct–April 9am–5pm • €2 • ☎ 0254 216 750, ⓦ mcdr.ro

In the park at the foot of the hill – beneath the Hollywood-style "Deva" sign on the citadel – is the **Magna Curia palace**, rebuilt in 1621 by *Voivode* Gábor Bethlen, who made Deva briefly capital of Transylvania. Since 1882, it has housed the **Muzeul Civilizaţiei Dacice şi Romane** (Museum of the Dacian and Roman Civilizations), now reopened after lengthy restoration. There are relics aplenty from the Dacian and Roman sites, very well presented, as well as displays of local costumes and ceramics, art and natural history.

ARRIVAL AND DEPARTURE   DEVA

By train All trains on the main line from Arad stop at Deva, making it a good place to pick up services to Budapest or the further corners of Romania; from the station, the town centre is just 5min south along B-dul Iuliu Maniu.

Destinations Arad (9 daily; 2hr 10min–3hr); Braşov (2 daily; 5hr 45min); Bucharest (3 daily; 8hr 30min); Budapest (2 daily; 7hr); Cluj (2 daily; 4hr); Sibiu (2 daily; 3hr 15min); Sighişoara (1 daily; 3hr 30min); Timişoara (4 daily; 3hr 30min–4hr 20min); Vienna (1 daily, summer only; 10hr).

By bus Deva is also a hub for bus services. From the old bus station east of the train station, services mainly serve local destinations such as Hunedoara, Brad, Călan and Orăştie while the PlusCom bus station just west serves remoter destinations such as Cluj, Sibiu, Oradea and Timişoara.

Destinations Alba Iulia (9 daily); Arad (8 daily); Bistriţa (2 daily); Brad (hourly); Câmpeni (3 daily); Cluj (8 daily Mon–Fri, 6 daily Sat & Sun); Hunedoara (every 15–20min); Oradea (3 daily); Orăştie (every 30min–1hr); Sarmizegetusa/Zeicani (2 daily Mon–Fri); Sibiu (10 daily); Târgu Jiu (1 daily); Târgu Mureş (2 daily); Timişoara (every 1–2hr).

ACCOMMODATION

Casa Alina Str. Horea 98 ☎ 0727 892 962; map p.172. To the west of town just beyond the Aqualand water park, this welcoming place, courtesy of the charming Alina herself – has four individually designed a/c rooms and a very spruce garden. **€33**

Gasthaus Catona Str. Ştefan cel Mare 9, Ilia ☎ 0254 282 678 or ☎ 0723 176 277; map p.172. Delightful German-run guesthouse, with excellent food and a lovely covered terrace, 25km west in a village bypassed by the DN7 (Prince Gábor Bethlen was born in 1580 in the mansion at the village's western exit). **€50**

Pensiunea Subcetate Str. 1 Decembrie 1918 37B ☎ 0766 377 373, ⓦ devacazare.ro; map p.172. Just behind the museum, this is a homely little guesthouse with a lovely, flower-filled garden and orchard, a fabulous spot to take breakfast in warmer weather. **€32**

Villa Castelul Maria Banpotoc no. 20 ☎ 0254 260 000, ⓦ castelulmaria.ro; map p.172. In an attractive village across the Mureş, this beautiful mansion offers large, colour-themed rooms with period-style furnishings, a good range of meals, and a lovely garden and orchard. **€40**

Vila Sarada Str. Horea 204 ☎ 0724 862 820 or ☎ 0763 150 220; map p.172. Near the westernmost junction to Deva from the DN7, this boutiquey guesthouse is in a slightly remote but quiet suburban area; the six large rooms are warm and colourfully furnished, and an excellent breakfast can be served on the terrace. **€31**

EATING

Capriccio Str. 1 Decembrie 1918 14 ☎ 0354 109 537; map p.172. A better than average Italian (and Romanian) restaurant, in a big courtyard where kids can play; lunch specials (Mon–Fri) include the likes of soup and maybe trout or *tochitură* for €3.50. Daily 11am–11pm.

Castelo Str. Aurel Vlaicu 1 ☎0254 213 883, ⓦrestaurantenuti.ro; map p.172. On the corner of Str. 1 Decembrie 1918, with a small terrace facing the park, this is a decent locals' restaurant serving Romanian and Italian dishes. Mon–Fri 8am–11pm, Sat 1–11pm, Sun 10am–11pm.

The Refresh Str. 1 Decembrie 1918 18 ☎0721 496 132, ⓦtherefresh.ro; map p.172. With pavement seating opposite the theatre, this is a great place to chill out with a shake, fresh juice (both fruit and veg), or good-quality coffee. Daily 8am–10pm.

Corvin Castle

March, April, Sept & Oct Mon 10.30am–5pm, Tues–Sun 9am–5pm; May–Aug Mon noon–7.45pm, Tues–Sun 9am–7.45pm; Nov–Feb daily 9am–4pm . March, April, Sept & Oct €5.50, May–Aug €6.50, Nov–Feb €4.50 • ☎0786 048 718, ⓦcastelulcorvinilor.ro

HUNEDOARA (Vajdahunyad/Eisenmarkt), 16km south of Deva, would be dismissed as an ugly, run-down industrial town were it not also the site of **Corvin Castle**, Romania's greatest fortress. Patrick Leigh Fermor found its appearance "so fantastic and theatrical that, at first glance, it looks totally unreal". Founded in the fourteenth century, it was rebuilt in 1440–53 by **Iancu de Hunedoara**, with a Renaissance-style wing added by his son Mátyás Corvinus and Baroque additions by Gabriel Bethlen from 1618. A remarkably long footbridge on tall stone piers leads across a 30m-deep moat to a mighty barbican, built by Iancu in 1440–4 and altered in the seventeenth century to replace the castle's original entrance; below are the dungeon (with a prisoner in a cage) and torture chamber, with the usual replicas of a rack, a chair of nails and execution axes. The castle is an extravaganza of galleries, spiral stairways and Gothic vaulting, most impressively the Knights' Hall (immediately to the right), with its rose-marble pillars, a display of weaponry and a statue of Iancu. To the southwest a long gallery bridge leads to the isolated **Neboisa Tower** (from the Serbian *nje boisia* or "be not afraid"), built by Iancu in 1446–56; to the east the Council Hall is similar to the Knights' Hall, divided by a row of columns. To the north, the **Mátyás wing**, which sports a fine Renaissance loggia, houses a display of costumes and sixteenth-century Florentine *cassone* chests. Viewpoints outside the fortifications give views of the fifteenth-century rhomboid pattern on the exterior of the Painted Tower, and of the steeple added in 1873, with a bronze knight on top.

Legend has it that Iancu de Hunedoara (in Hungarian Hunyadi János) was the illegitimate son of **King Sigismund**, who gave the castle to Hunyadi's nominal father Voicu, a Romanian noble, in 1409. Hunyadi, the "White Knight", rose largely by his own efforts, winning victory after victory against the Turks, and routing them at Belgrade in 1456. Appointed *voivode* of Transylvania in 1441, he was later regent of Hungary and a kingmaker, responsible for the overthrow of Vlad Dracul by his son, the Impaler (see page 398), while his own son, Mátyás Corvinus, became one of Hungary's greatest kings.

The reserves of iron ore in the Poiana Ruscă hills west of Hunedoara, known from Roman times, were exploited on an industrial scale from 1884; under communism a huge and ugly steel plant was deliberately placed right in front of the castle. The castle, however, has had the last laugh, as Romania's heavy industry has collapsed in the last three decades and the plant has been cleared (although the Arcelor-Mittal steelworks at the north end of town is still belching forth smoke).

ARRIVAL AND INFORMATION   HUNEDOARA

By bus Buses run every fifteen minutes between Deva and Hunedoara. There are also six minibuses a day from Hațeg, 45min south. From the train and bus stations, it's a 20min walk south to the castle: turn right onto the main B-dul Republicii, and right again onto B-dul Libertății until you reach the town hall and cathedral; turn right here to cross a bridge and follow the signs for 5min to the castle. Local maxitaxis run from the station as far as Parcul Libertății by the bridge.

Destinations Cluj (2 daily); Deva (every 15–20min); Hațeg (6 daily); Orăștie (4 daily).

By train There are three daily trains to Simeria (30min).

ACCOMMODATION

Maier B-dul Republicii 1A ☎0345 417 130, ⓦhotelmaier.ro. At the junction with B-dul Libertăţii, this is the closest hotel to the castle, a good modern place with spacious rooms that also houses a pizzeria. **€40**

Rusca B-dul Dacia 10 ☎0254 717 575, ⓦhotelrusca. ro. This much-improved communist block, with staid but perfectly acceptable rooms, is a 10min walk east of the station; head down Str. Avram Iancu, opposite the station, then turn right along B-dul Dacia. The decent *Park Place* restaurant (B-dul Dacia 6; ☎0354 882 341) is across the road. **€32**

Haţeg and around

HAŢEG, 20km southeast of Hunedoara, is the gateway to Transylvania's greatest Roman remains and to the north side of the Retezat mountains. You'll also find some interesting **Romanesque churches** in the surrounding area, all reachable by bus with a little effort. The area is also known for its dwarf dinosaur fossils and other geological features: the **Haţeg Country GeoPark** is an innovative scheme to use these for sustainable tourist development. From the central Piaţa Unirii a slightly odd one-way system (signed to Prislop) leads to the GeoPark's visitor centre (Str. Libertăţii 9A ☎0254 777 853, ⓦhateggeoparc.ro), where there's a Dragons and Dinosaurs exhibition (legend has it that the dragon Balauri was killed by the brave Cânde, lord of Sântămăria-Orlea and an ancestor of Prince Charles).

Hidden in the foothills of the Poiana Ruscă mountains 15km northwest of Haţeg, **Prislop monastery** was founded in 1400; it's one of the country's oldest convents but was very tranquil and little visited until a revered monk (and future saint) called Arsenie Boca was buried there in 1989, and is now overrun with Romanian tourists. It lies just off the direct road from Hunedoara to Haţeg, but most traffic goes via **Călan**, on both the train line and the DN66 (E79) south from Simeria, now just a crossroads where a huge steelworks used to rise; the town (a spa dating from Roman times) lies across the river to the east, with the lovely little church of **Streisângeorgiu** on a hillock on its southern fringe. This was built in 1313–4, with frescoes painted at the same time (call ☎0786 051 815 or ☎0746 613 624 to visit).

Sântămăria-Orlea and Densuş

Three kilometres south of Haţeg is **SÂNTĂMĂRIA-ORLEA** (Oraljaboldogfalva), site of a late thirteenth-century church which marks the transition from the Cistercian Late Romanesque to Gothic style and has a floor of Roman terracotta bricks and a fine collection of fourteenth-century frescoes; climb the tower (passing some Roman stonework in the gallery) for a great view of the Retezat range.

In **DENSUŞ**, 12km west of Haţeg, a very strange little church has been cannibalized from the mausoleum of a fourth-century Roman army officer – most of what you see dates from the early thirteenth century, with frescoes from 1443. If it's closed ask at no. 15 on the main road, east of the statue of the etymologist Ovid Densuşianu, or at the **tourist information centre** (Mon–Fri 8am–4pm).

Roman Sarmizegetusa

Museum Tues–Sun 9am–5pm; ruins daily 8am–8pm • Joint ticket €2 • Buses run from Târgu Jiu and Haţeg to Caransebeş (6 daily) and from Deva to Zeicani (2 daily Mon–Fri)

SARMIZEGETUSA, 15km southwest of Haţeg, is the site of the Romans' capital, Ulpia Traiana Sarmizegetusa, founded c.107 AD, but only part of the **Roman ruins** have been excavated. Just east of the village centre are the remains of the forum, the palace of the Augustales, and the elliptical amphitheatre – unlikely as it seems, this could seat over five thousand spectators. Start by visiting the **museum** in a neo-Brâncovenesc villa across the road from the ruins, which avoids mentioning that most of the Roman colonists believed to have interbred with the Dacians to create the Romanian race were probably of Greek or Semitic origin.

ARRIVAL AND DEPARTURE

By bus Haţeg's *autogară* is at Str. Progresului 84, on the main road south.

Destinations Caransebeş (6 daily); Cluj (3 daily); Densuş (2 daily); Hunedoara (6 daily); Petroşani (10 daily); Sarmizegetusa (8 daily Mon–Fri, 6 Sat & Sun); Timişoara (6 daily); Târgu Jiu (9 daily).

HAŢEG AND AROUND

By train Haţeg's station is at Subcetate, 6km east; it's served by local trains from Simeria (between Deva and Orăştie) to Petroşani and Târgu Jiu.

Destinations Deva (7 daily; 50min–1hr 20min); Simeria (8 daily; 35–55min); Petroşani (7 daily; 1hr 30min); Târgu Jiu (4 daily; 2hr 30min).

ACCOMMODATION AND EATING

HAŢEG

Art Motel B-dul Tudor Vladimirescu 15 ☎0746 022 447, ⓦgeraico.ro. Bang in the centre (and nothing like a motel), this small but modern place has stylish rooms above the beautifully designed *Bistro ArtGrill*, serving burgers and grills (€3–5). Bistro daily 8am–10.30pm. **€26**

Vila Belvedere Str. Progresului 59 ☎0722 230 391, ⓦvilabelvederehateg.ro. Probably the best of a group of larger places 1km south on the Petroşani road (at the Abator bus stop, served by buses to the Subcetate rail station), though rooms are functional at best. Their restaurant is often busy with weddings but pleasant and affordable otherwise; there's also an attractive garden with terrace and swimming pool. **€20**

SARMIZEGETUSA

Sarmis no. 82 ☎0744 794 051, ⓦpensiuneasarmis. ro. On the road south to the church (about 500m west of the ruins), this very smart place has an indoor pool, table-tennis and tennis facilities and a fishing lake, as well as a good restaurant. **€30**

Ulpia Traiana no. 153 ☎0744 984 613, ⓦulpiatraiana. webpro.ro. Also near the church, with four rooms and space for ten tents, this is owned by one of the resident archeologists, who offers guided tours as well as abundant home-cooked food; shared bathroom. **€25**

Zamolxe no. 60 ☎0740 111 601, ⓦzamolxe-sarmisegetusa.ro. More rustic than other guesthouses, but with varied sports facilities, this friendly guesthouse also has wooden chalets, and space for tents (€3) and caravans. **€18**

The Retezat mountains

Routes southeast from Haţeg skim the northern reaches of the **Retezat mountains**, although access is slightly harder here than in the other Transylvanian mountain ranges. Whereas in the Făgăraş or Piatra Craiului you generally find yourself following a ridge walk, with little opportunity to step aside and view the summits from a distance, here you'll find yourself surrounded by well-defined peaks, often reflected in clear alpine lakes. There is a large network of **hiking routes**, so you'll meet fewer walkers and have a better chance of seeing **wildlife** such as chamois and eagles. The northwestern part of the massif is a scientific reserve (Ceauşescu treated it as a private hunting ground) and entry is restricted.

The **Retezat National Park** (☎0254 779 969, ⓦretezat.ro) was set up in 1935, becoming a UNESCO Biosphere Reserve in 1980. To enter, you need a permit (€2.50 for a week), available from an entry post or from a patrol; you'll be given a rubbish bag and a ticket with a basic map – it's worth buying a more detailed one in advance. **Visitor centres** are at Ostrovel (entering Râu de Mori) and at the park's headquarters just north of Nucşoara; boards here and at Câmpu lui Neag give **information** in English and German on the trails and the park's dozen camping sites. **Guides** can be booked through the National Park.

Approaches to the Retezat

There are **three main approaches** to the Retezat: from Râu de Mori, to the west (a bus ride from Haţeg), where there are various guesthouses; from various points along the Subcetate–Petroşani road and railway to the northeast; and from the Jiul de Vest

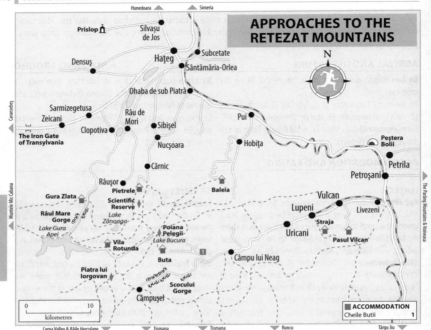

APPROACHES TO THE RETEZAT MOUNTAINS

N

Hunedoara ▲ ▲ Simeria

Prislop ⌂   Silvașu de Jos

Densuș   Hațeg   Subcetate
                 Sântămăria-Orlea

        Ohaba de sub Piatră

Sarmizegetusa   Râu de Mori   Pui
Zeicani   Clopotiva   Sibișel
The Iron Gate   Nucșoara   Hobița   Peștera Bolii
of Transylvania

Caransebeș

        Cârnic   Petrila

Râușor   Baleia   Petroșani
Pietrele
Gura Zlata   Scientific Reserve   Vulcan
Râul Mare Gorge   Lake Zănoaga   Lupeni   Livezeni
Lake Gura Apei   Poiana Pelegii   Straja   Uricani
        Lake Bucura   Pasul Vilcan
Vila Rotunda
        Buta   Câmpu lui Neag

Piatra lui Iorgovan

        Scocului Gorge

Câmpușel

Montele Mic Cabana

The Parâng Mountains & Voineasa

0 ___ 10
kilometres

■ ACCOMMODATION
Cheile Butii   1

Cerna Valley & Băile Herculane ▼   Tismana ▼   Tismana ▼   Runcu ▼   Târgu Jiu ▼

(West Jiu) valley. From **Râu de Mori** it's at least a three-hour walk south along the Râul Mare valley to the *Gura Zlata* cabana (see page 179) and campsite, from where you can strike out for the high peaks; alternatively, the paved road continues south to end at Lake Gura Apei. From **Ohaba de sub Piatră**, to the northeast, it's 18km (a five-hour trek, following blue stripes then blue triangles) to the *Pietrele* cabana, campsite, park information centre and first-aid post. The 2pm bus from Hațeg goes as far as Nucșoara, 7km short of the cabana, with summer services going a few kilometres further to the end of the road at Cârnic; alternatively, an information board at the Ohaba station gives phone numbers for taxis. Many hikers arrive this way, so the trail and cabana both get quite crowded; some therefore prefer to walk south from Râu de Mori to **Râușor** (2hr, following red triangles), where there are guesthouses, a campsite and a 1300m ski run; or from the campsite at Pui, east of Ohaba, hiking for six and a half hours up a steep and winding track (marked with red stripes) to the cabanas at Baleia (16km) and Stâne de Râu (6km further). Hiking is possible beyond these points (see page 179)

The final approach is from the grim mining towns of the **West Jiu valley**, principally **PETROȘANI**, served by trains and buses heading for Târgu Jiu (see page104); the only reason to stop here is to stock up on food before hiking, and most people head straight up the valley by frequent maxitaxis. Câmpu lui Neag is the main starting point for hiking (see page 179), but in summer buses continue about 3km further west to the excellent *Cheile Butii* hotel (☎0253 210 279, ⓦcheile-butii.ro), with various guesthouses nearby.

ACCOMMODATION   APPROACHES TO THE RETEZAT

RÂUL MARE VALLEY
Pensiunea Dumbrăvița ☎0374 001 033, ⓦpensiuneadumbravita.ro. In a delightful rural setting 5km south of Râu de Mori, this good modern guesthouse

has seven double rooms and four suites, and a lovely garden. €36

Vila Rotunda ☎088216 595 00150. Ceaușescu's former hunting villa, 6km to the east from where the road ends at

HIKING IN THE RETEZAT

FROM GURA ZLATA

Some popular hikes start from **Gura Zlata cabana**, south of Sarmizegetusa along the Râul Mare valley. A succession of coloured symbols marks the trail east to the *Pietrele* cabana, by way of Lake Zănoaga (campsite), Lake Tăul Portii and the Bucura Saddle (9–10hr). From Gura Zlata the road continues 12km south to **Lake Gura Apei**, from whose western extremity well-equipped hikers can follow a trail west across the mountains to the *Muntele Mic* cabana in the vicinity of Caransebeş, or south to Băile Herculane; allow two days for each. Heading east by the reservoir and up the **Lăpuşnic valley** takes you to either the *Buta* cabana or the Bucura valley in four hours. From Râuşor red-stripe markings lead south to Bucura.

FROM CÂMPU LUI NEAG

Also leading to the cabana at Buta are two of the most popular trails from **Câmpu lui Neag** and the *Cheile Butii* hotel in the south of the region. Red crosses mark the quickest route to the cabana (6–7hr), which offers great views of the "karst cathedrals" en route. Yellow stripes indicate the longer trail (10–12hr) to the cabana, via the strange formations of the Scocului gorge and the plateau of Piatra lui Iorgovan, where you may spot **chamois**. A forestry road continues southwest over the watershed from the Jiu into the Cerna valley, and on towards **Băile Herculane**, a good two days' walk (see page 336); another path, marked with blue triangles, heads south to Tismana, west of Târgu Jiu, in roughly six hours.

Buta lies in the **Little Retezat**, the limestone ridge south of the great glacial trough of the Lăpuşnic valley, which has an almost Mediterranean flora and fauna. However, the best hikes take you into the crystalline **Great Retezat** to the north, past serried peaks and alpine lakes. One trail, marked by blue stripes, follows a switchback path to the *Pietrele* cabana (7hr), dropping into the Lăpuşnic valley and leading up past the wonderful lakes of the Bucura valley before coming down from a pass of 2206m; another, marked by red stripes, yellow crosses then blue triangles, follows a trail to the **Stâne de Râu** cabana, via the Barbat springs and the Ciumfu waterfall (9hr).

3

Lake Gura Apei, is not nearly as grand as you might expect; in fact it's pretty basic, but still has a certain sinister something about it. There are seven doubles and one suite. **€30**

RÂUŞOR

Pensiunea Iris ☎0746 022 447, ⊛geraico.ro. Run by the owners of Haţeg's *Art Motel*, this is as stylish and

comfortable as you'd expect, aimed more at skiers than summer hikers. **€28**

Pensiunea Ancuţa ☎0256 438 713 or ☎0722 224 245, ⊕adrianpopescu@hotmail.com. A less glamorous option, this friendly guesthouse has five doubles with shared bathrooms plus a gym and table tennis, and offers good, filling meals. **€25**

The Székely Land

For most visitors the chief attractions of the **Székely Land** (Székelyföld) are the Székely culture and the scenery. Religion remains important here, as shown by the fervour of the Whitsun pilgrimage to Miercurea Ciuc (see page 189), the continuing existence of Székely mystics, and the prevalence of walled churches (less grimly fortified than the Saxon ones). Traditional architecture is well represented here, epitomized by tiny hilltop chapels and blue-painted houses with carved fences and gateways incorporating a dovecote above, the best examples being in Corund. The landscape gets increasingly dramatic as you move north through the **Harghita mountains**, particularly around the Tuşnad defile and St Anne's Lake to the south, and Lacu Roşu and the Bicaz gorges on the borders of Moldavia.

Odorheiu Secuiesc

ODORHEIU SECUIESC (Székelyudvarhely), roughly 50km from Sighişoara, Miercurea Ciuc and Sovata, is unusually prosperous, thanks to textile companies producing 1.5 million men's suits per year, as well as the furniture, leather and print industries. There's

> ### THE SZÉKELY
>
> In the ethnic patchwork of Transylvania, the eastern Carpathians are the home of the **Székely**, who speak a distinctive Hungarian dialect and cherish a special historical identity. For a long time they were believed to be descended from Attila's Huns, who entered the Carpathian basin in the fifth century. However, it's now thought that the Székely either attached themselves to the Magyars during their long migration from the banks of the Don, or are simply the descendants of early Hungarians who pushed ever further east into Transylvania. Whatever their origins, the Székely feel closely akin to the Magyars who, in turn, regard them as somehow embodying the finest aspects of the **ancient Magyar race**, while also being rather primeval. Today, their traditional costume is close to that of the Romanian peasants, the chief difference being that Székely men tuck their white shirts in while Romanians wear them untucked and belted.

a series of crafts, food and beer **festivals** culminating in the Fruit Festival in mid-September (ⓦgyumolcsfesztival.ro), while the excellent **Szejke** festival is held in late May out at the spa of the same name, 4km north by the Sovata road, when folk groups dance in front of a picnicking audience. There's also the Motion Festival of electronic music (ⓦmotionfestival.ro) at Szejke on the first weekend of July. The spa is known for its warm pools and its display of wooden Székely beam-gates; there's also a **Mineral Water Museum** here (May–Sept Tues–Fri 10am–6pm, Sat & Sun 10am–2pm), which looks back fondly on the spa's heyday with ceramic water jugs, minerals and rocks, and a superb buffalo cart (used for transporting water).

Piaţa Primăriei and Piaţa Márton Áron

The attractive town centre essentially consists of two conjoined squares, **Piaţa Primăriei** (Városháza tér) and the much smaller **Piaţa Márton Áron**, where three churches stand in a row: to the northwest, the former Franciscan monastery (1730–79); on the island between the two squares, the Reformed church (1781); and, on the hill beyond, the Catholic church of Sf Miklós (1787–93), between the Jesuits' building (1651) and the huge Tamasy Aron Gymnasium or high school, established in 1593 and now in a Secession building dating from 1911–2, set back from Piaţa Márton Áron. From Piaţa Primăriei, Strada Cetăţii leads to the fifteenth- and sixteenth-century **citadel**, known as the Székelytámadt Vár or Székely-attacked Fort, having been destroyed in 1599 by the townspeople protesting against the threatened loss of their freedoms. It houses an agricultural college, but you can go inside to stroll along the walls.

Muzeul Haáz Rezsó and around

Str. Bethlenfalvi 2–6 • April to mid-Sept Tues–Fri 9am–6pm, Sat & Sun 10am–6pm; mid-Sept to Oct Tues–Fri 9am–5pm, Sat & Sun 10am–2pm; Nov–Feb Tues–Fri 9am–4pm • €1.50 • ☎0266 218 375, ⓦhrmuzeum.ro

In the centre of town, the **Muzeul Haáz Rezsó** (town museum) has a fine ethnographic collection, with ceramics and Székely funerary posts, which may hark back to the days when a Magyar warrior was buried with his spear thrust into the grave. Used only by Calvinists and Unitarians, these bear carvings of the tools of the deceased's trade and a ring for each decade of life; a man's post is topped with a star and a woman's with a tulip. There's also a superb wooden gate, typical of those found throughout the region. It also includes the Korunk art gallery at Str. Kossuth 42 and a daylight photographic studio, established in 1906, at Str. Kossuth 24. The **Jesus Chapel** (Jézus-kápolna), 2km further down the road, is one of the area's oldest buildings, built in the thirteenth century, with a coffered ceiling fitted in 1667.

ARRIVAL AND INFORMATION

ODORHEIU SECUIESC

By bus The bus and train stations are about 1km north of the town centre along Str. Bethlen Gábor; trains stop first at Odorhei Sud halt (on Str. Tamasi Aron, the road north to Sovata), which is nearer the centre. There's also the new

Autogara Gas Tours, reached down an alley opposite the main bus station or by a riverside track from Str. Tompa László, north of the citadel.

Destinations (main terminal) Braşov (1 daily); Budapest (3 daily); Covasna/Târgu Secuiesc (2 daily); Gheorgheni (1 daily); Ghimeş/Oneşti (1 daily); Miercurea Ciuc (4 daily); Praid (11 daily); Sf Gheorghe (4 daily); Sovata (7 daily); Târgu Mureş (6 daily).

Destinations (Gas Tours terminal) Budapest (2 daily); Covasna (1 daily); Cristuru Secuiesc (7 daily); Miercurea Ciuc (4 daily Mon–Fri, 2 Sat & Sun); Mugeni (8 daily); Sovata/ Târgu Mureş (5 daily).

By train Sighişoara (3 daily; 1hr 30min).

Tourist information TourInfo, Str. Bethlen Gábor 43 (at Str. Uzinei; Mon–Fri 8am–4pm; ☎0751 126 278; ⌨ tourinfo.ro). Harghita county has information online at ⌨ visitingharghita.ro.

ACCOMMODATION

Europa Str. Kossuth Lajos 23 ☎0266 218 228, ⌨ europahotel.ro. In a Neoclassical block built as a bank in 1949, this has comfortable, if rather dated, rooms and two suites (with private jacuzzi and sauna), and includes the *Taverna* restaurant (10am–10pm). **€49**

Gondűző Str. Sântimbru 18 ☎0731 021 455, ⌨ gonduzo.ro. The best hotel in the centre, a 5min walk east of Piaţa Márton Áron, with 22 large, comfortable rooms featuring lovely wood furnishings, thick carpets and corner baths; tours can be arranged, including hunting and offroading. **€60**

Hostel Tranzit Str. Tompa László 36 ☎0744 753 650, ⌨ hotel-tranzit.ro. A pretty simple and cheap place that's popular with groups and families, with rooms for up to six with shared and private bathrooms; there's a bar but no restaurant. **€22**

Panorama Panzió Str. Móricz Zsigmond 76 ☎0266 212 345, ⌨ panoramapanzio.ro. To the north off the Sovata road, this is an upmarket guesthouse overlooking town (a pleasant walk) with just eight rooms and a sauna (which costs extra); excellent breakfasts made to order, but no other meals. **€40**

EATING

Alexandra Piaţa Márton Áron 1 ☎0266 218 300 or ☎0266 218 290. A fabulous, old-fashioned Hungarian-style *cukrászda* (patisserie) in the centre of town with marvellous coffee and cake, and very friendly service. Mon–Fri 7am–9pm, Sat & Sun 9am–9pm.

Kalapos Pub Str. Bethlen Gábor 4 ☎0745 895 338, ⌨ kalapos.ro. This is a genial little place with 2.5 litre tubes to guzzle Lobkowicz beer from, and pubby food choices such as burgers and quesadillas. Mon–Thurs 11am–11pm, Fri 11am–1am, Sat 6pm–1am.

Park Etterem Str. Mihail Kogălniceanu 1 ☎0755 082 484, ⌨ junglepub.ro. In the leafy park behind the Casa de Cultură (with plenty of outdoor seating), this excellent

pizzeria – also known as "the Jungle" – has dark Ciuc beer on tap. Mon–Thurs 10am–10pm, Fri 10am–3am, Sat & Sun noon–10pm.

Pethö Str. Rákóczi 21 ☎0745 923 055, ⌨ pethopanzio. ro. A little way south of the centre, in the pension of the same name, this is a super Hungarian restaurant with great service and huge portions – the cold soups, goulash and desserts are all excellent.

Petőfi Panzió Str. Petőfi 2 ☎0266 212 262, ⌨ petofipanzio.ro. On the corner of Str. Cetăţii, this busy guesthouse has a popular restaurant serving filling portions of Hungarian dishes such as tarragon soup or bean goulash. Daily 6am–10pm.

DRINKING

G Café Str. Szent Imre Utca 8 ☎0751 336 375. Mellow place with dinky wooden tables and bare-brick walls

adorned with prints, and often hosts live music and other arty events. Mon–Sat 8am–2am, Sun 8am–midnight.

Dârjiu, Mugeni and Cristuru Secuiesc

DÂRJIU (Székelyderz), 17km southwest of Odorheiu, has a particularly fine fortified church, now on UNESCO's World Heritage List, with frescoes dating from 1419. Built in the fourteenth century and walled and modernized in Gothic style in the fifteenth, it is now Unitarian. As in some Saxon villages, ham and grain are still stored inside the church walls, ready for the next siege. Ask for the key next door at no. 163 (☎0266 222 183), where the priest offers accommodation.

   MUGENI (Bögöz), 9km west of Odorheiu by road and rail (the station is 1km north), has a fine fourteenth-century Calvinist church with wonderful late-Romanesque frescoes and a coffered ceiling, plus charming guesthouses.

Continuing west towards Sighişoara, you'll pass through the larger village of **CRISTURU SECUIESC** (Székelykeresztúr), whose excellent **museum** (Tues–Fri 10am–5pm, Sat & Sun 10am–1pm; €1; ☎0266 242 580, ✉mimuzeum@gmail.com) on the elongated square, Piaţa Libertăţii, tells the story of the ceramic industry, established here by 1590, in addition to a natural history display. Through-buses stop in the main square, but those terminating here arrive at the train station, ten minutes' walk east. The best place to eat is the *Bonfini* restaurant on Strada Libertăţii (☎0266 244 499).

<table>
<tr><th>ACCOMMODATION</th><th>MUGENI AND CRISTURU SECUIESC</th></tr>
</table>

Ilyés Panzió Str. Principală 383, Mugeni ☎0266 245 505, ⊛ilyespanzio.ro. A modern bungalow in a pleasant garden, this friendly guesthouse prides itself on its traditional costume and authentic Székely food. The full board option is great value. Breakfast €4. **€20**

Kúria Vendégház (Vicarage Guesthouse) Rugăneşti 82, Cristuru Secuiesc ☎0749 331 324, ⊛kuriavendeghaz.ro. This well-established guesthouse has seven en-suite rooms (one triple), a kitchen, a large

balcony and a huge garden with barbecue (and car parking). Breakfast €4. **€18**

Székelykapu Panzió Templom Útca Str. Bisericii 176, Mugeni ☎0266 245 437, ⊛szekelykapupanzio.com. This delightful guesthouse – the "Carved Gate" – has tiny, traditionally furnished rooms and great food (half and full board available), and also space for tents and caravans. Breakfast €4. **€20**

Corund, Praid and Sovata Băi

CORUND (Korond), 25km north of Odorheiu, is famed for its green and brown pottery, as well as the cobalt blue introduced by the Germans in the eighteenth century. You'll see it for sale everywhere, but much is now made in Asia – for authentic products poke around the backstreet workshops or visit the colourful market on the weekend closest to August 10.

For something completely different, continue 12km north to the lively little resort of **PRAID** (Parajd), where the main attraction is the **Salina Praid** (☎0266 240 200, ⊛salinapraid.ro), comprising an underground salt mine (dating from 1762) and the Ştrand (daily 10am–8pm, plus July & Aug Thurs–Sun 9–11pm; Mon–Fri €5.50, Sat & Sun €6.50), with modern swimming pools in old salt pits. Ancient buses wait at the ticket office on Strada Salinei (with toilets and tourist information) to ferry visitors 120m below ground (entries every 20–30min 8am–2.50pm, exits 9.10am–4pm; Mon–Fri €6.50, Sat & Sun €7.50). You'll find an amusement park with playground, bouncy castle, climbing wall and ropes course, as well as a cinema and café; there's also a viewpoint (where you can taste wines) over the huge chamber.

Seven kilometres further north by road and rail is Sovata, with 1km east the larger **SOVATA BĂI** (Szováta Fürdő), a bathing resort amid beautiful forests on the shore of **Lacul Ursu** (Medvetó or Bear Lake). A surface layer of fresh water, 1m deep, acts as an insulator keeping the lower saltwater at a constant 30–40°C year-round; it rains a lot here, in short showers, but bathing is still pleasant. Its mineral waters are supposedly particularly effective for curing infertility. The resort's most distinctive feature is the array of wooden buildings lining the main street, Strada Trandafirilor: huge, extravagantly balconied pensions and twee Hansel and Gretel churches.

A 14km stretch of **narrow-gauge railway** from Sovata north to Câmpul Cetăţii has been reopened for a steam-hauled tourist train known as the Mocăniţa (☎0743 160 556, ⊛mocanitasovata.ro; May–Sept; €5.50, return €7.50), a two-hour jaunt through bucolic rolling hills; these are hauled by a relatively large tender locomotive rather than the gutsy little tank engines that work Romania's forest railways. The departure point is just north off Strada Lungă, the road to Reghin.

<table>
<tr><th>ARRIVAL AND DEPARTURE</th><th>CORUND, PRAID AND SOVATA BĂI</th></tr>
</table>

By bus Corund and Praid are served by the sixteen daily buses between Odorheiu Secuiesc and Sovata (6 continuing to Târgu Mureş), as well as six from Odorheiu as far as Praid. Sovata Băi's bus station is on Str. Trandafirilor.

Destinations Budapest (1 daily); Cluj/Oradea (1 daily); Covasna (1 daily); Gheorgheni (3 daily); Ghimeş/Oneşti (1 daily); Miercurea Ciuc (3 daily); Odorheiu Secuiesc (16 daily Mon–Fri, 8 Sat & Sun); Piatra Neamţ (2 daily); Reghin (2 daily Mon–Fri, 1 Sat & Sun); Sf Gheorghe (4 daily); Sibiu/Sighişoara (1 daily); Târgu Mureş (22 daily Mon–Fri, 14 Sat & Sun). **By train** Regiotrans runs two trains/day from Blaj to Sovata and Praid (3hr 30min).

ACCOMMODATION AND EATING

PRAID

Casa Telegdy Str. Principală 1173 ☏0751 010 017. Right opposite the junction to the Salina Praid, this is a good, if unspectacular restaurant serving up large portions of mid-priced Székely-influenced food. Daily 10am–10pm.
Hotel Praid Str. Principală 1098 ☏0266 240 686, ⊕ hotelpraid.ro. Just north of the bus stop and the junction to Gheorgheni, this nicely refurbished block has eleven simple rooms with balconies, a big terrace and a pizzeria. €28
Ice Italy Str. Principală 1093 ☏0266 240 461. At the central bus stop, this lively restaurant-pizzeria is popular with families, largely on account of its rather splendid ice-cream counter. Daily 8.30am–11pm.
Vendéghaz Maria Str. Principală 1161 ☏0744 483 112. On the main road just northwest of the hotel, this is similar to the many small guesthouses in the back streets that have a few en-suite rooms and offer use of the kitchen. €13

SOVATA BĂI

Danubius Str. Trandafirilor 111 ☏0265 570 151, ⊕ danubiushotels.com. Sovata Băi is dominated by the triumvirate of Hungarian-owned hotels: the *Danubius*, the *Fäget* and *Bradet* (both on Str. Vulturului; same contacts). Each has a pool and treatment facilities, while the *Danubius* also has an indoor saltwater pool. The *Fäget* is a rather tatty two-star (€38), the others are excellent four-star places. €86
Pacsirta Str. Trandafirilor 85A ☏0365 082 480, ⊕ hotelpacsirta.ro. A glorious old building with wooden balconies has been transformed into Sovata's finest boutique hotel, with large, beautifully-appointed rooms, heated bathroom floors and impeccable service; good mountain bikes are available to rent. The restaurant here is first class, its dishes above and beyond anything else hereabouts, for example vanilla and raspberry soup, buttered quails eggs with garlic, and grilled duck liver with parsnip puree (€12). €84
Perla Lacului Camping Str. Lacului 9 ☏0730 214 577, ⊕ ardeal.info.ro. Immediately behind the bus station, this has space for tents and camper vans, and also three double rooms in a modern chalet. €22
Szeifert Str. Bradului 28 ☏0265 570 108, ⊕ hotelszeifert.ro. Between the bus station and Lacul Ursu, this large villa offers cosy rooms, a sauna and hot-tub in the basement, and a good restaurant with a large terrace. €42
Tivoli Str. Tivoli 1 ☏0265 570 493. A few hundred metres beyond Lacul Ursu (turn left just beyond the strikingly modernist Catholic chapel), this attractive stone-clad hotel is surrounded by woods with deer foraging outside the windows – the rooms are pretty dated though. It's a 5min walk on to Lacul Tineretului (Lake of Youth), where you can rent pedaloes from the snack kiosks. Closed Nov–March. €33
Villa Klein Str. Trandafirilor 81 ☏0265 577 686. A good and very affordable guesthouse with pool and sauna; the main block is more atmospheric but the newer block behind is more comfortable. €18

Sfântu Gheorghe

SFÂNTU GHEORGHE (Sepsi-Szentgyörgy), 30km northeast of Braşov, is an industrial town which has become the heart of the Székely cultural revival. Originally the centre was around the walled church, but in the late eighteenth century it moved almost a kilometre south to the barracks area. It's now focused on the large green space of Erzsébet Park, on the east of which is the Arcaded House (Casa cu Arcade/Lábasház; 1812), now the tourist office; to the west of the park are a technical college designed by Kós (with his bust in front), and a library where the decision was taken in 1848 to fight the Austrians, local hero Gábor Áron announcing he would cast the necessary cannons. The **Zilele Sfântu Gheorghe festival** covers the week straddling St George's Day, April 23.

Székely National Museum

Str. Kós Károly 10 • June–Sept Tues–Sun 9am–5pm; Oct–May Tues–Fri 9am–4pm, Sat & Sun 9am–2pm • €2 • ⊕ sznm.ro

The town's highlight is the **Székely National Museum**, south of the centre. Built in 1910–12 to the design of **Kós Károly** (see page 185), it covers the archeology, history – focusing on the revolution of 1848–9 (see page 378) – natural science and ethnography

KÓS KÁROLY

Kós Károly (1883–1977) was the leading architect of the Hungarian National Romantic school, which drew inspiration from the village architecture of Transylvania and Finland. The Transylvanian style is reflected in the wooden roofs, gables and balconies of his buildings, while the Finnish influence appears in the stone bases and trapezoidal door frames. Fine examples of Kós's work can be seen in Sfântu Gheorghe and Cluj (notably the Cock Church), as well as in Budapest.

After the separation of Transylvania from Hungary, Kós, a native of Timişoara, was one of the few Hungarian intellectuals to accept the new situation, choosing to remain in Cluj (and his country home near Huedin) and to play a leading role in Hungarian society in Transylvania. He continued to work as an architect, and travelled around Transylvania, recording the most characteristic buildings (of all ethnic groups) in delightful **linocuts**; these were published in 1929 by the Transylvanian Artists' Guild (cofounded by Kós himself), with an English translation published in 1989.

of the area, with displays of ceramics, textiles and painted furniture. There's a small open-air section in front, centred on a house built in 1768.

3

ARRIVAL AND INFORMATION

SFÂNTU GHEORGHE

By bus Both the train and bus stations are 2km east of the centre: take bus #1 (every 20min to 10.40pm, Sat & Sun hourly), #2 or #3 (both hourly) or follow Str. 1 Decembrie 1918 to Piaţa Libertăţii. Maxitaxis to Braşov leave every 30min from the market and stop at the Banca Transilvania just beyond Piaţa Széchenyi (on Str. 1 Decembrie 1918). There's also the smaller Autogară Transbus Codreanu (B-dul Bălan 4) with departures to Miercurea Ciuc and Braşov (each 4 daily) and local villages.

Destinations Bacău (1 daily); Braşov (every 30min); Budapest (1 daily); Covasna (13 daily); Miercurea Ciuc (5 daily); Odorheiu Secuiesc (4 daily); Sovata/Târgu Mureş (4 daily); Târgu Secuiesc (11 daily).

By train Braşov (12 daily; 30–55min); Covasna (4 daily; 45min); Miercurea Ciuc (11 daily; 1hr–1hr 30min); Târgu Secuiesc (4 daily; 1hr 10min).

Tourist information The tourist office (Mon–Wed 7.30am–3.30pm, Thurs 7.30am–5pm, Fri 7.30am–2pm; ☎0267 316 474, ⓦsfantugheorgheinfo.ro) is on the east side of the park at Piaţa Libertăţii 7. They have a new multimedia show on the town's history (Mon–Fri 9am–5pm, Sat 9am–2pm).

ACCOMMODATION

Bobo Pánzio Str. Podului 12 ☎0753 522 022. A very friendly and helpful family run this new guesthouse with three rooms (the two upstairs sharing one bathroom); it's in a quiet area 500m from centre (and not much further from the walled church). **€30**

Ferdinand Panzió Str. 1 Decembrie 1918 10 ☎0740 180 502, ⓦrestatferdinand.ro. Off a dusty car park behind

the café of the same name, this has simply furnished but stylish rooms (including a single and two suites). **€38**

Sugás Str. 1 Decembrie 1918 12 ☎0267 312 171, ⓦsugaskert.ro. Behind the restaurant of the same name, this charming little place is the town's best hotel, its rooms (some on the ground floor) decorated with a mix of Székely and modern themes. **€38**

EATING

Cofetarie Aria Total Natural Str. 1 Decembrie 1918 41 ☎0267 311 808, ⓦariaice.ro. This is not a health-food café, as you might think, but a source of deliciously rich cakes and ice creams; it's air-conditioned and has a nice garden. Mon–Sat 9am–8pm, Sun 11am–8pm.

Eleven Street Food Str. Ciucului 11 ☎0367 404 145 Unassuming burger joint that rustles up the best patties in town, best enjoyedd with a side of fries or salad, and then washed down with a local beer. Daily 11am–10pm.

Szentgyörgy Pince Str. Gábor Áron 4 ☎0267 352 666, ⓦszentgyorgypince.ro. The rather lovely St George Cellar is by some distance the town's premier restaurant, offering classic, and exciting, Hungarian dishes such as catfish stew, and deer goulash with dumplings (€9). The low, brick-vaulted ceiling and subtle lighting ensure an intimate atmosphere. Daily 10am–midnight.

Covasna

Trains east from Sfântu Gheorghe to Târgu Secuiesc and Breţcu pass close to the spa of **COVASNA** (Kovászna), 30km away, although the DN11 (E574) lies well to the north.

The Valea Zânelor (Fairies' valley), just east, is popular with walkers, and gives easy access to the Vrancea and Penteleu mountains. At the end of the valley a spectacular inclined plane, built in 1886 as part of Romania's first narrow-gauge **forestry rail line**, has been restored and now carries a steam-hauled *mocăniţa* **tourist train** (April–Sept hourly Fri–Sun & holidays 9am–6pm; €2.50 return; ☎0745 363 780, ⓦcfi.ro) along the valley to the foot of the incline at Comandau, 7km distant; in Covasna, trains depart from in front of the Hotel Clermont. This is not to be confused with the *trenuleţ* or road-train that goes as far as the cardiology hospital, 4km from the centre of town and 2km short of the inclined plane (Wed–Fri 2pm, 4pm, & 6pm, Sat & Sun 10am, noon, 2pm, 4pm & 6pm; €0.50).

In the **town centre** are a park with *mofetas*, emitting health-giving gases, and an art gallery (Tues–Thurs 9am–4pm, Fri 9am–6pm, Sat 9am–2pm; free) on Strada Şcolii, its garden a busy cut-through to the bus station (which sits between the market and a cemetery with Székely grave-marker poles).

3

ARRIVAL AND INFORMATION   COVASNA

By bus The bus station is behind the market at Str. Ştefan cel Mare 48, just east of the road to the station; ten buses a day to Sfântu Gheorghe (six at weekends) start from opposite the hospital in the Valea Zânelor, most continuing to Braşov. Destinations Braşov (8 daily, Sat & Sun 4); Odorheiu Secuiesc (2 daily); Sfântu Gheorghe (9 daily); Sighişoara/Târgu Mureş (2 daily); Târgu Secuiesc (6 daily).

By train From the train station, buses take you the 2.5km to the town and continue 5km to the hospital in Valea Zânelor.
Destinations Sf Gheorghe (4 daily; 45min); Târgu Secuiesc (4 daily; 20min).
Tourist information The tourist office is south of the centre at Str. Unirii 2A (☎0267 340 344, ⓦvisit-covasna.com).

ACCOMMODATION

Bradul Aleea Zânelor 10 ☎0267 340 081, ⓦhotelbradul.ro. Near the cardiology hospital in Voineşti, this is a big communist block with nearly one hundred rooms and its own mineral pools. The rooms are nothing special but it makes a good base for walking in the hills. **€30**
Clermont Str. Eminescu 225A ☎0267 342 123, ⓦclermonthotel.ro. Opposite the hospital, this is a modern spa-hotel, with helpful staff and pool, sauna, indoor and outdoor sport facilities (bowling, archery, tennis/football/basketball courts), as well as a café-bar and restaurant. Better rooms have balconies. **€66**
★ **Mikes Kástely** Zăbala (Zabola) ☎0735 231 432, ⓦzabola.com. The Mikes Estate, 7km north of Covasna,

was confiscated by the communists and has been returned to the countess and her family, who have opened a six-room boutique hotel as well as self-catering accommodation in a hunting lodge. There's excellent bear-watching in what was one of the largest private forests in Transylvania, and boating on a large lake in a French-style park. **€80**
Pensiunea Pálma Reci (km42 DN13E). Midway between Covasna and Sfântu Gheorghe (not far east of the DN11) this pleasantly rustic campsite is across the road from a small fishing and boating lake; it has camping space, wooden chalets, a restaurant and a friendly little bar. **€16**

EATING

Krama Str. Dozsa Gyorgy 1 ☎0769 997 672. Next to the town hall, this low brick cellar offers coffee, beer, wine and soft drinks plus a range of pub meals, with outdoor seating as well in summer. Daily noon–midnight.

Târgu Secuiesc

The attractive small town of **TÂRGU SECUIESC** (Kezdivásárhely), 25km north of Covasna, is a stronghold of Székely culture, with little Romanian spoken – something of a backwater now, it was a major trading centre in medieval times, being the last stop before the Oituz Pass into Moldavia. It was the first Székely town to be granted a charter in 1427 (its Romanian name means Székely Market), and people still flock to its **Thursday market** today. There's also a **craft shop** just south of the museum at Curtea 11, and across the square from the museum is the splendid **Vigadó Theatre**, with occasional interesting events.

Museum of the Guilds

Curtea 10 • Tues–Fri 9am–5pm, Sat 9am–4pm, Sun 9am–2pm • €1 • ⊕ sznm.ro

One of the nineteenth-century merchants' houses lining the central Piața Gábor Áron now houses the **Museum of the Guilds** – in addition to the history of the guilds, there are surprisingly good displays of costumed dolls, fire engines and the history of photography, plus temporary art shows.

ARRIVAL AND DEPARTURE   TÂRGU SECUIESC

By bus Through buses between Brașov, Onești and Bacău stop on the ring road, Str. Fabricilor, just north of the train station, or at the Peco petrol station at the exit towards Brașov; there are two bus yards near the station at Str. Gării 52 and 89.

Destinations Bacău (6 daily); Brașov (12 daily); Covasna (6 daily); Sfântu Gheorghe/Miercurea Ciuc (2 daily).
By train It's a 10min walk north on Str. Gării from the station to the centre.
Destinations Covasna (4 daily; 20min); Sfântu Gheorghe (4 daily; 1hr 10min).

ACCOMMODATION AND EATING

Atrium Str. Abatorului 11A ☎ 0367 412 223, ⊕ atrium-hotel.ro. Under 10min from the main square (via Curtea 11, near the museum, and Str. Matko István), this fine modern hotel has a central courtyard with pleasant a/c rooms opening onto a terrace around it, and a bowling alley. **€45**

Jazz Bistro & Winery Gábor Áron tér 4 ☎ 0724 231 404, ⊕ jazzbistro.ro. Opposite the Calvinist church at Curtea 69, this serves soups, salads, pasta, meat and fish in a courtyard or pleasant barn-like hall; they also have good wines. Oh, and they stage some great gigs too. Mon & Sun noon–10pm, Tues–Sat noon–midnight

Székely Vendéglő Str. Școlii 1 ☎ 0267 364 513, ⊕ idolrestaurant.ro. Not far behind the church in a

nineteenth-century printing house with traditional painted furniture, this serves excellent Székely food such as goulash and kohlrabi. A covered courtyard hosts live music. Mon–Thurs 9am–midnight, Fri 9am–2am, Sat 10am–2am, Sun 10am–midnight.

Vörös Panzió Gábor Áron tor 19 ☎ 0267 360 789, ✉ office@perlaneagra.ro. The most central option, in an eighteenth-century house opposite the museum, this has charming rooms furnished in traditional Székely style, except for one in Swedish modern style and an apartment with a four-poster bed, and a restaurant. **€23**

Băile Tușnad and St Anne's Lake

To the north of Sfântu Gheorghe, the River Olt has carved the beautiful **Tușnad defile**, at the far end of which is **BĂILE TUȘNAD** (Tusnádfürdő), a spa set amid larch and fir woods. In addition to the hotel spas, there's Wellness Tusnad (Str. Ciucaș 7; ☎ 0756 118 479, ⊕ wellness-tusnad.ro), with modern facilities such as infrared saunas; salt room, jacuzzi, indoor and outdoor thermal pools, and a bar and buffet. Work up a sweat first at the nearby Club Aventură (Str. Oltului; ☎ 0730 345 004; daily 10am–5pm), which has a long and challenging ropes course.

There's good **walking** in the area, in particular on the steep trail that leads in two hours to **St Anne's Lake** (Lacu Sf Ana), following blue cross markings; you can also take an easier trail following blue stripes (4–5hr), or a bad road from the village of Bixad, just south (parking costs €4.50). In a crater on Mount Ciumatu, it's Europe's only intact volcanic lake; there's a restaurant and shop and you can swim or rent a boat. The *Lacul Sfânta Ana* cabana (☎ 0745 310 955) is set on the east rim of the crater, near the rare Tinovul Mohoș peat bog (in a secondary crater, with glacial relics such as *Drosera* insectivorous plants viewable from a new boardwalk).

ARRIVAL AND INFORMATION   BĂILE TUȘNAD

By bus Buses between Sfântu Gheorghe and Miercurea Ciuc (5 daily) stop in the car park of the InfoTur tourist office (Tues–Sun 2–7pm, summer daily 10am–10pm; ☎ 0266 335 150, ✉ bailetusnad@yahoo.com), which can arrange accommodation and tours, for instance to Lacul Sf Ana (€5).

By train From the train station follow the road up to the main DN12 (Str. Oltului) and continue a couple of hundred metres south to find InfoTur.

ACCOMMODATION AND EATING

Ciucaş Aleea Sf Ana 7 ☎ 0266 335 004, ⌨ hotelciucas.ro. Just above the main road at km4, this is probably the best of the big spa hotels, a modern place with spacious a/c rooms and balconies, a good restaurant/terrace and all kinds of spa treatments. **€52**

Csomád Panzió Str. Kovács 64 ☎ 0266 355 145 or ☎ 0744 586 929, ⌨ csomadpanzio.ro. To the north of the station, this has three buildings offering a range of room types, as well as a swimming pool and sauna. **€22**

Restaurant Apor Str. Oltului 124 ☎ 0722 532 638, ⌨ aporpizza.ro. At the south end of the village, this friendly place serves a good range of pizzas, spaghetti and salads. Mon–Fri & Sun 9am–10pm, Sat 9am–midnight.

Miercurea Ciuc

MIERCUREA CIUC (Csíkszereda/Szeklerburg), 100km north of Braşov, is an important transport hub and capital of Harghita county, though it is less charming than its other towns. Its main claim to fame these days is as the home of Ciuc, one of Romania's better beers (*Csiki sor* in Hungarian, pronounced "cheeky sure" – and now owned by Heineken). The city centre, with the windswept **Piaţa Libertăţii** at its heart, was extensively rebuilt in communist concrete, made worse by a rash of ugly modern churches, and aside from some Secession and Art Nouveau touches on Strada Petőfi,

3

MIERCUREA CIUC

ACCOMMODATION

Casa Genesini	3
Casa Lasarus Ház	4
Korona	2
Vardomb	1

EATING

Bandidos	4
Petőfi Kávéház	3
Renegade Pub & Pizza	1
San Gennaro	2

the Mikó citadel and the adjacent 1890s Law Courts and City Hall, there is little of architectural merit here.

Muzeul Secuiesc al Ciucului

Piața Cetății 2 • Tues–Sun 9am–5pm • €3.50 • ☎ 0266 372 024, ⓦ csikimuzeum.ro

The Mikó Citadel, built in Renaissance style in 1611–21, was rebuilt in 1714 and now houses an excellent county museum, the **Muzeul Secuiesc al Ciucului**, with exhibits on the castle's history and on Székely churches and traditional life. You can also see the Franciscans' printing press from Csiksomlyó (see box below) and an array of fine wooden beam-gates outside. There's multilingual information including videos and other high-tech presentations, and a good shop. The courtyard is the venue for the **Csíki Jazz Festival** (ⓦ jazzfestival.ro) in late July.

Galeria de Artă Nagy Imre

Str. Nagy Imre 175 • Mid-May to mid-Oct Tues–Sun 9am–5pm • €1.50

Two kilometres south in the suburb of Jigodin (Zsögödfürdő; buses #1 and #2) the **Galeria de Artă Nagy Imre** (Nagy Imre Art Gallery) displays a rotating selection of the forceful paintings of the Székely artist Nagy Imre (1893–1976); his former home, at the rear of the gallery, is exactly as he left it, with his collections of local textiles and Corund ceramics.

Roman Catholic Church and Millennium Templom

Near the train and bus stations on Strada Kossuth, the **Roman Catholic church** was built in 1751–8 in a simple Baroque style; behind it, the utterly weird **Millennium Templom**, also Catholic, is a vision of what Magyar nomads might have built a millennium ago if they'd had modern materials. Another huge and ostentatious Catholic church is now rising at the east end of Strada Kossuth.

ARRIVAL AND INFORMATION   MIERCUREA CIUC

By bus Miercurea Ciuc's bus station is west of the centre, off the Odorheiu road.

Destinations Bacău (2 daily); Băile Tușnad (8 daily); Brașov (3 daily); Budapest (2–3 daily); Odorheiu Secuiesc (8 daily); Piatra Neamț (3 daily); Sfântu Gheorghe (5 daily); Sovata (3 daily); Suceava (1 daily); Târgu Mureș (5 daily); Târgu Neamț (2 daily); Târgu Secuiesc (2 daily).

By train The railway station is immediately south of the bus station. Siculeni station, one stop north, is the junction for the line across the Eastern Carpathians to Adjud (trains between Cluj and Moldavia stop here without passing through Miercurea Ciuc).

Destinations Brașov (11 daily; 1hr 30min–2hr 15min); Budapest (1 daily; 14hr); Cluj (2 daily; 5hr 50min); Dej (2 daily; 4hr 45min); Gheorgheni (10 daily; 1hr–1hr 30min); Târgu Mureș (2 daily; 4hr 20min–5hr 15min).

Tourist information Csík-Info is upstairs in the city hall at Piata Cetății (Vár tér) 1 (Mon–Fri 8am–4pm, in theory; ☎ 0266 317 007, ⓔ csikinfo@szereda.ro).

THE PILGRIMAGE TO CSIKSOMLYÓ

The great **Catholic pilgrimage** on Whit Sunday gives a great insight into the Székely culture. It takes place at Șumuleu (Csiksomlyó; ⓦ csiksomlyo.ro), a Franciscan monastery 2km northeast of the city (buses #3, green, and #4, purple, and services to Șoimeni from the station). The complex was founded in 1442 by Iancu de Hunedoara in thanks for the Székely victory over the Turks at Marosszentimre (and rebuilt in 1733–79); a Baroque pilgrimage church was added in 1804–76. The festival, however, commemorates the 1567 victory of the Catholic Székely over János Sigismund Báthori, who was attempting to impose Calvinism on them. At least 200,000 black-clad pilgrims attend, singing hymns and queuing to touch the miraculous statue of the Virgin (carved in limewood in about 1515) behind the altar, before processing on to three chapels on a nearby hill top, which gives a good view of the plain, dotted with Székely villages.

ACCOMMODATION

Casa Genesini Ciba (Csiba) no. 9D ☎0745 325 041; map p.189. Isolated in the fields in the first village west on the Odorheiu Secuiesc road, this is a wonderfully welcoming Hungarian/Italian run guesthouse with five comfortable rooms and great Italian food. €30

Casa Lasarus Ház Str. Gál Sándor 9 ☎0266 310 497 or ☎0751 052 753, ⓦlasarushostel.ro; map p.189. This excellent HI-affiliated youth hostel has very tidy, en-suite four-bed rooms with TV, plus laundry facilities, internet and a kitchen. Per person €12

Korona Str. Márton Áron 40 ☎0266 310 993, ⓦkorona. panzio.ro; map p.189. The town's most appealing

accommodation, an attractive nineteenth-century building with sixteen large, delightfully coloured rooms and a good restaurant in the courtyard. €30

Vardomb Str. Câmpul Mare 50 ☎0744 812 638, ⓦvardomb.ro; map p.189. In a green and pleasant setting near the Şumuleu monastery, this is a delightful guesthouse, with ten ensuite rooms swathed in pinewood, and restaurant (mainly Hungarian dishes such as goulash, but with exotic touches such as Armenian caraway soup) with plenty of scope for outdoor activities. €28

EATING

Bandidos Str. Petőfi 25 ☎0266 314 749, ⓦbandidospizza.ro; map p.189. A lively and popular place with a terrace that in addition to the usual pizza and grilled meats offers Mexican dishes such as tacos, burritos and chimichanga (€5). Mon–Fri 10am–11.30pm, Sat & Sun 11am–11.30pm.

Petőfi Kávéház Majláth Gusztáv Károly tér 2 ☎0748 101 401; map p.189. A stylish glass-fronted café in a modern (but otherwise disused) cinema building. Mon–Thurs 8am–midnight, Fri 8am–1am, Sat 9am–1am, Sun 9am–midnight.

Renegade Pub & Pizza Str. Petőfi 3 ☎0266 372 700, ⓦrenegadepizza.ro; map p.189. It's pretty much pizza all the way at this convivial pizza-pub which has seating on the main pedestrianized street. Mon–Thurs 10am–1am, Fri 10am–2am, Sat 11am–2am, Sun 1pm–1am.

★**San Gennaro** Str. Petőfi 15 ☎0266 206 500, ⓦsangennarociuc.ro; map p.189. Run by an Italian chef who forages for black truffles and mushrooms in the local forests, shoots partridge and duck and imports other provisions from Italy, this offers the region's most authentic pasta, risotto and fish. Daily 10am–midnight.

The Upper Mureş valley

From Miercurea Ciuc both road and rail routes cross a low pass from the Olt to the Mureş valley and curve around to the city of **Târgu Mureş**. It's a leisurely route taking in the tranquil **Lacu Roşu**, the untamed **Căliman mountains** and a plethora of attractive villages. There are far fewer trains than south of Miercurea Ciuc, and you may need to change at Deda for Târgu Mureş; with your own transport you can take a short cut via Sovata, but there are few buses on either route.

Gheorgheni

GHEORGHENI (Gyergyószentmiklós), once a centre of Armenian settlement, is the jumping-off point for **Lacu Roşu** (see page 192) and for hiking in the area's thickly forested mountains. The road from the station, Bulevardul Frăţiei, meets the DN12 at a well-conserved synagogue and continues east as Bulevardul Lacu Roşu; one block south (opposite the splendid high school, completed in 1915) is Piaţa Libertăţii, ringed with tatty buildings redolent of Austro-Hungarian times.

Tarisznyás Márton Múzeum and the Armenian Catholic church

Museum Str. Rácóczi 1 • May–Sept Tues–Fri 9am–5pm, Sat & Sun 10am–5pm; Oct–April Tues–Fri 9am–5pm • €1.50 • ☎0266 365 229, ⓦtmmuzeum.ro

Strada Márton Áron leads east from Piaţa Libertatii past the Catholic church (1756), with its striking west gable, to Piaţa Petőfi and the **Tarisznyás Márton Múzeum**, housed in a former Armenian merchants' inn. It contains fascinating artefacts and costumes, including some from the Csángó region across the Carpathians, plus paintings by the Postimpressionists Sándor Ziffer and János Karácsony. Just north of the museum (on the Lacu Roşu road) rises a walled **Armenian Catholic church**; diaspora Armenians arrived here in 1671, and the church was built in 1733. The exterior is more interesting than the standard Baroque interior (although there is an icon of the Armenian King Tiridat III, produced in 1752 in Venice) but if you want the key it's held by the wonderfully named Zárug Aladár at B-dul Lacu Roşu 23 (☎0266 361 951 or ☎0752 839 137).

ARRIVAL AND DEPARTURE

By bus The bus and train stations are a 20min hike west of the centre; buses towards town (from Ambient to Botvar) run roughly hourly, usually passing the station at 10min past the hour; returning, they run at about 30min past the hour. You can also board eastbound buses on B-dul Lacu Roşu, just north of the centre; the only bus west on the DN13B leaves at 9.45am for Praid, Sovata and Târgu Mureş. Destinations Bacău (1 daily); Braşov (3 daily); Budapest (1 daily); Cluj (5 daily); Lacu Roşu (3 daily); Miercurea Ciuc (5 daily); Odorheiu Secuiesc (2 daily); Piatra Neamţ (4 daily); Reghin (4 daily); Sibiu (1 daily); Sovata (1 daily); Suceava (1 daily); Târgu Mureş (5 daily); Târgu Neamţ (2 daily); Topliţa (5 daily).

By train Braşov (7 daily; 2hr 40min–4hr 20min); Budapest (1 daily; 13hr); Cluj (2 daily; 4hr 50min); Miercurea Ciuc (9 daily; 1hr–1hr 40min); Târgu Mureş (2 daily; 3hr 30min).

GHEORGHENI

ACCOMMODATION

Astoria Str. Doua Poduri 2 ☎0266 163 698. A block south from the Roman Catholic church, this offers clean and simple en-suite rooms above a pizzeria (which also serves local specialities such as wild boar goulash). **€37**

Lázár Panzió Str. Băii 3 ☎0266 362 042, ⍟lazarpanzio. ro. Just off the southwest corner of the main square, this pleasant family-run guesthouse has attractive rooms above a restaurant and a large café terrace. Breakfast €3.50. **€24**

Motel Patru ☎0266 364 213. Along the road east towards Lacu Roşu there are various guesthouses giving access to hiking trails and the riverside; this place, 4km east of town, is a cheaper option, with rooms, two suites and wooden chalets. **€18**

Pensiunea Muskátli B-dul Frăţiei 15 ☎0266 365 477, ⍟muskatli.ro. Halfway to the stations, this is a modern place that prides itself above all on its restaurant but also has eight comfortable rooms with cheap laminated furniture. **€18**

Szilagyi Piaţa Libertăţii 17 ☎0266 364 591, ⍟szilagyivendeglo.ro. The town's oldest hotel (in a nice Secession building), this has relatively simple accommodation, with en-suite rooms for up to four, and a restaurant. **€24**

EATING

Cofetărie Marzipan Piaţa Libertăţii 15. In a courtyard off the south side of the square, this café also serves exquisite pastries and cakes. Mon–Sat 8am–9pm, Sun 9am–9pm.

DRINKING

Cziffra Kávéház Piaţa Libertăţii 5. On the north side of the square, this is a popular spot for coffee and tea and also for beers and cocktails. Mon–Thurs 7am–10pm, Fri 7am–11pm, Sat 10am–11pm, Sun 10am–10pm.

Lacu Roşu

In a small depression 25km east of Gheorgheni, **Lacu Roşu**, or the **Red Lake** (Gyilkostó, or Murderers' Lake, in Hungarian), was formed when a landslide dammed the River Bicaz in 1838; you can still see the tips of a few pines protruding from the water, which is rich in trout. Surrounded by lovely scenery and blessed by a yearly average of 1800 hours of sunshine, this is an ideal stopover if you're crossing the Carpathians into Moldavia through the wild Bicaz gorges (see page 236). It's also very busy and probably best avoided in August. The area is part of the Bicaz Gorges-Haşmaş National Park (⍟cheilebicazului-hasmas.ro), and the **Eco-Info-Center** (Tues–Sun 10am–6pm), in the paid car park by the lake, offers information on walks. The easiest option is the path around the lake itself, marked with red crosses, and boating is also popular.

ACCOMMODATION   **LACU ROŞU**

Camping Lacu Roşu km21.3 ☎0729 366 113. This simple campsite, with cabins, is at the eastern end of the resort, although there are other options and nobody seems to mind if you just pitch a tent discreetly. Cabin €10

Iasicon Str. Suhard ☎0266 380 081, ⓦhoteliasicon.ro. A sprawling, surprisingly good hotel in a quieter location (up a bad road to the left/north at the east end of the resort); it offers roomy doubles and suites, a restaurant and a coffee shop. €36

Topliţa and the Căliman mountains

The DN12 and the railway continue north for 36km (passing the Renaissance castle of Lăzarea) to **TOPLIŢA** (Maroshévíz), a logging town and minor spa and ski resort. The only real sights are a covered bridge south of town, and two wooden churches – Sf Ilie's, in beautiful gardens 1km north on the main road, built in 1847 and moved here in 1910, and the Doamnei Church in a lovely nunnery 10km further on, dating from 1658. From Topliţa, the road and rail routes head west into the Deda-Topliţa gorge, in which retreating German soldiers made a vain attempt to ambush the Red Army in 1944; it's now protected by the **Parcul Natural Defileul Mureşului Superior**. To the north, the wild, unpopulated **Căliman mountains** – the main volcanic zone of the Carpathians – are now a national park (ⓦcalimani.ro). It's a hikers' paradise, with routes (marked with blue crosses) leading north from the stations of Lunca Bradului and Rastoliţa (where there's a cute little eighteenth-century wooden church), over the peaks to the settlements in the huge crater beyond, and ultimately to Vatra Dornei in Moldavia. Near Lunca Bradului station the **Călimani Equestrian Centre** (c/o Transair, Piaţa Trandafirilor 32, ap. 58, Târgu Mureş; ☎0265 268 463, ⓦhorseriding.ro) offers great horseriding holidays as well as fine meals and accommodation.

ACCOMMODATION   **TOPLIŢA AND THE CĂLIMAN MOUNTAINS**

Cabana Şeştina ☎0266 341 178, ⓦcabanasestina. ro. This very rural guesthouse has fourteen rooms (mostly doubles but also rooms sleeping three-, four- and five people) and two chalets, facilities for sports such as badminton, tennis and archery and a swimming pool, plus a trout pool. €20

Pensiunea Denisa ☎0265 558 133, ⓦpensiunea-denisa.ro. Lovely guesthouse 3km west of Lunca Bradului station with ten very agreeable rooms furnished largely in dark wood, plus a sauna, jacuzzi and hammam (extra charge); you can also rent bikes. €30

Târgu Mureş

TÂRGU MUREŞ is still at heart the great Magyar city of **Marosvásárhely**, although recent Romanian and Gypsy immigration has diluted the Hungarian influence – just under half the city's 150,000-strong population is now Hungarian, although that figure probably includes the Gábor Roma, more visible and styishly dressed here than elsewhere. The city was briefly notorious for ethnic riots in 1990, but is better known as a centre of learning – its university is small, but both the medical and drama schools are renowned nationally; in fact foreign students now flock here for cheap English-language medical courses.

The Prefecture and Palatul Culturii

Prefecture tower Tues–Sun 11am & 2pm; book at the Palace of Culture ticket office, Mon–Fri 10am–1pm & 5–7pm • **Palace of Culture** May–Aug Tues–Fri 9am–5.30pm, Sat & Sun 9am–3.30pm; Sept–April Tues–Fri 9am–4pm, Sat & Sun 9am–2.30pm • €2.50 • ☎0365 451 034, ⓦpalatul-culturii.ro

The main square, **Piaţa Trandafirilor**, is lined with fine Secession-style edifices, the most grandiose being the adjacent Prefecture and Palace of Culture, built in 1907 and 1913 respectively and typical of that era when a self-consciously "Hungarian" style of architecture reflected Budapest's policy of "Magyarizing" Transylvania. The rooftops of the **Prefecture**'s clock tower blaze with polychromatic tiling, as do those of the **Palatul Culturii** (Palace of Culture), whose facade is richly ornamented with bronze bas-reliefs, ornately carved balconies and a splendid mosaic. Inside, the gloomy corridors are relieved by floral painted walls and and 50kg of gilding – working your way up the marble stairs, take a look at the many stained-glass windows illustrating eminent Hungarians, such as composer Franz Liszt, politician Lajos Kossuth and poet Sándor Petőfi. One flight up is the most spectacular room of all, the **Hall of Mirrors** (Sala de Oglinzi), with stained-glass windows illustrating local myths. Another flight up is the city's **History Museum**, which now mainly deals in temporary shows. You can also get a glimpse from the gods of the city's **concert hall**; the huge organ is often used

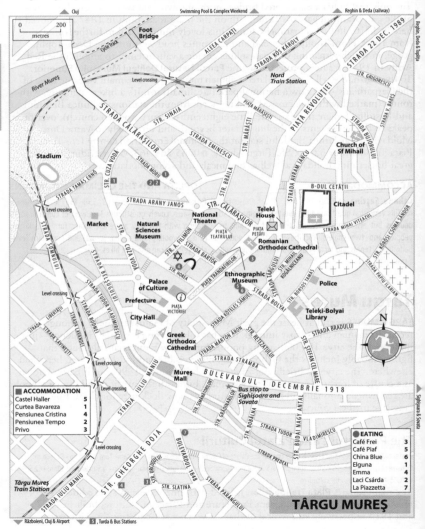

TÂRGU MUREȘ

■ **ACCOMMODATION**
Castel Haller	5
Curtea Bavareza	1
Pensiunea Cristina	4
Pensiunea Tempo	2
Privo	3

● **EATING**
Café Frei	3
Café Piaf	5
China Blue	6
Elguna	1
Emma	4
Laci Csárda	2
La Piazzetta	7

for recitals, and there are classical concerts on Thursdays. Another floor up is the **Art Museum**, with two galleries covering Classical Hungarian and Modern Romanian Art.

Muzeul de Etnografie

Piaţa Trandafirilor 11 • Tues–Fri 9am–4pm, Sat 9am–2pm, Sun 9am–1pm • €1

Two blocks north of the Palace of Culture, in front of the concrete plaza of Piaţa Teatrului, with its undistinguished modern sculptures, the fine Baroque Toldalagy House houses the **Muzeul de Etnografie** (Ethnographic Museum), freshly refurbished and with interesting collections pertaining to local industry, as well as a fine assemblage of colourful regional costumes, crafts and icons on glass.

Biblioteca Bolyai-Teleki

Str. Bolyai 17 • Tues–Fri 10am–6pm, Sat & Sun 10am–1pm • Free • ☎ 0265 261 857, ⓦ telekiteka.ro

Târgu Mureş takes great pride in its intellectual tradition; its greatest treasure, the **Biblioteca Bolyai-Teleki** (Teleki-Bolyai library), was amassed by the chancellor of Transylvania, Count Samuel Teleki (1739–1822), and consists of some forty thousand volumes, many of which were banned to ordinary mortals. The collection includes 67 incunabula (books printed before 1500) and the work of just about every significant Enlightenment philosopher, including Newton, Galileo, Franklin, Galvani, Linnaeus, Brahe, Kant, Hobbes, Rousseau, Descartes, Leibnitz and Voltaire, as well as two sixteenth-century atlases, first translations of the Bible in both Hungarian (1590) and Romanian (1688), the only copy of the first Hungarian encyclopedia, and copies of the

3

THE GYPSIES AND TZIGANIA

The **Rroma** or **Gypsies** (*ţigane* in Romanian, *cigány* in Hungarian) left northern India in the tenth and eleventh centuries and arrived in Europe around 1407, at the same period as the Tatar invasions. Almost at once many were enslaved and became *vătraşi* or "settled Gypsies", working as servants or farm labourers, as well as being musicians, while others were left to roam as nomads. Wallachia and Moldavia finally freed their Gypsies in 1837–56, as cheap grain imports from North America flooded Europe and the economic system that made slavery viable broke down. Many in fact stayed with their former owners, but many also **emigrated**, reaching Western Europe in the 1860s and North America by 1881.

World War II brought the Porajmos or Devouring, the Nazi attempt to wipe out the Gypsies; at least twenty thousand Gypsies were deported to Transnistria by Antonescu's regime, and a higher proportion died than in any other European country. The communist regime confiscated Gypsies' carts and forced them to settle on the edges of villages; in 1956, 38 percent of Gypsies over the age of 8 were illiterate, but by 1966 almost all their children at least went to elementary school. There are now over two million Gypsies in Romania (of eight million in Europe), almost 10 percent of the population and Europe's largest minority. Around forty percent of them no longer speak Romani and these consider themselves barely Rom; very few are still nomadic, and even these usually spend winters camped at a permanent settlement.

There is widespread **antipathy** towards Gypsies, given their great increase in numbers and visibility, and they have received very little international aid; discrimination, particularly in employment, has inevitably pushed many into crime. After the fall of communism there was an alarming rise in crime against the Rroma, with many instances of fights leading to mobs burning down Gypsy houses and driving them out of villages, with several cases of murder. In almost every case village authorities condoned the attacks, police kept away, and there have been no arrests.

Rroma people are highly visible in **Târgu Mureş** – particularly the very natty Gábors, but also the less fortunate residents of the Valea Rece shanty town on the south side of the city. As a rule it's not easy for tourists to see much of their culture, but one excellent solution is a **tour** organized by Tzigania (June–Oct; ☎ 0741 912 180, ⓦ tzigania.com). Day-trips go to nearby villages such as Vălenii or Glodeni for meals, or to Ceauş for music, and it's possible to stay overnight in Vălenii.

US Declaration of Independence, the *Supplex Libellus Valachorum Transylvaniae* (the 1791 petition of the Romanians to Leopold II) and Teleki's own will. Opened to the public in 1802, the library is an exquisite Baroque space; useful information cards are available in English and other languages.

Citadel and wooden church

Citadel: Tues–Fri 4.30–6pm, Sat & Sun 10am–8pm • Free

Just to the north of the Teleki-Bolyai library, beyond Strada Mihai Viteazul, the **citadel**, built in 1602–52, shelters the Calvinist church, the city's oldest building, built for the Dominicans in 1430 and later used by the Transylvanian Diet. After years of neglect, parts of the citadel have been restored (over-restored, in the case of the roofs), including the former barracks lining its eastern side, where local artists exhibit; the spacious grounds are also becoming a focus for open-air theatre and the like in summer months. On the north side of the citadel a beautiful cherry-tree-lined promenade runs down the centre of Bulevardul Cetăţii. From here, Strada Şaguna heads north to the **wooden church** of Sf Mihail (1794), set in a large cemetery; it has a shingled onion dome and a porch that is a virtual shrine to the national poet, Mihai Eminescu, owing to the fact that he slept in it in 1866 because there was no room at the inn.

ARRIVAL AND INFORMATION   TÂRGU MUREŞ

By plane Târgu Mureş's airport (☏ 0265 328 259, ⊚ aeroportultransilvania.ro) is busy with low-cost flights from Western Europe, including London Luton in the UK; 17km west, it's best reached by taxi, although Cluj and Mediaş buses do pass.

By bus In the centre of Transylvania, Târgu Mureş is a hub for bus services, with three terminals, all to the southwest beyond the train station. Most long-distance services use the Autogară Voiajor at Str. Gheorghe Doja 143 (on the Cluj road); the Silentina terminal, further southwest at Str. Bega 2 (and the terminal for many city buses), offers more frequent services to Turda and Cluj and the regular C&I maxitaxis to Bucharest, Braşov, Sibiu and Bistriţa. The TAM terminal at Str. Budului 101 handles the main services to Sighişoara and Sovata – these also stop on B-dul 1 Decembrie 1918, in front of Policlinic no. 2.

Destinations from Voiajor Alba Iulia (4 daily); Bacău (1 daily); Baia Mare/Satu Mare (1 daily); Bistriţa/Botoşani (1 daily); Braşov (2 daily); Câmpeni (1 daily); Cluj (7 daily); Covasna (2 daily); Iaşi (4 daily); Miercurea Ciuc (4 daily);

Odorheiu Secuiesc (10 daily); Piatra Neamţ (1 daily); Râmnicu Vâlcea (3 daily); Sibiu (6 daily); Sighet (1 daily); Sovata (3 daily); Timişoara (2 daily); Topliţa (5 daily).

Destinations from Silentina Bistriţa (8 daily); Braşov/ Bucharest (every 2hr from 5.30am); Cluj/Turda (7 daily); Oradea (2 daily); Sibiu (3 daily).

Destinations from TAM Sighişoara (16 daily Mon–Fri, 9 Sat & Sun); Sovata (17 daily Mon–Fri, 9 Sat & Sun).

By train On a secondary line between Razboieni and Deda, Târgu Mureş has poor connections to the south, and you're best off taking a bus or maxitaxi 55km south to Sighişoara and catching a train there. The train station is a 15min walk south of the centre – turn left for the city centre.

Destinations Deda (7 daily; 1hr–1hr 20min); Cluj (1 daily; 2hr 50min); Deva (1 daily; 4hr 20min); Războieni (12 daily; 1hr 20min–1hr 45min).

Tourist information The tourist office (June–Aug Mon 8am–4pm, Tues–Fri 8am–6pm, Sat 8am–4pm; Sept–May Mon–Fri 8am–4pm; ☏ 0265 404 934, cjmures.ro/turism) is at Str. Enescu 2 on the corner with Piaţa Trandafirilor.

ACCOMMODATION

Castel Haller Marosugra (Ogra de Mureş) no. 466 ☏ 0747 049 819, ⊚ castelhaller.ro; map p.194. To the west beyond the airport, this late Baroque palace is now a lovely hotel with huge rooms packed with period furnishings; the restaurant is elegant, and there's a less formal brick-arched wine cellar. This is great value all things considered. €52

Curtea Bavareza Str. Cuza Vodă 68 ☏ 0265 267 372; map p.194. The "Bavarian Court" is a friendly little guesthouse with eleven large, superbly equipped rooms

(with a/c and DVD player), and immaculate bathrooms with complimentary accessories. Good value. €40

Pensiunea Cristina Str. Piatra de Moară 1A ☏ 0265 266 490, ⊚ pensiunea-cristina.com; map p.194. Nothing fancy, but this welcoming little pension is convenient for the bus and train stations and has bright, tidy a/c rooms and a restaurant. €26

Pensiunea Tempo Str. Morii 27 ☏ 0265 213 552, ⊚ tempo.ro; map p.194. Upscale yet very affordable pension with a mix of modern and rustic rooms, the latter with timber ceilings and beautifully-crafted wooden beds, cupboards and seating areas painted in different colours; the restaurant is terrific too. **€31**

Privo Str. Gheorghe Doja 27 (entrance from Str. Urcuşului 1) ☎0365 424 442, ⊛hotelprivo.ro; map p.194. Set within a big park at the junction with Str. Slatina, this modernist L-shaped block conceals white, light-filled

rooms offset with a smattering of bold-coloured fittings, for example a red telephone. Just behind here is the stunning Art Nouveau *Villa Csonka* whose six gorgeous rooms are replete with Thonet or Art Deco furnishings; there's an *enoteca* (wine bar), a good restaurant and the *Lobby Bar*, which offers gourmet sandwiches. **€96**

EATING

Cafe Frei Piaţa Trandafirilor 49 ☎0365 424 721; map p.194. This looks like a pub but in fact serves the best coffee in town (at least sixty varieties, including with lemon, chilli etc) as well as hot chocolates and teas; there's lots more seating in the gallery and cellar. Mon–Thurs 8am–10pm, Fri 8am–midnight, Sat 9am–midnight, Sun 9am–8pm.

Café Piaf Str. Bolyai 8 ☎0771 525 526, ⊛piafcafe.ro; map p.194. An excellent and popular café with a range of attractive rooms and plenty of courtyard seating; offers a wide choice of drinks – from coffees and smoothies to beers and cocktails – and food, including breakfasts, burgers and desserts. Mon–Thurs 8am–1am, Fri 8am–3am, Sat 10am–3am, Sun 10am–1am.

China Blue Str. Bolyai 10 ☎0741 664 303, ⊛chinablue. ro; map p.194. Surprisingly, this is a pretty decent Chinese restaurant (also serving sushi), with seating indoors and in the courtyard the three-course menu of the day is cracking value at €4. Mon–Fri 10am–11pm, Sat & Sun 10am–midnight.

Elguna Str. Morii 8 ☎0265 216 944; map p.194. A standard pizza place (mainly for takeaways), but it also offers *produse ţărănesc* (peasant products) such as *palaneţ* or pancakes stuffed with cabbage or cheese. Mon–Fri 10am–10pm, Sat & Sun 11am–10pm.

Emma Str. Horea 6 ☎0265 263 021 or ☎0757 348 912; map p.194. A fine traditional Hungarian restaurant (*vendéglő*) offering lots of goulash and dumpling dishes (as well as pasta and pizza); their menu of the day (until 8pm) is excellent value at €3. Mon–Sat 8am–10pm.

Laci Csárda Str. Morii 27 ☎0265 213 552, ⊛tempo. ro; map p.194. This popular and lively place replicates a Hungarian-style inn (*csárda*) with lots of rustic trappings and great food, particularly the soups and bread; a Gypsy band plays most evenings. Daily 9am–10pm.

La Piazzetta Str. Crinului 4 ☎0265 262 072; map p.194. At the north end of B-dul 1848 this is a genuine Italian-run restaurant with a full range of *prime*, *secondi* (pastas, meat and fish) and excellent pizzas, fine wines from Villa Vinea and good music. Daily 10.30am–11pm.

Cluj

With its Baroque and Secession outcroppings and weathered *fin-de-siècle* backstreets, **CLUJ** (officially Cluj-Napoca; Klausenburg in German and Kolozsvár in Hungarian) looks every bit the Hungarian provincial capital it once was. The city's focal point is **Piaţa Unirii**, surrounded by shops, cafés and restaurants and dominated by the monumental St Michael's Cathedral. With a clutch of fine **museums** (especially the marvellous Ethnographic Museum), churches and buildings, and buzzing **nightlife**, Cluj could quite easily detain you for several days.

Brief history

The city was founded by Germans in the twelfth century, on the site of a Roman Municipium, and the modern-day Magyars – now under a fifth of the city's population – still regret its decline, fondly recalling the *belle époque* when Kolozsvár's café society and **literary reputation** surpassed all other Balkan cities. For Romanians, however, this was the city of the Hungarian landlords until 1920; most consider Ceauşescu's addition of Napoca to its name in 1974 as fair recognition that their Dacian forebears settled here 1850 years ago, long before the Magyars reached Transylvania. It's rightly said that Romanians live in Cluj and Hungarians still live in Kolozsvár, with separate schools and theatres, though relations between the two communities are healthy. Cluj is also the birthplace of the **Unitarian creed** and its centre in Romania, further adding to the multiethnic, multi-faith cocktail.

Under communism, Cluj was **industrialized** and became Transylvania's largest city, with a population of over 330,000. Nonetheless it retained something of its old languor, as well as a reputation for being anti-Ceauşescu. From 1992 to 2004, the city was run by **Gheorghe Funar**, the "Mad Mayor", former leader of the Romanian National Unity Party, and notorious for his anti-Hungarianism – park benches and litter bins were painted in the colours of the Romanian flag, while several absurdly expensive monuments were raised.

Unlike almost every other Romanian city of comparable size, Cluj avoided the construction of a Civic Centre and the widespread demolition of its historic centre, which remains largely unspoiled within the line of the **city walls**. It's increasingly being **pedestrianized**, allowing stylish new bars and restaurants to flourish; unfortunately the city's drivers haven't got the message and are trying to cram more and more cars into the remaining space.

Cathedral of St Michael

Free organ recitals Sat 5pm

Dwarfing the central Piaţa Unirii is the Roman Catholic **cathedral of St Michael**, built between 1349 and 1487 in the German Gothic style of the Saxons who then ruled unchallenged over the city. It's a superb example of a Central European hall church – like the Black Church in Braşov (see page 131) – with three capacious naves separated by mighty pillars that curve into austerely bare vaulting. To this great church the Hungarian aristocracy later added a sacristy, its amazingly ornate door (dated 1528) encapsulating the Renaissance style introduced under Mátyás Corvinus, a wooden pulpit flush with Baroque carving, and in 1859 a tapering bell tower like a massive rocket. Note, too, the fifteenth-century frescoes in the southwestern chapel and on the south wall, to the right as you enter.

Piaţa Unirii

South of the cathedral, the main square, **Piaţa Unirii**, covers the remains of the Roman town, recently excavated and covered up again. A clumsy but imposing equestrian statue of Mátyás Corvinus (raised in 1902) tramples the crescent banner of the Turks underfoot. His formidable Black Army kept Hungary safe from banditry and invasion for much of his reign (1458–90), but his reputation derives equally from his Renaissance attributes, for which the credit should be shared with his wife, **Beatrix of Naples**. She introduced him to the Renaissance culture of Italy, selecting foreign architects and craftsmen, and humanists like Bonfini to chronicle events and speeches, and personally commissioned many volumes in the Corvin Library.

In the southwestern corner of the square stand the **Shot Pillars**, seven bronze cylinders erected in 2003 to commemorate those gunned down in the 1989 revolution, some 26 in total. Across the road, the University Bookshop, another fine building, bears two plaques to those killed on December 21 and 22, 1989. Facing it, the **Hotel Continental** was built in 1895 in an eclectic style combining Renaissance, Classical and Baroque elements; this was where Patrick Leigh Fermor and the married woman he called "Angéla" famously enjoyed cocktails, as related in *Between the Woods and the Water* (see page 401), before it served as the German military headquarters in Transylvania at the end of World War II; although now cleaned up and repainted, it remains sadly defunct.

Muzeul de Artă Cluj-Napoca

Piaţa Unirii 30 • Wed–Sun 10am–5pm • €2 • ☎ 0264 596 952, ⓦ macluj.ro

The Bánffy Palace, built in 1774–85 to the design of Johann Eberhardt Blaumann, rises on the east side of Piaţa Unirii. The grandest Baroque monument in Transylvania, with a Rococo facade and a grand portal, it houses the **Muzeul de Artă Cluj-Napoca**, which, with its Bucharest counterpart (see page 46), offers the best survey of Romanian art. The collection is dominated by the largely French-influenced artists of the nineteenth and twentieth centuries, including Romania's foremost painter, Nicolae Grigorescu

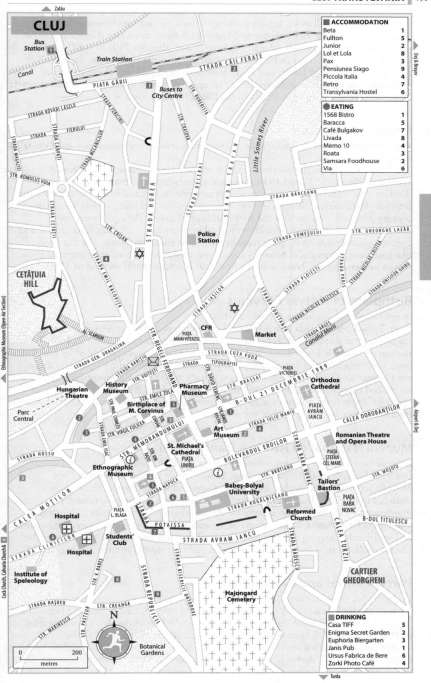

(1838–1907); as well as his superb landscapes, look out for some wonderful character paintings, such as *Turkish Prisoner* and *Gypsy with Bear*, and a rare self-portrait. Also well represented are Theodor Aman (1831–91) and Theodor Pallady (1871–1956), who spent several decades in Paris and was clearly inspired by Matisse. Some Székely painters, such as Nagy István and Nagy Imre, also get a look-in. There are lots of temporary shows, and in summer there's an **open-air bar** in the courtyard, and **concerts** by anyone from Gypsy brass bands to the Cluj Philharmonic.

Pharmacy Museum

Piaţa Unirii 28 • Mon–Wed & Fri 10am–4pm (and the last Sat of the month, closed the following Mon), Thurs noon–6pm • €1.50 • ☎ 0264 597 567, ⓦ mnit.ro

The Hintz House, on the northeast corner of Piaţa Unirii, housed Cluj's first apothecary from 1573 until 1949. Inside, the timewarp-like **Pharmacy Museum** displays a beautiful collection of ancient prescriptions, jars and vases stored inside the original glass cabinets, alongside more curious exhibits including some eighteenth-century Mummy powder and the anal glands of a beaver. The equipment room features a selection of brutal-looking medical implements, including some dental and gynecological devices that, quite frankly, don't bear thinking about. The dungeon-like basement, meanwhile, houses a laboratory, complete with an assortment of tools, pestles and containers. Note, too, the beautiful Baroque mural painted in 1766.

Birthplace of Mátyás Corvinus

Str. Sextil Puscariu 1 • mid-July to mid-Sept daily 10am–6pm • €2.50

From Piaţa Unirii, Strada Matei Corvin leads north to a small fifteenth-century mansion, **birthplace of Mátyás Corvinus**, Hungary's greatest king. Born in 1440, he was the son of Iancu de Hunedoara, and thus a Romanian, as a plaque added by Funar (see page 198) proclaims; however, Magyar myth makes his father the illegitimate son of the Hungarian King Sigismund, so this is equally significant for Hungarians. It's now an art and design college, but it's worth stepping inside to view the entry door and vaulted Gothic ceiling; otherwise, in the summer, artwork by a number of the college's teachers is displayed in several of the rooms.

Muzeul Naţional de Istorie a Transilvaniei

Str. Daicovici 2 • Tues & Thurs–Sun 10am–4pm, Wed noon–6pm • €2 • ☎ 0264 595 677, ⓦ mnit.ro

From the birthplace of Mátyás Corvinus, Strada Corvin continues north to Piaţa Muzeului, centre of the medieval city. At the west end of the square is the Franciscan church, built in 1247 but now Baroque, with side chapels housing the funerary monuments of the Hungarian aristocracy. At the other end of the square is the **History Museum of Transylvania**, where strange skulls and mammoth tusks are succeeded by arrow- and spearheads, charting progress from the Neolithic and Bronze Ages to the rise of the Dacian civilization, at its peak between the second century BC and the first century AD.

Parcul Central and Cetăţuia Hill

In the restful **Parcul Central**, just west of the centre, is a lake with pedaloes, and, at its far end, a casino (built in 1897 and now a cultural centre). East of here are Piaţa Mihai Viteazul, dominated since 1976 by a huge statue of Michael the Brave, and the busy **market** (see page 206); just north across the river, Strada Horea leads to the train station past the Mughal-style Neologue New Synagogue, built in 1886, sacked by the Legionaries in 1927, demolished in 1944 and rebuilt in 1951. Behind it, atop **Cetăţuia Hill**, the remains of a fifteenth-century **citadel** – converted in the eighteenth century into Transylvania's first Vauban-style fortification – ring the *Belvedere* hotel. Only a few gates remain and it's now a park overlooking the city. The plinth of the massive cross, raised here by the Uniate Church in 1997 (replacing one demolished in 1948), gives the best **views**. The Securitate used the hotel as its power base, and twelve people were supposedly gunned down on the steps in the 1989 revolution.

Babes-Bolyai University

From Piaţa Unirii, Strada Napoca leads west to the Students' Club and the old library on Piaţa Blaga, and Strada Universităţii heads south past the Piarist Church (Cluj's first Baroque church, built in 1718–24) to the **Babeş-Bolyai University**. Founded in 1581 as a Jesuit Academy, this has produced scholars of the calibre of Edmund Bordeaux Székely (translator of the Dead Sea Scrolls), but has also served as an instrument of cultural oppression. Long denied an education in their own language, the Romanians promptly banned teaching in Hungarian once they took over in 1919, only to hurriedly evacuate students and staff when Hitler gave Northern Transylvania back to Hungary in 1940. After liberation, separate universities were created to teach in the two languages, but in 1959 the authorities decreed a shotgun merger, enforced by a little-known cadre called **Nicolae Ceauşescu**, which led to the suicide of the Bolyai's pro-rector, and, more predictably, a rapid decline in its Hungarian-language teaching. Since 1989, however, the university seems to have found a genuinely **multicultural** vocation, with teaching in both languages as well as the first Jewish Studies courses in Romania.

Outside the university's main building (1893–1903) stands a statue of Samuil Micu, Gheorghe Şincai and Petru Maior, the leaders of the **Transylvanian School** (Şcoala Ardeleana) whose philological and historical researches in Blaj fuelled the Romanian cultural resurgence of the nineteenth century and the resistance to Magyarization. They inspired the "**generation of 1848**", including Avram Iancu, who lived as a student in 1841–44 at Str. Avram Iancu 17, and Nicolae Bălcescu and Gheorghe Bariţiu who were based at Str. Avram Iancu 20 during the revolution of 1848–49.

Botanical Gardens

Str. Republicii 42 • Daily 8am–8pm; glasshouses April to mid-Oct 9am–6pm; mid-Oct to March 9am–4pm (greenhouses closed first Mon of the month all year) • €2.50 • ☎ 0264 592 152, ⓦ ubbcluj.ro

Just south of the university are the **Botanical Gardens**, with more than ten thousand species, which are of course best in summer but lovely all year. They are very popular for wedding photos and student idling, and contain a museum and greenhouses with desert and tropical plants including Amazon waterlilies 2m across, and a small Japanese garden.

Reformed church

The tree-lined Strada Kogălniceanu runs east from the university to the Calvinists' **Reformed church**, built by Mátyás Corvinus for the Franciscans in 1486–1503. In front stands a copy of the statue of St George and the Dragon in Prague's Hradčany castle – one of the world's most famous equestrian statues – made in 1373 by the masters Martón and György of Kolozsvár (Martin and George of Cluj). The church's interior features plain late-Gothic stonework above the stalls, a pulpit added in 1646 and wooden funeral panels showing the coats of arms of Transylvania's leading Hungarian families. The ornate **organ** (1766) in the gallery above the west door is used for recitals. When the church is closed, get the **key** from Str. Kogălniceanu 21.

Orthodox Cathedral

Piaţa Avram Iancu 18 • Mon & Sat 6am–1pm & 5–8pm, Tues–Fri & Sun 6am–8pm • **Museum** Tues–Sat 10am–5pm, Sun noon–5pm • €1

UNITARIANISM

Founded in Cluj in 1556 by the hitherto Calvinist minister David Ferenc (1520–79), the **Unitarian Church** had its origins among the Italian and Spanish humanists and some of the more extreme Anabaptists. Unitarianism derives its name from its rejection of the doctrine of the Trinity, as well as other basic doctrines such as the divinity of Christ, his atonement for the sins of the world, and thus the possibility of salvation. However, its significance lies in its undogmatic approach – adherents are conspicuous for their **devotion to liberty and reason** in matters of religion and their exercise of tolerance to all sincere forms of religious faith.

By 1568 Unitarianism was already accepted as one of the four official churches of Transylvania; it spread **worldwide** and by the 1830s had mutated to become the religion, for instance, of the Boston/Harvard establishment, with an emphasis on scientific progress and material success. In Romania there are now around 75,000 Unitarians, almost all Hungarian-speaking.

The notorious statue of Avram Iancu – leader of the 1848 revolt against the Hungarians – on Piaţa Avram Iancu was raised by Funar in 1993. Behind it, the huge **Orthodox Cathedral** was built in 1923–33, also celebrating the Romanian triumph in Transylvania. It looks as if it fell through a time warp from Justinian's Constantinople, but the neo-Byzantine facade hides a concrete structure. The enormous chandelier was a gift from King Carol I, while much of the narthex and nave walls were decorated in 2001 with Murano mosaic from Venice, using over a hundred hues, including twenty different shades of gold.

On the right-hand side of the church (as you face the entrance), steps lead down to a small but fascinating museum holding numerous church treasures: chalices, monstrances, icons on wood and glass, plus lots more. Here, too, are a number of ostentatious marble tombs containing the bodies of prominent local bishops, including that of Nicolae Ivan (1855–1936), founder of the diocese of Cluj.

Muzeul Etnografic al Transilvaniei

Main museum Str. Memorandumului 21 • Wed–Sun 10am–6pm • €1 • Ⓦ muzeul-etnografic.ro • **Open-air section** Wed–Sun: mid-March to mid-Oct 10am–6pm; mid-Oct to mid-March 9am–4pm • €2 • It's a 30min walk from the centre, or take bus #37 from Piaţa Mihai Viteazul to Parcul Industrial Tetarom, or #27, #28 or #30 to Piaţa 14 Iulie (Cartier Grigorescu), and then walk 10min north up Str. Tăietura Turcului

The city's main east–west axis runs across the northern edge of Piaţa Unirii, continuing eastwards as Bulevardul Eroilor 21 Decembrie 1989 and westwards as Strada Memorandumului, where the late-Baroque Reduta Palace hosted the Transylvanian Diet in 1790–1 and the trial of the Memorandumists in 1894, as well as concerts by Franz Liszt. It now houses the main branch of the superb **Muzeul Etnografic al Transilvaniei** (Ethnographic Museum); displays start with the history of shepherding in the region, featuring finely crafted staffs, cattle horns used for carrying gunpowder and ferocious bear traps. The importance of traditional crafts is evident in a collection of carved gates from Maramureş, painted Saxon chests and wardrobes, and some exquisite glazed pottery. There's also an outstanding assemblage of musical instruments, such as flutes, alpenhorns and clarions, the last used throughout the Apuseni region to ward off predators.

Upstairs is probably Romania's finest collection of traditional carpets and **folk costumes** – from the dark herringbone patterns of the Pădureni region to the bold yellow, black and red stripes of Maramureş. Blouses and leggings are predominantly black or white, but women's apron-skirts, and the waistcoats worn by both sexes for special occasions, are brilliantly coloured. Peacock feathers serve in the Năsăud area as fans or plumes, and the love of complicated designs spills over onto cups, masks, distaffs (used as an application for marriage) and linked spoons (a charm against divorce). Afterwards, you can check out the excellent **craft shop**, then have a drink in the pleasant courtyard **café**.

The museum also has an excellent **open-air section** on the Hoia hill, northwest of town, with peasant houses and three wooden churches from the surrounding areas, notably one from Cizer (Sălaj county; 1773) which legend has it Horea helped to build.

Cock Church and Calvaria Church

Strada Memorandumului continues west from the museum to the splendidly towered city hall, where it becomes Calea Moților. At no. 84 the beautiful Calvinist **Cock Church** was built in 1913 by Kós Károly, who designed everything down to the light fittings, all with a cock motif symbolizing St Peter's threefold denial of Christ before cock's crow; ask for the key at the parish office behind the church. Kós's first house, built for his parents at Str. Breaza 14, north of the train station, now houses the architectural conservation group Utilitas. Further west, behind the Calea Mănăştur flyover, the **Calvaria Church** was built by the Magyars in the twelfth century and rebuilt by the Benedictines in 1466; it's a Gothic hall church, simple but surprisingly high, recently restored and with a new belfry.

ARRIVAL AND DEPARTURE · CLUJ

By plane The airport, 5km east (☎0264 307 500; ✆airportcluj.ro), is reached by bus #5 from the train station and #8 from Piaţa Mihai Viteazul (both lines operate roughly 5am–11pm); buses to Gherla also pass every 20min. There are one or two flights a day to Bucharest as well as international services.

By train From the station it's about a 20min walk down Str. Horea and Str. Regele Ferdinand to Piaţa Unirii. Across the road from the station, trolley buses #3, #4 and #9 stop on their loop route into the centre, going south on Str. Traian and returning along Str. Horea. Train tickets can be bought at Piaţa Mihai Viteazul 20 (Mon–Fri 8am–8pm; international bookings Mon, Wed & Fri 8.30am–3.30pm, Tues & Thurs 1–8pm).

Destinations Baia Mare (3 daily; 4hr 10min); Budapest (1 daily; 7hr); Miercurea Ciuc (2 daily; 5hr 50min–6hr 30min); Oradea (10 daily; 2hr 40min–4hr); Sfântu Gheorghe (2 daily; 7hr–7hr 40min); Sighişoara (4 daily; 3hr 40min–5hr 15min); Suceava (3 daily; 7hr).

By bus The bus station is just across the bridge to the north of the train station (bus #39).

Destinations Abrud (1 daily); Alba Iulia (every 30–60min); Athens (2 weekly); Baia Mare (11 daily); Bistriţa (9 daily); Braşov (3 daily); Bucharest (7 daily); Budapest (10 daily); Câmpeni (2 daily); Deva (7 daily); Gheorgheni (4 daily); Huedin (10 daily); Hunedoara (2 daily); Oradea (8 daily); Râmnicu Vâlcea (10 daily); Reghin (4 daily); Satu Mare (15 daily); Sibiu (15 daily); Sighet (3 daily); Târgu Jiu (5 daily); Târgu Lapuş (1 daily); Târgu Mureş (15 daily); Turda (every 10–15min).

GETTING AROUND

By bus and tram Operated by CTP Cluj-Napoca (✆ctpcj. ro), buses, trolley buses and trams provide frequent and reliable city transport; buy tickets (€1.20 for two rides) at kiosks or machines (which accept cash or cards, including contactless).

By taxi The most reliable taxis are Pritax (☎942), Diesel (☎946), ProRapid (☎948), Terra (☎944) and Nova (☎949).

By bike Bikes can be rented from Umibike, Str. Grapei 24 (Mon, Tues & Fri 9am–5pm, Wed & Thurs noon–8pm, Sat 10am–2pm; ☎0740 074 851, ✆umibike.ro).

By car An excellent local rental company is Pan Travel, Str. Grozăvescu 13 (☎0264 420 516, ✆pantravel.ro). There's also Autonom, Str. Inau 29B (☎0749 151 028, ✆autonom. ro) and Rodna Rentacar, Str. Regele Ferdinand 7, ap. 3 (☎0745 933 498, ✆rodna-trans.ro).

INFORMATION AND TOURS

Tourist information The city tourist office at B-dul Eroilor 6–8 (April–Oct Mon–Fri 8.30am–8pm, Sat & Sun 10am–6pm; Mov–March Mon–Fri 8.30am–6pm, Sat 10am–6pm; ☎0264 452 244, ✆visitcluj.ro) is very helpful. There's also the Cluj County tourist information office at the Ethnographic Museum (May–Sept Mon–Fri 9am–7pm, Sat & Sun 9am–5pm; Oct–April daily 9am–5pm; ☎0264 450 410, ✆clujtourism.ro). The City Card (€13) gives free access to eleven museums plus the Botanic Garden and free public transport for three days, and various discounts in some restaurants; buy it at the *Hotel Agape* Café Info Point, on Str. Babeş Bolyai at Str. Iuliu Maniu (☎0264 546 789, ✆topcitycard.com). Excellent maps of Cluj (including public transport routes), produced by Top-o-Gráf/Freytag

& Berndt and Schubert & Franzke, are available from the tourist office, bookshops and kiosks around Piața Unirii.

Tours Free guided tours take place daily at 11am and 6pm departing from the Corvinus Statue on Piața Unirii (☎ 0745 043 025, ⓦ cityguidedtour.ro).

Tour operators Adventure Center, Str. Cristea 13 (☎ 0743 119191, ⓦ adventurecenter.ro); Johan's Green Mountain, Str. Voievodul Menumorut 38 (☎ 0744 637 227, ⓦ greenmountain.ro); Pan Travel, Str. Traian Grozăvescu 13 (☎ 0264 420 516 or ☎ 0722 513 100, ⓦ pantravel.ro); Transybike (☎ 0746 891 741, ⓦ transybike.com).

ACCOMMODATION

Beta Str. Giordano Bruno 1 ☎ 0264 455 290, ⓦ hotelbeta-cluj.ro; map p.199. Refurbished hotel inside the bus station; rooms are dull and a little poky, but it's convenient for early departures. There are also hostel rooms (€15 bed) on the fifth floor, with washbasins in the rooms but shared showers and toilets. Breakfast €3. **€28**

Fullton Str. Sextil Pușcariu 10 ☎ 0264 597 898, ⓦ hotelfullton.ro; map p.199. Very elegant hotel tucked away behind an unattractive entrance near Corvinus's birthplace; the warm rooms – some with four-poster beds – are smartly furnished with thick pile carpets and arty decor, although there's no lift and it can be noisy. Good breakfasts. **€48**

Junior Str. Căii Ferate 12 ☎ 0264 432 028, ⓦ pensiune-junior.ro; map p.199. Dull-looking but quiet and welcoming establishment just 200m east of the train station, with 21 en-suite double and triple rooms; although the decor is a tad gaudy, rooms are spacious and spotless. Pleasant breakfast room and bar too. **€40**

★ **Lol et Lola** Str. Neagră 9 ☎ 0264 450 498, ⓦ loletlolahotel.ro; map p.199. This fantastic little hotel has injected a welcome dollop of colour onto the Cluj hotel scene, quite literally, courtesy of its twenty vibrantly painted rooms – each of which sports its own name, such Salt & Pepper, and Flower Power – and which come with patterned duvets, spotty cushions, and so on. Bathrooms are similarly imaginatively designed, with tea- and coffee making facilities a welcome bonus. **€65**

Pax Piața Gării 1 ☎ 0264 432 927, ⓦ hotelpax.ro; map p.199. Opposite the rail station, this long-time travellers' favourite has fourteen rooms – with and without bathrooms – that are rather sprightlier than the exterior

might suggest. Ultimately though, it serves as little more than a base if arriving late or leaving early. **€36**

Pensiunea Siago Str. Republicii 33 ☎ 0264 422 422, ⓦ vilasiago.ro; map p.199. This graceful nineteenth-century house just below the Botanic Gardens is excellent value, with nicely appointed a/c rooms (including triples and quads) offering welcome splashes of colour; in the hallway on each floor, there's a minibar with free fruit, biscuits, coffee and tea at any time, while meals can also be ordered. **€45**

Piccola Italia Str. Racoviță 20 ☎ 0264 536 110 or ☎ 0745 931 119, ⓦ piccolaitalia.ro; map p.199. Well-run little guesthouse on a quiet residential street, with breezy, modern rooms, including several triples, and a small kitchen. Breakfast €3.50. **€32**

★ **Retro** Str. Potaissa 13 ☎ 0264 450 452, ⓦ retro. ro; map p.199. In a brilliant central (but still remarkably quiet) location built up against the medieval city wall, this clean, friendly and well-run place is a charming warren with singles, doubles, triples and four- and six-bed dorms – tea, coffee, and breakfast are included, there are two kitchens, cellar lounge/bar and sauna, and laundry can be washed for an extra charge. The hostel can book bus tickets to Budapest (€18) as well as their own tours (ⓦ retrotravel.ro) and car rental. Dorms **€13**, doubles **€40**

Transylvania Hostel Str. Iuliu Maniu 26 ☎ 0264 443 266, ⓦ hostelcluj.com; map p.199. Charming backpackers' place with dorms for up to eight, a big kitchen and games room with pool, table tennis and musical instruments; there's an attractive garden in the courtyard. Breakfast included. Dorms **€14**, doubles **€38**

EATING

Cluj has a reasonable bunch of restaurants, including a couple of upmarket options, various pizzerias, for instance on B-dul Eroilor, and lots of fast-food options and snack bars, especially on Str. Napoca and Piața Blaga. Café life – and in particular the craft coffee scene – ranks second only to that of Bucharest, as does the bar and club scene, thanks to the city's large student population.

1568 Bistro B-dul 21 Decembrie 1989 14 ☎ 0720 856 588; map p.199. Occupying the former residence of the Unitarian Bishops, you could be forgiven for thinking that this sprawling, smartly-presented restaurant might be more style than substance, but in fact the food – traditional

dishes prepared in a modern way – is terrific, for example slow cooked beef cheeks in a coffee sauce with buttered spinach (€11). Mon–Wed 9am–11pm, Thurs & Fri 9am–midnight, Sat noon–midnight, Sun noon–11pm.

Baracca Str. Napoca 8A ☎ 0732 155 177, ⓦ baracca. ro; map p.199. There's seriously good international food here, like foie gras in a pear puree with wild rice, *coq au vin* (€10) and Argentinian tenderloin (€23), plus a wide range of wines and cocktails with and without alcohol. Daily noon–11pm.

Café Bulgakov Str. Inocențiu Micu Klein 17 ☎ 0264 450 156, ⓦ cafebulgakov.ro; map p.199. This literary

CINEMA IN CLUJ

Cluj is the unofficial capital of Romanian **cinematography** – it was here, in 1905, that the country's first film studio was inaugurated, and the city has more cinemagoers than any other Romanian city. Moreover, it's one of the few places where **city-centre cinemas** survive in addition to multiplexes in the new malls: notably the Cinema Florin Piersic, Piața Mihai Viteazul 11 (☎0264 433 477); and Victoria, B-dul Eroilor 51 (☎0264 450 143, ⓦcinemavictoria.ro). Cluj is also home to the country's premier film festival, the **Transylvanian International Film Festival** (TIFF; ⓦtiff.ro), a ten-day jamboree at the beginning of June that features a superb mix of domestic and world films shown at the cinemas listed above.

establishment (seat of The League of Hungarian Writers of Transylvania, and scene of regular book launches) offers a sophisticated take on Hungarian cuisine, such as trout fillet fried in cornflour, and stuffed cabbage rolls with pork shank and polenta (€6). Mon–Wed & Sun 11.30am–1am, Thurs–Sat 11.30am–5am; food to 11pm daily.

Livada Str. Clinicilor 14 ☎0722 111 115, ⓦrestaurantlivada.ro; map p.199. A large and stylish bare-brick place with a big garden; good breakfasts, pizza, pasta, burgers and other meat dishes, including plenty of vegetarian and salad options and a menu of the day (€4; Mon–Fri noon–4pm); they also like their music, with two, sometimes three, live gigs every week. Mon–Fri 9am–midnight, Sat & Sun noon–midnight.

Memo 10 Str. Memorandumului 10 ☎0727 892 831; map p.199. The best-value lunch spot in Cluj, this no-frills, canteen style joint is actually the City Hall's restaurant, with soups, salads and mains going for around €2–3 a pop, plus a cracking value menu of the day for €3.50. Mon–Fri 11am–6pm.

★ **Roata** Str. Alex Ciura 6A ☎0264 592 022; map p.199. Just off Str. Isac, this cosy, rustically styled restaurant – Transylvanian costumes and textiles draped over the walls, or a vine-shaded arbour – offers some of the city's best Romanian food; add sharp service and a convivial atmosphere, and it's a most enjoyable option. Daily noon–11pm.

★ **Samsara Foodhouse** Str. Cardinal Iuliu Hossu 3 ☎0364 889 278, ⓦsamsara.ro; map p.199. An absolutely sublime vegetarian resaurant serving a dazzlingly inventive array of dishes (some vegan and some raw), such as mango, tofu and coconut rolls (€5), goat's cheese and avocado, and chocolate and mint cake, alongside more conventional favourites like pizza. The drinks, especially, the homemade lemonades, are equally delicious – try the seabuckthorn. The light, sunny interior makes for an inviting setting, while the olive tree plonked right in the middle of the restaurant is a novel feature. Daily 11am–11pm.

Via Str. Inocențiu Micu Klein 6 ☎0264 593 220, ⓦviarestaurant.ro; map p.199. A small but excellent restaurant in a vaulted eighteenth-century house with crisply laid out tables and a menu that takes some beating; home made gnocchi with shiitake mushrooms in a ginger celeriac cream, lemon risotto with calamari (€7), and a lychee raspberry mousse (€4) are just a few of the sumptuous dishes one can salivate over. Daily noon–midnight.

DRINKING

Casa TIFF Str. Universității 6 ☎0745 252 452, ⓦcasatiff.ro; map p.199. At the home of the Transylvanian International Film Festival, everything here is movie-related, not least the big fat burgers (€6.50), sporting names such as the Whoopi Goldburger and the Arnold Schwarzenburger; the main reason to come, though, is the mellow *TIFF Bar*, its spacious brick courtyard a great spot to indulge in a craft beer or three. Mon–Thurs 9am–2am, Fri & Sat 11am–2am, Sun 11am–1am.

Enigma Secret Garden Str. Iuliu Maniu 12 ☎0752 104 642, ⓦenigmacaffe.ro; map p.199. Think *Mad Max* and *The Terminator* rolled into one and that's what this superb kinetic steampunk bar looks like, featuring seven striking dynamic statues; the music is unobtrusive, the food is good, and the vast, tree-shaded courtyard is lovely in warmer weather. Mon–Sat 8am–3am, Sun 10am–3am.

Euphoria Biergarten Str. Cardinal Hossu 23 ☎0756 393 333, ⓦeuphoriabiergartencluj.ro; map p.199. In a villa near the central park with a large garden, this is a great place to enjoy German beers and a range of foods such as goulash, *sarmale*, steak or pizza. Daily 9am–3am.

Janis Pub Piața Unirii 19 ☎0736 365 807; map p.199. Studenty club with a good mix of music for dancing and lots of cheap drinks (even free beer from time to time). Daily 8pm–6am.

Ursus Fabrica de Bere Calea Mănăștur 2–6 ☎0756 393 333, ⓦfabricadebereursus.ro; map p.199. The cavernous bare-brick hall of the Ursus brewery is usually packed with people enjoying its products (try the black or unfiltered beers); decent food (pizza and filling Romanian dishes) is served swiftly. Also here is the Euphoria Music Hall (☎0745 393 333, ⓦeuphoriamusichall.ro), with lots of live gigs. Food served till midnight. Daily 8am–late.

> ### CLUJ FESTIVALS
>
> Cluj's big one – and now the country's premier music festival – is **Untold** (ⓦuntold.com), which brings in some of Europe's biggest dance and techno acts over the first weekend of August; most concerts take place in the Cluj Arena and Polyvalent Hall immediately to the west. Second to Untold is **Jazz in the Park** (ⓦjazzinthepark.ro) , which actually takes place in multiple locations throughout the city over eleven days in late June and into early July; and then there's the **Cluj Blues Festival** in early November, which has variously been held at the Ethnographic Museum and the Student Cultural House. Cluj also stages Romania's premier film festival (see page 205).

Zorki Photo Café Str. Rațiu 10 ☎0264 595 970, ⓔzorkiphotcafe@yahoo.com; map p.199. Arty café, with photos on the walls and acoustic music, plays and book launches, and a quiz on Thurs (8pm); popular with students enjoying alcoholic and other drinks, including the café's own Zorki coffee. Mon–Fri 9am–late, Sat noon–late, Sun 5pm–late.

ENTERTAINMENT

Cluj has a strong cultural suit, partly due to the healthy mix of Romanian and Hungarian communities. Note that most venues close from around early July to mid-Sept.

Fabrica de Pensule Str. Barbusse 59 ☎0727 169 569, ⓦfabricadepensule.ro. Appropriately, this former paintbrush factory, northeast of the centre, is now a vast space for contemporary art, with galleries, studios and performance spaces. Visits include a free guided tour. Tues–Sat 3–7pm.

Filarmonica Transilvania Str. Kogălniceanu ⓦfilarmonicatransilvania.ro; box office Piața Lucian Blaga 1–3 ☎0264 430 060 (Mon–Thurs 10am–4pm, Fri & performance days 10am–2pm). Cluj's professional symphony orchestra.

Hungarian State Theatre and Opera (Kolozsvári Állami Magyar Színház; Kolozsvári Magyar Opera) Str. Emile Isac 26 ⓦhuntheater.ro or ⓦmagyaropera.ro; box office ☎0264 431 986 (daily 10am–2pm and from 90min before performances). A wide range of theatrical and operatic productions, mostly in Hungarian.

Opera Națională Română Cluj-Napoca Piața Ștefan cel Mare 2–4 ⓦoperacluj.ro; box office Piața Ștefan cel Mare 14 ☎0264 592 466 (Mon–Fri 11am–2pm & 3–5pm, to 6.30pm on performance days, 1hr before matinees). Romanian-language opera.

Teatrul Național Cluj-Napoca Piața Ștefan cel Mare 2–4 ⓦteatrulnationalcluj.ro; box office Piața Ștefan cel Mare 14 ☎0264 595 363 (Tues–Sun 11am–2pm & 3–5pm, and until performances start). Romanian-language theatre and a variety of concerts.

Teatrul de Păpuși Puck Str. Brătianu 23 ☎0264 595 992, ⓦteatrulpuck.ro. Fabulous puppet theatre for kids.

SHOPPING

English-language books Bookstory Librăria Independența, B-dul Eroilor 6 (Mon–Fri 9am–8pm, Sat 10am–8pm, Sun 10am–6pm; ⓦbookstory.ro); Cartureşti, in the Iulius Mall, Str. Vaida-Voievod 53 (daily 10am–10pm; ⓦlibrarie.carturesti.ro); Gaudeamus, Str. Iuliu Maniu 3 (Mon–Fri 10am–6pm, Sat 10am–2pm; ⓦlibriartis.ro); Librăria Humanitas, Str. Universității 4 (Mon–Fri 8.30am–8pm, Sat 10am–5pm, Sun 10am–4pm; ⓦlibhumanitas. ro); Librăria Universității, corner of Piața Unirii and Str. Universității (Mon–Sat 9am–9pm, Sun noon–8pm).

Malls The main shopping centre in the heart of the city is the Centrul Comercial Central at Str. Regele Ferdinand 22 (Mon–Sat 10am–8pm). There are also flashy malls (with multiplex cinemas, bowling and so on) further from the centre: Iulius Mall, Str. Vaida-Voievod 53 (daily 10am–10pm ⓦiuliusmall.com/cluj); Vivo!, Str. Avram Iancu 492 (daily 10am–10pm; ⓦvivo-shopping.com/ro/cluj); Sigma Center, Str. Republicii 109 (Mon–Sat 10am–8pm, Sun 10am–3pm ⓦsigmacenter.ro).

Market Piața Mihai Viteazul (daily 8am–9pm), with plenty of effectively organic food from village producers.

The Apuseni mountains

The **Apuseni mountains** lie largely between the Crişul Repede and the Arieş valleys, enabling easy access by public transport. The DN75 follows the Arieş west from **Turda** to Bihor county via Câmpeni, where the DN74 turns south to Alba, Brad and Deva. Câmpeni is the capital of the **Moți highlanders**, who repelled the Roman invaders, then moved into the hills in the eighteenth century when the Habsburgs attempted to conscript them into the army; their settlements are some of the highest in Romania, scattered groups of high-roofed, thatched cottages at up to 1400m.

Despite opposition from the forestry and other industries – although the uranium and gold mines are now closed – the **Apuseni Nature Park** (ⓦparcapuseni.ro) was established in 2004, alongside the revival of an excellent network of hiking trails. The Cluj-based Johan's Green Mountain tour operator (see page 204) organizes a range of activities (hiking, cycling, kayaking and horseriding) mainly in the Apuseni mountains; they can also provide information and arrange homestays throughout the Apuseni.

GETTING AROUND
THE APUSENI MOUNTAINS

By bus mostly run east along the Arieş valley to Turda and Cluj in the early morning, returning west more or less hourly through the afternoon; similarly, services head to Alba Iulia and Deva and return later.

By trains Along the Crişul Repede valley to the north, most fast trains stop only at Huedin, Ciucea and Aleşd, but slow services stop at every hamlet.

Turda

TURDA (Torda), 30km south of Cluj along the DN1 (E60/81), was once one of Transylvania's wealthiest towns, thanks to salt mining, and was the first Romanian town to be lit by gas, in 1917. Modern Turda, with large Magyar and Roma minorities, is ringed by defunct factories, but still has the surprisingly elegant centre which Patrick Leigh Fermor likened to a Devon market town – a slightly odd comparison perhaps. The main reasons to come are to visit the **salt mine** and to explore the spectacular **Turda gorge**, 8km west in the Apuseni foothills.

Salina Turda

Aleea Durgaului 7 (up Str. Avram Iancu then Str. Vlahuţa) • Daily 9am–5pm, last entry 4pm • €6.50 • ☎ 0364 260 940, ⓦ salinaturda.eu • Bus #17; alternatively, maxitaxis from Cluj, or bus #10 from the centre (every 10min Mon–Sat, every 15min Sun), can drop you at the leafy park shading the walled Calvinist church of Turda Nouă, at Piaţa Basarabiei 12; from here, Str. Tunel heads east to the old entrance at Str. Salinelor 54

The **Salina Turda** (Turda Salt Mine), the town's main attraction, is on its northern edge in Valea Sărată, where a new entrance allows access by modern panoramic lifts, instead of rickety wooden staircases. Gradually excavated over 240 years, the mine consists of several huge hangar-like chambers, the most impressive being the cavernous Rudolf Mine, some 80m long, 42m high and 50m wide. It is now a glitzy underground theme park, with a Ferris wheel, bowling, minigolf and table tennis among the many activities, though all of these do cost a little extra. You'll also pass through the Joseph Mine, known for its twenty or so echoes, and another with an altar sculpted from salt, allowing religious services and prayers before miners began their shifts. You can go boating in the Terezia Mine, 112m below the surface, while the Ghizela Mine is set up for health treatments (9am–2pm). It's under 12°C in the mine, so bring warm clothing. There are also salt pools on the surface and a modern Wellness Centre with a large pool and spa.

The Calvinist and Catholic churches

Two Gothic churches stand on the central Piaţa Republicii: the lower, built between 1387 and 1437, is a **Calvinist hall church**, and the upper is **Roman Catholic** (built in 1478–1504 and rebuilt in 1822 after a fire), with a Baroque interior and facade. It housed meetings of the Transylvanian Diet, including the promulgation of the 1568 Edict of Turda, which recognized the equality of four faiths – Calvinist, Lutheran, Roman Catholic and Unitarian – in Transylvania at a time when religious wars were all the rage in Europe. However, it merely tolerated Orthodoxy, the religion of the Vlachs, legitimizing discrimination against them. At the rear of the upper church the **municipal theatre** (1904) is a beautifully restored Eclectic edifice.

3

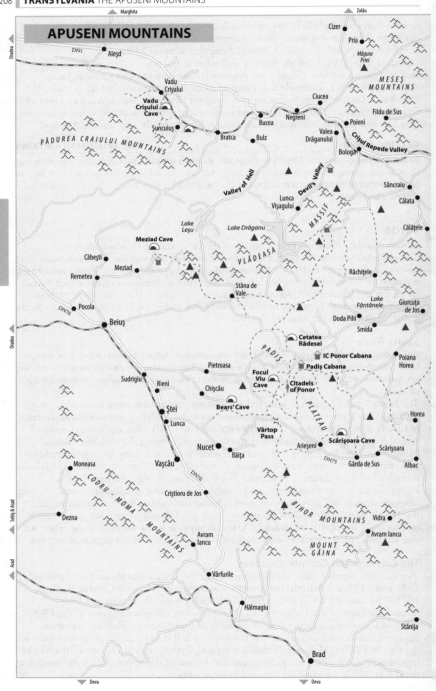

APUSENI MOUNTAINS

▲ Marghita   ▲ Zalău

◄ Oradea

DN1

Aleşd

Cizer
Pria
Măgura Priei ▲

MESEŞ MOUNTAINS

Vadu Crişului
Vadu Crişului Cave

Şuncuiuş

Ciucea
Negreni
Bucea
Bratca
Bulz

Fildu de Sus
Poieni
Valea Drăganului
Crişul Repede Valley
Bologa

PĂDUREA CRAIULUI MOUNTAINS

Valley of Hell

Devil's Valley

Lunca Vişagului

Săncraiu
Călata

MASSIF

Călăţele

Lake Leşu
Lake Drăganu

Meziad Cave

Căbeşti
Remetea
Meziad

Rămeţele

Răchiţele

VLĂDEASA

Lake Fântânele
Giurcuţa de Jos

Stâna de Vale

DN76
Pocola

Beiuş

Doda Pilii
Smida

Cetatea Rădesei

PADIŞ

Poiana Horea

Pietroasa

IC Ponor Cabana
Padiş Cabana
Focul Viu Cave
Citadels of Ponor

Sudrigiu
Rieni
Chişcău

Bears' Cave

PLATEAU

Horea

Ştei
Lunca

Vârtop Pass

Scărişoara Cave

Nucet
Băiţa

Arieşeni
DN75
Gârda de Sus

Scărişoara
Albac

Moneasa

Vaşcău

DN76

CODRU - MOMA MOUNTAINS

Cristioru de Jos

BIHOR MOUNTAINS

Vidra

Dezna

Avram Iancu

Avram Iancu

MOUNT GĂINA

Vârfurile

Hălmagiu

Stânija

Brad

◄ Oradea

◄ Sebiş & Arad

◄ Arad

▼ Deva   ▼ Deva

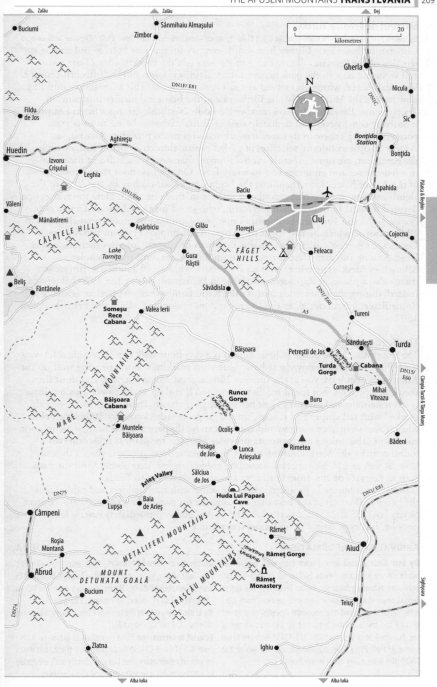

3

Muzeul de Istorie Turda

Str. Haşdeu 2 • May–Aug Tues–Fri 10am–5pm, Sat & Sun 11am–7pm; Sept–April Tues–Sun 10am–5pm • €1.50 • Ⓦ muzeu-turda.cimec.ro

Christianity has a long history here – fifth-century tombs have been found among the remains of the Roman military camp of Potaissa (on the western edge of the town), and some are now in the park between the Calvinist church and the fifteenth-century Voivodal Palace, which also served as a salt customs house. This magnificent building now houses the **Muzeul de Istorie Turda**, one of the best local history museums in Transylvania. Excellent displays start with Middle Neolithic ceramics (found during motorway construction immediately west of Turda), Potaissa being an important pottery-making centre in its time; artwork was also much prized in Potaissa, as evidenced by a wonderful selection of gilded bronze statuettes. Better still, down in the basement, are some superbly carved Roman altar stones, including a memorial to a hairdresser and an image of a funerary feast. On the first floor there's coverage of the Age of Migrations, including the beginning of salt trading by the Avars in the eighth century, and the first record of a fortress in Turda in 1075. Here too is a section devoted to local-born politician Ion Raţiu, who stood for the Christian Democratic National Peasant Party in the country's first post-Communist presidential elections in 1990, prior to which he had spent fifty years in self-imposed exile in Britain; one of Ceauşescu's fiercest critics, his wife was Elizabeth Pilkington, of glass-manufacturing fame. Among the many fascinating items on display are some of his scholarly belongings (desk, typewriter), and his distinctive white wool and black trim jacket; there's also a photo of Raţiu remonstrating in Parliament during the 1990 Mineriada. Indeed, during the nineteenth century the Raţiu family were involved in agitating for Romanian rights, above all in the Memorandum presented to Emperor Franz Joseph in 1892.

The Turda gorge

The impressive **Turda gorge** (Cheile Turzii) is a two-hour walk (or 7km cycle ride) west from Piaţa Romană, following red and blue cross markings. Buses heading west up the Arieş valley will leave you at the turning 2km beyond Mihai Viteazu; you must then continue north on foot for 5km. Either way, you'll end up at the *Cheile Turzii* cabana (with restaurant and campsite) just before the gorge itself. There's a narrow footpath, marked with red stripes and crosses, up the gorge, overshadowed by 300m-high cliffs where caves were once outlaws' hideouts; it can be slippery and the bridges are in poor condition. The unique **microclimate** provides a habitat for plant species otherwise found only by the Mediterranean or in Central Asia; there are more than a thousand here, as well as 111 bird species, including golden eagles. After about 3km, the path ends at **Petreştii de Jos**, from where occasional buses return to Turda.

There's a via ferrata (a protected climbing route with fixed ladders and cables) and the gorge is also one of the best sites in Romania for **paragliding** (*parapente*) – contact Skyfly (Ⓣ0727 802 248, Ⓦskyfly.ro). The Tureni gorge, immediately east, is less popular, but even narrower and more spectacular.

ARRIVAL AND INFORMATION	**TURDA**

By bus Turda is well served from Cluj, with four to six maxitaxis an hour from Piaţa Ştefan cel Mare 5 (at Str. Brătianu), returning from Str. Avram Iancu 4 at the top of Turda's main drag. All longer-distance services from Alba Iulia, Târgu Mureş and the southern Apuseni stop (even though the town is now bypassed by the motorway) at the Autogară Sens Vest (Ⓣ0264 313 431) below the town centre just off Piaţa Romană, the roundabout where the DN75 (the Arieş valley road) leaves town.

Destinations Abrud (1 daily); Aiud (every 30–45min); Alba Iulia (every 30–45min); Bistriţa (3 daily); Budapest (5 daily); Câmpeni (4 daily); Haţeg (4 daily); Râmnicu Vâlcea (12 daily); Sibiu (15 daily); Sighişoara (3 daily).

By train Trains stop at the town of Câmpia Turzii, 9km east; take bus #20 to Piaţa Republicii.

Tourist information Piaţa Republicii 45 (Mon–Fri 9am–5pm Ⓣ0744 678 674, Ⓦturdaturism.ro); there's not much by way of information here but the friendly staff are happy to assist with any queries or practical arrangements.

ACCOMMODATION

★ **Casa Raţiu** Piaţa 1 Decembrie 1918 1 ☎0732 670 178, ⍟casaratiu.ro. The Raţiu Centre for Democracy has opened up its lovely guesthouse to the public, and it exemplifies their values with historical photos, lots of worthy reading matter and superb, locally sourced food. The house, built by Ceauşescu's chef, has exquisite rooms, a small kitchen upstairs and leafy arbours to sit in outside. Delightful communal areas, including a splendidly comfortable lounge and a terrace where breakfast can be taken in warmer weather. **€35**

Castel Prinţul Vinator Str. Şuluţiu 4 ☎0264 316 850, ⍟huntercastle.ro. Just off Piaţa Republicii, the "Hunter

Prince Castle" is completely over the top, with its pointy turrets and loud decor, but the rooms – all completely different – are full of character, with cast iron beds, painted cupboards and colourful stone walls jutting out at odd angles. **€55**

Centrum Str. Avram Iancu 11 ☎0264 315 220, ⍟hotelturda.ro. This glass-fronted modern place just above the maxitaxi station, has a kitschy foyer, clean comfortable rooms and helpful staff. **€30**

Palace Piaţa Republicii 31 ☎0740 986 226, ⍟palace-turda.ro. Lovely Secession building on the (largely traffic-free) main square has large and spacious a/c rooms (either economy or standard), and a café-bar. **€33**

EATING

Castel Prinţul Vinator Str. Şuluţiu 4 ☎0264 316 850, ⍟huntercastle.ro. This hotel has the best restaurant in the town centre; despite its overcooked medievalism and the life-size model of Vlad Ţepeş in the Dracula Room (yes, really), both food (chicken with polenta (€5.50), wild boar with roast potatoes) and service are first-class. You can also eat on the terrace overlooking the pretty garden. 24hr.

La Papion Piaţa 1 Decembrie 1918 1 ☎0742 124 293. By the entrance to the Raţiu Centre for Democracy, this is a stylish literary café with books, newspapers and low-key jazz to go along with the excellent coffees, soup, snacks

(crepes, quiche) and cakes. Its name and the Warhol-esque paintings pay tribute to the bow tie that was politician Ion Raţiu's trademark. Mon–Thurs 8am–10pm, Fri & Sat 8am–11pm, Sun 8am–4pm.

Sarea-n Bucate ☎0730 632 792, ⍟sarea-nbucate.ro. By the main (Aleea Durgaului) entry to the salina, this is a fine restaurant-with-rooms where you can enjoy vegetables from their own garden, organic apple juice from their orchard and wine from the nearby vineyard, the Crama La Salina. Daily 8am–10pm.

Rimetea

West of Turda, the main DN75 follows the River Arieş through a succession of small villages. A poor road leads 8km south from Buru to **RIMETEA** (Torockó; five buses daily from Aiud, one/two at weekends), which is famed, at least in Hungary, as one of the loveliest and most authentic of Romania's Hungarian villages – although it was in fact inhabited by Saxons until most were killed by the Tatars. The village, prosperous due to iron mining, was rebuilt in Saxon style after a major fire in 1870, and even now furniture is painted in the Sighişoara style. The centre of the village is now a **conservation area** (⍟transylvaniatrust.ro), where almost every home has rooms to let, while big modern pensions (and two new monasteries) stand on the outskirts. Traditional dress is worn for festivals on February 22 and the first Sunday of March, and can also be seen in the **Ethnographic Museum** (Tues–Sun 9am–5pm; €1), upstairs in the *Primaria*, along with mining tools, locks and keys, women's red boots and an elaborate bridal headdress.

ACCOMMODATION AND EATING   RIMETEA

Aranyos Panzio no. 285 ☎0258 768 027. Opposite the Unitarian church, this welcoming guesthouse offers half board with a superb dinner of typically Transylvanian cuisine (perhaps *mămăligă* or goulash, home-baked bread and local desserts such as "ash-bake" or walnuts in dough). Half board per person **€15**

Gyopár Panzio-Camping no.157A ☎0744 542 563, ⍟gyoparpanzio.hu. At the village's north end, this has rooms in a wooden house and space (May–Sept) for camper vans and tents. Half board is available and recommended. Camping **€7**, room **€24**

Roşia Montană

The DN74A runs to Abrud, passing Gura Roşiei, the turning for **ROŞIA MONTANĂ**, 7km east (no buses). Transylvania has been a major source of gold ever since

THE GIRL FAIR OF MUNTELE GĂINA

The **Girl Fair** (Târgul de Fete) of Muntele Găina takes place on the closest Sunday to July 20 on the flat top of Mount Găina (Hen Mountain), roughly 33km west of Câmpeni, near the village of **Avram Iancu**, named after the leader of the 1848 revolt against the Hungarians who was born here in 1824. The region's largest festival, it was originally a means for young men who were away shepherding for two-thirds of the year to meet young women from other communities and to pursue matrimony. Prospective spouses made every effort to enhance their appeal, the girls being displayed in their finest attire, surrounded by linen, pottery and other dowry items – even carting along **rented furniture**. This aspect of the fair has all but disappeared, but thousands still come for the music and spectacle.

Buses bring visitors from Câmpeni to the fair, which is a large and lively event, but the real action is on the hill top, and you should really **camp** there the night before to catch the dawn chorus on *tulnics* (alphorns). A rough forestry road takes an 8km loop to reach the hill top, but you can find more direct routes on foot. The biggest names in popular traditional Romanian music appear here, with local dance ensembles, and there's plenty of food and drink, but little drunkenness.

the Dacians started digging here; the Romans and others followed more or less continuously until, in the 1970s, Ceauşescu's opencast mining demolished the entire Cetate massif. More recently, a Canadian mining company, initially with strong government backing, planned Europe's largest **opencast gold mine** beneath Roşia Montană, which was to be largely demolished, along with its attractive Baroque houses and Roman mining tunnels; however, Romania's most determined and successful civic campaign finally managed to block the project in 2015.

Muzeul Mineritului Aurifer Roşia Montană

Str. Principală 178 • Mon–Fri 8am–2pm (out of season to noon; reserved groups to 3.30pm) • €2

In the **Muzeul Mineritului Aurifer Roşia Montană** (Museum of Gold Mining) at the former Roşiamin mine, a guided tour (90min) takes you down 157 steps into a Roman gallery, with a characteristic trapezoid profile, just one of thirty or more adits running for over 6km into four separate volcanic masses. Outside the mine entry you'll see a range of mortars and stamps from the Roman period to the twentieth century (made by Fraser & Chalmers of Erith near London) and a chemical flotation plant; in the museum are Roman lamps, tombstones and wax tablets recording operational details, found both here and in the six Roman villages and cemeteries so far uncovered. There are also superb 1930s photos of Muntele Cetate, destroyed in the communist period.

INFORMATION ROŞIA MONTANĂ

Tourist information Cultural Foundation of Roşia Montană, no. 321 on the main square (☎ 0728 444 941, ⓦ fcrm.ro).

ACCOMMODATION

Casa Manu no. 421A ☎ 0746 583 343 or ☎ 0758 322 107. Beneath a rocky outcrop a 10min walk above the historic centre, this has big and comfortable wooden chalets and good food. €18

Hostel La Gruber Str. Principală 229 ☎ 0258 859 310 or ☎ 0741 473 414, ✉ lagruberromania@gmail.com. This attractive one-storey house just north of the Cetate mine has six rooms with shared bathroom and kitchen; the owners are very helpful and knowledgeable. Per person €10

Abrud

You can hike south from Roşia Montană (following red triangles) to **ABRUD** in about an hour. The Old Town is tatty but attractive, its Baroque buildings incorporating stones from earlier Roman structures and liberally adorned with plaques commemorating the many notables who visited when Abrud was the Moți capital. A **steam train** ambles back up the valley from the north end of Abrud to the junction of the DN75 and DN74, about 1km east of Câmpeni, and back (mid-June to mid-Sept 10am, 1 & 4pm; €6.50; ☎0754 055 632, ⓦcfi.ro).

ARRIVAL AND DEPARTURE
ABRUD

By bus Local buses leave from the central Piața Eroilor; longer-distance buses stop by the bridge on Str. Horea (the DN74A).

Destinations Alba Iulia (3 daily); Brad (3 daily); Câmpeni (8 daily); Cluj (1 daily); Oradea (1 daily).

ACCOMMODATION

Pensiunea Detunata Str. Avram Iancu 56 ☎0744 399 482. At the south end of Abrud this large guesthouse has seven rooms (four en-suite) and a large restaurant, plus plenty of space for camping. **€22**

Gârda de Sus and Ghețari

3

GÂRDA DE SUS is a pretty village featuring a part-wooden church built in 1792, with naïf paintings inside. More notably, it is the starting point for several excellent **hikes**, the most popular of which, marked with blue stripes, leads north through the Ordâncuşa gorges and reaches the village of **Ghețari** after three hours; from here you can continue, following blue stripes, to Padiş (see opposite). Until recently there was no drivable road to Ghețari but now there are two: it's best to go up by the much longer route to the right, via the Ordâncuşa gorge and the Poarta lui Ionele cave, and return down the steeper direct road. At the cave of **Poarta lui Ionele** (Wed–Sun 9am–6pm; €2), good metal steps and walkways lead from the high entry arch to a chamber up to 30m high. Immediately west of Gârda de Sus is the scattered village of **Arieşeni**, with many guesthouses along the road as it rises to the Vârtop Pass at the boundary of Bihor county (see page 318).

Scărişoara ice cave
Daily 9am–6pm • €3

At the west end of Ghețari a track leads to the **Scărişoara ice cave** (Peştera ghețarul), which contains the world's largest and oldest underground glacier, more than 75,000 cubic metres in volume, preserving evidence of climatic change over 4000 years. Steps descend from a large sinkhole into the main chamber, and you can continue to the "church", so-called because of its pillar-like ice formations; lower parts are open only to scientists.

ACCOMMODATION
GÂRDA DE SUS AND GHEȚARI

GÂRDA DE SUS

Mama Uța Str. Centrului 97 ☎0735 164 098, ⓦmamauta.ro. A busy pension-restaurant-campsite on the main road 2km west of the village with a selection of basic rooms (doubles and triples) in three wooden villas; there's also a short ski slope with chairlift across the river to the south. Breakfast €4. Camping per person **€3.50**, room **€25**

Pensiunea Danciu Str. Centrului 51 ☎0763 131 329, ⊜liviu_idanciu@yahoo.com. This pleasant riverside restaurant and terrace, 200m from the bridge and road junction, also has comfortable rooms, both with and without bathrooms. Breakfast €3. **€18**

GHEȚARI

Pensiunea Poiana Ghețar ☎0745 283 430, ⊜lavy_pasca@yahoo.com. This modern wooden chalet near the cave has four rooms with hydromassage showers and a kitchen. **€20**

Pensiunea Scărişoara no. 242 ☎0744 528 363, ⓦpensiuneascarisoara.ro. A 15min walk from the cave, this large and well-organized guesthouse serves its own home-grown food as far as possible; ten en-suite doubles and three triples with shared bathrooms. **€19**

The Padiş plateau

The **Padiş plateau** (Plateul Padiş) is at the heart of a classic **karst** area, with streams vanishing underground and reappearing unexpectedly, and dips and hollows everywhere, all promising access to the huge cave and river systems that lie beneath. The road from Sudrigiu (to the west in Bihor county) has now been paved, and the north–south route between Huedin and Albac via Padiş and Horea is largely paved; the plateau is at risk of uncontrolled development but there is still plenty of enjoyable **hiking** here on easy woodland trails that drop suddenly into gigantic sinkholes.

Buses (weekdays only) depart Huedin for Răchiţele, Doda Pilii and Poiana Horea, where there are guesthouses bookable through Johan's Green Mountain Holidays (see page 204); from here it's an easy day's hike to the *Padiş* cabana (☎0259 130 737 or ☎0788 561 223), focal point for the region's trails. Continuing west on the forestry road from the *Padiş* cabana for 3km you'll come to the park's Padiş visitor centre, not far south of the *Vărăşoaia* cabana (☎0788 601 815), a quieter (and cleaner) place to stay on the trail (marked with blue stripes) northwest towards Stâna de Vale, and the Padiş cave (by a trail marked with red stripes). It's a slightly shorter hike from Doda Pilii to Padiş via IC Ponor, where the *Sat de Vacanţa* (☎0744 272 465) consists of a cabana and eight biggish *casuţe*; there's also the *Pensiunea Alex* (☎0728 095 872, ⓦpensiunepadis.ro; €24), a comfortable place with a swimming pool.

The Crişul valley

From Cluj, the DN1 (E60) heads west along the verdant **Crişul valley**, shadowed most of the way by the railway. A dozen trains a day run from Cluj to Huedin and Oradea; buses are less frequent. The Dutch-owned *Camping Eldorado*, just west of Gilău at km496 (☎0745 930 945, ⓦcampingeldorado.com; mid-April to mid-Oct; €8.50), is one of Romania's finest campsites, also with wooden cabins and apartments, plus pool and café. You'll find a rich choice of other accommodation options along or just off this route, including in **Gura Răştii**, **Valea Ierii** and **Izvoru Crişului** (Körösfó) – this last

---

HIKES ON THE PADIŞ PLATEAU

Of the various **trails** from the *Padiş* cabana, the most popular, marked with blue dots, is a three-hour hike south to the **Cetăţile Ponorului** (Citadels of Ponor), where an 80m-high portal leads into a spectacular series of karst sinkholes up to 150m deep, which can be viewed from metal platforms. There's a good camping spot en route at Glăvoi and the wooden chalets of Cazare Padiş-Glăvoi (☎0725 863 653, ⓦpadis-glavoi.ro); a little further south is the excellent *Cetăţile Ponorului* cabana (☎0740 007 814, ⓦpadis.ro; €30) with two- and four-beds rooms, with and without bathrooms, plus eating possibilities. A trail from the Citadels (marked by yellow dots) leads north for 2km to the **Focul Viu ice cave** (viewed from a wooden balcony) and back to *Padiş*. Alternatively, head south from Ponor to Arieşeni (see page 213) in three hours following red stripes and triangles, or west from Focul Viu to Pietroasa (see page 318) in two and a half hours, following yellow dots and blue crosses.

North of the *Padiş* cabana, you can hike to the **Cetaţea Rădesei** cave; follow red stripes along a track to the forestry road and head north. Ten minutes beyond the Vărăşoaia Pass, take another path (red dots) to the right of the citadel itself. Here you follow the stream through a cave – slightly spooky but quite safe, although a flashlight helps – and return by the overground route (marked by red dots) to see the various skylights from above.

Other hikes simply follow forestry roads, west to Pietroasa (marked by blue crosses), east to Răchiţele or Poiana Horea (unmarked), or northwest to **Stâna de Vale** (red stripes). This last route continues from Vărăşoaia, climbing to the Cumpănăţelu saddle (1640m) and eventually turning right off the ridge to descend through forest to the resort (see page 317).

From the *Padiş* cabana you can also hike southeast to Scărişoara in five hours along a marked track, or southwest to Vârtop in three to four hours, following red stripes and triangles.

THE CULTURE OF THE KALOTASZEG

The area just west of Cluj is known to Hungarians as **Kalotaszeg**, and, since the great Hungarian Millennium Exhibition of 1896, they have revered it as the region where authentic Magyar culture has survived uncorrupted. It's common to see local people selling handicrafts by the roadside – particularly to Hungarian tourists on pilgrimages to the wellsprings of their culture.

The local **embroidery** is particularly famous, usually consisting of stylized leaves and flowers, in one bold colour (usually bright red) on a white background; the style is known as *írásos*, meaning "drawn" or "written", because the designs are marked on the cloth (traditionally with mixed milk and soot) before being stitched. The Calvinist churches are noted for their **coffered ceilings**, with square panels (known as "cassettes") beautifully painted in the eighteenth century, along with the pews and galleries, in a naïf style similar to the embroidery.

The composers **Béla Bartók and Zoltán Kodály** collected Transylvanian crafts, and Bartók's assortment of carved furniture from Izvoru Crişului (Körösfó) can be seen in his home in Budapest. Their main project, however, was to collect **folk music**. Starting in 1907, they managed to record and catalogue thousands of melodies, despite local suspicion of the "monster" (the apparatus for recording onto phonograph cylinders). They also discovered a rich vein of inspiration for their own compositions; Bartók declared that a genuine peasant melody was "quite as much a masterpiece in miniature as a Bach fugue or a Mozart sonata".

---

village is essentially one big bazaar selling Magyar crafts, and also has a seventeenth-century walled Calvinist church with an eighteenth-century painted ceiling.

Huedin and Sâncraiu

HUEDIN (Bánffyhunyad), 46km west of Cluj, is a small town with a largely systematized centre; it's notable for its huge Gypsy palaces by the main road to the west. At the central crossroads is a fifteenth-century church with a solid guard-tower and a fine (but delightfully wonky) painted ceiling (key from the parish office opposite). The chief reason for stopping here is to pick up buses to the surrounding valleys. Through buses stop on the main road while local buses leave from the train station, a five-minute walk north of the centre. Most nearby villages are served by two or three buses a day during the week, but there's virtually no service at weekends. The only **accommodation** in Huedin itself are the rooms above *R & R Pizzerie* (Piaţa Victoriei 40; ☎0744 609 740 or ☎0264 353 323; €16) on the main road just east of the centre; there's also the *Motel Montana* (☎0264 353 090, ⊚motelmontana.ro; €22) just east of town at km525. Homestays are a better option, with a dozen or so available just on the main street of **SÂNCRAIU** (Kalotaszentkirály), 6km south, and known for its strong Magyar folklore, celebrated by a week-long dance festival in August and the Rosehip Festival in late October. It's also known for its thirteenth-century church, with a cassette ceiling and cute embroidered hymnbook covers. Signs for Tourist Information bring you to the excellent **Davincze Tours** opposite the church at no. 291 (☎0264 257 580, ⊚kalotaszeg-davincze.ro; €24), where you can stay in rooms with lovely painted furniture and enjoy excellent traditional meals. They also book rooms in guesthouses across the region and run tours, including visiting local craftsmen and musicians Bikes can be rented here or from the Juhász family at no. 123 (☎0745 764 150 or ☎0747 018 350).

Ciucea, Negreni and Şuncuiuş

CIUCEA (Csucsa), 20km west of Huedin by road and rail, is notable for a **museum** (Tues–Sun 10am–5pm; €1; ☎0264 259 003, ⊕muzeu.goga@yahoo.com) dedicated to

---

THE MEASUREMENT OF THE MILK FESTIVAL

The practice of shepherds spending summer in the high pastures protecting the flocks from bears and wolves while making cheese gave rise to **Measurement of the Milk Festivals** (*Măşurisul Laptelui*), the best known of which are held in the villages around Ciucea on the slopes of Măgura Priei, the highest ridge in the Meseş range. At dawn on the first or second Sunday in May, the flocks are brought to a glade outside the village, where the "measurement" takes place. The nanny goats are milked by women and the ewes by shepherds – the yield of each family's animals is measured to determine the share of cheese that they will receive that season. The ritual is followed by much feasting and dancing. Măgura Priei is just 10km or so north of Ciucea, and the festival is reached by buses from Huedin.

3

Octavian Goga, poet and prime minister in 1937 for six chaotic weeks; it's at the east end of the village, by the church (km548.5). This Neo-Gothic house belonged to the wife of Endre Ady, the great figure of early modernist poetry in Hungary, who lived here until 1917; Goga bought it after Ady's death in 1919 and moved a **wooden church** (built in 1575) here from Gălpâia in order to preserve it – old frescoes are faintly traceable in the otherwise blackened interior. Goga's own **mausoleum**, ostentatiously decorated with bright blue mosaics on a silver and gold background, was later built in the grounds.

Just west at km557 is **NEGRENI**, renowned for its huge fair, held since 1815 on the second weekend of October, and also for the best *mici,* with rows of trucks pulled up at roadside shacks.

Local trains stop at **ŞUNCUIUŞ** (Vársonkolyos), 23km west of Ciucea and a short walk from the **Peştera Vântului** (Cave of the Wind), the country's longest cave, with 52km of passages discovered so far; this is now open to visitors (☎0264 597 634, ⍵ pesteravantului.ro), and rafting and climbing are also becoming popular here. You can walk west between the river and railway to the next halt, Peştera, and the **Vadu Crişului** cave (Tues–Sun 9am–5pm; €1; ☎0744 512 926), discovered in 1903 and around 1km-long, around 700 metres of which are visited on a guided tour; it's known in particular for its fine stalactites. It's another kilometre through the limestone gorge to the village of Vadu Crişului (Rév), with a station and guesthouses.

| ACCOMMODATION | CIUCEA, NEGRENI AND ŞUNCUIUŞ |

CIUCEA

Pensiunea Ruta 60 ☎0264 259 051, ⍵ route60.ro. By the highway just west of town, this busy restaurant has a large car park and decent modern rooms; the food is good but service can be poor and rushed. €22

Perla Ardealului ☎0264 258 022. Alongside the Ruta 60, this has a pleasant restaurant with a terrace, and attractive rooms with a lounge area on each floor. €18

VADU CRIŞULUI

Cabana Roua Munţilor no. 76A ☎0723 479 352, ⍵ pensiunearouamuntilor.ro. At the east end of Vadu Crişului, this triangular peach-coloured block has ten comfortable en-suite rooms, a restaurant and bar, jacuzzi and an outdoor pool. €28

Pensiunea Cori-Men Str. Haltii 69A ☎0740 242 118. Just 50m from the station (and 2km south of the E70) this friendly place has two houses each with two bedrooms and a shared bathroom. €16

Northern Transylvania

The counties of Sălaj and Bistriţa-Năsăud (and the northernmost part of Cluj county), stretching from the Apuseni mountains to the Eastern Carpathians, are historically referred to as **Northern Transylvania**. Travelling from Cluj to Maramureş, or eastwards over the Carpathians into Moldavia, the roads are fast and direct (the railways less so), but it's worth considering detours in this little-visited region. To the west, the chief attraction is the idyllic rural scenery of unspoiled Sălaj county, with its many old wooden churches.

Bonțida

From Cluj, the DN1C (E576) and a rail line head north to Gherla and Dej, passing **BONȚIDA** (Bonchida), site of **Bánffy Castle** (daily 8am–8pm; €2), once known as "the Versailles of Transylvania". A Renaissance mansion was built in 1437–1543, with a large U-shaped Baroque palace added in the mid-eighteenth century by the great Austrian architect Fischer von Erlach the Younger. In 1944 its owner was Miklos Bánffy, a Hungarian diplomat who was sent to make peace with the advancing Red Army; in revenge, the retreating Germans virtually destroyed the palace. In 2001, two years after the World Monuments Fund placed Bonțida on its list of the world's one hundred most endangered monuments, a Built Heritage Conservation Training Centre was established here, whereby craftsmen and architects could be trained while rebuilding the palace, which is ongoing and will be for years. One of the first buildings to be renovated was the old kitchen block, now housing the pleasant little Cultural Café. Entry is through a small gatehouse with a small exhibition and visitor reception area. There is also a community cultural centre in the chapel, and workshops and other facilities in the stables and the Miklós building.

The **Bonțida Cultural Days** attract up to six thousand people on the last weekend of August to see craft demonstrations and classical and traditional music and dance from Romanian, Hungarian Jewish and Rroma groups; however, Bonțida is now best known for Electric Castle (@electriccastle.ro) in mid-July, when over 150 dance acts perform on six stages, and thousands of festival-goers camp in the grounds.

ARRIVAL AND DEPARTURE   **BONȚIDA**

The **train** halt is near the main road at the entrance to the village, from where it's a long (about 4km) but pleasant walk to the palace.

Buses between Cluj and Gherla (every 20min) will also leave you at the turning.

Destinations By bus Bistrița (3 daily; 2hr 20min); Cluj (every 20–30min; 45min); Dej (10 daily; 50min); Gherla (every 20–30min; 25min).

Gherla

GHERLA (Szamosujvár/Neuschloss) has been a centre of Armenian settlement since 1672; their houses have fine gateways topped by carved family crests, but the population is now assimilated with the local Hungarians. The town is also synonymous with its **prison**, in the sixteenth-century Martinuzzi citadel just north of the centre, which held political detainees during the communist era; in one notorious incident in 1977, the prison flooded, but wardens refused to open the cells, resulting in the deaths of some inmates. From the train station, it's under five minutes' walk west along Strada Avram Iancu to Piața Libertății and the Baroque Armenian-Catholic **cathedral**, built in 1748–98. Its greatest treasure is a painting of the *Descent from the Cross*, supposedly by Rubens, in a small chapel to the left of the choir – you may have to ask to see it. The tower, meanwhile, has had a colourful existence, having collapsed no less than three times. Just to the northeast of the square, at Str. Mihai Viteazul 6, the town **museum** (Mon–Fri 9am–2.30pm; €1) houses its collection of icons on glass and musty Armenian vestments behind the superb gateway of a seminary built in 1725; relics from the Roman castrum 1km southwest of town and the ethnographic collection from Sic (see page 218) have also been moved here.

3

By bus BusTrans has departures every 20min between Cluj and Gherla, most terminating at the bus station on Str. Romană, just north of the centre.
Destinations Baia Mare (5 daily); Bistrița (3 daily); Bonțida (every 20–30min); Sic (14 daily).
By train Lying on the Banat–Moldavia axis, Gherla has surprisingly good long-distance connections.

Destinations Baia Mare (3 daily; 3hr 20min); Bistrița (3 daily; 2hr); Cluj (16 daily; 50min–1hr 10min); Dej (20 daily; 20min); Iași (3 daily; 8hr); Sighet (2 daily; 6hr); Suceava (3 daily; 6hr); Timișoara (2 daily; 7hr 40min–9hr 45min).
Tourist information The helpful Gherla Information and Promotion Centre is located at Libertății 3 (☎0264 241 925, ⓦgherla.ro).

ACCOMMODATION AND EATING

Hayak Pub & Café Str. 1 Decembrie 1918 1 ☎0770 471 453. On the main road immediately south of the Armenian cathedral, this warm and stylish café offers good coffee, real Armenian brandy and snacks; there's a garden with a small terrace perched in a tree. Mon–Thurs 8am–midnight, Fri 8am–3am, Sat 10am–3am, Sun noon–midnight.
Mariflor Str. Rebreanu 56 ☎0372 731 777. This big modern place 1km out of town (on the road to Nicula and

Târgu Mureș) has fine rooms and gardens and the area's best restaurant. €36
Pensiunea Ioana Str. Clujului 4 ☎0264 243 173, ⓦpensiuneaioana.ro. Conspicuous, glass-fronted place about 15mins southwest of the centre with fifteen comfortable rooms, a couple of apartments, and a fairly simple restaurant. €18

Nicula and Sic

The monastery of **NICULA**, 7km southeast of Gherla, is the oldest and best-known centre of painting icons on glass, a Transylvanian speciality since the seventeenth century. There's an eighteenth-century wooden church, moved here after the monastery burned down in 1973, and a miraculous icon of the Virgin and Child painted in 1681, which shed tears in 1699 and is the object of a huge pilgrimage on August 15 (the Assumption of the Virgin Mary).

One of the best villages to hear **traditional music** in this area is **SIC** (Szék), 20km southeast of Gherla, with a number of churches and municipal buildings testifying to its importance as a salt mining centre since Roman times. Every street in Sic seems to have its own band (normally just three musicians, on violin, viola and double bass), typically playing ancient Magyar and Romanian melodies woven in with Gypsy riffs. The village **festival** is on August 24, when the largely Magyar population wear their distinctive costumes – men in narrow-brimmed, tall straw hats and blue waistcoats, and women in leather waistcoats, red pleated skirts and black headscarves embroidered with flowers.

There are a dozen or so **buses** a day from Gherla to Sic, six of them coming from Cluj.

ACCOMMODATION

Sóvirág Panzió Str. I 504 ☎0760 237 678, ⓦsoviragpanzio.ro. A charming guesthouse at the entry

to Sic, with ten rooms and two suites featuring authentic painted furniture, and good local food. €25

Bistrița

BISTRIȚA (Bistritz), 68km east of Gherla, and the forested **Bârgău valley** beyond, are the setting for much of Bram Stoker's **Dracula**; it was in Bistrița, on his way to Dracula's castle in the Borgo (Bârgău) valley, that Jonathan Harker received the first hints that something was amiss. The town was first recorded in 1264, when Saxon settlers arrived; they built fine churches in many villages (less fortress-like than those further south) but the bulk of the Saxon population left after World War II. Bistrița was heavily fortified, but nineteenth-century fires have left only vestiges of the citadel along Strada Kogălniceanu and Strada Teodoroiu, including the fifteenth-century **Coopers' Tower** (Turnul Dogarilor), now housing a collection of folklore masks and puppets.

The central square and church

From the train and bus stations, it's about ten minutes' walk to the centre, passing a typically hideous Centru Civic before reaching a more attractive townscape, with arched pedestrian alleys linking mostly north–south streets. The main square, **Piața Centrală**, is dominated by a great Saxon Evangelical **church** (Tues–Sat 10am–noon & 2–5pm, Sun 3–5pm). The fourteenth-century Gothic church was given Renaissance features in 1560–3 by Petrus Italus da Lugano, who introduced the style to Moldavia. A 76m tower was added in 1478–87, the highest stone church tower in Transylvania (although Cluj claims that its is higher, including the cross); rebuilt after fires in 1857 and 2008, there's now a lift up, allowing great **views** of the town and surrounds.

On the northwest side of Piața Centrala, the arcaded **Sugălete** buildings were occupied by merchants from the fifteenth century; you can pop in for a look at the gallery of the **Union of Plastic Artists** (Tues–Sat 11am–2pm & 4–7pm; free). At Str. Dornei 5, the Renaissance **Casa Argintarului** (Silversmith's House) has a gateway supposedly added by Petrus Italus; it's now a German cultural centre (Mon–Fri 8am–4pm; free), including a display of paintings by Bistrița-born Norbert Thomae (1887–1977).

The House of Ion Zidaru and the County Museum

From the central church, it's a pleasant stroll up the pedestrianized main thoroughfare, **Strada Rebreanu** (Holzgasse); with its cafés and sunny lemon- and mint-green-coloured

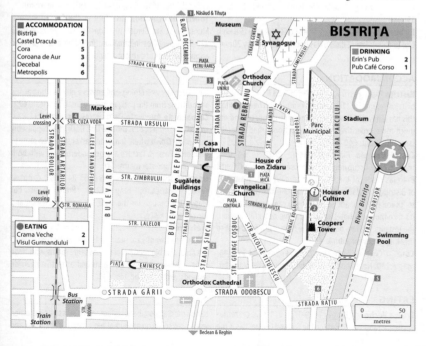

BISTRIȚA FESTIVALS

Bistrița hosts various enjoyable festivals, namely the **Bistrița Medieval Festival** in mid-June, the **International Folklore Festival** in the second week of August, the Brass Band Festival in September and **Bistrița Folk** in mid-November. There are also some interesting festivals in the villages of the Bârgău valley to the east of Bistrița; Prundu Bârgăului, 22km distant, is host to the **Festival of Regele Brazilor** (King of the Fir Trees), traditionally in late June but now in mid-August. This is an opportunity to hear traditional songs and the part-improvised lamentations (*bochet*) telling of a deceased person's life and deeds. Also here are the **Raftsmen's Festival** on the last weekend of March, when unmarried men crown their usual attire of sheepskin jackets with a small hat buried beneath a plume of peacock feathers, and the **Toamnă Bârgăuană** (Bârgău Autumn) in early November.

---

townhouses, the most notable being the **House of Ion Zidaru**, at the southern end. Built in the fifteenth century in late Gothic style, it was given Renaissance features early in the next century by Johannes Murator (John the Mason, or Ion Zidaru in Romanian) and is now a restaurant. Just north is Piața Unirii, where a church built for the Franciscans in 1270–80 was handed to the Orthodox Church in 1948. Just beyond is the synagogue (now an arts centre) and then the **County Museum** (Tues–Sun: April–Sept 10am–6pm; Oct–March 9am–5pm; €1.50) with a collection of Thracian bronzeware, Celtic artefacts and products of the Saxon guilds, mills and presses, as well as a smallish wooden church at the rear.

ARRIVAL AND INFORMATION   BISTRIȚA

By train Trains run from Cluj via Gherla to Bistrița Nord; heading south you'll have to change trains at Sărățel, on the Brașov–Dej line.

Destinations Cluj (3 daily; 3hr 10min); Sărățel (10 daily; 15min).

By bus Baia Mare (2 daily); Borșa (1 daily); Brașov (5 daily); Cluj (8 daily); Iași (2 daily); Năsăud (Mon–Fri every 30min, Sat & Sun 6 daily); Suceava (3 daily); Târgu Mureș (8 daily); Vatra Dornei (6 daily).

By bike The Real Bike rental shop is just north of the centre at B-dul 1 Dec 1918 20 (☎0744 126 487, ⌨realbike.ro).

Tourist information An office in the Centrul Cultural Municipal at Str. Berger 10 (Mon–Fri 9am–5pm; ☎0263 219 919) gives free information (including maps) and can arrange all sorts of outdoor activities.

ACCOMMODATION

Bistrița Piața Petru Rareș 2 ☎0263 231 154, ⌨hotel-bistrita.ro; map p.219. Near the centre (with free parking), this has renovated "business" rooms far superior to (and not much more expensive than) the older ones, and a decent large restaurant. **€40**

Castel Dracula Piatra Fântanele ☎0263 264 010; map p.219. Occupying the supposed location of Count Dracula's castle, at the Tihuța (or Bârgău) pass, 50km east of Bistrița, this place wallows in vampire kitsch, with visits to "Dracula's tomb" and so on – if you can overlook all this, it's a comfortable hotel in an attractive peaceful location; the restaurant is less good, but the terrace is a good spot to break a journey for a drink. **€50**

Cora Str. Codrișor 23 ☎0263 221 231 or ☎0744 957 746; map p.219. Not the most attractive or upmarket place, but it is extremely welcoming, and enjoys a quiet setting across a footbridge from the park; rooms are small but clean. **€22**

Coroana de Aur Piața Petru Rareș 4 ☎0263 211 872, ⌨hcda.ro; map p.219. Dracula fans flock here, supposedly the *Golden Crown* where Jonathan Harker stayed en route to the Borgo Pass; in fact it's a large modern place with both three- and four-star rooms. **€48**

Decebal Str. Cuza Vodă 2B ☎0263 212 568, ⌨hotel-decebal-bistrita.ro; map p.219. Pretty basic but reasonable enough for the price; it's near the market and the rail lines. **€22**

Metropolis Str. Parcului 19 ☎0263 205 020, ⌨hotelmetropolis.ro; map p.219. Easily the best hotel in the area, this big modern place has large rooms with huge beds, a swimming pool and gym and attractive riverside grounds; excellent food, too. **€30**

EATING

Crama Veche Str. Berger 10 ☎0730 011 812, ⌨crama-veche.ro; map p.219. Behind the Cultural Centre, this is the town's most atmospheric restaurant, thanks to its costumed waitresses scuttling around at high speed in the cellar and the vast park-side terrace; the food, mostly grilled meats, is superb, and there's draft beer too. To round it off, there's live folk or ancient music several evenings a week. Daily noon–midnight.

Visul Gurmandului Str. Rebreanu 45 ☎0752 225 554, ⓦpizza20.ro; map p.219. A commendable pizzeria on the corner of Piața Unirii, under the arch and upstairs; pizza aside, there's plenty else on the menu including pasta, grilled meats and some terrific soups. Mon–Sat 10am–11pm, Sun 1–11pm.

DRINKING

Erin's Pub Str. Șincai 19 ☎ 0743 123 124, ⓦerinspub. ro; map p.219. A cheery Irish pub with a busy kitchen that churns out everything from burgers and pizza to a full menu of *ciorbă*, pasta and grilled meats. Mon–Thurs 9am–midnight, Fri 9am–2am, Sat 2pm–2am, Sun 2pm–midnight.

Pub Café Corso Piața Mică 33 ☎0753 074 959; map p.219. An attractive café, with a secluded mezzanine gallery, that turns into a late-night bar. Mon–Wed 8am–1am, Thurs–Sat 8am–5am, Sun noon–midnight.

3

Moldavia

GHIMEŞ-FĂGET, BACĂU COUNTY

Moldavia

A large swathe of land covering the easternmost portion of Romania, Moldavia used to be twice its present size, having at various times included Bessarabia (the land beyond the River Prut) and Northern Bucovina (on the edge of the Carpathians). Both territories were annexed by Stalin in 1940, severing cultural and family ties, though these have been revived since the fall of communism, especially between Moldavia and the former Bessarabia (now the sovereign Republic of Moldova).

Moldavia's complex history is best understood in relation to the cities of **Iaşi** and **Suceava**, the former capitals of the region. The former is one of the country's most appealing destinations, with numerous churches and monasteries retained from its heyday as the Moldavian capital, and a strong cultural scene. Suceava, meanwhile, is symptomatic of many towns and cities in Moldavia, a typical new-town development marred by hideous concrete apartment blocks and factories, though it does retain some significant historical associations. Suceava also acts as the main base for the jewels in the Moldavian crown, the **painted monasteries of southern Bucovina**, secluded in lush valleys near the Ukrainian border. Their medieval frescoes of redemption and damnation blaze in polychromatic splendour – Voroneţ and Suceviţa boast peerless examples of the Last Judgement and the Ladder of Virtue, while Moldoviţa is famous for its fresco of the Siege of Constantinople. The unpainted Putna monastery, final resting place of Stephen the Great, draws visitors interested in Romanian history.

Elsewhere, the countryside looks fantastic, with picturesque villages dwarfed by the flanks of the Carpathians. Just over halfway to Suceava, Neamţ county's principal towns are **Piatra Neamţ** and **0 Neamţ** which, though nothing special, serve as bases for Moldavia's historic convents – **Neamţ**, **Agapia** and **Văratec** – the eclectic **Neculai Popa Museum** in Tărpeşti, and the weirdly shaped **Ceahlău massif**, whose magnificent views and bizarrely weathered outcrops make this one of Romania's most dramatic hiking spots. Backwaters such as **Ghimeş** in the Magyar-speaking **Csángó region** are worth investigating if you're interested in rural life, and there are also numerous local **festivals**.

GETTING AROUND   **MOLDAVIA**

By train and maxitaxi Public transport in the region is fairly good, with decent rail and bus (maxitaxi) links between all the major centres and many of the smaller towns – however, without your own transport, getting to the monasteries will prove difficult.

The Csángó region

The name "**Csángó**" is thought to derive from the Hungarian for "wanderer", referring to those Székely (see page 180) who fled here from religious persecution in Transylvania during the fifteenth century, to be joined by others escaping military conscription in the seventeenth and eighteenth centuries. There is evidence that Hungarians have been present in this area for even longer than that, however; the true origin of the Csángó remains a subject of contentious debate. Once, there were some forty **Csángó villages** in Moldavia, a few as far east as present-day Ukraine, but today their community has contracted into a core of about five thousand people living between Adjud and Bacău, and in **Ghimeş** at the upper end of the Trotuş (Tatros) valley; this is the largest and most rewarding of the Csángó settlements, and the only one that can be visited with any ease.

Highlights

❶ Ghimeş An isolated Hungarian enclave perched on the old Habsburg-Ottoman border, this quiet village is surrounded by rolling green hills. See page 227

❷ Agapia monastery This picture-perfect convent, where over four hundred nuns live in trim cottages, is one of the spiritual centres of the Romanian Orthodox Church. See page 233

❸ Neculai Popa Museum A delightful collection of folk sculpture and other curiosities, set in the rugged village of Tărpeşti, south of Târgu Neamţ. See page 234

❹ The Ceahlău massif Bucovina is the most forested region of Romania, and the hills and rock formations of the massif offer wilderness on an impressive scale. See page 235

❺ Iaşi The old Moldavian capital is full of surprises, not least some superb religious architecture and a vibrant cultural scene. See page 237

❻ Bucovina pensions Stay at least a night in one of the dozens of hospitable Bucovina guesthouses such as *Casa Cristian* in Gura Humorului, where you can eat traditional meals made from home-grown produce. See page 258

❼ The Ladder of Virtue, Suceviţa monastery This splendid, richly detailed ensemble is just one of the unforgettable frescoes of Bucovina's painted monasteries. See page 263

HIGHLIGHTS ARE MARKED ON THE MAP ON PAGE 226

Most rural Csángó are fervently religious and fiercely conservative, retaining a distinctive folk costume and dialect; their music is harsher and sadder than that of their Magyar kinsfolk in Transylvania, although their dances are almost indistinguishable from those of their Romanian neighbours. Mutual suspicions and memories of earlier injustices and uprisings made this a sensitive area in communist times. While allowing them to farm and raise sheep outside the collectives, the Party tried to dilute the Csángó and stifle their culture by settling Romanians in new industrial towns like Oneşti. Things are a lot freer now, and the idyllic upper valley of the Csángó region is frequently visited during the summer by tour groups from Budapest, as well as a few independent travellers. The tourist infrastructure in these parts, however, remains fairly poor, so bring what supplies and money you're going to need with you.

HIGHLIGHTS

1 Ghimeş
2 Agapia Convent
3 Neculai Popa Museum
4 The Ceahlău massif
5 Iaşi
6 Bucovina pensions
7 The Ladder of Virtue, Suceviţa monastery

Ghimeş

Nearly all of the residents of **GHIMEŞ** (Ghimeş-Făget or Gyimesbükk) are Hungarian, though there is a small Gypsy population, which, unusually, is well integrated into village life. This helps to account for the strong musical tradition, most in evidence at the **winter fair** held annually on January 20–21. Ghimeş' appeal lies in its tranquil setting, but the town does have a few modest sights. The village itself, divided in two by the Trotuş River, is also an inviting place to take a walk – its houses are neat and colourful, with many boasting intricately carved eaves and flower gardens, and its streets are enlivened by the various farm animals wandering about. Ghimeş's handful of commercial establishments are all in the centre of town, opposite the vast train station, built in the nineteenth century to handle customs and immigration formalities.

Otherwise, the area's remoteness makes it ideal for **hiking**, and a series of little-used trails, including several longer routes into Transylvania, is delineated on the 1:60,000 DIMAP map of the area, sold at the *Deáky Panzió* pension (see below).

Customs house and Castle

1.5km east of the train station

The village's principal monument, at least for those who wish to contemplate the injustices of the Trianon Treaty after World War I (under which Hungary was forced to cede Transylvania to Romania), is the derelict nineteenth-century **customs house** that marked the old border of Transylvania and Moldavia and, earlier, the Habsburg and Ottoman empires. It's just off the main road, 1.5km east of the station. The steps behind it lead up to the insubstantial ruins of **Rákóczi Castle**, built in 1626 by Prince Gábor Bethlen – more than the ruins, though, it's the **view** of the Trotuş valley from here that makes the climb worthwhile. This is also the beginning of the path that leads up the ridge of Papoj mountain (1271m).

Gyimesi Hazimuseum, church and chapel

Opposite the train station, the tiny **Gyimesi Házimúseum** (no set hours; free; call at the house to the rear) displays a jumble of rural memorabilia, including pottery, textiles and local photographs. The main **church**, rebuilt in 1976, is 200m up from the station; more interesting, and a good place to picnic, is the small wooden **chapel** that overlooks the town from a hilltop meadow across the river. Reaching it entails scaling a few fences, but nobody seems to mind. East towards the head of the valley, Lunca de Jos (Gyimesközeplok) and Lunca de Sus (Gyimesfelsólok) are Csángó villages just across the border in Transylvania.

ARRIVAL AND DEPARTURE   GHIMEŞ

By train Adjud is the junction on the main Bucharest–Suceava line for the branch line west to Oneşti, Ghimeş and Transylvania. However, if you're coming to Ghimeş from the north, rather than riding all the way down to Adjud, it may be quicker to disembark at Bacău, catch a bus to Comăneşti, and wait there for the next train up the valley. The train station is smack bang in the centre of town.

Destinations Adjud (6 daily; 3hr–3hr 15min); Miercurea Ciuc (4 daily; 1hr 30min); Siculeni (5 daily; 1hr 10min).
By bus What few buses stop here drop off along the main street, Str. Principală.
Destinations Bacău (4 daily; 2hr 30min).

ACCOMMODATION AND EATING

Deáky Panzió Str. Principală 40 (from the station, turn left and follow the main road downhill for about 1km, past the post office until you see the sign on your right) ☎ 0234 385 621, ✉ deakyandras@xnet.ro. An attractive pension on a large converted farm by the river, this is the main place to stay in the village. Spread around the neat grounds are small wooden bungalows, each containing en-

suite rooms sleeping two or three people. The pension's very good restaurant is pretty much the only place in the village to eat, with excellent food and wine from local farms. If you stay for a few days, your visit is likely to coincide with a group of Hungarian tourists coming for dinner and an evening of wine, dancing and Csángó and Gypsy music. May–Oct. **€25**

4

Vár campsite Str. Principală 2 ☎ 0234 385 655. Located 200m further along from the *Deáky Panzió*, this tidy little site also has small wooden huts, though they're somewhat more basic. Camping **€6**, hut **€18**

Piatra Neamț

Hemmed in by the Carpathian foothills, **PIATRA NEAMȚ** is one of Romania's oldest settlements, once inhabited by a string of Neolithic and Bronze Age cultures, as well as the Dacians, whose citadel has been excavated on a nearby hilltop. The town was first recorded in Roman times as Petrodava, and in 1453 under the name of Piatra lui Craciun (Christmas Rock); its present title may refer to the German ("Neamț") merchants who once traded here, or may derive from the old Romanian word for an extended family or nation ("Neam"). As the county seat, the town is a lively place, and retains a surprisingly large number of important historical and religious sites, notably up on **Piața Libertății** (effectively the remains of the old town), which retains a fantastic ensemble of medieval-inspired architecture.

Biserica Sf Ioan and Turnul Clopotniță

Piața Libertății

The spireless **Biserica Sf Ioan** (Church of St John) originally formed part of a Princely Court (Curtea Domnească) founded in 1468, of which only vestiges remain. Erected by Stephen the Great in 1497–98, hard on the heels of his seminal church at Neamț monastery, it set a pattern for Moldavian church architecture thereafter. The upper part is girdled by niches outlined in coloured brick, in which it was probably intended to paint saintly images. Beside the door, a votive inscription by his son Bogdan the One-Eyed presages a host of tacky modern paintings of Stephen inside the almost blackened interior.

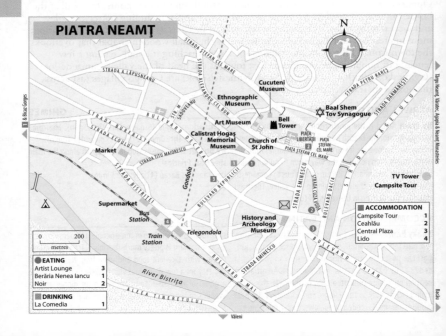

MY HEART BELONGS TO DADA

The magazine *Simbolul* ("The Symbol") was founded in 1912 by three Jewish schoolboys in Bucharest: Ion Vinea, Marcel Iancu and Samuel Rosenstock. All three were to play leading roles in the development of avant-garde art, but it was Rosenstock, calling himself **Tristan Tzara** (1896–1963), who was to achieve greatest fame. A poet and playwright, he was a central figure in the absurdist **Dada movement**, founded at Zürich's *Cabaret Voltaire* in 1916; he moved to Paris in 1920 but broke with Dadaism in 1923 when its French leaders, such as André Breton and Louis Aragon, turned to Surrealism. Iancu, better known as **Marcel Janco** (1895–1984), also went to Zürich, returning in 1922 to Bucharest and, with **Ion Vinea** (1895–1964), founding the magazine *Contimperanul* ("The Contemporary") which ran until 1932. Its manifesto (similar to that of the Dutch group De Stijl) was more Constructivist than Dadaist. Janco also became the leading architect of Cubist and International Style buildings in Bucharest; after World War II he emigrated to Israel, dying there in 1984.

A younger artist, and perhaps the most important, was **Victor Brauner** (1903–66) who was born in Piatra Neamț and studied briefly at the Bucharest School of Fine Arts; he was involved with the Constructivists before leaving for Paris in 1930. André Breton saw him as "the quintessential magic artist"; a painter of premonitions, as well as a sculptor and print-maker, he was obsessed by blindness, painting figures without eyes, even in a self-portrait. Ironically, at a Surrealist party in 1938 a glass was thrown and smashed, putting out his left eye. He spent World War II in the French Alps, returning to Paris in 1945 and breaking from the Surrealists in 1948.

A few paces from the church stands the sturdy **Turnul Clopotniță** (Bell Tower; daily 9am–5pm; €1), a magnificent Gothic structure with a fantastic witch's hat brim raised in 1499, also by Stephen the Great; lit up at night, it looks suitably spooky against the backdrop of the forested hills. If the tower is closed, ask someone at the Cucuteni Museum (see page 229) to let you in.

Muzeul de Etnografie and Muzeul de Artă

Piața Libertății 2 • Both Tues–Sun: April–Sept 10am–6pm; Oct–March 9am–5pm • Both €1 • ☎ 0233 216 808

In a building that combines folk architecture with Art Nouveau is the **Muzeul de Etnografie** (Ethnographic Museum), which has four rooms of nicely presented exhibits on the folk culture of Neamț county – with good English translation – as well as a number of masks made by Neculai Popa (see page 234), typically used during winter carnivals. Next door, a Brâncovenesc mansion with ceramic studs echoing those on the church houses the **Muzeul de Artă** (Art Museum). Works are mostly by local painters, like Constantin Stahi, whose rural landscapes (*Peasants Ploughing*) are not dissimilar to Grigorescu's. There's also an impressive set of sculpture by Ion Jalea (see page 361), notably the sizeable *Dragos and the Bison*.

Muzeul de Artă Eneolitică Cucuteni

Str. Ștefan cel Mare 3 • Tues–Sun: April–Sept 10am–6pm; Oct–March 9am–5pm • €1 • ☎ 0233 226 471

The **Muzeul de Artă Eneolitică Cucuteni** (Cucuteni Museum) is so named after the Cucuteni culture, one of the most important late Neolithic civilizations, which flourished from 4500 to 2500 BC and comprised some three thousand settlements scattered throughout eastern Romania, Moldavia and southeast Ukraine. Most characteristic of the Cucuteni is its ceramic work, a superb collection of which is on display here – painted bowls, vases, amphorae and statuettes. The museum's most celebrated pieces are *Soborul Zeițelor* (The Goddess Council), a group of 21 seated female statuettes, and the wonderfully expressive *Gânditorul* (The Philosopher), one of only two ever discovered – the other resides in Bucharest's National Museum.

Sinagoga Baal Shem Tov and Sinagoga Noua

Str. Dimitrie Ernica 7 • Sinagoga Baal Shem Tov Mon–Fri 8am–1pm; Sinagoga Noua normally closed • ☎ 0233 223 815

Baal Shem Tov, the founder of Hasidism (a branch of Judaism based on the omnipresence of God and man's communion with Him), was for a short time supposed to have lived close to Piatra Neamț, occasionally visiting to pray at the eighteenth-century wooden **Sinagoga Baal Shem Tov** (Baal Shem Tov Synagogue). This is almost the only survivor of hundreds of similar buildings that were found across Eastern Europe until World War II. Following extensive renovation in 2009, it was revealed that the synagogue was likely built on an earlier stone one, possibly dating from the sixteenth century. The synagogue is completely surrounded by other buildings, so that you would have no idea of its existence were it not for the stone tablets on the roof. It seems like an annexe to the adjacent newer wing, and both are overshadowed by the late nineteenth-century white-stone **Sinagoga Noua** (Temple Synagogue), which houses frescoes representing Jerusalem and the Holy Land.

Muzeul Memorial Calistrat Hogaş

Str. Calistrat Hogaş • Tues–Sun: April–Sept 10am–6pm; Oct–March 9am–5pm • €1

The unassuming former home of writer Calistrat Hogas (1848–1917) is now **Muzeul Memorial Calistrat Hogaş**, a memorial museum to a man who praised the charms of Piatra Neamț when it consisted largely of Alpine-style chalets; he came to the city in 1869, living in the house from 1871 until his death. The lack of English captioning doesn't diminish the enjoyment of this charming little exhibition, which includes first editions, various bits of attire, and his chess set and pistol (Hogaş being a keen hunter).

ARRIVAL AND DEPARTURE   PIATRA NEAMȚ

By train and bus From the train and bus stations, side by side on Str. Bistritei, it's a 10min walk up B-dul Republicii to Piața Libertății.

Destinations (train) Bacău (8 daily; 1hr 10min–1hr 30min); Bicaz (3 daily; 40min); Bucharest (2 daily; 6hr 40min).

Destinations (bus) Bacău (hourly; 1hr 10min); Bicaz (hourly; 30min); Brașov (3 daily; 6hr); Bucharest (7 daily; 6hr); Comănești (2 daily; 2hr 10min); Gheorgheni (3 daily; 2hr 20min); Iași (hourly; 2hr 15min); Poiana Largului, for Durău (3 daily; 2hr); Suceava (4 daily; 3hr 30min); Târgu Mureș (1 daily; 4hr); Târgu Neamț (hourly; 1hr); Vatra Dornei (2 daily; 5hr).

GETTING AROUND

By telegondola Located directly in front of the train station (see above), the gondola (Mon, Tues & Thurs–Sun 10am–8pm, Wed noon–8pm; €5) transports passengers on a 6min ride up to Cozla mountain (657m).

ACCOMMODATION

Campsite Tour Aleea Tineretului (1km west along Str. Bistriței until you reach the footbridge) ☎ 0233 217 835, ⓦ campsitetourpiatraneamt.ro; map p.228. Well-kept site just across the river, which also has simple wooden cabins with shared bathrooms. Camping **€6**, cabin **€15**

Ceahlău Piața Ştefan cel Mare 3 ☎ 0233 219 990, ⓦ hotelceahlau.ro; map p.228. Hulking concrete block concealing rooms that won't particularly set the pulse racing, though the jet showers might; fairly priced though. **€38**

Central Plaza Piața Petrodava 1 ☎ 0233 216 230, ⓦ centralplazahotel.ro; map p.228. The best of the town's accommodation, a renovated high-rise with consummate, light-filled rooms in fetching brown and beige colours. **€70**

Lido B-dul Piața Gării 5 ☎ 0233 226 349, ⓦ pensiune-lido.com; map p.228. Smack bang in between the train and bus stations, this outwardly dowdy building conceals better than expected rooms, with decent furnishings, wood-effect vinyl and spotlessly clean bathrooms. Breakfast €4. **€25**

EATING

Artist Lounge Piața Mihail Kogălniceanu 2 ☎ 0233 219 663, ⓦ artistlounge.ro; map p.228. Despite the slightly pretentious name, this brazenly colourful restaurant is not bad at all, offering a prodigious and appealing menu featuring the likes of pumpkin cream soup with bacon, and duck breast with vanilla parsnip puree (€10). Mon–Thurs 9am–midnight, Fri 9am–2am, Sat 10am–2am, Sun 10am–midnight.

Berăria Nenea Iancu B-dul Republicii 5 ☎0233 213 114; map p.228. Cool, industrial-styled interior where you can chomp away on spicy sausages or burger and fries, all washed down with one of several draught beers on offer, including the delicious, unfiltered *Nenea Iancu* from Bucharest, in addition to dozens of bottled varieties. Mon–Fri 9.30am–midnight, Sat & Sun 11am–midnight.

★ **Noir** Piaţa Mihail Kogălniceanu ☎0233 211 886, ⓦrestaurantnoir.ro; map p.228. One of the best restaurants in Moldavia, *Noir* offers a terrific menu with smart but simple dishes like pan-fried perch fillet in a lemon caper sauce with cherry tomatoes (€10) keeping a loyal band of punters happy. The sleek decor, combining wood-panelled walls and a jet-black painted ceiling, alongside moody lighting, adds further poise to proceedings. Daily noon–11pm.

DRINKING AND NIGHTLIFE

La Comedia B-dul Republicii 20 ☎0744 676 369, ⓦlacomedia.ro; map p.228. Occupying a grand old villa, this comedy- and music-themed bar (the walls are arrayed with lots of vinyl and photos of comedy legends such as Chaplin and Laurel and Hardy) is the best spot in town for a drink, with occasional live music on summer weekends. Mon–Thurs & Sun 10am–10pm, Fri & Sat until midnight.

Târgu Neamţ and around

TÂRGU NEAMŢ, with its systematized concrete centre, is far smaller and duller than Piatra, and therefore a less attractive stopover. However, it does possess Moldavia's finest ruined castle, as well as a couple of worthy memorial houses.

Cetatea Neamţului

1km west along Str. Ştefan cel Mare; from the *La Cetate* pension (see page 232), itself the limit for car access, it's a stiff 15min climb to the entrance • Daily 9am–7pm • €1 • ☎0233 222 011

Visible from the road to Neamţ monastery, but far more impressive at close quarters, the **Cetatea Neamţului** (Neamţ citadel) was founded by Petru I Muşat in 1359 and beefed up by Stephen the Great just in time to withstand a siege by the Turkish Sultan Mohammed II in 1496. Later it was partly demolished on the orders of the Turks, but again saw service in 1691 in the war between Moldavia and Poland. Its military importance waned thereafter, and in 1717 it was almost totally destroyed on the orders of Mihai Racoviţa, erstwhile Prince of Moldavia. Subsequent renovation has quashed much of its historical charm, but it remains a mightily impressive sight. Once you've reached the entrance the approach to the citadel is over a long, curving **wooden bridge** raised on pillars high above a dry moat; the final stretch was originally designed to flip enemies down into an oubliette. Within the **bailey**, a warren of roofless chambers that used to be an arsenal, courthouse and baths surrounds a deep well, ringed by battlements that offer superb views of the Neamţ valley for kilometres around.

Casa Memorială Veronica Micle

Str. Ştefan cel Mare 33 • Tues–Sun: April–Sept 10am–6pm; Oct–March 9am–5pm • €1 • ☎0233 790 594

Somewhat out of kilter with its unprepossessing surrounds, the small and pretty **Casa Memorială Veronica Micle** (Veronica Micle Memorial House) – built in 1834 by Neamţ monastery as a school for monks – was where the eponymous poet, and muse of Mihai Eminescu, lived for three years from 1850 before moving to Iaşi. The three small rooms remain beautifully furnished, as well as holding a wealth of personal possessions, including her binoculars, a mirror, clocks and a desk. Micle, a bust of whom stands in front of the lovely balconied porch, is buried in the grounds of Văratec monastery (see page 232).

4

Casa Memorială Ion Creangă

Str. Ion Creangă 8 • Tues–Sun: April–Sept 10am–6pm; Oct–March 9am–5pm • €1 • ☎ 0233 663 320

South of town, out on the road to Tărpești, stands the **Casa Memorială Ion Creangă** (Ion Creangă Memorial House), birthplace of the eminent nineteenth-century writer. A neat, whitewashed wood-and-clay construction, it manifests a superb shingled roof (which slopes almost all the way down to the ground on one side) and three simple rooms; the largest of these is decked out in peasant furnishings, with another displaying various items belonging to Creangă, including first editions. Together with Eminescu, Creangă was a prominent member of the Junimea literary society in Iași, which is where his cottage is to be found (see page 245).

ARRIVAL AND DEPARTURE TÂRGU NEAMȚ

By bus There are a couple of bus stations in Târgu Neamț; the main bus station (Autogară Mondotour) is a few minutes from the centre on Str. Cuza Vodă, while there's another (Autogară Flozampet) south of the centre out on the road to Piatra Neamț; buses to the Agapia, Neamț and Văratec monasteries depart from the latter.
Destinations Agapia (10 daily; 15min); Bacău (5 daily; 2hr); Bicaz (1 daily; 1hr 45min); Brașov (1 daily; 6hr 30min); Iași (hourly; 2hr); Neamț monastery (7 daily; 20min); Piatra Neamț (hourly; 1hr); Rădăuți (4 daily; 3hr 20min); Suceava (4 daily; 1hr 30min); Târgu Mureș (3 daily; 5hr); Văratec (10 daily; 25min); Vatra Dornei (2 daily; 4hr).
By train The train station is a 20min walk east off the main bus station at the end of Str. Cuza Vodă. There is just one line to Pascani, where you change for trains to Bacău, Iași and Suceava.
Destinations Pascani (6 daily; 40min).

ACCOMMODATION

Pensiunea La Cetate Str. Cetății 33 ☎ 0233 660 249, ⓦ pensiuni-neamt.ro. Just below the citadel, this is the town's one decent place to stay; generously sized rooms with lovely wooden bedsteads and sparkling bathrooms, in addition to a row of tidy little huts, each with double bed and bathroom plus heating. The restaurant here is equally accomplished and makes for a lovely spot to eat, or just for a beer, after viewing the citadel. Huts **€16**, doubles **€26**

Victoria Str. Mihail Kogălniceanu 6 ☎ 0233 790 270, ⓦ hotelvictoria-targuneamt.ro. A dull glass building that offers no visual appeal whatsoever but the rooms are clean and decently furnished. It's located behind the main church on B-dul Ștefan cel Mare, 400m east of the central crossroads in the direction of Iași. **€38**

Mănăstirea Văratec

14km southwest of Târgu Neamț • Open access • Free; museum €1

Hedgerows, alive with sparrows and wagtails, line the narrow road winding through Văratec to the pretty nuns' village and **Mănăstirea Văratec** (Văratec

---

WALKS FROM VĂRATEC

In fine weather, it's an agreeable **walk** through the woods from **Văratec monastery** (see opposite) to Agapia; the 7km trail takes about an hour and a half, starting by house no. 219, back down the road from Văratec Convent. It's also possible to walk along the road connecting the two convents (from Văratec, walk about 1km back towards the main road, then turn left; from Agapia take the asphalt road across the bridge at the end of the nunnery village). Picnic tables are provided, but camping is not allowed. Another beech-tree-lined trail from Văratec, marked by blue dots, leads west to **Sihla hermitage** (2hr), built into the cliffs near the cave of St Teodora, and hidden by strange outcrops. A back road turns off the main road from Târgu Neamț to the Ceahlău massif, 2km west of the turn-off for Neamț monastery (see page 234), and passes the **Sihastria and Secu hermitages** en route to Sihla – an easy 10km hike. The Sihastria hermitage was founded in 1655 and subsequently built over with a new stone church in 1734; the Secu hermitage dates from 1602 and has Renaissance-style paintings inside as well as the grave of Bishop Varlaam, who in 1634 printed *Cazania* ("Romania's teaching book"), the first book written in Romanian.

monastery), its whitewashed walls and balconies enclosing a lovely garden shaded by cedars. The novices inhabit two-storey buildings named after saints, while the older nuns live in cottages. Văratec was founded in the eighteenth century, around a church that no longer exists; the site of its altar is marked by a pond with a statue of an angel. The present **church**, built in 1808, is plain and simple, culminating in two bell-shaped domes. To cope with the harsh winters, the nuns have sensibly installed stoves by the columns dividing the narthex from the nave, so that both chambers are heated. The gilt pulpit and the gallery over the entrance to the narthex are unusual, but the interior painting is not great. There's a **museum of icons** to the south, and an **embroidery school** established by Queen Marie in 1934. It's an odd but not unfitting site for the **grave of Veronica Micle**, the poet loved by Eminescu, who couldn't afford to marry her after the death of her despised husband (see page 245); she killed herself two months after Eminescu's death.

ARRIVAL AND DEPARTURE

MĂNĂSTIREA VĂRATEC

Regular **buses** (10 daily; 15min) from Târgu Neamţ (see opposite) drop off right outside the monastery.

ACCOMMODATION

Pensiunea Alina Str Mihai Eminescu 137, Filioara 282 ☎ 0233 244 861. The road between Agapia and Văratec passes through the pretty village of Filioara, where you'll find this friendly place with eight rooms (some triples) and serving excellent meals with produce from the garden. Breakfast €4. **€26**

Mănăstirea Agapia

13km southwest of Târgu Neamţ • Open access • Free; museum €1

An easy, and very lovely, 7km walk from Văratec, **Mănăstirea Agapia** (Agapia monastery) actually consists of two convents a few kilometres apart; most visitors are content to visit only the main complex of **Agapia din Vale** ("Agapia in the valley"), at the end of a village with houses with covered steps. The walls and gate tower aim to conceal rather than to protect; inside is a whitewashed enclosure around a cheerful garden. At prayer times a nun beats an insistent rhythm on a wooden *toaca* while another plays the panpipes; this is followed by a medley of bells, some deep and slow, others high and fast. The convent **church** – much smaller than the one at Văratec – was built in 1644–47 by Prince Basil the Wolf's brother, Gavril Coci. Its helmet-shaped cupola, covered in green shingles, mimics that of the gate tower. After restoration, the interior was repainted between 1858 and 1861 by Nicolae Grigorescu, the country's foremost painter at the time (see page 90); he returned to stay at Agapia from 1901 to 1902.

Grigorescu's close attachment to the convent can also be seen in the **museum**, which stars an entire room of the painter's Renaissance-style work – the most celebrated of which is a large canvas entitled *The Laying of Christ's Body in the Tomb* – as well as portraits of the Vlahuţă family. Icons, vestments and embroidery from the seventeenth and eighteenth centuries complete a sizeable collection. An enticing variety of breads, jams and syrups, all harvested by the nuns, is available from the kiosk outside the convent entrance.

Casa Memorial Alexandru Vlahuţă

Up past the nuns' cottages • Tues–Sun 10am–6pm • €0.50 • ☎ 0233 662 136

Beyond the convent walls is the **Casa Memorial Alexandru Vlahuţă**, the small house where the author (1858–1919) spent summers visiting his mother and sister, who were both nuns here. As well as two traditionally furnished bedrooms, the third room keeps books, photos and mementoes, plus a painting of Vlahuţă and one of his sister

Elizabeta, by Octav Băncila. Downhill by the Topolniţa stream stands a wooden church with three shingled domes and a modern gate tower.

Muzeul Vivant

Roughly 100m back down the road from the convent • Mon–Sat 9am–7pm, Sun 11am–7pm • Free • ☎ 0233 244 848

The **Muzeul Vivant** (Living House) is a neat complex comprising the monastic house, trim gardens and a pottery workshop; you may even catch some of the nuns at work. Despite its dark and dingy interior, the candlelit house – with two cells on each of the upper and lower floors – has some lovely stuff on display, including furnishings, textiles and icons, and, best of all, some fabulous black-and-white photographs depicting the nuns' participation as nurses during the two World Wars.

ARRIVAL AND DEPARTURE   AGAPIA

By bus Buses from Târgu Neamţ drop off outside the Muzeul Vivant, a short walk down from the monastery. From Agapia, buses continue on to Văratec.

Destinations Târgu Neamţ (10 daily; 15min); Văratec (10 daily; 10min).

ACCOMMODATION

Pensiunea Maria At the far end of the village, towards the monastery but still 3km away ☎ 0233 245 004, ⓦ pensiuni-agapia.ro. Decent pension with six tidy, pinewood-furnished rooms and two apartments, a lovely garden and a good restaurant that doubles up as the best place to eat hereabouts. Breakfast €4. Doubles €30, apartments €45

Mănăstirea Neamţ

12km northwest of Târgu Neamţ • Open access • Free • Buses from Târgu Neamţ (7 daily); also frequent services along the main road to the turn-off at km33, with 4km walk to the monastery

The twelfth-century **Mănăstirea Neamţ** (Neamţ monastery) is the oldest in Moldavia and is the region's chief centre of Orthodox culture; it is also the largest men's monastery in Romania, with seventy monks and dozens of seminary students. It was founded as a hermitage, expanded into a monastery in the late fourteenth century by Petru I Muşat, and then rebuilt in the early fifteenth century by Alexander the Good, with fortifications that protected Neamţ from the Turks. It also had a printing house that spread its influence throughout Moldavia. The new church, founded by Stephen the Great in 1497 to celebrate a victory over the Poles, became a prototype for Moldavian churches throughout the next century, and its school of miniaturists and illuminators led the field.

Outwardly, Neamţ resembles a fortress, with high stone walls and its one remaining octagonal corner tower (there used to be four). On the inside of the gate tower, a painted Eye of the Saviour sternly regards the monks' cells with their verandas wreathed in red and green ivy, and the seminary students in black tunics milling around the garden. The sweeping roof of Stephen's church overhangs blind arches inset with glazed bricks, on a long and otherwise bare facade. Its trefoil windows barely illuminate the interior, where pilgrims kneel amid the smell of mothballs and candlewax. At the back of the compound is a smaller church dating from 1826, containing frescoes of the *Nativity* and the *Resurrection*. Outside the monastery stands a large, onion-domed **pavilion** for *Aghiastmatar*, the "blessing of the water", to be taken home in bottles to cure illness.

Muzeul Neculai Popa

Str. Neculai Popa 305, Târpeşti • Daily 8am–8pm • €2 • ☎ 0233 785 111, ⓦ muzeulpopa.ro • Buses from Târgu Neamţ (4 daily; 15min) drop off in the centre of the village; there are many signs indicating the whereabouts of the museum

About 10km southeast of Târgu Neamţ, the ramshackle village of **TĂRPEŞTI** is the location for the delightful **Muzeul Neculai Popa** (Neculai Popa Museum), the family home of the eponymous folk artist (1919–2010).

Set in Popa's own yard, the museum's diverse works (all collected by Popa himself) are displayed with care and wit. The main building is devoted to Popa's folk art collections, including paintings by Romanian artists – starring some delightful Naïve paintings – an unusually good set of icons and old Moldavian handicrafts such as thick leather belts and painted trousseaux. The colourful masks and folk costumes on display in the second building, made by both Popa and his wife, Elena, are occasionally used in children's pageants recounting legends such as that of Iancu Jianu, an eighteenth-century forest bandit known as the Robin Hood of Wallachia. Popa's son, Damian, now runs the museum, and is only too happy to show visitors around (his English is excellent); there is also a gallery where folk art and icons are sold. His life-size wooden sculptures in the garden are of various family members, including a wonderful one of Popa himself, with tools in hand.

Ceahlău National Park

West of Târgu Neamţ, 60km beyond the turning to Neamţ monastery • €2, also applicable for stays in Durău (see below) and payable at the gate uphill from the resort or in the cabanas; free leaflet map, though more detailed versions available to buy

The **Ceahlău massif**, now protected as the **Ceahlău National Park** (ⓦceahlaupark.ro), is aptly designated on local maps as a *zona abrupt*, rising above neighbouring ranges in eroded crags whose fantastic shapes were anthropomorphized in folk tales and inspired Eminescu's poem, *The Ghosts*. The Dacians believed that Ceahlău was the abode of their supreme deity, Zamolxis, and that the gods transformed the daughter of Decebal into the Dochia peak. The massif is composed of Cretaceous sediments – especially conglomerates, which form pillar-like outcrops – and covered with stratified belts of beech, fir and spruce, with dwarf pine and juniper above 1700m. Its **wildlife** includes chamois, lynx, capercaillie, bears and boars, and the majestic Carpathian stag. Ceahlău's isolation is emphasized by the huge, artificial **Lake Bicaz** (Lacul Izvoru Muntelei) that half-encircles its foothills. A hydroelectric dam, built in 1950, rises at the lake's southern end, 3km beyond the small, systematized town of **BICAZ**, which has a small **Muzeul de Istorie Bicaz** (History Museum; Tues–Sun 9am–5pm; €1), just north of the centre at Str. Barajului 3, with a display on the building of the dam and a small art exhibit.

ARRIVAL AND INFORMATION

CEAHLAU NATIONAL PARK

By bus You can get to the dam from Piatra Neamţ by hourly maxitaxis (30min), which terminate halfway between Bicaz and the dam.

By train The train station in Bicaz is a 10min walk from the centre on Str. Republicii.

Destinations Bacău (3 daily; 2hr); Piatra Neamţ (3 daily; 40min).

Tourist information The Ceahlău National Park visitor centre, in Izvorul Muntelui (Tues–Sun 9am–5pm; ☎0233 256 600, ⓦceahlaupark.ro), has plenty of useful practical information as well as an exhibition and film about the park.

ACCOMMODATION

Bicaz Tourist Complex 500m beyond the dam ☎0748 110 400, ⓦbicazlac.ro. A cobbled road winds down to the lakefront and this tidy complex comprising the *Pension Pescăruş*, the *Lebăda* floating hotel (closed in winter), four-

bed huts and space for camping. Pleasure boats sail from here in summer (€2.50/30min). Camping €4, huts €22, pension double €22, floating hotel double €22

HIKES FROM DURĂU

From the resort, it's a 45-minute walk to the *Fântânele* cabana (1220m; ☎0730 603 803), on the steep, red-striped trail starting at the end of the road. A two-hour route (marked by blue crosses, then red crosses and finally yellow triangles) also runs there via the lovely **Duruitoarea cascade**, 2km from town, which falls a total of 25m in two stages. From Fântânele, the red-striped route (2hr) ascends within sight of the Panaghia rocks and Toaca peak to a plateau with glorious views and, in a further two hours, to the *Dochia* cabana (1750m; ☎0730 603 801). You can also follow red crosses direct from the cascade to Dochia. The route then continues south via several massive rock pillars, passing Ocolaşu Mare – at 1907m, the massif's highest peak – on its way to Poiana Maicilor, where the red-striped route turns downstream to the *Izvoru Muntelui* cabana (☎0233 247 039), while another, less frequented, trail marked with blue crosses runs on to Neagra village, on the road to the Bicaz gorges. Both routes take about two hours from Dochia.

Durău

The main base for hiking (and winter skiing) in the Ceahlău massif is **DURĂU**, on its northwestern side, though it's not reachable by public transport. From the turn-off 7km west of Poiana Largului (and 67km east of Topliţa in Transylvania) it's 12km up a dead-end road to the resort, passing through the village of Ceahlău, where there are various guesthouses. Durău's major draw is the **Ceahlău Feast**, on the second Sunday in August, an opportunity for shepherds to parade in their finery and an attraction for many tourists. It also boasts a small **hermitage** built in 1833, overwhelmed by a modern monastery.

ACCOMMODATION   DURĂU

Bradul 300m to the left from the main crossroads ☎00233 256 501. This is the largest and best of Durău's several hotels, though that doesn't mean it's particularly exciting; still, it's a well-established place with respectable rooms and courteous staff. **€35**

Into Transylvania and north to Vatra Dornei

To the north and south of the Ceahlău massif, narrow valleys enable two routes **into Transylvania**. The northern one crosses the 1112m-high Borsec Pass beyond the alpine spa of Borsec, before descending to Topliţa, in the upper Mureş valley (see page 193). It's a scenic route, with buses heading west to Borsec and some continuing to Topliţa. A better route runs through the **Bicaz gorges** (Cheile Bicazului), 25km upriver from Bicaz, past the lovely village of **Bicaz Ardelean**, which has a wooden church dating from 1829. Sheer limestone cliffs rise as high as 300m above the river, pressing so close around the Gâtul Iadului ("Neck of Hell") that the road is hewn directly into the rockface. The *Cheile Bicazului* cabana, amid the gorges, marks the start of several **hiking** trails, and a longer one ascends from Lacu Roşu (see page 354) to the *Piatra Singuratică* ("Lonely Rock") cabana (☎0744 156 566).

Alternatively, you can head north from Târgu Neamţ via Poiana Largului to Vatra Dornei (see page 270). By bus the 136km journey takes four hours, following the River Bistriţa through a narrow, twisting valley hemmed in by fir-covered peaks. About 20km before Vatra Dornei, you'll see the well-signposted, though now closed, *Zugreni* cabana across the river, from where a trail leads to the heart of the Rarău massif (see page 269).

Iaşi

IAŞI (pronounced "yash"), in the northeast of Moldavia, is the region's cultural capital and by far its most attractive city, the only one where you're likely to want to stay a while. Its university, theatre and resident orchestra rival those of Bucharest – which was merely a crude market town when Iaşi became a princely seat – and give it an air of sophistication enhanced by a large contingent of foreign students. Cementing its place in the nation's heart, Romanians associate Iaşi with the poet Eminescu, and Moldavians also esteem it as the burial place of St Paraschiva.

The majority of Iaşi's sights are strung along a north–south axis through the city, with the anonymous main square, **Piaţa Unirii**, joining the two halves. To the north of the square, beyond the excellent **Museum of the Union**, lie the university district of **Copou**, home to the enlightening **University Museum** as well as parks and gardens, and the residential district of **Ţicău**, location for a couple of memorial houses. South of the square, Iaşi's traditional interplay of civil and religious authority is symbolized by a parade of edifices along Bulevardul Ştefan cel Mare şi Sfânt, where florid public buildings face grandiose churches, not least the magnificent **Church of the Three Hierarchs**. This in turn leads down to the huge **Palace of Culture**, housing several museums, and beyond here, the Nicolina quarter, where you'll find a trio of fabulous hilltop **monasteries**.

Brief history

Iaşi's ascendancy dates from the sixteenth century, when the Moldavian princes (*hospodars*) gave up the practice of maintaining courts in several towns, and settled permanently in Iaşi. This coincided with Moldavia's gradual decline into a Turkish satellite, ruled by despots who endowed Iaşi with churches and monasteries to trumpet their earthly glory and ensure their eternal salvation. **Basil the Wolf** (Vasile Lupu, 1634–53) promulgated a penal code whereby rapists were raped and arsonists burned alive; he also founded a printing press and school, which led to the flowering of Moldavian literature during the brief reign, from 1710–11, of the enlightened **Dimitrie Cantemir**.

After Cantemir's death, Moldavia fell under the control of **Greek Phanariots**, originally from the Phanar district of Constantinople (Fener in modern Istanbul), who administered the region on behalf of the Ottoman Empire, chose and deposed the nominally ruling princes (of whom there were 36 between 1711 and 1821), and eventually usurped the throne for themselves. The boyars adopted Turkish dress and competed to win the favour of the Phanariots, the sole group that advised the sultan whom among the boyars he should promote.

Alexandru Ioan Cuza

As Ottoman power weakened, this dismal saga was interrupted by the surprise election of **Prince Alexandru Ioan Cuza**, who clinched the unification of Moldavia and Wallachia in 1859 with the diplomatic support of France. In the new Romania, Cuza founded universities at Iaşi and Bucharest, introduced compulsory schooling for both sexes, and secularized monastic property, which at the time accounted for one-fifth of Moldavia. Finally, his emancipation of the serfs so enraged landowners and military circles that in 1866 they overthrew Cuza and restored the status quo ante – but kept the union.

Literary life and nationalism

The latter half of the nineteenth century was a fertile time for intellectual life in Iaşi, where the Junimea literary circle attracted such talents as the poet **Mihai Eminescu** and the writer **Ion Creangă**, who, like the historian **Nicolae Iorga**, became national figures. This was also the heyday of Jewish culture in Iaşi (or Jassy, as it was called in Yiddish), and in 1876 local impresario **Avrom Goldfadn** staged the world's first Yiddish theatre performance at the Pumul Verde ("Green Tree") wine garden, facing

Botanic Garden

Airport

IAŞI

French Cultural Centre
University Museum
Ai Cuza University
Hospital
Casa Pogor
Eminescu Library
Student House
Museum of Union
Old University
Nat. History Museum
Moldavian Philarmonic
Great Synagogue
Golia Monastery
Bârboi Monastery
Armenian Church
Church of St Sava
Central Market Hall
National Theatre Vasile Alecsandri
Metropolitan Cathedral
Old Metropolitan Church of St. George
Roman Catholic Cathedral
Church of the Three Hierarchs
Casa Dosoftei
Church of St Nicholas
Barnovschi Monastery
Luceafărul Theatre
Palace of Culture
Palas Shopping Mall

Maxitaxi
Iaşi Train Station

Mihail Kogălniceanu Memorial House
Cottage of Ion Creangă

TICĂU

Bus Station

Iulius Mall
Autogara Eurovoyage
Bus Station & Chişinău
Vaslui

NICOLINA

Nicolina Train Station

Galata Monastery

Frumoasa Monastery

Vaslui   Cetăţuia Monastery   Chişinău

● EATING
The Box	4
Casa Bolta Rece	6
Chef Galerie	10
Cuib	7
La Conac	2
Fika Café	8
Jassyro	9
Little Texas	1
Meru	3
Tuffli	5
Vivo	11

■ DRINKING & NIGHTLIFE
Acaju	2
Corso	1
The Trumpets	3

0   200
metres

■ ACCOMMODATION
Bicycle Hostel	6
Continental	5
International	9
Little Texas	1
Moldova	7
Ramada	8
Select	4
Traian	2
Unirea	3

● SHOPPING
Cărtureşti	3
Galeriile Anticariat	1
Humanitas	2
Palas Shopping Mall	3

THE IRON GUARD AND ROMÂNIA MARE

Moldavia and Iaşi have long been associated with the far right of Romanian politics. The most ardent member of Iaşi's League of Christian National Defence was **Corneliu Codreanu**, who went on, in the early 1930s, to found the Legion of the Archangel St Michael, better known as the **Iron Guard** (Garda de Fier). Wearing green shirts with bags of Romanian soil around their necks, the Legionari chased away village bailiffs to the delight of the peasantry, and murdered politicians deemed to be insufficiently nationalistic, until Marshal Antonescu jailed its leaders and Codreanu was shot "trying to escape". His followers fled to Berlin, returning with the Nazis to help carry out their genocidal "Final Solution" in Romania.

After the war, the communists employed ex-Legionari as thugs against the socialists and the National Peasant Party, whom they regarded as their real enemies. Following the 1989 revolution, fascism made a comeback with the **România Mare** ("Greater Romania") party (PRM) of **Corneliu Vadim Tudor**, who ascribed all the nation's problems to a conspiracy of Jews, Magyars, Gypsies and everyone else who wasn't a "pure" Romanian. However, the 2016 parliamentary elections saw the PRM gain little over one percent of the vote, the lowest since its foundation, while Tudor himself died in 2015.

the present National Theatre. The Junimea brand of nationalism was more romantic than chauvinist, but unwittingly paved the way for a deadlier version in the Greater Romania that was created to reward the Old Kingdom (Regat) for its sacrifices in World War I, when most of the country was occupied by the Germans, and the government was evacuated to Iaşi. With its borders enlarged to include Bessarabia and Bucovina, Moldavia inherited large minorities of Jews, Ukrainians and Gypsies, aggravating ethnic and class tensions in a region devastated by war.

During the 1920s, Iaşi became notorious for **anti-Semitism**, spearheaded by a professor whose League of Christian National Defence virtually closed the university to Jews, then over a third of the population, and later spawned the Iron Guard (see box). Their chief scapegoat was **Magda Lupescu**, Carol II's locally born Jewish mistress, widely hated for amassing a fortune by shady speculations; in 1940 she fled abroad with Carol in a train stuffed with loot.

Muzeul Unirii

Str. Lăpuşneanu 14 • Mid-April to Oct Wed–Sun 10am–5pm • €3 • ☎ 0232 314 614

Alexander Ioan Cuza's former mansion now houses the absorbing **Muzeul Unirii** (Museum of the Union). Cuza actually rented the property between 1859 and 1862, after which time the building served as the headquarters for King Ferdinand during World War I. While the ground floor is largely given over to the history of the union, the first floor reveals more about Cuza himself; the richly furnished rooms where he and his wife, Elena, lived, worked and entertained contain many personal items, such as Cuza's oak bureau, pipe and briefcase in the cabinet office, his royal chair and diplomat's suit and Elena's ball gown in the glittering salon, as well as a pristine billiard table alongside his cue in the games room. Look out, too, for the many Grigorescu paintings, as well as a coffee set emblazoned with an imperial "N", indicating Napoleon III's support for unification between Wallachia and Moldavia.

The rather comic tale of Cuza's downfall in 1866 is glossed over. Bursting into his bedroom, soldiers found Cuza making love to the King of Serbia's daughter-in-law; when pressed to sign a decree of abdication, he objected, "But I haven't got a pen". "We have thought of that," they said, producing a pen and ink, whereupon Cuza complained of the lack of a table. "I will offer myself," said a colonel, presenting his back to forestall further procrastination, and so Cuza signed and went into exile. He died in Heidelberg in 1873.

Catedrala Mitropolitana

B-dul Ştefan cel Mare 16 • Free • ☎ 0232 215 300

The huge, colonnaded **Catedrala Mitropolitana** (Metropolitan Cathedral) was begun in 1833 and completed in 1887, though is still undergoing various stages of refurbishment. The largest Orthodox church in Romania, it dwarfs worshippers with its cavernous interior, painted by Tattarescu, and dominates the neighbouring Metropolitan's Palace and Theological College. In 1641, Basil the Wolf spent the country's entire budget for the next year and a half to acquire the **relics of St Paraschiva** of Epivat (c.980–1050), which were moved to the cathedral in 1889. Venerated as the patron saint of Moldavia, households, harvests, traders and travellers, St Paraschiva seems to be a conflation of four Orthodox martyrs of that name. There are pilgrims here throughout the year (some crawling the last 100m or so), but on October 14 (the saint's day) the cathedral overflows with thousands of worshippers who come to kneel before the blue and gold bier containing the relics.

Biserica Sf Gheorghe

B-dul Ştefan cel Mare • Free

Immediately to the south of the cathedral stands the **Biserica Sf Gheorghe** (Old Metropolitan Church of St George), built in 1761; the pillars of its glassed-in porch are carved with symbolic animal reliefs, in the post-Brâncoveanu style of Wallachia. Inside it's like a mini-Sistine chapel, the large nave painted in a neo-Byzantine style and enhanced by effective uplighting. From 1999 to 2000 neo-Byzantine mosaics were added in the porch, with four scenes of paradise and one of the arrival of the relics of St Andrew the Apostle in Iaşi in 1996.

Teatrul Naţional Vasile Alecsandri

Str. Agatha Bârsescu 18 • ☎ 0232 117 233

East of the elegant Pumul Verde Park is the French-eclectic-style **Teatrul Naţional Vasile Alecsandri** (National Theatre Vasile Alecsandri), built by the Viennese architects Fellner and Helmer in the 1890s and named after Vasile Alecsandri (1821–90), who cofounded the company in 1840; however, owing to a lack of plays in Romanian, Alecsandri had to write much of its initial repertory himself. It retains one of the most beautiful auditoriums in the country, and it's well worth attending a performance if you can.

Biserica Trei Ierarhi

B-dul Ştefan cel Mare 28 • Church daily 9.30am–noon & 3–5pm; museum Tues–Sun 10am–4pm (ask in the church if the door is locked) • Free • ☎ 0232 216 349, ⓦ manastireasftreiierarhi.ro

Iaşi's landmark site is the famous **Biserica Trei Ierarhi** (Church of the Three Hierarchs), its exterior carved all over with chevrons, meanders and rosettes as intricate as lace. When it was completed in 1639 – perhaps by the Armenian master builder Ianache Etisi – Basil the Wolf had the exterior gilded, desiring it to surpass all other churches in splendour. Aside from its unique carvings, the church follows the classic Byzantine trilobate plan, with two octagonal drums mounted above the naos and pronaos in the Moldavian fashion. Over the following two centuries, the church was damaged by fire and six earthquakes, but was rebuilt by the French architect Lecomte de Noüy during the period 1882 to 1887. Inside the formidably dark interior – currently a tangle of scaffolding – you can just make out the **sarcophagi** of its founder Basil the Wolf, Dimitrie Cantemir and Alexandru Ioan Cuza. Since 1994 this has once more been a working monastery. The adjacent abbot's house, in which Basil the Wolf set up

SUCEVITA MONASTERY, BUCOVINA

Moldavia's first printing press in 1644, is now a modest museum containing a display of religious icons.

Palatul Culturii

Piaţa Ştefan cel Mare 1 • **Museums** Tues–Sun 10am–5pm • €3 each or €8.50 for all four • ☎ 0232 275 979, ⓦ palatulculturii.ro

At the southern end of Ştefan cel Mare, an equestrian **statue of Stephen the Great** and a cross commemorating the martyrs of the revolution are overshadowed by the stupendous **Palatul Culturii** (Palace of Culture) – a Neo-Gothic pile built between 1906 and 1925 as a government centre, and which, after years of painstaking restoration, now houses four of the city's museums. The palace's spired tower and pinnacled wings presage a vast lobby awash with mosaics, stained glass and armorial reliefs, dominated by a magnificent double staircase. If time is limited, you may have to be selective when it comes to the museums: first up on the ground floor is the **Museum of Science and Technology**, with sections devoted to energetics, telecommunications, computers and the like, but best of all are the displays of music boxes, symphonia and orchestrions, which staff may be willing to demonstrate. Also on the ground floor, the **Museum of Moldavian History** is particularly strong on local archaeology, though the numismatics collection is surprisingly impressive. Upstairs, the **Ethnography Museum's** collection includes two-metre long alpine horns, hollow trunks used as beehives, an enormous oil press, and some dazzling costumes. The **Museum of Art** is divided into Romanian and European galleries, the former featuring all the big hitters including Grigorescu and Aman. There's also a fine collection of post-1919 Colourist painters, such as Luchian and Pallady, while portraits of bearded boyars in Turkish fur hats, and scenes of Jewish life by Octav Băncila give more colour.

Muzeul Literatură Veche and Biserica Sf Nicolae

Str. Anastasie Panu 54 • Tues–Sun 10am–5pm • €1 • ☎ 0232 261 070

Marooned on its own little island and with traffic coursing by, the superbly arcaded **Casa Dosoftei**, built between 1677 and 1679, is a fitting home for the **Muzeul Literatură Veche** (Museum of Old Moldavian Literature) – it once housed a press that spread the words of the cleric and scholar Metropolitan Dosoftei, a statue of whom sits outside. The Phanariot policy of using Iaşi's presses to spread Greek as the language of Orthodox ritual had the unintended result of displacing the ossified Old Slavonic tongue from this position, clearing the way for intellectuals to agitate for the use of their own language, Romanian. As impressive as the seventeenth- and eighteenth-century manuscripts are (some by Cantemir), there's nothing by way of English explanation, which make a visit a little frustrating; in any case, the museum is currently closed pending renovation, and there's no way of knowing when it might reopen. A few paces away is the courtly **Biserica Sf Nicolae** (Church of St Nicholas), in theory the oldest building in Iaşi, erected by Stephen the Great in 1492 but pulled down and rebuilt by Lecomte de Noüy from 1885 to 1897; its svelte facade now masks a hermetic world of carved pews and gilded frescoes.

Mănăstirea Bărboi

Str. Bărboi 12 • Open access • Free

Housed in a tranquil walled garden with a tall neo-Byzantine gate tower, the **Mănăstirea Bărboi** (Bărboi monastery) still bears the name of Urşu Bărboi, who founded it in 1613, although the present Church of Peter and Paul, with an overhead gallery for the choir, was built from 1841 to 1844 by Dimitrie Sturdza, who is buried in the pronaos in a tomb covered with Greek inscriptions. It's a large open church, painted throughout, with a magnificent, if ostentatious, gilt iconostasis.

Sinagoga Mare

Str. Sinagogilor 7

Secreted away beyond the busy Strada Sărărie, you can see the Star of David atop the **Sinagoga Mare** (Great Synagogue) – somewhat of a misnomer for this low-domed edifice built between 1659 and 1671 and restored after an earthquake in 1977, shortly before most of its congregation left for Israel. Supposedly Romania's oldest synagogue, it is currently undergoing a painstakingly slow renovation programme, though the exterior restoration is more or less complete. Outside is an obelisk to the victims of the pogrom of June 28–29, 1941.

Mănăstirea Golia

Str. Cuza Vodă 51 • **Monastery** Daily 6am–6pm • Free • **Tower** Mon–Fri 9am–5pm, Sat & Sun 10am–4pm • €1.50

Mănăstirea Golia (Golia monastery) is a peaceful haven in the heart of Iași whose fifteen monks enjoy a rose garden dotted with shrines and protected by a 30m-tall gate tower and rounded corner bastions. Founded in the 1560s by Chancellor Ion Golia, when the capital was moved from Suceava, the monastery was rebuilt and fortified by Basil the Wolf, who began a new **Church of the Ascension** within the monastery's grounds, completed by his son Ștefăniță in 1660. The walls and towers were built in 1668 (with the gate tower added in 1855). It was burnt three times and damaged by an earthquake, but survived to become the Metropolitan Cathedral in 1786; however, by 1863 it was a ruin, being rebuilt only in 1947. A striking mixture of Byzantine, Classical and Russian architecture, with the traditional Moldavian domed plan but Corinthian capitals on the exterior, the church boasts of its associations with Tsarist Russia, since it was visited by Peter the Great in 1711, and serves as the burial place for the **viscera of Prince Potemkin**, Catherine the Great's favourite. These were removed so that the rest of his body could be preserved and returned home after he died in 1791, after catching a fever in Iași and defying doctors' orders by wolfing down huge meals, starting at breakfast with smoked goose and wine. He actually died across the border in present-day Moldova. The unfurnished interior was painted in 1838 and retains frescoes and an iconostasis not dissimilar to the one in Bărboi monastery.

It's possible to climb the superbly restored, 30m-high **Turnul Golia** (Golia Tower), whereupon you're rewarded with superlative views of the city, and, on a clear day, the Ceahlău mountains some 100km to the west; meanwhile, the arcaded eighteenth-century house to the east of the church was home to dean Ion Creangă from 1866 to 1871.

Copou

Copou, the university district, lies northwest of the centre, out along the Bulevardul Carol I, where trams (#1, #11 and #13) and buses (#28 and #41) toil uphill. The foot of the hill is distinguished by a Stalinesque **Student House** to the right, with bas-reliefs of musical youths, alongside a small park overlooked by statues of Moldavian princes, and the colonnaded **Biblioteca Centrală Universitară Mihai Eminescu** (Mihai Eminescu Central University Library) on the opposite side of Bulevardul Carol I. Working as a librarian in an earlier incarnation of this building, Eminescu could nip across the road (in the middle of which stands a statue of him sage-like in a cloak) for meetings of the Junimea literary society in the Casa Pogor (see below), just north of the Student House.

Muzeul Vasile Pogor

Str. Vasile Pogor 4 • Tues–Sun 10am–5pm • €2 • ☏ 0232 267 701

Built in 1850 by Vasile Pogor, three-time mayor of Iași, **Casa Pogor** was the headquarters of the Junimea society (1863–85), of which Pogor was a cofounder. Today it houses the **Muzeul Vasile Pogor**, which re-creates the atmosphere of Iaşi's burgeoning literary world at that time. The ground floor is laid out with furnishings belonging to both the Pogor family and the former prime minister, Mihail Kogălniceanu; of special interest are the wonderful ceramic stoves in each room. The second floor is largely devoted to the activities of the society itself, including first editions of *Convorbiri Literare* (Literary Conversations), the society's literary review magazine, though the star exhibits are Eminescu's death mask and his gold ring and watch – indeed, Eminescu (see box) lived here for a very brief period in 1874 – brooches owned by Veronica Micle (Eminescu's muse) and a pocketwatch belonging to Ion Creangă, another founding member of the Junimea.

Muzeul Universităţii

Str. Titu Maiorescu 12 • Tues–Fri 9am–4pm, Sat & Sun 10am–3pm • Free • ☎ 0232 201 102 • ⓦ muzeul.uaic.ro

The **Universitatea A.I. Cuza** is an Empire-style edifice built in the 1890s, which acts as an umbrella for 26 faculties and eight research institutes of the Romanian Academy. Just to the north is the Titu Maiorescu Dendrological Park, as well as fine 1880s villas housing the Goethe Zentrum and Chamber of Commerce. The university's illustrious history is proudly documented in the excellent **Muzeul Universităţii** (University Museum), courtesy of a wide assortment of exhibits including the hammer and trowel used to lay the first stone, paintings of various alumni, first research papers, sporting trophies and so on. Better still, though, is a sumptuous collection of ceramics from the Cucuteni culture (see page 229), unearthed by professors from the university's institute of archeology. A genuinely exciting hoard, it comprises cups, dishes, bowls and stemmed pots, variously painted or patterned in red, black and white motifs, alongside an exquisite collection of male and female statuettes.

Parcul Copou: Muzeul Eminescu and Muzeul Teatrului

Muzeul Eminescu and Muzeul Teatrului Tues–Sun 10am–5pm • €2.50 (joint ticket)

The tranquil **Parc Copou** (Copou Gardens) is where Eminescu meditated under a favourite lime tree, itself now squat and ugly and boxed in by a low hedge. In the centre of the park a small cultural centre houses the small and intermittently interesting **Muzeul Eminescu**; while there are no personal effects on show, there are photos of the poet alongside Creangă and Pogor, as well as first editions. Upstairs, the **Muzeul Teatrului** (Theatre Museum) exhibits an array of original costumes used in performances of plays by Romania's greatest playwrights, such as Matei Millo and Vasile Alecsandri.

Casa Memorială Mihail Kogălniceanu

Str. Kogălniceanu 11 • Tues–Sun 10am–5pm • €1 • ☎ 0232 258 422

Ţicău is a pretty, hilly, old residential quarter, east of the university area, with lime trees, some modernist houses (1930s–50s) and two memorial museums that provide an excuse for a ramble. On the street that now bears his name, the **Casa Memorială Mihail Kogălniceanu** (Mihail Kogălniceanu Memorial House) commemorates the orator and journalist who was banned from lecturing for lambasting "oppression by an ignorant aristocracy". He fled to Habsburg Bucovina in 1848, returning in the 1850s to help secure Cuza's election and serve as foreign minister. The rooms are lavishly furnished, predominantly in Louis XVI style, though the undoubted centrepiece is the gorgeous oval room, today used for piano recitals. In Kogălniceanu's study, there are numerous personal effects on display, including his attaché case, a cup he used while travelling and a marble ashtray.

MIHAI EMINESCU

Mihai Eminescu, Romania's national poet, was born in 1850 in Botoşani, east of Suceava, and schooled in Cernăuţi, the capital of Habsburg Bucovina. At the age of 16, he gave his surname, Eminovici, the characteristic Romanian ending -escu and became a prompter for a troupe of actors, until his parents packed him off to study law in Vienna and Berlin. Returning to Iaşi in 1874, he found a job as a librarian, joined the Junimea literary society, and had a tortured affair with Veronica Micle, a poet and wife of the university rector. After the rector's demise, Eminescu decided that he was too poor to marry her and took an editorial job in Bucharest to escape his grief. Overwork led to a mental breakdown in 1883, and from then on, until his death from syphilis six years later, periods of madness alternated with lucid intervals. He is best remembered for *Luceafărul* (*The Evening Star*), a 96-stanza ballad of love.

Bojdeuca Ion Creangă

Str. Simion Bărnuţiu 4 • Tues–Sun 10am–5pm • €1 • ☏ 0747 499 488

Dating from 1850 at the latest, the small wood-clad **Bojdeuca Ion Creangă** (Cottage of Ion Creangă) displays first editions and prints of his works, including stills from films based on them. A defrocked priest and failed teacher, Creangă (1837–89) wrote *Recollections of Childhood* and fairy tales such as the *Giants of Irunica*, finally achieving success just before he died. The pretty, stepped garden in front of the house is used as an amphitheatre for local productions.

The southern monasteries

An ambitious way to stretch your legs is to visit the **monasteries** in the Nicolina district, south of the city centre. Catch bus #9 or a southbound maxitaxi downhill past the Palace of Culture and out along Strada Nicolina; cresting the flyover, you'll see the Cetăţuia and Galata monasteries on separate hilltops to the east and west, and a modern Roman Catholic church with a prow-like spire in the valley, which is where you should alight. From here, either follow Strada Tudor Neculai west up the hill and past a cemetery to Galata monastery, or cross the main road and head east through apartment buildings and under the tracks to find Frumoasa monastery and the trail south to Cetăţuia. If you're intending to visit all three, it's best to see Cetăţuia first and work your way back to the others, as the hike to Cetăţuia requires the most effort.

Mănăstirea Galata

Str. Mănăstirii • Daily 8am–6pm • Free • ☏ 0232 224 545

Architecturally, **Mănăstirea Galata** (Galata monastery) is the most interesting of the three monasteries south of town. The church – its handsome exterior manifesting alternate bands of red brick and an enormous overhanging eave – was built between 1579 and 1584 to a typically Moldavian plan, with an enclosed porch and narthex preceding the nave, which was painted in 1811. Its founder, Prince Petru Şchiopul, is buried in the nave with his daughter, Despina. To the right of the gate tower, beside a newer building in use today, are the ruins of the original monks' quarters and a Turkish bath.

Mănăstirea Frumoasa

Str. Radu Vodă 1 • Daily 8am–6pm • Free • ☏ 0232 279 457

Entered through a sturdy but badly decrepit gate tower, **Mănăstirea Frumoasa** (Frumoasa monastery) stands on a hillock surrounded by low walls. Formerly a barracks and military hospital, the complex stood derelict for decades, but after recent restoration is close to living up to its name – meaning "beautiful" – once more. Largely built by Grigore II Ghica from 1726 to 1733, Frumoasa differs from the other monasteries thanks to the ponderous form of Neoclassicism in favour when the

4

complex was reconstructed in the 1830s; the interior, too, is markedly different in style, with thick columns topped with gold and blue stucco capitals. On the north side are Ghica's summer garden and court, beyond a grand marble Neoclassical tomb built in 1842 by Francesco Vernetta for the family of Prince Mihail Sturdza.

Mănăstirea Cetăţuia

Str. Cetăţuia 1 · Daily 8am–6pm · Free · ☎ 0744 647 957 · From Frumoasa monastery, turn left out of the gate onto Str. Cetăţuia and after 5min cross B-dul Poitiers, along which runs bus #43; on the far side the road climbs through woods for 1.5km to a hilltop

Far smaller and more atmospheric than Frumoasa, **Mănăstirea Cetăţuia** (Cetăţuia monastery) – whose name means "citadel" – seems remote from Iaşi; on misty days, the city is blotted out, and all you can see are the surrounding ridges. Its high walls conceal a harmonious ensemble of white stone buildings with rakish black roofs, interspersed by low conifers and centred on a church that's similar to the Church of the Three Hierarchs in town, but hardly carved, except for a cable moulding and Renaissance window frames. The interior frescoes, meanwhile, are blackened to the point of being almost invisible. Prince Gheorghe Duca and his wife, now buried in the pronaos, founded the monastery in 1669, with a royal palace that served as a refuge for the ruling family in time of war.

ARRIVAL AND DEPARTURE   IAŞI

By plane Iaşi's airport (☎ 0232 271 590, ⓦ aeroport-iasi. ro), currently with flights to London Luton and a growing number of other European destinations, is 7km northeast of the centre. Bus #50 makes the journey to Piaţa Unirii (8–10 daily); otherwise, a taxi will cost around €6.

By train Iaşi's main train station (Nicolina) is on Str. Silvestru, from where it's a 15min walk to Piaţa Unirii; alternatively you can catch trams #3, #6 or #7. You can make bookings at the CFR office at Piaţa Unirii 10 (Mon–Fri 7.30am–8.30pm; ☎ 0232 147 673), including for the overnight *Prietenia* to Chişinău in Moldova (see box).

Destinations Bucharest (5 daily; 6hr 50min–7hr 30min); Chişinău (2 daily; 4–6hr); Cluj (4 daily; 9hr 30min); Paşcani, for Târgu Neamţ (11 daily; 1hr 10min–1hr 30min); Suceava (7 daily; 1hr 50min–2hr 30min).

By bus Most buses and maxitaxis arrive and depart from Autogară Codreanu across the street from the train station, though you might also arrive at the basic Autogară Iaşi Vest, behind the Autocenter, 1km northwest of the train station on Şoseaua Moara de Foc (tram #2 or bus #30 to Iaşi centre); or the Autogară Eurovoyage, at Str. O. Teodoreanu 49, 100m south of Calea Chişinăului in an industrial wasteland to the southeast of the centre (trams #2, #7, #15).

Destinations Bicaz (3 daily; 3hr); Bucharest (8 daily; 7hr); Câmpulung Moldovenesc (4 daily; 3hr 40min); Chişinău (hourly; 3–4hr); Comăneşti (3 daily; 3hr 20min); Durău (4 daily; 4hr); Galaţi (7 daily; 5hr); Gura Humorului (7 daily; 3hr 30min); Piatra Neamţ (hourly; 2hr 15min); Suceava (14 daily; 2hr 45min); Târgu Mureş (3 daily; 6hr 45min); Târgu Neamţ (hourly; 2hr).

GETTING AROUND

By bus and tram Buses and trams rock and roll their way to most parts of the city (every 10–15min, 5am–10pm); fares are €0.50 for a single ride, €1 for two, and €2.20 for a day; tickets can be purchased from machines located at bus stops or from kiosks.

By taxi The most reliable companies are Delta Taxi (☎ 0232 222 222) and Pro-Taxi (☎ 0232 218 584); expect to pay around €0.40/km (€0.50/km after 10pm).

Car rental Avis, at the airport (☎ 0728 228 923, ⓦ avis.ro); Autonom, Str Pacurari 130 (☎ 0748 127 981, airport ☎ 0748 127 981, ⓦ autonom.ro); Sixt, at the airport (☎ 0745 062 158, ⓦ sixt.ro).

INFORMATION

Tourist information The tourist information office, at Piaţa Unirii 12 (Mon–Fri 8.30am–4.30pm; ☎ 0232 261 990,

ⓦ turism-iasi.ro), has a limited stock of information, but the staff are friendly and willing to help with any queries.

ACCOMMODATION

Iaşi has a healthy stock of **hotels**, with some decent mid-range options alongside the typically more expensive business-like establishments, most of which have pools; there are a few budget options too.

Bicycle Hostel Str. Silvestre 18 ☎ 0754 699 195, ⓦ iasi. bicycle-hostel.ro; map p.238. Little more than a five-minute walk from the stations, this smart, well-run hostel has a mixture of spacious and colourful four-bed dorms

CROSSING TO MOLDOVA

Maxitaxis to **Chişinău** in **Moldova** leave more or less hourly from the terminal opposite the train station in Iaşi, arriving either at the Gara Centrala (at the central market) or the Gara Sud (2km south) in Chişinău, where a range of hostels and decent hotels are now available. There's one direct train (the *Prietenia*), which departs from Iaşi's main station each morning at 3.19am, arriving in Chişinău at 9.27am; in addition, another train departs Iaşi each day at 1.18pm, though this requires a change in Ungheni before arriving in Chişinău at 7.17pm

and private doubles, with spankingly clean bathrooms (all shared) and a fab lounge with games, instruments and the like. No breakfast. Dorms, **€11**, doubles **€30**

Continental Str. Cuza Vodă 4 ☎0232 267 744 , ⓦcontinental-iasi.ro; map p.238. Cheapest of the central hotels. The rooms, in what is otherwise a fine old building, are really quite old-fashioned and rather clumsily furnished, but they're clean enough and all have bathrooms. Air-conditioned rooms cost a little extra. **€40**

International Str. Palatului 5A ☎0332 110 072, ⓦhotelinternationaliasi.ro; map p.238. A few hundred metres downhill from the Palace of Culture near the Podu Ros transit interchange, this impressive, imposing block of a building more than merits its four-star rating; slick, light-filled rooms with cream and beige decor jazzed up with occasional splashes of purple, plus soft, patterned carpets under foot, and dazzling bathrooms. Gorgeous spa too. **€90**

Little Texas Stradela Moara de Vânt 31 ☎0232 272 545, ⓦlittletexas.ro; map p.238. Beautifully set on a hilltop out on the road towards the airport, this small and gracious American-run hotel is a cut above anything else in Iaşi. The well-appointed rooms (Cowboys & Indians Room, Wild West Room and so on) incorporate custom-made US furniture and offer great views from the balconies; you'll also receive a typically hearty American breakfast. **€70**

Moldova Str. Anastasie Panu 31 ☎0232 260 240; map p.238. This communist high-rise is by no means a thing of beauty, but its rooms are infinitely more appealing than

the exterior suggests; moreover, it's central, decently priced, and the rooms on the higher floors afford splendid citywide views; sauna, gym and indoor swimming pool. **€60**

Ramada Str. Grigore Ureche 27 ☎0232 256 070, ⓦramadaiasi.ro; map p.238. Hidden behind the *Moldova*, this is one of the city's classiest outfits, as you'd expect from this well-heeled chain; supremely comfortable rooms with high beds and thick duvets, plush red carpets and glassed-in bathrooms; tea- and coffee-making facilities too. **€90**

Select Piaţa 14 Decembrie 1989 2 ☎0232 216 440, ⓦselectgrup.ro; map p.238. This handsome building sports wonderfully cool rooms, combining smooth wood furnishings, soft grey carpets and bright, crisp drapes. Good-sized, sparkling bathrooms too. **€80**

Traian Piaţa Unirii 1 ☎0232 266 666, ⓦgrandhoteltraian.ro; map p.238. Atmospheric establishment designed by the Eiffel company in 1882 featuring sky-blue and cream coloured rooms furnished in classic French period style; there are some neat touches too, such as wrought-iron wall lamps, old-style phones, and tea- and coffee-making facilities. **€99**

Unirea Piaţa Unirii 5 ☎0232 205 006, ⓦhotelunirea. ro; map p.238. Although somewhat less glamorous than the adjacent *Traian*, this large 1960s high-rise conceals very modern, sunny and solidly furnished rooms; the pool and spa facilities are among the best in the city. **€70**

EATING

Iaşi's **restaurant** scene is steady rather than spectacular though there are now a number of stylish places offering Romanian interpretations of various world cuisines, in addition to the many traditional establishments where you can try Moldavian cooking.

CAFÉS

Fika Café Piaţa Unirii 7 ☎0745 154 608; map p.238. The immediately identifiable Swedish blue and yellow colour scheme makes for a decidedly chilled vibe in this great looking spot; the folk here, led by the affable Daniela, are certainly giving *Jassyro* (opposite) a run for their money, with tip-top coffee and a wicked selection of pastries and desserts. Mon–Fri 8am–10pm, Sat & Sun 8.30am–10pm.

★ **Jassyro** Str. Ştefan cel Mare 1C ☎0747 771 771, ⓦjassyro.ro; map p.238. You'll know you've hit upon this gem of a coffee shop by the long queue of punters lining up outside for their daily fix. More outlet than café (though there is seating on small cushioned benches outside), *Jassyro* has charming staff who prepare lovingly crafted coffee using single origin or blended beans from the fabulous *Origo* café in Bucharest. Mon–Fri 7.30am–5pm, Sat & Sun 9.30am–5pm.

Meru B-dul Carol I 3 ☎0332 401 312; map p.238. Chilled out, art-themed coffee bar occupying an old, hall-style room with happily careworn furnishings and bits of artwork scattered all around. Tricky to find, as there's no sign, it's in the building just behind and to the right of *The*

4

IAŞI FESTIVALS

Iaşi's big annual event is the **St Paraschiva festival week** (Sarbatorile Iaşului) starting on October 14, when people from all over Moldavia flood into town to pay homage to the saint buried in the Metropolitan Church. The **Festival of the Three Hierarchs** is celebrated on January 30, when literally a million pilgrims come to worship in the presence of the church's relics. Musically, the city's key event is the four-day **Afterhills Music and Arts Festival** at the end of May (w afterhills.com), featuring a terrific cross section of musical genres, including some pretty big names (Tricky in 2018), as well as comedy, theatre and performance art. Another fun event is **Cucuteni 5000**, a mammoth ceramics fair on the last weekend of June, when potters from all over the country come to display their wares in Copou Park.

Box (see below), then up the flight of stairs. Mon–Thurs 10am–midnight, Fri 10am–1am, Sat & Sun noon–1am.
Tuffli Str. Lăpuşneanu 7 ☎ 0721290 812; map p.238. A fixture on this lively pedestrianized street for years, this excellent coffee house and patisserie offers a wide range of beverages, cakes and pastries. Park yourself inside or on one of the terrace's squidgy sofas. Mon–Thurs 8am–10.30pm, Fri & Sat 8am–midnight, Sun 9am–10.30pm.

RESTAURANTS

The Box B-dul Carol I ☎ 0751 737 585; map p.238. Occupying a customized shipping container, this is street food at its best; although catering mostly to the nearby student population, it makes for a cracking little lunch munch en route to or from Copou Park; burgers, sausages and quesadillas all going for around €3–4 a pop. Daily 11am–9pm.

Casa Bolta Rece Str. Rece 10 ☎ 0232 212 255, w casaboltarece.ro; map p.238. Secreted away in a quiet residential area, this legendary restaurant and wine garden dates back to 1786. The food is decent traditional Romanian, while the kitsch peasant decor, allied to live folk music most evenings, really makes this one for the tourist parties. Daily 8am–midnight.

Chef Galerie Str. Palat 3 ☎ 0747 858 353, w chefgalerie. ro; map p.238. Large, modern diner with floor-to-ceiling windows and nicely spaced tables arrayed around an open kitchen. The food is a mix of international flavours, though is inclined towards Italian; for example, black spaghetti with white wine and jumbo shrimps (€11), and pear, blue cheese and walnut risotto. Daily noon–11pm.

★ **Cuib** Str. Gavril Musicescu 14 ☎ 0747 485 053, w incuib.ro; map p.238. Easy-going *Cuib* – which translates as the Urban Centre for Good Initiatives – is

a gem of restaurant serving great vegetarian food; for example, baked pancakes with red pepper, beet salad and horseradish, and tagliatelle with spinach and mushroom (€4). The line-up of beer is terrific too, including the super-tasty *Zăganu*, and several unfiltered varieties. Mon 1–11pm, Tues–Thurs & Sun 10am–11pm, Fri & Sat 10am–midnight.

La Conac Str. Nicole Gane 27 ☎ 0746 279 893, w laconac-traditie.ro; map p.238. This ostentatious-looking *conac* (a fortified manor house) harbours a rather lovely, family-run restaurant furnished with beautiful hand-carved tables and chairs, and walls adorned with peasant textiles, icons and other knick-knacks; the adventurous menu concentrates mainly on Moldavian specialities such as *sărmălute mămăligă*, while beer is served in ceramic jugs. Daily 11am–11pm.

Little Texas Stradela Moara de Vânt 31 ☎ 0232 272 545, w littletexas.ro; map p.238. At the hotel of the same name (see page 247), this American establishment offers exemplary burgers (each one named after a movie star), steaks, chicken platters alongside mouthwatering Tex-Mex specialities such as chilli Colorado burrito (€8); if you can, round it off with apple pie and vanilla ice cream. Either dine inside, amid the more or less tasteful Wild West decor, or on the fabulous garden terrace. Daily 8am–midnight.

Vivo Str. Zimbrului 5 ☎ 0332 417 727, w vivofoodbar. com; map p.238. Fusion street food is the strapline here, which effectively means burgers, but what burgers they are: the Italian (the "Goodburger"), Cheese ("Breaking Gouda") and Vivo ("Games of Dijons") are just some of the cleverly titled morcels on the menu (around €6). The interior, with its exposed brick and jet-black walls, and industrial-style ceiling pipes, looks terrific. Daily noon–11pm.

DRINKING AND NIGHTLIFE

Thanks in part to its large student population, Iaşi's reputation for its diverse **nightlife** is well deserved, though it's cool and laidback rather than particularly energetic.

Acaju Str. Sf Sava 15 ☎ 0727 255 514; map p.238. If you want a serious chill-out, this delightful café/bar is perfect;

sup a beer or take tea inside the two artily painted rooms, furnished with low wooden bench seating and 70s retro-style accoutrements. They occasionally stage evenings of a cinematic or literary bent. Daily 10am–1am.

Corso Str. Lăpuşneanu 11 ☎ 0728 920 092, w corsoterasa.ro; map p.238. Massive semicircular terrace bar set around lush lawns that looks like an MTV dance set; relaxing by day, it becomes a somewhat more invigorating venue at sundown. Daily 8am–12.30am.

★ **The Trumpets** Esplanada Teatrul Luceafarul ☎ 0786 364 316; map p.238. A banging, good-time party place with high ceilings, long wooden bar tables and stools, and all manner of brass instruments lining the walls – oh, and a London phone box; live music on most Thurs (€5), with DJ sets on Fri. Men should (and probably will) check out the loos, where you're obliged to pee into a trumpet, so aim straight. Daily 9am–2.30am.

ENTERTAINMENT

Luceafărul Theatre Str. Grigore Ureche 5 ☎ 0332 407 218, ⓦ luceafarul-theatre.ro. Excellent, long-standing youth theatre that offers an inventive programme, mostly for younger children, including puppetry.

Moldavian Philharmonic Str. Cuza Vodă 29 ☎ 0232 212 509, ⓦ filarmonicais.ro. Lovers of classical music should try to attend a performance of this orchestra, the country's best outside Bucharest. Box office Mon–Fri 10am–1pm & 5–7pm.

National Theatre Str. Agatha Bârsescu 18 ☎ 0232 255 999, ⓦ teatrulnationaliasi.ro. Romania's oldest theatre is also one of its grandest, with a fabulous repertoire, as well being used by the highly regarded Opera Naţională Româna Iaşi (ⓦ operaiasi.ro).

SHOPPING

Cărtureşti Level 1 of the Palas Mall (see below) ☎ 0734 554 439; map p.238. This airy, beautifully lit bookshop is lovely for browsing, and also has a little coffee/seating area; good for music and souvenirs too. Daily 10am–10pm.

Galeriile Anticariat Str. Lăpuşneanu 24 ☎ 0748 515 374; map p.238. Selling antiques, icons and secondhand books in several languages, this is easily the best shop of its kind in Moldavia. Mon–Fri 9am–9pm, Sat & Sun 10am–7pm.

Humanitas Piaţa Unirii 6 ☎ 0232 215 568; map p.238. Directly opposite the *Traian* hotel (see page 247), this tiny but friendly little shop is the best place for new books in English. Mon–Fri 9am–6pm, Sat 9am–5pm.

Palas Shopping Mall Str. Palas 7A ☎ 0232 209 920, ⓦ palasiasi.ro; map p.238. Occupying part of the newly landscaped area behind the Palace of Culture, this thoroughly shiny mall is the city's main, and most appealing, shopping centre; there are cheap dining possibilities here too. Daily 10am–10pm.

DIRECTORY

Hospital Urgenţe (emergency) admission is on the corner of Str. L. Catargiu and Str. G. Berthelot (☎ 0232 216 584).

Internet The British Council library, Str. Păcurari 4 (Mon & Tues 1–7pm, Wed–Fri 10am–4pm, ☎ 0232 316 159, ⓦ britishcouncil.ro/iasi), is the best place to log on if you don't have access to wi-fi; the entrance is actually on B-dul Carol I.

Left luggage Both the train station and the main Autogară have nonstop facilities (€1.50/24hr).

Pharmacy The best and most central of the city's several 24hr pharmacies is Ropharma, behind the *Unirii* hotel at Piaţa Unirii 3 (☎ 0232 220 549). There's also Rosmarin, Str. Tudor Vladimirescu 44 (☎ 0232 263 365).

Post office Str. Cuza Vodă 3 (Mon–Fri 8am–7pm, Sat 9am–1pm).

Suceava

Crossing the industrial sprawl between the stations and the city centre, it's difficult to imagine **SUCEAVA**, 150km northwest of Iaşi, as an old princely capital. The city's heyday more or less coincided with the reign of **Stephen the Great** (1457–1504), who warred ceaselessly against Moldavia's invaders – principally the Turks – and won all but two of the 36 battles he fought. This record prompted Pope Sixtus IV to dub him the "Athlete of Christ" – a rare accolade for a non-Catholic, which wasn't extended to Stephen's cousin Vlad the Impaler (see page 398), even though he massacred 45,000 Turks during one year alone.

While Stephen's successors, **Bogdan the One-Eyed** and **Petru Rareş**, maintained the tradition of building a new church or monastery after every victory, they proved less successful against the Turks and Tatars, who ravaged Suceava several times. Eclipsed when Iaşi became the Moldavian capital in 1565, Suceava missed its last chance of glory in 1600, when **Michael the Brave** (Mihai Viteazul) completed his campaign to unite Wallachia, Moldavia and Transylvania by marching unopposed into Suceava's Princely Citadel. In terms of national pride, Suceava's nadir was the long period from 1775 to 1918, when the **Habsburgs** ruled northern Moldavia from Czernowitz (Cernăuți), although Suceava was able to prosper as a trading centre between the highland and lowland areas. Under communism, this role was deemed backward and remedied by hasty **industrialization** – the consequences of which long blighted the town.

Save for the lovely **ethnographic museum** and a clutch of churches, there are few real sights in town itself; instead, Suceava's principal attractions are a good twenty minutes' walk from the centre, namely the superb **Village Museum** to the east, and the **Zamca monastery** to the west. For visitors though, Suceava is primarily a base for excursions to the **painted monasteries** (see page 259).

Biserica Sfântul Dumitru

Str. Curtea Domnească

Built in 1534–35 by Petru Rareș, the **Biserica Sf Dumitru** (Church of St Dumitru) is typical of Moldavian churches of the period, with a double row of niche-bound

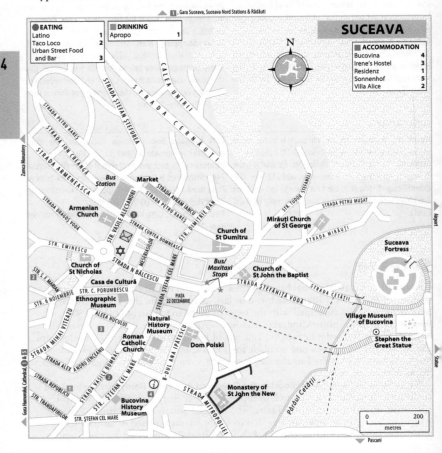

saints (sadly now largely effaced) under its eaves, and coloured tiles ornamenting its drum. The interior frescoes of gruesome martyrdoms date from the sixteenth to the nineteenth centuries and have recently been restored. Inside lies the tomb of Bogdan, son of Rareş. Meanwhile, the freestanding, 40m-high bell tower, added in 1561, bears the Moldavian crest (see page 252); it's currently closed pending renovation.

Biserica Sfântul Ioan Botezatorul and Curtea Domnească

B-dul Ana Ipătescu

Built as his court chapel by Basil the Wolf in 1643, the **Biserica Sf Ioan Botezatorul** (Church of St John the Baptist) is an atmospheric little church with whitewashed walls and a lovely wood-shingled roof. Its large exterior belies a tiny, attractive interior (it was originally a church for children), which gradually slopes downwards to a darkened iconostasis somehow jammed in between the two side walls. At weekends, visitors may witness funerals here, where the deceased is laid out in an open coffin, amid candles and loaves of bread, while a horse-drawn hearse waits outside. Across the road from the church are the overgrown ruins of the **Curtea Domnească** (Princely Court), rebuilt twice (by Stephen the Great and Vasile Lupu) before finally being abandoned in the late seventeenth century.

Biserica Mirăuţi Sfântul Gheorghe

Str. Mirăuţi 17

The **Biserica Mirăuţi Sf Gheorghe** (Mirăuţi Church of St George) is the oldest in Suceava. Founded by Petru I Muşat in about 1390, this was the Metropolitan cathedral, where the early princes of Moldavia were crowned, including Stephen the Great. Its facade is decorated with blind arches and a sawtoothed cornice sandwiched between thick cable mouldings, while below the eaves are frescoes of saints, added when it was heavily over-restored between 1898 and 1903 by Emperor Franz Jozef I.

Hanul Domnesc and Muzeul Etnografic

Str. Ciprian Porumbescu 5 • Tues–Sun 10am–6pm • €1.50 • ☎ 0230 216 439

Providing some welcome respite from the concrete monotony is the **Hanul Domnesc** (Princely Inn), a superb half-timbered building originally dating from around the early seventeenth century, which makes it the oldest civil edifice in Suceava county. Formerly a hunting lodge for members of the Habsburg family, it also served as the court guesthouse, but these days houses the **Muzeul Etnografic** (Ethnographic Museum). Its half a dozen or so vaulted rooms are crammed with furnishings typical of that era; the guest room is notable for its gorgeous stove, plastered with green-and-yellow painted tiles depicting scenes from the hunt and everyday folk life, while the bedroom features an unusually high, hand-carved wooden bedstead. Upstairs you'll find a fine display of pottery, in particular the famous black pottery from Marginea and glazed vessels typical of the area around Rădăuţi (see page 266), alongside some beautifully patterned textiles – woollen blankets and wall towels – plus incredibly thick fur coats that shepherds wore to withstand the biting winters of yore.

Mănăsteria Sfântul Ioan cel Nou

Str. Ioan Vodă Viteazul 2 • Open access • Free

Easily identified by its colourful steeple striped with blue, black and yellow chevrons, the **Mănăsteria Sf Ioan cel Nou** (Monastery of St John the New) was started by Bogdan the One-Eyed in 1514 and finished by his son Ştefăniţă in 1522. Its monumental **Church of St George** was intended to replace the Mirăuţi Church as Suceava's

PRINCE DRAGOŞ AND THE AUROCHS

Throughout Moldavia, churches display the emblem of the medieval principality, often over the main gateway: an aurochs' head and a sun, moon and star. This symbolizes the legend of **Prince Dragoş**, who is said to have hunted a giant **aurochs** (the *zimbru* or European bison) all the way across the mountains from Poland, until he cornered it by a river and slew the beast after a fight lasting from dawn to dusk – hence the inclusion of the Sun, Moon and Morning Star in the emblem. Dragoş's favourite hunting dog, **Molda**, was killed in the fight, and the prince named the River Moldova in her honour, adopting the aurochs, the mightiest animal in the Carpathians, as his totem. The last wild aurochs in Romania was killed in 1852 near Borşa, although captive-breeding populations survive, notably at Vânători Neamţ, just west of Târgu Neamţ.

Metropolitan cathedral, so no expense was spared. In 1534 it was painted inside and out with frescoes like those of the painted monasteries of Bucovina, but only the *Tree of Jesse* on the south wall (the far side) and a fragment of the *Last Judgement* on the west end remain; both are barely discernible. The interior's mostly dark blue painted frescoes are more or less intact, save for the odd missing patch. The relics of St John the New rest here, to the right of the nave, and are taken on a grand procession through the city each year on June 24, the feast of St John the Baptist (the feast of Sânziene). St John the New's martyrdom is depicted inside a small chapel near the church, where nuns now run a shop selling religious paraphernalia. Arrested for preaching in Turkish-occupied Moldavia in 1332, he was dragged through the streets of Cetăţii Alba behind a horse, and slashed to death by enraged Muslims. There's also a pavilion housing a 230-litre drum of holy water, for the faithful to take away in bottles.

Cetatea de Scaun a Sucevei

Aleea Cetăţii • Tues–Sun: Jan, Feb, Nov & Dec 10am–6pm; March 9am–6pm; April 9am–8pm; May–Aug 9am–10pm; Sep 10am–10pm; Oct 10am–9pm • €2.50 • ☎ 0230 216 439

Overlooking the city from a hill to its east stands the impressive **Cetatea de Scaun a Sucevei** (Suceava Fortress), built by Petru I Muşat (reigned 1375–91), who moved the Moldavian capital from Siret to Suceava; it was subsequently strengthened in the fifteenth century by Alexander the Good. Stephen the Great added the moat, curtain walls and bastions that enabled it to defy the artillery of Mohammed II, conqueror of Constantinople, in 1476. Although blown up by Dumitrascu Cantacuzino (as ordered by the Turks) in 1675, much of the three-storey keep and the outlying chambers remain. Modern accretions may have quashed much of the fortress's historical charm, and there's little of substance to see inside, but it's fun to wander the various underground rooms, and the views from the ramparts are terrific.

Muzeul Satului Bucovinean

Aleea Cetăţii • Mid-April to mid-Oct Tues–Sun 10am–6pm; mid-Oct to mid-April Mon–Fri 9am–4pm • €1.50 • ☎ 0230 216 439, ⓦ muzeulsatuluibucovinean.ro

In a former pasture opposite Suceava Fortress (see above), you'll find the superb **Muzeul Satului Bucovinean** (Village Museum of Bucovina), a work in progress currently displaying some two dozen wooden buildings, all removed from Bucovina villages and reassembled on the site. Most are late nineteenth- or early twentieth-century structures, uniformly constructed from fir beams and reinforced with whitewashed clay, then topped off with shingled roofs. Some buildings, including a family house from Roşu (near Vatra Dornei) and a sizeable tavern from Şaru Dornei, have been furnished with colourful textiles, handmade furniture and housewares, while many of the region's traditional crafts and industries are also represented – a potter's workshop from Marginea and a flour mill from Humor. There's also a wooden church from Vama, a chunky stone and wood edifice dating from 1783 and which is still used for services – alongside it stands an octagonal bell tower. Throughout the summer various shows are performed on the open-air stage just inside the entrance; the main event is the **Folk Handicraftsman Fair** taking place in August.

To reach the fortress and the museum, head east from Piaţa 22 Decembrie through the park and across the bridge into the woods, where rather steep steps lead up to a giant equestrian **statue of Stephen the Great**, unveiled in 1977; the bas-reliefs on the pedestal depict his victory over the Turks at Vaslui in 1475. From here a road leads around the Village Museum to the car park and cafés between it and the fortress.

Mănăstirea Zamca

Str. Zamca 30

The neglected ruins of the Armenian **Mănăstirea Zamca** (Zamca monastery) straddle a plateau on the northwest edge of town, twenty minutes' walk from the centre along Strada Armenească or a short walk from Strada Mărăşeşti. The Armenian diaspora had reached Moldavia by 1350, and Alexander the Good founded the Armenian bishopric of Suceava in 1401; in 1551, the diaspora fell foul of the Rareş family, leading to a pogrom, but in 1572 an Armenian actually became ruler of Moldavia. The buildings here, which combine Gothic and classical elements with oriental motifs, were founded in 1606 and later fortified with ramparts and a gate tower. The three-storey gate tower and guesthouse, where dignitaries were once accommodated, is currently closed as part of a long and slow restoration project, as is the plain white church, which is home to a few lovely **frescoes**; unfortunately, it's anyone's guess as to when it might reopen. Though not much from a monumental standpoint, the site has a desolate grandeur, particularly at dusk, when you can walk around the earthworks.

4

ARRIVAL AND DEPARTURE   SUCEAVA

By plane Suceava's Ştefan cel Mare airport (☎ 0230 529 999, ⊕ aeroportsuceava.ro), currently with flights to London Luton, Bucharest and a few Italian cities, is 12km east of town; it's accessible only by taxi (around €15).

By train Suceava has two main stations: Gara Suceava, some 4km north of the centre in Burdujeni (bus #2 to the centre) a grand, Italian-built edifice dating from 1868 and modelled on the station in Turin; and Suceava Nord, 6km northwest of the centre in the suburb of Iţcani (bus #5 to the centre); most trains stop at both stations.

Destinations Bucharest (6 daily; 6hr 50min–7hr 20min); Câmpulung Moldovenesc (8 daily; 1hr 30min–2hr); Cluj (4 daily; 6hr 40min–7hr 15min); Gura Humorului (8 daily; 50min–1hr 10min); Iaşi (8 daily; 2hr–2hr 50min); Rădăuţi (2 daily; 1hr 30min); Vatra Dornei (6 daily; 2hr 30min–3hr 20min).

By bus The bus station is just northwest of the town centre on Str. V. Alecsandri, from where it's a 5min walk into the centre.

Destinations Câmpulung Moldovenesc (10 daily; 1hr 30min); Gura Humorului (every 30min–1hr; 40min–1hr); Iaşi (hourly; 2hr 45min); Pătrăuţi (Mon–Fri 7 daily; 30min); Piatra Neamţ (2 daily; 3hr 30min); Rădăuţi (every 30min; 50min); Solca (5 daily; 1hr); Târgu Neamţ (3 daily; 1hr 30min); Văratec (5 daily; 30min); Vatra Dornei (7 daily; 2hr 15min–3hr 45min).

By taxi Eurotaxi (☎ 0230 511 111) and Cris Taxi (☎ 0230 522 222) are reliable taxi companies.

SUCEAVA FESTIVALS

Suceava's principal annual event is the **Stephen the Great Medieval Festival**, in mid-August, a three-day jamboree of theatre, music, dance and, naturally enough, medieval games, all held within the suitably appropriate surrounds of Suceava Fortress; just a week or two later, in the same venue, is the **Bucovina Rock Castle Festival**, a three-day gathering of mostly Romanian, and occasionally international, bands.

INFORMATION

Tourist information The excellent tourist office is at Strada Mitropoliei 4 (Mon–Fri 8am–4.30pm, Sat 9am–1pm; ☎ 0230 551 241), a few paces along from the *Bucovina* hotel (see below). They run free guided walks of the town and its main sights every Friday and Saturday at 9am. Staff here can also assist with information on visiting the painted monasteries, though for information on agencies providing tours of the monasteries, see page 259.

ACCOMMODATION

Bucovina B-dul A. Ipătescu 5 ☎ 0230 520 250, ⓦ hotelbucovina.ro; map p.250. Still bearing all the trappings of the communist era, this ugly high-rise on the centre's southern fringe still retains its rather shabby (but very cheap) older rooms, but does now possess some far more appealing renovated ones too, which don't cost that much more. Breakfast €4. **€20**

Irene's Hostel Aleea Nicului 1 ☎ 0721 280 100, ⓦ ireneshostel.ro; map p.250. Tricky to find – it's actually on the ground floor of an apartment block just behind Str. Bumbac – this small and tidy hostel has a total of ten beds in rooms ranging from a single up to a four-bed dorm; breakfast is not included but there is a kitchen for use. The owners of this hostel also offer trips to the monasteries (see page 259). Dorm **€11**

Residenz Str. N Iorga 6A ☎ 0230 251 734, ⓦ hotelresidenz.ro; map p.250. Although some way from the centre, this is an excellent station hotel, located just 250m from the Gara Suceava (turn right as you exit); rooms are immaculate, decently sized and well furnished. **€48**

Sonnenhof B-dul Sofia Vicoveanca 68 ☎ 0230 220 033, ⓦ hotelsonnenhof.com; map p.250. Located 3km southwest of town out on the E85, this is Suceava's most appealing hotel, an attractive low-rise concealing accomplished rooms with solid wood furnishings but offset with plenty of colour; the buffet breakfast will keep you going well into the afternoon. **€75**

Villa Alice Str. Simion Florea Marian 1 bis ☎ 0230 522 254, ⓦ villaalice.ro; map p.250. Centrally located but very peaceful pension with a variety of differently priced rooms, though all represent exceptional value; the more expensive ones have Louis XV style furnishings and marble tiled bathrooms with baths, a/c, DVD player and balcony. Breakfast €6. **€32**

EATING

Latino Str. Curtea Domnească 9 ☎ 0230 523 627, ⓦ restaurant-latino.ro; map p.250. Located opposite the bus station, this busy, hectic place is the best restaurant in town, offering a superb Italian-inspired menu (risotto with salmon and asparagus), plus an appetizing steak menu. Add to the mix a terrific selection of wines, and a professional and friendly service, and you've got yourself a pretty good evening. Daily 9am–11pm.

Taco Loco Str. Vasile Bumbac 5 ☎ 0230 220 032, ⓦ tacolocosv.ro; map p.250. Although this place casts itself as a Mexican, the emphasis is most definitely on Romanian food, with Moldavian specialities such as *tochitură bucovineană* and *tochitură moldovenească* forming the mainstay of a lengthy and varied menu. It's nothing to get excited about, but it will fill you up. Bizarrely, though quite usefully, it's open round the clock. Daily 24hr.

Urban Street Food and Bar Bulevardul 1 Mai 8 ☎ 0330 803 230; map p.250. It's a little trek from the centre, but well worth it for its scrumptious burgers (Double Italian, Big Boy; €5–6) and ribs, washed down with a cold Zaganu beer. The place looks great too, with its brick lined walls and bar, and ultra colourful decor. Mon–Fri 8am–midnight, Sat & Sun 10am–midnight.

DRINKING

Apropo Str. Republicii 10 ☎ 0330 111 725; map p.250. Easy-going, lounge-style café with a vaguely arty vibe that serves both the best coffee and best pastries in town. Good wi-fi and obliging staff rounds things off nicely. Mon–Fri 8am–11pm, Sat & Sun 9am–11pm.

ENTERTAINMENT

Ciprian Porumbescu Dance Ensemble (Ansamblul Artistic Ciprian Porumbescu) Str Universitatii 17 ☎ 0230 531 280. This excellent folk dance troupe, named after the nineteenth-century Romanian composer, performs in the Centre for the Traditions of Bucovina Suceava. The ensemble tours extensively around Bucovina, but do keep an eye out for any appearances here.

Mănăstirea Dragomirna

Mitocul Dragomirnei • Open access • Free • ☎ 0230 533 839, ⓦ manastireadragomirna.ro

The nearest of the Bucovina monasteries to Suceava is the (unpainted) Dragomirna Convent, 3km beyond the village of **Mitocul Dragomirnei**, which is 12km north of Suceava. Massively walled like a fortress, the **Mănăstirea Dragomirna** (Dragomirna monastery) was founded in 1602 by Metropolitan Anastasie Crimca, who designed its **church**, which is dramatically proportioned at 42m high but only 9.6m wide. There's a cable moulding around the exterior, and Renaissance windows. The octagonal tower, set on two star-shaped pedestals, is carved with meanders and rosettes, like the Church of the Three Hierarchs in Iaşi. Inside, it doesn't seem so high and thin, gradually rising by steps to the pronaos and naos, with an unusual star-vault and a very ornate Baroque iconostasis. Crimca himself is buried in the pronaos; his portrait is visible on the pillar to the left as you walk through.

The complex's solid walls and towers were added in 1627 owing to the threat of foreign invasions – these were so frequent that wooden village churches were sometimes mounted on wheels so that they could be towed away to safety. The complex is in excellent condition, with living quarters on two sides for the nuns who farm much of the surrounding land, and a **museum** harbouring a number of the original 26 manuscripts of the school of illuminators founded here by Crimca, himself a talented artist; one 1602 manuscript features Crimca's self-portrait, the earliest known by a Romanian. Also on display is an exquisite three-armed cross carved in cedar wood and containing 32 biblical scenes in miniature, and an enormous candle first lit for the monastery's consecration in 1609. The tiny original church is in the cemetery, to the left as you leave by the gateway, but it is usually locked.

From Dragomirna, it's a lovely, well-signposted 6km hike (the road is closed to cars) to Pătrăuţi and the Church of the Holy Cross (see below).

4

ARRIVAL AND DEPARTURE   DRAGOMIRNA

By maxitaxi and bus There are five maxitaxis (#31) a day on weekdays (three at weekends) from Piaţa 22 Decembrie in Suceava to the monastery, with the same number making the return journey. Alternatively, if you fancy a long and pleasant ramble, then it's do-able; take bus #5 to Iţcani, get off under the road bridge by the railway, and walk across the tracks to the right-hand or east side of the main road, Str. G.A. Ghica. The turn-off is on the right, 50m ahead, from where it's 4km to the start of the village and 4.5km more to the monastery, which is hidden from view by rolling plains until the last moment. You may have to walk from the village, but you'll pass a couple of sheepfolds along the way.

Biserica Sfântu Cruce

Pătrăuţi • Open access • Free • ☏ 0740 057 712, ⓦ biserica.patrauti.ro

Some 11km north of Suceava, just off the main DN2/E85 turning, the village of **Pătrăuţi** is the location for the **Biserica Sfântu Cruce** (Church of the Holy Cross), the first church founded by Stephen the Great, in 1487. On UNESCO's World Heritage List, the church was the prototype for subsequent Moldavian churches, and also contains the oldest paintings in Moldavia; save for a few bare patches, the tiny interior is frescoed throughout. Notable are the paintings of Stephen the Great, with a big red beard, on the south wall, and a splendid *Emperor Constantin and the Great Cavalcade* on the west wall. Alas, save for some fragments of a *Last Judgement*, and a band of painted squares under the eaves and the central tower, the exterior is devoid of ornamentation. A few paces away, the two-tiered wooden bell tower keeps a collection of haphazardly arranged wooden crosses. If the church is locked, ask at the museum just across the road, which itself contains a standard collection of vestments, icons and the like.

From the church, signs show that it's just 6km to Dragomirna monastery; the road is closed to cars, but it makes a lovely easy **hike**, once you're past the Gypsy area on the edge of the village and into the state forest. An easier option is to start from Dragomirna and then fork left to return via Lipoveni to Mitocul Dragomirnei, a loop of about 5km.

Southern Bucovina

The **painted monasteries of Southern Bucovina**, in the northwest corner of Moldavia, are rightfully acclaimed as masterpieces of art and architecture, steeped in history and perfectly in harmony with their surroundings. Founded in the fifteenth and sixteenth centuries, they were citadels of orthodoxy in an era overshadowed by the threat of infidel invaders. **Grigore Roşca**, Metropolitan of Moldavia in the mid-fifteenth century, is credited with the idea of covering the churches' outer walls with paintings of biblical events and apocrypha for the benefit of the illiterate faithful. These **frescoes**, billboards from the late medieval world, are essentially Byzantine, but infused with the vitality of the local folk art and mythology. Though little is known about the artists, their skills were such that the paintings are still fresh after 450 years of exposure. Remarkably, the layer of colour is only 0.25mm thick, in contrast to Italian frescoes, where the paint is absorbed deep into the plaster.

Perhaps the best of these are to be found at **Voroneţ**, whose *Last Judgement* surpasses any of the other examples of this subject, and **Suceviţa**, with its unique *Ladder of Virtue* and splendid *Tree of Jesse*. **Moldoviţa** has a better all-round collection, though, and **Humor** has the most tranquil atmosphere of them all. Nearby **Putna monastery**, though lacking the visual impact of the painted monasteries, is worth a visit for its rich historical associations.

The monasteries are scattered across a region divided by **rolling hills** – the *obcine* or "crests" which branch off the Carpathians – and by the legacy of history. Although settlers from Maramureş arrived here in the mid-fourteenth century, the area remained barely populated for two centuries until Huţul shepherds moved south from the Ukrainian mountains. They lived in scattered houses in the hills, and the region was a sort of free republic until the Habsburgs annexed northern Moldavia in 1774, calling it Bucovina, a Romanianized version of their description of this beech-covered land (Büchenwald). Soon the place was organized and the Huţuls moved into villages such as Argel, Raşca, Moldoviţa and Ciocăneşti, where they could better be taxed and drafted into the army. Bucovina remained under Habsburg rule until the end of World War I, when it was returned to Romania, only to be split in half in 1940 – the northern half being occupied by the Soviet Union and incorporated into Ukraine, where it remains today. Thus, Romanians speak of **Southern Bucovina** to describe what is actually the far north of Moldavia – implying that Bucovina might be reunited one day. Names aside, the scenery is wonderful, with misty valleys and rivers spilling down from rocky shoulders heaving up beneath a cloak of beech and fir. The woods are at their loveliest in May and autumn.

Gura Humorului

A small logging town some 40km west of Suceava, **GURA HUMORULUI** has more than enough facilities to make a satisfactory base for visits to the monasteries, in particular Voroneţ and Humor, both of which lie just a few kilometres either side of town and are within walking distance. In the nineteenth century its population was seventy to eighty percent Zipser German and twenty percent Jewish; the Germans left after 1945 and the last Jew died in 2006, so the population is now all ethnic Romanian.

Muzeul Obiceiurilor Populare din Bucovina

Piaţa Republicii 2 • Tues–Sun 8am–4pm • €1 • ☎ 0230 231 108

The **Muzeul Obiceiurilor Populare din Bucovina** (Bucovina Museum of Folk Customs), by the huge new Orthodox church, displays temporary shows of art, usually by émigré Romanians, on the ground floor, and ethnographic displays upstairs. These are built around tableaux of Christmas, New Year and Easter scenes, showing carol singers, masque costumes (such as the king and queen, bears, witches and Gypsies), fish

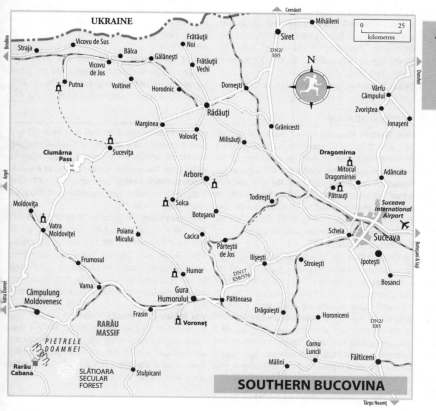

SOUTHERN BUCOVINA

traps, beehives, a smithy and a sheepfold; as interesting as it is, the absence of English captioning makes this a pretty frustrating visit.

ARRIVAL AND INFORMATION

GURA HUMORULUI

By train Be sure to leave the train at Gura Humorului Oraş station, a 10min walk west of the town centre on Str. Gării, and not Gura Humorului station amid the fields to the east. Destinations Câmpulung Moldovenesc (7 daily; 40–50min); Suceava (8 daily; 45min–1hr 10min); Vatra Dornei (7 daily; 1hr 50min).

By bus The main bus station is adjacent to the train station.

Destinations Câmpulung Moldovenesc (hourly; 45min); Iaşi (7 daily; 3hr 30min); Rădăuţi (5 daily; 1hr 15min); Solca (1 daily; 50min); Suceava (12 daily; 45min); Vatra Dornei (8 daily; 1hr 45min).

Tourist information In the small park across from the *Best Western Bucovina* hotel, you'll find the tourist information hut (Mon–Fri 8am–4pm; ☎0330 100 394), though it's just as likely to be closed as it is open.

ACCOMMODATION

Best Western Bucovina Piaţa Republicii 18 ☎0230 207 000, ⓦbestwesternbucovina.ro; map p.258. A ten-storey block towering over the roundabout at the centre of town, this is the finest large hotel in this part of Romania. Although the rooms are on the small side, they are well appointed, with ash wood furnishings and stylish bathrooms, while those from the sixth floor upwards have balconies offering superb views to the distant Bucovina hills; additional facilities include sauna, jacuzzi and Turkish bath, and a kids' play area. **€85**

★**Casa Cristian** Str. Victoriei 22 ☎0230 230 864, ⓔcristianhouse@yahoo.com; map p.258. Just off the road to Humor, 1.5km north of the centre, this magnificent four-star pension is a class above anything else in town, with individually designed rooms and Austrian-style glassed-in balconies. Cristian's top-class facilities are complemented by gracious hospitality, scrumptious organic meals and a manicured garden with over a hundred varieties each of roses and tulips. The house also hosts regular Sun morning concerts by some of Europe's finest classical musicians. **€90**

★**Hilde's Residence** Str. Şipotului 2 ☎0230 233 484, ⓦlucy.ro; map p.258. Fabulous boutique guesthouse just off the main road to Voroneţ, with sixteen rooms of varying

degrees of comfort spread between three buildings; each room is conceived in a different style, and may include, for example, wrought-iron or bamboo framed bedsteads, wicker chairs, floral textiles, French-style mirrors and wall-mounted artwork. A lovely flower garden with gazebo and a top-notch restaurant (see opposite) round things off superbly. Breakfast €6. **€50**

Pensiunea Lions Str. Ştefan cel Mare 39 ☎0230 235 226, ⓔpensiunea.lions@yahoo.com; map p.258. Situated at the turning to the train station, this vaguely Alpine-looking place possesses twelve cosy and quirkily designed rooms, furnished with lovely hand-carved wooden beds; although it's bang on the main road, it's well insulated. Breakfast is extra (€5) but this is still terrific value. **€20**

Vila Fabian Str. Câmpului 30 ☎0230 232 387; map p.258. Out on the road towards Voroneţ, this is a clean and friendly mid-range option, offering good food, saunas and massages, plus billiards and other games; another good reason to stay here is that they offer good painted monastery tours (see box). **€30**

EATING

Hilde's Residence Str. Şipotului 2 ☎0230 233 484, Ⓦlucy.ro; map p.258. As accomplished as the hotel it's housed in (see above), *Hilde's* gorgeous restaurant serves up scrummy food using ingredients plucked from their own garden and orchard; the wine card is superb too. Daily noon–10pm.

Mănăstirea Voroneţ

Ion Neculce's chronicle records that Stephen the Great founded **Mănăstirea Voroneţ** (Voroneţ monastery) in 1488 to fulfil a pledge to his confessor, the hermit Daniil, who had previously assured the despondent *hospodar* that, should he undertake a

---

VISITING THE PAINTED MONASTERIES

TOURS

Given that almost everyone comes to Southern Bucovina to visit the **painted monasteries** but public transport to them is limited, it's not surprising that many visitors opt for organized **tours**, which can be arranged either in Suceava or Gura Humorului. In **Suceava**, tourist agencies will provide a comfortable car with a driver for between €70 and €90, depending on the number of sights, and charge an additional €5–10 for an English-speaking guide. The price is generally for the car (or minibus), not per person, and doesn't usually include entrance fees; the best agencies in Suceava are Axa Travel (☎0330 102 680, Ⓦaxatravel.ro), which offers a rate of €35 per person (minimum of three people), and Hello Bucovina (☎0744 292 588, Ⓦhellobucovina.com), which offers a full-day tour of the main four monasteries for €40 per person; this also includes lunch (minimum three people). You'll have more time to see the monasteries if you choose to stay in **Gura Humorului**, where *Vila Fabian* (see opposite) runs tours for between €50 and €60 (for the car, up to a maximum of four people). The higher prices for tours from both Suceava and Gura Humorului include Putna monastery, which is out of the way and thus more expensive to visit (and also makes for a long, rushed day).

ON YOUR OWN

By making the trip independently, you'll be able to spend more time at each monastery and stay in Bucovina's charming **pensions**, many of which serve terrific home-cooked, organic meals. There's not much choice at Moldoviţa, but plenty at and around the other monasteries. The route entails striking out from Suceava and following a circular course that requires some backtracking, although this can be avoided by hiking across the hills at certain points. It can be done in reverse, but it's most convenient to head first to **Gura Humorului**, the jumping-off point for Voroneţ and Humor. From Gura Humorului, it's relatively easy to reach Vatra Moldoviţei, site of Moldoviţa monastery, but from here travel becomes more difficult; the road that leads from here to Suceviţa monastery is traversed by three or four buses a day (the Campulung to Rădăuţi bus), and light traffic makes hitching uncertain. The road continues from Suceviţa monastery to Rădăuţi, from where there are hourly maxitaxis back to Suceava. A good compromise is to make Gura Humorului your base, see Voroneţ and Humor on your own, and then either book a tour to the rest with *Vila Fabian* or commandeer a taxi for the day. Alternatively, and if you don't have your own wheels, there are plenty of **car rental** companies in Suceava, such as Autonom (☎0748 295 660, Ⓦautonom.ro) and Auto Boca (☎0733 508 484, Ⓦautoboca.ro); expect to pay around €30 per day.

OPENING TIMES AND PRICES

Though the monasteries have no set **visiting hours**, you can assume they'll be open daily from 8am to 8pm, all year round. There is usually a modest **admission charge** (€1.50), which includes entrance to the **museums** attached to the monasteries, plus a surcharge of around €2 for cameras or videos (which are usually not allowed inside the churches anyway). As working convents or monasteries, they prohibit smoking and ask that visitors dress appropriately; a few robes are kept on hand for those who arrive in shorts. The small markets set up outside the monastery entrances in summer are among the best places in the country to buy **traditional handicrafts**.

4

campaign against the Turks, he would be successful. The Turks were duly forced back across the Danube, and Voroneţ was erected in three months; chronologically, it comes between Putna and Neamţ monasteries. Its superb **frescoes** – added at the behest of Metropolitan Roşca between 1547 and 1550 – have led to Voroneţ being dubbed the "Oriental Sistine Chapel", and put "Voroneţ blue" into the lexicon of art alongside Titian red and Veronese green. Obtained from lapis lazuli, this colour appears at its most intense on a rainy day, just before sunset. Voroneţ is by far the most visited of the painted monasteries – as the crush of tourist stalls leading up to the entrance suggests – so try and time your visit for early morning or late afternoon.

The church

The **church** was designed to be entered via a door in the southern wall, with a closed exonarthex replacing the usual open porch, thus creating an unbroken surface on the western wall (at the far end). Here is painted a magnificent *Last Judgement*, probably the finest single composition among the painted monasteries. Fish-tailed bulls, unicorns and zodiacal symbols form a frieze below the eaves, beneath which Christ sits in majesty above a chair symbolizing the "Toll Gates of the Air", where the deceased are judged and prayers for their souls counted. On either side are those in limbo, the Turks and Tatars destined for perdition. Beneath them, devils and angels push sinners into the flaming river that sweeps them down to hell. In response, graves open, a sunken ship is returned from the deep, and wild animals come bearing the limbs of those they have devoured – all except the deer (a symbol of innocence) and the elephant (no threat in Romania). Amusingly, there's a crush of righteous souls at the gates of the Garden of Heaven.

The south wall, seen as you enter, is covered by three compositions: comic-strip scenes from the lives of St Nicholas and St John on the buttress; a *Tree of Jesse*; and a register of saints and philosophers where Plato is depicted with a coffin-load of bones. There are more saints and philosophers on the curved east end. Weather has largely effaced the frescoes along the north-facing wall, but you can still distinguish Adam and Eve (clothed in the Garden of Eden, semi-naked and ashamed thereafter), the first childbirth, the discovery of fire and the invention of ploughing and writing. Also notice *Adam's Deed*, illustrating the myth that Adam made a pact with Satan.

Inside, the walls and ceiling of the exonarthex are painted with martyrdoms and miracles. The second row from the bottom on the left depicts Elijah in his "chariot of fire" (like a standard Romanian *caruţa*), intent on zapping devils with his God-given powers. According to local folklore, God promptly had second thoughts and restricted Elijah's activities to his name day. On the right-hand sides of the narthex and star-vaulted sanctuary are the **tomb of Daniil** the **Hermit**, and, facing the altar, a fresco of Stephen, his wife Maria Voichiţa and their son Bogdan presenting the monastery to Christ. After 1786, the monastery was dissolved and the surrounding monks' cells disappeared, but are now being rebuilt; the **bell tower** also survives.

ARRIVAL AND DEPARTURE
VORONEŢ

By taxi From Gura Humorului to Voroneţ a taxi shouldn't cost more than €2–3; grab one from the rank just outside the tourist information hut.

By car The car park (€0.50/hr) is a 5min walk down from the monastery.

On foot On a fine day it's no hardship to walk the 4km from Gura Humorului Oraş train station (where you can leave baggage); head left along the main road, Str. Ştefan cel Mare, for 750m to the clearly signposted turn-off. There's no chance of going astray on the valley road – fork right after 3.5km to the monastery, entered by a gate near the cemetery.

ACCOMMODATION

With Gura Humorului so close, you'll probably not need to **stay the night**, but there are some reasonable options if you do. As well as those places listed below, you'll find plenty of houses offering rooms (*cazare*) throughout the village.

Casa Elena Str Voronet 8, at the entrance to the village (the north end) ☎ 0230 235 326, ⓦ casaelena.ro. This is a large complex of villas with smart double rooms largely furnished in thick pinewood; facilities include a spa centre, billiards room and a restaurant. **€45**

Voroneţ Residence Aleea Piatra Pinului (1.3km from the main road; turn left after the bridge) ☎ 0230 231 024, ⓦ voronet-residence.ro. This modern, if slightly lacklustre, place has eighteen well-kept rooms furnished in standard brown colours; it also has a handful of rooms in an older, cabana-style building just across the way. Breakfast €5. **€26**

Mănăstirea Humor

In another valley 4km north of Gura Humorului, beyond the Jewish cemetery, the tranquil village of **Mănăstirea Humor** straggles towards its namesake, the sixteenth-century **Humor monastery**. Unlike the other complexes, Humor is protected by a wooden stockade rather than a stone rampart (although the ruins of the stone wall can be seen), and lacks a spire over the naos – indicating that it was founded by a boyar, in this case Teodor Bubuiog, Chancellor of Petru Rareş, in 1530; he is now buried here with his wife Anastasia. The **frescoes** were painted by Toma of Suceava; the prevailing hues are reddish brown (from oriental madder pigment), but rich blues and greens also appear.

The *Last Judgement* on the wall beneath the unusual open porch is similar to that at Voroneţ, with the significant difference that the Devil is portrayed as the Scarlet Woman, though this patch is now so faint that you can't actually tell. Such misogyny had its counterpart in the peasant conception of hell, which was said to be a cavern upheld by seven old women who had surpassed Satan in wickedness during their lifetimes. Since the women are mortal, the legend goes, the Devil (Dracul) must constantly search the world for replacements – and he never fails to find them. The *Tree of Jesse* along the northern wall has been virtually effaced by weathering, but restorers have touched up the *Hymn to the Virgin* on the south front (with a wonderful *Adoration of the Virgin and Child* in the middle). As at Voroneţ, this depicts her miraculous intervention at the siege of Constantinople by the Persians – although the enemy was changed into Turks for propaganda purposes. Morale may have been stiffened, but neither murals nor the stone watchtower added by Basil the Wolf could save Humor from marauding Turks, and the monastery was eventually declared derelict in the eighteenth century. The interior is also fully painted with the usual calendar of saints and martyrdoms, as well as St Luke painting the Virgin and Child. It is now a small convent – the villagers use another church, on a nearby hillock.

Twelve kilometres further up the Humor valley, three **trails to Suceviţa monastery** have their starting point at the long, strung-out, Slovak-populated village of **Poiana Micului**; the easiest (marked by blue stripes) follows a forestry track and takes about five hours.

ARRIVAL AND DEPARTURE   HUMOR

By maxitaxi Maxitaxis leave for Humor from Gura Humorului's Piaţa Republicii (every 20–30min), next to the *Best Western Bucovina* hotel, though it's a pleasant walk in warm weather. If you don't want to walk back, wait for a maxitaxi at the bench just below the fork in the road. The monastery is 200m to the left of the cemetery.

ACCOMMODATION

The village is awash with **pensions**, as well as places advertising rooms (*cazare*), most of which are in close proximity to the monastery.

Casa Ancuţa Str. Ştefan cel Mare 154 ☎ 0744 638 749. Located 150m north of the monastery (there's no sign, it's next to the pharmacy), this cosy farmhouse has six snug, rustically furnished rooms (some with shared bathroom), some of which have lovely ceramic stoves; the hosts also serve delicious meals. Breakfast €3. **€16**

Casa Marion Str. M. Sadoveanu 3 ☎ 0230 572 815. Welcoming, family-run place next to the village church, offering two rooms and two apartments, all of which are en suite. Home-cooked meals can be prepared for just €7. Breakfast €3. Double **€16**, apartment **€22**

4

Mănăstirea Moldoviţa and around

Approaching from Gura Humorului, you'll find the **Mănăstirea Moldoviţa** (Moldoviţa monastery) a couple of hundred metres to the right shortly after entering the village of **Vatra Moldoviţei**, the most isolated and picturesque of the monastery villages. It's also the highest, and the air here feels cleaner than elsewhere in Bucovina. The monastery is a far smaller complex than Suceviţa but equally well defended, its ivy-clad walls enclosing white stone buildings with lustrous black-shingled roofs. It was founded in 1532 by Stephen the Great's illegitimate son, Petru Rareş, during whose reign the Turks finally compelled Moldavia to pay tribute and acknowledge Ottoman suzerainty. The monastery was painted (inside and out) by Toma of Suceava in 1537, at a time when Petru Rareş still hoped to resist the Turks, despite the inexorability of their advance following the fall of Constantinople in 1453.

To raise morale, the Turkish siege was conflated with an earlier, failed attempt by the Persians in 626 AD. A delightfully revisionist *Siege of Constantinople* along the bottom of the south wall depicts Christians routing the infidel with arrows and cannons, and miraculous icons being paraded around the ramparts. Illustrated above this is the *Hymn to the Virgin*, composed by Metropolitan Sergius in thanksgiving for her intervention, while to the right is a lovely *Tree of Jesse*, with dozens of figures entwined in foliage. All the compositions are set on an intense blue background. There's a parade of saints and philosophers on the east end, but little remains on the north wall.

The open porch contains a fine *Last Judgement*, showing a crowd of dignitaries growing agitated as a demon drags one of their number, said to be Herod, by his beard towards the fires below, where Satan sits on a scaly creature – defaced with oddly formal German graffiti, left during the years 1786 to 1931 when the monastery was closed down by the Austrians. Within the church, saints and martyrs are decapitated en masse around the narthex, nave and the intervening tomb chamber, whose doorway bears an expressive *Virgin and Child*. Although built on a Byzantine plan, the church has Gothic windows and Renaissance internal doors. Note the charming mural of Petru Rareş with his wife and sons, dutifully presenting the monastery to Jesus, on the right as you enter the nave, and the superb Crucifixion and Pentecost in the conches (virtually side apses) of the nave.

Nuns' cells line the south side of the compound, while in the northwest corner rises an imposing two-storey *clisarniţa*, a guesthouse for passing dignitaries, with a circular tower. Built in 1612, this contains a **museum** of monastic treasures including a silver-chased Evangelistry presented by Catherine the Great and the wooden throne of Petru Rareş, a bust of whom stands outside. Shepherds' trails in the surrounding hills offer ample opportunities for **walking**, with the added incentive of a view of the monastery from above.

Mocăniţa Huţulca

Moldoviţa • July & Sept daily 10am & 2pm; rest of the year plus holidays Sat & Sun 10am & 2pm; Aug daily 10am, 2pm & 5pm • €7 return • ☎ 0755 0865 618, ⊛ cfi.ro

Some 3km north of Vatra Moldoviţa, Moldoviţa is the terminus of the delightful **Mocăniţa Huţulca** (Mocăniţa Steam Train), a newly restored narrow gauge that chugs its way north to the hamlet of Argel, some 12km distant. The line – originally 24km in length – was built in 1888 to transport timber from the forest to the sawmills, a function it served until 2001; these days, its half a dozen or so carriages provide passengers with a lovely, slow ride amid gorgeous mountain scenery.

Muzeul Ouălor Lucia Condrea

Str. Stadionului 87, Moldoviţa • Daily 9am–5pm • €1 • ☎ 0230 336 312, ⊛ muzeuloualorluciacondrea.ro

Just up from the big white church in the centre of Moldoviţa is the delightful, one-of-a-kind **Muzeul Ouălor Lucia Condrea** (Museum of Painted Eggs), named after the eponymous local artist who has spent her lifetime practising this popular Romanian folk custom; indeed, such is her standing in the art that she has participated in exhibitions all over the globe. On display are a staggering five thousand eggs, made of ceramic, stone or wood and decorated with a remarkable range of geometric motifs. If Lucia is around, she's quite likely to be giving demonstrations, while in summer she hosts an international summer school for egg painting.

ARRIVAL AND DEPARTURE

VATRA MOLDOVIŢEI

By bus The train line is now defunct, and so Vatra Moldoviţei can only be reached by a limited number of bus services; even hitching is likely to take a while, as there's not much traffic over the Ciumârna Pass, which separates the two monasteries. This is a very scenic route, built only in the

1950s by the army, with a viewpoint at the pass over the low, parallel Obcinele Bucoviniei ridges. For buses to Gura Humorului, you'll have to change in Vama.
Destinations Câmpulung Moldovenesc (hourly; 45min); Rădăuţi (3–4 daily; 1hr 20min); Vama (hourly; 30min).

ACCOMMODATION

Vila Crizantema Str. Mănăstirii 284A ☎ 0230 336 116, ⓦ vilacrizantema.ro. Just off the main road on the way to the monastery, this is a friendly, comfortable pension with small, heavy pine-furnished en-suite doubles and simple, delicious meals. Closed Nov–Feb. **€24**

Vila Lulu 1.5km north of Moldoviţa monastery on the road to Suceviţa ☎ 0744 396 685, ⓦ vilalulu.ro. Chalet-style pension which also has dinky wooden huts sleeping two, and a basic field for camping; there's a modern shower block and toilets for both campers and those staying in huts. Camping **€4**, huts **€14**, doubles **€23**

Mănăstirea Suceviţa

Mănăstirea Suceviţa (Suceviţa monastery) – the last and grandest of the monastic complexes to be built in Bucovina – is a monument to Ieremia Movilă, Prince of Moldavia, his brother and successor Simion, and his widow, Elisabeta, who poisoned Simion so that her own sons might inherit the throne. The family first founded the village church in 1581, followed by the monastery church in 1584, and its walls, towers and belfry in stages thereafter. The fortified church's massive, whitewashed walls and steep grey roofs radiate an air of grandeur; its **frescoes** – painted in 1596 by two brothers – offset brilliant reds and blues with an undercoat of emerald green.

The church

Entering the monastery through the formidable gate tower, you're confronted by a glorious *Ladder of Virtue* covering the northern wall, which has been largely protected from erosion by the building's colossal eaves. Flights of angels assist the righteous to paradise, while sinners fall through the rungs into the arms of a grinning demon. The message is reiterated in the *Last Judgement* inside the unusual fully closed porch – reputedly left unfinished because the artist fell to his death from the scaffolding – where angels sound the last trumpet and smite heathens with swords, Turks and Jews can be seen lamenting, and the Devil gloats in the bottom right-hand corner. Outside the south porch, you'll see the two-headed Beast of the Apocalypse, and angels pouring rivers of fire and treading the grapes of wrath. The iron ox-collar hanging by the north doorway is a *toaca*, beaten to summon the nuns to prayer.

The *Tree of Jesse* on the south wall symbolizes the continuity between the Old Testament and the New Testament, being a literal depiction of the prophecy in Isaiah that the Messiah will spring "from the stem of Jesse". This lush composition on a dark blue background amounts to a biblical Who's Who, with an ancestral tree of prophets culminating in the Holy Family. *The Veil* represents Mary as a Byzantine empress, beneath a red veil held by angels, while the *Hymn to the Virgin* is illustrated with Italianate buildings and people in oriental dress. Along the bottom is a frieze of ancient philosophers clad in Byzantine cloaks – Plato bears a coffin and a pile of bones on his head, in tribute to his meditations on life and death. The paintings on the rounded east wall are no less impressive, depicting the *Prayer of All Saints*; cast over seven levels is a procession of angels, preachers and apostles, alongside – on the third level just above the window – the Virgin Mary holding the infant Jesus, and, above her, Jesus depicted as the Great Bishop and Judge.

Inside the narthex, the lives of the saints end in burning, boiling, spit-roasting, dismemberment or decapitation – a gory catalogue relieved somewhat by paintings of rams, suns and other zodiacal symbols. Ieremia and Simion are buried in the small tomb chamber (*camera mormintelor*) between narthex and naos, in marble tombs carved with floral motifs. The frescoes in the tomb chamber are blackened by candle smoke, but those in the nave have mostly been restored and you can clearly see a votive picture of Elisabeta and her children on the wall to the right. Ironically, her ambitions for them came to naught as she died in a Sultan's harem – "by God's will", a chronicler noted sanctimoniously.

The museum

Sucevița's **museum**, to the east in what was once the council chamber, displays a collection of richly coloured tapestries, including sixteenth-century tomb covers featuring the portraits of founder Ieremia Movilă and his brother Simion, as well as icons, an ancient wooden lectern and illuminated manuscripts bound in silver. More impressive, however are some exquisite wood-sculpted crosses, and more unusually, a collection of miniature ivory-sculpted icons, each featuring twelve remarkably detailed scenes from the bible.

Walks from Sucevița

By climbing the **hill** behind the village church's graveyard, you can see the complex as a whole, and appreciate its magnificent setting at the foot of the surrounding hills, carpeted with firs and lush pastures. The **trail to Humor** (8hr) starts next to the *Pensiunea Memory*, about 1km north of the village. It's not well marked, but heading southeast from here it should take about five hours to reach **Poiana Marului**, 12km north of Humor along a logging road that's busy enough to make hitching feasible. Opposite the monastery a forestry road leads north, continuing over the watershed (as a trail marked with blue crosses) to Putna (5hr).

ARRIVAL AND INFORMATION   SUCEVIȚA

By bus Buses stop right outside the monastery gates, by the car park.
Destinations Câmpulung (3–4 daily; 1hr 20min); Rădăuți (every 30min–1hr; 30min).

Tourist information The owners of *Casa Felicia* (see below) also run the *Reteaua Verde* ("Green Network") information centre, and can provide assistance on local crafts, architecture and walking trails, for instance to Putna or Humor.

ACCOMMODATION

Casa Felicia Str. Fierăriei 478 ☎ 0745 560 253, ✉ cazac. dana@yahoo.com. Set back from the main road a short walk east of the monastery, this restful guesthouse has seven gorgeous bedrooms decked out wall to floor with local textiles; if you can, try and bag one of the two rooms in the traditional wooden house, which retains its two beautiful ceramic stoves. Closed Oct–March. **€26**

Complex Turistic Bucovina Str. Calea Movileștilor 305 ☎ 0757 065 700, 🌐 popas.ro. Located 1.5km southwest of the monastery, out on the road to Moldovița, this wide-ranging complex has rooms in four modern villas, plus a charming wood-panelled house with its own communal area. There's also space here for camper vans (with electrical hook-ups), but not tents, plus tennis courts and a good restaurant. Doubles **€40**, villas **€45**

Mănăstirea Putna

Mănăstirea Putna (Putna monastery) may lack the external murals of the painted monasteries, but as the first of the great religious monuments of Southern Bucovina and the burial place of Stephen the Great, it is rich in historical associations and is as important to Romanian patriots as to the Orthodox faithful. Putna's relative remoteness, and absence of murals, means that it receives far fewer visitors than other monasteries, which is a shame, because there's much to savour here, and it enjoys a fabulous setting.

In 1466, Stephen chose the site of Putna monastery by firing an arrow from the steep hill that now bears a white cross. The monastery was burnt down and rebuilt in 1484, 1536 and 1691, ravaged by war three times in the seventeenth century, and repaired in the eighteenth (by Metropolitan Iacob Putneanu, who was born here and is buried in the porch), only to be damaged by an earthquake and restored again in 1902 and from 1955 to 1988. Its walls and bell tower were plainly intended for defence; in these less troubled times, they emphasize Putna's status as a patriotic reliquary. The bust of Eminescu inside the entrance (to the right) identifies the national poet with Moldavia's national hero Stephen the Great, and commemorates the speech he gave here in August 1871, on the occasion of the monastery's quadricentennial: "Let us make Putna the Jerusalem of the Romanian people, and let us also make Stephen's grave the altar of our national conscience". The Pan-Romanian Festival he organized in 1871 was followed by others in 1904 and 2004. Behind Eminescu's bust stand three **bells**, the largest of which, cast in 1484, was only used to herald events such as royal deaths, and was last rung in 1918, when it was heard as far away as Suceava. Hidden from the communists for almost fifty years, it only reappeared after the 1989 revolution. The middle bell traditionally served for everyday use, while the smallest one was the gift of an archimandrite who repaired its sixteenth-century precursor.

The church

The **church** itself is plain and strong, its facade defined by cable mouldings, blind arcades and trefoil windows, while the interior follows the usual configuration of three chambers: the sanctuary, containing the altar, at its eastern end, separated by the iconostasis from the nave, and the narthex, just inside the *pridvor* or porch – although at Putna this has also been enclosed to form an exonarthex. Prince Bogdan the One-Eyed, the wife of Petru Rareş and Stephen's daughter and nephew are buried in the narthex, which is separated from the nave by two thick, cable-moulded columns, both appearing ever so slightly wonky. Here, a graceful arch and a hanging votive lamp distinguish the **tomb of Stephen the Great** from those of his two wives, both called Maria, and two sons, Bogdan and Petru, and their family members. The frescoes, dazzling throughout and illuminated by stained-glass windows, have been repainted with gold leaf.

Treasury Tower and museum

At the rear of the yard stands the **Treasury Tower**, the only building surviving intact from Stephen's time; it kept safe one of the world's most important collections of Byzantine embroidery, now in the Abbot's House to its north. The Abbot's House was converted in 1976 to a **museum** and displays a wealth of icons, holy vessels, carved wooden crosses and illuminated manuscripts, as well as a fourteenth-century carved chest that once held the relics of St John the New. The star exhibit, however, is a magnificent collection of antique embroidery, all of which was crafted by monks from Putna; the most revered piece is the tomb cover of Stephen the Great. Indeed, an embroidery school and scriptorium still function here at Putna. The monks' cells along the wall date from 1856 (the other Bucovina monasteries now house nuns, but Putna is still all male).

Chilia lui Daniil Sihastrul

Around 1.5km east of Putna monastery (it's well signposted), there's a curious hollowed-out rock with a door and window, reputedly once the **Chilia lui Daniil Sihastrul** (Cell of Daniil the Hermit) – Stephen's confessor, whose prediction led to the foundation of Voroneţ monastery. There's nothing inside the grotto save for a simple stone table, which can be viewed through the sealed door.

Walks from Putna

You can **hike** to Suceviţa in about five hours, a route now dubbed "the Prince Charles hike" after he walked it. Pick up the route (marked by blue crosses) from (the disused) Putna station and follow the main valley for about an hour; ignore the turn-off to the left near a hut and a bridge, but take the next turning right, cross another bridge and carry on round to the left, which will bring you out at a forestry hut called *Canton Silvic 13*. From here, stick to the track up to another forestry hut, *Strulinoasa Sud*, which deteriorates into a pony trail as it approaches the watershed, but improves once it descends into an open valley. You should reach the monastery about an hour and a half after crossing the watershed. If in doubt, take the major route at every junction, turning left at the only really ambiguous one.

ARRIVAL AND DEPARTURE
PUTNA

By bus The train line to Putna is now defunct, but there are four or five maxitaxis a day from Rădăuţi (45min), where you need to change to a bus or maxitaxi to reach Suceviţa and the other monasteries.

ACCOMMODATION

Aga Str. Mănăstirii 165 ☎0230 414 223. Just below the monastery gates, on the right-hand side, this most basic of pensions has twin-bedded rooms (with shared bathrooms) in the main house, in addition to four cabins; those staying in cabins are free to use the bathroom in the house. No breakfast. Cabins **€10**, doubles **€18**

Pensiunea Muşatini Str. Mănăstirii 513A ☎0230 414 444, ⓦpensiuneamusatini.ro. A big modern place on the main road, with reasonably serviced en-suite rooms, some with balcony. There are cheaper rooms with shared bathroom in the attic. Indoor pool too. The restaurant here is pretty much the only place to eat in the village. **€28**

Rădăuţi

The market town of **RĂDĂUŢI** plays a key role in the local transport network as the junction for roads to Suceava, Putna and the painted monasteries of Suceviţa and Moldoviţa. If you find yourself with a wait between connections, you could visit a few sights of interest in the town centre, and there's some decent accommodation here.

Biserica Bogdana
Str. Bogdan Vodă

Named after its founder, Bogdan I, **Biserica Bogdana** (Bogdana Church), facing the roundabout just south of the centre of town, makes a welcome refuge on a hot day. It's the oldest stone church in Moldavia, a sturdy structure with a steeply pitched roof and large overhanging eaves, built between 1359 and 1365, and still in its original state except for the addition of a closed porch in 1559 and a semi-fortified bell tower in 1781. Inside, and unlike the monasteries, it has aisles alongside the nave. Unfortunately, the interior is so dark that it's virtually impossible to make out the remaining frescoes, themselves blackened by years of smoke. Bogdan is buried inside, along with other family members.

Muzeul Etnografic
Piaţa Unirii 63 • Daily 8am–4pm • €1 • ☎0230 562 565

On the corner of Str. Republicii (the Suceviţa road), the **Muzeul Etnografic** (Ethnographic Museum) has a comprehensive, if rather dull, collection of local costumes and artefacts. It is worth visiting, however, for its displays of **black pottery** from Marginea, a village 10km west of Rădăuţi renowned for its ceramicists, and the colourful Kuty pottery, typically green and yellow painted vases and plates decorated with floral and zoomorphic designs.

By train Rădăuți's semi-derelict train station is some 750m west of the centre on Str. Gării. Exiting the station, turn right and walk for 100m, round the bend in the road, and up to the main road, Str. Ștefan cel Mare; turning right here will bring you into town.

Destinations Suceava (2 daily; 1hr).

By bus Bewilderingly, there are some half a dozen bus/maxitaxi stations in town, most of which are located along Str. Ștefan cel Mare, so you've really just got to scour them for the right destination.

Destinations Arbore (5 daily; 25min); Câmpulung Moldovenesc (6 daily; 2hr); Putna (6 daily; 45min); Solca (10 daily; 30min); Suceava (every 30min; 50min); Sucevița (every 30min–1hr; 30min); Târgu Neamț (2 daily; 2hr 45min); Vatra Dornei (4 daily; 2hr 45min).

ACCOMMODATION

Fast Str. Ștefan cel Mare 80 ☎0230 560 060, ✉rezervari@fast-radauti.ro. Convenient for the stations, the rooms here are quite poky, and the furnishings are a bit plastic, but it's clean enough and cheap; it also has a small but decent bistro. €26

Gerald's Hotel Piața Unirii 3 ☎0330 100 650, ⊛geraldshotel.com. The stark, rather unprepossessing exterior aside, this large hotel overlooking leafy Piața Unirii is top drawer, its rooms furnished in gorgeous softwood lumber (spruce) and with fetching lime green and chocolate brown decor. Both the classy restaurant and the cool, colourful bar are creditable places to eat and/or have a drink. Restaurant daily noon–10pm; bar daily 7am–midnight. €85

Arbore

Though the church at **ARBORE** is often grouped together with the painted monasteries by virtue of its external frescoes, it is in fact merely a village church. This quibble aside, however, its kinship in form and spirit is undeniable. Opposite the cemetery, 1km east of Arbore's central crossroads, stands the **church**, built in 1503 by Luca Arbore, lord of the village and Marshal of Moldavia, who defended Suceava for forty years before he was treacherously killed in 1523. While its wooden stockade and stone bell tower are rustic enough, its frescoed walls and sweeping roof are as majestic as any monastic edifice. Like the painted monasteries, its **murals**, dating from 1541, follow iconic conventions inherited from Byzantium, which designated subjects for each wall, arranged in rows according to their hierarchical significance. This is obvious on the apses, where the angels and seraphim appear at the top, archangels and biblical saints below, then martyrs, and lastly a row of cultural propagators or military saints.

The best-preserved **frescoes** are found on the relatively sheltered south and west walls. The west wall has eight rows of scenes from Genesis and the lives of the saints, while the eaves and buttresses have protected half of the battered *Last Judgement* at the east end of the south wall, which consigns "heathens" awaiting hell to the top right-hand corner. Along the south wall lie two heavy, hollowed-out stone slabs used for mixing dyes to paint the walls, after they had been rendered with charcoal and lampblack. The founder now lies in the pronaos, under a Gothic baldachino with his wife and family members. The **iconostasis**, brought here in 1777 and blackened by centuries of smoke and incense, is at last being cleaned, together with the frescoes of the naos.

By bus Arbore lies on a back road about 35km northwest of Suceava, and public transport from the city is intermittent, so you'll be lucky to get any further than Sucevița or Gura Humorului the same day.

Solca

From Arbore, it's 7km west to a road junction 2km north of the centre of **SOLCA**, where a road leads 500m west to a **church** founded in 1614 by Ștefan Tomșa II. The church was a monastery until 1785 and like other Bucovina monasteries was fortified and used as a garrison in times of crisis. It is tall and heavily buttressed, with the characteristically Moldavian octagonal belfry on a double star-shaped base. The exterior is plain except for its Renaissance doors and windows; the church is unpainted but there are strong cable mouldings inside and a score of processional crosses and banners, as well as a horse-drawn hearse and bier outside.

ACCOMMODATION   SOLCA

Hanul Solca Str Tomşa Vodă 18, a short walk down from the church ☎ 0230 477 508. If for any reason you need to stay in the village, this friendly local inn has a mix of very simple but good-sized doubles and triples, all en suite. No breakfast. €20

Cacica

The old salt mine of **CACICA**, 12km south of Solca, was founded in the late eighteenth century by Austrian emperor Franz Josef II. The first miners to be settled here were Polish, and they named the village after wild ducks (*kaczki* in Polish) found nesting in nearby swamps. Workers of other nationalities followed, and by the mid-nineteenth century Cacica was known for its ethnic mix and nicknamed "little Austria". The Czechs, Germans and Slovenes who once laboured here are long gone, but there is still a sizeable Polish community – around twenty percent of the population – and lots of Polish visitors to the Roman Catholic church (a Minor Basilica) and summer events.

The Cacica air is said to be beneficial for those suffering from respiratory diseases. However, the salt vein here is mixed with clay and needs to be heated to the point of evaporation to crystallize: for many years, fuel oil was used in this process, and today a strong odour of petroleum acts as a deterrent to would-be convalescents.

Mina de Sare Cacica
Adjacent to the modern mine in the heart of the town • Daily 9am–5pm • €3

An enjoyable visit for adults and kids alike, the **Mina de Sare Cacica** (Salt Mine) is accessed by a moderately treacherous, salt-encrusted staircase down to a large chamber some 30m below the surface; also known as the St Barbara chapel (St Barbara being the patron saint of miners), it is where salt was first extracted in 1803; communions are still occasionally held here. Further steps lead down a long hallway to a tiny, recessed chapel with a cross sculpted in salt rock, discovered in 1971; carved into the wall are a series of life-size salt reliefs depicting biblical figures such as Adam and Eve. Another descent brings you to an enormous cavern taken over by a football pitch, before you emerge into the Brine Lake, where you'll also see the original, now heavily salt-encrusted raft which was used to transport guests to the adjacent Sala del Bal (ballroom) – it's believed that King Carol I once attended a ball here; relaid with wooden flooring and lit by chandeliers, this is still used for the occasional function. The rest of the more than 50km of underground passages are off limits to the public.

Câmpulung Moldovenesc

The logging town of **CÂMPULUNG MOLDOVENESC**, 70km west of Suceava on the main road and rail line to Cluj, is chiefly of interest as a base for **hiking** in the Rarău and Giumalău massifs, and as a way station en route to Transylvania or Maramureş. A longish block east by the tracks brings you to memorials to the Red Army soldiers killed in 1944 and to political prisoners under communism (a telling conjunction) at Strada D. Cantemir. Left of here is a **riverside park** with embankment paths and decent footbridges east and west; right is the main pedestrianized plaza on Calea Bucovinei – don't miss the impressively kitsch bronze **statue of Prince Dragoş** and the aurochs (see page 252).

Muzeul Artei Lemnului
Calea Transilvaniei 10 • Tues–Sun 9am–5pm • €1 • ☎ 0230 311 378

Next to the gaudy pseudo-Byzantine church, the **Muzeul Artei Lemnului** (Museum of Wooden Art) demonstrates the absolute ubiquity of wooden products in traditional life here. The displays upstairs include fish and rat traps, log beehives, a honey centrifuge, a butter churn and mould, wooden ploughs, hayforks, ceremonial hatchets, carved shepherds' staves, musical instruments, plates, spoons and mugs, and everything else from limebark sandals up to oil and fruit presses and carts and sleighs, with black-and-white photos of them in use. Many are intricately carved, but all have the beauty of functionality and some are very imaginative. There are also some sculptures inside the front door, as well as portrait plaques and modern abstract sculptures; in the yard at the rear are a few wooden houses and gateways. There are captions in English, French and German, but sadly no mention of which kinds of wood are used.

Colecţia de Linguri din Lemn

Str. Gheorghe Popovici 1 • Tues–Sun 9am–5pm • €1 • ☎ 0230 311 315

Thrills of the wooden variety are to be had at the late Professor Ion Tugui's vast **Colecţia de Linguri din Lemn** (Collection of Wooden Spoons), a bizarre delight that's said to be the only one of its kind in Europe. Lining every spare inch of the walls, ceilings and stairwells of this small house are some five thousand spoons, crafted in all manner of shapes, sizes and colours, many intricately painted and some even encrusted with jewels. Identifiable by its colourful plates affixed to the exterior, it's located just west of the centre (and near the station).

ARRIVAL AND DEPARTURE CÂMPULUNG MOLDOVENESC

By train Câmpulung Moldovenesc has two train stations: Câmpulung Est is 2km east of town – alight here only if you want to hike straight off up Rarău (or are staying at the *Eden* hotel); and Câmpulung Moldovenesc – to reach the centre from here, exit left and walk along Str. Viitorului for 100m, whereupon you reach the bus station; turn right here, past the market (with a small Ukrainian bazaar) and up to the main street, Calea Transilvaniei (which becomes Calea Bucovinei east of the town centre).

Destinations Cluj (4 daily; 5hr 40min); Gura Humorului (7 daily; 40–50min); Iaşi (3 daily; 3hr 40min); Suceava (7 daily; 1hr 30min–2hr); Vatra Dornei (8 daily; 1hr 10min).

By bus The bus station is just behind the market on Str. Vitorului, from where it's a 5min walk into the centre.

Destinations Cluj (5 daily; 5hr); Gura Humorului (10 daily; 50min); Iaşi (4 daily; 4hr); Piatra Neamţ (1 daily; 5hr); Rădăuţi (6 daily; 2hr); Suceava (hourly; 1hr 30min); Vatra Dornei (7 daily; 1hr); Vatra Moldoviţei, then Moldoviţa (hourly; 45min).

ACCOMMODATION

Eden Calea Bucovinei 148 ☎ 0230 314 733, ⓦ hoteledengardenspa.ro. Despite its dowdy exterior, this three-star, 1km west of the Câmpulung Est station, is perfectly acceptable; there's also a tightly packed row of bungalows sleeping two to four people. Pool, sauna and fitness facilities. Hotel year round; bungalows closed Oct–April. **€45**

Pensiune Bucovina Calea Transilvaniei 13 ☎ 0230 311 111, ⓦ pensiunebucovina.ro. Occupying a communist-era apartment block, the six rooms here are in fact smartly presented, with modern furnishings and tasteful decor; reception is in the large and lively restaurant, itself the best place to eat in town, though that's not really saying much. **€38**

The Rarău massif

The **Rarău massif** to the south of Câmpulung is a popular **hiking** spot, with its dense spruce forests harbouring lynx, bears, roebuck and other **wildlife**. Most visitors base themselves at the *Rarău* cabana (☎ 0758 852 959; 1520m), 14km and three to four hours' walk up the road from Câmpulung Est station. From the cabana, a four-hour trail marked by red triangles leads past the **Pietrele Doamnei** ("Princess's Rocks"), three huge Mesozoic limestone towers, to reach the ancient **Slătioara Secular Forest** of 50m-high firs and spruces. Another route (red-striped) runs southwest from *Rarău* to the *Giumalău* cabana (3–4hr; ☎ 0748 359 121), from where you can hike on to Vatra Dornei via the Obcina Mică peak (5–6hr). None of these trails is feasible in winter.

ACTIVITIES AROUND VATRA DORNEI

There are fine **hikes** on all sides of Vatra Dornei, as shown on maps available at the tourist office. One of these (approximately 22hr), to the Rotunda Pass in the Rodna mountains (marked by blue stripes), begins at the Băi station. It then runs up Strada Luceafărului and west along Strada Eminescu, past an abandoned Moorish-style synagogue, and leaves town past a self-styled motel (actually a bar full of hunting trophies) and the campsite; you'll need your own camping gear for this hike as there are no cabanas along the route. A shorter trail (marked with blue then red stripes), with more dramatic scenery and a choice of mountain cabanas, heads east from the Băi station to Giumalău (5hr 30min), Rarău (9–10hr from Băi station) and Câmpulung Moldovenesc (11–13hr from Băi station). The **chairlift** at the top of Str. Negreşti is open year-round (daily 10am–5pm but sometimes closed 1–3pm; €5 return); from Strada Republicii, walk up Strada G. Coşbuc or Strada Negreşti, following the *telescaun* signs. The lift takes 25min to ascend to the peak of Dealul Negrii (1300m), where ravens circle over alpine meadows. Bring provisions as the café at the top of the lift is frequently closed. There's also a shorter ski-drag, the Teleschi Parc, immediately west of the park, that operates only in winter, with ski rental shacks and a bar at its foot. An Olympic cross-country ski centre is near the campsite at the top of Strada Runc. Dorna Adventure (☎0744 332 378, ⦿dorna-adventure.ro) can arrange guided hiking, ice-climbing, cross-country skiing, mountain biking and rafting among many other activities.

The road **to Vatra Dornei** crosses the lovely Mestecăniş Pass (1096m), by way of two villages with Ukrainian-style **wooden churches**, to enter the Bistriţa valley. The *Mestecăniş* cabana is here, 8km east of the large village of Iacobeni, the site of a murder by poison recounted in Gregor von Rezzori's *The Snows of Yesteryear* (see page 402), and where trains usually halt after emerging from a tunnel below the pass. Accommodation is available at the *Roşan* cabana (☎0742 469 589) in the village of Mestecăniş.

Vatra Dornei

Forty kilometres west of Câmpulung Moldovenesc, the former logging town of **VATRA DORNEI** has been better known as a spa since Habsburg times, and has dabbled in skiing and other outdoor activities since the 1970s. The skiing facilities in particular have developed in recent years, and though the slopes themselves are not challenging, Vatra Dornei is an increasingly popular winter destination for Romanians and Ukrainians, and is rich in hotels and pensions, if not sights. Across the river by a footbridge from Vatra Dornei Băi train station, you'll see the ochre and white Baroque casino, once the focal point for visitors but now derelict and awaiting its fate. Behind this is the spa's large and lovely **park**, home to a few red squirrels, a mineral spring piped through a mock-Gothic tower, and a neo-Byzantine church opposite an onion-domed bandstand.

ARRIVAL AND INFORMATION

VATRA DORNEI

By train There are two stations in town, the most useful of which is Vatra Dornei Băi, right in the centre of town on Str. Dornelor; the other, Vatra Dornei, is north of town.

Destinations Câmpulung Moldovenesc (7 daily; 1hr); Cluj (4 daily; 4hr 30min); Gura Humorului (6 daily; 1hr 50min); Iaşi (3 daily; 4hr 40min); Ilva Mică (7 daily; 1hr 35min–2hr 10min); Suceava (6 daily; 2hr 35min–3hr 10min).

By bus Vatra Dornei's main bus station is on Str. 22 Decembrie, 100m east of the train station, on the south side of the River Dorna; some buses also depart from Autogară Sincarom, 100m west of *Carol* hotel (see opposite).

Destinations Bistriţa (8 daily; 2hr 15min); Câmpulung Moldovenesc (7 daily; 1hr); Cârlibaba (2 daily; 1hr 15min); Cluj (4 daily; 4hr 45min); Gura Humorului (8 daily; 1hr 45min); Piatra Neamţ (3 daily; 4–5hr); Poiana Largului (4 daily; 2hr 30min); Rădăuţi (4 daily; 3hr); Suceava (7 daily; 2hr 30min); Târgu Neamţ (2 daily; 3hr 50min); Vişeu de Sus (1 daily; 2hr 45min).

Tourist information The tourist information office, across from Vatra Dornei Băi station at Str.Gării 2 (Mon–Fri 9am–5pm; ☎0230 372 767, ⦿vatra-dornei.ro), has town maps as well as a map of local hiking trails.

ACCOMMODATION AND EATING

Most of Vatra Dornei's many **hotels** are located on the spa (south) side of the river, with a cluster of pensions located in the maze of side streets between the ski lifts.

Bristena Str. Eminescu 34 ☎ 0230 372 338. Fabulous patisserie with a delectable selection of cakes, pastries and chocolates, plus pretty decent coffee too. Mon–Sat 7am–11pm, Sun noon–11pm.

Carol Str. Republicii 3 ☎ 0751 214 844, ⓦ hotelcarol.ro. Distinctive, Austrian-styled building with corner turrets and wooden balconies just a few paces along from the casino, whose elegantly furnished rooms come with brass fixtures

and fittings, chandelier lighting and old-style telephones; the very reasonable price includes use of sauna and jacuzzi. **€45**

Casa Bucovineană Str. Vasile Deac 2 ☎ 0230 372 588, ⓦ casa-bucovineana.ro. Although it's 1.5km west of town, it's worth the short trek to eat in this convivial, faux-rustic restaurant. Serves a lengthy list of Romanian standards in addition to veal steak, grilled chicken liver, beer sausages and the like. Decent house beer too. They've got perfectly competent rooms too. Restaurant daily 8am–midnight. **€22**

Routes to Maramureş and Transylvania

From Vatra Dornei, you can head southeast towards **Neamţ county**, northwest into **Maramureş**, or west into **Transylvania**. Four buses a day follow the scenic Bistriţa valley down to Poiana Largului, at the northern end of Lake Bicaz and in the vicinity of the Ceahlău massif (see page 235); three of them carry on to Piatra Neamţ or Târgu Neamţ.

The route to Maramureş heads up the valley past such lovely villages as **Ciocăneşti**, where Huţul houses with decorated facades are perched on hillocks. There are ski-drags here and hiking trails on both sides of the valley, and facilities for equestrian tours. Around Easter, the village holds the **National Festival of Painted Eggs**, one of the most important and popular of its kind in the country; there is also a trout fishing festival in July or August. If you wish to stay, you can choose from various guesthouses dotted around.

Just north, **Botos** has a **wooden church** in the Ukrainian style: very broad and square, with one large and four small cupolas. Eight kilometres north of **Cârlibaba** (founded by Zipser German foresters in the late eighteenth century), the road forks towards the Rotunda Pass into Transylvania, and the Prislop Pass into Maramureş, where the **Horă at Prislop Festival** occurs on the second Sunday in August. One bus daily (leaving Vatra Dornei at 1.30pm) crosses the mountains to Vişeu de Sus in Maramureş, while another runs as far as Cârlibaba, from where you could probably hitch over the pass. Heading north instead of west from Cârlibaba, a battered road that ends at the Ukrainian border passes through the tiny Huţul hamlet of Moldova Suliţa. From there it's 7km up a dirt path to the **Lucina Stud**, where the famous Hutzul horses, used for cavalry in Austrian times, are bred.

Of the three routes into Transylvania, the most dramatic is via the **Tihuţa Pass** – otherwise known as the Bârgău Pass, where Bram Stoker located Dracula's castle. Along the way, you'll find accommodation in a number of pensions in **Poiana Ştampei**. Eight buses a day from Vatra Dornei run through the pass en route to Bistriţa. Travelling by train, you'll take a more northerly route via Ilva Mică. The third route, only possible if you're driving, crosses the 1271m-high **Rotunda Pass**, which is prone to blizzards.

4

Maramureş

ROMANIAN WINTER FESTIVAL, MARAMURES

5 Maramureş

Romania has been described as a country with one foot in the industrial future and the other in the Middle Ages – that's still true enough of Maramureş, crammed up against the borders with Hungary and Ukraine and little changed since Dacian times. Within 30km of industrial Baia Mare, forested mountains and rough roads maintain scores of villages in almost medieval isolation, amid rolling hills with clumps of oak and beech and scattered flocks of sheep.

The county's main attraction is its **villages**, with their superb wooden houses and churches, and traditional way of life. Every family occupies a compound with its livestock, fenced with timber, brush or latticework, and entered via a beamed gateway (*poarta*), the size of which indicates the family's status and prosperity. Nowhere else in Europe do **folk costumes** persist so strongly, men wearing tiny *clop* straw hats and medieval rawhide galoshes (*opinchi*) or archaic felt boots bound with thongs, and women weaving boldly striped *catriniţa* aprons of cloth from the water-powered fulling mills. It is the women who embroider the wide-sleeved cotton blouses worn by both sexes – most conspicuously during markets and **festivals**. Villagers have retained their traditional **religion** (Orthodox rites alloyed with pagan beliefs), myths and codes of behaviour.

Most interesting of all is the marvellous **woodwork** of Maramureş: the gateways, many elaborately carved with symbols such as the Tree of Life, sun, rope and snake, continue to be produced today, and are rivalled only by the *biserici de lemn* or **wooden churches**, mostly built during the eighteenth century when this Gothic-inspired architecture reached its height – Maramureş has the finest examples in all of Eastern Europe (see page 283), their fairy-tale spires soaring from humpbacked roofs. While some wooden churches are in a poor state, around twenty of the most valuable have been restored in recent years, and eight are on UNESCO's World Heritage List. In recent years many new **monasteries** have also been constructed, in a modern version of the traditional style. Wooden houses, on the other hand, are vanishing from Maramureş villages, as modern homes are built and old timbers sold off to panel bars across Western Europe.

It's particularly worth making the effort to see the towering wooden church at **Şurdeşti**, the beautiful church paintings at **Bârsana**, **Rogoz** and **Deseşti**, the frescoes and icons of **Călineşti** and **Budeşti**, the superb prison museum in **Sighet** and the quirky "Merry Cemetery" at **Săpânţa**. Further afield in the Iza valley, the visions of hell painted inside the church at **Poienile Izei** are the most striking images you'll see in Maramureş, while the frescoes at **Ieud** are the most famous. There's also good hiking in the peaceful **Rodna** and **Maramureş mountains** on the borders with Bucovina and Ukraine.

GETTING AROUND   MARAMUREŞ

Getting around can be tricky, as side roads are rough and public transport is patchy, especially at weekends. Other than buses and maxitaxis, the alternatives to renting a car are cycling – especially given the short distances between villages – or hitching, though be prepared for intermittent lifts or rides in the back of carts or vans. Hotel accommodation is generally limited to towns, but there are many village guesthouses. In fact, Maramureş is leading the way in developing rural tourism, with homestay schemes and cycle circuits (including a Greenway trail south and west from Ocna Şugatag to Budeşti and Deseşti, over half of its 88km on forestry roads). Bikes can be rented from guesthouses in Sighet, Vadu Izei, Breb, Deseşti, Ocna Şugatag and elsewhere.

BARSANA MONASTERY

Highlights

❶ Wooden churches With their magnificent spires, wooden churches are an integral part of the Maramureş landscape and several are now on UNESCO's World Heritage List. See page 283

❷ Prison Museum, Sighet Illuminating and moving tributes to the victims of communism in Sighet's notorious prison. See page 289

❸ Winter Customs Festival, Sighet Lively Christmas spectacle featuring folk music, wacky costumes and traditional customs. See page 289

❹ Merry Cemetery, Săpânţa Exuberantly coloured and beautifully crafted wooden grave markers in one of Romania's most unusual attractions. See page 293

❺ Logging train, Vişeu de Sus Jump aboard the early-morning mocăniţa for a picturesque ride up the Vaser valley. See page 302

❻ Rodna mountains Beautifully unspoiled mountain range offering some of the country's most enjoyable and secluded hiking. See page 304

HIGHLIGHTS ARE MARKED ON THE MAP ON PAGE 276

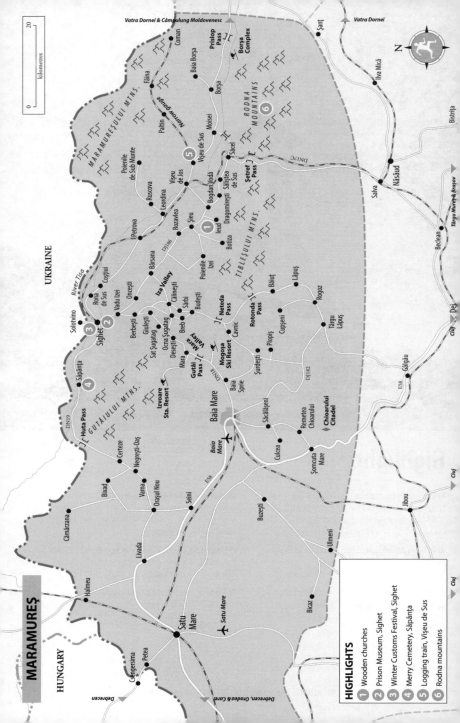

MARAMUREŞ

HUNGARY

UKRAINE

River Tisa

MARAMUREŞULUI MTNS.

Narrow gauge

RODNA MOUNTAINS

TIBLEŞULUI MTNS.

GUTÂIULUI MTNS.

Vatra Dornei & Câmpulung Moldovenesc

Vatra Dornei

Şanţ

Ilva Mică

Coman

Prislop Pass

Borşa Complex

Baia Borşa

Borşa

Moisei

Făina

Paltin

Poienile de Sub Munte

Vişeu de Sus **5**

Săcel

Setref Pass

Salva

Năsăud

Bistriţa

Ruscova

Leordina

Vişeu de Jos

Bogdan Vodă

Săliştea de Sus

Dragomireşti

DN17C

Petrova

Rozavlea

Şieu

Ieud **1**

Botiza

DN18G

Bârsana

Poienile

Izei

Izel

Iza Valley

Vadu Izei

Rona de Sus

Oncești

Costiui

Solotvino

Sighet **2 3**

Berbeşti

Giulești

Sârbi

Budeşti

Neteda Pass

Băiuţ

Lăpuş

Rogoz

Ocna Şugatag

Breb

Călineşti

Rotonda Pass

Sat Şugatag

Deseşti

Vama Valley

Cavnic

Cupşeni

Târgu Lăpuş

Săpânţa **4**

Mara

Gutâi Pass

Mogoşa Ski Resort

Plopiş

Şurdeşti

DN18

Izvoare Sta. Resort

Huta Pass

Baia Sprie

Baia Mare

Certeze

Negreşti-Oaş

Orașul Nou

Seini

Săcălăşeni

Remetea Chioarului

Chioarului Citadel

DJ182

Gălgău

Dej

Cluj

Biсаz

Camârzana

Bixad

Vama

Livada

Buzeşti

Culcea

Şomcuta Mare

Ulmeni

Ibou

Halmeu

Satu Mare

Satu Mare

Petea

Cehegesima

DN19

E58

Baia Mare ✈

Debrecen, Oradea & Carei

Debrecen

Târgu Mureş & Braşov

Bistriţa

N

kilometres

0   20

Baia Mare

5

To the south of the Gutâi and Igniş mountains, **BAIA MARE**, the largest town in Maramureş, makes a good base for forays into the surrounding countryside. Mining has been important here since the fourteenth century when, under its Magyar name of Nagybánya ("big mine"), it was the Hungarian monarchs' chief source of gold, but it remained a small town until the communists turned it into a major nonferrous metals centre in the 1950s, diluting its largely Hungarian population to just fourteen percent of the total. The town has an attractive old core, now largely restored, and some worthwhile museums, in particular the **Art Gallery** and **Village Museum**.

The heart of Baia Mare's **old town** is **Piaţa Libertăţii**, a beautifully restored square lined with sixteenth- to eighteenth-century houses; it is now pedestrianized, along with parts of the neighbouring streets, and there are plenty of bars along its south side. At no. 18, the thick-walled **Casa Elisabeta** was begun by Iancu de Hunedoara, fifteenth-century Regent of Hungary, for his wife, and completed by their son, Matei Corvin; next door is the house where the great Hungarian actor Lendvay Márton was born in 1807. On the west side of the square a lovely Secession hotel is now the newly refurbished Cinematograful Minerul, albeit this is now only used for the occasional art exhibition. To the south of the square rises the 40m-high **Stephen's Tower**, built in 1442–46 and all that remains of a Roman Catholic cathedral that burned down in 1769; the adjacent Baroque pile, built by the Jesuits in 1717–20, then became the city's cathedral. Immediately north of Piaţa Libertăţii, at the junction of Strada Monetăriei and Strada Podul Viilor, is the landmark **Reformat church**, built in 1809 and topped by what seems to be a giant red diver's helmet, which appears in many paintings by the Nagybánya School. Other than the museums listed in this account, the modern **Muzeul de Mineralogie** (Museum of Mineralogy; B-dul Traian 8; Tues–Sun 9am–5pm), towards the stations, is also worth a quick look.

The **Chestnut Festival** (Sărbătoarea Castanelor), held over the last weekend of September, celebrates – naturally – the chestnut season, with exhibitions, a riotous beer festival and traditional music on the Sunday.

Muzeul Satului and Muzeul de Etnografie şi Artă Populară

Str Dealul Florilor 1 • Tues–Sun: May–Sept 10am–8pm; Oct–April 10am–6pm • €1 • ☎ 0262 276 895, ⓦ etnografie-maramures.ro

Baia Mare's main attraction is its **Muzeul Satului** (Village Museum), ten minutes' walk north of the centre, where many peasant houses, wine presses, watermills and other structures from the surrounding region are preserved. In particular look out for the wooden church – raised in 1630 in Chechiş, just south of Baia Mare – and, close by, the homestead from Berbeşti, with its fine carved gate with the Tree of Life motif.

A five-minute walk away from the Village Museum, and under the same management, the **Muzeul de Etnografie şi Artă Populară** (Museum of Ethnography and Folk Art) presents a neat array of agricultural and viticultural implements, ceramics, textiles and garments from the four ethnographic regions of Maramures: Chioar, Lăpuş, Codru and Historic Maramureş.

Muzeul de Artă

Str. 1 Mai 8 • Tues–Sun 10am–4.30pm • €1.50 • ☎ 0262 213 964

The **Muzeul de Artă** (Museum of Art) contains eighteenth- and nineteenth-century paintings on wood and glass, and a number of canvases by artists of the **Nagybánya School** (see page 279). Much of the work is now in Hungary, however, and the stuff here is attributed – in a somewhat nationalistic gesture – to the "Baia Mare School". While the usual big-hitters of Romanian art are absent from this particular gallery, this by no means makes it any less interesting.

5

Colonia Pictorilor and Galeria Oliver Thurman

Colonia Pictorilor Str. Victoriei 21 • Mon–Fri 8am–3pm • **Galeria Oliver Thurman** Piaţa Libertăţii 17 • Tues–Sat 2–6pm, Sun noon–4pm • Free • **Library** Mon–Fri 8am–7pm, Sat 9am–2pm

The villa that housed the Nagybánya School in 1910–12 is now the **Colonia Pictorilor** gallery, staging temporary exhibitions. Another exhibition venue is the **Galeria Oliver Thurman** on the east side of Piaţa Libertăţii, which also has a permanent display of works by the renowned local wood sculptor, Géza Vida. Vida made a name for himself after World War II – exhibiting at the Venice biennial in 1958 – with his themes of mythology and realism; the pieces on show here are a constant delight. You're also quite likely to find exhibitions held in the modern **library** next to the House of Culture.

Muzeul de Istorie şi Arheologie

Str. Monetăriei 1 • Tues–Sun 10am–5pm • €1 • ☎ 0262 211 924, ⓦ muzeubaiamare.ro

Housed in the old mint (1734–42), the **Muzeul de Istorie şi Arheologie** (Museum of History and Archeology) covers the local mining industry, with Bronze Age metalwork, coins – some produced in this very building – and around three hundred clocks, the undoubted highlight of the collection. There are also sixteenth- to nineteenth-century religious books, and medieval ceramics.

Strada Dr Vasile Lucaciu to the Butchers' Bastion

Butchers' Bastion exhibition Mon–Fri 8.30am–4pm • Free

Strada Dr Vasile Lucaciu has some interesting old buildings whose cellars are entered from the street, and an attractive Hungarian Lutheran church. The road leads to the Orthodox Cathedral, built by the Greek Catholics in 1905–11 (there was no Orthodox church in Baia Mare until 1926). From here, Strada Olarilor follows the line of the

BAIA MARE

N

● EATING	
Barbarossa	1
Bizo	3
Buonissimo	5
Il Padrino	6
Pur şi Simplu	4
Sandwich House	2

■ DRINKING	
The Cellar	2
Log Out	3
Podul Viilor	1

■ ACCOMMODATION	
Diafan	2
La Fontana	5
Pensiunea Pictorilor	1
Pensiunea Union (Casa Rusu)	4
Rivulus	3
Sport	6

Village & Ethnographic Museums • Ethnographic Museum • Village Museum

STRADA TUDOR VLADIMIRESCU • ALEEA N. GRIGORESCU • Stadium • STRADA MINERILOR • STR. PODUL VIILOR

STRADA IULIU MANIU • Satu Mare • STRADA VICTORIEI • Colonia Picturilor • Museum of Archeology and History • Orthodox Cathedral • STRADA DR. VASILE LUCACIU • Sighet

CFR • House of Culture • MINERVA • House of Iancu de Hunedoara • PIAŢA LIBERTĂŢII • Stephen's Tower • Evangelical Church

BULEVARD INDEPENDENŢEI • River Şasar • Prefecture ℹ • STR. CERBI • PIAŢA PĂCII • STR. ŞTEFAN • Cathedral • STRADA OLARILOR

Observatory • STR. G. COŞBUC • STRADA GH. ŞINCAI • STRADA MUREŞAN • STRADA CULTURII • Art Gallery • STR. TM.

Train and Bus Stations • PIAŢA REVOLUŢIEI • Butchers' Bastion

BULEVARD BUCUREŞTI • STRADA 22 DECEMBRIE • Market • PIAŢA IZVOARELOR • TAROM

STR. 9 MAI • STR. PROGRESULUI • Maxitaxis To Târgu Lăpuş ★ • STRADA MIHAI EMINESCU

Museum of Mineralogy • B-DUL TRAIAN • BULEVARD UNIRII • STR. ŞUIULUI • STR. VASILE ALECSANDRI • Jewish Cemetery • Dej

0 — 300 metres

Greek Catholic Church

▼ Târgu Lăpuş

5

THE NAGYBÁNYA SCHOOL

The **Nagybánya School** (using the Hungarian version of the city's name) was responsible for transforming Hungarian art at the close of the nineteenth century. Its founder was **Simon Hollósy** (1857–1918), born of Armenian stock in Sighet and trained in Munich, where he was influenced by the refined naturalism of Jules Bastien-Lepage. In 1886 he set up his own school in Munich, and from 1896 brought his students to a summer school in Baia Mare. An exhibition in 1897 of the school's paintings was seen as marking the start of a new era in Hungarian art and the school became known as the "Hungarian Barbizon", although the area's motifs and colours were closer to those of Provence.

In 1902, Hollósy suffered a creative crisis, and the leadership of the school was taken over by **Károly Ferenczy**; tuition fees were abolished, and the embittered and jealous Hollósy left to set up a rival school in Técső, now the Ukrainian town of Tyachiv, just downstream of Sighet. Ferenczy suffered a similar crisis in 1910, and did little work thereafter. Of the second generation of artists, the most gifted was Cavnic-born Jenő Maticska (1885–1906). After his untimely death, Béla Czóbel, Csába Vilmos Perlrott, Sándor Ziffer and others revolted against creeping stagnation; their 1906 exhibition, influenced by Cézanne, Matisse and German Expressionism, again marked the start of a new era in Hungarian art. After World War I the school was opened to both Hungarian and Romanian students – up to 150 a year – but interest faded in the 1930s and the school closed its doors.

old city walls south to Piaţa Izvoarelor, where the fifteenth-century **Butchers' Bastion** (Bastionul Măcelarilor) overlooks the market place in which Robin Hood-style outlaw Pintea Viteazul (Pintea the Brave) was shot in 1703 during the Rakóczi rebellion; it now houses craft displays.

ARRIVAL AND INFORMATION
BAIA MARE

By plane Maramureş airport (☎0262 293 444, ⓦaimm. eu), with just a handful of flights to Bucharest, is 9km west on the Satu Mare road. A taxi will cost around €7.

By train The station, 2km west of town on Str. Gării, is linked to the centre by buses #1, #2, #9 and #50.
Destinations Braşov (2 daily; 9hr 30min–11hr); Bucharest (2 daily; 12–14hr); Cluj (3 daily; 4hr 20min); Dej (3 daily; 2hr 30min); Satu Mare (4 daily; 1hr 45min).

By bus The Imperativ bus station is immediately north of the railway station some 2km west of town, and is reached by buses #1, #2, #9 and #50. Buses for Săcălăşeni and Culcea (5 Mon–Fri, 3 Sat & Sun) leave from the Piaţa Izvoarelor

market; those to Târgu Lăpuş leave from Str. Eminescu, just south of the market.
Destinations Bicaz (2 daily); Borşa (14 daily); Bucharest (2 daily); Cavnic (5 daily); Cluj (12 daily); Hoteni (6 daily); Negreşti-Oas (4 daily); Oradea (every 2hr); Satu Mare (12 daily); Sighet (15 daily); Târgu Lăpuş (3 daily); Vişeu (10 daily); Budapest (2 daily).

Tourist information Maramureş InfoTurism is in the Prefectura (County Hall) at Str. Şincai 46 (Mon–Thurs 9am–4pm, Fri 9am–2pm); ☎0262 206 113, ⓦvisitmaramures.ro.

GETTING AROUND

By car Rental companies include Rent a Car Maramureş, Str. Bogdan Vodă, Block 3 staircase E (☎0744 705 873, ⓦrentacarbaiamare.ro), and Logicar Motors, B-dul Independenţiei 28A (☎0745 704 837).

By bike Ski & Bike Centre, Str. Victoriei 3 (Mon–Fri 10am–6pm, Sat 10am–5pm; ☎0362 412 576, ⓦbike-ski.ro).

ACCOMMODATION

★**Diafan** Piaţa Libertăţii 14 ☎0362 402 702, ⓦhoteldiafan.ro; map p.278. Comfortably the pick of Baia Mare's hotels, this stylish outfit occupies a superbly restored medieval building in the heart of the old town and offers eleven attractive, colourfully decorated rooms. €55
La Fontana Str. Closca 11 ☎0362 402 777, ⓦla-fontana.ro; map p.278. Just south of the historic centre, this is a good budget option, with warm, well furnished

rooms and comfortable beds, alongside a reasonably priced Italian restaurant. €30
Pensiunea Pictorilor Str. Pictorilor 1 ☎0756 420 992, ⓦpensiuneapictorilor.ro; map p.278. The "Painter's" guesthouse is a remarkably good value place near the Colonia Pictorilor, with twelve simple en-suite rooms, some of which are named after the painters themselves; there's a pleasant café too. Breakfast €4. €20

Pensiunea Union (Casa Rusu) Str. Crişan 9 ☎0262 215 752; map p.278. In the courtyard of a fine Neoclassical townhouse, just south of the city centre (ask at the RMN Clinic in the same courtyard if in doubt), this place has very quiet and simple rooms that are also amazingly cool in summer. €22

Rivulus Str. Culturii 3 ☎0262 216 302, ⊚hotelrivulus. ro; map p.278. A slightly pricier option but all rooms here have been well refurbished, with a/c, wi-fi and a balcony; there's a lift and a decent restaurant (see below), and it's right in the modern city centre. €55

Sport B-dul Unirii 14a, but actually one block west on Str. Transilvaniei ☎0262 226 869; map p.278. A classic (for which read: very basic and very cheap) sport hotel intended for visiting teams but open to all. Plenty of space, unless there's a big tournament on. €7 per person.

EATING

Barbarossa Piaţa Libertăţii 12 ☎0262 212 517, ⊚barbarossabm.ro; map p.278. A well-established terrace right on the main square, with pub-style food and service – a prolific menu includes excellent pork ribs (€4) and trout (€4.50), plus there's pasta and pizza. Breakfast is served until 1pm. Mon–Fri 8am–midnight, Sat & Sun 11am–midnight.

Bizo B-dul Bucureşti 8 ☎0262 220 068, ⊚bizo.ro; map p.278. Upmarket patisserie serving superb French-style pastries, cakes, breads and sandwiches, as well as a terrific selection of beverages including espressos, juices and lemonades; takeaway downstairs and seating above. Mon–Fri 7am–8pm, Sat 7am–4pm.

Buonissimo Str. Şcolii 3A ☎0262 221 015, ⊚buonissimo.ro; map p.278. Very stylish pizza and pasta joint that's equally worth a visit for its coffee, cakes and ice cream. Mon–Sat 10am–10pm, Sun 1–10pm.

Il Padrino Str. Şcolii 9 ☎0262 275 629; map p.278. The best Italian restaurant in town, with a pleasant terrace and also a deli. Mon–Sat 8am–10pm, Sun 11am–10pm.

Pur şi Simplu Str. Şcolii 1/7 ☎0746 822 111; map p.278. "Pure and Simple" serves chicken, pork and beef dishes (€4–4.50) as well as pasta and pizza (€2.50–4) and salads (€4); breakfast includes omelettes (€2–4) and a full English (€3). Mon–Fri 7am–midnight, Sat 8am–midnight, Sun 10am–midnight.

Sandwich House Str. Şincai 24 ☎0262 211 105, ⊚sandwichhouse.ro; map p.278. Excellent salads, sandwiches, soups and even sushi, plus an appealing menu of fresh juices and smoothies; to takeaway or eat in. Mon–Fri 7.30am–9pm, Sat 8am–5pm.

DRINKING AND ENTERTAINMENT

The Cellar Str. Podul Viilor 2 ☎0262 217 473, ⊚thecellar.ro; map p.278. The best place in town if you fancy a decent glass of Romanian wine rather than beer, with the bonus of a nice terrace on the main square from which to enjoy your beverage. Daily 6–10pm.

Log Out Pub Str Lucaciu Vasile 1 20 ☎0748 667 252; map p.278. This boho-tatty bar in the sixteenth-century Casa Schreiber has a pleasant *gradina de vară* at the rear hosting live music most weekends; also serves burgers and pizzas (€2.50–6). Daily 10am–midnight.

Podul Viilor Podul Viilor 9 ☎0362 730 932; map p.278. Attractive cellar-bar with a rear garden, and good jazz and blues music; pizza available Thurs–Sun evenings. Mon–Thurs 8am–11pm, Fri 8am–2am, Sat noon–3am, Sun noon–11pm.

Southern Maramureş

The southwestern corner of the present Maramureş county, beyond the River Someş, is known as **Codrul**; immediately south of Baia Mare is **Chioarul**; and further east lies **Lăpuş**. While the rolling green landscape is not as dramatic as in the north, it is delightful, and you could easily spend a couple of days pottering around the region's fine **wooden churches** (see page 283). Folk costumes here are similar to those of historic Maramureş, although the tall straw hats are unique to the region.

Buzeşti and Bicaz

The most accessible village in Codrul is **BUZEŞTI**, 30km west of Baia Mare. Its wooden church, built in 1739, has a bulbous steeple bearing witness to the penetration of Baroque influences into this area, while its four corner pinnacles echo the Gothic towers of both Transylvania and Hungary. Far more remote, at the county's western extremity, is **BICAZ**, whose Orthodox church dates from 1723 and was soon painted inside with images of hell in the pronaos and the life of Jesus in the naos. As in Buzeşti, a new church has been built and the old one, though repaired, is disused.

ARRIVAL AND DEPARTURE   **BUZEŞTI AND BICAZ**

Two **buses** a day run from Baia Mare to Bicaz (7am, 3.30pm) and once daily to Buzeşti (at 1.30pm).

Săcălăşeni, Culcea and Remetea Chioarului

Many of the villages of Chioarul have old churches, but the most interesting is at **SĂCĂLĂŞENI**, 10km south of Baia Mare. There has been a church on the site since 1442; it was rebuilt at the end of the seventeenth century, while its carved doorway and paintings date from 1865. Just 2km southwest, in **CULCEA**, is an early eighteenth-century wooden church with plastered walls, hidden on a small rise just beyond the ugly modern church. A further 5km south is the larger village of **REMETEA CHIOARULUI**, also with a fine church, dating from 1800 – for entry, find the caretaker of the adjacent modern church.

ARRIVAL AND DEPARTURE   **SĂCĂLĂŞENI, CULCEA AND REMETEA CHIOARULUI**

By bus Five buses a day (three on Sat and Sun) run from Piaţa Izvoraele in Baia Mare to Culcea via Săcălăşeni. Three buses a day from Baia Mare's autogară continue to Remetea Chioarului.

ACCOMMODATION

Moara Veche Str. Unirii 137, Săcălăşeni ☎0262 289 353, ⓦmoaraveche.ro. A good motel near the church – simple, but clean and modern, with two-, three- and four-bed rooms, and a swimming pool. **€16**

Şurdeşti and around

Heading east out of Baia Mare you'll pass the tallest structure in Romania, the 352m-high Phoenix Copper Smelter chimney, and come to the old mining town of Baia Sprie, 10km from Baia Mare; from here, it's another 10km to **ŞURDEŞTI**, where a magnificent Uniate wooden church stands just beyond the village on a hill overlooking a stream. Built in 1721, it boasts a 54m-high **tower** – three times the length of the church itself – which was Europe's tallest wooden structure until it was topped by the new monasteries at Bârsana and then Săpânţa (see pages 298 and 293). Inside the church, which someone from the house three doors back up the road will unlock for you, there are remarkable wall paintings dating from 1810, and some fine late eighteenth-century icons.

Plopiş

PLOPIŞ, 1km or so south across the fields, has a similar though slightly smaller church to Şurdeşti's, built between 1796 and 1811; it is also on UNESCO's World Heritage List. It follows the usual plan with a pentagonal apse to the east and a porch to the west, but unusually it has very small windows in vertical pairs. You can still see the Holy Trinity and the Virgin Mary, painted in 1811, in the central vault.

ARRIVAL AND DEPARTURE   **ŞURDEŞTI AND AROUND**

For Şurdeşti, take one of the five **buses** daily from Baia Mare towards Cavnic (45min).

ACCOMMODATION

Pensiunea Amethyst Str. Cavnicului 455, Şurdeşti ☎0262 298 530, ⓔcostin_gavrila@yahoo.com. Friendly guesthouse with comfortable rooms and rather crazy wooden balconies; good meals from their own garden and orchard. **€22**

5

Secret Garden no. 61, Şurdeşti ☎0262 298 036, ⓦsecret-garden.ro. On the Baia Sprie road, this is a modern resort with large rooms, indoor and outdoor swimming pools, gym and sauna (all free to guests), and a stylish restaurant. **€54**

Târgu Lăpuş and around

Buses from Baia Mare run southeast only as far as the nondescript little town of **Târgu Lăpuş**, the hub of the Lăpuş area where many villages have wooden churches. There are various places to stay in Târgu Lăpuş, making it a good base for exploration.

Rogoz

The finest wooden churches in Lăpuş are the two in **ROGOZ**, 6km east of Târgu Lăpuş, which, despite the arrival of a modern church, remain well maintained: the Uniate church, built around 1695 in Suciu de Sus and moved here in 1893, stands in the grounds of the larger Orthodox church of the Archangels Michael and Gabriel, built of elm in about 1663. The latter is unique thanks to its naturalistic horse-head cantilevers supporting the roof at the west end, and its asymmetric roof, with a larger overhang to the north sheltering a table where paupers were fed. It's one of the most beautifully decorated churches in Maramureş, with paintings by Radu Munteanu, notably a *Last Judgement*, to the left inside the door, and the *Creation* and the *Good Samaritan*, on the naos ceiling. Next to the church is a **museum house** created by the very entertaining priest (☎0745 590 625; he speaks some French), displaying clothes, rugs and tools.

Lăpuş and Cupşeni

LĂPUŞ, 7km east of Rogoz, boasts a village museum and a seventeenth-century wooden church with carved and painted walls. The church's oldest murals date from the early eighteenth century, and its icons include the first works of Radu Munteanu (see box). **CUPŞENI**, 11km north of Rogoz, is one of the region's most idyllic villages and home to some of its best carpenters. The upper church, built in 1600, has a fine tower but badly damaged paintings, and the tiny lower church, moved here from Peteritea in 1847, was beautifully painted in 1848 by Radu Munteanu. A cycle trail, marked with a blue "C", makes a fine 46km loop from Târgu Lăpuş via Cupşeni and Rogoz.

ARRIVAL AND DEPARTURE
TÂRGU LĂPUŞ AND AROUND

By bus Buses from from Piaţa Eroilor in the centre of Târgu Lăpuş serve Baia Mare (3 daily); Rogoz/Baiuţ (4 daily); Cluj (1 daily). Maxitaxis to Baiuţ via Rogoz and Lăpuş leave regularly from the far/east side of the bridge (and go occasionally to Cupşeni).

ACCOMMODATION

Hostel Lăpuşul Piaţa Eroilor 2 ☎0762 943 646. Just before the bridge on the Rogoz road, this friendly little place has bog standard but perfectly acceptable rooms, plus a gym and sauna, and café with terrace. **€18**

Hotel Casa Preturii Piaţa Eroilor 21 ☎0720 600 820, ⓦhailanoi.ro. Renovated late nineteenth-century building offering big pleasant rooms with modern bathrooms and coffee-/tea-makers; amenities include restaurant/bar, billiards and table tennis. **€22**

Pensiunea Aurica Str. Tibleşului 54 ☎0262 385 082. This modern four-storey block about 1km out on the Rogoz road has seven large a/c rooms with balconies, decent food and a nice garden with swimming pool. Ping pong too. **€18**

Northern Maramureş

The historic county of Maramureş – heart of the present-day county – lies north of Baia Mare, beyond the Gutâi Pass. You'll find idyllic rolling countryside, still farmed in the traditional manner, together with some of the region's finest **churches**, in picturesque villages where customs have remained virtually unchanged for centuries.

WOODEN CHURCHES

A swathe of **wooden churches** stretches across Eastern Europe, from northern Russia to the Adriatic, but in terms of both quality and quantity the richest examples are in Maramureș. From 1278, the Orthodox Romanians were forbidden by their Catholic Hungarian overlords to build churches in stone, and so used wood to ape Gothic developments. It was long thought that most were rebuilt after the last Tatar raid in 1717, acquiring large porches and tall towers, often with four corner-pinnacles, mimicking the masonry architecture of the Transylvanian cities. However in 1997 a tree-ring study showed that the wood used in many churches – notably those of Cornești (see page 285), Breb (see page 286) and Oncești (see page 297) – was far older, the oldest dating from 1367.

In general, the walls are built of blockwork (squared-off logs laid horizontally), cantilevered out in places to form brackets or consoles, supporting the eaves. However, Western techniques such as raftering and timber framing enabled the development of characteristic high roofs and steeples in Maramureș. Following the **standard Orthodox ground plan**, the main roof covers the narthex and naos and a lower one the sanctuary; the naos usually has a barrel vault, while the narthex sits beneath the tower, its weight transmitted by rafters to the walls and thus avoiding the need for pillars. The main roof is always shingled and in many cases double, allowing clerestory windows high in the nave, while the lower roof may be extended to the west to form a porch (exonarthex or *pridvor*).

Inside, almost every church has a choir gallery above the west part of the naos, always a later addition, as shown by the way it is superimposed on the **wall paintings**. These extraordinary works of art were produced by local artists in the eighteenth and early nineteenth centuries, combining the icon tradition with pagan motifs – such as ropes and suns – and topical propaganda against the invading Turks. They broadly follow the standard Orthodox layout, with the *Incarnation* and *Eucharist* in the sanctuary (for the priest's edification), the *Last Judgement* and moralistic parables such as the *Wise and Foolish Virgins* in the narthex (where the women stand), and the *Passion* in the naos.

The first of the major painters was **Alexandru Ponehalski**, who worked from the 1750s to the 1770s in Călinești and Budești, in a naïf post-Byzantine style with blocks of colour in black outlines. From 1767 to the 1780s, **Radu Munteanu** worked around his native Lăpuș and in Botiza, Glod and Desești, painting in a freer and more imaginative manner. A more Baroque style developed in the first decade of the nineteenth century, with **Toader Hodor** and **Ion Plohod** working in Bârsana, Cornești, Văleni, Nănești and Rozavlea.

Since 1989, there has been a renaissance of the **Uniate** or Greco-Catholic faith, repressed under communism and forcibly merged with the Romanian Orthodox Church: many parishes have reverted to Greco-Catholicism, reclaiming their churches; in others, one church is now Orthodox and the other Uniate, while in some villages the congregations even manage to share one church. Many villages have built large, new churches, making it more likely that you'll find the wooden churches locked – even on a Sunday. Finding the key-holder can be problematic, but ask around and someone is bound to help out. People **dress conservatively** here, and wearing shorts is not appropriate for visiting churches.

Of about a hundred wooden churches in Maramureș, 35 are left in the north of the county and thirty in the south. Eight were placed on **UNESCO's World Heritage List** in 1999: Bârsana, Budești (Josani), Desești, Ieud (Deal), Sisești, Plopiș, Poienile Izei and Rogoz.

Mara, Desești and Hărnicești

Winding down from the Gutâi Pass into the Mara valley, the DN18 passes through **MARA**, with its splendidly carved gateways and the excellent Alex trout farm and restaurant (☎0726 254 276), and soon enters **DESEȘTI**, where a lovely wooden church hides among trees to the left. Built in 1770, it's a fine example of the "double roof" or clerestory style, with high windows to give more light; nowadays, electric lighting allows you to fully appreciate the marvellous **wall paintings**. Executed by Radu Munteanu in 1780, these seem more primitive and less stylized than those in the Moldavian monasteries, painted two centuries earlier. Boldly coloured in red, yellow and white, saints and martyrs are contrasted with shady-looking Jews, Turks,

5

Germans, Tatars and Franks. There are also folk-style geometric and floral motifs, and inscriptions in the Cyrillic alphabet – Old Church Slavonic remained the liturgical language of Romanian Orthodoxy until the nineteenth century.

Some 2km along the road, in **HĂRNICEȘTI**, the church, built in 1770, houses a number of fine icons; the apse was widened in 1942 and a porch added in 1952, so that the tower now seems disproportionately short.

ARRIVAL AND DEPARTURE   MARA, DESEȘTI AND HĂRNICEȘTI

By bus and maxitaxi Almost all services between Baia Mare and Sighet follow the DN18 through the Mara valley stopping wherever required. In addition, seven buses a day (two on Sun) from Baia Mare to Ocna Șugatag take this road.

ACCOMMODATION

Pensiunea Irina no. 259 Deseşti ☏0262 372 603, ⓦpensiuneairina.weebly.com. At the south end of Deseşti, this friendly and well-established place has eight comfortable, colourful rooms – one of which has a wood stove – and also serves up great home cooking; bikes to rent. Breakfast €5. **€25**

Pensiunea La Marie de la Rascruce no. 12A ☏0742 221 226, ⓦlamariedelarascruce.weebly.com. Although it's modern, this place – with four en-suite rooms – is very much focused on traditional Maramureş life, with lashings of filling food. Breakfast €4. **€13**

Pensiunea Mara no. 322 Deseşti ☏0749 445 331, ✉pensiuneamaradesesti@yahoo.com. Just off the main road at the north end of Deseşti, this welcoming guesthouse has pleasant rooms with balconies offering lovely views, and terrific home-grown food. **€16**

Hoteni, Sat-Șugatag and Mănăstirea

HOTENI, 2km east of the Baia Mare road at Hărniceşti (and 3km west of Ocna Şugatag), has its day in the spotlight on the first or second Sunday of May. The **Tânjaua festival** is a celebration of the First Ploughman, a fertility rite dating back at least to Roman times: a dozen youths adorn bulls and lead them to the house of the chosen First Ploughman, the hardest-working farmer in the village, for him to plough the first field of the season, before dunking him in water and commencing the feasting and dancing. Hoteni also has a wooden church, built in 1657 and brought here in 1788.

Some 2km north on the Baia Mare–Sighet road lies **SAT-ȘUGATAG**, where a wooden church sits, unusually, on flat land by the road. A finely carved wooden gate leads to a graveyard with stout wooden crosses; the beautifully compact church, built in 1642 (painted internally in 1783), features a twisted rope motif just below the eaves. A right turn 2km north leads to **MĂNĂSTIREA**, a tiny village with a tiny church, founded in 1653 and now shared by Orthodox and Uniate congregations; it boasts fine paintings from 1653 and 1783, as well as late eighteenth-century icons by Alexandru Ponehalski.

ARRIVAL AND DEPARTURE   HOTENI, SAT-ȘUGATAG AND MĂNĂSTIREA

By bus Sat-Şugatag is on the Baia Mare–Sighet road, served by fifteen buses daily; Mănăstirea is a short walk from this road. Hoteni is served by the five buses a day (two on Sun) from Baia Mare to Ocna Şugatag.

ACCOMMODATION

Pensiunea Maramureş no. 35, Hoteni ☏0746 984 943. This big modern house has seven rooms and an apartment, all sharing a balcony and lounge (featuring a massive TV); no English is spoken, but they compensate with lots of great food and hospitality. **€28**

Ocna Șugatag

A former salt-mining centre that is now a booming spa, **OCNA ȘUGATAG** is also the commercial centre for the surrounding villages, with a post office, bank and ATMs, and a market on Thursday mornings. Various salt pools are now lively **spas**, notably the Lacul Sarat (8am–8pm daily; ☏0764 013 067), just west from the central crossroads, which has an indoor salt-water pool and two outdoor pools as well as pedalos on the lake (€7/hr). There's also the odd pizzeria and café-bar at the central crossroads.

ARRIVAL AND DEPARTURE OCNA ŞUGATAG

Six **buses** a day from both Sighet and Baia Mare.

ACCOMMODATION

Lacul Sarat ☎ 0764 013 067. A lively bar/restaurant at the salt lake, with nine rooms, cabins and tent space; the owners speak English. Tent space **€7**, rooms **€22**

Pensiunea Manolo Str. Vulcan 405 ☎ 0749 383 525. This excellent and very friendly guesthouse has ten rooms and a large garden with four four-person camping cabins, barbecue and a swimming pool. **€13**

Popasul din Deal Str. Unirii 1D ☎ 0262 374 133, ⓦ popasul.ro. At the north end of the village, this large place has twelve comfortable, if uninspiring, rooms as well as indoor and outdoor pools, tennis courts and bikes for rent It's home to the Maramureş Greenways tour agency (☎ 0262 374 133 or ☎ 0741 773 683, ⓦ maramuresgreenways.ro) which runs hiking trips in the Gutâi mountains. **€38**

The Cosău valley

Between Giuleşti and Berbeşti a road leads east up the **Cosău valley**, the most interesting of all in Maramureş. Just 2km southeast of Fereşti (where the wooden church was raised in the 1790s) is tranquil little **CORNEŞTI**, where the church (painted in 1775) dates in part from 1406, making it the second oldest in Maramureş; there's a **watermill** here, beside which women beat clothes with carved wooden laundry bats by the river, often improvising songs and verses as they work, using a distinctive local technique called singing "with knots" (*cu noduri*), in which the voice is modulated by tapping the glottis while the singer doesn't breathe for lengthy periods.

Continuing south, you come to three villages about 4km apart, with two **wooden churches** apiece. At sprawling **CĂLINEŞTI**, the beautiful Susani (Upper) or Băndreni church, high above the road just north of the junction, was built and painted in the 1780s. The Josani (Lower) or Caieni church, built in 1628, is one of the loveliest in Maramureş, with its huge nineteenth-century porch and beautiful internal paintings by Ponehalski. It's best reached by the path across the fields next to house no. 385, on the road east to Bârsana. There are also wooden *vâltoare* or whirlpools (used for giving woollen blankets back their loft) and **horincă** stills at nos. 96 and 129.

SÂRBI has two unassuming little wooden churches – the Susani to the north, built in 1638 and painted by Ponehalski in 1760, with icons by Radu Munteanu and a beautifully carved door frame; and the Josani, to the south, built in 1703 – and some fine examples of traditional technology. At no. 181 you can visit a fine watermill, two fulling mills, a **vâltoare (whirlpool)** and a *horincă* still, as well as various workshops; it's signposted as "Ansamblul de arhitectură tehnică populară" and is now rather overtouristy, with a bar – better to stop immediately north at no. 173, where the family are happy to show you their fulling mill, *vâltoare* and still, as well as the loom in the house. There's also a maker of *opinci* (sandals) at no. 143, at the village's south end.

Finally, **BUDEŞTI** is a large village but remarkably unspoiled, with even its new houses largely built in the traditional style. In the centre, the Josani church, built in 1643, contains the chain-mail coat of the outlaw Pintea the Brave (see page 279). Its frescoes are among Alexandru Ponehalski's finest, especially the *Last Judgement*. The Susani church, dating from 1586, has particularly fine paintings from the 1760s, also by Ponehalski, and has been gradually extended westwards, so that the tower is now almost central.

ARRIVAL AND DEPARTURE THE COSĂU VALLEY

Buses run (Mon–Fri 7 daily) from Sighet to Budeşti via Corneşti and Călineşti.

5

ACCOMMODATION

Pensiunea Bontos Str. Principală 299A, Budeşti ☎ 0751 521 021. A very friendly place with seven en-suite rooms and shared balcony and kitchen. The home-cooked meals are fantastic, and the delightful hosts will talk until the early hours, with a *tuica* or several to hand. **€18**

Pensiunea Borodi Ileana Str. Principală 829, Budeşti ☎ 0262 373 683. This friendly young family offers accommodation in two double rooms plus meals; no English but some French spoken. **€18**

Pensiunea Casa Opris Călineşti no. 62A ☎ 0745 359 090 or ☎ 0744 700 154. On the road to Ocna Şugatag, this modern house offers comfortable rooms, and is also the only place in these villages to get a decent lunch (€4.50), using entirely home-grown produce. **€16**

Pensiunea Cosau ☎ 0262 373 311 or ☎ 0742 098 941, ✉ pensiuneacosau@gmail.com. In a lovely rural setting midway between Călineşti and Corneşti (6km north of Ocna Şugatag), this guesthouse has plenty of space for a swimming pool, other sports and fishing facilities, and a large restaurant. **€26**

Pensiunea Poieniţa Str. Poieniţei 258, Budeşti ☎ 0740 816 955, ⓦ pensiuneapoienita.weebly.com. Set in wide lawns at the south end of the village, there's one building here with six rooms and another with three four-bed apartments. **€16**

Breb

From Budeşti, there's a particularly fine 10km walk through idyllic countryside to Hoteni (see page 284) via **BREB**, a small village with a very lovely and tranquil Uniate wooden church (1531) hidden away in the valley. It's becoming known as something

---

MARAMUREŞ FUNERALS

The **Cult of the Dead** is central to the culture of Maramureş, where rituals are fixed and elaborate; if anything is omitted, it's believed that the soul will return as a ghost or even a vampire. There are several phases, covering the separation from the world of the living, preparation for the journey, and entry into the other world. A dying person asks forgiveness of his family and neighbours, who must obey his last wishes. Black flags are hung outside the house where the deceased lies for three days, while the church bells are rung thrice daily, neighbours pay their respects and women (but not men) lament the deceased in improvised rhyming couplets.

The wailing reaches a climax on the third day when the priest arrives and blesses a pail of water, extinguishes a candle in it, and consecrates the house with a cross left etched on the wall for a year. The coffin is carried by six married men, stopping for prayers (the priest being paid for each stop) at crossroads, bridges and any other feature along the way, and then at the church for absolution. The funeral itself is relatively swift, with everyone present throwing soil into the grave and being given a small loaf, a candle and a **red-painted egg**, as at Easter; these must also be given to passers-by, including tourists (be aware it would give great offence to refuse it). The knot-shaped loaves or *colaci* bear the inscription NI KA ("Jesus Christ is victorious"), stamped in the dough by a widow or some other "clean woman" using a special seal called a *pecetar*. The seal's wooden handle is often elaborately carved with motifs such as the Endless Column, the Tree of Life, wolf's teeth or a crucifix.

Three days later there is another *pomană* or **memorial meal**, when bread is again given to all present. After nine days, nine widows spend the day fasting and praying around the deceased's shirt; six weeks and then six months after the funeral, the absolution is repeated with another meal, as the dead must be given food and drink, and after a year a feast is given for all the family's dead. Until this time the close family may not attend weddings or dances and women wear black. As elsewhere in Romania, *cergare* (embroidered napkins) are hung over icons in the church or over plates on house walls in memory of the dead. The Uniates also remember their dead on All Souls' Day.

Marriage is seen as essential, so much so that if a person of marriageable age (in fact from 8 years old, the age of first confession) dies unmarried, a **Marriage of the Dead** (Nunta Mortului) is held, with a stand-in bride or groom (as appropriate), and a bridesmaid or best man dressed in wedding costume, although everyone else wears mourning garb.

of a **museum village**, due to wooden houses threatened with collapse elsewhere being rebuilt here (one is traditionally furnished – ask for Maria alui Gheorghe din Zavoia, who has the key). It's a great place to visit craftsmen, such as woodcarver Petru Pop at no. 370. It was in Breb that the author, William Blacker, lived for several years in the late 1990s, and it was his experiences here, and in Transylvania, that informed his superb book *Along the Enchanted Way* (see page 401).

ARRIVAL AND DEPARTURE
BREB

By bus There are two buses a day from Sighet (opposite the railway station) to Breb. From Baia Mare the five daily buses (two at weekends) to Borşa will leave you at the Breb turning, about 15min walk from the village.

ACCOMMODATION

Babou Maramureş no. 149 ☎0362 402 558, ⓦbaboumaramures.com. A delightful Dutch-owned campsite (1.5km north through the village; or 3km south from Hoteni) that also has five dorm beds in a renovated barn, with a kitchen and bathrooms; guests of the campsite are free to avail themselves of these facilities. Fires also permitted on site. Dorms €11, camping €5.50

Pensiunea Lucia no. 285 ☎0262 374 584, ⓦpensiunealucia.com. About 250m to the right from the entrance to the village, this welcoming, traditional-style guesthouse serves meals made from their own produce; lunches and picnics can be arranged too. €16

Pensiunea Maramu' no. 290 ☎0760 149 552, ⓦpensiuneamaramu.weebly.com. Facing the new church, about 200m to the right from the entry to the village, this guesthouse has two traditional-style rooms, sharing a bathroom, and, upstairs, two more modern en-suite rooms. Meals are largely made with their own produce. Price is per person, half board. €22

Pensiunea Mărioara no. 346 ☎0262 374 593 or ☎0768 597 158, ⓔpensiuneamarioara@yahoo.com. At the entry to the village, you can stay in the big modern pension or (recommended) the old wooden house. They also offer bike rental and minibus tours/transfers. Price is per person, half board. €24

★ **Village Hotel** no. 349 ☎0723 223 059, ⓦvillagehotelmaramures.com. Guests at the British-run *Village Hotel* sleep in traditional wooden houses that have been taken down and re-erected in the centre of Breb (and fitted with modern showers and kitchens) – it's more a miniature village than a hotel, really. The energetic owners also organise all manner of activities, including guided hikes and walks (including wildlife walks), meals with shepherds, and horse and cart rides. €45

Vadu Izei

At the junction of the Iza and Mara valleys, **VADU IZEI** has plenty of guesthouses, making it an alternative base to Sighet; it's also the headquarters of the Fundaţia Agro-Tur-Art, which aims to bring tourists and local craftspeople together; their office is on the main road just north of the village centre (Str. Principală 161 Mon–Fri 9am–3pm ☎0262 330 171, ⓦovr.ro). There's also a **tourist office** (daily 9am–4pm, summer 9am–8pm) at the north end, just south of the bridge to Sighet. Right at the heart of the village, at the road junction, *La Petre* restaurant (☎0745 849 697) provides a simple alternative to guesthouse meals.

ARRIVAL AND DEPARTURE
VADU IZEI

All **buses** from Sighet towards Baia Mare and the Cosău and Iza valleys serve Vadu Izei.

ACCOMMODATION

Casa Muntean Str. Dumbrava 505 ☎0262 330 091, ⓦcasamuntean.ro. This excellent guesthouse, 1.5km east on the Bârsana road, has seven twin rooms and is a great choice for independent travellers and backpackers. Meals, free *horincă*, bike rental, free pick-ups in Sighet, and excursions and transfers are available; English and French are spoken. Per person €9

Casa Tradiţională Borlean Str. Zăvoi 689 ☎0262 330 228, ⓦpensiunea-casa-traditionala-borlean.ro. The manager of Fundaţia Agro-Tur-Art (see above) runs this collection of beautifully restored wooden houses, each with several rooms. There's also a gallery of his paintings on glass (traditional small icons and more complex larger pieces) and his wife's weavings. Breakfast €4. €22

5

Pensiunea Doina Str. Şugău 75 ☎ 0262 330 602, ⓦ pensiune-doina.ro. There's excellent food and a huge garden here, in a lovely rural setting 3km west of Vadu Izei, with accommodation in either a modern or a traditional house. Bikes are available to rent. €35

Sighet

Sighetu Marmatiei, or **SIGHET** as it's generally known, is just 1km from the Ukrainian border and was a famous smuggling centre before World War I when the territory to the north was called Ruthenia. History is repeating itself today; the bridge to Solotvino (Slatina to Romanians), destroyed in World War II and reopened in 2006, is now busy with traffic crossing into Ukraine to buy cigarettes and petrol for resale in Romania. A peaceful town of around 42,000 inhabitants, it has always been highly multi-ethnic, with a plethora of churches and schools catering for Ukrainians, Hungarians and others. You can see residents of the surrounding villages in local costume on Wednesdays and especially on the first Monday of the month, when a livestock market is held 1km out on the Baia Mare road. The key attractions are the **Village Museum**, the memorial house dedicated to Holocaust survivor Elie Wiesel, and the superb **Memorial Museum**, which ranks among the country's finest museums. The town is also famed for its **winter carnival** on December 27 (see page 289), when many of the participants wear extraordinary shamanistic costumes and masks.

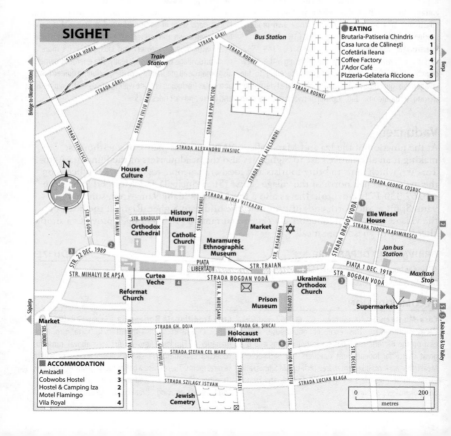

5

WINTER CUSTOMS FESTIVAL

Held on December 27, Sighet's **Winter Customs Festival** (Festivalul Datinilor de Iarna) is a vibrant display of music, costumes and customs, illustrating the enduring influence of pre-Christian beliefs. It opens with brightly decorated horses galloping down the main street, followed by up to fifty groups from villages all over Maramureş, Bucovina, Transylvania and Ukraine slowly making their way down the street to present their song or skit to the mayor. Thereafter, a rather mishmash **play** begins with soldiers arriving to tell King Herod about the rumour of a saviour, while bears roll around the ground to raise the earth spirits. Horsemen are called to find the infant child and men bring heavy iron cowbells to drive away evil spirits, represented by multicoloured, animist *dracus*. Active throughout is the clapping wooden goat (*capra*), warding off **evil spirits** to ensure the return of spring. In the afternoon there are concerts both on the streets and in the theatre, lasting until early evening when more impromptu celebrations take over.

From the train and bus stations, it's a ten-minute walk south down Strada Iuliu Maniu to the **Reformat church**, a fourteenth-century structure rebuilt just before World War I on an unusual ground plan. The town centre, to the east, comprises two one-way streets, both of which change their names and are linked by several squares, so it can be hard to make sense of addresses. Immediately east of the Reformat church is the **Curtea Veche**, the Baroque county hall of 1691, now housing a restaurant and shops. Beyond here is Piaţa Libertăţii, with the Baroque **Roman Catholic church**, built by the Piarist order in 1730–34, on its northern side. On the east side of the church at Piaţa Libertăţii 22, the **Ukrainian high school** is a splendid piece of Art Noodle, as some jokingly refer to the Hungarian version of Art Nouveau.

Muzeul Etnografic Maramureşului

Piaţa Libertăţii 15 • Tues–Sun 10am–6pm • €1 • ⓦ muzeulmaramuresului.ro

The **Muzeul Etnografic Maramureşului** (Maramureş Ethnographic Museum) has an above-average collection of local pottery and woodwork – including some beautifully carved gates and gateposts – as well as a selection of costumes and masks worn by participants in the town's winter carnival.

Memorial Victimelor Comunismului şi Rezistenţei

Str. Coposu 4 • Mid-April to mid-Oct daily 9.30am–6.30pm; mid-Oct to mid-April Tues–Sun 9.30am–4.30pm • €2.50 • ☎ 0262 319 424, ⓦ memorialsighet.ro

To the south of the Ethnographic Museum stands the former prison (see above), which opened in 1997 as the **Memorial Victimelor Comunismului şi Rezistenţei** (Memorial Museum of the Victims of Communism and of the Resistance). The cells have been converted into exhibition spaces, covering the oppression of the communist era; little is in English but the general outlines are clear enough. In addition to memorials to Iuliu Maniu and Gheorghe Brătianu, the prison's two most famous inmates, there are displays on collectivization, forced labour on the Danube–Black Sea Canal, the deportations to the Bărăgan and the demolition of the heart of Bucharest during the 1980s. There's fascinating coverage of the feared Securitate, and another cell-full of Ceauşescu-oriented memorabilia (aptly entitled "Communist Kitsch"), including paintings, busts, lists of honorary doctorates and photos of him lording it with world leaders such as Castro and Nixon. In the **courtyard** is an underground memorial hall, its walls inscribed with the names of some eight thousand people imprisoned under communism, and a dozen or so uninspiring bronze statues. The museum also cares for the Paupers' Cemetery (see page 292).

Muzeul Culturii Evreieşti din Maramureş

Str. Tudor Vladimirescu 1, corner with Str. Dragoş Vodă • Mid-April to mid-Oct Tues–Sun 10am–6pm; mid-Oct to mid-April Mon–Fri 8am–4pm • €1 • ☎ 0742 015 169

5

THE REMAINS OF JEWISH SIGHET

One block west of the Memorial Museum along Strada Şincai you'll find a monument to the 38,000 **Maramureş Jews** rounded up by Hungarian gendarmes and deported in 1944; there's also a plaque to them at the railway station, where they were herded into cattle trucks. Not far from the monument, on Strada Izei, is the **Jewish cemetery** (Mon–Thurs & Sun 9am–7pm, Fri until 5pm; €3; ☎0757 341 955), where pilgrims still visit the graves of Hasidic elders. One **synagogue**, dating from 1904, survives at Strada Basarabia 10, on the far side of Piaţa Libertăţii (Mon–Fri & Sun 9am–2pm; ☎0262 319 703 or ☎0740 486 931). Note that neither the cemetery nor the synagogue open reliably and you may need to contact the **Jewish Community Center** (Comunitatea Evreilor din Sighet) at Str. Basarabia 8 (☎0262 311 652). There is also the Tarbut Foundation at Str. Gheorghe Doja 67 (☎0744 145 351, ◫ftsighet.com), who offer walking tours of the city, as well as excursions elsewhere in the region.

A plain house a block north of the main drag was the childhood home of **Elie Wiesel**, Auschwitz survivor and winner of the 1986 Nobel Peace Prize for his work in helping to understand and remember the Holocaust. It's now an impressive memorial house and the **Muzeul Culturii Evreieşti din Maramureş** (Museum of Jewish Culture in Maramureş), with books, furniture and religious items donated by local Jewish families; there are documents on the Jewish and other communities in Sighet before World War II, along with photos of the deportation of the Jews, Wiesel's liberation from Buchenwald, and his many visits to Sighet, including one in 2002 to open the house. Photo captions are in English and French, but otherwise the texts, including quotations from Wiesel, are in Romanian only.

Muzeul Satului

Str. Dobăieş 40 • Tues–Sun 10am–6pm • €1 • ☎0240 513 249, ◫ muzeulmaramuresului.ro • The museum is a 30min walk from the centre, or take bus #1 to the bridge (the Podul Ronişorii stop), then walk northeast for 5min up Str. Muzeului

Set on Dobăieş hill on the town's eastern outskirts, the open-air **Muzeul Satului** (Village Museum) preserves dozens of houses, farm buildings and churches relocated from villages across Maramureş – worth viewing if you'll miss the real thing, although there's not a lot of information displayed. The oldest building is a sixteenth-century church from Onceşti, while the Jewish, Schwab and Ukrainian minorities are represented too.

ARRIVAL AND INFORMATION   SIGHET

By train The railway station (☎0262 310 952) is a 10min walk north of town on Str. Gării.

Destinations Braşov (1 daily; 11hr 45min); Bucharest (1 daily; 15hr); Cluj (1 daily; 6hr 15min–6hr 45min); Salva (1 daily; 4hr); Vişeu de Jos (3 daily; 2hr 10min).

By bus Sighet has several bus stations (and other pick-up points). The most important is the Mara terminal at Str. Gării 10, although the older Autogară Tur, opposite the railway station, still sends buses to Cluj and various villages; there's also the private Autogară Jan on Piaţa 1 Decembrie 1918 (for Satu Mare, Oradea, Arad, Poienile Izei and other villages). Buses from the Mara and Tur terminals also pick up south of the Str. Unirii roundabout and in front of the Kaufland hypermarket, about 500m further south; some also stop by the supermarkets opposite the Autogară Jan. Connections to the surrounding villages are good, if sporadic – the remotest are reached by a single departure at about 4pm. It's also worth considering transfers organized by guesthouses (stopping at various sights) to connect with fast/overnight trains at Sighişoara or Suceava.

Destinations Baia Mare (15 daily); Borşa (10 daily); Budeşti (8 daily Mon–Fri); Cluj (4 daily); Costiui (8 daily); Mara (2 daily); Oradea/Arad/Timişoara (2 daily); Poienile de sub Munte (2 daily); Poienile Izei (3 daily Mon–Fri); Satu Mare (4 daily); Săpânţa (10–13 daily); Vişeu de Sus (10–12 daily).

Tourist information The Centrul de Informare Turistică is at Piaţa Libertăţii 26 (Mon–Fri 9am–5pm; ☎0371 347 133, ◫turismsighet.ro). Look out too for Teo Ivanciuc's English/Romanian map of Maramureş, sold at major bookshops (such as the Libreria Luceafarul, Str. Bogdan Vodă 10; Mon–Fri 9am–5pm, Sat 9am–1pm), the Memorial Museum and the Merry Cemetery in Sapânţa.

MERRY CEMETERY OF SAPANTA

5

THE PRISON OF THE MINISTERS

Sighet prison operated from 1898 until 1977, achieving a notoriety gained by few others. Its nadir was between 1950 and 1955, when political prisoners (former government ministers, generals, academics and bishops) were held here so that they could be "protected" by the Red Army or rapidly spirited away into the Soviet Union if the communist regime was threatened. The 72 cells held 180 members of the prewar establishment, at least two-thirds of them aged over 60; they were appallingly treated and, not surprisingly, many died. The most important figure to perish here was **Iuliu Maniu**, regarded as the greatest living Romanian when he was arrested in 1947 (at the age of 73) and now seen as a secular martyr – the only uncorrupt politician of the prewar period, opponent of the 1944 coup, and notably reluctant to pursue revenge against Transylvania's Hungarians after the war.

The leading Hungarian victim was **Áron Márton**, Roman Catholic bishop of Alba Iulia, who opposed the persecution of the Jews in 1944 and of the Uniates in 1949, and was imprisoned from 1950 to 1955, surviving until 1980. Others who died in Sighet included two of the three members of the Brătianu family imprisoned here – Dinu, president of the National Liberal Party and Finance Minister (1933–34), and Gheorghe, historian and second-division politician – as well as Mihail Manoilescu, theoretician of Romanian fascism, and Foreign Minister in 1940. Their graves can be seen at the Cimitrul Săracilor or **Paupers' Cemetery**, a couple of kilometres west on the Săpânţa road, where fir trees mark out the outline of Romania, with an altar and cenotaph on the spot representing Sighet. In 2012, the **Portal of Memory**, a bell tower evoking an open book, was built nearer the road, with a viewing platform.

ACCOMMODATION

Sighet has a good range of reasonably priced hotels, though none really excels; alternatively, homestays (see page 28) are available in nearby villages such as Vadu Izei or Rona de Jos, from where you can easily visit Sighet.

Amizadil Str. Mocăniţei 51A, Valea Cufundoasă ☏ 0744 289 461, ⊕ amizadil.com; map p.288. Local guide/author Teofil Ivanciuc has restored this traditional wooden house and offers three rooms, without TV or internet access but in a delightful rural setting out beyond the Village Museum (4km from the station, with transfers included). Closed mid-Oct to mid-April. Two-night minimum stay. Per night **€40**

Cobwobs Hostel Str. 22 Decembrie 1989 42A ☏ 0740 635 673, ✉ cahul1@yahoo.com; map p.288. British-run, this is a genuine backpackers' hostel, in a modern house with very spacious dorms (equipped with lockers, proper duvets and big towels) and good showers, as well as bikes, laundry, kitchen and a large garden. They also organize village tours and evenings camping at a farm. Dorms **€9**, doubles **€22**

Hostel & Camping Iza Str. Popa Luca 64 ☏ 0740 230 861; map p.288. This place has six rooms with four single beds each, shared bathrooms and a kitchen, as well as camping facilities. Camping **€8.50**, rooms **€18**

Motel Flamingo Str. Coşbuc 36 ☏ 0371 026 161, ⊕ flamingopension.ro; map p.288. A slightly pricier option, but just about worth it for the eight good-sized, well-kept rooms; the stylish restaurant serves beautifully presented Romanian food and there's a relaxing garden too. **€52**

Vila Royal Str. Mihaly de Apşa 1 ☏ 0262 311 004, ⊕ vilaroyal.ro; map p.288. Although little more than rooms above a bar (with entry from the side alley), *Vila Royal* is nicely designed, offering a/c rooms with balconies, and parking at the rear. It's very central but not noisy, with a decent breakfast served in the bar. **€28**

EATING

Brutaria-Patiseria Chindris Str. Simion Bărnuţiu 6 ☏ 0742 884 787; map p.288. Excellent café near the Memorial Museum, with good coffee, pastries, cakes and snacks. Mon–Fri 7am–6pm, Sat 8am–3pm.

Casa Iurca de Călineşti Str. Dragoş Vodă 14 ☏ 0262 318 882, ⊕ casaiurca.ro; map p.288. Well regarded but a bit touristy, serving Western dishes like chateaubriand, schnitzel and "roast beef anglaise" as well as Maramureş cuisine; portions are big but service can be poor. Traditional music and dance shows at 8pm Wed–Sun. Daily 7am–10pm.

Cofetăria Ileana Piaţa 1 Decembrie 1918 35 ☏ 0754 024 420, ⊕ cofetariaileana.com; map p.288. Come for pastries and coffee, either in the large wood-panelled interior or on the small terrace in this deservedly popular place. Daily 7am–10pm.

Coffee Factory Str. Bogdan Voda ☏ 0758 454 033; map p.288. Something more akin to the new wave of coffee houses in Bucharest or Cluj, which can only be a good thing, this energetically staffed place serves first class espressos, iced coffees and the like in colourful, contemporary

surrounds. Cracking cakes too. Mon–Fri 7.30am–10pm, Sat & Sun 8am–10pm.
J'Ador Café Str. Iuliu Maniu 1 ☎0744 251 607; map p.288. With terrace and courtyard seating, and excellent coffee, lemonade and cocktails, you could a lot worse than chill out here for an hour or so. Mon–Fri 7am–11pm, Sat & Sun 10am–11pm.

Pizzeria-Gelateria Riccione Piața 1 Decembrie 1918 ☎0745 551 073; map p.288. At the south end of Str. Dragoș Vodă, this is a stylish modern place for genuine Italian-style pizza and ice cream. Mon–Fri 7.30am–midnight, Sat & Sun 9am–midnight.

Săpânța

Eighteen kilometres northwest of Sighet, **SĂPÂNȚA** has achieved widespread fame thanks to the work of the woodcarver Stan Ion Pătraș (1908–77) and his disciples Vasile and Gheorghe Stan Colțun, Viorel and Dumitru "Tincu" Pop, and Toader Turda, in the village's **Merry Cemetery**. You can find more of Pătraș' artistry in his modest wooden cottage some 300m along the dusty road behind the cemetery (it's signposted). The barn where he worked is adorned with some spectacularly colourful fixtures and fittings, as well as highly unusual wood-carved portraits of the Ceaușescus. Săpânța is also known for its traditional *cergi* or woollen blankets, and the village, lined with handicraft stalls, has become accustomed to busloads of tourists making a thirty-minute stop before rushing on.

Merry Cemetery
500m south of the main road • €1

The **Merry Cemetery** (Cimitir Vesel) is a forest of beautifully worked, colourfully painted wooden grave markers carved with portraits of the deceased or scenes from their lives, inscribed with witty doggerel (in Romanian) composed by Pătraș as he saw fit. Some are terse – "who sought money to amass, could not Death escape, alas!" – while a surprising number recall violent deaths, like that of the villager killed by a "bloody Hungarian" during World War II, or a mother's final message to her son: "Griga, may you pardoned be, even though you did stab me". Pătraș himself is buried right in front of the church door, his carved portrait flanked by two white doves ("Ever since a lad I was, I have been Stan Ion Pătraș…").

Peri monastery
Follow the main road east from the Merry Cemetery junction for 200m across the Râul Săpânța bridge then (at an ATM) head left for 500m; if you're on foot, take the path diagonally through the Pădurea Parc Livada forest reserve

Săpânța's most recent claim to fame, the world's highest wooden tower, is at the **Peri monastery**, north of the village. The church, though wooden, is not at all traditional in detail, set on a very high concrete base and with a 38m-high tree trunk inside its tower, which soars to a height of 75m.

ARRIVAL AND INFORMATION
SĂPÂNȚA

By bus Ten to thirteen buses a day come here from Sighet, three continuing to Negrești and Satu Mare.

Tourist information There's limited information at ⓦ sapantamaramures.ro.

ACCOMMODATION AND EATING

Casa Ana & Camping Poiieni no. 638 ☎0740 593 380, ⓔ campingpoieni@gmail.com. At a trout farm 2.5km south of the cemetery, there's a good restaurant here (serving trout, naturally) with rooms as well as wooden cabins and camping space. Camping €6.50, rooms €25
Casa Vlad Alex no. 1088 ☎0755 488 085 or ☎0744 927 789, ⓔ irinastan35@gmail.com. On the main road just east of the Peri junction, this friendly place

has two en-suite rooms and two with shared bathroom. €17
Pensiunea Anca no. 106 ☎0262 372 148 or ☎0746 145 012, ⓔ ion.braicu@yahoo.com. Just off the main road to the east, with three doubles and three triples, all en-suite; there's free use of a swimming pool and kitchen. €21
Pensiunea Ileana Ștețca no. 656 ☎0745 491 756, ⓔ sapantaileana@yahoo.com. Opposite the cemetery,

5

with six simple rooms and a display of local costumes and crafts; the excellent food comes from their pigs, hens and a vegetable garden. **€30**

Pensiunea Montana no. 910 ☎ 0744 208 112. Midway between the main road and the cemetery, this very

hospitable family has five en-suite rooms, including a triple, along an upstairs balcony; you can order meals or use their kitchen. **€17**

The Oaş depression

Beyond Săpânţa, heading towards Satu Mare, the road winds up to the Huta Pass (587m) to enter the **Oaş depression**. Oaş was once billed as an "undiscovered Maramureş", but so many local men now work abroad that the roads are lined with new bungalows and imported Mercedes, and traditional costume is little worn except at festivals and in the remotest villages such as Cămărzana, where you'll find just about the only wooden houses left in Oaş. The region's shepherds assemble in the hills above various villages on the first or second Sunday of May for the **festival of Sâmbra Oilor**, when the milk yield of each family's sheep is measured. Whether this process – known as *Ruptul Sterpelor* – occurs in May (as here) or June or early July (as it does further south), the participants dress for the occasion in waist-length sheepskin jackets (*cojoc*) covered in embroidery and tassels, or fluffy woollen overcoats called *guba*, and heartily consume fiery *horincă* (double-distilled plum brandy) and sweet whey cheese.

Negreşti-Oaş

Oas Museum Str. Victoriei 140 • Tues–Fri 9am–4pm, Sat & Sun 9am–2pm • ☎ 0261 854 839, ⓦ oasmuseum.ro • **Ethnographic display** Str. Livezilor 3 • Mon–Fri & Sun 9am–5pm, Sat 9am–2pm; Dec–Feb by reservation only • ☎ 0261 854 860

NEGREŞTI-OAŞ, some 35km southwest of Săpânţa, is the largest settlement in the region of Oaş. Just north of the systematized centre, the **Oaş Museum** has displays of costumes, tools, furniture, pottery from Vama and paintings of local landscapes. The more worthwhile open-air **ethnographic display**, to the south beyond the bridge, includes half a dozen blue-painted houses, mostly from the nineteenth century, and a wooden church, built in 1600, from Lechinţa; its interior was painted in 2006. You'll also see a pottery workshop, a smithy and costume displays.

ARRIVAL AND INFORMATION   NEGREŞTI-OAŞ

By bus In addition to four buses and hourly maxitaxis from Satu Mare, there are three a day from Sighet via Săpânţa, and four a day from Baia Mare.

Tourist information Centrul de Informare Turistică is at Strada Victoriei 59 (daily 10am–5pm; ☎ 0261 884 652, ⓦ turism-taraoasului.ro).

ACCOMMODATION

Hotel Dallas Str. Creangă 110 ☎ 0742 118 158, ⓦ dallas.ro. A couple of kilometres northwest of town on the Călineşti road, this stately pile mostly caters for weddings in its large restaurant, but it also has twelve comfortable, if slightly overpriced, rooms. **€55**

Motel Mujdeni Oraşul Nou ☎ 0261 830 077, ✉ dor_ghe@yahoo.com. By a lake just north of the pass into Satu

Mare county, 12km west of Negreşti, this is a big modern block with a spa and swimming pool. **€33**

Pensiunea Diana Str. Victoriei 108 ☎ 0261 855 010. With just nine rooms, this is a more pleasant place to stay in Negreşti than the larger hotels, although it also specializes in weddings and other big events. **€26**

Satu Mare

When the diplomats at Versailles signed the Trianon Treaty, they dismembered Hungary's Szabolcs-Szatmár county, handing its capital Szatmárnémeti to Romania, since when its Hungarian population has fallen from about 75 percent of the total to about 30 percent. Renamed **SATU MARE** ("Big Village" in Romanian) and shorn of its historic links with the Great Plain, the town lost its role as a trading post, shipping salt from Ocna Dejului down the River Someş; today, its position near the border means that it's relatively prosperous again. Although there's little to detain you, it's a handy spot to break a journey to or from Oradea or Hungary.

The central **Piața Libertății** is a pleasant green space dominated by the Neoclassical **Roman Catholic cathedral** (1785–93) on its east side. Just north of the square, off the alley alongside the stunning *Hotel Dacia* (built in 1902, and currently closed), you'll see the **fire tower** (Tues–Fri & Sun noon–7pm, Sat noon–4pm; €1), a slender 45m-high redbrick structure like a Turkish minaret, raised in 1904. Further north, in the middle of Piața Păcii, the Calvinist **"Church with Chains"** is a long and relatively low Baroque buiding (1793–1802); from here you can return to the square along Strada Ștefan cel Mare, lined with interesting if tatty turn-of-the-century buildings. From the square Strada Decebal continues south, past the twin synagogues that served the city's thirteen thousand Jews (one still active, the other now a cultural centre), to the **river**; here you'll find the run-down plaza of the 1980s Centru Civic, dominated by the moribund Casa de Cultură and the striking tower of the prefecture.

Art Museum

Piața Libertății 21 • Tues–Sat 9am–5pm, Sun 9am–2pm • €0.70 (€1 with County Museum)

In a Neo-Gothic mansion on the south side of the main square, the **Art Museum** features local artist Aurel Popp (1879–1960), who produced sun-dappled Postimpressionist views of Baia Sprie, and much darker images of World War I and the death of capitalism. The collection also includes artists of the Baia Mare School (see page 279) and other twentieth-century Romanian painters.

County Museum

Piața Vasile Lucaciu 21 • Tues–Sat 9am–5pm, Sun 9am–2pm • €0.70 (€1 with Art Museum)

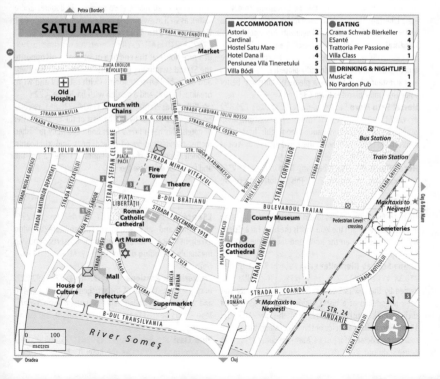

5

The **County Museum**, some 500m east of the centre, has both ethnographic and archeological exhibitions. The former contains standard rural implements and folk costumes, as well as brightly coloured ceramics from Hollóháza in Hungary and Vama in Oaş, while the beautifully presented archeological exhibitions feature fine Daco-Roman remains, clay vessels and grave goods, including some intricate jewellery kept in the treasury.

ARRIVAL AND INFORMATION SATU MARE

By plane Ten kilometres south of the city, Satu Mare Airport (☎0261 768 640, ⊛aeroportulsatumare.ro) currently has flights to London Luton and Bucharest; it's reached by bus #9 from Piaţa Libertăţii and buses towards Zalău and Cluj. Taxis cost around €3.

By bus The bus station is 1km east of the centre on Str. Griviţei (a continuation of B-dul Traian, running east from Piaţa Libertăţii), and is connected to town by bus #1 (every 15–20min). Buses for Baia Mare, Arad, Timişoara and Deva leave from Str. Luceafarului 25 (☎0259 471 690). Buses for Cluj and Bucharest leave from the Autogar FANY south of the river at Str. Closca 14 (☎0736 909 080). Maxitaxis to Negreşti-Oaş leave from Piaţa Romană and head north on Str. Botizului.

Destinations Baia Mare (12 daily); Bucharest (2 daily); Budapest (6 daily); Carei (every 30min); Cluj (every 2 hr); Negreşti-Oaş (hourly); Oradea (8 daily); Sighet (6 daily Mon–Fri, 3 daily Sat & Sun); Timişoara (6 daily).

By train The railway station is opposite the bus station 1km east of the centre on Str. Griviţei and is connected to town by bus #1 (every 15–20min).

Destinations Baia Mare (5 daily; 1hr 15min–1hr 45min); Braşov (1 daily; 12hr 30min); Bucharest (1 daily; 15hr 30min); Cluj (1 daily; 5hr 20min); Oradea (3 daily; 2hr 10min–2hr 50min).

Tourist information Limited information is available from hotels and at ⊛viziteaza-satumare.com/en.

ACCOMMODATION

Astoria Str. Kogălniceanu 1 ☎0261 806 185, ⊛hotel-astoria.ro; map p.295. At the northwestern corner of Piaţa Libertăţii, this hotel has large rooms, good bathrooms and wi-fi – but no lift (staff will help with luggage). €49

Cardinal Piaţa Eroilor Revoluţiei 5 ☎0261 706 906, ⊛hotelcardinal.ro; map p.295. Near the centre but in a quiet residential area, this friendly place has 25 a/c rooms and a restaurant, as well as a pleasant courtyard; better value than most places in town €36

Hostel Satu Mare Str. 24 Ianuarie 17 ☎0261 750 472 or ☎0741 190 544, ✉djtsatumare@gmail.com; map p.295. By the Ştrand swimming pool, this hostel has comfortable rooms with hot water and large TVs, as well as cheaper *căsuţe*. €18

Hotel Dana II Piaţa Libertăţii 5 ☎0261 806 230, ⊛dana-hotel.ro; map p.295. This historic city-centre building has been refurbished in a somewhat blingy style with fairly small rooms (two singles, six doubles and a suite), as well as swimming pool, sauna and hot tub. €52

Pensiunea Vila Tineretului Str. Tinereteului 13 ☎0753 219 341, ⊛vilatineretului.ro; map p.295. In a nice house at the end of a quiet dead-end opposite the Ştrand swimming pool, this "youth hotel" has two- and three-bed en-suite rooms (with cable TV and wi-fi; breakfast extra) and a garden with barbecue. €22

★ **Villa Bódi** Piaţa Libertăţii 5 ☎0261 710 861, ⊛villa-bodi.ro; map p.295. By far the best of the central cluster of hotels, this has a lovely foyer and beautifully furnished rooms manifesting wood-carved beds and cupboards, wooden floors and chandelier lighting; there's a hot-tub and sauna for guest use too. €50

EATING

There are few decent places to **eat** in Satu Mare other than in the hotels, of which the *Villa Bódi* is the best. For a **drink**, try the terrace bars on the north and south sides of Piaţa Libertăţii.

Crama Schwab Bierkeller Piaţa Lucaciu 9 ☎0361 402 318 or ☎0746 427 225; map p.295. This cellar-pub, owned by the town's Swabian (German) community, has been remodelled as a bistro, serving Schwab specialities such as pork knuckle; the menu of the day (Mon–Sat 11am–8pm) offers a choice of three soups and three main courses, plus dessert, for just €4. Mon–Fri 8am–11pm, Sat 8am–midnight.

ESanté Str. Decebal 2 ☎0261 716 468; map p.295. A bright and airy vegan/vegetarian café, serving excellent juices, sandwiches and desserts, and an invariably intriguing dish of the day. Mon–Fri 11am–6pm.

Trattoria Per Passione Str. Decebal 2 ☎0720 092 302; map p.295. Just north of the synagogue, this is a stylish and authentically Italian cellar restaurant with terrace. Mon–Thurs 8am–11pm, Fri 8am–midnight, Sat 9am–midnight, Sun 5–11pm.

Villa Class Str. Rebreanu 11 ☎0261 715 400, ⊛vila-class.ro; map p.295. Like the hotel it's housed in, *Class* is a cut above anything else in town; both the food (goose liver, deer medallions, pork hock) and setting – there's a lovely garden to dine out in – is top drawer. Daily 10am–midnight.

DRINKING AND NIGHTLIFE

Music'at Str. Hám 4 ☎0743 933 541; map p.295. On the corner of Str. Petőfi, this Hungarian café and music pub offers gigs, DJs and karaoke in its redbrick cellar. Mon–Wed 8.30am–10.30pm, Thurs 8.30am–midnight, Fri 8.30am–2am, Sat noon–2am.

No Pardon Pub Str. Corvinilor 11 ☎0261 768 206, ⓦnopardon.ro; map p.295. Halfway to the station, this lively pub also serves some of the best food in town from a meat-heavy menu (€11 for goose). Food Mon–Sat 11am–midnight, Sun 11am–11pm.

Carei

The small town of **CAREI** (Nagykároly), near the border 35km west of Satu Mare, was the fiefdom of the Károlyi family, one of the oldest and most distinguished branches of the Hungarian aristocracy, and more than half of its population is still Hungarian-speaking. From the eighteenth century, the town was also home to Schwab and Jewish communities, and was capital of Szatmar county from 1760 to 1920.

Károlyi Castle

B-dul 25 Octombrie 1 • Tues–Sat 9am–5pm, Sun 10am–2pm; park daily 6am–11pm • Free • ☎0261 864 981, ⓦvisitcarei.ro

The **Károlyi Castle** in the town centre was built as a fortress in the fourteenth century and was heavily involved in the wars of the sixteenth and seventeenth centuries. It was rebuilt in Baroque style in the 1790s and transformed in 1896 into a Neo-Gothic mansion (notably the chapel projecting from the outside wall); it has recently been renovated and houses **two museums**. Four ground-floor rooms cover the history and archeology of Carei, while ten rooms upstairs have been beautifully furnished to illustrate nineteenth-century aristocratic life; there's also a display of weapons and African hunting trophies. The castle is set in a lovely **dendrological park** (with trees marked on a map), which is likely to be taken over by weddings at weekends.

ACCOMMODATION
CAREI

L'Art Hotel Carei Str. 1 Decembrie 1918 2 ☎0361 809 999, ⓦarthotelcarei.ro. Across the road to the east of the castle, this is an expensively design-led new place with handcrafted cherry wood furnishings, wall art (naturally) and tea-and coffee-making facilities, alongside a classy, Art Nouveau inspired restaurant. €62

Motel Select Str. Progresului 1 ☎0261 861 595, ⓦhotelincarei.ro. To the northwest of town, this modern hotel's rooms and restaurant are functional and unexciting – but remarkably good value. €21

The Iza valley

Some of the loveliest villages and wooden churches in Maramureş are in the **Iza valley**, extending roughly 60km from Sighet to the Rodna mountains, on the frontier with Bucovina. Smaller villages nestle in side valleys, enticing visitors to walk across the hills between them.

ARRIVAL AND GETTING AROUND
THE IZA VALLEY

There are regular **buses** from Sighet to Vişeu de Sus and Borşa – most following the DJ186 along the Iza valley, although some take the DN18 along the Rona and Vişeu valleys – and a daily bus from Sighet to most of the villages in the Iza's side valleys.

Onceşti

Despite being on the main Iza valley road, **ONCEŞTI**, 11km from Sighet, is perhaps the Maramureş village that has best preserved its folk customs, with many people wearing traditional dress on Sundays. It's been inhabited since ancient times, and the ruins of a medieval fortress remain on Dealul Cetăţeaua. It still boasts many carved wooden gates and two fine groups of **wooden houses**, one by Str. Principală 241 (just east of the school), but the sixteenth-century wooden church is now in Sighet's Village Museum (see page 277). There are also some fine guesthouses.

ARRIVAL AND DEPARTURE

ONCEŞTI

By bus All buses from Sighet towards Botiza, Borşa and Săcel via the Iza valley serve Onceşti (25min).

ACCOMMODATION

Pensiunea Bud Mariana no. 360 ☏ 0262 348 448, ⊚ agrotur.ro/bud. Towards the east end of the village, there's wonderful family hospitality here, with six rooms, huge and delicious meals and the chance to try on local costumes or see *ţuica* being made. There's also space for camper vans. Per person. **€8**

Pensiunea Sub Cetate la Matei no. 480 ☏ 0262 348 498 or ☏ 0742 342 328. At the west end of the village, this pension has eight rooms with TV, friendly service, good home-grown food and traditional furnishings, as well as a small museum including tools saved from a blacksmith's forge. **€20**

Bârsana and Rozavlea

The wooden church of **BÂRSANA**, 19km southeast of Sighet on the DJ186, is small and neat and perfectly positioned atop a hillock to the west of the village centre. It was built in 1720, and its florid **paintings**, among the best in Maramureş, date from 1720 and 1806. Hodor Toador and Ion Plohod were responsible for the later set, with icons on wood by the former – the narthex is adorned with saints and processional images, while the naos is painted with Old and New Testament scenes, each in a decorative medallion. Don't miss the images of angels covered in eyes. At the east end of the village, 4km from the centre, stands the new **Bârsana monastery**, a large complex of wooden buildings, all in traditional style, including the wooden church which, unusually, has a pentagonal *privdor* and two apses, as well as a 57m steeple, briefly the world's highest but now overtaken by that at Săpânţa (see page 293). The original monastery was closed by the Austrians in 1791; construction of a new one (in fact a nunnery) began in 1993, and it has expanded steadily since. Just east of the Călineşti junction, at no. 605, you can visit the splendid woodworker Teodor Bârsan, with carvings big and small for sale.

As a border region, Maramureş remained vulnerable to attacks by nomadic tribes until the eighteenth century, and the wooden church just east of the centre of **ROZAVLEA**, 20km further along the valley, was one of many rebuilt after the last Tatar invasion in 1717. Its magnificent double roof, recently restored, is now weathering nicely; its paintings by Ion Plohod, including an unusual exterior painting of the *Beheading of St. John the Baptist* in the porch, have been cleaned.

ARRIVAL AND DEPARTURE

BÂRSANA AND ROZAVLEA

All **buses** from Sighet towards Botiza, Borşa and Săcel via the Iza valley serve Bârsana (35min) and Rozavlea (45min).

ACCOMMODATION

BÂRSANA

Cabana Iza no. 281 ☏ 0262 331 212, ⊚ izamaramures. ro. An attractive place, decorated in traditional style, with seven spacious rooms sleeping between one and four; swimming pool and spa, and bikes can be rented too (€8/day). **€22**

Camping Bradova no. 803 ☏ 0746 993 061, ⊚ camping-bradova.ro. In a rural setting 2.5km north

from the west end of Bârsana, this has modern chalets as well as space for tents and motorhomes. **€11**

Pensiunea Cerbul Carpatin no. 279 ☏ 0262 331 212 or ☏ 0765 497 836, ✉ marcflorent@yahoo.fr. In a slightly older building near the monastery, this is less grandiose than most Bârsana guesthouses, with five doubles and a quad, sharing two bathrooms. **€14**

Pensiunea Fraţii Paşca no. 1338A ☎ 0762 609 352, ⓦ fratiipasca.ro. To the east of the village, this tidy complex consists of three cottages, variously accommodating rooms with and without bathrooms, as well as kitchens and dining rooms; there's also a pool, jacuzzi, table tennis and a playground. €15

Pensiunea Pop no. 442 ☎ 0262 331 064, ⓔ ghpop1@ yahoo.fr. A cozy traditional house with spacious rooms and shared bathroom. The owners offer wonderful hospitality and there's plenty of filling food on offer. €13

ROZAVLEA

Casa Tomşa no. 961 ☎ 0262 333 155 or ☎ 0751 758 416, ⓔ ionut_tomsa2005@yahoo.com. This motel-style place, with large swimming pool, is an alternative to the various homelier guesthouses dotted around the village. €14

Şieu and Botiza

Şieu, 2km east of Rozavlea, has a fine wooden church (500m south on the Botiza road), built in 1760. From here a side road leads 10km south to **BOTIZA**, a growing centre for agritourism, with many good guesthouses. The **wooden church** here, beautifully set on a hillside, was built in 1699 in Vişeu de Jos and moved to Botiza two hundred years later. Beyond a few blackened frescoes of the Apostles and some floral motifs, there's little to see inside, but if you want a look, ask for the key at no. 743. There are several **mineral springs** along the Poienile Izei road, notably a sulphurous well at a ruined spa by the bridge about 1km from the village centre. From the second bridge below the church there's a delightful (but unmarked) **hike** to Ieud; turning right onto a lovely path across fields, it takes thirty minutes to a low pass, after which you need to keep to the right. In the other direction, start on a side road 1km south of the Val church in Ieud. The "Pentru Mândra din Botiza" ("For my Darling from Botiza") **folk festival** takes place over a weekend in mid-August.

ARRIVAL AND DEPARTURE
ŞIEU AND BOTIZA

There are **buses** from Sighet towards Botiza (7 daily from Autogar Jan), Borşa and Săcel via Iza valley serve Şieu (50min).

ACCOMMODATION

★ **Casa Berbecaru** no. 743, Botiza ☎ 0262 334 107, ⓦ agrotur.ro/berbecaru. Victoria Berbecaru, renowned for her carpet-making using natural dyes, offers rooms in a modern house and also in the charming wooden house – built around 1790 and right in front of the church – where she has her weaving studio. Per person €9.

Casa Maria Poienar no. 429, Botiza ☎ 0744 901 311, ⓔ mariepoienar@yahoo.com. South of the centre, two houses offer seven doubles with shared bathrooms, and excellent home cooking. Per person €6.50

Pensiunea Ancuţa Valea Sasului 222, Botiza ☎ 0262 334 079. A couple of kilometres west of the centre, friendly owners offer six rooms sharing two bathrooms, and also sell traditional textiles. Per person €11

Pensiunea Manţa no. 407, Botiza ☎ 0262 334 132 or ☎ 0727 684 148, ⓔ casa.manta@yahoo.com. This guesthouse has six comfortable rooms, some en suite; you can also buy Doamna Manţa's weavings. Per person €7

Poienile Izei

Although there's a good road from Şieu to **POIENILE IZEI** ("the meadows of the Iza"), from Botiza only an unpaved road leads 6km northeast to this charming little village, famous for its old **wooden church**, which is on UNESCO's World Heritage List. Lovers of traditional music will enjoy staying at the *Pensiunea Ion de la Cruce*.

Poienile Izei church

Mon–Fri 9am–1pm, Sat 2–6pm, Sun noon–4pm • €1 • ☎ 0762 608 235

Built in 1604–32, **Poienile Izei church** is filled with nightmarish paintings of hell. On the red walls to the left dozens of demons (*draci*) with goat-like heads and clawed feet are depicted torturing sinners and driving them into the mouth of hell – an enormous bird's head with fiery nostrils. These pictures constitute an illustrated rule book too terrifying to disobey: a huge pair of bellows is used to punish farting in church; a

5

woman guilty of burning the priest's robes while ironing them is herself pressed with a hot iron; adulteresses are courted by loathsome demons, and a woman who aborted children is forced to eat them. These hell scenes presumably formed the nasty part of a huge *Day of Judgement* in the narthex, the other half of which has, ironically, not been saved. Opposite are paintings of gardens and distant cityscapes in a sort of Gothic Book of Hours style, executed around 1793–94. The nave's murals are badly damaged and soot-blackened, but from the gallery you can recognize *Adam and Eve*, *The Fall* and episodes from the lives of Christ and John the Baptist.

ARRIVAL AND DEPARTURE   POIENILE IZEI

From the Autogar Jan in Sighet three **buses** a day run to Poienile Izei (6.45am, 11.30am & 4pm).

ACCOMMODATION

Pensiunea Ileana Petreuş no. 130 ☎0751 932 825 or ☎0724 619 163, ⍟pensiuneaileanapetreus.ro. This traditional-style house 700m north of the centre has seven en-suite rooms with balconies; it's also a working farm and uses its own fresh produce for meals. Half board per person **€14**

Pensiunea Ion de la Cruce no. 15 ☎0262 334 365 or ☎0726 387 108. This very welcoming and comfortable guesthouse 1km east on the road to Şieu is strongly recommended for the traditional music played virtually every night – Ion is a particularly accomplished violinist; prices are for half board with shared bathroom. **€31**

Pensiunea La Domniţa Str. Dubului 135 ☎0262 334 383 or ☎0724 764 036, ✉domnitailies@yahoo.com. Some 700m north of the centre, the thirteen rooms here, spread across two buildings, are not the most luxurious, but the welcome and the home cooking are great. French is spoken and there are lots of costumes for you to try on. Per person **€10.50**

Ieud

Continuing along Iza valley, and 4km southeast of the Botiza turning, a turn-off at Gura Ieudului leads upstream to the village of **IEUD**, 2.5km south. It was Ieud artisans, supervised by master carpenter Ion Ţâplea, who restored Manuc's Inn in Bucharest (see page 60), and master carpenter Gavrilă Hotico is currently building new wooden churches all over Maramureş and beyond.

Hill Church

Summer Mon–Sat 9am–2pm & 3–8pm, Sun 1–4pm & 5–8pm; winter Sun 1–4pm & 5–8pm • €1

The village's tradition of woodworking has been maintained since the superb Orthodox **Hill Church** (Biserica din Deal) was first raised here in 1364. Long thought to be the oldest church in Maramureş (though largely rebuilt in 1620 and the eighteenth century), with a double roof and tiny windows, it once housed the Ieud Codex (1391–92) – now in the Romanian Academy in Bucharest – the earliest-known document in the Romanian language. It has perhaps the most renowned **paintings** of any Maramureş church, executed by Alexandru Ponehalski in 1782; look out for Abraham, Isaac and Jacob welcoming people in their arms, in the pronaos. And don't miss the ingenious removable ratchet that opens the bolt in the main door.

Lower church

Key available from Matuşa Juji across the road • €0.50

No less splendid than the Orthodox church is the Uniate **lower church** (the Val or Şes church, also dubbed "the cathedral of wood"), built in 1718 with a magnificently high roofline, though, unusually, no porch; few wall paintings survive, but the iconostasis and icons on glass (including an image of St George on a blue horse) are artistically valuable.

Muzeul Pleş

No. 909 • Daily 8am–noon & 1–8pm • €1 • ☎0262 336 104

5

The **Muzeul Pleș**, 150m before the Hill Church, consists of a couple of traditional buildings, almost 200 years old, stocked by the Pleș family with traditional clothing, wooden tools and furniture, all handmade. There's no English spoken, but the owners are still keen to show everything including their own wedding costumes.

ARRIVAL AND DEPARTURE   IEUD

All **buses** from Sighet towards Borșa and Săcel via the Iza valley pass Gura Ieudului (55min), from where you can walk or hitch a ride to the village.

ACCOMMODATION

Pensiunea Casa Dăncuș no. 539 ☎0262 336 126 or ☎0765 249 899. With thirteen rooms in a big new house facing the lower church, this is a more upmarket option than most in the village, with good traditional food. €15

Pensiunea Casa Tradiţilor no. 794A ☎0763 768 648, ⌨casatraditiilor.ro. Just 1km south from the main

Iza valley road, this is called "the house of traditions" not because it's a traditional wooden house, but because of the authentic furnishings, food and hospitality found within. Six highly original en-suite rooms with names like House of Judges, and It Floats from Above. €25

Bogdan Vodă

BOGDAN VODĂ, stretching east from Gura Ieudului, is one of the valley's main villages, with long-standing ties to Moldavia. It was known as Cuhea until the late 1960s, when it was renamed in honour of the local *voivode*, Bogdan, who left in 1359, supposedly to hunt bison, but ended up founding the Moldavian state (see page376). The influence of Stephen and other Moldavian rulers lent a semi-Byzantine style to the frescoes inside Bogdan Vodă's **wooden church**, though the materials used in 1718 were typical of eastern Maramureș – thick fir beams rather than the stone used in the Bucovina monasteries, or the oak of western Maramureș. Unfortunately, it's now dwarfed by a huge modern successor erected far too close to it.

Dragomirești

The main road east out of Bogdan Vodă leads to **DRAGOMIREȘTI**, where the worthwhile **Muzeul Tarancii Romane** (Museum of the Romanian Peasant Woman; daily 9am–7pm; €0.50), just west of the centre in an eighteenth-century house, displays a wide range of domestic and other implements, almost all wooden, showing that a Maramureș woman's work is never done. You can buy crafts here, too. Just west of this is a Uniate **wooden church** (on a concrete base), completed in 2000 to replace the village's original church, now in Bucharest's Village Museum (see page 65).

ARRIVAL AND DEPARTURE   BOGDAN VODĂ AND DRAGOMIREȘTI

All **buses** from Sighet towards Borșa and Săcel via the Iza valley serve Bogdan Vodă (55min) and Dragomirești (1hr).

Săliștea de Sus and Săcel

SĂLIȘTEA DE SUS, 4km east of Dragomirești, boasts two old **wooden churches** on either side of the river, both rebuilt after the Tatar raid of 1717. The Baleni or Valley church has icons painted by Radu Munteanu in 1775 and an unusual central tower, while the Nistorești church has a second tower on a porch added after World War II. At **SĂCEL**, 53km from Vadu Izei, the Iza valley road meets the railway and the DN17C, which heads northeast to Moisei (11km) and south to Salva and Bistriţa (44km and 71km) in Transylvania. The village is known for its unglazed red **ceramics**, but only Tănase Burnar (Str. Bistriţiei 362; ☎0748 244 490 or ☎0747 900 352) is still using the same technique as the Dacians two millennia ago, with a 300-year-old kiln.

5

ARRIVAL AND DEPARTURE

All **buses** from Sighet towards Borşa and Săcel via the Iza valley serve Săliştea de Sus (1hr 5min) and Săcel (1hr 15min).

ACCOMMODATION

Pensiunea Maria Str. Centru 235, Săcel ☎ 0262 339 064 or ☎ 0745 844 372, ✉ psusca@umfcluj.ro. Just east of the centre (west of the main road junction) this is a simple and welcoming little place with good food and traditional decor (although many rugs use lurid artificial dyes). **€18**

Pensiunea Seky Str. Ciresilor 1, Săliştea de Sus ☎ 0742 776 304, ⓦ seky.ro. Offers six doubles with a gym, sauna

and restaurant; further rooms in two nineteenth-century wooden houses, and a treehouse. **€22**

Pensiunea Vasilica Str. Buleasa 58, Săliştea de Sus ☎ 0742 243 308. Only Romanian is spoken, but staying here is a delightful and authentically rural experience; there are four traditionally furnished en-suite rooms and a garden with swing seats. Half board **€31**

The Vişeu valley

The railway east from Sighet follows the River Tisza for 25km before heading up the beautiful **Vişeu valley**; the hills between the Tisza and Vişeu valleys are inhabited by Huţul or Ruthenian people, the archetypal inhabitants of the Carpathians, who speak a dialect of Ukrainian incorporating many Romanian words. Local buses from Sighet run along the DN18 through the Ukrainian-populated village of **Rona De Jos** to terminate at the tiny spa of **Coştiui**, 22km from Sighet, which has a motel and *căsuţe*. Beyond the turning to Coştiui the road climbs to a pass in lovely beech forest; from Leordina (once home to Harvey Keitel's parents), 28km southeast of Rona de Jos, a rough side road follows the River Ruscova north into a Huţul enclave. There's still a synagogue in **Ruscova**, once home to British politician Michael Howard's father, while in **Poienile de sub Munte**, the centre of the area, there's a Ukrainian-style wooden church dating from 1788 and a couple of guesthouses. Back in the Vişeu valley, trains continue 10km east from Leordina to **VIŞEU DE JOS**, then turn south towards Transylvania; from Vişeu de Jos, passenger trains no longer run up the branch line to Borşa, but there are regular buses as far as Vişeu de Sus, and fewer on to Borşa.

Vişeu de Sus

Just east of Vişeu de Jos is **VIŞEU DE SUS**, a logging town that's growing into a tourist town thanks to the popularity of the **steam train** from here up the steep Vaser valley, with new guesthouses that appeal more to Romanians in search of comfort than foreigners seeking a wooden-house-and-farm-animals experience. Diagonally across the main Strada 22 Decembrie from the museum is a **wooden Uniate church** built in 1993–5 by Gavrilă Hotico of Ieud. There's also the big new **Aqua Park** on the main road (Str. Rândunelelor 6; ☎ 0744 565 478 or ☎ 0744 470 012, ⓦ mirage-resort.ro), for those with kids to placate.

Muzeul de Istorie şi Etnografie

Str. Libertăţii 7 • Mon–Fri 9am–5pm • €1

Although the **Muzeul de Istorie şi Etnografie** (Museum of History and Ethnography) is a work in progress, there's worthwhile coverage of the ethnography of the Romanian, Ruthenian, Jewish and Zipser communities. The Zipsers (Ţipţerai in Romanian) were German foresters who until World War II lived here in some numbers, trading mainly with Jewish timber merchants.

Mocăniţa Narrow-Gauge Railway

Train Leaves at 9am daily June–Sept from the yard on Str. Cerbului, 1km north of the centre; head up Str. Carpaţi, opposite Str. I. Maniu; trains return from Paltin between 2.30 and 3.30pm • €15 return; late March–May & Oct to mid-Nov Thurs–Sun €12 • ☎ 0262 353 381 or ☎ 0744 686 716, ⓦ cffviseu.com • **Café** Daily 8–10am & 2–5pm

The **narrow-gauge railway** up the wild Vaser valley, towards the Ukrainian border, is still used by diesel-hauled logging trains; in addition, tourist trains run as far as Paltin, 21km up the valley. These are hauled by small steam locomotives – known as *mocăniţa*, meaning "little mountain shepherd" – which have been restored by enthusiasts, the oldest dating from 1910.

There's a pleasant **café** in a typical wooden house at the departure point, with a small exhibition on the town's vanished Jewish community (about forty percent of the population in 1940). There are also three preserved steam locomotives here, including a huge standard-gauge beast (a 2-10-0) near the train-hotel (see below).

Along the route, you may see deer drinking from the river, unperturbed by the trains. The River Vaser, rich in trout and umber, descends rapidly through the 50km-long valley; its whirling waters have begun to attract kayakers to logging settlements like **Măcârlău**, also the start of a rugged trail over the Jupania ridge of the Maramureş mountains to the former mining centre of Baia Borşa, just north of Borşa. You can also take bikes and cycle the 9km back from Novăţ station.

ARRIVAL AND INFORMATION
VIŞEU DE SUS

By bus Maxitaxis for Moisei (continuing to Borşa Mon–Fri) start from km125 on the main road just east of the centre; longer-distance buses pick up here and at a layby opposite the hospital at the bottom of Str. 22 Decembrie 1989. Destinations Baia Mare (9 daily); Borşa (8 daily); Sighet (10–12 daily).

Tourist information Fundaţia ProVişeu (Mon–Sat 9am–5pm; ☎0262 352 285, ⑩turismviseu.ro) at Str. Libertăţii 1, on a corner with the main Str. 22 Decembrie, offers information and can organize private rooms here and in the surrounding area.

ACCOMMODATION AND EATING

Carpatia Express Str. Cerbului 5 ☎0262 353 381, ⑩cffviseu.com. This "train-hotel" at the *mocăniţa* station has two sleeping cars, with twenty compartments, each with two beds and a washbasin. There are two toilets on board but showers (and more toilets) are located outside the train; breakfast is served in the dining car, where a good candlelit dinner is available (€15). You can also park a camper van here (€9). Great fun. **€30**

Hotel Gabriela Str. Rândunelelor 1 ☎0262 354 380, ⑩hotel-gabriela.ro. About 1km east at km127.5 on the Moisei road, this is the most upmarket place here, offering spacious rooms with balconies, tennis courts, a spa and a decent restaurant (although this often hosts weddings). **€31**

Pension Agnes Str. Spiru Haret 10 ☎0742 153 808 or ☎0744 332 730. Tucked behind the hospital (down a rough track), immediately west of the town centre, this charming guesthouse features a delightful riverside garden, with

camping and barbecue. Owners speak excellent English. **€20**

Pensiunea Bârsan Str. A.I. Cuza 69B ☎0748 600 492, ⑨pensiunea_barsan@yahoo.com. Rail enthusiasts should stay at this guesthouse, 600m beyond the station: run by the wife of one of the engine drivers, it has a balcony with views of passing trains and a gate onto the track. Four triple rooms and one quad, and meals by arrangement. **€22**

Magnolia Guesthouse Str. Arşiţa 90A ☎0757 104 341, ⑩magnoliaresort.ro. From 126km on the Moisei road it's 1km west to this fabulous complex of three wooden houses and a chalet beautifully sited in an orchard, where they grow much of their own food. The hosts, who speak English and German, are utterly charming. **€33**

Vila Landhaus Str. Grigorescu 1B ☎0748 916 527. Just north beyond the Ţipţerai Quarter, this lovely large chalet, run by delightful young owners, has six tidy rooms and a garden on the edge of the forest. **€20**

Moisei

The straggling village of **MOISEI**, 12km west of Vişeu de Sus, lies below the Rodna massif, whose peaks are often still snowy while fruit is ripening in the village's orchards.

HORĂ AT PRISLOP FESTIVAL

At Prislop Pass, close to the *Cabana Alpina*, and a new (stone) monastery, the **Horă at Prislop festival** takes place on a Sunday in mid-August, attracting thousands of participants and spectators for traditional music, dance, food and drink.

5

> ## ROUTES ON TO MOLDAVIA AND TRANSYLVANIA
>
> From Borşa Complex, a hairpin road heads up to the **Prislop Pass** at the border of Maramureş with Bucovina – 2km away as the crow flies, but a dozen kilometres by this tightly twisting road. Just before the pass you'll see a **monument** marking the site where the last Tatar raid was finally driven off in 1717. Beyond the pass the road follows the lovely Bistriţa Aurie valley to Iacobeni, from where you can reach Suceava and several of the **painted monasteries** by rail; just two buses a day come this way from Borşa (at 7.44am and 11.19am). Travelling to **Transylvania**, three trains a day link Vişeu de Jos with Salva, 61km to the south and a junction on the busier line from Cluj to Vatra Dornei and Suceava; there's also a daily bus from Borşa to Bistriţa, and four from Sighet to Cluj via the Iza valley and Săcel.

Though today it seems tranquil, October 1944 saw Moisei suffer an atrocity that became a symbol of martyred innocence throughout Romania, when retreating Hungarian troops machine-gunned 29 locals and set the village ablaze – a massacre commemorated by a circle of twelve **stone figures** by Vida Geza, with faces modelled on two of the victims and on the masks worn during Maramureş festivals. The memorial is 5km east of the centre, opposite a small museum at km141. A couple of kilometres along a side valley south of the village (off the Săcel road) stands a monastery that sees a 40km **pilgrimage** on August 15, the Feast of the Assumption.

ARRIVAL AND DEPARTURE   MOISEI

By bus Local maxitaxis run from Mosei to Vişeu de Sus and to Borşa (combined as a through service Mon–Fri); longer-distance buses from Sighet, Baia Mare and Transylvania to Borşa pass through Moisei.

Borşa Complex and the Rodna mountains

The eastern border of Maramureş is formed by the **Rodna mountains**, one of Romania's best **hiking** areas, largely because you're sure to have them virtually to yourself. Routes converge on the grubby mining town of **Borşa**, 5km east of Moisei, with some buses continuing for 10km to the small ski resort (beginners and intermediates only) of **Borşa Complex** on the mountain flanks. Naturally, there's a **wooden church** in Borşa, hidden away north of Strada Libertăţii, west of the centre; it was rebuilt in 1718 and painted internally by Zaharia Zugrav in 1765.

The easiest way into the mountains is either by the **chairlift** from Borşa Complex (daily 9am–5pm, although you may have to wait until a dozen or so people have gathered; €2) or by hiking south from the 1416m **Prislop Pass** on the road from Maramureş to Moldavia; you can also head north into the Maramureş mountains, wild and largely unvisited, although scarred by mining and forestry. Heading south into the Rodnas, following red triangle markings then blue stripes, it should take two hours at most to reach the main crest at the **Gârgălău saddle**; from the Complex you can get here in no more than four hours following blue stripes. Then you can follow red stripes east to the Rotunda Pass and ultimately (camping wild en route) to Vatra Dornei (see page 270), or head west along the main ridge to the highest peaks. This will get you to La Cruce in four and a half hours, from where you can turn right to follow blue stripes up to the weather station on the summit of **Mount Pietrosul** (2303m), ninety minutes away. There are great views in all directions, particularly deep into Ukraine to the north. Borşa is 1600m below, another two and a half hours away, or you can return to the Complex (a loop of 22km in all). Well-equipped hikers can continue west to the Şetref Pass (south of Săcel), or south towards the Someş Mare valley and Năsăud in two days, camping wild en route.

Alternatively, follow red stripes from the Complex up the Fântana valley to the **Cascada Cailor** (Horses' Waterfall; Romania's highest at 90m), which takes ninety minutes. You can continue to the Şaua Ştiol (at the top of the chairlift) and on to the Prislop Pass, following red triangles (4–5hr), and return to the Complex in at most three hours following yellow stripes.

ARRIVAL AND INFORMATION BORŞA

By bus Buses run to Baia Mare (10–12 daily), Bistriţa (1 daily), Sighet (10–12 daily) and Vatra Dornei (2 daily). Maxitaxis west to Moisei (continuing to Vişeu de Sus Mon–Fri) leave from the west end of the bridge (just west of the centre); those east to Borşa Complex leave (usually every 40min) from the hospital, just east of the centre.

Tourist information The Rodna National Park is based on the south side of the mountains (☎0263 377 175,

@parcrodna@email.ro), but there's an office in Borşa at Str. Zorilor 2B (☎0362 412 953 or ☎0740 002 125, @pnmrborsa@ddcnet.ro); the Maramureş mountains Natural Park has its headquarters in Vişeu de Sus, at Str. 22 Decembrie 20 (☎0262 352 216, ⓦmuntiimaramuresului.ro). Munţii Rodnei hiking maps (look for the Schubert & Franzke 1:55,000) are available in shops and tourist agencies.

ACCOMMODATION

Hotel Roman Str. Brădet 2A ☎0758 362 384, ⓦromanhotel.ro. At the Complex's central junction, 1km from the main road, this modern ski hotel has a panoramic bar-restaurant and swimming pool. **€32**

Motel Rodna Str. Libertăţii 37 ☎0262 344 961 or ☎0744 699 052. Down an alley by the market, just 300m west of the centre, this is the best accommodation in Borşa itself, with small but neat and good-value rooms, and a restaurant and pizzeria (Mon–Sat 8am–10pm, Sun 10am–10pm). **€11**

Pensiunea Borşa Turism Str. Pietroasei 9 ☎0745 271 576, ⓦborsa-turism.com. Towards the mountains to the south immediately east of the hospital, a Belgian-Romanian couple owns this attractive guesthouse with chalets in the garden, plus space for tents. Camping **€7**, rooms **€24**

Pensiunea Fântana Str. Fântana 36B ☎0745 932 523 or ☎0755 584 194. More a hotel than a guesthouse, this has ten rooms (some with shared bathrooms) and two suites, plus a busy bar-restaurant. It's at the junction midway between the main road and the chairlift. **€22**

Pensiunea Fulg de Nea Str. Fântana ☎0262 343 685 or ☎0745 693 304. At the bottom of the Complex, near the main road and several other pensions in older wooden houses with orchards, this fairly simple place has six en-suite rooms and a restaurant. **€16**

Pensiunea Hantig-Lucian Str. Cascada 6 ☎0262 343 663. Ideal for hikers, this pension is 1.3km up the unpaved track to the Cascada Cailor (see above). It has three en-suite rooms and five with shared bathrooms, plus a kitchen, and a barbecue in the garden. **€18**

The Banat and Crişana

TIMIŞOARA ORTHODOX CATHEDRAL

The Banat and Crişana

The Banat (Bánság) is the historical term for the western marches of Romania between the Timiş and Mureş rivers, but it has also come to include the Crişana, to the north between the Apuseni massif and the Hungarian border. With its largely featureless scenery, great rivers, historical sites and intermingled ethnic groups, the Banat has much in common with its neighbours, Hungary's Great Plain and Serbia's Vojvodina region. The frontiers were supposedly settled according to the principle of national self-determination at the Versailles conference of 1918–20, each country's delegates bringing reams of demographic maps and statistics to support their claims, but in truth the region's ethnic tangle could not be unpicked. Communist policies towards minorities were comparatively fair until the 1960s, when an increasingly hard line led to a haemorrhaging of the Banat's population, particularly of Magyars. In both 1988 and 1989, around eighty thousand left, as liberalization gained pace in Hungary but things went downhill fast in Romania. The Schwab Germans, who colonized this area when the marshes were drained after the expulsion of the Turks, have almost all emigrated to Germany since 1989. Nevertheless, many Slovaks, Serbs, Magyars and other minority groups remain.

Key attractions are the cities of **Oradea**, **Arad** and **Timişoara**, each of which also dominates a route between Transylvania and Hungary or Serbia, and gives access to most other places of interest in the region. Timişoara, in particular, is hugely enjoyable, and the city not to miss should you have to choose just one in the region. There are also rural temptations aplenty, such as the western ranges of the **Apuseni mountains**, with their stalactite caves and wooden churches, and the spas at **Băile Herculane** and **Băile Felix**; moreover, there are some terrific **festivals** in the smaller villages.

Oradea and around

The congenial city of **ORADEA**, capital of the Crişana, is close to the site of Biharea – the capital of the Vlach *voivode*, Menumorut, who resisted Hungarian claims on the region during the tenth century. Founded around a monastery, the medieval town of Nagyvarad (as the Magyars still call it) prospered during the reign of **Mátyás Corvinus** (raised at the Bishop's Palace here) and later acquired a mammoth Vauban-style citadel and the wealth of charming Secession buildings (built in the decade before World War I) which are today Oradea's most characteristic feature. The city sits astride the **Crişul Repede river**, north of which are the main shopping area and a couple of small museums, while to the south are the city's most interesting buildings and the citadel. Aside from being a useful place to break a journey to or from Hungary, Oradea is just a short bus ride away from the spas at **Băile Felix** and **Băile 1 Mai**. They're enjoyable places to spend an afternoon relaxing, and can also make a good base for visiting Oradea itself; treatments for muscular pain and rheumatic diseases (available at hotels) include healing baths in sapropelic fossil mud and dips in pools fed by the warm and slightly radioactive River Peţa.

Highlights

❶ Oradea Charming town, rampant with Secession architecture and near a couple of small spa resorts. See page 308

❷ Chişcău and Meziad caves Take a tour through these atmospheric caves, featuring stunning stalactite and stalagmite formations. See page 317

❸ Timişoara Birthplace of the 1989 revolution, this vibrant, engaging city is characterized by colourful squares, green parks and lively nightlife. See page 326

❹ Băile Herculane Elegant Habsburg-era buildings and bathing opportunities aplenty in this once fashionable spa. See page 336

❺ Crivaia Attractive alpine resort, from where you can partake in any number of hikes to the hills and caves of mountainous Banat. See page 337

HIGHLIGHTS ARE MARKED ON THE MAP ON PAGE 310

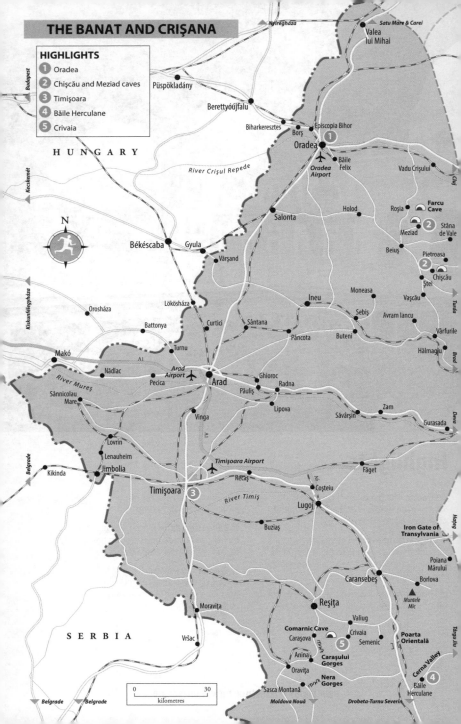

Roman Catholic Cathedral and Bishop's Palace

In the large leafy park just west of the train station, the **Roman Catholic Cathedral**, reputedly the largest Baroque building in Romania, was built in 1752–80 by countless serfs. It has a striking facade and is decorated inside with gold leaf and marble, and accommodates a huge organ – posters advertise regular concerts. The serfs' labour was also doubtless exploited to construct the vast U-shaped **Bishop's Palace** adjacent to the cathedral; built by Franz Anton Hillebrandt in 1762–77, it was modelled on Lucas von Hildebrandt's Belvedere Palace in Vienna. The composer Michael Haydn, brother of the more famous Joseph, worked here as the bishop's music director from 1760 to 1762. The palace is currently undergoing a huge programme of restoration which, when complete (2020 at the earliest), will showcase a new museum for the Catholic diocese of Oradea, together with enhanced features within the park itself.

Calea Republicii and Piaţa Regele Ferdinand

Turning south towards the river, **Calea Republicii** becomes a pedestrianized promenade, lined with shops, cafés, fast-food joints and many ostentatious Secession buildings in various states of refurbishment. Of particular interest are the buildings at the intersection of Calea Republicii and Strada Eminescu; although missing much of their original plasterwork, no. 10 and no. 12 (the former Apollo Palace, which is currently being restored to something like its former glory) have retained some outstanding features, notably heavily stuccoed facades and corner turrets.

Calea Republicii leads to **Piaţa Regele Ferdinand**, dominated by the State Theatre, a typically pompous design by the Viennese duo Helmer and Fellner completed in 1900. Just behind the theatre stand two fine Secession buildings: the Adorján tenement houses at Str. Patrioţilor 4 and 6, built in 1903 and 1904, and each sporting a flurry of rosettes.

The Endre Ady, Aurel Lazăr and Iosif Vulcan Museums

Muzeul Ady Endre Tues, Thurs & Sat 10am–3pm, Wed, Fri & Sun 10am–2pm & 4–6pm • €0.50 • ☎ 0259 412 724 • **Museul Aurel Lazăr** Str. Aurel Lazăr 13 • Same times and price • ☎ 0259 442 112 **Muzeul Iosif Vulcan** Str. Vulcan 16 • Same times and price • ☎ 0259 463 755

Just to the east of Strada Republicii are three small memorial houses: in the tiny Traian Park the lovely **Muller building** commemorates the Magyar poet **Endre Ady** (1877–1919) who lived in Oradea for four years and, unusually for his era, opposed Hungarian chauvinism towards the Romanians. Formerly a society café where Ady and his pals would gather for evenings of drinks and bonhomie, it now keeps a handful of personal effects and Ady-era furnishings, including a neatly arranged editorial suite complete with beautiful oak bureau – to the rear is a cool, shaded terrace café and basement bar.

One block south is the family home of **Aurel Lazăr** (1872–1930), one of the leaders of the movement for the union of Transylvania with Romania in 1918. In the attractive Secession house, built at the end of the nineteenth century, are documents, photos and family items; there are some intriguing furnishings and artwork too, including a three-door cupboard containing several volumes of Lazăr's books, and a vase with two elephant's heads.

Another block south is the museum remembering poet and novelist **Iosif Vulcan** (1841–1907), who lived here from 1880 to 1906. Vulcan published the best writers of his day in the literary journal *Familia*, which survives to this day – it was in this magazine that Mihai Eminescu made his debut in 1866 with the poem *De-aş avea* (*If I Had*), a copy of which is on display. The museum seeks to re-create the atmosphere of a late nineteenth-century literary salon, with period pieces of furniture, including Vulcan's Biedermeier desk. Across the road at Str. Vulcan 11, the Darvas-La Roche house (1909–10) is the best example of a Secession-style private house in Oradea; at the time of writing, work was ongoing to convert the house into a museum illustrating the city's Art Nouveau movement.

6

Piaţa Unirii

City Hall tower: Str. Tudor Vladimirescu 2 • April–Oct Tues–Fri 12.30–6pm; Sat & Sun 12.30–7pm; Nov–March Tues–Sun 12.30–4pm •
☎ 0731 212 284

Across the Crişul Repede from Piaţa Regele Ferdinand is the newly pedestrianized **Piaţa Unirii**, a vast open space which, beyond the nondescript Catholic church (1720–41) half-blocking the square's north side, is replete with fanciful Secession buildings. The **City Hall** in the northwestern corner is, however, a monumental restatement of well-worn classical themes to which the architects added a fun touch: chimes that play the *March of Avram Iancu* every hour. Given that the Habsburgs were still in control when the building was raised in 1902–03, it seems odd that they allowed this commemoration of Iancu, a Romanian revolutionary who inspired the protest on the "Field of Liberty"

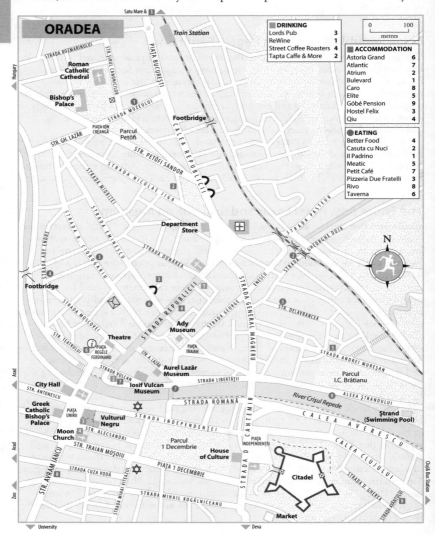

at Blaj in 1848 (see page 380), and who then took to the hills with a guerrilla band, harassing Magyar troops and landlords and urging the serfs to revolt. There are viewing platforms 50m up in the City Hall's tower, offering great views of the city (as well as the clock mechanism). Just south of City Hall is the **Greek Catholic Episcopal Palace** (1905), a spectacular pile spotted with all manner of protrusions and jutting towers.

Vultural Negru, Moskovits Palace and Moon Church

On the east side of Piaţa Unirii is the splendidly named **Vulturul Negru** (Black Eagle), an astonishingly ornate Secession-style edifice dating from 1908. Running through it is an arcade, notable for its beautiful stained-glass roof connecting three streets; recently renovated, the arcade is now lined with cafés and bars, making it one of the most enjoyable places in town for a drink. Part of the complex is occupied by what was once one of Romania's most historic hotels – an ill-lit labyrinth of rooms and corridors inhabited by brooding staff and a furtive clientele. It did reopen as a luxury hotel, but alas soon closed again.

Immediately south, on the corner of Strada Alecsandri, the **Moskovits Palace** (1911) is another enduring Secession edifice – cut into the brickwork on the upper half of the green-and-yellow checked facade are several fine reliefs of men and women tackling their daily chores. Beyond here, Oradea's main Orthodox church, built in 1784–92, marks the stylistic transition from Baroque to Neoclassical; it is better known as the **Moon Church** after the large sphere mounted beneath its clock, which rotates to indicate the lunar phases in a 28-day cycle.

Synagogues

Just east of Piaţa Unirii, Strada Traian Moşoiu was the heart of Oradea's Jewish quarter, once Hungary's second largest. In 1927, Codreanu's League of the Archangel Michael, soon to become the Iron Guard (see page239), held a congress here, and wrecked four of the city's eleven **synagogues** before leaving. There are still three imposing synagogues nearby: one (still functioning) just east of Piaţa Unirii at Str. Mihai Viteazul 2, one on Piaţa Rahovei, and one at Str. Independenţei 22 near the Vulturul Negru, which belonged to the wealthy Neolog or Reformed congregation. Recently refurbished, this is now a cultural space and tourist information centre.

At a tram interchange at the far end of the spacious Parcul 1 Decembrie, immediately east, is a preserved four-wheel electric **locomotive**, constructed in Austria in 1905, which operated at a maximum 6km/h until 1994.

Citadel

Tues–Sun 9am–5pm • €1 • ☎ 0359 191 096

To the east of Piaţa Unirii rises the sprawling bulk of Oradea's **citadel**, founded in 1092 by the Hungarian King László I, who had been hunting nearby; angels supposedly told him in a dream to build a monastery here by the warm waters of the Petea stream, and he then raised a wooden stockade too. This was replaced in the fourteenth century by a episcopal fortress, rebuilt as a pentagonal citadel by Italian engineers in 1569–98, and given its final shape in 1775–6 – it has survived at least eight sieges, but was also an important centre of Humanism in the fifteenth century. The Gothic cathedral, in which five Hungarian kings were buried, was destroyed in 1565, while the present Fortress Church was built in 1775–6 by Lodovico Marini.

A lengthy **refurbishment** of its dilapidated walls and buildings was finally completed in 2015; guided tours don't cover all the 468 rooms of the eight buildings inside the citadel, but you'll see parts of the Princely Palace (built in 1620–29 by Giacomo Resti), the bakery and officers' barracks, both dating from 1692, and the food store and administration block, built in 1775. There's also an open-air theatre in the sixteenth-century Ciunt ("mangled") Bastion, to the northwest; an attractive **park** (always open), with good information panels, occupies the area outside where the moat was.

ARRIVAL AND DEPARTURE
ORADEA

By plane The airport (☎0259 416 082, ⊛aeroportoradea. ro), with flights to Bucharest and a couple of European destinations, is just 4km south on the Arad road; a taxi should cost no more than €5.

By train From the train station on Piaţa Bucureşti, trams run south along Calea Republicii towards the city centre (those with black numbers #1N and #3N run from the station and those with red numbers #1R and #3R run north to it), past the Crişul department store and southeast along Str. Gen. Magheru. To reach the city centre proper, alight at the department store stop and walk on along Str. Republicii. Destinations Arad (5 daily; 2hr 10min–3hr 15min); Baia Mare (1 daily; 3hr 30min); Beiuş/Ştei (8 daily); Bucharest (1 daily; 13hr); Budapest (1 daily; 4hr 30min); Ciucea (8 daily; 1hr 20min–2hr 10min); Cluj (8 daily, 2hr 40min–4hr); Iaşi (1 daily; 12hr 30min); Satu Mare (3 daily; 2–3hr); Suceava (1 daily; 10hr); Timişoara (4 daily; 3hr–4hr 45min).

By bus The bus station is southeast of the centre at Str. Războieni 81, 200m west of the Oradea Est train halt (bus #17 to Gara de Est); take bus #10 into town (every 30–40min), or it's a 30min walk. Maxitaxis to Arad, Cluj, Satu Mare, Baia Mare and Timişoara run from immediately north of the railway station.

Destinations Abrud/Alba Iulia (2 daily); Arad (every 90mins); Bistriţa/Suceava (2 daily); Budapest (6 daily); Cluj (10 daily); Debrecen, Hungary (1 daily); Deva (4 daily); Kecskemét, Hungary (1 daily); Sibiu (2 daily); Sighet (1 daily); Târgu Mureş (2 daily); Timişoara (12 daily).

Tourist information The national tourist office is at Str. Patrioţilor 2 (daily 9am–5pm; ☎0259 427 697, ⊛travelbihor.ro), just north of the *Hotel Astoria* and opposite the theatre. The city's tourist office is at the citadel, Piaţa Emanuil Gojdu, 41 corp J (⊛oradea.travel), while there are also offices at the City Hall Tower and the synagogue at Str Independenţei 22. An excellent source of information on outdoor (and underground) activities is the Centru pentru Arii Protejate Dezvoltare Durabila (Centre for the Sustainable Development of Protected Areas) at Piaţa 1 Decembrie 4–6 (Mon–Fri 9am–5pm; ☎0359 410 556, ⊛capdd-bihor.org); at the same address, Apuseni Experience (☎0745 602 301 or ☎0747 962 482, ⊛apuseniexperience.ro) can arrange visits to the Chişcău and Meziad caves (see page 317), as well as a range of hiking, biking and ski-touring trips in the Apuseni, and cultural tours.

GETTING AROUND

By bike The Ivelo bike-sharing station is on the north side of Parcul 1 Decembrie (April & Oct Mon–Fri 11.30am–7.30pm, Sat & Sun 9.30am–7.30pm; May & Sept Mon–Fri 11.30am–8.30pm, Sat & Sun 9.30am–8.30pm; June–Aug

Mon–Fri 11.30am–9pm, Sat & Sun 9.30am–9pm; €1.50/hr, €6/24hr; ⊛ivelo.ro).

By car Autonom, Calea Aradului 4 (☎0751 010 710, ⊛autonom.ro).

ACCOMMODATION

Astoria Grand Str. Teatrului 1 ☎0359 101 039, ⊛astoriaoradea.ro; map p.312. A striking Secession building (1902) that's been beautifully refurbished, although it's not really a four-star – the spacious rooms have big windows and efficient a/c, and there's an attractive café-restaurant on the street corner. Breakfast €5. **€40**

Atlantic Str. Iosif Vulcan 9 ☎0359 172 263, ⊛hotelatlantic.ro; map p.312. Decent, if hardly exciting, four-star place with good-sized, a/c rooms decorated in different primary colours; the restaurant's worth a punt and there's a cracking bar here (see page 315). **€43**

Atrium Str. Republicii 38 ☎0259 414 421, ⊛hotelatrium.ro; map p.312. Exceptional, very good-value hotel with windows opening onto an airy atrium. The rooms are very stylish, while the bathrooms come with cute little corner tubs. Home to a quality restaurant, too. **€39**

Bulevard Str. Ştefan cel Mare 34 ☎0770 909 202, ⊛hotelbulevardoradea.ro; map p.312. Just north of the station, this budget hotel has fairly utilitarian a/c

rooms, though they are spotless; there's free parking but no restaurant (except for breakfast). **€36**

Caro Str. Kogălniceanu 21A ☎0359 405 204, ⊛caro-oradea.ro; map p.312. This self-styled boutique hotel (it's not really) has attractive minimalist decor and helpful staff, but rooms are small and the heating is underpowered; there's a pleasant *terasa* and restaurant plus basement spa facilities. **€37**

Elite Str. Brătianu 26 ☎0259 414 924, ⊛hotel-elite. ro; map p.312. Classy small hotel with sumptuous rooms in four categories, furnished in belle époque style; facilities include heated pool, gym, sauna and jacuzzi, not to mention an enchanting little restaurant. **€60**

Góbé Pension Str. D. Gherea 26 ☎0259 413 513, ⊛gobe.ro; map p.312. Just east of the citadel on the corner of Str. Avântului, this is a gem of a guesthouse, with fittings in the style of a Hungarian *csárda*, such as brightly coloured hand-woven duvets and wooden furniture painted with Hungarian peasant motifs. Friendly owners and very reasonably priced, too. **€35**

Hostel Felix Str. Eminescu 11 ✆0259 437 011, ✉tineret_bh@yahoo.com; map p.312. This simple and centrally located hostel has beds in spacious four-bed rooms (with or without bathroom). **€10** per person

Qiu Str. Republicii 15 ✆0733 666 555, ⓦqiu.ro; map p.312. This small seven-room hotel is most unusual from the off, in that there's no reception. The rooms themselves – some of which have balconies overlooking the pedestrianized street – are refreshingly modern and funky, with LED mood lighting, reading lamps and iPhone charging docks. In another unusual concept for Romanian hotels, there's a little kitchenette where you can help yourself to tea and coffee. All in all, remarkably good value. **€45**

EATING

Better Food Str. Ady Endre 41A ✆0736 244 505, ⓦbetterfood.ro; map p.312. With simple Scandinavian-style decor (seating only on stools), this place offers vegetarian and non-vegetarian menus of the day from about €5 (and posts them on Facebook); there are also usually a couple of tempting desserts on offer, as well as coffee, juices and smoothies. Mon–Fri 9am–4pm.

Casuta cu Nuci Str. George Enescu 57 ✆0259 268 742, ⓦcasutacanuci.ro; map p.312. Homely, Hungarian-style *csárda* – which rather amusingly translates as House of Nuts (or The Nut House) – with lots of peasant-style décor and serving authentic Magyar dishes such as catfish paprika with cottage cheese, and roasted duck leg with red cabbage and potatoes. Mon–Wed noon–10pm, Thurs & Fri noon–midnight, Sat 1pm–midnight, Sun 1–10pm.

Il Padrino Str. Muzeului 7 ✆0740 100 099, ⓦilpadrino-oradea.ro; map p.312. Not far from the station (towards the museum), this is far better than the snack bars there, with a pavement terrace. Daily 7am–10pm.

Meatic Str. Delavrancea 3 ✆0754 991 133, ⓦmeatic.ro; map p.312. Clean, bright space with minimalist décor, *Meatic* is, as the name suggests, one for the carnivores – you name it and they've probably got it: steaks, ribs, homemade sausages, duck and so on, though their pizzas (and desserts) are worth considering. Mon 5–11pm, Tues–Sun noon–11pm.

Petit Café Parc Libertății ✆0359 418 968; map p.312. At the north end of the footbridge, this is a delightful spot to sip coffee under the trees on a summer's day; pastries and snacks available too. Daily 8am–10pm.

Pizzeria Due Fratelli Str. Roman Ciorogariu 39 ✆0359 194 194, ⓦdue-fratelli.ro; map p.312. Far and away the best pizzeria in town, in part because most of the ingredients are sourced from Italy; they've a terrific range of thin crusts, as well as an equally tantalizing menu of pasta dishes. Mon–Thurs 10am–11pm, Fri 10am–midnight, Sat & Sun noon–midnight.

Rivo Aleea Strandului 3 ✆0359 444 445, ⓦrivorestaurant.ro; map p.312. Overlooking the river just east of the city centre, this is a fine-dining restaurant offering perfectly cooked and presented main courses such as pork knuckle roulade with white bean puree and caramelized onions (€8), but do leave space for the chocolate fondant with vanilla ice cream. Daily 11am–midnight.

Taverna Str. Eminescu 2 ✆0745 144 604, ⓦtavernaoradea.ro; map p.312. With traditional Romanian fare (and vegetarian options) and waitresses in local costume, this is an entertaining and reliable choice. Cheap (€4) two-course menu of the day too. Mon–Fri 10am–midnight, Sat & Sun noon–midnight.

DRINKING

Inside the Vulturul Negru arcade and in front on Piața Unirii there's a clutch of very lively late-night (or all-night) music pubs.

Lords Pub Piața Unirii 2–4 ✆0733 961 221, ⓦlordspub.ro; map p.312. Located at the entry to the Vulturul Negru arcade, with draught Guinness, regular parties and DJ nights. Mon–Thurs 9am–6am, Fri 9am–7.30am, Sat noon–7.30am, Sun noon–6am.

ReWine Str. Republicii 31 ✆0772 277 777, ⓦrewine.ro; map p.312. A good all-rounder this place, from scrummy early morning breakfasts or mid-morning coffee to late afternoon wine and tapas, a theme that continues well into the evening; they've got an impressive selection too, both from Romania and abroad.

Mon–Thurs 8am–midnight, Fri 8am–1am, Sat & Sun 4pm–1am.

Street Coffee Roasters Piața Unirii 12 ✆0728 244 435; map p.312. There's now no shortage of places in town to get a decent caffeine fix, but this cracking venue is top dog: delicious single origin coffee prepared by enthusiastic, well-informed baristas who really do know their beans (which are roasted on the premises), and an easy-going vibe to boot. Takeaway too. Mon–Fri 7am–5pm, Sat 8am–4pm, Sun 9am–2pm.

Tapta Caffe & More Str. Iosif Vulcan 9 ✆0722 159 010, ⓦtapta.ro; map p.312. A delightful café in the *Atlantic hotel* that's ideal for a quiet drink or a light lunch; closed Aug. Mon–Wed 7am–10pm, Thurs & Sun 7am–midnight, Fri & Sat 7am–2am.

ENTERTAINMENT

Arcadia Children's Theatre Str. Alecsandri 8 ✆0259 433 398 & ✆0745 642 305. Children will enjoy performances (often puppet shows), at the end of the Vulturul Negru arcade.

Filarmonica de Stat Str. Moscovei 5 ☎0259 430 853, ⓦoradeaphilharmony.com. The city symphony orchestra. Box office Mon–Fri 11am–5pm, and one hour before performances.

Teatrul Regina Maria Piața Regele Ferdinand 4 ☎0372 368 475, ⓦteatrulreginamaria.ro. Well-regarded theatrical and operatic performances (in both Romanian and Hungarian). Box office Tues–Fri 10am–6pm, Sat & Sun 10am–1pm, and one hour before performances.

Băile Felix and Băile 1 Mai

Just 8km southeast of Oradea along the DN76, **BĂILE FELIX** is a compact village whose residential core is overlooked by an ugly jumble of concrete high-rise hotels. The resort centres on the attractive **Parc Felix**, with several warm pools in which the **thermal lotus** (Nymphaea lotus thermalis), otherwise found only in the Nile Delta, has survived several ice ages, along with a tiny fish and a snail; there's also a **wooden church** by the market on the edge of the park. To the north at the entry to Felix, the year-round Ștrand Apollo (Mon 8am–7pm, Tues–Fri 8am–8pm, Sat & Sun 7am–8pm; €6.50) has a large **thermal pool** surrounded by mock-rustic buildings (built around 1900) plus indoor pools (from 30–33°C to 37–39°C) and also offers saunas and massages. The *Lotus Therm Spa & Luxury Resort*, a gleaming spa and aqua park with a five-star hotel, opened in 2015.

The much smaller and less developed spa of **BĂILE 1 MAI** (Ântâi Mai) is reached by a turning off the DN76 just before Băile Felix, or a 1km walk east across the fields. The aqua parks here are more modern and family-oriented than in Felix.

ARRIVAL AND DEPARTURE   BĂILE FELIX AND BĂILE 1 MAI

To reach Băile Felix, take tram #3N from Oradea's train station or bus #12 from Piața Unirii to the Nufărul terminal on the city outskirts, and then minibus #511 (every 15–30min; €0.50), which makes a clockwise loop past the communist hotel blocks before returning through the centre. Bus #512 runs two or three times an hour to Băile 1 Mai.

ACCOMMODATION AND EATING

BĂILE FELIX

Most of the dozen or so hotels are bland and not particularly good value, but there are some good guesthouses.

Camping Apollo ☎0359 464 484, ⓦcampingapollo. ro. At the north end of the spa, this small campsite is open all year; the thermal water showers are lovely. Per person **€4.50**, plus per caravan/camper **€4.50**

Casa Românească Str. Primăverii 42 ☎0744 546 494, ⓦcasaromaneasca.ro. Just off the main drag, this is comfortably the best place in the resort, serving traditional Romanian food including rabbit and boar (€6) as well as pasta and pizza (€3–6); service is not the best but portions are big and very affordable, and there's often live folk music. Daily noon–11pm.

Nufărul Str. Victoria 26 ☎0359 089 930, ⓦhotelnufarul. ro. A large communist-era block now well renovated with bright enough rooms plus a large thermal pool and a generous breakfast buffet. Half board. **€65**

Pension Sebastian Str. Primăverii 112B ☎0359 809 355, ⓦpensiuneasebastianfelix.cabanova.com. This bright little guesthouse near the market is a homely and convenient option; guests are free to avail themselves of the lounge and kitchen, and there's bike hire too. **€35**

Pensiunea Topaz Str. Primăverii 73A ☎0259 318 116, ⓦpensiuneatopaz.ro. On the main drag just south of the centre, this stylish chalet-style guesthouse has an indoor thermal pool and 21 comfortable rooms, including triples and family rooms plus some with balconies. **€38**

Rustic Str. Primăverii 27 ☎0770 131 018, ⓦrusticrestaurant.ro. An excellent traditional-style restaurant serving a huge variety of meat-based dishes (poultry, beef, game) plus a good value three-course menu of the day (€5) between noon and 4pm – there's also live music from 7pm Mon–Fri. Daily 9am–midnight.

Termal Str. Victoria 24 ☎0359 089 930, ⓦhotel-termal. ro. The best of the formerly state-owned places, in a tower west of the centre, well refurbished, with thermal pool, massages and treatments, sauna and solarium. Half board. **€95**

BĂILE 1 MAI

Allegria no. 88G ☎0259 318 317, ⓦpensiuneallegria. ro. A relatively grand pension-restaurant with the very attractive Allegria Spa across the road (Mon–Thurs 3–10pm, Fri–Sun 9am–10pm); a restaurant and wine cellar round things off nicely. **€40**

Pensiunea Mona Lisa no. 19 ☎0259 318 253 or ☎0722 470 231. A friendly modern guesthouse, with six double rooms and a suite, and kitchen and barbecue available to guests. **€12**

Perla no. 65B ☎0259 318 230, ⓦperla1mai.ro. The
best hotel here, with fairly swish rooms complemented by
various indoor and outdoor pools, hot tubs, gym and sauna,
as well as a good restaurant-pizzeria. **€66**

The western Apuseni mountains

The **Apuseni mountains** lie predominantly in Transylvania (see page 206), but their
westernmost massif, the Pădurea Craului or Király-erdő, is within easy reach of Oradea.
The Centre for the Sustainable Development of Protected Areas in Oradea (see page
314) is developing a network of four **show caves**, open to the general public, and also
of ten technical caves, restricted to guided groups, that will give access to magnificent
karst features (ⓦcapdd-bihor.org).

The small town of **Beiuș**, 55km southeast of Oradea, is the main jumping-off point for
the impressive stalactite **caves** of Farcu, Meziad and Chișcău, while the village of **Roșia**,
16km north of Beiuș on a newly surfaced road to Bratca and Bucea (with buses from
Beiuș on weekdays), and the modest alpine resort of **Stâna de Vale**, 30km east of Beiuș,
are bases for **hiking** and **mountain biking** in the unspoiled Pădurea Craiului. Mountain
bikes can be rented in Remetea (☎0744 296 308) and Roșia (☎0741 119 020), with
routes, including GPS tracks, available to download from ⓦpadureacraiului.ro. From
Stâna de Vale it's about six hours' walk to the *Padiș* **cabana** (see page 214), taking a path
marked with red stripes via the Poieni peak, the Cumpănățelu saddle and the Vărășoaia
clearing. Experienced hikers might prefer the more challenging trail to Meziad (6–8hr,
marked by blue triangles, not recommended in winter or bad weather); with many
twists and turns around karstic features, this follows the ridge above the Iad valley,
surmounting the Piatra Tisei peak. If you plan extensive hiking in the mountains, arm
yourself with either the 1:200,000 *Munții Apuseni* or the 1:35,000 *Valea Arieșului* **map**.

Farcu cave

April–June & Sept Wed–Sun 10am–4pm; July & Aug daily 10am–5pm; Oct & March Wed–Sun 10am–3pm; Nov–Feb call • €4.50 •
☎0744 426 272

From Roșia it's a few kilometres east to the Crystal Cave of **Farcu**, known for its
wonderful calcite crystals – indeed, this is perhaps the only cave in Romania where
it's possible to see such features. The half-hour **tour** starts in a disused bauxite mine,
with exhibits of old equipment, then moves into the cave, with modern lighting and
walkways leading through two of its nine chambers.

Meziad cave

April–June & Sept Wed–Sun 10am–4pm; July & Aug daily 10am–5pm; Oct & March Wed–Sun 10am–3pm; Nov–Feb call ☎0744 426
272 • €4.50 • ⓦpestera-meziad.ro

From the village of **Meziad**, 10km northeast of Beiuș (and reached by four buses on weekdays only), it's a further 2.5km east to the famous **Meziad cave**, with its huge entrance
arch. The cave was first explored in 1859, and after a road was built in the 1960s it was
visited by some 25,000 people a year until its popularity was usurped by the opening of
the even more spectacular cave at Chișcău in 1980. Hour-long **tours** start on the hour
and cover 1.1km of this warren, whose total length is almost 5km, the guide pointing out
the stalactites and other features of chambers up to 30m wide and 20m high.

Chișcău cave

Tues–Sun 10am–5pm • €4.50 • ⓦpesteraursilor.ro

There are bus services (Mon–Sat 2 daily) from Beiuș via Sudrigiu to **Chișcău**, some
25km southeast, where in 1975 quarry workers discovered a cave containing dozens

of Neolithic bear skeletons – hence its name, **"Bears' Cave"** (Peştera Urşilor). It's atmospherically lit, making the forty-five minute **tour** an unmissable experience. It starts in the Bones Gallery, where over one hundred bears were trapped by a rockfall fifteen thousand years ago and ended up eating each other, as the bones marked by bear teeth show. The extraordinary range of stalagmite and stalactite formations of the 488m-long upper gallery – shaped like castles, wraiths and beasts – are accompanied by the sound of water crashing into subterranean pools.

Pietroasa and around

From Beiuş the DN76 continues southeast towards the grimy industrial town of **Ştei**, known as Dr Petru Groza under communism (see box), from where the DN75 runs east through the heart of the Apuseni towards Turda. Buses turn east 11km south of Beiuş and run another 12km to **PIETROASA**, a picturesque village on the upper reaches of the River Crişul Pietros, where water-powered sawmills remain operational and older residents still wear traditional Bihor costume. The forest road up to the Padiş plateau (see page 214) is now asphalted, and the hiking trail to the *Padiş* cabana, marked with blue crosses, follows the road for the most part, with a path diverging south after about 5km (marked by yellow triangles) to the Focul Viu cave and Cetăţile Ponorului.

Just south of the turning to Pietroasa is Sudrigiu, where you'll find the headquarters of the Apuseni Nature Park; a couple of kilometres further south, **Rieni** is worth a look for its **wooden church**, just west of the village by the train halt. Built in 1753, this is now slightly run-down, with lots of woodpecker damage, but interesting for its doorway and its spire, typical of this area.

The village of **Băiţa**, 10km east along the DN75 through lovely beech forest, has several caves nearby and holds a lively **fair** on the last Sunday in September. At the Vârtop Pass (1160m) is a small ski resort (with a new 1.1km chairlift), from where hiking trails head south to a TV tower and north to Focul Viu (see page 214). Beyond, the road descends through Arieşeni to Gârda de Sus, both of which are southern entry points to Padiş (see page 214).

ACCOMMODATION   WESTERN APUSENI MOUNTAINS

Iadolina Stâna de Vale ☏0744 599 334, ⓦ hoteliadolina.ro. At 1100m, this excellent three-star hotel is a good base for skiing and for hiking; there are also guesthouses, cabins and a campsite here. **€42**

Traditional Casa Roşia ☏0744 603 706, ⓦ traditionalcasa.ro. This "tourist village" has rudimentary accommodation (ie on mattresses) in beautifully restored houses, as well as in a boarding house and on a peasant farm. They also offer unusual features such as a climbing wall and furniture workshop, as well as horseriding, mountain bikes and great sunsets. **€11**

DR PETRU GROZA

A delegate at the Assembly of Alba Iulia in 1918, **Dr Petru Groza** (1884–1958) was an important politician before and after World War II. With the Communist Party banned since 1924, it was he who, in 1933, founded the Ploughmen's Front, actually a cover for the communists; as a prosperous lawyer and landowner, Groza was well camouflaged. He was imposed as prime minister in 1945 – after communist *agents provocateurs* had gunned down communist demonstrators to discredit the democratic parties then leading the government – and organized elections in 1946 to establish the communists in power. The people voted overwhelmingly against them but to no avail: the result was falsified, and in mid-1947 the remaining leaders of the democratic parties were arrested.

Groza sought reconciliation with Hungary and tried to moderate the nationalism of the Communist Party leader Gheorghiu-Dej; his dismissal in 1952, along with Ana Pauker's Hungarian acolyte Vasile Luka, was a harbinger of the regime's crackdown on Romania's Magyar minority.

Turul Panzío Remetea no. 8 ☎0744 296 308, ⓦremeteturul.ro. This excellent guesthouse, 6km from the Meziad cave, also has a very good campsite, with cabins (sleeping two- to four) and tent space and a big cooking/ eating area, as well as mountain-bike rental. Breakfast €5. **€30**, cabins **€20**, camping **€14**

Arad and around

One of the Banat's oldest towns, **ARAD** has fewer sights than Oradea or Timişoara, and lacks their vibrancy. However, it can showcase an impressive number of Habsburg-era buildings as well as an eighteenth-century citadel, while its position on the road and rail routes between these two cities, and from Transylvania into Hungary, makes it a convenient place to stop off for an afternoon. It's also a good base from which to strike out towards **villages** in the foothills of the Apuseni mountains.

In summer, most townsfolk head across the river by the footbridge to the **park** (daily 8am–5pm; May–Sept €1; Oct–April free), which is rammed with swimming pools (May–Sept Mon 1–10pm, Tues–Sun 8am–10pm), cafés, bars and open-air discos. The city **festival** is the Zilele Aradului (Arad Days), spanning the second half of August.

Bulevardul Revoluţiei

Spearing southwards from the train station is **Bulevardul Revoluţiei**, its wooded central park bisected by busy tram lines. Of the many impressive buildings lining the boulevard, the standout is the brilliant white **City Hall** at no. 75, a wedding-cake-like edifice raised in 1872–4; a mix of late-Baroque and Neo-Renaissance, its most notable feature is the clock tower. A plaque in front commemorates those who died during the 1989 revolution, while opposite, in the middle of the road, is a simple monument to the same martyrs. Closing off the street's southern end is the **State Theatre**, also dating from 1872–4, while close by is the massive **Roman Catholic church** (1902–4), with an impressive domed entrance hall.

Piaţa Avram Iancu and Old Arad

A large green square to the rear of the theatre, **Piaţa Avram Iancu** is fringed by numerous two- and three-storey Secession buildings, many adorned with interesting stucco work and motifs. East of the square, at Str. Gheorghe Lazăr 2, is the semi-derelict **Old Theatre**, built in 1817 – Eminescu and many famous actors worked here – while to the west lies the main **market** and the Baroque Romanian Orthodox cathedral (1862–5). The jumble of dusty streets south of the square once comprised **Old Arad**, and was also home to a large Serb minority, served by the **Serbian Orthodox church** (1698–1702), a standard Habsburg structure on Piaţa Sârbească.

Citadel

Commanding a loop of the River Mureş, Arad's huge **citadel** faces the town on the west bank. A six-pointed star with ramparts and bastions angled to provide overlapping fields of fire, it was the state of the art in fortifications when it was constructed, in the style of Vauban, between 1762 and 1783. The Turks, against whom it was ostensibly raised, had already been pushed out of the Pannonian basin in 1718, but its underground casements provided the Habsburgs with a ready-made prison following the suppression of the 1784–5 and 1848–9 rebellions, as well as for Napoleonic prisoners of war, and for Gavrilo Princip after triggering World War I. With the army having recently vacated the citadel, it is due to become a museum complex, though this could take some time.

After 1718, the Habsburgs drained the marshy southern Banat, an area known as the Partium, and colonized it with Swabians, Slovaks, Serbs and Romanians; in 1848, Arad's population joined the Hungarian revolt against Habsburg rule, finally crushed

6

with the help of Tsarist Russia. The Habsburgs made an example of the ringleaders by executing thirteen generals, mostly Hungarian, outside the fortress walls, causing international scandal – a monument was placed there, but was moved after World War I to a less conspicuous site. In 2000, Iliescu (needing Hungarian votes) promised to move it back to the city centre, but dragged his feet, and failed to show up in 2004 for the inauguration of the **Plaza of Romanian-Hungarian Reconciliation** (just west from the market on Strada Goldiş), which the Statue of Liberty, with the Hungarian generals' busts around the base, had to share with a mini-Arch of Triumph with Avram Iancu, Bălcescu and a crowd of other Romanian heroes of 1848 marching through.

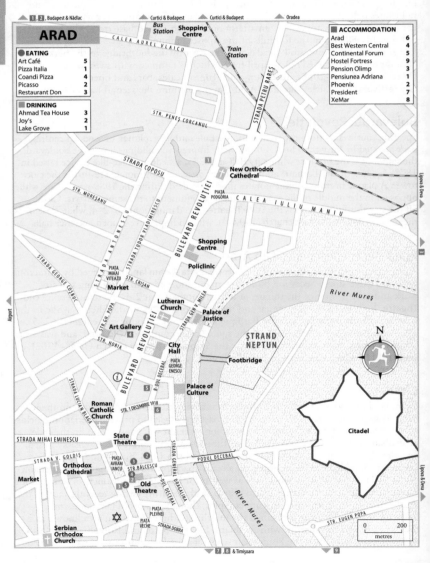

ARAD

● **EATING**
Art Café	5
Pizza Italia	1
Coandi Pizza	4
Picasso	2
Restaurant Don	3

■ **DRINKING**
Ahmad Tea House	3
Joy's	2
Lake Grove	1

■ **ACCOMMODATION**
Arad	6
Best Western Central	4
Continental Forum	5
Hostel Fortress	9
Pension Olimp	3
Pensiunea Adriana	1
Phoenix	2
President	7
XeMar	8

0 — 200 metres

County History Museum and Art Gallery

County History Museum Piaţa George Enescu 1 • Tues–Sun 9am–5pm • €0.50 • ☎ 0257 281 847 **Art Gallery** Str. Gheorghe Popa 2 • Same hours and price

The eclectic **Palace of Culture** (1913) behind the City Hall on Piaţa George Enescu houses a concert hall (in which the likes of Richard Strauss, Bartok and Enescu performed), a run-of-the-mill Natural Science Museum and the **County History Museum**, which has good coverage of the 1848–9 revolt and decent archeological, ethnographical and natural history displays. Far more engrossing is an exhibition on the **1989 revolution** – there are some moving exhibits, such as a blood-soaked jacket and a trainer with a bullet hole through it (and the offending bullet), in addition to some superb photos. Officially, nineteen people died here, relatively few compared to other cities.

On the opposite side of Bulevardul Revoluţiei, in the library building (1913), the **Art Gallery** features furniture from the seventeenth century on, as well as the odd painting by the likes of Grigorescu, Aman and Tonitza, and Hungarians such as Munkácsy Mihály and members of the Nagybánya School.

6

ARRIVAL AND INFORMATION
ARAD

By plane Arad's tiny airport (☎ 0722 111 998, ⊛ aeroportularad.ro) is only 3km west of town, though you'll have to rely on taxis (around €5) as there's no public transport.

By train The train station is about 1km north of the City Hall on Calea Aurel Vlaicu; take tram #1, #3 or #6 for the city centre. There's a separate Regiotrans ticket office for their trains to Brad, Nădlac and Sânnicolau Mare. Some trains from Timişoara halt only in the southern suburb of Arad Nou, from where tram #3 and bus #19 head into the centre. Destinations Brad (5 daily; 4hr); Braşov (3 daily; 8hr 15min–8hr 45min); Bucharest (3 daily; 10hr 30min–11hr 45min); Budapest (3 daily; 4hr 15min); Deva (8 daily; 3hr–4hr); Oradea (4 daily; 2–3hr); Radna (8 daily; 30–40min); Sânnicolau Mare (5 daily; 1hr 45min); Sibiu (1 daily; 5hr 40min); Sighişoara (1 daily; 5hr 30min); Timişoara (11 daily; 50min–1hr 30min); Vienna (1 daily, summer only; 8hr 30min).

By bus The main bus station (☎ 0257 270 097) is 500m beyond the train station at the corner of Calea Aurel Vlaicu and Calea 6 Vânători; international buses mostly leave from in front of the train station, where there's also the small Autogară JRC at which services from Timişoara to Brad and Moneasa call.
Destinations Abrud (2 daily); Budapest (7 daily); Câmpeni (2 daily); Cluj (4 daily); Deva (6 daily); Lipova (8 daily); Moneasa (3 daily); Oradea (12 daily); Satu Mare (8 daily); Timişoara (15 daily).

By car Cars can be rented from Autonom, Calea Radnei 115 (☎ 0751 016 444, ⊛ autonom.ro).

Tourist information The tourist office is at B-dul Revoluţiei 84 (Mon–Fri 9am–5pm, Sat 10am–2pm; ☎ 0257 270 277, ✉ centru.de.informare.turistica.arad@t-i.ro).

ACCOMMODATION

Arad B-dul Decebal 9 ☎ 0257 280 894, ⊛ hotel-arad. com; map p.320. This decent place, in a fairly quiet central location, has large, high-ceilinged rooms in kitschy colours, with and without bathroom; there's secure parking but no lift. Good value. **€25**

Best Western Central Str. Horia 8 ☎ 0257 256 636, ⊛ bwcentral.ro; map p.320. This modern, central hotel has generously-sized, polished rooms and apartments, plus a restaurant with terrace, sauna and gym; the welcoming staff also makes this one of the better places to stay. **€72**

Continental Forum B-dul Revoluţiei 79 ☎ 0257 281 700, ⊛ continentalhotels.ro; map p.320. Much like the others in the *Continental* chain, the *Forum* is a slick but ultimately charmless place aimed at business visitors; it does, though, offer great online deals. **€55**

Hostel Fortress Str. Cetăţii 34 ☎ 0745 357 989, ✉ fortress_arad@yahoo.com; map p.320. South of the citadel in the Subcetate suburb, this is more like a drab youth hotel, with en-suite rooms rather than dorms. **€21**

Pension Olimp Str. Vrancei 36 ☎ 0257 279 443, ⊛ pensiuneaolimp.ro; map p.320. A sweet little pension in the eastern suburbs with fifteen clean and inviting rooms (with up to six beds), all with TV and bath; laundry facilities too. **€25**

Pensiunea Adriana Str. Fraţii Neumann 7 ☎ 0257 289 120, ⊛ pensiuneaadriana.ro; map p.320. Immediately west of the UTA Stadium, this simple but cosy option is handy for the bus and rail stations. **€21**

Phoenix Calea Aurel Vlaicu 267 ☎ 0723 800 439, ⊛ hotelphoenix.ro; map p.320. Striking modern place northwest of the centre aimed at business travellers, with uninspiring but well-kept rooms and a half-decent restaurant if you don't fancy traipsing into town; weekend rates are cheaper. **€42**

President Calea Timişorii 164 ☎ 0257 278 804, ⓦ hotel-president.ro; map p.320. This large and slightly tacky place, 2km south in Aradul Nou, is yet another aimed at business visitors, but its rooms are neat, colourful and airy; there's also a swimming pool, gym and sauna. Tram #3 or #5. **€40**

XeMar Piaţa Eroilor 1 ☎ 0257 242 427, ⓦ xe-mar.ro; map p.320. Just across the bridge 1.5km south of town, this smart hotel has lovely, warmly decorated rooms; they've also got a simple, homely little pension 200m down the road at no. 13 (same tel. no). **€38**

EATING

Art Café Piaţa Avram Iancu 10 ☎ 0721 120 550; map p.320. This café, with a wide mix of paintings on its walls, from seventeenth-century reproductions to current local artists, knick-knacks on its shelves and gentle jazz, doubles up as a pretty competent restaurant with dishes that might include sushi, salad, chicken liver pâté (€6) or a burger (€4.50). Mon–Thurs 8.30am–11pm, Fri–Sun 9am–midnight.

Coandi Pizza Str. Bălcescu 5 ☎ 0257 281 514, ⓦ pizza-coandi.ro; map p.320. Near *Pizza Italia*, this is more of a takeaway place, with pizzas, salads and desserts forming the mainstay of the menu; *Geletaria Coandi* (☎ 0257 287 777; daily 10am–10pm) is across the road. Daily 11am–11pm.

Picasso B-dul Decebal 22 ☎ 0722 222 199, ⓦ ristorantepicasso.ro; map p.320. By some distance the classiest (and most expensive) place to eat in Arad, Picasso's prolific menu includes the likes of baked sea bream, and pasta ravioli with salmon and spinach (€12), as well as more expensive steak dishes. Mon–Sat noon–11.30pm.

Pizza Italia B-dul Decebal 14 ☎ 0772 002 201, ⓦ pizzaitaliaarad.ro; map p.320. The *Coandi* mini-empire includes this excellent Italian restaurant which offers much more besides pizza and pasta, for example barbequed pork and filet mignon. Mon 1pm–midnight, Tues–Sun 11am–midnight.

Restaurant Don Str. Bălcescu 1 ☎ 0357 431 788, ⓦ restaurant-don.ro; map p.320. Apart from its rather average pizza, this Italian restaurant is excellent – try the fish stew – with good service, led by the Brazilian-Italian chef. Daily 11am–midnight.

DRINKING

Ahmad Tea House Piaţa Avram Iancu 9 ☎ 0730 030 130; map p.320. Among a lively group of bars, this is a lovely place to relax with a range of unusual teas, and events such as quizzes and karaoke at weekends. Mon–Thurs & Sun 9.30am–11pm, Fri & Sat 9am–5am.

Joy's Str. Lazăr 1 ☎ 0257 211 918; map p.320. On the southeast corner of Piaţa Avram Iancu, this bookish café (with occasional readings and events) is actually named for James Joyce. Mon–Fri noon–midnight, Sat & Sun 5pm–1am.

Lake Grove B-dul Revoluţiei 20B ☎ 0357 439 700, ⓦ lakegrove.uv.ro; map p.320. With a large terrace overlooking an artificial lake, this is a pleasant spot for a bite or a beer. Mon 2pm–3am, Tues–Fri 10am–3am, Sat 10am–5am, Sun 10am–midnight.

Sânnicolau Mare

The area to the west of the Arad–Timişoara route is the quintessence of the Banat – originally marshy plains drained after the expulsion of the Turks and settled with a patchwork of diverse ethnic groups, some of whom still remain. One of the largest towns here is **SÂNNICOLAU MARE** (Nagyszentmiklós), known for the Nagyszentmiklós Hoard; 23 golden vessels, made for an Avar chieftain and buried at the time of the Magyar invasion of 896, were found here in 1799 and removed to Vienna, where they still reside in the Imperial collection. The town is also famed as the birthplace of the Hungarian composer **Béla Bartók** (1881–1945), some of whose personal effects can be seen in the Nako conac, a manor house built in 1864 and now the **House of Culture** (Tues–Sun 9am–5pm), at the start of the pedestrianized Strada Republicii. A plaque marks the site of his birthplace, a good walk west of town at Str. Brediceanu 17.

As you return towards Arad, the **Parcul Natural Lunca Mureşului** (Mureş Floodplain Natural Park; ⓦ luncamuresului.ro) protects an area of backwaters with islands covered in luxuriant vegetation, home to around two hundred species of birds – a sort of miniature Danube Delta. It's best seen by **kayak**, which can be rented (€2/hour, €12/day) from the Ceala visitor centre (April–Oct: Mon –Thurs 8am–4.30pm, Fri 8am–

VILLAGE FESTIVALS NORTHEAST OF ARAD

From Arad, it's possible to reach a number of villages noted for their **festivals**. The formerly Schwab village of **Sântana**, 7km east of the Arad–Oradea highway (30min by train from Arad towards Oradea or Brad, then a 15min walk), hosts the Sărbătoarea Iorgovanului festival (an excuse for dancing, music and dressing up in traditional costumes), on the last Sunday of May, a Schwab Kirchweih (church fair) on August 1, and a Pumpkin Festival (Festivalul Dovleacului) at the end of October.

Another 100km east (114km from Arad), Vârfurile is on the DN76 from Oradea to Brad; just west, a minor road runs 6km north to the small village of **Avram Iancu** (not to be confused with the other village of the same name just over the mountains), where people from thirty mountain villages gather on the second Sunday of June for the **Nedeia of Tăcaşele mountain festival**. In addition to trading and socializing, this large fair is an excellent opportunity to hear musicians playing *cetera* (fiddles), *nai* (panpipes) and *bucime* or *tulnic* (alpine horns). The connection between new life and stirring lust probably underlies a good many spring festivals, including the delightfully named **Kiss Fair** (Târgul Sărutului) at **Hălmagiu**, 10km southeast of Vârfurile. Traditionally, the event enabled young people to cast around for a spouse while their elders discussed the fecundity of livestock and crops; it takes place in March, but the exact date varies from year to year so check with the tourist office in Arad first.

2pm, Sat & Sun 10am–5pm; ☏0257 258 010), just west of Arad off Calea Bodrogului, and returned at Pecica, some 22km downstream.

ARRIVAL AND DEPARTURE SÂNNICOLAU MARE

By train Private Regiotrans trains arrive at the station 2km south, a long trudge along the main road.

Destinations Arad (6 daily; 1hr 40min); Timişoara (5 daily; 2hr).

ACCOMMODATION AND EATING

Celesto Str. Republicii 9 ☏0256 370 711. Friendly bar-pizzeria in the heart of the pedestrianized zone offering pasta, pizza and salads, plus a terrific value lunch of the day (€3.50). Daily 9am–midnight.

Timişoara Piaţa 1 Mai 6 ☏0356 108 790, ⌨hotelsannicolaumare.ro. A less grand offshoot of the *Timişoara* hotel in Timişoara itself, this is a decently refurbished block; no restaurant but breakfast is available (and included in the price). €35

Vila Albatros Str. Republicii 13A ☏0722 516 477, ⌨vila-albatros.ro. This solid nineteenth-century building on the main drag has fifteen large doubles with heavy furniture and old-fashioned beds. €30

Pauliş, Radna and Lipova

In 1934, Patrick Leigh Fermor (see page 401) walked from Arad into Transylvania, staying with Magyar aristocrats whose run-down mansions spoke eloquently of the decline in their fortunes since the Trianon Treaty. Nowadays, you're more likely to make the journey by road or train, but be warned that fast services stop at few places of interest. At **Sâmbăteni**, 17km from Arad, you'll see huge Gypsy palaces with colonnaded and pedimented fronts, built with the proceeds of sanction-busting trade with former Yugoslavia.

Arad's unique interurban tram line (routes #11/#12/#14) runs alongside the DN7 through Sâmbăteni before turning northeast to terminate at Ghioroc; it's another 4km to **PAULIŞ**, reached by six local trains daily from Arad. Full-bodied dark red **wine** has been produced from the iron-rich soil of the Podgoria Miniş-Măderat, stretching 35km north from the DN7, since 1023 at latest (when Queen Gizella gave a vineyard to the abbey of Bakony), and was particularly well known in the mid-eighteenth century, when it was Empress Maria Theresa's favourite. The **Balla Geza winery**, 1.5km north of Pauliş (☏0744 520 645, ⌨ballageza.com), was set up in 1999 and over eighty percent of its area is planted with the red Kadarka grape (well known in the Balkans

6

MOVING ON INTO HUNGARY AND GERMANY

Arad, like Oradea, 117km north, lies just inside the border from Hungary. The crossing at Nădlac, some 50km west, is on the new **motorway** from Szeged to Lugoj, eventually continuing to Sibiu and, one day, Bucharest. Cars and buses can also use a new, quieter route off the DN7 (E68) to Turnu, 17km from Arad, to Battonya in Hungary. Travelling **by train** from Arad, you'll cross over from Curtici, 12km north, to Lőkösháza in Hungary. All international **bus services** to Budapest and most of those to Germany run from the station forecourt. Tickets for Budapest can usually be bought on the bus, but travel to Germany should be booked in advance.

---

but only grown in this area in Romania), along with Fetească Neagra, Kékfrankos (Blaufränkisch), Pinot Noir, Cabernet Sauvignon, Cabernet Franc and Merlot. Wines are made in modern stainless-steel tanks but then kept in oak barrels for eighteen months to two years to make them less astringent. Busloads of mainly Hungarian visitors come for **tastings** with traditional food (Mon–Sat 8am–8pm; call in advance), and there's also the *Wine Princess* guesthouse with eleven double rooms and eleven triples (€35).

The next stop is **RADNA**, 35km from Arad, where Leigh Fermor played skittles with a Franciscan monk, until "we were both in a muck-sweat when the bell for vespers put an end to play". The **Abbey of Maria-Radna** is an old pilgrimage site, where many churches were built, then destroyed by the Turks; the current Baroque edifice was built in 1756–67, with 30m-high concrete extensions added to the two towers in 1991, and became a Minor Basilica in 1992. It houses a miraculous image of the Virgin Mary, painted in Italy in 1650, and silver ex votos on either side of the altar give thanks for her help. To the left of the church, corridors on three floors (lined with sacred hearts and thanksgiving images) link it with the **monastery**, built between 1727 and 1823 and used as an old people's home until 2012. It has since been restored in a huge EU-funded project; there are displays (with English text) on the abbey's history and a full museum will soon open.

Radna station, served by slow trains from both Arad and Timişoara, is actually nearer to **LIPOVA**, a quaint little town on the south bank of the Mureş that's the main stopping point between Arad and Deva. Its main sight is the lovely Orthodox **Church of the Annunciation**, with its classical facade and rather eccentric spire; these belie the interior, which dates from 1338 and contains the most important murals in the Banat – in pure Byzantine style, though painted in the early fifteenth century. Fragments of old murals are also visible on the exterior of the north wall. Having served as a mosque from 1552 to 1718, the church was rebuilt in 1732 in the Baroque style; the lower two levels of the iconostasis were painted in 1785 by the famous Serb painter Stefan Tenetski, showing Italian Renaissance influence. Ask at the parish house, immediately north, for access. The **museum** (Tues–Sun 9am–5pm; €0.50) at Str. Bălcescu 21 is identified by casts of Trajan's Column over the door and cast-iron lanterns either side, and holds a painting apiece by Grigorescu, Aman and Tonitza, some old Bibles and bits of sculpture, porcelain and silver- and glassware. The luxurious interiors include parquet flooring, Vienna faience stoves, crystal mirrors and chandeliers. The museum is on the main street one block south of the **iron bridge** across the Mureş to Radna, now open only to pedestrians.

ACCOMMODATION   RADNA AND LIPOVA

Băile Lipova ☎0257 563 139 or ☎0723 537 715 or ☎0740 191 443, ✉sbc@dntar.ro. At the spa 4km south of Lipova there are swimming pools and a campsite with solid two-bed huts, a restaurant and terrace bar with wi-fi. Huts **€18**

Motel-Restaurant Anna-Magdalena Str. Morilor 257, Radna ☎0257 563 032 or ☎0722 367 219, 🌐maggie. ro. At the Radna end of the road bridge across the Mureş, there are comfortable rooms here, behind an attractive

nineteenth-century building housing a restaurant, coffee shop and a garden terrace with interior courtyard. **€27**

Pensiunea Faleza Str. Petru Maior 13 ☎0257 561 702. This is a perfectly decent guesthouse just northeast of central Lipova, with a good restaurant and terrace with river views. **€25**

Route Roemenie Miniş no.298 ☎0745 372 072, ⊚routeroemenie.nl. This attractive Dutch-run campsite is a great spot to rest up; amenities include shower blocks, launderette, restaurant and playground, and, best of all, campfires are allowed. April–Sept. **€15**

6   The Mureş defile and Săvârşin

Just 3km east of Radna, the ruined castle of **Şoimoş** sits atop a rocky crag above the river. Built in the thirteenth century, and beefed up by Iancu de Hunedoara and his son Mátyás Corvinus in the fifteenth century, it guards the entry to the **Mureş defile** between the Zărand and Poiana Ruscă mountains. It's most impressive from the south bank, but it's worth taking the rough path up from the bridge on its southwestern side. From here, and from Ghioroc, Pauliş and Radna, **hiking routes** lead north into the Zărand range. At the narrowest point of the defile is **SĂVÂRŞIN**, which hosts fairs on January 30 and November 27; a modest **mansion** immediately east of the centre of the village, rebuilt in Neoclassical style in the nineteenth century, has been restituted to the royal family (Ocolul Regal Savarsin; ☎0257 557 447, ⊚familiaregala.ro/resedinte/domeniul-regal-savarsin). The grounds are occasionally opened to the public, and the garages (on Strada Vlad Ţepeş, just north of the main square) display the royal car collection. From here the railway and the DN7 continue eastward towards Deva, Cluj and Sibiu, a route described more or less in reverse order in Chapter 3.

Timişoara

The engaging city of **TIMIŞOARA** has long been the most prosperous and advanced of the Banat's cities, claiming to be the first place in Romania to have a public water supply, the first in Europe to have electric streetlighting and one of the first in the world to have horse-drawn trams. It still boasts Romania's premier technical university.

Timişoara grew up around a Magyar fortress in the marshes between the Timiş and Bega rivers, and in 1315, Charles Robert of Anjou, king of Hungary, established the capital of the Banat here; it played a crucial role during the 1514 uprising and Hunyadi's campaigns against the Turks, who occupied the city from 1552 until 1716. The Habsburgs who ejected them proved relatively benign masters over the next two centuries, when Temeschwar, as they called it, acquired many of its current features. The draining of the marshes created the **Bega Canal**, which now separates the old town from the newer quarters to the south. These days, Timişoara is best known as the birthplace of the 1989 revolution, and still sees itself as the true guardian of the revolution's spirit, swiftly hijacked by the neo-communists of Bucharest.

Close to the borders with Serbia and Hungary, and with flights from all over Europe and Romania, Timişoara is also a major transport hub. The city's sights are clustered around the two large main squares, **Piaţa Victoriei** and **Piaţa Unirii**.

Piaţa Victoriei

A wide, pedestrianized boulevard flanked on either side by shops and cafés and sliced down the middle by an attractive strip of greenery, **Piaţa Victoriei** was where, in December 1989, the Romanian revolution gathered momentum; demonstrators came out in force and the tanks rolled in for a series of bloody and tragic battles. There's now little sign of those events, save for the odd memorial or pockmarked building, such as the one above *McDonald's* at the square's northern end. Opposite this is the **Opera**

House, built in 1872–75 by the Viennese duo Helmer and Fellner, with a charmless neo-Byzantine facade added in 1923–28.

Romanian Orthodox Cathedral

Daily 6.30am–7pm

Between Piața Victoriei and the Bega Canal stands the monumental **Romanian Orthodox Cathedral**, constructed from 1936–46. Blending neo-Byzantine and Moldavian styles, it is best known for the children and young people gunned down on its steps in the 1989 uprising; there are memorials and candles to the victims outside. With its 83m-high middle dome, it can be a startling sight when lit up at night.

South of the Bega Canal

The willow-shaded banks of the Bega Canal have been beautified, especially the Rose Garden and adjacent summer theatre. To the south of the canal, the **Tőkés**

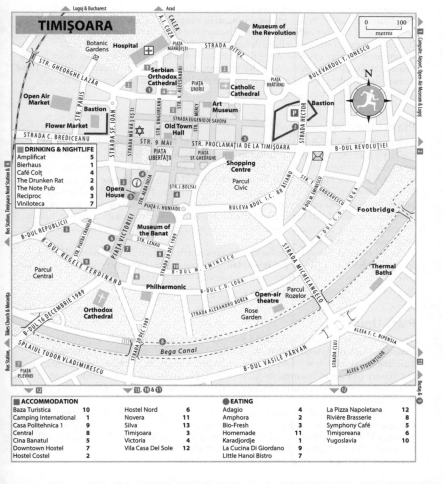

■ ACCOMMODATION						● EATING			
Baza Turistica	10		Hostel Nord	6		Adagio	4	La Pizza Napoletana	12
Camping International	1		Novera	11		Amphora	2	Rivière Brasserie	8
Casa Politehnica 1	9		Silva	13		Bio-Fresh	3	Symphony Café	5
Central	8		Timișoara	3		Homemade	11	Timișoreana	6
Cina Banatul	5		Victoria	4		Karadjordje	1	Yugoslavia	10
Downtown Hostel	7		Vila Casa Del Sole	12		La Cucina Di Giordano	9		
Hostel Costel	2					Little Hanoi Bistro	7		

6

Reformed Church is where László Tökés ignited the 1989 revolution (see page 329). A plaque marks the plain apartment building at Str. Timotei Ciprariu 1 (left off Bulevardul 16 Decembrie 1989), where his eviction took place – Tökés's church was on the first floor and its stained-glass windows can just about be seen from the street.

To the east, beyond the university area, the **Fabric** suburb was laid out from 1718 and inhabited by Germans and Serbs; there's a fine synagogue at Splaiul Coloniei 2, built in 1899 by the well-known Budapest architect Lipot Baumhorn (or Leopold Baumhorn), and you can also see the beer factory on Strada Ştefan cel Mare, electric power plant, tram garage and water tower. The similar **Iosefin** suburb, to the west towards the bus station, was laid out in 1744 and settled by Germans (with Roman Catholic churches), remaining semirural until the arrival of the railway in 1857; both Iosefin and Fabric are known for their Secession architecture, now rather tatty.

Museum of the Banat

Piaţa Iancu Huniade 1 • Tues–Sun 10am–4pm • €1 • ☎ 0256 491 339, ⓦ mnab.ro

The Huniade Castle, raised for the Hungarian monarch Charles Robert in 1307–15 and extended by Hunyadi in 1443–47, houses the **Museum of the Banat**, but is currently closed for major refurbishment; when it does reopen expect to see a voluminous display of archeological and historical exhibits. Outside, two street lamps boast that Timişoara was the first city in Europe to have electric streetlighting, in 1884. Temporary displays, including an exhibit of the month, can be seen in the Bastion Theresia at Str. Martin Luther 4.

Piaţa Libertăţii

Leaving Piaţa Victoriei to the north, you'll come to **Piaţa Libertăţii**, the middle of the city's three squares, newly paved in concentric rings. This was the setting for the gruesome execution of György Dózsa (Gheorghe Doja), leader of the peasant uprising that swept across Hungary and Transylvania in 1514; an iron throne and crown for the "King of the Serfs" were heated until red-hot, then Dózsa was seated and "crowned" before his body was torn asunder by pincers. Some of his followers were starved, compelled to watch his torture and then force-fed parts of the charred corpse, before themselves being executed, while others were hanged above the gates of Oradea, Alba Iulia and Buda as a deterrent.

The substantial Baroque pile on the square's north side, on the site of the Turkish baths, was built in 1734 as the **Town Hall** and now houses the university's music faculty. Just west at Str. Mărăşeşti 6, the Synagogue was built in 1863–5 by Ignatz Schumann of Vienna, in a largely Moorish style.

Piaţa Unirii

Two blocks north and east of Piaţa Libertăţii is the vast **Piaţa Unirii**, a splendid traffic-free showpiece of Baroque urban design lined with delightful yellow, green and red buildings, though a few could still do with sprucing up. At the heart of the square is the Trinity or **Plague Column**, with carvings of plague victims, which was raised in 1740 following a particularly virulent attack of the disease (there's a smaller one on Piaţa Libertăţii).

On opposing sides of the square are two monumental churches: the **Roman Catholic Cathedral**, on the eastern side, was built between 1736 and 1754 to the design of the younger Fischer von Erlach and is a fine example of the Viennese Baroque style; the **Serbian Orthodox Cathedral** to the west was built at the same time (1744–48), with beautiful paintings by local artist Constantin Daniel.

LÁSZLÓ TÖKÉS AND THE REVOLUTION OF 1989

Despite doubts about the authenticity of the events of **December 1989** in Bucharest, Timişoara's popular uprising is still regarded as the catalyst of the revolution. The spark was lit just southwest of the centre, when crowds gathered to prevent the internal exile of the Reformat pastor **László Tökés**.

Tökés came from a distinguished dynasty of Reformed (Calvinist) churchmen in Cluj. Born in 1952, he followed his father into the priesthood, but was soon in trouble for teaching Hungarian culture and history to his parishioners in Dej; after two years without a job, he was posted to Timişoara in 1986. Here, he became increasingly outspoken in his criticism of the government and the church authorities, while stressing that he spoke not only for Hungarians but also for the equally oppressed Romanians. In particular, he protested against the **systematization programme**, denouncing it on Hungarian television in July 1989. This led to an increasingly vicious campaign against him by the Securitate, who spread slanderous rumours about him, smashed his windows and harassed his family and friends, culminating in the murder in September 1989 of one of the church elders.

László Papp, Bishop of Oradea, a government placeman, agreed that he should be transferred to the tiny village of Mineu, north of Zalău, but he refused to leave his parish and resisted legal moves to evict him. Being officially deemed unemployed, he lost his ration book, but his parishioners brought him food despite continuing harassment. Eventually, he was removed to Mineu on December 17, and stayed there until the 22nd; the fact that it took so long for a police state to shift him, and that the eviction was so clearly signalled and then delayed for a day or two, is cited as evidence that plotters against Ceauşescu were deliberately trying to incite an uprising. After Tökés's removal, **riots** erupted on the streets of Timişoara, culminating in Ceauşescu's ordering the army to open fire, and eventually his overthrow.

The new National Salvation Front (FSN) tried to co-opt Tökés onto its council, along with other dissidents, but he soon asserted his independence; appropriately, in 1990 he took over the job of Bishop Papp, who fled to France. Romanian nationalists have accused him of being an agent of the Hungarian government and of the CIA, and he continues to be a hardliner, pushing for autonomy for the Magyar-dominated areas. Having cofounded the **National Council of Transylvanian Hungarians**, he was elected to the European Parliament in 2007, serving as vice-president in 2010–12.

Art Museum

Piaţa Unirii 1 • Tues–Sun 10am–6pm • €2.50 • ☎ 0256 491 592, ⓦ muzeuldeartatm.ro

The **Art Museum**, on the south side of the square in a palace built in 1752 and expanded in 1786 and 1886, features paintings – notably four portraits of George Enescu – by most major Romanian artists, such as Nicolae Grigorescu, Gheorghe Tattarescu, Theodor Aman, Ştefan Luchian and Nicolae Tonitza, and sculptures by Oscar Han, all with useful Romanian/English texts. There's also work by lesser-known Italian, German and Flemish masters, a collection of icons from the seventeenth century onward and some decorative art too, but of more interest are the rotating temporary exhibitions – often photographic.

At the rear of the museum, on the corner of stradas Eugeniu de Savoya and Augustin Pacha, a plaque marks the house in which Cuza apparently spent his last two nights in Romania on his way to exile (see page 378) – as the Banat was not part of Romania until 1918, he was presumably under the impression that he was already in exile.

Museum of the Revolution

Str. Oituz 2B • Mon–Fri 8am–4pm, Sat 10am–2pm • €2.50 • ☎ 0256 294 936, ⓦ memorialulrevolutiei.ro

A section of the Berlin Wall stands outside the marvellous **Museum of the Revolution**; inside, a tiny chapel remembers the 93 or so (the actual number is unknown) martyrs gunned down in the city, while photos, newspaper cuttings and a moving set of paintings by local school children illustrate vividly those extraordinary few days, as well as recalling the communist propaganda that was omnipresent until 1989. Equally gripping is a documentary **film** (subtitled in English; 30min) containing some remarkable footage, such as Ceauşescu's final, fatal, speech on the balcony of the Communist Party Headquarters building, and the moment when he and his wife Elena were informed of their impending execution.

Bastions

In 1868, the city purchased the redundant citadel from the Habsburg government, and demolished all but two sections, built in the 1730s and loosely known as the **Bastions**, to the west and east of Piaţa Unirii. Today, the western section contains a **market**, named Timişoara 700, in honour of the city's 700th anniversary in 1969, and the eastern section, known as the Bastion Theresia, houses wine bars and **restaurants**.

Muzeul Satului Bănăţean and Zoo

Muzeul Satului Bănăţean Aleea Avram Imbroane 1 • May–Sept Tues–Sat 10am–6pm, Sun noon–8pm; Oct–April Tues–Fri 9am–4pm, Sat & Sun 10am–5pm • €1 • ☎ 0256 225 588, ⓦ muzeulsatuluibanatean.ro • **Zoo** Aleea Avram Imbroane 90 • Tues–Sun: mid-April to Sept 10am–8pm; Oct to mid-April 10am–5pm • €0.70 • ☎ 0356 004 152, ⓦ carpatzoo.ro

About 5km east of town in the **Pădurea Verde** (Green Forest), old Banat homesteads and workshops have been reassembled in the open-air **Muzeul Satului Bănăţean** (Museum of the Banat Village) – take bus #46 from the Bastion Theresia to the end of the line. Just beyond is the city's **zoo**, which has been transformed into a spacious and attractive home for animals from around the world, including wallabies, guanacos, maras, bears, monkeys and many kinds of birds.

ARRIVAL AND INFORMATION TIMIŞOARA

BY PLANE

The airport (☎ 0256 386 089, ⓦ aerotim.ro), with flights to a number of European destinations including London Luton, is 12km east of the city; express bus #E4 goes to Bastion in the city centre, while #E4/ goes to the Gara de Nord (both hourly; €.60); a taxi should cost no more than €8 (call ☎ 940, ☎ 942, ☎ 945 or ☎ 949).

BY CAR

The new motorway from the Hungarian border to Lugoj passes close to the airport, which is where most car rental companies are to be found. Parking in the centre must be paid Mon–Fri 8am–5pm (SMS #1210, ⓦ timpark.ro).
Rental companies Avis, Timişoara airport (☎ 0256 203 234, ⓦ avis.ro); AW Rentacar, Piaţa Regina Maria 1 (☎ 0256 202 410, ⓦ awrentacar.ro); Autonom, Calea Dorobantilor 86 (☎ 0749 033 322, ⓦ autonom.ro); Budget, Timişoara airport (☎ 0256 386 022, ⓦ budget.ro); Europcar, Timişoara airport (☎ 0747 770 648, ⓦ europcar.ro); Sixt, Timişoara airport (☎ 0742 106 778, ⓦ sixt.ro).

BY TRAIN

From the main train station, Timişoara Nord, it's a 20min walk east to the centre along B-dul Republicii (or trolley buses #11, #14 or #18, tram #1). There's a separate ticket office for Regiotrans trains to Sânnicolau Mare.

Destinations Arad (11 daily; 50min–1hr 25min); Bucharest (2 daily; 8–9hr); Budapest (1 daily; 5hr); Buziaş (6 daily; 45min–1hr 25min); Caransebeş (7 daily; 1hr 30min–2hr 10min); Lugoj (12 daily; 55min–1hr 30min); Oradea (4 daily; 3–4hr 30min); Reşiţa (5 daily; 2hr 30min); Sânnicolau Mare (4 daily; 2hr 10min); Vršac, Serbia (2 daily; 2hr).

BY BUS

The bus station is across the canal from the train station and one block west, at Str. Iuliu Maniu 54, next to the main market (trams Tv2 and Tv7 towards Dâmboviţa). Normandia buses to Târgu Jiu and Bucharest leave from near the former abattoir on B-dul Eroilor de la Tisa.
Destinations Arad (hourly); Băile Herculane (10 daily); Caransebeş (14 daily); Câmpeni (3 daily); Cluj (4 daily); Lipova (2 daily); Lugoj (every 30–60min); Moldova Nouă (daily Mon–Sat); Oradea (12 daily); Oraviţa (4 daily); Reşiţa (3 daily); Sibiu (6 daily); Târgu Jiu (8 daily).

TOURIST INFORMATION

The helpful tourist office is at Str. Alba Iulia 2 (April–Sept Mon–Fri 9am–7pm, Sat 10am–4pm; Oct–March Mon–Fri 9am–6pm, Sat 10am–3pm; ☎ 0256 437 973, ⓦ timisoara-info.ro).

GETTING AROUND

By bike RATT operate a bike hire scheme called VeloTM (@ratt.ro/velo_tm.html), whereby you register (ID and email required), before collecting a bike (free of charge) from one of 25 stations around the city; the catch, though, is that you must return the bike (to any station) within an hour.

Tickets Tickets for RATT buses, trolley buses and trams can be bought at Piaţa Timişoara 700 (Mon–Fri 6am–8.30pm; @ratt.ro; bus €0.50, express €0.60).

ACCOMMODATION

Baza Turistica B-dul Eminescu ☎0256 490 469, ✉djt. timis@yahoo.com; map p.327. The DJT (County Youth Organization) has clean and simple three-bed rooms right in the city centre (between Str. 20 Decembrie 1989 and Str. Miron Cristea); book in advance. **€11**

Camping International Calea Dorobanţilor 63 ☎0256 217 086, @campinginternational.ro; map p.327. Basic campsite 4km east of the city in the Green Forest with well-equipped cabins sleeping one to four people and space for camping (€7) and caravans/motorhomes (€9). Trolley bus #11 terminates at Arena-Aquasport, opposite the campsite, or take bus M30 towards Pod Ghiroda. May–Sept. **€27**

Casa Politehnica 1 B-dul Regele Ferdinand 2 ☎0256 496 850, ✉casapoli1@yahoo.com; map p.327. A student residence – through the black door – with decent single and double rooms and breakfast included; also a restaurant with a menu of the day (€4.50). Doubles **€33**

Central Str. Lenau 6 ☎0256 490 091, @hotel-central. ro; map p.327. In a wonderfully central location, this has simple but clean, modern and a/c rooms, and extremely welcoming staff; parking has to be paid for except at weekends. **€45**

Cina Banatul B-dul Republicii 7 ☎0256 490 130, @hotelcina.ro; map p.327. One of the cheapest city-centre options, this completely renovated hotel has rather gloomy rooms and small bathrooms, but it's perfectly acceptable. Breakfast is extra; wi-fi in the foyer only. **€33**

Downtown Hostel Piaţa Victoriei 3, et 3, ap 15 ☎0721 001 081, @downtownhostel.ro; map p.327. This small but pleasant hostel occupies a nice little flat with one eight-bed dorm, one twin and one en-suite double, and a tiny kitchen/common space. Dorm, **€12**, doubles **€35**

Hostel Costel Str. Petru Sfetca 1 (former Str. Vidra) ☎0356 262 487, @hostel-costel.ro; map p.327. Just south of the river off Str. Abrud (take tram #1 to the 3 August 1919 stop, or the airport bus E4 to Badea Cârţan), this colourful house has three dorms (grey, green and purple) and one private room, a kitchen and a pleasant garden. Dorms **€11**, rooms **€30**

Hostel Nord B-dul Gen. Dragalina 47 ☎0256 497 504, @hostelnord.ro; map p.327. Cheerless and functional but very cheap and suffices if arriving late or departing early from the train station which is bang opposite. **€22**

Novera Str. Ripensia 29A ☎0256 466 156, @hotelnovera.ro; map p.327. Handy for the university and stadium, this modern place has rather flashy large rooms and a restaurant with Murano-style chandeliers; good value, especially at weekends. **€82**

Silva B-dul V. Babeş 25 ☎0256 201 406, @hotel-silva. ro; map p.327. One of the city's best small hotels, this very modern place is nicer in than out, with comfortable, bright and spacious rooms. **€50**

Timişoara Str. Mărăşeşti 3 ☎0256 498 852, @hoteltimisoara.ro; map p.327. In a plum location overlooking Piaţa Victoriei (entry to the north), this grand hotel has slickly furnished rooms which, although they retain a somewhat business-like feel, are among the most well-appointed in town. **€75**

Victoria Str. Lucian Blaga 3 ☎0256 431 602, @victoria-hotel.ro; map p.327. Well-renovated hotel in a lovely old building with large if fairly bare rooms, friendly staff and a decent breakfast, but no lift or parking. **€59**

★ **Vila Casa del Sole** Str. Romulus 12 ☎0356 457 771, @hotel.casadelsole.ro; map p.327. A lovely new boutique hotel around a beautiful courtyard, whose colourful, classically-furnished rooms pretty much hit the mark; a swimming pool, restaurant and cocktail bar round things off in delightful fashion; south of the Bega by a park and tram stop (#8). **€58**

EATING

For such a large and cosmopolitan city, Timişoara has a surprisingly slim selection of restaurants, although there are some particularly good Italian and Serbian places. Conversely, there's no shortage of drinking venues, particularly down by the canal in the summer, and, during term-time, around the lively student area – principally Aleea Studenţilor, where there's also plenty of fast food.

Adagio Str. Victor Vlad Delamarina ☎0746 182 381, @adagiofood.com; map p.327. Just off Piaţa Libertăţii, this Italian-owned *gelateria* serves excellent home-made ice cream with no additives or preservatives, as well as chocolates. Mon–Thurs 9am–midnight, Fri–Sun 9am–10pm.

Amphora Str. Hector 4 ☎0732 970 181, @enotecaamphora.ro; map p.327. This *enoteca*-restaurant (one of a group of rather slick restaurants in the Bastion Theresia) offers a wide range of Romanian wines and a terrifically varied menu including the likes of foie gras with fig jam, grilled trout (€6) and rabbit haunch (€11). Daily 10am–midnight.

Bio-Fresh Str. Griselini 2 ☎ 0256 221 747, ⊚ biofreshtm. ro; map p.327. A good (if drab) vegetarian restaurant, serving dishes such as aubergine gratin or stuffed pumpkin with pesto (both €5.50), or pasta (€2.50–4) as well as lots of shakes and organic wine and beer. There's also a branch south of the canal at Str. Miron Costin (Piaţa Maria; Mon–Fri 10am–5pm, Sat noon–4pm). Mon–Fri 10am–10pm, Sat & Sun noon–10pm.

Homemade Str. Gheorghe Doja 40 ☎ 0730 832 299; map p.327. A short stroll south of the centre, beyond the Bega Canal, this place offers something a little bit different to anywhere else in town, at least in terms of its setting, which is an apartment concealing a couple of cozy rooms adorned with rugs, potted plants, wall pictures and the like; the food, meanwhile (asparagus and lemon risotto, tenderloin pork with polenta; €7) is well presented and tasty. Daily noon–11pm.

Karadjordje Str. Lazăr 2 ☎ 0256 430 712; map p.327. A full-blooded Serbian place just off Piaţa Unirii serving lashings of meat, such as grilled chicken or *pleşcaviţa* (both €4.50), Kara Djordje schnitzel (€5.50) and a menu of the day (€3.30). Mon–Sat noon–11pm.

★ **La Cucina Di Giordano** Str. Daliei 14 ☎ 0256 490 298, ⊚ lacucinadigiordano.ro; map p.327. Genuinely excellent and extremely popular trattoria, run by Italians, near the student quarter, just behind the OMV station off B-dul Eroilor de la Tisa. Among the usual suspects are some intriguing dishes such as perch fillet with sausage sauce (€9) and spaghetti with clams and asparagus (€8.50). Daily 11am–midnight.

La Pizza Napoletana Str. Argeş 18 ☎ 0722 234 345; map p.327. Hands-down the best pizzeria in town, this ordinary-looking outfit south of the Bega doles out superb wood-fired, thin crust pizzas (but with lovely puffy edges),

including a number of more unusual creations, such as *Voichi* (pumpkin cream, fennel and prosciutto). Daily noon–midnight.

Little Hanoi Bistro Str. Johann Wolfgang von Goethe 2 ☎ 0256 224 683, ⊚ littlehanoi.ro; map p.327. A cute little hangout, which, as the name suggests, specializes in Vietnamese cuisine, and rather fine it is too; pho (beef, chicken), spring and summer rolls (duck, shrimp) form the mainstay of a concise but appealing and keenly-priced menu. Daily 11am–10pm.

Rivière Brasserie Parcul Justitiei 1 ☎ 0746 095 573, ⊚ riviere.ro; map p.327. A delightful waterfront venue with a large terrace under the weeping willows, and water sprays instead of a/c (more pleasant than it might sound); service is usually fast and cheery, dishing up pasta, steaks and the like. Daily 10am–midnight.

Symphony Café Str. Alba Iulia 2 ☎ 0256 292 699; map p.327. Next to the opera, this has the best terrace in town for people-watching, and a good range of hot and cold drinks such as lemonades. Daily 9am–11pm.

Timişoreana Piaţa Victoriei 2 ☎ 0256 295 421; map p.327. Owned by the brewery of the same name (founded in 1718, and now part of the SAB-Miller comglomerate), this wood-panelled cellar serves cheap and delicious local food such as *sarmale* and *papanasi*. On Str. Ştefan cel Mare in the Fabric district, there's also the Timişoreana Brewery restaurant, with unfiltered draught beer (trams #5, #7 and #8 to the Fabrica de Bere stop). Daily 10am–midnight.

Yugoslavia Str. G. Dragomir 10 (Piaţa Bălcescu) ☎ 0737 394 794, ⊚ restaurantyugoslavia.ro; map p.327. Hugely enjoyable, and typically hospitable, Serbian restaurant in the south of town, opposite the *Perla II/IV* hotel, serving specialities such as *ćevapi* (minced spiced meat rolls) and *sarma* (cabbage leaves wrapped around rice and meat). Vegetarians need not bother. Daily 11am–11pm.

DRINKING AND NIGHTLIFE

Amplificat Str. Vasile Alecsandri 7 ⊚ amplif.ro; map p.327. Lively venue for underground culture, with urban and electronic music the speciality. Thurs–Sat 9pm–6am.

Bierhaus Str. Ungureanu 15 ☎ 0721 279 039, ⊚ bierhaus.ro; map p.327. A real pub with a good range of drinks (although the draught beers may only be available in bottles), with very quiet rock music, a mezzanine gallery and fussball (no food). Mon–Fri 11am–1am, Sat 4pm–3am, Sun 4pm–1am.

Café Colţ Piaţa Unirii 4 ☎ 0732 229 933; map p.327. At the corner of stradas Ungureanu and Lazăr, this is a vibrant café-cum-bar on two floors with a grand chandelier. Daily 9am–midnight.

The Drunken Rat Str. Cosbuc 1 ☎ 0756 143 050; map p.327. On the northeastern corner of Piaţa Unirii, this busy little pub has good beer, tasty ribs and music. Mon–Thurs & Sun 8am–3am, Fri & Sat 24hr.

The Note Pub B-dul Mihai Eminescu 2 ☎ 0256 488 958; map p.327. A lively pub with a pleasant deck at the rear that does pretty average food (burger and chips, or menu of the day €4) and hosts live bands and cabaret. Mon–Wed & Sun 8am–midnight, Thurs–Sat 8am–5am.

Reciproc Str. Mărăşeşti 14 ☎ 0756 081 961, ⊚ lareciproc. ro; map p.327. A lovely little café with a good range of coffees, tea, juices and lemonade, beer and wine, also selling snacks and products from local organic suppliers such as jams and cakes. Mon–Thurs 8am–midnight, Fri 8am–2am, Sat 10am–2am, Sun 10am–11pm.

Viniloteca Str. Gen. Berthelot 6 ☎ 0256 707 107; map p.327. Just off Piaţa Maria, this small cellar bar is owned by a beer-loving DJ, so there's a great range of bottled beers from Belgium and elsewhere (from €3.30) and a deck playing vinyl LPs, but not too loud. Mon–Fri 8am–10pm, Sat noon–10pm.

TIMIŞOARA FESTIVALS

The city stages several terrific music **festivals**; first up, in early May, there's the **Timişoara Muzicală Festival** (⊛timisoaramuzicala.ro), a series of classical concerts and opera at the Opera House, followed by the **Revolution Festival** (⊛revolutionfestival.com) at the end of May, a three-day jamboree of rock, dance and dub, among other genres, taking place within the grounds of the Village Museum. **JazzTM** (⊛jazztm.ro) takes place on the first weekend of July, then it's the turn of the well established **Plai** world music festival (⊛plai.ro), held at the Village Museum in mid-September, which attracts some of the best performers from around the globe.

6

ENTERTAINMENT

Banat Philharmonic B-dul C.D. Loga 2 ☎0256 492 521, ⊛filarmonicabanatul.ro (box office Mon, Wed & Fri 10am–2pm, Tues & Thurs 2–7pm and 1hr before concerts. Timişoara's excellent symphony orchestra often performs in the open air or other unusual venues.

Opera House Str. Mărăşeşti 2 ☎0256 201 286, ⊛ort.ro. The city's main concert venue, also housing two theatres staging plays in German and Hungarian; box office daily 10am–1pm & 5–7pm; opera tickets from €6.

The Timiş valley

The main rail line and the DN6 follow the River Timiş southeast from Timişoara towards Băile Herculane and Wallachia, passing through the small Habsburg towns of **Lugoj** and **Caransebeş**. Caransebeş offers easy access into the mountains, either west into the Semenic massif or east to Muntele Mic, Ţarcu, Godeanu and, ultimately, the Retezat range.

Cramele Recaş

Tastings and shop Mon–Fri 9am–6pm, Sat 10am–6pm • ☎0256 330 100, ⊛cramelerecas.ro

Wine has been made in **Recaş**, 23km east of Timişoara, since at least the mid-fifteenth century; privatized in 2000 and now a Romanian-British business, the **Cramele Recaş** winery, 4km north of Recaş station, produces excellent red and white vintages, as well as a sparkling *spumant*. In fact, their range may now be too wide: it's best to concentrate on their authentic Schwab German wines (using Riesling and Traminer grapes). **Visits** are welcome, and well organized, but should be booked at least two days in advance – they usually do require a minimum of four people however; they range from a one-hour tasting of seven wines (€10) to a full three-course meal accompanied by an unlimited supply of your preferred wine (€36).

Lugoj

LUGOJ, 63km east of Timişoara, is notable as the birthplace of several Romanian musicians, including the operatic tenor Traian Grozăvescu (1895–1927), and the composers Tiberiu Brediceanu (1877–1968), Filaret Barbu (1903–84) and Ion Vidu (1836–1931). Its non-Romanian sons are less likely to be remembered by plaques, but Béla Ferenc Dezső Blaskó (1882–1956) immortalized his birthplace's Hungarian name when he became Béla Lugosi, Hollywood's most famous Dracula and the nearest yet to a genuinely Transylvanian Count; fittingly, the cinema next to the *Hotel Dacia* is now the Cinema Béla Lugosi. Across the street, the unassuming Old Theatre dates from 1835.

Exit left from the train station and head up Strada Al. Mocioni – soon pedestrianized – towards the Iron Bridge, thrown across the Timiş in 1902 to link the formerly Schwab town to the Romanian quarter. On the corner of Strada Bălcescu is the **Galeria**

Pro Arte, with free shows of local artists, and just beyond at Str. Bălcescu 2, the **town museum** (Tues–Sun 9am–5pm; €0.50) has good displays of local costumes (including the heavy sheepskin coats that are the town's speciality) and ceramics plus excellent old photos of costumes and jewellery and of wooden churches; upstairs is the history section, with various weapons and displays on the town's musical personalities and the poet Laura Vlad Rădulescu and Béla Lugosi.

Cross the river to Piaţa Republicii, where the **Uniate Cathedral** (1843–54) has a rough cement exterior and some fine neo-Byzantine paintings inside. Nearby, on Piaţa Victoriei, is the **Orthodox Church of the Assumption**, a hall-church built in 1759–66 by the younger Fischer von Erlach, which is one of the most important Baroque buildings of the Banat, with a very ornate interior. The stumpy tower of the church of St Nicholas (1726) stands alongside, while across Strada 20 Decembrie 1989, the Hanul Poştei (Gasthof Post) was built at about the same time.

ARRIVAL AND DEPARTURE   LUGOJ

By bus The bus station by the river on Splaiul Morilor has become a major interchange for buses making their last stop in Romania before striking out all over Western Europe. Destinations Băile Herculane (9 daily); Câmpeni (2 daily); Caransebeş (12 daily); Deva (9 daily); Drobeta Turnu Severin (7 daily); Orşova (7 daily); Sibiu (3 daily); Târgu Jiu (6 daily); Timişoara (20 daily). **By train** Băile Herculane (2 daily; 2hr 10min); Caransebeş (7 daily; 30–45min); Craiova (2 daily; 5hr 15min); Deva (2 daily; 2hr 20min); Timişoara (12 daily; 1hr–2hr).

ACCOMMODATION AND EATING

Brutăria Sudriaş Str. Someşului 5. This neat little bakery serves light lunches including sandwiches, burgers and grilled pork or chicken and chips (€2.20). Mon–Fri 7am–4.30pm, Sat 7am–2.30pm.
Dacia Str. Mocioni 7 ☎ 0256 352 740, ⓦ hotel-dacia.ro. A hotel of sorts since 1835, this has individually designed but slightly cramped and pricey rooms; the entry is around the corner on Str. Cuza Vodă, with a marble foyer and some nice Deco touches. €38
Pensiunea Dariana Str. Caransebeşului 4B ☎ 0256 352 704, ⓦ dariana.ro. A fairly ugly block 3km south, this has pleasant if functional rooms with balconies and offers a good breakfast. €30

Caransebeş

CARANSEBEŞ lies beneath the mountains at the confluence of the Timiş and Sebeş rivers, where Gypsies of the Zlatari tribe used to pan for gold. Having been the Banat's judicial centre in medieval times and commanding communications through the Eastern Gate, Caransebeş inevitably became a Habsburg garrison town – hence, the outcrops of *belle époque* buildings among the prefabricated structures of the socialist era. There's little to distract you from heading into the mountains, other than the **County Museum of Ethnography and the Border Regiment** (Tues–Sat 10am–4pm; €1), in the former barracks, an imposing Baroque pile (1739) on Piaţa Dragolina, with some impressive artefacts from central and south Banat. The **Galeria de Arte Corneliu Baba**, with free exhibitions of local artists, is just south of Piaţa Dragolina at the top of the pedestrianized Strada Episcopiei, which leads to the foundations of a medieval (probably thirteenth-century) church squeezed between the modern Orthodox cathedral and Roman Catholic church.

ARRIVAL AND DEPARTURE   CARANSEBEŞ

By train From the main train station, north of town, maxitaxis run into the centre; otherwise, it's at least 20min walk. Some local services also stop 2km further south at the Caransebeş halt, west of the centre. On the railway line from Timişoara to Orşova and Turnu Severin on the Danube (see page 109) and onwards into Wallachia, Caransebeş is the junction for a branch line west to Reşiţa (see page 337). Destinations Băile Herculane (6 daily; 1hr 20min–2hr); Bucharest (3 daily; 3hr 30min–8hr 10min); Craiova (1 daily; 4hr 15min); Drobeta-Turnu Severin (3 daily; 2hr 15min–3hr); Lugoj (11 daily; 30–50min); Orşova (6 daily; 1hr 45min–2hr 30min); Reşiţa (7 daily; 1hr); Timişoara (10 daily; 1hr 30min–2hr 15min).

By bus The small private Autogară Nadina is at the north end of the bridge on Calea Severinului, south of the centre, from where maxitaxis run to Reşiţa and Borlova; otherwise, through buses stop at the station and south of the bridge.

Destinations Borlova (9 daily); Craiova (3 daily); Hunedoara (1 daily); Râmnicu Vâlcea (2 daily); Reşiţa (8 daily); Sarmizegetusa/Haţeg (7 daily); Târgu Jiu (7 daily); Timişoara (12 daily).

ACCOMMODATION

Armando Str. Libertăţii 35 ☎0255 517 308, ⓦ hotelarmando.ro. Easily the best of the town's hotels, with beautifully furnished boho-chic rooms and car parking in the courtyard; has a reasonable restaurant too. **€36**

GeAS I Str. Bălcescu 59 ☎0255 511 637, ⓦ hotelgeas. ro. On the corner of Str. Crişan, this is a fairly simple place with a restaurant, gym and sauna, though it does have a superior sister hotel, Geas IV at Str. Bălcescu 35 (☎0255 515 228; €30). **€20**

Borlova and the Muntele Mic

Borlova, 13km east of Caransebeş, is noted for its embroideries and peasant weddings, and holds a **Measurement of the Milk festival** around April 23 every year. Most visitors, however, pass straight through en route to the **Muntele Mic** (Little Mountain) resort, where you can ski between December and March – there are a number of guesthouses and cabanas here. There are also good **hiking** trails in the Ţarcu mountains, high open moorland of which a large area protected by a Natura 2000 site (ⓦ tarcu.ro). You can walk north to the Muntele Mic itself in an hour, or south to the weather station (2190m) atop Mount Ţarcu in three hours. Well-equipped hikers can take trails eastwards towards Lake Gura Apei and the Retezat mountains in four hours (following red stripes), or southwards to Godeanu and the Cerna valley in six hours (red dots). From Muntele Mic, there's also a route (following blue stripes) to Poiana Marului, to the east, from where there are hourly buses to Otelu Roşu, with connections to Caransebeş.

Some 28km southeast of Borlova, in the remote Ţarcu Mountains (see above), European **bison** have recently been reintroduced, some two hundred years after disappearing from the area. Also known as Bison Hillock, there are currently 36 free-roaming bison, the aim being to reach 100 in the not too distant future. In the village of **Armeniş**, around 16km southwest of the Ţarcu Mountains (or roughly halfway between Caransebeş and Băile Herculane on the DN6/E70), the Bison Interpretation Centre (also known as the Centrul de Informare Turistică Armeniş; no official opening times; ☎0757 810 905) offers insight into the project. The Bison Hillock Association (based at the Interpretation Centre) offers opportunities to visit Bison Hillock, though you must contact them at least two weeks in advance.

The Cerna valley

The road and rail routes south from Caransebeş pass through the **Poarta Orientalis** or Eastern Gate of Transylvania before reaching **Băile Herculane** and its spa at the bottom of the **Cerna valley**. The middle and upper reaches of the valley itself, now protected by the **Domogled-Valea Cernei National Park**, are much as Patrick Leigh Fermor described them in the 1930s: "a wilderness of green moss and grey creepers with ivy-clad water-mills rotting along the banks and streams tumbling through the shadows [illuminated by] shafts of lemon-coloured light". Among the butterflies and birds that proliferate here are bright blue rollers, which the Romanians call *dumbrăveancă*, "one who loves oakwoods".

6

Băile Herculane

BĂILE HERCULANE gets its name from the Roman legend that Hercules cured the wounds inflicted by the Hydra by bathing here, and the nine springs, with their varied mineral content and temperature (38–60°C), are used to treat a wide range of disorders. The Roman baths were rediscovered in 1724, and royal patronage made Herkulesbad, as it was then known, one of Europe's most fashionable watering holes. The old spa, centred on Piața Hercules, was still elegant when Patrick Leigh Fermor came here but is now in a terrible state of decay and only slowly being restored to its former glory. There's far more life in the ugly but livelier satellite spa of **Pecinișca**, 2km towards the train station and dominated by half a dozen or so grim high-rise hotels.

Other than a wallow in the renowned **baths**, Băile Herculane's chief attraction is its surroundings – soaring limestone peaks clothed in lush vegetation and riddled with caves. You can bathe in the **Seven Hot Springs** (Șapte Izvoare Calde) just beyond the Cerna rapids about 35 minutes' walk upstream from Piața Hercules, from where a path (marked with red dots) climbs east to the Cascada Cociu (or Cascada Roșeț), a 120m-high waterfall. Another two hours' hiking up the Cerna valley brings you to **Gisella's Cross**, from where there are magnificent views. From here, an unmarked path leads in thirty minutes to a forest of black pines, dotted with boulders, and a spectacular 300m precipice. Other paths provide access to the vaporous **Steam Cave** on Ciorci Hill (1hr 30min), the **Outlaws' Cave** where Stone Age tribes once sheltered (30min), and **Mount Domogled**, which has trees and flowers of Mediterranean origin and more than 1300 varieties of butterfly (4hr).

It's roughly 40km from Băile Herculane to the watershed of the River Cerna, on a forestry road that continues to Câmpușel and the Jiu valley. A path marked with red stripes runs parallel along the ridge to the north to Piatra lui Iorgovan in the **Retezat mountains** (see page 177) – allow one or two days.

ARRIVAL AND DEPARTURE BĂILE HERCULANE

By train From Băile Herculane's lovely train station (built in 1878), 5km from the spa, buses run on the hour and half-hour to Piața Hercules from 6am to midnight.
Destinations Bucharest (3 daily; 6hr 15min–6hr 45min); Caransebeș (7 daily; 1hr 20min–2hr 10min); Craiova (3 daily; 3hr); Drobeta Turnu Severin (4 daily; 55min); Lugoj (6

daily; 1hr 50min–3hr); Orșova (7 daily; 30min); Timișoara (6 daily; 2hr 50min–4hr 30min).
By bus Caransebeș (11 daily); Craiova (5 daily); Drobeta Turnu Severin (7 daily); Orșova (9 daily); Timișoara (11 daily).

ACCOMMODATION AND EATING

There are not many decent hotels in the old spa, or among the group of huge communists blocks just south, but there are a number of reasonable pensions towards the station in Pecinișca, as well as signs advertising cheaper private rooms. The best restaurant (which isn't saying a lot) is in the *Ferdinand* hotel, while there are also two popular pizza places, the Greek *Pizza Dimitrios*, near the *Cerna* hotel at Piața 1 Mai 4 (☎0255 560 691) and the *Restaurant-Pizza Cristal* at Str. Castanilor 7 (☎0255 560 000).
Camping Hercules DN6 km382 ☎0255 523 458. Hidden beside a bright green motel about 800m north of the train station on the Timișoara road, this excellent little site also has a handful of rooms available, as well as a restaurant. Camping €3, rooms €18
Cerna Piața 1 Mai 1 ☎0255 560 436, ⬩hotelcerna. ro. The best-value of the few hotels in the old spa is this renovated place next to the open-air thermal baths (1871), which has rooms with and without bathroom. €40

Ferdinand Piața Hercules 1 ☎0255 561 121, ⬩hotel-ferdinand.ro. A well-restored building (dating from 1811) with a good restaurant and its own baths, but poor service and a slightly tacky vibe. €55
Hostel Sara's Sons Str. Aleea Teilor 2A ☎0255 560 577, ⬩sarassons.ro. Overlooked by the huge communist *Dacia* and *Diana* hotels, this is a more pleasant place with sizeable, accomplished rooms, three large pools of sulphurous healing waters, spa, gym and restaurant. €32
Roman ☎0255 560 394, ⬩hotelroman.eu. Beyond the little octagonal Catholic church (1838) at the end of Piața Hercules, a one-way road continues 400m to the remains of a Roman aqueduct and this communist block which straddles the road and the Imperial Roman Baths (daily 8am–6pm; €2.50). Renovated and partially renovated rooms, with either a forest or river view, plus a thermal pool. €30

The mountainous Banat

Various low massifs run south parallel to the Serbian border, all the way to the Danube, their limestone rocks opening into lovely caves and their warm climate fostering semi-Mediterranean flora and fauna; there's also some interesting industrial heritage here.

Reşiţa

People have been beating iron into shape around **REŞIŢA**, 40km southwest of Caransebeş, since Dacian times. The foundry can trace its history back to 1771, and steam locomotives were manufactured here from 1872 until 1964. It's now one of Europe's largest bicycle factories, but the town is largely communist concrete and has a depressed feel to it. Arriving at the grubby bus station on Strada Lalescu, walk west past the post office and theatre, over the footbridge and under the ropeway, and you'll come to the windswept central plaza, **Piaţa 1 Decembrie 1918**, with a massive rotating fountain.

By the river north of the centre (on Bulevardul Revoluţiei din Decembrie, the main road north), the **Parcul Triaj** is an open-air collection of Reşiţa-built steam locomotives, notably *Resicza no.2*, the first steam loco made in present-day Romania in 1872; all are in decent condition and there's information in English. The **Museum of Mountainous Banat**, at B-dul Republicii 10 (Tues–Sat 9am–5pm; free), not far from the next station north, Reşiţa Nord, mainly hosts temporary shows by local artists and the like, due to lack of funds, although there are some Roman funerary and votive monuments by the entrance. The town does stage a couple of festivals: steelworkers take pride of place in the **Spring Parade** (Alaiul Primăverii), normally in the first week of April, while there's also the **Bârzava Song Festival** in August. At other times you may as well continue straight on to the mountains.

ARRIVAL AND DEPARTURE   REŞIŢA

By train Trains terminate at Reşiţa Sud station, just across from the plaza by a footbridge.
Destinations Caransebeş (7 daily; 1hr); Timişoara (1 daily; 2hr 40min).
By bus There are two rather run-down bus stations (Transmontana and BusTrans) just east of the centre on the main road, Str. Libertăţii.

Destinations Băile Herculane (2 daily); Caransebeş (9 daily); Crivaia/Văliug (Sun–Fri 4 daily); Deva (Mon–Sat 1 daily); Drobeta (1 daily); Moldova Nouă (Mon–Sat 2 daily); Oraviţa (4 daily); Timişoara (3 daily Mon–Sat).

ACCOMMODATION AND EATING

There's also cheaper accommodation outside town at Semenic or Crivaia (see page 337) or at one of the guesthouses 13km east on Lake Secu. There are a couple of adequate pizza places, *Soho House* and *Nera*, on Piaţa 1 Decembrie 1918, actually just to the west off the main plaza. If you're planning to hike in the Semenic mountains, Reşiţa is the last chance to stock up on food; there's a good covered market just east of the Sud train station.
Intim Str. Republicii 2 ☎ 0255 252 595, ⍵ intimhotel. ro. To the north in the newer town, handy for the

museum, this bland, office-like block has eight rooms and a suite, all a bit purple but perfectly comfortable. **€35**
Rogge Str. Caragiale 12 ☎ 0355 411 111, ⍵ hotelrogge. ro. This relatively long and low modern block on the main through-road has very decent rooms that are not huge but come with comfortable, wood-framed beds and large plasma TVs. It also has the town's best restaurant, with dishes including trout. **€60**

The Semenic mountains

Văliug, 23km southeast of Reşiţa, sits at the north end of Lacul Gozna, with **Crivaia** 6km south at the other end; both have a range of guesthouses and are starting points for excursions into the **Semenic mountains**. From Văliug another road climbs through

6

beautiful beech forest to mountain-top **Semenic** (also reached by chairlift from Crivaia), which has chalet-style accommodation and two hotels. **Skiing** is possible here from November to April – pistes range from very easy to difficult.

Although the massif is lower and less rugged than others in the Carpathians, it still offers good **hiking**. One of the most popular trails heads west from Semenic to the Comarnic Cave and on to the Carașului gorges (9–10hr; red cross markings). Just before the eastern entrance to the gorges, the **Comarnic Cave** is the Banat's largest grotto, with a spectacular array of rock "veils" and calcite crystals distributed around its 400m of galleries on two levels (guided tours Sat & Sun 10am–6pm, Mon–Fri call ☎0763 276 349; €2). It can also be reached by taking the road from north of Carașova to Iabalcea (3km) then hiking for 7km.

The gorges themselves are wild and muddy and harbour several more caves. If you don't fancy hiking here from Semenic or Crivaia, the gorges can also be entered from the west (following blue triangle markings) near the Croatian-populated village of **Carașova**, on the main road 16km south of Reșița.

ACCOMMODATION — THE SEMENIC MOUNTAINS

Aquaris Hotel ☎0374 210 210, ⊕aquaris.com.ro. This luxury lakeside resort 4km south of Văliug on the Crivaia road has a fancy restaurant and rooms, and has boats, bikes and ATVs available for rent. **€42**

Cabana Andra Semenic ☎0725 963 388. At the resort's highest point, 500m from the ski slopes, this has simple double rooms (some with balcony) and a restaurant serving traditional food. **€30**

Cabana Claris Crivaia ☎0745 999 339, ⊕hotel-claris. ro. Really a small hotel, most rooms here have a balcony, and the restaurant has a pleasant terrace; bikes and table-tennis facilities are available. **€29**

Vila Baraj Valiug Str. Bolnovat 12, Văliug ☎0728 941 868. Near the Lacul Gozna dam, and also known as the *Kreiter Haus*, this consists of some stylish modern rooms beneath a circular café-restaurant at the foot of a chairlift. **€18**

Oravița

ORAVIȚA, 66km south of Reșița via Anina (a delightful drive in beech-covered mountains) and 110km south of Timișoara, was a prosperous centre of mining and metal-working from early in the Habsburg occupation, as shown by its museums and also the area's railways – the line from the Danube port of Baziaș to Oravița, opened in 1854, was the first in present-day Romania, followed in 1863 by the Oravița–Anina line, known as "the Semmering of the Banat" for its mountain scenery and the engineering feats (including fourteen tunnels and ten viaducts) required to forge a way through it. One train a day still winds its way over the line at a giddy 30km/h.

From the station, on the edge of the new town, it's a winding couple of kilometres to the **historic centre**, where a Roman Catholic church built in 1732 stands in front of the **Eminescu Theatre** (Str. Eminescu 18; Tues–Sun 11am–7pm; €2), Romania's oldest. Inaugurated in 1817 in the presence of the Austrian emperor Franz I and his wife, it's named after Romania's national poet Mihai Eminescu, who came here as prompter to a touring theatre company in 1868. The theatre is still occasionally in use. You can see its charming interior and the upstairs room where the gentry gathered, with the piano that Liszt played. Just down the road, the **Knoblauch Pharmacy** (Str. Eminescu 17; Tues–Sun 11am–7pm; €2) has been perfectly preserved, and on the other side of the road, the former **Imperial Mint** (Str. Eminescu 24; Tues–Sun 11am–7pm; €2) displays an impressive range of coins, the oldest minted in Vienna in 1502, as well as Romanian coins and war bonds, and contracts and other documents issued by the various banks established here. The museum also plans to open examples of Hungarian and German shops.

| **ARRIVAL AND DEPARTURE** | **ORAVIȚA** |

By bus The bus station is in the new town on the Timișoara road; a white minibus shuttles to the old town (€0.40).

Destinations Moldova Nouă (Mon–Sat 1 daily); Reşiţa (4 daily); Timişoara (Mon–Fri 4 daily, Sat 2).

ACCOMMODATION

Caraș Calea Timisorii 2 ☎0255 573 323, ⓦhotelcarasoravita.ro. Near the entry from Timișoara, this modern place has forty a/c rooms and three suites, plus a spa and thermal pools. **€31**

Condor Str. Cloşca 33C ☎0744 785 729, ⓦcazareoravita. ro. Just up the road from the *Caraș* and handy for the train

to Anina, this is of a similar standard, although service can be variable. **€34**

Pensiunea-Cabana Şapte Brazi Str. Nucilor 1 ☎0788 554 464/65. By the dam at the entry to Oravița from Anina (5km from the centre), this has 32 beds and a restaurant specializing in game. **€28**

The Nera Gorges-Beuşniţa National Park

At the southern limit of the Banat, approaching the Danube, mining (for copper, silver and lead) was first recorded in 120AD in the villages of Sasca Montană and Sasca Romană, 140km from Timişoara; they're now a base for hiking in Romania's warmest mountains, where trails lead up limestone gorges to sights such as the **Beuşniţa waterfalls**, up to 15m in height, on the Beu River above the Ochiul Beului (Eye of the Beu) lake, or the **Lacul Dracului** (Devil's Lake), the largest karst lake in Romania, formed as an underground chamber whose ceiling later collapsed.

The **National Park** office (and tourist information centre; Mon–Thurs 8am–4.30pm, Fri 8am–2pm; ☎0255 206 108, ✉apnchnerei@gmail.com, ⓦinfocheilenerei.ro) is in **Sasca Română**, 1km east of Sasca Montană, from where red stripes follow the Nera river east to the Cheile Nerei (Nera gorges), then north up the Beu to emerge on the DN57B south of Steierdorf (east of Oraviţa). It's a good forest track as far as the Ochiul Beiului and the Cascada Beuşniţa (6km), then an easy trail.

From about 2km south of Sasca Montană, a track forks left, marked with blue crosses to the Şuşara waterfall (45min); **longer hikes** lead to Anina via Sasca Romană (yellow stripes/blue crosses; 8–9hr), to the Beuşniţa waterfall via Carbunari, Lacul Dracului and Lacul Ochiul Beului (yellow stripes/blue crosses; 9–10hr), or from Lacul Dracului to Sasca Montană (red crosses; 9–10hr). Continuing south, the partly unpaved road climbs into lovely forest and eventually descends to the former mining centre of **Moldova Nouă** and the port of **Moldova Veche** on the Danube, 25km from Sasca Montană. From here the road west leads back to Oraviţa and Timişoara, while to the east there's a delightful drive (the DN57, with very little traffic and just one bus, at 2pm daily) along the Danube to the Kazan gorges in Wallachia (see page 110) and up to Băile Herculane.

| **ACCOMMODATION** | **THE NERA GORGES-BEUȘNIȚA NATIONAL PARK** |

La Vechea Moară Sasca Montană no. 530 ☎0726 307 762, ⓦvechea-moara.ro. The Old Mill Pension, towards the southern end of the village, is an atmospheric little German house with just three double rooms and excellent home cooking. **€35**

Pensiunea Cheile Nerei Sasca Romană no. 55 ☎0721 095 591, ⓦcheilenerei.ro. Near the entry to the gorges, this modern guesthouse has tidy, pine-furnished en-suite double and triple rooms, and is also an adventure centre, offering paintball, rafting and archery; there's also a craft shop. **€32**

Pensiunea Casa cu Roţi Sasca Romana no. 74 ☎0721 108 777, ⓦcasacuroti-cheilenerei.ro. Another restful option, here there are four rooms in traditional wooden cottages, an apartment in a stone built house, and a convivial restaurant-cum-bar. **€31**

Rocker's Inn Sasca Montană no. 763 ☎0726 179 062, ⓦrocker-s.ro. This big modern block at the south end of the village seems unattractive, but is well run, with rock-themed rooms (BritPop, Black Metal, Punk and the like) and a decent restaurant; they can provide guides for rafting, climbing and ziplining. **€48**

6

The Delta and the coast

NIGHT HERON ON THE DANUBE DELTA

The Delta and the coast

Nearly 3000km downstream from the Black Forest, the Danube Delta is a vast network of reeds and shifting land clinging to the far eastern side of Romania. Rich in wildlife, the Delta provides a unique habitat for 330 species of bird, many of which are found nowhere else in Europe. To really appreciate the diversity of birdlife, however, you're best off taking a tour or paying one of the local fishermen to row or motor you into the backwaters and lakes; travel in the Delta can be time-consuming, so if you're seriously bent on birdwatching, be prepared to spend at least a week here.

To the south, Romania's **Black Sea coast** is blessed with abundant sunshine, warm water and sandy beaches, but due to the popularity of summer resorts such as **Mamaia**, **Neptun** and **Venus** it's best to book a package holiday from home, or head to one of the prettier former fishing villages near the Bulgarian border: **Doi Mai** is quiet and family-oriented, while the more independent-minded resort of **Vama Veche** grows more fashionable by the year. For a drop of culture amid all this sea and sand, the port city of **Constanţa** offers a splendid array of museums and historical riches, particularly throughout its atmospheric old quarter. The remainder of the region is often bypassed, though it's not without its attractions, not least Roman remains at **Adamclisi** and **Histria**, as well as the superbly sited citadel at **Enisala**.

The Danube Delta

Every year, the River Danube dumps forty million tonnes of alluvium into the **Danube Delta** (Delta Dunării), the youngest, least stable landscape in Europe, abutting the oldest, the heavily eroded Hercynian hills immediately south. Near **Tulcea**, the river splits into three branches (named after their respective ports, Chilia, Sulina and Sfântu Gheorghe), dividing the Delta into more than 4000 square kilometres of reeds and marsh, half of which is flooded in spring and autumn. The **grinduri**, tongues of accumulated silt supporting oak trees, willows and poplars, account for the five percent of the Delta that remains permanently above the water. The distinction between these and the **plauri** (floating reed islands) is a fine one, since flooding continually splits, merges and often destroys these patches of land, making any detailed map of the delta outdated almost as soon as it's drawn. Although fishing communities have lived here for centuries, it's an inhospitable environment for humans: a Siberian wind howls all winter long, while in summer the area is inundated with mosquitoes. If you just want to take a trip down to the sea and back, **Sfântu Gheorghe** is probably the best choice; it's prettier than Sulina, has a more tranquil beach, and is within easy reach of several good birdwatching spots. **Sulina** is more crowded and built-up, but richer in historical associations.

GETTING AROUND   THE DANUBE DELTA

By ferry NAVROM-Delta (ⓦnavromdelta.ro) operates regular ferries (Nava Clasica) from Tulcea (see opposite), the jumping-off point for journeys into the heart of the Delta. The ticket office (open sailing days only 11am–1.30pm) is in the Gara Fluviala on the waterfront; tickets can only be bought on the day of travel and cost €10–12. There's a 30kg baggage limit and departures are always 1.30pm. Note that the summer schedule runs May–Sept and winter schedule Oct–April.

Destinations Periprava (summer Mon, Tues & Fri, also stopping at Chilia Veche, returning Tues, Wed & Sun at 6am; winter Fri, returning Sun; 5hr 30min); Sfântu Gheorghe (summer Wed, Thurs, Fri & Sat, also stopping at Mahmudia, returning Mon, Thurs, Fri & Sun at 7am; winter Wed returning Thurs; 4hr 30min); Sulina (summer Mon, Wed,

Highlights

❶ **Birdlife in the Delta** Even visitors without a special interest in winged fauna will be taken aback by the abundance and diversity of birdlife on view in the Danube Delta. See page 350

❷ **Fresh fish** All over the Delta, meals consist of the day's haul: carp, pike or catfish, usually served with juicy tomatoes from local gardens. See page 354

❸ **Sfântu Gheorghe** This cluster of brightly painted houses of mud and reed is one of the prettiest of the Delta's fishing villages. See page 354

❹ **Halmyris** The ancient Roman city of Halmyris is an archeological work in progress

that recently saw the discovery of the remains of legendary martyrs Epictet and Astion. See page 355

❺ **Constanţa** Romania's principal port is rich in historical associations, and offers an attractive mix of places to stay and eat. See page 359

❻ **Mamaia** The epicentre of Black Sea tourism, brash Mamaia might not be sophisticated, but it has fine beaches and vigorous nightlife. See page 364

❼ **Vama Veche** This charming small retreat on the Bulgarian border remains the most untouched and free-spirited of the Black Sea resorts. See page 372

HIGHLIGHTS ARE MARKED ON THE MAP ON PAGE 344

Fri & Sat, also stopping at Maliuc and Crişan, returning Tues, Thurs, Sat & Sun at 7am; winter Mon, Wed & Fri, returning Tues, Thurs, Sat & Sun; 4hr 30min).

By catamaran NAVROM-Delta also operates a pair of fast catamarans, *Delta Expres 1* and *2*, which traverse all three branches of the Delta, and depart at 1.30pm. Tickets are priced at €13–15.

Destinations Periprava (year round Wed, returning Thurs at 6am; 3hr); Sfântu Gheorghe (summer Mon & Sat, returning Tues & Sun at 7am; winter Mon & Fri, returning Tues & Sun; 3hr); Sulina (summer Tues, Thurs & Sun, returning Mon, Wed & Fri at 7am; winter Thurs & Sat, returning Mon & Fri; 2hr).

By hydrofoil There's also the privately run Nava Rapida Diana hydrofoil (☏ 0737 259337, ⩊ navarapidadiana.ro), a business-like craft with opaque windows. Tickets cost €16.

Destinations Sulina (year round 2 daily at 9.30am & 1pm, returning at 6.50am & 11.30am; 90min).

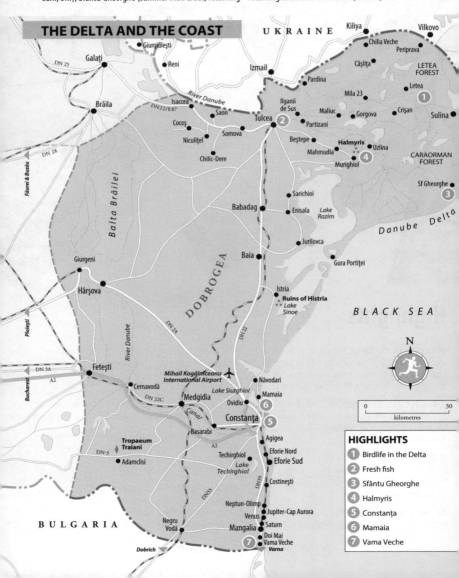

THE DELTA AND THE COAST

HIGHLIGHTS
1. Birdlife in the Delta
2. Fresh fish
3. Sfântu Gheorghe
4. Halmyris
5. Constanţa
6. Mamaia
7. Vama Veche

TULCEA FESTIVALS

Tulcea is busiest in August, when its two main festivals take place, namely the **International Folklore Festival**, a week-long jamboree of music, dance and colourfully patterned costumes taking place at the beginning of the month, and on the last weekend, the wonderfully entertaining **Rowmania Fest**, in which competitors participate in river races on *canotca*, specially crafted wooden boats (a cross between a canoe and a dinghy) set against a backdrop of live music, and food and drink along the promenade.

Tulcea

Clustered around the south bank of a bend in the Danube, **TULCEA** has been tagged the "Threshold of the Delta" ever since ancient Greek traders established a **port** here. Its maritime significance was slight until the closing stages of the period of Ottoman domination (1420–1878), when other powers suddenly perceived it as commercially and strategically important. Nowadays, the outskirts of the town are heavily industrialized, and the port is too shallow for large modern freighters, but it's still the chief access point for passenger vessels entering the Delta, which is why most people end up here. Otherwise, the largely systematized, hence mostly uninspiring, town centre has enough attractions to fill a few hours, not least a cluster of enjoyable museums around Piaţa Republicii. Moreover, there's plenty of accommodation here should you wish to stay before pushing on into the Delta; note that ferries to the Delta's three channels all depart at 1.30pm (see page 342).

Centrul Muzeul Ecoturistic Delta Dunării

Str. 14 Noiembrie 1 • Tues–Sun 9am–6pm • €4 • ☎ 0340 105 562, ⓦ icemtl.ro

With its extensive use of interactive maps and some thoughtfully presented dioramas, the bulk of the **Centrul Muzeul Ecoturistic Delta Dunării** (Danube Delta Ecotourism Museum Centre) is given over to the formation and evolution – both natural and man-made – of the Biosphere Reserve. Among the many fascinating items on display is a *Gheţărie*, a subterranean ice-house made of reeds which was traditionally used in winter months for the storing of fish. The highlight of the museum, however, is the basement aquarium, featuring local aquatic species – including some magnificent specimens of eel, catfish and sturgeon – as well as Whitetip Reef and Port Jackson sharks, and a smaller collection of tropical fish.

Muzeul de Etnografie şi Artă Populară

Str. 9 Mai 2 • Tues–Sun 9am–5pm • €1.50 • ☎ 0240 516 204, ⓦ icemtl.ro

Housed in a former bank building, the modest little **Muzeul de Etnografie şi Artă Populară** (Museum of Ethnography and Folk Art) has displays on the multifarious groups that have long inhabited the region; most of the minority groups are represented, such as the Lipovani, Russians and Tartars, courtesy of some lovely items, not least a terrifically colourful assemblage of decorative woven fabrics. In a large L-shaped barn to the rear of the building is a sizeable collection of equipment and tools representing the various crafts and trades that have long been prominent in Dobrogea, not least the agricultural and viticultural industries.

Muzeul de Artă

Str. G. Antipa 2 • Tues–Sun 9am–5pm • €2.50 • ☎ 0240 513 249, ⓦ icemtl.ro

Built by Ismail Pasha in 1870, the **Muzeul de Artă** (Art Museum) houses a fine collection of paintings, including Impressionistic female nudes by Pallady, a couple of offerings from Aman, and the obligatory contribution from Grigorescu, including an unusually vibrant *Peasant Woman on the Road*. Refreshingly though, Delta landscapes dominate proceedings, with evocative works by local boy Gheorghe Sârbu (*Port Tulcea*) and Stavru Tarasov (*Landscape in Danube Delta*), while you'll also see Igolesco's

7

Balchik, a depiction of the thriving artistic community in southern Dobrogea, a village so loved by Queen Marie that she asked for her heart to be buried there. When the area was handed over to Bulgaria, the queen's heart was brought back in a casket that now rests in the National History Museum in Bucharest (see page 52). There's also a selection of avant-garde works, including the country's best collection of paintings by the Romanian Surrealist Victor Brauner (1903–66), and a few pieces by the renowned sculptor Frederic Storck (see page 54).

Muzeul de Istorie şi Arheologie and around

Str. Gloriei • Tues–Sun: May–Oct 9am–5pm; Nov–April 8am–4pm • €1 • ☏ 0240 513 626

Although it's a bit of trek to get to, the **Muzeul de Istorie şi Arheologie** (Museum of History and Archeology) offers up one of the most absorbing archeological collections anywhere in the country. Among the highlights is a cache of treasure found inside a fourth-century incineration grave at Enisala (see page 356) – including bronze mirrors and bone tools, and a number of beautifully painted *skyphos* (small, double-handed wine pitchers) and *askos* (miniature, kettle-like clay vessels). Even more exquisite is the stash of wood-and-bone carved jewellery (buckles, combs, hair pins and necklaces), and ceramic game pieces (chips and die). There's a superb numismatic collection too, the most impressive of which is the so-called Uzum Baiir hoard, comprising some 21,000 Tatar dirhams and seventy silver bars. Next to the museum is the **Parcul Monumentului Independenţei**, where you'll find an **obelisk** to the dead of the 1877–78 war and some **Roman remains**. There are some fantastic views of the Danube from up here.

ARRIVAL AND DEPARTURE   TULCEA

By train Tulcea's futuristic train station is on Str. Portului, from where it's a short walk along the waterfront to the centre. To get to either Bucharest or Constanţa, you'll need to change at Medgidia, a painfully slow journey in itself.
Destinations Medgidia (2 daily; 3hr 10min).

By bus The bus station is also on Str. Portului, but a few paces closer to the centre. Travelling onwards to Brăila and

Galaţi in Moldavia, you'll have to take a bus or maxitaxi from Smârdan and I.C. Brătianu respectively, from where ferries shuttle back and forth across the Danube.
Destinations Brăila (5 daily; 2hr 20min); Bucharest (8 daily; 4hr 30min); Cocoş monastery (4 daily; 50min); Constanţa (every 30–45min; 2hr 10min); Galaţi (15 daily; 1hr 30min); Iaşi (1 daily; 6hr 40min); Jurilovca (1 daily; 1hr 30min);

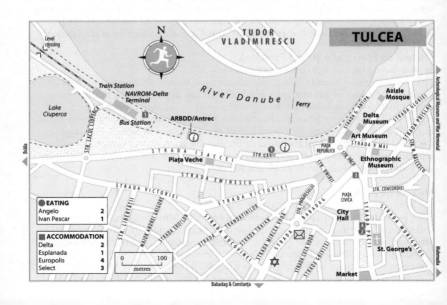

DELTA TOURS

A host of agencies offer **day-trips** into the Delta – typically up the Sulina channel to Crişan and Mila 23 – for around €40–45 per person, including a fish lunch; outfits worth trying are Amatour (☎ 0744 320 394, ⓦ amatour.ro), on the waterfront near the *Delta* hotel (see opposite), which itself runs trips (☎ 0240 514 720, ⓦ hoteldelta.eu). There's also Escape Travel (☎ 0240 516 649 or ☎ 0743 609 626, ⓦ godanubedelta.com), inside the *Europolis* hotel (see opposite). Most of these agencies also offer two-, three- and four-day trips. Smaller and less formal outfits along the Tulcea waterfront charge anywhere between €20 and €50 per group per hour, depending on the size of the boat.

Most travel agencies in Tulcea also offer packages to **floating hotels** (*hotel plutitoare*) in the heart of the Delta, though these are often aimed at groups; expect to pay around €75 per night, including all meals.

Mahmudia (4 daily; 40min–1hr); Murighiol (12 daily; 50min).

By ferry The NAVROM-Delta ferry terminal (Gara Fluviala; tickets daily 11am–1.30pm; ☎ 0240 519 008, ⓦ navromdelta.ro) is located next to the bus station on Str.

Portului. Further along the waterfront, ferries (every 15min from dawn to dusk; €1) shuttle across the river to the largely Russian suburb of Tudor Vladimirescu, where there's a sandy bank for sunbathing.

INFORMATION

Tourist information The tourist office is on the waterfront at Str. Gării 26 (Mon–Fri 8am–4pm; ☎ 0240 519 130, ⓔ tourisminfo_tulcea@yahoo.com), though it actually faces Str. Portului, next to the Port Captain's headquarters (Căpitănia Portului).

Danube Delta Biosphere Reserve Administration (ARBDD) Big, blue-glass-fronted building located between the ferry terminal and the tourist office at Str. Portului 34A (Mon–Thurs 8am–4.30pm, Fri 8am–2pm; ☎ 0240 518

945, ⓦ ddbra.ro). This is the place to come for everything pertaining to travel within the Delta; they've got good maps of the region, as well as information on accommodation, trips and permits. Indeed, this is the only place where you can obtain permits, if required. In the same building you'll also find the Antrec office (Mon–Fri 8am–5pm, Sat & Sun 9am–4pm; ☎ 0755 360 463, ⓦ antrec.ro), where you can make reservations for homestay and pension accommodation in the Delta.

ACCOMMODATION

Delta Str. Isaccei 2 ☎ 0240 514 720, ⓦ hoteldelta. eu; map p.346. Sprawling place overlooking the Danube, which has both three- and four-star rooms, though it's worth paying the minimal extra for the infinitely more polished four-star ones; either way, try to bag a room with a river view. There's an indoor pool, too. **€70**

Esplanada Str. Portului 1 ☎ 0240 506 607, ⓦ hotelesplanada.ro; map p.346. In a plum location on the waterfront, opposite the ferry departure point, this large, impressive hotel has good-sized, airy and colourfully decorated rooms, all with tea- and coffee-making facilities.

Try and bag one of the river-facing rooms, which are the same price as the street-facing ones. **€85**

Europolis Str. Păcii 20 ☎ 0240 512 443, ⓦ europolis.ro; map p.346. Slightly bland and colourless hotel just south of Piaţa Civică, but there's a range of different rooms available, including some cheaper ones without bathroom. **€35**

Select Piaţa Civică 1 ☎ 0240 506 180, ⓦ calypsosrl.ro; map p.346. Unmissable bright red building concealing solid, as opposed to inspiring, rooms, though they're decently sized with a/c and some bathrooms have big corner tubs. Breakfast €5. **€40**

EATING

Angelo Str. Păcii 20 ☎ 0240 511 717; map p.346. Next door to the *Europolis* hotel (see above), this shiny *cofetariă* does the job for all things sweet and sticky with its prodigious selection of cakes and pastries; alternatively grab an ice cream and sit in the park opposite. Daily 8.30am–9pm.

Ivan Pescar Str. Gării 26, though it actually faces the waterfront on Str. Portului ☎ 0240 515 861; map p.346. This fabulous fish bar is Tulcea's one credible restaurant,

its short menu offering the likes of roasted Black Sea whelks, mussels in white wine, and carp with sauerkraut, all of which are served in oval clay dishes; the restaurant itself, with its big bay windows and fetching aquatic-blue furnishings, looks terrific. Tues–Sun 1–10pm.

7

DELTA ESSENTIALS

To enter the **Danube Delta Biosphere Reserve (RBDD)**, you need a **permit**, which gives access to everywhere except the strictly protected reserves, of which there are twenty. If you're taking a tour, this will be handled by the company; independent travellers can get permits (€1.50/day, €4/week) from the ARBDD information centre in Tulcea (see page 347). The ARBDD recommends electric boats and a 10km/hr speed limit, both generally ignored. Expensive organized tours are limited to seven routes; if you're planning to explore further, take a compass and a detailed **map** – the best is the *Danube Delta in Europe* map (free from the ARBDD centre). Here, you can also pick up the excellent *Danube Delta Biosphere Reserve Visitor Guide*, a detailed handbook with maps at the back. There are very few **hotels** in the Delta, though this is compensated for by plentiful **resort complexes** and **pensions** (most open May–Sept). Alternatively, you can try cheaper **B&B** accommodation in a **private home**. Either way, Antrec, in Tulcea, should be able to help you find some form of accommodation (see page 347). **Camping** is possible in Crişan, Maliuc, Murighiol, Partizani, Sulina, Sfântu Gheorghe and on the shore of Lake Roşu, but buy **essential supplies** like canned food, fruit and cheese in Tulcea; candles and mosquito repellent are also useful. Most Delta villages have a bakery, but fresh bread sells quickly. Wherever you stay, expect generous fish dinners and fresh salads; most pensions offer full board – indeed, you are most likely to eat here as restaurants are few and far between.

Braţul Chilia

The **Chilia arm** of the river (Braţul Chilia), which branches off upstream from Tulcea and marks the border with Ukraine, carries more than half of the Danube's water, but very little tourist traffic, mainly because boats will only carry you as far as Periprava (100km from Tulcea but still 30km from the Black Sea), where there's a total lack of tourist facilities.

Chilia Veche

In the days when the entire Delta was part of Moldavia, **CHILIA VECHE**, 35km from Periprava, was merely a suburb of Chilia (now Ukrainian Kiliya) across the river. When the town repelled a Turkish invasion in 1476, Chilia was just 5km from the coast – today, it's 40km. Chilia takes its name from the time when it was a Greek colony called Achillea, after which time it became a major port, linking Europe with the Orient.

INFORMATION   **CHILIA VECHE**

Tourist information The ARBDD's information centre is right on the waterfront (May–Oct Tues–Fri 8am–4pm, Sat 8am–noon; Nov–April Mon–Fri 8am–4pm; ☎0759 180 725, ⓦ ddbra.ro).

ACCOMMODATION

Limanul Resort Str. Dunarii 97 ☎0730 909 035, ⓦ limanul.com. Wonderfully relaxing retreat offering twelve beautifully coloured, predominantly wood-furnished rooms, with custom-made furnishings and traditional rugs; some have their own little terrace. There's a lovely pool, as well as bikes and canoes for rent, plus regular barbecues in the pretty garden. €65

Pensiunea Vital 200m south of Limanul Resort ☎0744 276 435, ⓦ vital-chiliaveche.ro. Somewhat more basic, but nevertheless very hospitable, this agreeable pension has a mix of accommodation in the house itself and in neighbouring wooden huts; there's also a fancy outdoor swimming pool on site. Breakfast is extra (€4) while other meals are available. Boat rental, hunting and fishing trips are also possible. Huts €18, pension €25

Lacul Roşca, Periprava, Pădurea Letea and Ceatalchioi

Lacul Roşca (Lake Rosca), roughly 10km south of Babina on the Cernovca tributary between Chilia Veche and Periprava, is one of the larger strictly protected reserves, harbouring geese, egrets, storks and Europe's largest **white pelican colony**; it's estimated that some three thousand breeding pairs arrive here in early April, staying until

October or early November. Immediately to the east is **PERIPRAVA**, a largely Lipovani village and the site of a notorious labour camp during the communist regime of Gheorghe Gheorghiu-Dej, when prisoners would spend summers making dams to prevent flooding and the winters transporting wood from **Pădurea Letea** (Letea Forest) to the south; another protected zone, this is a richly forested area of white and black poplar, elm, ash and oaks tangled with lianas, and provides a haven for falcons, white-tailed eagles, boar and wildcats. Surrounding the forest are **sand dunes** inhabited by tortoises, lizards and the horned viper.

One way of seeing a little of the Brațul Chilia route is to travel as far as **Ceatalchioi**, 20km north of Tulcea, where the reeds (*stuf*) that are used to build Delta houses are gathered in winter, when it's possible to drive tractors on the ice. Not far beyond Ceatalchioi (due north as the river flows), boats pass **Izmail**, the main Ukrainian city in the Delta, whose bloody recapture from the Turks in 1790 is described in Byron's *Don Juan*.

7

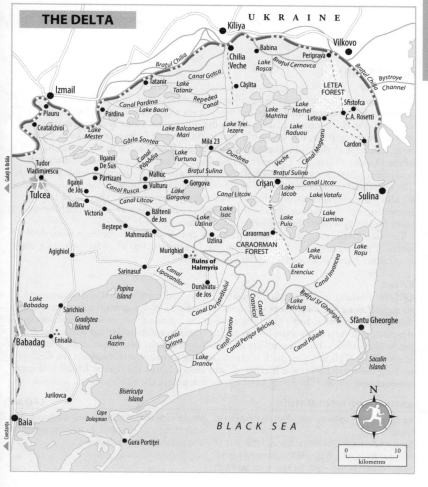

DELTA WILDLIFE

The Danube Delta is a paradise for **wildlife**, and after years of environmental neglect culminating in Ceauşescu's plan to drain the Delta for agricultural use, it was declared a **Biosphere Reserve** in 1990, with over 500 square kilometres strictly protected, and a UNESCO World Heritage Site the following year. The reserve is also a member of DANUBEPARKS, a network of seventeen protected areas along the length of the Danube, which was formed in 2009.

The area is particularly important for **birds**, which pass through during the spring and autumn migrations, or come from Siberia to winter here or from Africa to breed in summer. Besides herons, glossy ibis, golden eagles, avocets, shelduck and other Mediterranean breeds, the Delta is visited by reed buntings, white-tailed eagles and various European songbirds, as well as whooper swans, arctic grebes and half-snipes from Siberia, saker falcons from Mongolia, and egrets, mute swans and mandarin ducks from China. Its lakes support Europe's largest colonies of pelicans, which come from Africa to breed. The best time to see birds is from April to early June (the latter being the wettest month of the year), and September. Some 135 species of **fish** have also been catalogued in the Delta, with healthy stocks of carp and pike, as well as a resurgence in sturgeon; the best time to fish is September and October. The Delta is also home to otters, mink, boars, wolves and other **animals**, while at night streets in the Delta villages are alive with frogs, beetles and hawk moths.

Braţul Sulina

Between 1862 and 1902, the **Sulina arm** of the river (Braţul Sulina) was shortened from 84km to 63km by the digging of long straight sections, now paralleled by a communist-era power line. Distances from the sea were marked in **nautical miles**, as opposed to the kilometres later used on the other arms. Constant dredging and groynes running 10km out to sea still enable 7000-tonne freighters to take this route from Tulcea; with the additional tourist traffic, this is the busiest and least serene of the Danube's branches. However, it does have a tourist infrastructure and several settlements that offer a fair chance of renting boats to visit a variety of wildlife habitats. The revitalized town of **Sulina** itself is now the Delta's most popular tourist destination; it's also the most built-up, and the only one with streets and cars. There are a few interesting sights in Sulina, but the fishing villages along the way make much better bases for seeing wildlife and exploring the wetlands.

Travellers attempting to explore the Delta **by canoe** will face turbulence from the wakes of passing ships on the main waterway, but beyond **Ilganii de Sus** you can escape into calmer backwaters leading to the inland lakes.

Crişan

CRIŞAN, a fishing settlement that consists of a single dirt path, lined with houses and straggling along the south bank of the shoreline for 7km, is the main tourist centre in this part of the Delta, and a good place to see the region's most common bird species; the ditch that runs behind the houses shelters herons, egrets and other waders, and you're likely to find hoopoes, rollers and goldfinches in the brushland at the west end of the village. Pelicans glide high overhead in long formations throughout the day, making their way from Lake Merhei to Lake Iacob. Across the river at Mila 13, there is a **monument** unveiled by Carol I in 1894 to inaugurate the new short-cut sections.

ARRIVAL AND INFORMATION   CRIŞAN

By ferry Ferries stop on the south bank, in the centre of Crişan.

Tourist information On the north bank, before Mila 14 near the *Lebăda* hotel, is the ARBDD's information centre (May–Oct Tues–Fri 8am–4pm, Sat 8am–noon; Nov–April Mon–Fri 8am–4pm; ☎0728 281 466, ⊛ddbra.ro), with plenty of materials and advice on travelling around the Delta, plus an excellent viewing tower.

ACCOMMODATION

Delta Boutique and Carmen Resort Str. Principală 195 ☎0723 315 021, ⓦdeltaboutique.ro. Stunning wood-clad waterfront lodge comprising two luxury guest houses (*Delta Boutique* and *Carmen Silva*); twenty-one supremely comfortable, oak-furnished rooms are complemented by a beautiful pool, hot-tub and sauna as well as a games room, pool bar and restaurant. Boat, bike and canoe rental available, as well as transfers and local excursions. **€120**

Doi Căpitani On the DC2, 300m east of Delta Boutique and Carmen Resort ☎0755 116 652, ⓦpensiunedeltadunarii.ro. Gorgeous, family-run hotel with whitewashed walls and thatched roofing set around a sparkling little pool. The ten split-level rooms are thoughtfully designed, with wicker framed beds and furnishings, blue-mosaic tiled bathrooms and wooden balconies. The restaurant, meanwhile, is the best place to eat in the village, and there's a fabulous winery here too. **€69**

Sunrise Str Babadag 140 ☎0748 870 412, ⓦhotelsunrise.ro. A decent third option after *Delta* and *Doi Căpitani*, this largish complex offers simple, agreeable rooms in the hotel itself as well as bungalows right on the waterfront. Pool, playground, playroom and restaurant round things off. Bungalow **€68**, hotel **€62**

Pădurea Caraorman

South of Crişan, the forest of **Pădurea Caraorman** (Caraorman Forest), now a strict reserve, is the best area of dunes in the Delta, striped with unusual linear dunes of ancient oaks, poplar, ash and willow, and protecting wildlife such as Ural owls, white-tailed eagles, kestrels, wildcats, boars and wolves. The dyke that runs south from Crişan leads to a dead end; to get to the forest, catch the boat that meets ferries at Crişan to take passengers to the predominantly Ukrainian village of **CARAORMAN**. Half a dozen unfinished skeletal apartment blocks are testament to plans, under Ceauşescu, to remove the dunes en masse; the 1989 revolution intervened.

Letea, C.A. Rosetti and Sfistofca

Three remote and very different settlements lie to the north of Crişan, on the south side of the Letea forest: **LETEA**, a village of Lipovani/Ukrainian fisherfolk, where there's a rangers' house and birdwatching tower; neighbouring **C.A. ROSETTI**, home to Romanian cattle breeders and the Delta's last windmill; and **SFISTOFCA**, an even smaller Lipovani village. You may get a room in these places on the spot, but it's best to check with the ARBDD or Antrec in Tulcea (see page 347) before setting out. The **Letea forest**, just north of Rosetti and Letea, is strictly off-limits, but the **Sfistofca forest**, to the south, is almost as good, a maze of trees up to two hundred years old, tangled with lianas and orchids.

Sulina

Ever since it was recorded as a port by a Byzantine scribe in 950, **SULINA** has depended on shipping. Genoese vessels used to call here during the fourteenth century, while throughout the Ottoman period it was not so much a trading port as a nest of pirates who preyed on traffic in the Black Sea. Devastated during the Crimean War – only the church and lighthouse survived after the British, driving out the Russians, burned the place down – Sulina was rebuilt and went on to prosper as the headquarters of the

7

THE LIPOVANI

Descendants of the Old Believers who left Russia around 1772 to avoid religious persecution, the **Lipovani** (identifiable by their blond hair, blue eyes and, among the men, beards) were once dispersed all over the Delta but are now found only at Periprava, Mila 23, Mahmudia and Letea, as well as Jurilovca and Sarichioi on Lake Razim.

Adapting to their environment, the Lipovani became skilled **fishermen** and gardeners, speaking a Russian dialect among themselves but equally fluent in Romanian. Since you're likely to rely on Lipovani boatmen to guide you through the confusing side channels (*gârla*), smokers should be prepared for their fundamentalist abhorrence of the "Devil's weed", tobacco; their consumption of vodka, however, is legendary.

European Commission of the Danube, established in 1856 to regulate free passage along the waterway. In 1900 it became a free port, and its freewheeling multinational life was captured in the novel *Europolis* by Jean Bart (pseudonym of the Romanian sea captain Eugeniu Botez, 1874–1933). Within a decade, however, larger vessels and worldwide recession had emptied Sulina, so that by 1940 the writer John Lehmann found "a hopeless, sinking feeling" in a place where "people get stranded, feel themselves abandoned by civilization, take to drink, and waste into a half-animal existence". Today, expensive annual dredging is required to enable even small-capacity ships to enter, while larger freighters can now bypass the Delta altogether by taking the Danube–Black Sea Canal. Tourism is succeeding where trade failed, and, drawn by the long sandy beach 2km from the port, a small but growing contingent of Romanians has chosen Sulina as an alternative to the more established resorts further south. There's plentiful accommodation here, and a few bars, though the principal evening activity is strolling the promenade eating ice cream.

Farul Vechi

Str. II 15 • Tues–Sun: May–Sept 10am–6pm; Oct–April 8am–4pm • €2

A taste of the ambience of Sulina's golden days survives in the nineteenth-century houses along the waterfront, and at the **Farul Vechi** (Old Lighthouse), two blocks south of the ferry landing; built in 1870 by the Ottomans, it is now a history museum, with a room dedicated to Jean Bart and the conductor George Georgescu (born in Sulina in 1887), and another to the European Commission of the Danube.

Cemetery and beach

Some 500m southeast of the Old Lighthouse, between the town and the sea, is the **cemetery**, which provides an evocative record of all the nationalities who lived and died here in the town's days as a free port. Greeks dominated business, but there was also a large British contingent, some now resting beneath dignified Victorian tombstones in the Anglican plot, directly behind the chapel. Like so much of the Delta, the cemetery is full of birds – this is one of the best places to see hoopoes, and possibly cuckoos and orioles. From the cemetery, it's a 1km walk to the **beach** (maxitaxis also run this route). Also look for two **churches** from the nineteenth century: the Greek Church of St Nicholas on the waterfront, and the Russian church near the west end of town.

INFORMATION
SULINA

Tourist information The ARBDD information centre is near the dock in the centre of town on Str. I (May–Oct Tues–Fri 8am–3pm, Sat & Sun 8–11am; ☎ 0728 281 467, ⓦ ddbra.ro).

ACCOMMODATION

Complex Class Sulina Str. VI 72 ☎ 0749 111 455, ⓦ complex-class-sulina.ro. The unattractive, slightly unwieldy name doesn't particularly inspire, but this hostel-like pension suffices for a cheap stay, with its mix of cheap two- and three-bedded rooms. Here too are some attractive gardens, a courtyard with pool and a kids playground. €50

Pensiunea Casa Coral Str. I 195 ☎ 0742 974 016, ⓦ casacoralblog.wordpress.com. Attractively sited waterfront pension with decent, if a little old-fashioned, rooms, including triples; it does also harbour one of the settlement's better restaurants. €40

Pensiunea Delta Miraj Str. I 21 ☎ 0744 368 238, ⓦ pensiunedelta-sulina.ro. West of the village centre, this is the most appealing (though overpriced) pension in the village, its nineteen modernish rooms complemented by a good restaurant and swimming pool. €65

Braţul Sfântu Gheorghe

The Delta's oldest, most winding arm, **Braţul Sfântu Gheorghe**, is the least used by freighters and fishing boats; it's wider but shallower than the Sulina arm. It carries a fair amount of tourist traffic and, unlike other parts of the Delta, some of its settlements can be reached by bus from Tulcea. If you plan to visit these, it's easiest to go direct to

Sfântu Gheorghe, then head by boat to **Murighiol**, from where you can make a boat trip to the fishing village of **Uzlina** or visit the ruins of **Halmyris**. There's plenty of parking in Murighiol; if you've come by car, it's better to leave it there rather than in Tulcea.

Sfântu Gheorghe

SFÂNTU GHEORGHE, 75km downriver from Murighiol, is a small village of brightly painted Lipovani and Ukrainian cottages that has subsisted on fishing since the fourteenth century. Most prized is the **sturgeon**, whose eggs, *icre negre* or black caviar, once drew thousands of Romanian tourists here on shopping trips. However, a combination of overfishing and loss of suitable habitat has led to a sharp decline in numbers, and there is now a ban in place on sturgeon fishing, though illegal activity does still occur. The **reed and mud houses**, most of which support colonies of swallows, are the main attraction of the village itself, but most tourists come for the relatively untouched **beach** (stretching 38km north to Sulina) or to make trips into the surrounding **marshes**. A large tractor, one of the two or three motorized land vehicles in the village, carries tourists the 2km to and from the beach in a trailer, departing every hour or so from the centre – the schedule should be posted on one of the information boards near the main square. These days, the village is best known for hosting the fabulous **Anonimul Film Festival** (w festival-anonimul.ro) in early August, a week-long celebration of independent films from around the world, with screenings at the *Green Village* (see below).

ACCOMMODATION AND EATING   **SFÂNTU GHEORGHE**

There are stacks of pensions in the village, as well as other villagers offering private **accommodation**, many of whom are likely to meet you at the ferry upon arrival.

Casa Galbena Str. Principală ☏ 0744 374 951, w ineditdelta.ro. Otherwise known as the Yellow House, this warm little pension has ten rooms, some of which have shared bathroom facilities; the hosts offer delicious lunches and dinners. **€26**

Green Dolphin Camping 700m east on the road to the beach ☏ 0241 487 093, w dolphincamping.ro. A large part of the *Green Village* is given over to *Green Dolphin Camping*, a vast site with excellent amenities (indoor and outdoor showers, volleyball and football, restaurant and outdoor bar), plus fifty or so simple but neat wooden cabins, all sleeping two, though shower facilities are shared with campers. The site is also the setting for the Anonimul Film Festival (see above). Camping **€6.50**, cabin **€20**

Green Village 700m east on the road to the beach ☏ 0241 487 093, w greenvillage.ro. This smart resort offers a range of high-class villas accommodating a mix of beautifully finished rooms and apartments fashioned from local materials and all with terrace views, either to the Danube or the Black Sea. Outdoor pool, organic garden, restaurant, beer house and a kids club are just some of the first-rate facilities. **€75**

Lesser Sacalin Island and Greater Sacalin Island

During July and August, the Sfântu Gheorghe tractor (see above) makes occasional day excursions to **Sulina** (1hr 30min) – look for a sign in the town centre or ask around if you're interested. Otherwise you can take an informal **boat trip** (just ask around and negotiate with the fishermen) north to **Lake Roșu**, or south down the Gârla de Mijloc canal to **Lesser Sacalin Island** (Insula Sacalinu Mic) at the river's mouth, which is inhabited by all three species of marsh tern, stilts, ibis and other waders, as well as goosanders, red-breasted geese and goldeneyes. This is one of the oldest parts of the Delta and a strictly protected reserve, so boats are not allowed to moor: to get to the beach on the island, you'll have to wade through the ankle-deep mud at the canal's end. Depending on the wind, the trip takes an hour or more; the motorboat is faster but, at €10 per hour, at least twice as expensive. Look for kingfishers along the way. Further south still is **Greater Sacalin Island** (Insula Sacalinu Mare), while to the west, on Lake Lejai and near the Crasnicol sand bank, is the remote area where the Delta's three hundred or so Dalmatian pelicans breed. The trip to **Lacul Roșu** (Pink Lake) is longer than that to Lesser Sacalin Island, but you're likely to see white pelicans.

Murighiol and Halmyris

The main settlement en route to Tulcea is **MURIGHIOL**, which, though connected to the outside world by road as well as water, still has some of the isolated feeling of an interior Delta village. Murighiol has its natural attractions – namely black-winged stilts, red- and black-necked grebe, Kentish plover, avocets, red-crested pochards and Romania's only colony of Mediterranean gulls, all nesting around the late-freezing **salt lakes** (Sărături Murighiol) nearby, but the principal reason to come here is to visit the ruin at **Halmyris** or the fishing village of **Uzlina**. There are dozens of places around the village offering boat trips.

The ruins

Two kilometres out from Murighiol, on the road to Dunavatu de Jos, lies the ruined Roman city of **HALMYRIS**. One of the most important ancient sites in Romania, Halmyris was continuously inhabited from the sixth century BC to the seventh century AD, when a combination of marauding barbarians, climatic changes and dwindling imperial support led to its demise. Originally a small seafront fort – in ancient times, a Danube channel met the Black Sea only a few hundred metres to the east – it grew in size and importance until it became the permanent home to Roman troops and a station for the Danube fleet, *Classis Flavia Moesica*, serving as a stopping point on the road that connected the major Roman settlements of the Delta.

Today, Halmyris is best known for the **tomb of Epictet and Astion**, two Christians from Asia Minor who were tortured and executed here on July 8, 290, after refusing to renounce Christianity, thus becoming the earliest Romanian martyrs (and earning a place on the Romanian Orthodox calendar). One of their judges was said to have been converted by the resolve with which Epictet and Astion met their fates, and to have secretly buried their remains, which were then kept hidden until the conversion of Constantine, when they were interred in Halmyris's **basilica**. The story seemed to be the stuff of legend until 2001, when a **crypt** containing two skeletons was discovered beneath the basilica's altar, along with a **fresco** bearing the name "Astion".

In addition to the basilica and the crypt, the two-hectare site also features extensive remains of an L-shaped private **bathhouse**. The Western Gate, which dates from the sixth century AD, was constructed largely of stones carved with honorary inscriptions that had in earlier times adorned the homes of the town's more prominent citizens. Much of Halmyris, as well as the surrounding cornfields that cover its harbour, remains unexcavated (digging only began here in 1981), and its greatest attraction is not the ruins themselves, or the tombs of Epictet and Astion, but the chance to see an ancient city still in the process of being uncovered.

ARRIVAL AND DEPARTURE

MURIGHIOL

By bus Buses run to and from Tulcea, on a circular route via either Mahmudia or Sarinasuf.
Destinations Tulcea (12 daily; 50min).
By ferry Ferries from Tulcea to Sfântu Gheorghe call at Mahmudia, some 10km back down the river. However, you will find numerous boatmen touting for business down by the landing stage, which is 5km northeast of the centre of the village, near the *Puflene Resort*; follow the forested road that begins just before here, and it's around 1.5km further on.

ACCOMMODATION

Camping Lac Murighiol Str. Mahmudiei 10 ☏ 0744 175 581, ⊕ campinglacmurighiol.ro. Located 200m along from *Pensiunea La Tavi*, this small but neat and well-kept private campsite comes with a modern shower block and laundry. Closed Oct–April. **€5**

Pensiunea La Tavi Str. larga 19 ☏ 0742 058 447, ⊕ pensiunealatavi.ro. Almost the first house at the entrance to the village (coming from Tulcea), this is not a pension at all but instead nine handsomely constructed and well-equipped two-bed huts pitched among trim lawns; there's a kitchen available for guest use. The bus from Tulcea can set you down right outside. **€22**

Puflene Resort Str. Portului 7 ☏ 0241 487 080. Nestled in between Lake Murighiol and the Bratul Sfântu Gheorghe, some 2km east of the village, this sprawling resort offers a range of accommodation, with either lake or park views, alongside comprehensive sporting facilities (volleyball and tennis courts and an Olympic-size pool). **€78**

7

Uzlina, Dunavatu de Jos and Mahmudia

Murighiol is also the jumping-off point for the tiny fishing village of **UZLINA**, the site of the scientific centre of the Biosphere Reserve and the Cousteau Foundation. North of Uzlina, the Isac and Uzlina lakes are home to a protected **pelican colony**, which you can see from a respectful distance. Heading downstream, the new channel is edged by high levees, but the meanders of the old channel are tree-lined and populated by deer, boar, foxes, water snakes, black ibis and egrets. **Lake Belciug**, roughly halfway back towards Sfântu Gheorghe, is one of those least affected by algal blooms and deoxygenation, and retains the submerged vegetation once typical of the Delta, as well as a colony of glossy ibis.

To the southeast, 8km beyond Murighiol, the road ends at **DUNAVATU DE JOS**, on a channel between the Sfântu Gheorghe arm and Lake Razim. Ferries also call at **MAHMUDIA**, on the Tulcea road 7km west of Murighiol. Down by the landing stage, at the far end of the village, you'll find numerous fishermen offering boat trips.

ACCOMMODATION	DUNAVATU DE JOS AND MAHMUDIA
Casa Teo Str. Portului, Mahmudia ☎ 0240 545 550, ⓦ pensiuneacasateo.ro. A handsomely constructed wood- and white-stone building on the waterfront near the ferry landing stage, *Casa Teo* conceals a collection of thoughtfully designed rooms – lots of wood and exposed stone – and it's worth paying the minimal extra for a river-facing room. A useful place to stop if catching the 9am ferry back to Tulcea. Breakfast €5. **€46**	**Egreta** Str. Egretei, Dunavatu de Jos 7 ☎ 0742 828 831, ⓦ newhotelegreta.ro. At the very end of the village, near the landing stage, this accomplished hotel boasts sleek rooms with underfloor heating, and sparkling bathrooms with big walk-in showers; there's a lovely kidney-shaped pool, too. **€76**

Lake Razim

South of the Delta proper, **Lake Razim** is separated from the Black Sea by two long, tongue-like *grinds*. Like other parts of the Delta, Razim has been adversely affected by development: the western shores were reclaimed in 1969 for fish farming, and in 1974 a sluice at Gura Portiței cut the lake off from the sea, causing it to fill with fresh water, which has led to frequent algal blooms, deoxygenation and a steady decline in fish yields and biodiversity. It's still a good spot for birdwatchers, however, particularly in November and December, when the western shoreline is invaded by a million white-fronted and red-breasted geese from arctic Russia, which stay here and on Lake Sinoe just south until the reedbeds freeze. In the north of the lake, Popina island is now a closed reserve.

Enisala

A quiet, attractive village of reed-thatched cottages, **ENISALA** lies 8km east of Babadag, which is itself some 27km south of Tulcea.

Gospodăria Țărănească

Centre of the village • Mon–Fri 8am–4pm • €1

Gospodăria Țărănească is a traditional peasant home superbly preserved as a museum, and easily identified by its neatly thatched roof and red and blue trim. Indeed, this striking, sea-blue colour is typical of the Dobrogea region, and quite distinct from the slightly lighter blue hues traditionally associated with the Lipovani. The three earthen-floored rooms are adorned with brightly coloured tapestries and textiles, ceramics and rugs woven from Danube reeds. Completing the ensemble is a large barn packed with various agricultural and viticultural implements – including painted carts – a shed, corncrib and an outdoor kitchen.

Cetate Medievală

About 1km north of the village • April–Sept Tues–Sun 10am–6pm • €1.50

Commanding a superb spot atop a dry rocky outcrop overlooking Lake Razim is the **Cetate Medievală** (Medieval Fortress), built by Genoese merchants late in the thirteenth century at the behest of the Byzantine emperor, on the site of a seventh-century Byzantine fort. Taken by Sultan Mehmet I in 1417, it was held by the Ottomans until they abandoned it around the sixteenth century. The views out to the lake, and beyond to the Black Sea, are fantastic. This area is one of Europe's prime birdwatching sites, thanks to a mix of habitats: a vast area of reedbeds along the shoreline, stretching back to open land and the Babadag forest. You're likely to spot white-fronted and red-breasted geese, terns, waders, pelicans, herons and warblers. If you're coming from Tulcea, watch the left side of the road: shortly before passing the citadel, you'll see an apiary that supports a sizeable colony of bee-eaters.

Jurilovca and Gura Portiței

The tiny fishing village of **JURILOVCA** was founded by the Lipovani at the beginning of the nineteenth century, and it's one village where traditional customs remain strong; it still retains one of the coast's largest fishing communities.

From Jurilovca (where there's guarded parking; €1.50), boats (see below) sail to **GURA PORTIȚEI**, on a spit of land between Lake Razim and the sea. Before 1989, this was one of the few remote corners of Romania where it was possible to escape the Securitate for a week or two; today, it consists of a few Lipovani huts and, primarily, the *Gura Portiței Holiday Village* (see below). Both rowing and motor boats are available in addition to fishing and birdwatching excursions to the **Periteașca-Leahova reserve**, just north, where twenty thousand red-breasted geese (half the world's population) spend the winter. Continuing towards Constanța, you'll rejoin the main DN22 at the north end of **BAIA**, better known as **Hamangia**, site of Romania's most famous Neolithic finds.

ARRIVAL AND DEPARTURE

JURILOVCA AND GURA PORTITEI

By boat Regular boats cross from Jurilovca to Gura Portiței in summer (May–Sept daily at 9am, 2pm & 6pm; returning at noon, 4pm & 8pm; €13 return)

By bus There's one daily bus to Tulcea (1hr 30min).

ACCOMMODATION

Gura Portiței Holiday Village ☎ 0724 214 224, ⓦ guraportitei.ro. Large holiday village accommodating a variety of rooms in villas as well as wooden cabins (each with two beds and shared bathrooms) and space to camp. Closed Oct–April. Camping **€10**, cabin **€35**, double **€57**

Pension Anastasia Str. Portului 12, Jurilovca ☎ 0747 065 286, ⓦ anastasia-jurilovca.ro. Some 200m up the road from the harbour/port, this bright little six-room pension does the job for an overnight stay; all rooms are en suite, with TV and a/c, and while no breakfast is served, guests are free to use the kitchen facility. **€38**

Cetatea Histria

8km east of Istria (and 35km north of Constanța), on the shores of Lake Sinoe • Daily: May–Sept 9am–8pm; Oct–April 9am–5pm • €3.50 • A handful of maxitaxis a day run from Constanța as far as Istria village; from here you're quite likely to be successful in hitching a ride; the Istria train stop is on the DN22, too far west to be of use

Heading south from Babadag and Baia and turning left at Mihai Viteazul, you'll pass through the village of **Istria**, jumping-off point for **CETATEA HISTRIA** (ruined city of Histria), with its shattered Greek temples to diverse deities, as well as Roman baths and other Romano-Byzantine edifices. The **ruins** cover a fairly small area, despite the fact that this was long the most important of the ancient Greek settlements along the coast. It was founded in 657 BC, though none of the remains dates from before 300 BC. Histria's decline began soon after that, but it was inhabited until early in the seventh century AD, when the port was smothered in silt and the town abandoned after attacks by Avar-Slavic tribes.

The **museum**, in an ugly glass building next to the entrance, holds an exceptional hoard of Greek and Roman finds, the first of which were unearthed in 1914 by the eminent historian Vasile Pârvan; prominent among the display are dozens of pillars, altars and funereal stones (*stelae*), some beautifully sculpted marble friezes with reliefs of Greek deities (Apollo, Poseidon, Aphrodite and so on), superb Roman Corinthian capitals, terracotta statuettes and ceramics.

Another very good reason to head out this way if you have wheels is for the birdlife; this bleak but beautiful wilderness is one of Europe's best areas for birdwatching, with more than two hundred species making an appearance in the winter months.

The Dobrogea and the Danube–Black Sea Canal

The overland approaches to Constanţa cross one part or another of the bleak northern **Dobrogea**, a poor area where donkeys still haul metal-wheeled carts. While there's no reason to break your journey here, the changes wrought over the last forty years certainly merit some explanation. Driving on the DN2A, you'll cross the Danube at **Giurgeni** and see orchards and fields planted on what used to be pestilential marshland; this transformation is nothing compared to the great works further to the south, starting at **Cernavodă**, where the Danube is spanned by what was, when it opened in 1895, Europe's longest bridge (4037m, with a main span of 1662m); trains now run alongside on a bridge built in 1987. A road bridge was added in the same year, linking the DN3A and the DN22C to provide the most direct road route to Constanţa, parallel to the rail line and the **Danube–Black Sea Canal**. The motorway bridge passes diagonally under the 1895 rail bridge, with its carriageways continuing on either side of the railway.

Tropaeum Traiani

Just north of the DN3 and the village of Adamclisi • Wed–Sun: June–Sept 9am–8pm; Oct–May 9am–5pm • €2 • Buses run from Cernavodă and Medgidia (heading for Băneasa and Ostrov), and a few daily maxitaxis from Constanţa via Băneasa stop here on their way to Oltina

The armoured, faceless warrior gazing over the surrounding plateau from a height of 30m is an arresting marble reconstruction of the **TROPAEUM TRAIANI**, a trophy-statue erected here in 109 AD to celebrate Trajan's conquest of the Dacians. Every facet reflects unabashed militarism, not least the dedication to Mars Ultor. Carved around the side of its 32m base are 49 bas-reliefs or **metopes** portraying the Roman campaign. Each of the six groups of metopes comprises a marching scene, a battle and a tableau representing victory over the enemy, an arrangement identical to the one that underlies

---

CERNAVODĂ AND THE CANAL

CERNAVODĂ, whose name rather ominously translates as "Black Water", was chosen in the late 1970s to be the site of Romania's first nuclear power station, but it's better known as the western entrance to the **Danube–Black Sea Canal**. Opened to shipping in 1984, the canal put Cernavodă a mere 60km from the Black Sea, offering obvious savings in time and fuel. However, realizing a profit on such a huge investment remains dependent on European economic revival and on the success of the Rhein–Main and Nürnberg–Regensburg canals. Charlemagne's vision of a 3000km-long waterway linking Rotterdam with the Black Sea finally came to fruition in 1993, although environmental protests in Bavaria and soaring costs had stalled the final stage of the project for ten years.

INTO BULGARIA

Sixty kilometres west of Adamclisi along the DN3 is the small border town of **OSTROV**, where you can cross over to the Bulgarian town of **Silistra** (also accessible on a ferry across the Danube from Călăraşi). Although the **Vama Veche** crossing (see page 372) is more suitable if you're driving down the coast to Varna, it's also possible to enter Bulgaria from **NEGRU VODĂ** at the south end of the DN38 (57km southwest of Constanţa), a crossing that's also used by three local trains a day from Medgidia. All three crossings are open 24 hours a day; if you need a visa, make sure you get it either before leaving home or in Bucharest (see page 79).

---

scenes XXXVI–XLII of Trajan's Column in Rome, a copy of which is in Bucharest's National History Museum (see page 52). Around the statue are **ruins** of buildings once inhabited by the legionary garrison or serving religious or funerary purposes.

The coast

7

Romania's **Black Sea coast** (the *litoral*) holds the promise of white beaches, dazzling water and an average of ten to twelve hours of sunshine a day between May and October. Travelling from Bucharest or the Delta, your first stop on the coast will almost certainly be **Constanţa**, a relaxed seaport-cum-riviera town, dotted with Turkish, Byzantine and Roman remains, which has always seemed to keep a discreet distance from the surrounding resorts.

North of Constanţa, **Mamaia** is indisputably the coastal hot spot, swarming with hotels and buzzing with nightlife, while the multiplicity of resorts to the south, merging imperceptibly with one another, are more uniform; their seasons are also much shorter. **Mangalia** is the only town of any real size south of Constanţa and the one place not dependent upon tourism, beyond which lie the twin resorts of **Doi Mai** and **Vama Veche**. Located just a few kilometres from the Bulgarian border, they offer a more relaxed vibe and a welcome escape from the crowds.

GETTING AROUND   THE COAST

By train Trains from Bucharest to Constanţa are reasonably fast and frequent, but get very overcrowded in season, when many services continue to Mangalia.

By maxitaxi Maxitaxis run regularly between Bucharest and Constanţa, and between Constanţa's train station and the various resorts, in effect north to Mamaia and south as far as Mangalia; you'll have to change in Mangalia to get to Doi Mai or Vama Veche.

By car Driving from Bucharest, you can take the A2 motorway, which now goes all the way to Constanţa; a toll of €3 is payable at Feteşti.

Constanţa

Most visitors first encounter the Black Sea coast at **CONSTANŢA**, a busy riviera town and Romania's principal port. Its ancient precursor, Tomis, was supposedly founded by survivors of a battle with the Argonauts, following the capture of the Golden Fleece; centuries later, the great Roman poet Ovid was exiled here for nine years until his death in 17 AD. These days, the town is an attractive mix of Greco-Roman remains, Turkish mosques and crisp modern boulevards, home to several interesting museums and a lively restaurant scene.

The oldest area of Constanţa, centred on **Piaţa Ovidiu**, stands on a headland between what is now the tourist port and the huge area of the modern docks to the south and west. Walking up the shore from the tourist port, you'll find Constanţa's passable **beach**, and inland, beyond the remains of the walls of ancient Tomis, the modern **commercial area**, along boulevards Ferdinand and Tomis. Further north, nearing the resort of **Mamaia**, are various sights designed to appeal to children, including a dolphinarium. Pilot cutters mounted by the road at the town's northern and southern entries attest to its status as a port, as does its biggest festival, **Navy Day** on August 15, when up to ten thousand people watch the parade.

Piaţa Ovidiu

Piaţa Ovidiu, the central square of the old quarter, is dominated by a mournful statue of Ovid, a rather fine bronze piece sculpted by Italian Ettore Ferarri in 1887. Exiled here from Rome by Emperor Augustus in 8 AD, and marooned in backwater Tomis, the poet spent his last years unsuccessfully petitioning emperors for his return, and composing his melancholy *Tristia*.

Muzeul de Istorie Naţională şi Arheologie

Piaţa Ovidiu 12 • May–Sept daily 9am–8pm; Oct–April Wed–Sun 9am–5pm • €4.50; €5.50 with the Roman mosaic (see below) • ☎ 0241 618 763, ⓦ minac.ro

Housed in the imposing former city hall, Constanţa's **Muzeul de Istorie Naţională şi Arheologie** (Archeological and National History Museum) harbours one of the country's most significant archeological collections; among the exhibits is a quite brilliant assemblage of marble and limestone friezes, reliefs and statues, the most eye-catching of which is one of Fortuna and Pontus, the patron deities of Tomis (albeit with a few missing appendages). The museum's signature piece, however, is the extraordinary **Glykon Serpent**,

CONSTANŢA

BLACK SEA

Tulcea, Mamaia & Airport — Mamaia

Hospital ✛

Beach

Opera/Ballet Theatre

Art Museum

Church of the Transfiguration

Tomis Mall

Ruins of Tomis

Ethnographic Museum

Tomis Harbour

National Theatre

Tourist Port

Museum of the Romanian Navy

Archeological Museum

Genoese Lighthouse

Roman Mosaic

Mascheea Carol

Ion Jalea Collection

Cathedral Church

Aquarium

Casino

Bucharest →

Train Station, Autogară Sud & Agigea Sud (ferry terminal) →

STRADA CALARAŞI
BULEVARDUL TOMIS
STRADA MIRCEA CEL BĂTRÂN
STR. DECEBAL
STRADA PUŞKIN
STRADA MIHAI EMINESCU
STRADA TUDOR VLADIMIRESCU
BULEVARDUL MAMAIA
STRADA MIHAI VITEAZUL
STRADA RĂSCOALEI DIN 1907
BOLINTINEANU
STRADA DECEBAL
STRADA DIMITRIE
STRADA DACIA
STR. SARMIZEGETUSA
STRADA CONSTANTIN BRĂTESCU
STRADA GRIVIŢEI
STRADA ŞTEFAN CEL MARE
STRADA CUZA VODĂ
BULEVARDUL FERDINAND
BULEVARD TOMIS
STR. MIRCEA CEL BĂTRÂN
STR. E. VARGA
STR. V. ALECSANDRI
STRADA CALLATIS
PIAŢA OVIDIU
STR. TRAIAN
STRADA TRAIAN
ALEEA V. CANARACHE
STRADA TERMELE ROMANE
BDUL MARINARILOR
STRADA REMUS OPREANU
STRADA LEBEDEI
PIAŢA OVIDIU
STR. REVOLUŢIEI
STR. AMZEI
STR. REMUS
22 DEC
STR. OPREANU
STRADA DUCA

● EATING	
Arabica	7
Asado	2
Byblos	4
Haute Cup	3
Marco Polo	1
On Plonge	5
Pizzico	6

■ ACCOMMODATION	
Chérica	2
Dali	1
Ferdinand	4
Guci	3
Tineretului	6
Voila	5

■ DRINKING & NIGHTLIFE	
Club Phoenix	1
Irish Pub	2

0   250
metres

7

a unique creation about the size of a squatting toddler, with an antelope's head, human hair and eyes, and a gracefully coiled serpentine body ending in a lion's tail, which dates from the second or third century BC; it was discovered in 1962 just a few hundred metres from the square. There are more similarly dazzling treasures up on the first floor – not least an exceptional collection of *stelae*, funerary slabs ornamented with scenes from the life of the deceased – as well as oil lamps and amphorae dredged up from the Black Sea. The top floor, meanwhile, is devoted to a largely forgettable history section.

Edificiul Roman cu Mozaic

To the rear of the the Archeological and National Museum (see opposite) • May–Sept daily 9am–8pm; Oct–April Wed–Sun 9am–5pm • €2; €5.50 with the Archeological and National Museum • ☎ 0241 614 562

An ugly glass and concrete structure encloses extensive remains of the fine **Edificiul Roman cu Mozaic** (Roman mosaic). The mosaic originally consisted of some 2000 square metres, of which around 800 square metres survives, and although much of it has been effaced, there are still some remarkably well-preserved sections, typically featuring geometrical and floral motifs. The series of large holes is where marble plates would have been affixed to the wall by crampons. Discovered 5m below street level in 1959, it may have once graced the upper hall of the Roman baths, whose outer walls can be seen from Aleea Canarache. Built in the late fourth century AD, this was part of a three-storey structure linking the upper town to the port, which also incorporated warehouses and shops.

Moscheea Carol

Str. Crângului 1 • Daily 9am–6pm • €1

An austere edifice manifesting neo-Egyptian and neo-Byzantine elements, the **Moscheea Carol** (Carol Mosque) was so named after King Carol I, who had it rebuilt in 1910 in acknowledgement of the local Muslim community – the original mosque dated from 1834. Designed by Romanian architect Victor Ştefănescu, its most unusual aspect is its dome, which was the first structure in the country to be built using reinforced concrete. It's now the seat of the Mufti, the spiritual head of Romania's 55,000 Muslims (Turks and Tatars by origin), who live along the coast of the Dobrogea. Climbing the 140 steps leading up through the 47m-high minaret is worth it for the great **view** of the town and harbour.

Muzeul Ion Jalea

Str. Arhiepiscopiei 26 • May–Sept daily 10am–6pm; Oct–April Wed–Sun 9am–5pm • €2 • ☎ 0241 618 602

Down towards the waterfront, opposite some ruins of ancient Tomis, the **Muzeul Ion Jalea** (Ion Jalea collection) houses an assortment of conventional and academic sculptures by the eponymous artist in a lovely neo-Brâncovenesc villa. While not in the class of Brâncuşi, or his mentor, Frederic Storck, Jalea (1887–1983) was certainly no slouch, particularly when you consider that his best work came after he lost his left arm during World War I; displayed here are bronze, marble and stone busts of eminent Romanians like Eminescu and Aman, family members, mythical and saintly figures, and a series of nudes. Below the museum, on a small grassy bank leading down to the promenade, stands a statue of the poet Carmen Sylva (the pen name of Queen Elisabeta, wife of King Carol), and sitting at her feet is a harpist, sculpted by Jalea.

Cazino

Midway along the pedestrianized waterfront

Jutting out on a rounded promenade is the once magnificent **cazino**. Originally erected as an Art Nouveau pavilion for Queen Elisabeta in 1904–10, it became a favoured haunt for European royalty, before being closed down in 1990, since when it has been slowly decaying – that said, its badly crumbling facade can't quite disguise the still superb clamshell-shaped windows and beautiful stuccowork. Sadly though, there's little sign that the city authorities are willing to rekindle the building's past glories any time soon.

Farul Genovez

At the end of the promenade

The **Farul Genovez** (Genoese Lighthouse) is a squat grey limestone structure erected in 1860 by workers of the Danubius and Black Sea Railway company, in memory of the thirteenth- and fourteenth-century mariners who tried to revive the port. Standing at just 8m, the lighthouse continued to function until 1913, since which time the Carol I lighthouse in the harbour has carried out duties.

Ruins of Tomis

Junction of B-dul Ferdinand and B-dul Tomis

The focal point of the new town is an archeological park displaying sections of ancient walls, serried amphorae and other **ruins of Tomis**. Tomis was settled by Greeks from Miletus in the sixth century BC as an annex to Histria, which it later superseded before being incorporated into the Roman empire at the beginning of the Christian era. The most prominent remains are those of the defensive wall, created in the third and fourth centuries, and the Butchers' Tower, raised in the sixth century by Byzantine colonists who revived the city and renamed it to honour the emperor's sister Constantia.

Muzeul Marinei Române

Str. Traian 53 • Wed–Sun 9am–5pm • €2.50 • ☎ 0241 619 035

Occupying the one-time premises of the city's naval academy and appropriately overlooking the north end of the commercial *port maritim*, the **Muzeul Marinei Române** (Museum of the Romanian Navy) offers a thoroughgoing trawl through Romania's illustrious maritime history, the navy itself being founded in 1860. Despite its name, the museum includes models of Greek triremes that sailed long before Romania existed, and photographs recording the unexpected visit of the battleship *Potemkin*, whose mutinous sailors disembarked at Constanța in July 1905 and scattered. Little is said about the role of Romania's own navy during World War II, when it supported the occupation of Odessa and aided the Nazi fleet.

Among the many superb items on display are the enormous lenses from old lighthouses in Sfântu Gheorghe and Tuzla, a magnificent 10m-long barge (*monoxila*) carved from a tree trunk, wooden figureheads retrieved from the Black Sea, and an array of fine model ships, including one of the supertanker, MT *Independența*, sunk by a Greek freighter in 1979; standing next to it is the champagne bottle used by Elena Ceaușescu to launch the vessel in 1977, leading many to suggest that because the bottle had not broken the ship was inevitably doomed. Today's Romanian navy counts around seven thousand servicemen and women, with three frigates, of which one, *Regele Ferdinand*, was formerly HMS *Coventry*, and another, *Regele Maria*, was formerly *HMS London* and served in the Gulf.

Lake Tăbăcăriei and Delfinariu

Dolphinarium B-dul Mamaia 255 • Daily: June–Aug 9am–9pm; Sept–May 9am–5pm; shows at 11am, 3pm & 7pm • Adults €8, children €4; includes tickets for the planetarium and micro-reserve • ☎ 0241 481 230, ⓦ delfinariu.ro

Visitors with children or a low tolerance for provincial museums head straight for the **beach** north of the tourist port, spread beneath a terraced cliff behind the art museum, or the park at Lake **Tăbăcăriei**, between Constanța and Mamaia. Serenely set on the lake's southern shore, and easily detected thanks to its enormous 41m-high spire poking up through the thicket of trees, is the fabulous **Biserica Sfîntul Mina** (St Mina Church; free). A huge all-wooden structure built in 1994 by carpenters from Maramureș, the church boasts a magnificent, almost sheer, double-tiered eave, a lovely sunny porch and an equally elaborate wood-carved interior, including the iconostasis.

The nearby **delfinariu** is most certainly one for the kids, with three daily shows lasting around twenty minutes; there also a **planetarium** here, but better than both is the **microrezervatie** (micro-reserve), a lovely, landscaped park replete with all manner of animal life, including antelope, boar, dingos, pelicans, ostriches and a collection of exotic birds.

ARRIVAL AND DEPARTURE

CONSTANȚA

By plane Constanța, with flights to London Luton among other destinations, is served by Mihail Kogălniceanu airport (☎0241 255 100, ⌨mk-airport.ro), 25km northwest of town, and connected by shuttle bus to the centre (from the airport every 20min, 5.25–9.05am, then hourly until 8.05pm; from Constanța pretty much hourly 5.30am–8pm; 30min; €6.50). A taxi should cost no more than €10.

By train The train station is 2km west of the centre at the southern end of B-dul Ferdinand.

Destinations Bucharest (7–12 daily; 2hr–3hr 30min); Mangalia (7–10 daily; 1hr 20min); Medgidia (12 daily; 1hr 10min).

By bus The grotty main bus station (*Autogară Sud*) is 200m north of the train station on Str. Theodor Burada, though,

confusingly, some buses (principally those to Bucharest) also depart from a spot in front (and to the left) of the train station.

Destinations Athens, Greece (2 daily; 17hr); Brăila (hourly; 3hr); Bucharest (every 45min; 3hr 15min); Cernavodă (every 30min; 1hr 30min); Chișinău, Moldova (2 daily; 8hr); Galați (12 daily; 3hr 30min); Hârșova (hourly; 1hr); Istanbul, Turkey (2 daily; 10hr); Mihai Viteazu (for Istria, hourly; 1hr); Jurilovca (1 daily; 1hr 40min); Mangalia (every 30min; 45min); Medgidia (hourly; 1hr); Oltina (for Adamclisi, 2 daily; 3hr 30min); Tulcea (every 30min; 2hr 10min); Varna, Bulgaria (1 daily; 3hr).

ACCOMMODATION

The city has a large stock of central **hotels**, and while there's very little to differentiate between them (in fact, with one exception, they're a pretty unexciting bunch) they are all reasonably priced. Otherwise, locals with **private rooms** sometimes wait by the train station, holding signs reading *cazare*. Another other option is to head up to Mamaia (see page 364), where there are hotels by the dozen. Moreover, you'll see plenty of people standing by the roadside rattling their keys; these are perfectly acceptable options, but do check where the accommodation is before accepting.

★ **Chérica** Str. Ștefan cel Mare 4 ☎0241 617 174, ⌨cherica.ro; map p.360. A fine late nineteenth-century building and one-time residence of Princess Chérica Sturdza, this impeccably serviced hotel is a class above anything else in town; the eighteen rooms, effectively mini-suites, are cool and beautifully furnished in dark hardwood, with wood-framed bedsteads, leather sofas and armchairs, and fetching grey-and-white tiled bathrooms. By no means cheap, but worth the splurge. **€135**

Dali Str. Smărdan 6A ☎0241 619 717, ⌨hotel-dali.ro; map p.360. Popular and well-appointed three-star hotel with pastel facade and comfortable, spacious rooms, even if the furnishings err on the side of old-fashioned; the eight apartments are only marginally more expensive than the

rooms, but in any case try and bag one with a sea view. Double **€75**, apartment **€85**

Ferdinand B-dul Ferdinand 12 ☎0241 407 761, ⌨hotelferdinand.ro; map p.360. A classic mid-twentieth-century Deco-style building concealing fifteen well-furnished, if slightly bland, burgundy-coloured rooms, some of which have balconies. Try to avoid those facing the noisy road. **€77**

Guci Str. Răscoalei din 1907 23 ☎0241 695 500, ⌨guci-hotel.ro; map p.360. Although not quite as classy as the name might suggest, this compact hotel, just off the main pedestrianized area, offers smoothly furnished rooms, laminate flooring and attractive wall lamps and pictures. There's also a basement sauna and jacuzzi. **€45**

Tineretului B-dul Tomis 20–26 ☎0241 613 590; map p.360. Constanța's youth hotel is not a particularly pretty sight – rough-hewn stone walls, small beds and antiquated bathrooms – but it's clean, well located and very cheap. Breakfast is included in the price. **€17**

Voila Str. Callatis 22 ☎0241 508 002, ⌨hotelvoila.ro; map p.360. In a pleasantly secluded spot on the edge of the old town, and near the harbour, this small four-star hotel is idiosyncratically decorated with pseudo-Roman mosaics; the pretty rooms are furnished in deep burgundy, with big cast-iron beds and cast-iron chandeliers and mirrors. **€82**

EATING

Arabica B-dul Tomis 3 ☎0728 674 276; map p. 360. Even if the staff are a bit grumpy here, this great-looking café is well worth seeking out for the unusual ways in which they prepare their Turkish-style coffee, typically heated in small copper vessels over hot sand and then served in small china cups on copper-plated trays together with a silver bowl of sugar; you can also choose from a variety of French Press and filter coffees. Daily 8am–midnight.

Asado Str. Smărdan 12 ☎0728 348 990, ⌨asado.ro; map p.360. Contemporary steakhouse serving

meat imported from Argentina, Texas and Scotland. The possibilities are mouthwatering: Black Angus burger with foie gras (€13), boneless rib-eye (€28) and Tomahawk steaks (€18), plus cheaper options such as spicy chicken wings. Daily 11am–1am.

Byblos B-dul Tomis 48 ☎0341 172 416, ⌨byblos-constanta.ro; map p.360. Noisy location and kitschy decor aside, this lively Lebanese outfit is worth a visit for its well-cooked and colourfully presented staples such as *tabouleh*, falafel and Arayes lamb (pita stuffed with barbecued lamb;

€5). Round off the evening with a hookah pipe. Daily 9am–1am.

★ **Haute Cup** Str. Grivitei 20 ☎0734 660 088, ⓦhautecup.ro; map p.360. The third-wave coffee movement in Constanța comes courtesy of this fabulous coffee house, discreetly (though unfortunately) hidden from view behind the Tomis Mall. Run by an enthusiastic, happy team of young baristas, who'll whip you up the finest flat white this side of the Black Sea. Daily 8am–11.30pm.

Marco Polo Str. Sarmisegetuza 2 ☎0241 617 357; map p.360. Above-average Italian restaurant, as impressive for its decor – cool chocolate-brown tables and chairs, and crisp white tablecloths – as it is for its food; in warmer weather, the wood-decked, tree-shaded terrace is rather fine too. Daily 11am–midnight.

On Plonge Portul Turistic Tomis ☎0241 601 905; map p.360. One of Constanța's better restaurants, not only because of its lovely harbourside setting, but also for the array of both fresh and saltwater items on the menu – carp, trout, crab, cuttlefish, mussels and mackerel, to name just a few; service could be better, though. Daily 10am–11.30pm.

Pizzico Piața Ovidiu 7 ☎0241 615 555, ⓦpizzico.ro; map p.360. Just about the only worthwhile place to eat down in the old quarter, this large, fashionable restaurant offers a lot more besides pizza; the vast menu also incorporates steak and a host of seafood dishes including *bouillabaisse*, grilled octopus and baked bream in a white wine sauce (€12). Alternatively, park yourself down on the sunny terrace with a coffee after visiting the Archeological Museum opposite. Daily 9am–midnight.

DRINKING AND NIGHTLIFE

The city's **nightlife** can't match that of many of the coastal resorts, particularly Mamaia (see below), but that's no bad thing here; note, also, that many bars close down during the summer, when the action moves up to Mamaia.

Club Phoenix Str. Capitan Dobrila Eugeniu 1, near the Ciresica complex in the suburb of Tomis Nord ☎0730 617 787; map p.360. Constanța's main live music venue hosts jazz, blues and rock on a regular basis, plus evenings of stand-up. Bus #42 or #43.

Irish Pub Str. Ștefan cel Mare 1 ☎0241 550 400, ⓦirishpub.ro; map p.360. Despite the dreadfully dull name, this massively popular pub-restaurant is actually rather good. A dark, predictably wooden interior gives way to a fine covered terrace offering lovely views across the port, and is ideal for both a daytime coffee or a bout of more serious evening drinking. Many people come here for the food, which is surprisingly accomplished (grilled red tuna fillet with pesto sauce and asparagus €10). Daily 8am–1am.

DIRECTORY

Consulate Turkey, B-dul Ferdinand 82 (Mon–Fri 9am–noon; ☎0241 60 79 10).

Hospital B-dul Tomis 145 (☎0241 516 800 or 961).

Left luggage At the train station, in the subway under the tracks (daily 7am–9pm; €2).

Pharmacy Constanța has four 24hr pharmacies: Eurosantis, Str. Ecaterina Varga 55 (at B-dul Ferdinand); Minifarm, B-dul Tomis 133; Dumifarm, in the Tomis Mall at Str. Ștefan cel Mare 49 (at Str. Mihai Viteazul); and one inside the train station building.

Post office B-dul Tomis 79 (Mon–Fri 7am–8pm, Sat 8am–1pm) and Str. 22 Decembrie 1989 (Mon–Fri 9am–4.30pm).

Shopping The city's largest shopping mall (with associated cinemas, leisure facilities and restaurants) is the Maritimo Center (daily 10am–10pm) at B-dul Aurel Vlaicu 120, closely followed by City Park (same hours), out by Lake Tăbăcăriei on the road to Mamaia. In the centre, Str. Ștefan cel Mare is the main shopping street – especially the pedestrianized stretch from Str. Răscoalei din 1907 to Str. Duca – in the centre of which is the Tomis Mall (daily 10am–10pm) and its basement Mega Image supermarket (daily 7.30am–10pm), the best in town.

Mamaia

MAMAIA, 6km north of Constanța, is Romania's best-known coastal resort, and the place where the majority of package tourists end up. Legend has it that the gods created the **beach** to reunite a kidnapped princess with her daughter, who was abandoned on the seashore wailing "Mamaia, Mamaia!"; its fine, almost white sand, fringed with wild pear trees, is the resort's greatest asset, especially since its gentle gradient and the absence of currents and strong tides make it particularly safe for children.

As late as the 1930s, Mamaia was, in the words of Gregor von Rezzori, "an empty expanse, excepting two or three bathing huts and a wooden pier, of miles of golden sand and tiny pink shells"; a far cry from what you'll find here today. Ranged along a narrow spit of land between the Black Sea and Lake Siutghiol, the resort's **main street**

curves away around the shore of the lake. The southern stretch of the beachfront promenade is dominated by fast-food stands, mini-markets, pharmacies and shops selling all manner of beach paraphernalia and other accessories, but, beyond the **casino** (which is more or less the heart of Mamaia), the resort is more restrained. The **telegondola** (Mon noon–11.30pm, Tues–Sun 10am–11.30pm; €4.50) will whisk you the 2km from near the Aqua Magic park at the southern end of Mamaia to just north of the casino. There's a big plaza on the inland side of the casino, with a small stage and rows of family restaurants (mostly pizza places, all with big *terasas*). Mamaia's main summer festival is the (biannual) **Sunwaves Festival** (⟨w⟩sunwaves-fest.ro), which is held alternately in May and mid-August and features a world class line-up of electronic acts performing across several stages on Kazeboo beach in the north of the resort.

Ovid's Island and Lake Siutghiol

Boat trips May–Sept daily 11.30am–midnight • €6 return • ☎ 0720 265 599

From Mamaia, regular **motorboats** (either the *Ovidius* or the smaller *Sabrina*) shuttle between the Tic-Tac dock opposite the casino to **Ovid's Island** at the northern end of **Lake Siutghiol**. Also known as Lake Mamaia, **Lake Siutghiol** was formed when a river's outlet silted up, and for many centuries it was a watering hole for herds of sheep and cows brought down from the Carpathians – hence the name, meaning "Lake of Milk" in Turkish.

ARRIVAL AND INFORMATION — MAMAIA

By bus/maxitaxi To get to Mamaia from Constanța, take one of the regular maxitaxis (#23) to Năvodari, which leave from in front (and to the left) of the train station (€0.50); otherwise, bus #100 also leaves from in front of the train station (directly in front by the RATC booth) and goes as far as the Sat de Vacanță (holiday village) just south of Mamaia; tickets, which you can purchase from the booth, cost €0.40 for one journey and €0.80 for two trips. A one-day ticket (for use on buses, not maxitaxis) costs €1.20. Buses run from 5.15am (5.45am at weekends) to 11pm.

By taxi General Taxi (☎ 0241 617 844) and Romaris (☎ 0241 690 000) are trustworthy taxi companies; a trip up to Mamaia should cost no more than €4–5.

Tourist information Predictably enough, information is scant, but you could pop into the Mistral Tours agency (Mon–Fri 9am–6pm, Sat 9am–1pm; ☎ 0728 281 679, ⟨w⟩mistraltours.ro), next to the telegondola, who will be only too happy to furnish you with maps and literature.

MAMAIA ACTIVITIES

Mamaia has ample **facilities** for those wanting to play on the **water**, most of which take place on Lake Siutghiol – waterskiing (€12/10min), jet-skiing and wakeboarding (€25/10min) and kayaking (€5/hr/one person, €8/hr/two people) are all possible; or you can just thrash about on a banana boat (€4/15min). The best facilities are at the *Nautica Blue Club* (☎ 0241 607 000), attached to the *Club Scandinavia* hotel, and *Club Nautic Pinguin* (☎ 0722 258 187), opposite the *Hotel Majestic*.

    Bikes and various pedal carts can be rented from the promenade in front of the *Iaki* hotel (€4/hr). There are several excellent **tennis** clubs in Mamaia, the best of which are *Break Tennis Club* (☎ 0722 630 518, ⟨w⟩breaktennisclub.ro), to the north of the resort opposite the *Hotel Regal*; and *Tenis Club Idu* (☎ 0241 831 225, ⟨w⟩tenisclubidu.ro), to the west of the main road south of the casino, opposite the *Ovidiu* hotel; both have indoor and outdoor courts – expect to pay around €6–8 per hour at both.

    Easily the best place in Mamaia to take **children** is the gleaming **Aqua Magic water park** (daily: June & Sept 10am–6pm; July & Aug 9am–7pm; €15 adults, €7 children; ☎ 0241 831 183, ⟨w⟩aqua-magic.ro), at the southern entrance to Mamaia, which has all the requisite slides and chutes. If all of the above seems far too energetic and you just fancy chilling out on the beach, there's assorted equipment for rent, including sunbeds (*sezlong*; €4.50/day) and umbrellas (*baldachin*; €11/day).

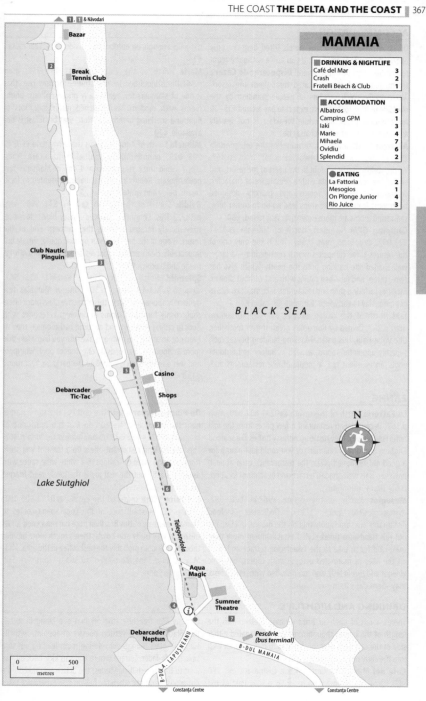

MAMAIA

DRINKING & NIGHTLIFE	
Café del Mar	3
Crash	2
Fratelli Beach & Club	1

ACCOMMODATION	
Albatros	5
Camping GPM	1
Iaki	3
Marie	4
Mihaela	7
Ovidiu	6
Splendid	2

EATING	
La Fattoria	2
Mesogios	1
On Plonge Junior	4
Rio Juice	3

7

Bazar

Break
Tennis Club

Club Nautic
Pinguin

BLACK SEA

Debarcader
Tic-Tac

Casino

Shops

Lake Siutghiol

Telegondola

Aqua
Magic

Summer
Theatre

Debarcader
Neptun

Pescărie
(bus terminal)

B-DUL A. LĂPUȘNEANU

B-DUL MAMAIA

N

0 — 500
metres

Constanța Centre   Constanța Centre

& Năvodari

7

ACCOMMODATION

Unless otherwise stated, the hotels listed here are only open between May and Sept. If you arrive without a room reservation, try one of the several **Dispecerat de Cazare** (room allocation) offices located throughout the resort. Alternatively, you'll see lots of people standing by the roadside touting for business; expect to pay around €15–20 for a double room, and while breakfast is not usually available, the use of a kitchen may be.

Albatros By the northern terminal of the telegondola ☎0241 831 381, ⓦhotelalbatros.ro; map p.367. Warm, welcoming hotel right in the heart of the resort, and one of the few in Mamaia with a semblance of character; comfortable, colourful rooms and quirkily designed bathrooms featuring little steps leading up to corner tubs; sea-facing rooms are more expensive. Year round. **€80**

Camping GPM Năvodari, north of Mamaia ☎0241 831 002, ⓦgpm.ro; map p.367. This is the only one of the resort's three campsites worth considering – a large, well-shaded site backing onto the beach, which also has two-, three- and four-bed cabins with and without shower. Facilities include a shop and restaurant. Take maxitaxi #23 to get here. May to early Sept. Camping **€8**, cabin **€36**

Iaki North of the casino ☎0241 831 025, ⓦiaki.ro; map p.367. Owned by Romania's greatest ever footballer, Gheorghe Hagi, this palatial-looking building boasts cool, superbly appointed rooms, as well as indoor and outdoor pools, an excellent spa, a couple of fine restaurants and,

naturally enough, an outdoor five-a-side pitch. Year round. **€150**

Marie North of the casino ☎0341 731 731; map p.367.Undistinguished-looking three-star low-rise that is one of Mamaia's few realistically priced options; bright rooms with modern, well-matched furnishings, lots of light and sparkling bathrooms. Note that breakfast is not available. **€70**

Mihaela South of Aqua Magic in the Zona Perla ☎0749 995 029, ⓔhotelmihaela.mamaia@gmail.com; map p.367. Solid three-star option and one of Mamaia's few newer hotels. Rooms are immaculately presented in fresh cream, beige and white colours. **€75**

Ovidiu South of the casino ☎0241 831 590; map p.367. This brightly painted navy-blue low-rise, conveniently located towards the southern end of the resort, is one of the best two-star options going; simple but impeccably clean singles, doubles and triples, all with TV, fridge and balcony. **€51**

Splendid North of the casino ☎0341 412 541, ⓦsplendidhotel.ro; map p.367. One of Mamaia's few genuinely appealing hotels, this attractive glass block offers cool, crisply furnished rooms in different categories with floor to ceiling windows and dazzling bathrooms – they've even got an adults only wing; make sure you bag a lakeside room as opposed to a roadside one. Indoor pool, whirlpool and wet and dry saunas complete the package. Year round **€130**

EATING

La Fattoria North of the casino ☎0241 831 010; map p.367. Decent Italian restaurant a few paces from the *Iaki* hotel (see above). They rustle up unfussy dishes like seafood linguine and grilled calamari, or you could just plump for a good old-fashioned pizza; the restaurant's chief appeal, however, is its well-shaded terrace and beachfront location. Daily 10am–midnight.

Mesogios North of the casino ☎0341 820 082, ⓦmesogios.ro; map p.367. Dedicated seafood restaurants are surprisingly thin on the ground in Mamaia, but this handsome Greek-styled establishment more than makes up for it; take to the lake-facing terrace and feast on the likes of marinated octopus with capers, balsamic vinegar and *rucola* (€9), and squid stuffed with feta cheese. May–Sept daily 1pm–midnight.

On Plonge Junior Inside the hotel of the same name, near the Debarcader Neptun dock at the south end of Mamaia ☎0724 036 633, ⓦonplongejr.ro; map p.367. This fine-looking restaurant offers up a feast of wet stuff, from pike egg salad to scallops in a white wine sauce with asparagus (€8), but the real joy is the lovely reed-fringed terrace. Daily 10am–midnight.

Rio Juice 100m south of the casino ☎0732 505 101; map p.367. A small slice of the Copacabana comes to Mamaia courtesy of this Brazilian juice bar renowned for its fresh and very fruity acai bowls; there's much more besides though, including probably the best coffee in the area. Mid-May to mid-Sept Mon–Wed 10.30am–7pm, Fri–Sun 10.30pm–9pm.

DRINKING AND NIGHTLIFE

There's a raft of open-air **bars** running pretty much the length of the beach, though most are congregated either side of the casino; expect most places to rock on until well into the early hours, typically 3 or 4am.

Café del Mar 100m south of the casino ☎0745 980 980, ⓦcafedelmarmamaia.ro; map p.367. Part of the

Café del Mar franchise (the original one being in Ibiza), this Black Sea coast version doesn't disappoint, with its swish all-glass lounge-cum-dining room leading out to a smart, sofa-laden terrace where you can kick back all day long to Balearic chill-out tunes; the action is cranked up a notch post midnight when the full-on club experience takes

over. The food's pretty good too. Mon–Wed & Sun 9am–midnight, Thurs–Sat until 5am.
Crash 100m north of the casino ☎0724 918 623; map p.367. Ostentatious, timber-framed beachfront bar with an enormous wood-decked terrace that packs them in on a nightly basis. Although nothing particularly exciting happens here, it's a terrific spot for just hanging out with a beer while DJs spin the decks. Daily 10am till late.

Fratelli Beach & Club 500m north of the casino ☎0722 115 115, ⓦfratelli.ro; map p.367. Just like its sister club in Bucharest, *Fratelli* is one for the beautiful people, though it's not quite as pretentious as all that; while the club is all glitz and glam, the *Beach Bar* lounge serves good food, including a gut-busting brunch on Sat and Sun (1–5pm). Club Fri & Sat 11.30pm–5am; beach bar daily 11.30am–1am.

Eforie Nord and Lake Techirghiol

Founded in 1899 by Bucharest's Eforia hospital as a spa for convalescent patients, **Eforie Nord** extends along a cliff top above the rather narrow **beach**, Plajă Belona, which, as far as coastal beaches go, is not at all bad, and rarely gets overcrowded; there's also an **Aqua Park** here (daily 9am–6pm; €8). The resort is, however, best known for the therapeutic **black mud** scooped from the shores of **Lake Techirghiol**, whose mineral-saturated waters gave the lake its name, derived from *tekir*, Turkish for "salt" or "bitter". **Baths** by the lake (a few minutes' walk south of the train station) specialize in treating rheumatic disorders and the after-effects of polio, while on the lake's single-sex nudist beaches, people plaster themselves with mud, wait until it cracks (happily exposing themselves to passing trains) and then jostle good humouredly beneath the showers.

ARRIVAL AND DEPARTURE   EFORIE NORD

By train The train station is located to the south of the resort on Str. Gării.
Destinations Constanța (7–10 daily; 25min); Mangalia (7–10 daily; 45min).

By bus Buses and maxitaxis drop off along B-dul Republicii. Destinations Constanța (every 30min; 30min); Mangalia (every 30min; 45min).

ACCOMMODATION

Europa B-dul Republicii 13 ☎0241 702 801, ⓦanahotels.ro. A towering, steel-blue four-star hotel with extensive lawns sloping down to a gorgeous pool and a private beach. Each and every one of the two hundred or so rooms has a sea view, while guests receive a fifty percent discount to the Ana Aslan Health Spa, one of the country's best. April–Oct. €104

Lucas Str. Andrei Mureşanu 2 ☎0341 444 941, ⓦlucashotel.net. It almost comes as a shock to find such a refreshingly smart, contemporary hotel located along this

part of the coast, but this boutique establishment is just that; minimalist grey and beige furnished rooms, gorgeous stone- and marble-clad bathrooms and wrought-iron balconies all add up to more than a touch of class. April–Sept. €80

Vera B-dul Republicii 42 ☎0241 742 200, ⓦhotelvera.ro. A large, modernish complex with three categories of rooms, ranging from standard upwards, though it's worth paying the slight extra for a Superior, which features high-end showers. April–Sept. €65

Neptun and Olimp

Sixteen kilometres south of Eforie Nord, **NEPTUN** was built in 1960 between the Comorova forest and the sea, ensuring a lush setting for the artificial lakes and dispersed villas. Originally enclaves for the communist *nomenklatura*, today Neptun and its classier, but much quieter, satellite of **OLIMP**, just north, are patronized by relatively affluent Romanian families and some Western tourists.

Both resorts are strung out along Strada Trandafirilor; in Neptun, about halfway along near the main complex of shops, Aleea Steagurilor leads down between a couple of lakes to the **beach**, with waterslides, beach bars and restaurants, and paths leading around the lakes; to the north are both government-owned and private villas – from the path you can see albino peacocks in one garden.

Paradis Land

Str. Plopilor, which runs parallel to Str. Trandafirilor • Daily 10am–6pm • €12/2hr 30min, including equipment; €2.50 or one zipline run; €4.50 for archery or rifle shooting • ☎ 0756 166 611, ⓦ paradisland.ro

If the beach thing doesn't appeal, then you could visit **Paradis Land**, a brilliantly designed adventure park secreted away in the forest; there are fourteen self-guided tracks, each one graded according to difficulty and age group, but expect high ropes, zip wires and climbing walls among the many other challenges. They've also got archery and air rifle shooting, as well as bikes for hire if you fancy nipping off around the forest for a bit.

ARRIVAL AND INFORMATION

By train Arriving at the train station (*halta*) just north of the *Albert* hotel (see below) it's a 5min walk down Str. Gării to Aleea Trandafirilor, which is the main road running through both Neptun and Olimp.

Destinations Constanţa (7–10 daily; 1hr 10min); Mangalia (7–10 daily; 15min).

By bus Note that if you're travelling to or from Constanţa by bus, services drop off on the highway and it's a walk of nearly 3km to Neptun.

NEPTUN AND OLIMP

Destinations Constanţa (every 30min; 1hr); Mangalia (5–8 daily; 10min).

Tourist information Information is available from Agenţia de turism Neptun-Olimp (May–Sept daily 9am–6pm; ☎ 0341 147 312, ⓦ neptun-olimp.com), located at the bottom of Str. Gării on Aleea Trandafirilor. They can also help out if you're without accommodation and need somewhere to stay.

ACCOMMODATION AND EATING

Café Efendi Str. Trandafirilor ☎ 0722 304 157. Nicely pitched among the greenery of Neptun Park Gardens, this is possibly the only Tatar hostelry you'll ever experience; the food (and coffee) is delicious, as is the setting, with low wooden tables and stools, oriental rugs and hookah pipes. April–Sept daily 10am–midnight.

Cocor Spa Hotel Str. Trandafirilor ☎ 0341 112 500, ⓦ cocorspahotel.ro. At the southern edge of Olimp, this is one of the most appealing hotels anywhere along the coast; its first-class rooms and facilities are complemented by two cool clamshell bars by the swimming pool, lush gardens and a superb spa. €70

Insula Str. Delta 1 ☎ 0241 731 722, ⓦ insulaneptun.ro. Perched down on the lakeshore, this smart, vine-clad hotel

is one of the few establishments that doesn't conform to the monotonous communist architecture that characterizes most places, hence its rooms do retain some semblance of character. The hotel's restaurant, a thatch-roofed floating terrace, is certainly worth trying for its fish, such as smoked carp fillet with polenta and garlic sauce (€7). April–Sept. €88

Q Str. Gării 1 ☎ 0372 794 486, ⓦ qhotel.com A 5min walk south of the train station, this place has been completely renovated, and while it'll hardly get the juices flowing, the light-filled rooms are tidily furnished and have balconies; there's a good-sized outdoor pool too. May–Sept. €70

Jupiter and Venus

The resorts to the south of Neptun are more uniform, less lively and likely to have fewer hotels open outside July and August. The first, immediately abutting Neptun, is **JUPITER**, between the forest and the artificial Lake Tismana, beyond which is a gently sloping beach with fine sand. Southeast of here is **Aurora**, set on the cape of the same name and dominated by several pyramidal hotel complexes. There's a minimal gap before you hit **VENUS** – broadly similar to Jupiter, but quieter and more family-oriented; Venus also has the most appealing accommodation along this stretch of coast. To the south of Venus is a sulphurous **spa** and, just inland, the Herghelia Mangalia **stables** (☎ 0241 751 325) where you can hire horses to explore the forest, inhabited by roe deer, grouse and pheasants.

ACCOMMODATION AND EATING

Camping Palace-Venus To the south of the Venus resort near the stables ☎ 0241 731 148. This is a large, well-shaded site, albeit a little scruffy in places. Huts with

JUPITER AND VENUS

and without bathrooms are also available. May–Sept. Camping €6, hut €23

Complex Hercules Str. Brindisi 8A, Jupiter ☎ 0341 566 905, ⓦ hotelhercules.ro. Occupying a prime beachfront location beside a lovely rocky bay, this nautically themed hotel is comfortably the most appealing place to stay in Jupiter. The hotel's ship-shaped restaurant is a fun place to eat and has the added bonus of terrific sea views. Mid-Sept to April. **€65**

Dana Str. Dem Rădulescu, Venus ☎ 0241 731 503, ⓦ hotel-dana.ro. A sprawling low-rise complex some 200m west of the beach, incorporating a range of smart villas, a delightful kidney-shaped swimming pool with bar, and an open-air restaurant set in gorgeous gardens. May–Oct. **€66**

Turquoise On the beachfront, Venus ☎ 0241 731 222, ⓦ hotelturquoise.ro. Superbly located beachfront hotel with beautifully designed rooms and snazzy bathrooms with enormous walk-in showers; you can almost dive into the sea from the hotel's gorgeous outdoor pool. Although pricey, rates do drop heavily out of high season. May to mid-Sept. **€150**

Zodiac Camping Str. Trandafirilor ☎ 0341 566 240, ⓦ campingzodiac.ro. One of the coast's more agreeable sites, *Zodiac* is actually as close to Neptun as it is to Jupiter; a large grassy site with decent amenities, including a pool, sports field and playground. Mid-April to Oct. **€8**

Mangalia

7

The modern suburbs of **MANGALIA** are close to swallowing up the small resort of Saturn, and in fact Mangalia's train station is nearer to Saturn than to the centre of town. As with Constanța, Mangalia's appearance of modernity belies its ancient origin – the Greeks founded their city of **Callatis** here during the sixth century BC, when population pressure impelled them to colonize the Black Sea coast. In Byzantine times it was renamed **Pangalia**, meaning "most beautiful". These days it's anything but that, though if you find yourself with an hour or two to spare, you will find a couple of small attractions to help pass the time.

Muzeul de Arheologie Callatis

Şoseaua Constanței 23 • Daily: May–Sept 8.30am–7.30pm; Oct–April 8.30am–4.30pm • €1 • ☎ 0341 146 763

Located north of town near the main roundabout, the **Muzeul de Arheologie Callatis** (Archeological Museum) exhibits some wonderful riches, which include a fabulous collection of grave goods, not least some spectacular jewellery, as well as Hellenic and Roman pottery, decorative friezes and, best of all, an assemblage of delicate ceramic statues. Don't miss, either, the superb fragments of a bronze age chariot unearthed in Doi Mai (see page 372). Elegantly preserved within the *Hotel President* at Str. Teilor 6 (though it's currently closed for renovation), are sections of wall from Callatis as well as other finds uncovered during the hotel's construction in 1993–94.

Moscheea Esmahan

Str. Oituz 1 • €1

Apart from the museum, the town's one other sight of note – indeed its sole remaining medieval monument – is the **Moscheea Esmahan** (Esmahan Mosque), Romania's oldest. Founded in 1575 by the eponymous daughter of the Ottoman ruler, Selim II (himself the son of Suleiman the Magnificent), the mosque is constructed from stone cut from the ruins of Callatis – though the porch retains its original oak pillars – and is surrounded by a three-hundred-year-old Muslim graveyard. It's possible to climb the chunky minaret, at the top of which is a small door which you can stick your head through for some rather splendid views.

ARRIVAL AND DEPARTURE   **MANGALIA**

By train The train station is a 10min walk north of the small town centre.
Destinations Constanța (6–11 daily; 1hr 10min).
By bus The main bus terminus is in front of the train station and to the left.

Destinations Doi Mai and Vama Veche (every 20–30min; 15min–25min); Saturn-Olimp (frequent; 10min).

7

ACCOMMODATION AND EATING

Nordiana Şos. Constanţei 57 ☎0241 756 266, ⓦnordiana.ro. An unprepossessing, modern glass building immediately to the left of the train station, this smallish three-star hotel is purely functional, with somewhat gaudy decor, but the rooms have modern furnishings and are spotlessly clean; moreover, it's absurdly cheap. Breakfast €4. €31

Peach-Pit Patisserie Şos. Constanţei 18 ☎0722 260 180. Located at the top of the pedestrianized section of the town's main through street, this oddly named patisserie is a cracking little place for a sweet or savoury snack and a cup of coffee. Daily 7am–10pm.

Pensiunea Oituz Str. Oituz 11 ☎0772 091 092, ⓦpensiuneaoituz.ro. A short walk west of the mosque, this simple pension's seven bright and modern a/c rooms represent good value for money; reception is in the Anna travel agency below. Breakfast (€4) is taken in the *Callatis* restaurant opposite. €35

Doi Mai

Ten kilometres south of Mangalia is the laidback village of **Doi Mai** (2 May), so named after Alexandru Ioan Cuza's coup d'état on this day in 1864. Despite lying in the shadow of the massive yellow cranes of Mangalia's shipyard, it's a peaceful and relaxed little resort, and extremely popular with families, thanks to its small but neatly formed and well-kept **beach**, part of which is for nudists; there's the odd low-key beach bar here too. The **Doi Mai-Vama Veche Marine Reserve** begins just south of the Mangalia port and extends to the border. Loggerhead turtles can be seen here, as well as sea horses, dolphins and corals.

ARRIVAL AND DEPARTURE   DOI MAI

By maxitaxi Maxitaxis shuttle north to Mangalia and south to Vama Veche (summer roughly every 30min; winter hourly; 15min), dropping off at various stops along Str. Mihail Kogălniceanu, the main through street.

ACCOMMODATION

There's a fair bit of **accommodation** in the village, most of it along Str. Falezi, the narrow street running along the cliff top above the beach.

Camping 2 Mai Up on the northern end of the beach ☎0724 196 505, ⓦcamping2mai.ro. This is a wonderfully relaxing option, with possibilities to camp, stay in a beach bungalow (sleeping two or three), or rent a caravan; shower facilities (€2) are available for campers too. May–Oct. Camping €8, caravan €32, bungalow €45

Casa Margo Str. Mihail Kogălniceanu 501 ☎0723 249 405, ⓦcasamargo.ro. Located along the main through road, *Margo* possesses thirteen comfortable air-conditioned rooms alongside a rose-filled garden where you can dine on freshly caught seafood prepared in the more than passable kitchen. €30

Vama Veche

Under communism, **VAMA VECHE** (Old Customs Post), just short of the border with Bulgaria, was closed to all but staff of Cluj University or those who could claim some vague affiliation with it; it became a haven for artists, intellectuals and nonconformists looking for an escape from the surveillance of the Securitate. In recent years, locals and investors have begun to capitalize on Vama Veche's countercultural reputation, and there's now an attractive assortment of accommodation on offer, ranging from low-key hotels and offbeat hostels to wild camping on the beach. While tourist facilities here continue to grow at a steady pace, fortunately the new developments have been planned with consideration for their surroundings, and the town still retains an air of bohemian sophistication not found elsewhere on the coast. Vama Veche's nightlife is also some of the best along the coast, with open-air dancing till dawn and live music in some great little bars on the beach, most wooden-walled and thatch-roofed. The **beach** itself is a long, wide expanse and tends to be more secluded the further south you go, while there's an area for nudist bathing up towards the northern end. The centre of the village, such as it is, is Strada Ion Creangă, a busy and colourful little street leading down from the main road to the beachfront; here you'll find most things of a practical nature, including an ATM and the village's small supermarket.

The village's main annual event, taking place during the last week of August, is **Vama Under Oscar Lights** (ⓦvslo.ro), whose main focus is film and photography, with numerous exciting screenings and exhibitions, but there's lots more besides, including painting workshops, theatrical performances and concerts; these mostly occur on or near the beach, and are free.

ARRIVAL AND INFORMATION
VAMA VECHE

By maxitaxi Maxitaxis shuttle north to Doi Mai and Mangalia (summer every 30min; winter hourly; 15–25min), with the main stop at the top of Str. Ion Creangă.

Tourist information There's no tourist office as such, but the reception in the *BazArt Hostel* (see below) pretty much acts as the village's go-to information centre (April–Sept daily 8am–10pm; ☏0722 889 087).

Diving The coast of Vama Veche is a great spot for diving, so if you fancy a go, head to Marine Explorers in the centre of the beach (☏0723 650 260, ⓦscubadivingcenter.ro; €32/2hr, including all equipment).

ACCOMMODATION

Wild **camping** on the beach has long been one of the main attractions for visitors to Vama Veche; it's easiest south of the main part of the beach, although it's also possible to camp to the north.

BazArt Hostel Str. Ion Creangă ☏0722 889 087, ⓦbazarthostel.ro. Eternally popular hostel featuring sweet, hut-like four-bed dorms and double rooms (with and without bathrooms). All have TV and a/c, and are arranged around a pretty courtyard. Breakfast is not available but there is a kitchen for use and bikes for rent. Mid-April to mid-Sept. Dorms €20, doubles €32

Elga's Punk Rock Hotel On the right as you enter the village ☏0241 858 070. It's not really that punk rock, but *Elga's* is still very cool, with cabin-like, en-suite rooms (all doubles) furnished in pine; the slightly more expensive Comfort A category rooms have a/c and TV. No breakfast but a small kitchen for use. May–Sept. €22

La John Down by the beachfront ☏0720 806 450. This is one of the village's few conventional hotels, a sensitively designed place with two storeys of wooden galleries containing large, slightly old-fashioned rooms with and without bathrooms; some come with balconies. €52

★ **Sandalandala** Str. Delfinului ☏0754 071 131, ⓦsandalandala.ro. Very much in keeping with the spirit of the village, this alternative hangout is the coolest campsite on the coast; there's ample room to pitch your tent on the lush lawn, itself sprinkled with a curious array of recycled furnishings (piano, bathtub and so on), while the super-cool terrace bar offers books, films and oven-baked pizzas; in short this is the best chill-out venue going. They've also got tents to rent (sleeping two- to four), and the rate for these includes breakfast. Closed mid-Sept to April. €10, rented tents from €28

EATING

Papa la Soni Str. Falezei ☏0365 424 490. An enterprising, multi-functional restaurant-bar and concert venue occupying a large and very colourful wood- and stone-built shack just above the beach; steaming bowls of soup and goulash are served up from enormous vats against a backdrop of easy-going music, while in summer there's a cracking programme of live music most nights. Daily 10am–late.

DRINKING AND NIGHTLIFE

Expirat Str. Falezei ☏0733 974 728, ⓦexpirat.org. Quite frankly, you could take your pick from any number of the village's groovy bars, but this long-standing party place towards the southern end of the beach just about trumps the lot; it comprises a host of different drinking areas (cocktail bar, wine bar, pizza bar and so on) all cleverly culled from shipping containers, while DJs ramp it up nightly. Daily 11am–late.

AN ETCHING OF 19TH-CENTURY ROMANIA

Contexts

History

Although inhabited since prehistoric times, Romania achieved statehood only in the nineteenth century, and Transylvania, one-third of its present territory, was acquired as recently as 1918. Hence, much of Romania's history is that of its disparate parts – Dobrogea, the Banat, Bessarabia, Maramureş and, above all, the principalities of Moldavia, Wallachia and Transylvania.

Greeks, Dacians and Romans

Despite the discovery of bones and tools in Carpathian caves (up to 35,000 years old), little is known about the hunter-gatherers of the early **Stone Age**. With the retreat of the glaciers, humans seem to have settled first in the Banat, where a people known as the **Criş Culture** was farming by around 5800 BC; followed by the **Hamangia Culture** in Dobrogea and the **Cucuteni Culture** in Moldavia. Other societies developed in the Bronze and Iron Ages, with Celts arriving from Asia in the last millennium BC.

During the seventh and sixth centuries BC, **Greek traders** established ports along the Black Sea coast; the chronicler Herodotus reported in the sixth century BC that of the various **Thracian tribes** (including the Getae on the Danube, the Dacians to their north, the Thracians proper to the south and the Illyrians in present-day Albania), the "bravest and most righteous" were those later known as the Geto-Dacians. Eventually these tribes coalesced, with Burebista (82–44 BC) ruling a short-lived **Dacian empire** stretching from the Black Sea to Slovakia, with its capital at **Sarmizegetusa**.

This kingdom was reunited by **Decebal** (87–106 AD), but the **Romans** were already on the Danube and expanding northwards. Decebal held them off until the Emperor Trajan conquered Dacia in two campaigns (in 101–102 and 105–106 AD), with the exception of the Apuseni mountains, Maramureş and Moldavia. The province of **Dacia** grew so rich from mining salt, silver and gold that it was known as Dacia Felix (Happy Dacia), but with increasing incursions by nomadic Asian tribes, its defence became too costly, and in 271 AD, Emperor Aurelian withdrew Rome's presence from the region.

The Age of Migrations and Daco-Romanian Continuity

The **Age of Migrations** was defined by the arrival of nomadic peoples sweeping out of Asia, including the Vandals (second century), Goths (third century), Huns (fourth and fifth centuries), Alans (fifth century), Gepids and Avars (sixth century), Slavs (seventh century) and Bulgars (seventh century, along the coast en route to Bulgaria). They left few traces and did nothing to undermine the **Daco-Romanian Continuity theory**, which holds that the Romanians are descendants of the Roman settlers and indigenous Dacians. Romanian philologists point to numerous Latin-derived words in their language; yet many of the settlers would have been not free Romans but former slaves and soldiers, many Greek and Arab. Cities were abandoned by the early fifth century, but coins found in the area now called Transylvania, protected by mountains, show continuing trade with the empire.

35,000 years ago	5800 BCE	7th century BCE	335 BCE	82–44 BCE
First traces of humans in Carpathian caves	First settled Neolithic culture	Greek settlements on the coast	Alexander the Great fought the Getae	Burebista creates Dacian empire

This would be of purely academic interest were it not entwined with the centuries-old dispute between Magyars and Romanians over the **occupation of Transylvania**. Romanians claim uninterrupted residence, while Magyars say their occupation (around 997) met little resistance, and that the indigenous people were Slavic. According to some Magyar historians, **Vlachs** (Romanians) are first mentioned in Transylvania around 1222 as nomadic pastoralists from a homeland in Macedonia and Illyria.

The medieval principalities

The Hungarian kings invited foreign settlers to bolster their control of **Transylvania** from the twelfth century; groups of Germans – subsequently known as **Saxons** – built up powerful self-governing market towns like Hermannstadt (Sibiu) and Kronstadt (Braşov). Another ethnic group, the **Székely**, colonized the eastern marches, also enjoying relative autonomy. These colonists had to withstand frequent invasions by the **Tatars** (or Mongols), who devastated much of Eastern Europe in 1241–42 and 1285 and continued wreaking havoc for another five centuries.

The Hungarian nobles dominated the **feudal system**, sitting alongside the Saxons and Székely on the Diet that advised the Hungarian governor. Romanian-speaking Vlachs, already possibly the majority of Transylvania's population, were initially represented on Diets, but from the mid-fourteenth century they faced increasing **discrimination**, due in part to being Orthodox (barring a few apostate nobles) rather than Catholic.

Beyond the Carpathians, the first record of **Wallachia** (Vlahia or the Ţara Românească), in a gap between Hungarian and Mongol rulers, dates from 1247, but chronicles attribute its foundation to either Negru Vodă (the Black Prince) or his son Radu Negru (1310–52), usually credited as founder of the Basarab dynasty, who established Wallachia's independence from Hungary at the Battle of Posada in 1330. The shift in Wallachia's capitals over the centuries – from Câmpulung in the highlands down to Curtea de Argeş and Târgovişte in the foothills and then Bucharest on the plain – expressed a cautious move from the safety of the mountains to the financial opportunities of the trade routes with Turkey.

Attempts to enforce Hungarian rule in Maramureş led some of the indigenous population to follow **Bogdan Vodă** eastwards in 1359 to found a new principality, **Moldavia**, but the process of occupying the hills and steppes beyond the Carpathians had begun centuries earlier, with groups of Romanian-speaking pastoralists and farmers gradually expanding to the Dnestr.

Ottomans, Nationes and Phanariots

From the mid-fourteenth century the **Ottoman empire** of the Seljuk Turks spread inexorably northwards, shattering the Serbian Empire at Kosovo Polje in 1389 and subjugating Bulgaria in 1393. They were briefly halted by **Mircea the Old** (Mircea cel Bătrân; 1386–1418) at the Battle of Rovine in 1394, but he was compelled to acknowledge Ottoman suzerainty in 1417. By surrendering the fertile **Dobrogea** region and paying tribute, outright occupation was avoided, although there was always the threat of overwhelming attack. Wallachia, Moldavia and Transylvania were now Christendom's front line of resistance to the Turks – throughout the fifteenth century,

87–106 AD	106	271	997	1211–25
Decebal reunites Dacian kingdom	Roman conquest of Dacia	Roman withdrawal from Dacia	Magyars settle Transylvania	The Teutonic Knights settle around Braşov

their history is overshadowed by this struggle and by four remarkable military leaders. First was Transylvanian *voivode* **Iancu de Hunedoara** (Hunyadi János), who defeated the Turks near Alba Iulia and Sibiu in 1441–43 and led a multinational army to victory at Belgrade in 1456. Iancu's son **Mátyás Corvinus** (also known as Hunyadi Mátyás or Matei Corvin), Hungary's great Renaissance king (1458–90), continued to resist the Turks, who were dislodged from southern Bessarabia by **Stephen the Great** (Ştefan cel Mare) of Moldavia. However, their resurgence under Bajazid II presaged the demise of Moldavian independence, as was apparent to Stephen by the end of his embattled reign (1457–1504). Due to Wallachia's greater vulnerablity, its rulers generally preferred to pay off the Turks rather than resist them – **Vlad Ţepeş** (Vlad the Impaler; see page 398) being a notable exception from 1456 to 1476.

In **Transylvania**, the least exposed region, the **Bobâlna peasant uprising** of 1437–38 rocked the feudal order. To safeguard their privileges, the Magyar nobility concluded a pact known as the **Union of Three Nations** with the Saxon and Székely leaders, whereby each of these three ethnic groups (Nationes) agreed to recognize and defend the rights of the others, effectively prohibiting Vlachs from holding public office or residing in Saxon and Magyar towns. Increasing exploitation of the Magyar peasantry led in 1514 to an uprising under György Dózsa (Gheorghe Doja), savagely repressed by governor **János Zápolyai** (Johann Zapolya, 1510–40).

The crushing defeat of Hungary by Suleiman the Magnificent at **Mohács** (1526) and the Turkish occupation of Buda (1541) exacerbated the isolation of the principalities. Although Austria's Habsburg dynasty claimed what was left of Hungary after Mohács, Zápolyai and successors such as István Báthori (1571–81) and Zsigmond Báthori (1581–97) maintained a precarious autonomy for Transylvania; in Moldavia, however, **Petru Rareş** could only hold his throne (1527–38 and 1541–56) by breathtaking duplicity and improvisations, while his successors plumbed even further depths.

Short-lived unification

Understandably, Romanian historiography prefers to highlight more successful leaders such as **Michael the Brave** (Mihai Viteazul, often known in Wallachia as Mihai Bravul), ruler of Wallachia from 1593. His defeat of the Turks in 1595 was followed by the overthrow of Andrew Báthori in Transylvania in 1599 and the seizure of the Moldavian throne in 1600. This opportunist **union of the principalities** – which fragmented immediately following his murder in 1601 – is presented as a triumph of Romanian nationalism, but it was only between 1604 and 1657 that Transylvania enjoyed real independence from both Habsburgs and Ottomans (although there were regular Turkish raids, with 100,000 killed in 1658).

Moldavia and Wallachia avoided Turkish occupation by accepting Ottoman "advisers", known as **Phanariots**, from the 1630s; a period of relative stability allowed a minor cultural renaissance until 1711 in Moldavia and 1714 in Wallachia. The Turks then dispensed with native rule, instead appointing Phanariot rulers whose greed, combined with more than seventy changes of ruler in Moldavia and Wallachia until 1821, crippled both regions.

1241–42 & 1285	1247	1280	1330
Tatar invasions	First record of Wallachia	Curtea de Argeş becomes Wallachia's second capital	The Battle of Posada establishes Wallachian independence from Hungary

The struggle for independence and unification

Habsburg power grew after the failure of the Turkish siege of Vienna in 1683; after the collapse of a Hungarian revolt in 1704–11, led by Ferenc II Rákóczi, Austrian governors were imposed on Transylvania. Some Orthodox clergy were persuaded to accept papal authority, with the promise that Vlachs who joined the **Uniate Church** (see page 170) would be granted equality with the Nationes. This promise was retracted in 1701, but Bishop Inocenţiu Micu and the intellectuals of the Transylvanian School agitated for equal rights and articulated the Vlachs' growing consciousness of being **Romanians**. Thus Joseph II's reforms came too late to prevent the great peasant rebellion led by **Horea**, **Crişan** and **Cloşca** in 1784–85. Its crushing only stimulated efforts to attain liberation by constitutional means, however.

The development of liberal and nationalist factions in **Moldavia and Wallachia**, driven by the ideals of Romanticism and the French Revolution, the success of Serbian and Greek independence movements and the emergence of capitalism, indicated that Turkish dominance was declining. A major uprising in Wallachia in 1821, led by **Tudor Vladimirescu**, was defeated, but it persuaded the Turks that it was time to end Phanariot rule, and power was restored to native boyars in 1822.

The rise of Russia and World War I

As the Ottoman empire declined, **Russia** expanded. Fired by imperialist and Pan-Slavist ideals and a fear of Habsburg encroachment (manifest in 1774, when Austria annexed the region henceforth known as **Bucovina**), Russia presented itself as guardian of the Ottomans' Christian subjects. In 1792, Russian forces reached the River Dnestr; one Russo-Turkish war led to the annexation of Bessarabia in 1812, and another to Moldavia and Wallachia becoming Russian protectorates from 1829 to 1834, allowing access to Western European trade and ideas at last. Assemblies were introduced in both principalities, but, given their domination by the boyars, economic development took precedence over the political and social reforms demanded by bourgeois liberals such as Nicolae Golescu, Ion Brătianu, Nicolae Bălcescu and Mihail Kogălniceanu, whose **democratic movement** briefly came to power in 1848, the **Year of Revolutions**.

The build-up to the Crimean War again saw Russia occupying Moldavia and Wallachia and fighting the Turks along the Danube. The Congress of Paris, ending the war in 1856, reaffirmed Turkish rule, but in 1859 the assemblies of Moldavia and Wallachia proclaimed their **unification** under a single ruler, **Alexandru Ioan Cuza**. He abolished serfdom and introduced agrarian reform, provoking landowners and other conservatives to overthrow him in 1866, inviting a German prince, Karl von Hohenzollern, to rule in his place as **Carol I**. Yet another Russo-Turkish war led to Rumania (as the United Provinces had renamed themselves in 1862) declaring independence on May 9, 1877, recognized the next year by the Treaty of Berlin.

Transylvania followed a different course, with support for Hungary's 1848 revolution split along ethnic lines; Magyars greeted Transylvania's unification with Hungary with enthusiasm, while the Romanian population objected and the Saxons were lukewarm. Following protest meetings at Blaj, **Avram Iancu** formed Romanian guerrilla bands to oppose the Hungarians; attempts by Kossuth and Bălcescu to compromise over Romanian rights came too late to create a united front against the Russian armies which invaded Transylvania to repress the revolution on behalf of the Habsburgs.

1359	1394	1415	1417	1437–38
Bogdan Vodă establishes the principality of Moldavia	Mircea the Old defeats the Turks at Rovine	Târgovişte becomes Wallachia's third capital	Mircea the Old accepts Turkish suzerainty	Bobâlna peasant revolt in Transylvania

The Ausgleich (Compromise) of 1867 established the Dual Monarchy of Austria-Hungary; Transylvania became part of Greater Hungary, ruled directly from Budapest, with a policy of **Magyarization** making Hungarian the official language and undermining Romanian culture (Bucovina and Maramureş, still under Austrian rule, avoided the worst of this). The cultural association **ASTRA**, founded in 1861, and the **National Party**, founded in 1881, defended the Romanians, maintaining close links with kindred groups across the Carpathians.

The influence of foreign capital increased enormously around the turn of the century, drawn by Rumania's mineral wealth – particularly its oil. While the Liberal and Conservative parties squabbled ritualistically and alternated in power, the peasantry got ever poorer, exploding in the **răscoala** of 1907 – a nationwide uprising that was savagely crushed (with around 11,000 deaths) and followed by ineffectual agrarian reforms.

Rumania's acquisition of northern Dobrogea, south of the Danube, in the Treaty of Berlin was one of the many causes of the **Balkan Wars** that embroiled Rumania, Bulgaria, Serbia, Macedonia and Greece. Rumania sat out the first Balkan War (1912–13), but joined the alliance against Bulgaria in 1913, thus gaining southern Dobrogea. King Ferdinand, who succeeded his uncle Carol in 1914, was married to Marie, granddaughter of both Queen Victoria and Tsar Alexander II, so, when Rumania entered **World War I** in 1916, it joined Britain, France and Russia and invaded Transylvania. This was a total fiasco, and only desperate defence at Mărăşeşti prevented the loss of the whole of Rumania. An onerous peace treaty was imposed in May 1918, but by October the disintegration of the Central Powers reversed this situation entirely, and Rumanian armies advanced into Transylvania, and then on into Hungary to overthrow the short-lived communist regime of Béla Kun in August 1919. On December 1, 1918, **Transylvania's union with Rumania** was declared in Alba Iulia; the Romanian population of Bessarabia, freed by the Russian Revolution, had already declared their union with Rumania in March 1918, followed in November by Bucovina. The **Trianon Treaty** in 1920 upheld Rumania's gains and the nation doubled in size, while Hungary lost half of its populace and two-thirds of its land – a source of resentment ever since.

Greater Romania

The enlarged country was dignified with the name **Greater Romania**; Hungarian estates in Transylvania were expropriated, and many Hungarian employees were dismissed, with Romanian immigrants brought in to replace them. Ferdinand favoured the **National Liberal Party**, which pursued damaging nationalist and populist policies; on his death in 1927, it was replaced by the **National Peasant Party**, led by **Iuliu Maniu**, which in 1928 won the only remotely fair election of this period. Despite a parliamentary majority and genuinely reforming policies, Maniu took a conservative line, constrained by the world economic crisis of 1929, vested interests and entrenched corruption.

However, it was a moral issue that led to the government's fall: in 1930, after a three-year regency, **Carol II** took the throne on condition he leave his divorced Jewish mistress, Magda Lupescu. He broke the promise, and the puritan Maniu and his

1441–43	1514	1568	1600–01
Iancu de Hunedoara defeats the Turks	Revolt led by György Dózsa in Transylvania	Edict of Turda recognizing equality of four non-Orthodox faiths	Wallachia, Moldavia and Transylvania briefly united under Michael the Brave

government resigned. Carol then exploited his right to dissolve parliament and call elections at will; a corrupt system developed whereby the government would fix elections by every means possible, only to be dismissed and replaced by the opposition when the king had tired of them. Between 1930 and 1940, there were no less than 25 separate governments, leading ultimately to the collapse of the political parties themselves; Carol set up his own "youth movement" and began routine phone-tapping by the **Siguranţa**, the Securitate's predecessor, enabling him to blackmail the entire political establishment except for Maniu.

The Iron Guard and World War II

A **fascist movement** also established itself, particularly in Bessarabia, which had a long tradition of anti-Semitism. The main fascist party, founded in 1927 and taking much of the National Peasant Party's rural support, was the Legion of the Archangel Michael; its green-shirted paramilitary wing, the **Iron Guard** (see page 239), extolled the soil, death and a mystical form of Orthodoxy, fought street battles against Jews and political rivals, and murdered four current and former prime ministers. In 1937, the anti-Semitic National League of Christian Defence and National Christian Party were installed in office by the king, but the prime minister, the poet Octavian Goga, insulted Lupescu and was dismissed in February 1938, after just six weeks in power. This at last provoked Carol to ban all political parties (other than his own National Rebirth Front) and set up a royal dictatorship.

Germany demanded a monopoly of Romanian exports in return for a guarantee of its borders, agreeing an oil-for-arms deal in March 1939, while Carol obtained feeble guarantees from Britain and France. The equilibrium was shattered by the Nazi-Soviet Non-Aggression Pact and the Soviet annexation of Bessarabia and northern Bucovina in June 1940; in August, Hitler forced Carol to cede Northern Transylvania to Hungary and southern Dobrogea to Bulgaria. Unable to maintain his position after giving away such huge portions of Romanian territory, Carol fled with Lupescu and his spoils in September, leaving his son **Mihai**, then 19 years old, to take the throne.

Mihai accepted the formation of a government led by **Marshal Ion Antonescu**, who styled himself Conducator ("leader", equivalent to Führer) but had little control over legionary groups who launched an orgy of violence against Jews and liberals. Antonescu eventually moved to disarm the Iron Guard, provoking an armed uprising in January 1941, only suppressed by the army after a fierce struggle.

Romania entered **World War II** in June 1941, joining the Nazi invasion of Russia with the objective of regaining Bessarabia and northern Bucovina. Romanian troops took Odessa and participated in the battles of Sevastopol and Stalingrad, taking heavy casualties. Opposition to the war mounted as the Russians drew nearer, and a **royal/military coup** on August 23, 1944 overthrew the Antonescu regime – a date commemorated until 1989 as **Liberation Day**, although it took a further two months to clear the Germans from the country.

The People's Republic

The first postwar government was a broad coalition, with **communists** only playing a minor role. With Soviet backing, however, their influence grew, and in March

1659	1687	1688–1714	1700
Bucharest becomes Wallachia's fourth capital	Habsburgs take control of Transylvania	Constantin Brâncoveanu presides over a cultural revival in Wallachia	Creation of Uniate (Greco-Catholic) church in Transylvania

THE HOLOCAUST IN ROMANIA

In 1939, Romania had the third-largest **Jewish population** in Europe after Poland and the Soviet Union. Most lived in Bessarabia, Bucovina and parts of northern Moldavia. In June 1940, Bessarabia and northern Bucovina were ceded to the Soviet Union, as demanded by Hitler, and at least fifty Jews were killed in Dorohoi by retreating Romanian troops. A year later troops carried out an awful pogrom in Iaşi, killing about eight thousand Jews, leading the Germans to comment, "we always act scientifically ... we use surgeons, not butchers". The attack on the Soviet Union led to many more massacres; at least 33,000 Jews died in Bessarabia and Bucovina between June 22 and September 1, 1941, and, in fact, the worst single massacre of the Holocaust was committed by Romanians as they took Odessa.

Deportations to Transnistria, the conquered territory beyond the River Dnestr, began in earnest on September 16; around 150,000 Jews were taken, of whom 18,000 to 22,000 died in transit. Up to ninety thousand more died from starvation, disease and general mistreatment. Between November 21 and 29, 1941, all 48,000 Jews in the Bogdanovka camp in southern Transnistria were killed; another eighteen thousand were killed in the Dumanovka camp.

In July 1942, the Germans began to press for the Jews of Wallachia, Moldavia and southern Transylvania to be deported to the camps, following the 120,000 already taken to Auschwitz from Hungarian-controlled Northern Transylvania. This was blocked after diplomatic lobbying, although it was probably more due to the fact that the Jews were still vital to the functioning of the economy. In November 1942, it was decided that Romanian Jews in Germany should be sent to the death camps.

When Romania was thinking of changing sides, the **World Jewish Congress** proposed a plan to save seventy thousand Romanian Jews, and possibly 1.3 million more in Eastern Europe, by paying the Romanian government twelve shillings per head to allow them to leave by ship for Palestine. This plan was blocked by opposition from anti-Semites in the US State Department and Britain, worried about Arab reaction to further Jewish immigration to Palestine, as well as by the practical implications of sending money to a Nazi ally. Thirteen ships did leave, with thirteen thousand refugees, but two sank (with 1163 on board) and others were stopped by Turkey, under pressure from both Britain and Germany.

Antonescu began a **limited repatriation** from the camps of Transnistria, bringing back 1500 in December 1943 and 1846 orphans by March 1944. He warned the Germans not to kill Jews as they retreated; nevertheless, a final thousand were killed in Tiraspol jail. On March 20, 1944, the Red Army reached the Dnestr, and the worst of the nightmare ended. In Antonescu's trial in 1946 he claimed to have saved about 275,000 Jews by his policy of keeping them for extermination at home; however, this did not save him from execution. Overall, between 264,900 and 470,000 Romanian Jews, and 36,000 Gypsies, died in the war; 428,000 Jews survived.

1945 the king was forced to accept a government led by **Dr Petru Groza**, with key posts held by communists. Land reform in 1945 benefited millions of peasants at the expense of the Saxons and Swabians, while women voted for the first time in 1946, supposedly contributing to the election of another ostensibly balanced government. In fact, virtually every device ever used to rig an election was brought into play and the takeover steamed ahead.

Groza's second administration also included other parties, who were then forcibly merged with the communists. On December 30, 1947, King Mihai was forced to abdicate and Romania was declared a **People's Republic**. Antonescu and up to sixty thousand were executed after highly irregular trials; eighty thousand arrests followed

1704–11	1711	1774	1784–85
Revolt led by Ferenc II Rákóczi in Transylvania	Imposition of Phanariot rule in Wallachia and Moldavia	Austrian annexation of Bucovina	Peasant rebellion led by Horea, Crişan and Cloşca in Transylvania

in an effort to impose **collectivization** (a reversal of the earlier agrarian reform), with around 180,000 more from 1948 in the campaign to "liquidate" the Uniate Church. **Police terror** was used against real or potential opponents, with victims imprisoned or sent to work on the Danube–Black Sea Canal, the "Canal Morţii" (see page 358) that claimed over 100,000 lives.

By 1952, **Gheorghe Gheorghiu-Dej** had taken control of the Communist Party, with Stalin's backing; he ignored reformist trends in the USSR after Stalin's death in 1953 and stuck grimly to the true faith, developing heavy industry and claiming the impossible growth rate of thirteen percent per year. The USSR, having again annexed Bessarabia, had given some of it to Ukraine and absorbed the rest as the puppet **Republic of Moldova**; therefore, his increasing refusal to follow the Moscow line was a great success domestically, tapping into a vein of popular nationalism. Gheorghiu-Dej died in 1965 and was succeeded by a collective leadership, but by 1969 the little-known **Nicolae Ceauşescu** had outmanoeuvred his rivals and established undisputed power.

The Ceauşescu era

There's little doubt that for a few years **Ceauşescu** was genuinely popular: he allowed a cultural thaw, put food and consumer goods into the shops, denounced secret police excesses (blaming them on Gheorghiu-Dej), and above all condemned the Warsaw Pact invasion of Czechoslovakia in 1968. His independent **foreign policy** gained Romania the reputation of being the Eastern bloc's "maverick" state, building links with the West and maintaining ties with countries with which the USSR had severed contact.

However, **economic failure** soon forced him to revert to tried and tested methods of control. Ceauşescu stuck throughout to a Stalinist belief in heavy industry, and during the 1970s his **industrialization programme** absorbed thirty percent of GNP and $10.2 billion in foreign loans.

With living standards plummeted, Ceauşescu was convinced that the key to industrial growth lay in a larger workforce, and in 1966 banned abortions and contraception for any married woman under 40 with fewer than four children (in 1972, the limits were raised to 45 and five); by 1989 eleven thousand women had died due to illegal abortions. In 1984, when his developing paranoia and personality cult were putting him increasingly out of touch, he introduced the **Baby Police** and compulsory monthly gynaecological examinations, and higher taxation for the childless.

Ceauşescu also **discriminated against the minorities**: it became increasingly hard to get an education or to buy books in Hungarian or German, or to communicate with relatives abroad. The damage to relations with Hungary didn't bother Ceauşescu, but he tried to keep on the right side of the German and Israeli governments, which purchased exit visas for ethnic Germans and Jews in Romania for substantial sums.

Human rights abuses worsened through the 1980s, including the **systematization** programme for rural redevelopment and constant repression by the **Securitate** (secret police), which produced an atmosphere of fear and distrust even within families, as up to one in four people was rumoured to be an informer. Living standards were falling fast, as the truth about economic collapse was hidden from Ceauşescu by his wife and subordinates. Absolutely everything was in short supply, but Nicolae and Elena pushed

1812	1821	1822	1829–34
Annexation of Bessarabia by Russia	Revolt in Wallachia led by Tudor Vladimirescu	End of Phanariot rule in Wallachia and Moldavia	Russian occupation of Wallachia and Moldavia

on with megalomaniac projects such as the Palace of the People in Bucharest and the Danube–Black Sea Canal (again).

The revolution

By **December 1989**, it seemed impossible for Ceaușescu not to bow to the wave of change sweeping across Eastern Europe. A series of strikes and riots culminated on December 20 with 100,000 people in Timişoara demanding Ceaușescu's resignation; despite his orders to fire, the army withdrew rather than launch a massacre. In Bucharest the next day, another crowd of 100,000, brought from their workplaces to show support, gathered in Piața Republicii (now Piața Revoluției) to hear him speak, but he was soon interrupted by heckling. The police and Securitate opened fire but were unable to drive the crowds away, partly because the Minister of Defence, **General Vasile Milea**, ordered the army not to fire. On the morning of December 22, Ceaușescu had Milea shot, but this merely encouraged more army units to defect to the side of the protestors. By noon, the crowds had broken into the Party's Central Committee building, and the Ceaușescus fled by helicopter from the roof. After going to their villa at Snagov and on to a military airfield near Titu, they hijacked a car before being arrested in Târgoviște. When news of their capture failed to stop loyal Securitate units firing on the crowds, they were summarily tried and **executed** on Christmas Day.

Meanwhile, street fighting broke out in many cities, with army and police units changing sides; it's unclear at what point their leadership had decided to abandon Ceaușescu. Nor is it clear at what stage the **National Salvation Front** (Frontul Salvării Naționale or FSN), which took power from December 22, had been formed; supposedly created in the Central Committee building that very afternoon by people who had gathered there independently, it's now clear many of them were already in contact. The key figures were Party members who had been sidelined by Ceaușescu, led by **Ion Iliescu** as president; his prime minister was **Petre Roman**.

Around 1100 people died in the revolution and the "terrorist" phase that lasted until January 18, although both the new government and the Hungarian media initially published inflated death tolls of ten thousand or more.

Free Romania

Within a month of the revolution it was clear that the former elite had no intention of losing power, as the FSN reversed its pledge not to run as a party in May's elections, and even shipped in ten thousand miners to deal with **protests** in Bucharest, leaving seven dead and 296 injured. The nation went into shock, and the economy collapsed.

The FSN easily won Romania's **first free election**, with Iliescu becoming president. The process was deemed fair enough by international observers, even though a million more votes were cast than were registered, supposedly "due to the people's enthusiasm for democracy". People began referring to December 1989 as the "so-called revolution", and it was increasingly taken for granted that nothing much had changed.

Economic reform got under way slowly. Food subsidies were cut and **prices** increased, while **inflation** reached almost three hundred percent in 1993. In 1991 the miners were

1848	**1859**	**1861**	**1866**
The Year of Revolutions (revolt in Transylvania to 1849)	Unification of Wallachia and Moldavia	Establishment of the ASTRA cultural association	Replacement of Alexandru Ioan Cuza by Carol I as prince of Rumania

brought back to force Roman to resign; he was replaced by **Teodor Stolojan**; the FSN soon split.

A **second general election** was held in 1992, after the adoption of a new constitution establishing a **presidential democracy**. Iliescu kept the presidency, installing a coalition government under **Nicolae Văcăroiu**; it needed support from the ultranationalists, but the need for aid and fear of international isolation kept it on a seemingly reformist course. Particularly welcome (and rewarded by substantial loans) was Iliescu's support for the tight **fiscal policies** of the National Bank's governor **Mugur Isărescu**. In 1995 taxes were cut to the lowest levels in East-Central Europe and the economy continued to improve, with unemployment falling and wages rising; however, this wasn't enough to keep Iliescu in power as a series of **scandals** alienated voters.

Constantinescu and the return of Iliescu

The 1996 election was won by the sixteen-party Democratic Convention of Romania, and geology professor **Emil Constantinescu** became president, appointing the youthful mayor of Bucharest, Victor Ciorbea, as prime minister. Their government was genuinely liberal-democratic and Western-oriented, concentrating on economic reform and attacking corruption. They found the coffers empty due to Iliescu's attempts to buy re-election, and the result was the most radical "shock therapy" campaign anywhere in East-Central Europe. Subsidies and price controls were abolished and in January 1997 alone fuel prices doubled and rail fares rose by eighty percent.

Ciorbea, unable to control the scheming coalition partners, was forced to resign early in 1998 to be replaced first by **Radu Vasile** and then by the central bank's Mugur Isărescu. However, the government was increasingly seen as failing, particularly in the war against corruption and in reforming and reviving the economy.

In the **general elections of 2000**, angry voters returned Iliescu and his Social Democratic Party (PSD; the FSN's latest incarnation) to power. **Adrian Năstase**, who had been successful as foreign minister, became prime minister; although various scandals led to resignations, the government proved remarkably stable, and in 2002 the **EU** announced that Romania could join in 2007. Romania also joined **NATO** in 2004. The EU knew that Romania (and Bulgaria) were not ready to join, but judged that letting them in to encourage the reformers was better than further delaying modernization. The PSD saw that it only had to make a show of fighting corruption, and did all it could to entrench its position by patronage and abuse of power.

President vs. prime minister

Romania's 1991 constitution virtually guarantees conflict between president and prime minister. In the November 2003 elections a PNL/PD alliance, **Justice and Truth**, took 31 percent of the vote, while the PSD and allies took 37 percent; widespread outrage at blatant vote-rigging led to a relatively clean run-off for the presidency, allowing a narrow win by the PD's **Traian Băsescu**, mayor of Bucharest. PNL leader **Calin Popescu-Tariceanu** became prime minister and was able to form a coalition government, but not before the smaller parties had joined the PSD to install its former prime ministers

1867	1877	1916–18	1918
Dual Monarchy of Austria and Hungary	Declaration of independence of Rumania on May 9	War against Austria-Hungary	Union of Transylvania with Rumania on December 1

THE KING OF ROMANIA

In the 1990s, many people looked to the **King** for an escape from the intrigues of the politicians. Born in 1921, **Mihai** reigned from 1940 to 1947; he earned respect due to his role in the coup of August 23, 1944, when he dismissed Antonescu, and his attempts to resist communism thereafter. When forced to abdicate by the communists, he went into exile in England and then Switzerland. He was not allowed to return after the revolution, until a brief visit in 1992 which drew large crowds. The situation changed totally with Constantinescu's election; Mihai began to visit Romania frequently and in 2001 returned to live. From 1997 he was an active ambassador for Romanian entry to NATO and gained in stature, with even Iliescu belatedly calling him "Majesty". Nevertheless, royalism has faded as a political force, although his daughter Princess Margareta is popular.

A castle at **Săvârşin** and the **Elisabeta Palace** in Bucharest have been restored to Mihai; the issue of Peleş was trickier, but in 2005 parliament voted to pay him €30m for the main castle while handing him Pelişor (both remain open as museums).

In March 2016 Mihai withdrew from public life after a diagnosis of cancer, appointing Margareta "Crown Custodian", and he died in December 2017.

Adrian Năstase and Nicolae Văcăroiu as speakers of the House of Deputies and the Senate respectively.

The oligarchs realized that Băsescu was the first Romanian leader to be serious about tackling corruption; once the country was safely in the EU (which was promising up to €1.2 billion per year in poorly supervised aid), on 1 January 2007, the PSD applied to the Constitutional Court for Băsescu's impeachment on grounds of interfering with cabinet government and the judiciary. The court rejected this, and parliament voted the next day to **suspend Băsescu** pending a referendum on impeachment.

Certainly Băsescu, a bluff former sea captain, was often tactless and impulsive, while his opponents were far suaver, but he had widespread popular support. Efforts to fix the referendum rules failed, meaning that he was always going to win, despite being largely banished from television, and the stand-off continued. Appalled by how thoroughly it had been hoodwinked, the EU set up a Co-operation and Verification Mechanism to monitor legal reforms and the anticorruption campaign.

The constant infighting of Romania's political parties continued, with PNL defectors forming a **Liberal Democrat** party which merged in 2008 with the Democrats as the Democrat-Liberal Party (PD-L). The 2008 elections produced a government headed by the PD-L's **Emil Boc**; in the November 2009 presidential elections, Băsescu just managed to beat the PSD's Mircea Geoana, who responded with bizarre accusations of parapsychological mind control, and Boc remained prime minister.

An **economic boom** began in 2001, with GDP growing by an average six percent annually from 2004 to 2008, until halted by the global crisis – in 2009 the economy shrank by seven percent and inflation rose to six percent (the highest in the EU), the economy kept afloat by IMF loans. In February 2012 the Boc government was forced to resign by mass protests, partly against swingeing austerity measures, but also against the government's practice of handing its backers contracts for vital infrastructure such as skating rinks and stadiums in villages without running water and sewage. Băsescu

1928–30	1940	1941	1944	1947
Iuliu Maniu prime minister	Soviet annexation of Bessarabia and northern Bucovina	Romania joins the Nazi invasion of Russia	Antonescu's fascist regime overthrown on August 23	King Mihai forced to abdicate

nominated spy chief **Mihai Razvan Ungureanu** as prime minister, but the opposition voted him out after three months and installed the hardline leftist **Victor Ponta**.

The EU blocked Romania from joining the Schengen zone in 2011 largely because not one high-profile politician had been jailed since the end of communism despite rampant corruption. Finally, the **National Anti-Corruption Directorate** (DNA), founded in 2003, began to get convictions, aided by the secret services; one of the first was **Adrian Năstase**, sentenced to jail in June 2012 for illegally raising €1.6m for his failed 2004 presidential campaign, who then shot himself in a bizarre fake suicide attempt. At this point the corrupt establishment decided to fight back. Having gained a parliamentary majority thanks to defections from the PDL, Ponta set about dismantling every check on his power, ruling by **emergency ordinance** and taking control of institutions from the presidency (including state television). Then parliament voted to suspend Băsescu again for thirty days, pending another referendum on impeachment. Ponta tried to change the referendum rules, cutting the threshold from half the electorate to a majority of those voting, but the constitutional court rejected this. Thus Băsescu survived by having his supporters stay at home to keep the turnout below fifty percent; he remained in office, and the country remained in crisis.

Parliamentary **elections** in December 2012 were marked by apathy and an inept campaign by the PDL, and Ponta's PSD/PNL coalition won a large majority, in the most corrupt parliament in recent Romanian history – twenty of its 588 members were under investigation, and two had already been convicted. Likewise, before the November 2014 presidential elections a host of prominent figures were arrested, including previously untouchable political barons like PSD leader Viorel Hrebenciuc. Ponta and Băsescu signed a **power-sharing deal**, giving the president pre-eminence in the areas of foreign policy, security and defense, and the prime minister in the areas of economic and domestic policy; this worked well until Băsescu vetoed the 2014 budget, objecting to a gas tax which would jeopardize aid from the EU and IMF. Again, in April 2015 the government announced a cut in **VAT** from 24 percent to twenty percent (to just nine percent on food), opposed by the EU and IMF and by Mugur Isărescu (still running the central bank), all warning that it was a populist move that risked hard-won economic stability; the president rejected the law but it was pushed through by emergency ordinance and triggered the expected short-term boom in consumption.

A backlash against the independent prosecutors was expected if Ponta won the presidency in November 2014 (Băsescu was ineligible for a third term). However it was an independent candidate, the Saxon mayor of Sibiu **Klaus Iohannis**, who made it to the run-off against Ponta; in the first round the government had tried to block the 3–4 million expatriates from voting, with inadequate facilities and massive queues, and public outrage forced the resignation of the foreign minister. In the run-off there was a high turnout, both in Romania and abroad, and Iohannis became president, promising pro-business policies, reform of the justice and voting systems, and of course continuing war on corruption; but it was Ponta, still prime minister, who held effective power.

In April 2015 Romania's second-richest man **Ioan Niculae**, worth over €1 billion, was jailed for illegally donating €1m to Geoana's 2009 presidential campaign; by August 2015 half of county council presidents and a third of city mayors were under investigation, and Ponta himself was indicted on charges of tax evasion, money

1952–65	1969	1989	1996	2000
Gheorghe Gheorghiu-Dej leads a Stalinist regime	Nicolae Ceauşescu takes power	Nicolae and Elena Ceauşescu executed on Christmas Day	Centre-right government takes over from former communists	Ion Iliescu becomes president for the second time

laundering, conflict of interest and making false statements (although parliament refused to lift his immunity from prosecution), but refused to resign. In September Bucharest's mayor Sorin Oprescu was arrested on bribery charges linked to the French-controlled Apa Nova company which was given a monopoly on Bucharest's water supply and sewage services until 2025 and massively raised prices. The most astounding news came in October 2015 when Iliescu was charged with **crimes against humanity** for the *mineriad* of June 1990.

Colectiv responsibility and the anti-corruption movement

Ponta survived four no-confidence votes in parliament but was no longer really in power. But it was a fire in the *Colectiv* nightclub in Bucharest on October 30, 2015 that killed 64 (27 at once, the rest dying of burns over several weeks, many from infections acquired in hospitals) that led to the resignations of Ponta, interior minister Gabriel Oprea and the mayor of Bucharest's Sector 4 after mass protests against a system totally oriented around bribery, in which it was more or less impossible to legally obtain **fire safety permits**. The crowds on the streets doubled in size after Ponta's resignation, demanding the whole corrupt system be swept away. Iohannis consulted the leaders of the political parties and of civil society before asking **Dacian Cioloş**, a former European Commissioner for Agriculture, to lead a non-party technocratic government. One side effect was that a ban on smoking in public places, which had been stuck in parliament, was finally voted through, coming into force in March 2016. A situation also arose in which €1.7 billion of European funding for **infrastructure projects** could not be delivered because politicians were too afraid of the prosecutors to sign the contracts; Romania was already failing to use seventy percent of allocated EU funds, and its infrastructure remains the worst in the EU.

Romania's **resident population** has now fallen below twenty million and may drop to fifteen million by 2050, with an ageing population and a shrinking tax base. For the present, the **economy** remains sound, helped by some €4 billion remitted annually by up to four million Romanians working abroad. The economy grew by nearly five percent in 2016, and seven percent in 2017, among the fastest growth rates in the EU; it's a trend that is likely to continue for the foreseeable future. Unemployment, meanwhile, is relatively low, having hovered around the five percent mark in recent years, and wages are rising fast.

Romania's chief hope of positive change is that several million younger people working in Western Europe have seen how genuine democracies can actually work for the people. Indeed, the **anti-corruption** movement gathered pace throughout 2017 and 2018, with mass street protests in Bucharest and elsewhere, many of which were supported by Romania's vast diaspora community; unsurprisingly, these were brutally suppressed by the police. As ineffective as these demonstrations appear to have been – and the battle to clean up Romanian politics clearly has a very long way to run – there is tangible hope, among the younger generation at least, that change really is afoot.

2007	2007 & 2011	2015	2017 & 2018
Romania joins the European Union	Attempts to impeach President Traian Băsescu	*Colectiv* nightclub fire (October 30); installation of technocrat government	Widescale demonstrations – the largest since the end of Communism – against government corruption

Wildlife and environmental issues

Thanks to its wide areas of untouched native forest, meadow and wetland, Romania is uniquely important for wildlife. This is a world where pesticides and fertilizers have never been used and that's home to an amazing variety of birds and wild flowers – a landscape typical of Europe two or three centuries ago.

That said, **industrial plants** have caused immense local pollution. While the bulk of the damage occurred under communism, notably from power stations at Deva, Rovinari and Turceni (all still among the EU's dozen worst pollution sources), some of the worst offenders, such as Copşa Mică's carbon-black plant and the Valea Călugărească fertilizer plant (near Ploieşti), were built in the capitalist period, while the Reşiţa and Hunedoara steelworks and the Zlatna copper smelter date back to the eighteenth century. With the end of communism and the return of woodland to the families of pre-communist owners, more than five thousand square kilometres have been logged. Coupled with extreme weather, this has led to disastrous **flooding and landslides**.

Habitat

One third of Romania is mountain, largely forested, and this is where most of the more interesting flora and fauna are to be found. One third of the country is hill and plateau, and one third is plain, mostly intensively farmed.

At lower levels (up to around 800m) of the arc of the **Carpathian mountains** the natural vegetation is forest of oak, hornbeam, lime and ash; above 800m, beech becomes more common, and at around 1400m it forms an association with silver fir and sycamore known as Carpathian Beech Forest (*Fagetum carpaticum*). Spruce dominates above this; above 1700m comes the lower alpine zone, characterized by dwarf pine, juniper and low-growing goat willow, and then, above 1900m, the higher alpine zone of grass, creeping shrubs, lichen, moss and ultimately bare rock.

Elsewhere, particularly on the **Transylvanian plateau**, there is oak and beech forest, although much has been cleared for farming. Large areas of eastern Romania – particularly southern Moldavia and Dobrogea – were covered by grassy steppes, until almost all went under the plough after World War II. In the **southwest** of the country, the Turda, Cerna and Nera gorges are notable for a more Mediterranean climate, with Turkey and downy oaks, Banat pine and sun-loving plant species on limestone rocks.

The **Danube Delta** is a unique habitat, Europe's most extensive wetland, the world's largest continuous reedbed and a uniquely important breeding area for birds. **Nature reserves** have existed in Romania since the 1930s, and some 7.5 percent of the country is now protected. The Retezat and Rodna mountains and the Danube Delta have been named as part of UNESCO's worldwide network of Biosphere Reserves, and there are twelve other national parks and seventeen natural parks.

Flora

In springtime, Romania's **meadows** are a riot of wild flowers, twelve percent of which are endemic to the Carpathians. You'll find spectacular scenes of clover, hawkweed, burdock, fritillary and ox-eye daisy covered in butterflies and, at higher levels, gentians, white false helleborine, globeflower and crocus. **Alpine plants** include campanulas, saxifrage, orchids, alpine buttercup, pinks and, in a few places, edelweiss.

The **Danube Delta** is home to more than 1600 plant species. The characteristic floating islets (*plaur*) are largely composed of reeds (mostly *Phragmites australis*), with sedge, Dutch rush, yellow water-flag, water fern, water dock, water forget-me-not, water hemlock and brook mint. Water plantain, arrowhead, duckweed, water soldier, waterlilies, frog bit and marsh thistle float on the backwaters, above underwater weeds such as water-milfoil, hornwort and water-thyme. Banks are lined with white willow and poplar, with isolated stands of alder and ash, while the more mature forests of Letea and Caraorman also contain oak, elm, aspen and shrubs such as blackthorn, hawthorn and dog rose; the Romanian peony can be found in woodlands such as Babadag Forest, just to the south.

Birds

Europe's most important wetland, the **Danube Delta**, serves as a breeding area for summer visitors, a staging post for migrants between Africa and the Arctic and a wintering ground for wildfowl; permanent residents are relatively few. Dedicated birders come from the end of March to early June, and from late July to October – but it's worth a visit with binoculars at any season.

Springtime, especially May, is an excellent time to visit, with the rare breeding species – black-winged pratincole, pygmy cormorant, glossy ibis, white and Dalmatian pelicans and warblers – all arriving. These are accompanied by large numbers of waders on passage to wetlands far to the north, such as little stints, five species of sandpipers and vast flocks of ruff. The great colonies of waders, herons (night, grey and squacco herons, great white and little egrets), and of both species of cormorant reach a peak of activity; the lower Danube holds most of the world population of the endangered pygmy cormorant.

In **high summer** there are more waders, as well as formation-flying white pelicans, and birds of prey such as the colonial red-footed falcon, lesser spotted eagle, marsh harrier and long-legged buzzard. In **winter**, the number of visiting birds is reduced but still impressive. Visitors include most of the European population of great white herons (or egrets), at times the entire world population of red-breasted geese (around seventy thousand birds) and up to a third of a million white-fronted geese.

On the **inland plains**, some steppe species persist, such as short-toed and calandra larks, while summer visitors include the hoopoe, lesser-spotted and booted eagles, red-footed falcons, European rollers, bee-eaters and lesser grey shrikes – the last three often seen on roadside wires.

Elsewhere, the most worthwhile nature reserves are in the **mountains**, where golden eagles are now rare, but ravens are common. At the tree line, black and three-toed woodpeckers and (in summer) ring ouzels can be found, while on the crags there are alpine accentors, wallcreepers, black redstarts, water pipits, alpine swifts, crag martins and rock buntings. There are also birds usually associated with more northerly regions, such as shore larks and dotterel (breeding only in the Cindrel mountains).

Mountain forests are home to the very shy capercaillie, as well as hazel grouse and (in the north) black grouse. Relatively healthy conifer forests favour some birds now rare elsewhere, notably the white-backed woodpecker, as well as nutcracker, crossbill and crested, willow and coal tits. The forests are also home to raptors, including buzzards, honey buzzards, sparrowhawks and goshawks, and the Ural, eagle, pygmy and Tengmalm's owls, among others.

Romania's extensive **lowland deciduous forests** harbour huge numbers of common European woodland birds – chaffinches, hawfinches, nuthatches, song thrushes, treecreepers and long-tailed, great, marsh and blue tits. Oak woods are home to the middle-spotted woodpecker, joined in summer by nightingales, wood warblers, chiffchaffs and common redstarts.

The white stork (actually black and white) characteristically builds its large nests in the heart of human habitations, on telephone poles and chimneys. The much shyer and rarer black stork breeds in forested areas near water, for example along the Olt in southern Transylvania.

Animals

Romania has Europe's most important populations of **large carnivore species** – bear, wolf and lynx. Having been protected under Ceauşescu for his own personal hunting, there are now around six thousand **brown bear** in Romania, particularly in the eastern Carpathians. They are generally afraid of humans and will keep well clear unless you come between a female and her cubs in April or May. While they will take prey as large as red deer (and indeed sheep, cattle and horses), they are omnivores, famously raiding wild bees' and wasps' nests not only for honey but also for the larvae.

Around three thousand **wolves** live in Romania's forests. They prey almost entirely on deer, occasionally boar and chamois, and the odd sheep, and pose no danger to humans. They are hunted, especially in winter when their tracks can be followed in the snow. There are 1200–1500 **lynx** in hill forests, but they're very hard to spot; highly specialized predators, they take roe deer in forest areas and chamois above the tree line.

Above the tree line in the Transylvanian Alps and the Rodna, the most visible mammal is the **chamois**, grazing in flocks with a lone male perched on the skyline to keep watch; **red deer** can be found mainly in spruce forest in hill areas. **Wild boar** are also widespread, from the Delta and lowland forests to the tree line and above in the mountains, and appear mostly at night; they have a reputation for aggression when protecting their young in the springtime.

Other mammals include the European bison, kept in a semiwild state in several areas; the golden jackal, now spreading from the southeast; the wild cat, in lowland forests as well as up to the highest mountain forests; and red fox, badger, three species of polecat, pine and beech martens, stoats, weasels and bats.

The Danube Delta, one of the last refuges of the European mink, is also home to enot (or raccoon dog), coypu and muskrat, North American species that have escaped from fur farms in the former Soviet Union. European beaver was native to Transylvania and has recently been reintroduced there. Romania's predators depend to a large extent on rodents for their prey; in steppe areas (especially in Dobrogea) it is impossible to miss the charming European souslik. Three kinds of hamster and four kinds of dormouse occur, and hikers in the Făgăraş, Retezat and Rodna will encounter the alpine marmot.

The most frequently seen **amphibians** are the abundant little bombina toads; in addition the exotic-looking green toad (with its trilling call) is frequently seen on village streets feeding on bugs that are attracted by lights, while the amazingly loud frog chorus of the Danube Delta and other lakes and reedbeds is produced by male marsh frogs. Less common are two species of spadefoot toad, the moor frog and the agile frog. Newt fanciers will love Romania's myriad ponds and watercourses; as well as the familiar warty, smooth and alpine newts there is the endemic Montandon's newt, restricted to the Eastern Carpathians. Fire salamanders with their vivid black and orange colouring are easily seen in the woods in wet weather.

The commonest **snake** is the grass snake, found in the Danube Delta and up to some altitude in the mountains. Other non-venomous species include the fish-hunting dice snake, the smooth snake, four-lined snake and the impressively large whip snake. Europe's most venomous snake, the horned viper, occurs near Băile Herculane, and the steppe (or Orsini's) viper survives in the Delta. The common viper (or adder) is more widespread, particularly in hill areas.

The warmer climate of the southern Banat and Dobrogea suits some exotic-looking lizards, such as the Balkan green lizard and Balkan wall lizard. More everyday species, such as the sand lizard and viviparous lizard, are widespread. The aquatic European pond terrapin is common around lowland lakes and in the Danube Delta, and there are two species of tortoise: the rare Hermann's tortoise, found only in the southwest, and the spur-thighed tortoise, fairly common in woods in Dobrogea.

With little industrial pollution, fertilizers or pesticides in most hill areas, there are impressive populations of **fish** – for instance grayling – in Carpathian hill streams. Six species of sturgeon occur in the Danube, and the picture for these is less rosy, as the

Iron Gates Dam blocks migration upstream; the endemic Danube salmon or huchen is now very rare. It is scarcely possible to avoid fish when in the Danube Delta; the common species caught are common and crucian carp, pike (especially in autumn) and pike-perch or zander. Catfish around 2m long are often caught, with confirmed accounts of even larger specimens. Several fairly rare goby species also occur, especially in lakes and lagoons south of the Delta. Most of these species have declined due to pollution, overfishing and eutrophication of the water due to algal blooms.

Wildlife section by: James Roberts, a true friend of Romania, who died far too young.

The environment

The main current problem is illegal timber cutting and **deforestation**, perhaps 135 square kilometres per year, at a cost to society of €52 million in 2013–14; in May 2015 protests were organized on Facebook, mainly against the Austrian group Schweighofer Holzindustrie (active in Romania since 2002 and linked to huge amounts of illegal forestry in previously untouched areas such as the Retezat), and at the end of the year a new forestry police was created. **Rubbish**, too, is a developing problem, as Western-style packaging takes over; recycling bins were introduced in 2015.

The most polluted sites are Copşa Mică, Zlatna and Baia Mare, where smelters produced acid rain and a cocktail of heavy metals that ran straight into the water system; life expectancy remains up to ten years below average in all three places. Almost as bad were the fibre, fertilizer and petrochemical plants in Arad, Brăila, Dej, Făgăraş, Piteşti, Ploieşti, Suceava and Târgu Mureş. Emissions halved after 1989, due to industrial recession, but are rising again with increasing prosperity; pollution is estimated to have cost Romania €80 billion in 2008–12.

The use of **fertilizers**, **pesticides** and **insecticides** has damaged nine thousand square kilometres of land. In 2000, a dam at a goldmine near Baia Mare gave way, releasing water containing a hundred tonnes of cyanide which made its way into Hungary, killing everything in the Someş and Tisa rivers; the mine's Australian owners claimed the fish had died of cold. Later that year, there was a spill of sludge contaminated with heavy metals from a mine at Baia Borşa, which also made its way into the Tisa.

Furthermore, the damming of the Iron Gates and the dyking of the Danube flood plain has led to a dramatic cut in the **Danube's flow** through the Delta, bringing algal blooms and lower fish yields; unless flows can be speeded up, the Delta may die. The Black Sea is one of the most polluted areas in the world – toxic wastes, overfishing and a one-fifth fall in freshwater inputs combining to disastrous effect. Surfeits of nutrients cause plankton blooms (red tides), leading to loss of light and dissolved oxygen, and thus decimating fish stocks.

Ceauşescu was determined to have his own **nuclear power station** at Cernavodă, on the Danube. However, construction standards were so appalling that it had to be almost totally rebuilt, entering service in 1996. The second reactor entered service in 2007, and the complex now produces eighteen percent of Romania's power; Chinese investment from 2013 should see the final two completed. Thirty percent of power comes from hydroelectric dams, and renewable energy capacity reached 5127MW at the end of 2015, including 3 129MW from wind power.

The protection of **historical monuments** was upheld until 1977, when the Historical Monuments Administration was disbanded for daring to oppose Ceauşescu's plans for Bucharest's Civic Centre. There was no effective protection from then until 1989, and many towns were simply gutted; now there is legislation in place but historic buildings in Bucharest in particular are being illegally demolished. Most conservation to date has been achieved with funding from the Church, or, in the case of Saxon monuments, from Germany. **Biertan**, the **Bucovina** and **Horez monasteries**, and a group of wooden **Maramureş churches** have all become UNESCO World Heritage Sites.

Music

The Carpathians trace the cultural fault line separating Central Europe from the Balkans, sharply dividing the musical styles on either side. Of course such borders are rarely impermeable; the Romanian language is spoken on either side and there is plenty of cultural and musical cross-fertilization. Romanian music preserves almost archeological layers of development, from the "medieval" music of Ghimeş and Maramureş to the "Renaissance" sounds of Mezőség and the more sophisticated music of Kalotaszeg.

Transylvania

With its age-old ethnic mix, **Transylvania's music** is extraordinary, with wild melodies and dances lasting all night. While recognizably part of a Central European tradition, it also springs from a distinctly Transylvanian culture – the composers Bartók and Kodály found this the most fertile area for their folk-song collecting trips in the early twentieth century. Music is social, with weekly dances in some places, but everywhere music is played around Christmas, at weddings, sometimes at funerals and at other occasions.

The **Romanians** and **Hungarians** share many melodies and dances and it takes a very experienced ear to tell the difference (and even then, a tune may be described as Hungarian in one village and Romanian in another just over the hill). Romanian dances may have a slightly less regular rhythm than the Hungarian, but often the only difference between one tune and another is the language in which it is sung.

The music of Transylvania sounds much less Balkan than that from over the Carpathians. The traditional ensemble is a **string trio** – a violin, playing the melody, and a rhythm section of viola (*contra*) and double bass, plus in certain parts of Transylvania, a cimbalom. The *contra* has just three strings and a flat bridge so it only plays chords, and it's the deep sawing of the bass and the rhythmic spring of the *contra* that gives Transylvanian music its particular sound.

Wedding customs and Gypsy bands

Wedding customs vary slightly from region to region but generally the band starts things off at the bride's or groom's house, accompanying the processions to the church and possibly playing for one of the real emotional high spots – the bride's farewell song (*cântecul miresei*) to her family and friends, and to her maiden life. While the marriage takes place in the church, the band plays for the young people, or those not invited to the feast, to dance in the street outside. Then there's another procession to the wedding feast where the musicians will play all night, alternating dances with songs to accompany feasting; there are even particular pieces for certain courses of the banquet.

Late in the evening comes the bride's dance (*jocul miresei*) when, in some villages, the guests dance with the bride and offer money. Dances are strung together in sets up to twenty minutes long, starting with slow tunes and picking up speed. Things usually wind down by dawn on Sunday; people wander off home or collapse in a field somewhere, and then around lunchtime the music starts up again.

With the trend towards larger weddings, all sorts of **instruments** have started to find their way into bands. Most common is the piano-accordion, which, like the *contra*, plays chords, though it lacks its rhythmic spring. You'll often hear a clarinet or the slightly deeper and reedier *taragot*, which sounds wonderful in the open air. While there's an increasing tendency towards guitars, drums and electric keyboards, there are still many groups that stick unswervingly to the traditional line-up, one of which is the marvellous **Pălatca** band, from Pălatca (Magyarpalatka).

Like most village musicians in Romania, the band from Pălatca are **Gypsies**. Gypsy communities all tend to live along one particular street in the village outskirts, often called Strada Muzicanților or Strada Lăutari – both meaning "Musicians' Street". Gypsy musicians will play for Romanian, Hungarian and Gypsy weddings alike and they know almost instinctively the repertoire required. Children grow up with the music in their blood, often playing alongside their parents from an early age. It's difficult to highlight the **best bands** – there are dozens of them – but in addition to Pălatca, the following central Transylvanian villages have excellent bands (the names are given in their Romanian form with the Hungarian in brackets): Vaida-Cămăraş (Vajdakamarás), Suatu (Magyarszovát), Sopuru de Câmpie (Mezőszopor), Sângeorz-Băi (Oláhszentgyorgy) and Sic (Szék), one of the great treasure houses of Hungarian music.

The Hungarians

The music of the **Hungarian minority** has made most impact outside Transylvania, as the Hungarians consciously promoted the culture of their brethren in the region. Hungaroton, the state label, produced many excellent recordings, while Budapest-based groups such as **Muzsikás** and the **Ardealul Ensemble** are splendid ambassadors for the music.

Transylvania has always held a special place in Hungarian culture as it preserves archaic traditions and medieval settlement patterns that have disappeared in Hungary itself. Communist repression led the Hungarians to wear their traditional costumes, sing their songs and play their music as a statement of identity, even protest. National costume and dances are still more visible among the Hungarian minority than the majority Romanians (other than in Maramureş).

Regional styles

Within the overall Transylvanian musical language, there are hundreds of local dialects: the style of playing a particular dance can vary literally from village to village. But there are some broad musical regions where the styles are distinct and recognizable.

Bartók gathered much material around **Hunedoara**, an area still musically very rich. Further north is the area the Hungarians call **Kalotaszeg**, home to some truly beautiful music. It straddles the route from Cluj (Kolozsvár) to Hungary and Central Europe, and the influence of Western-style harmony shows itself in sophisticated minor-key accompaniment, a development of the last thirty or forty years. Kalotaszeg is famous for its men's dance, the *legényes*, and the slow *hajnali* songs performed in the early morning as a wedding feast dies down, which have a sad and melancholy character all their own. One of the best of all recordings of Transylvanian music includes both these forms, featuring the Gypsy *primás* **Sándor Fodor** from Baciu (Kisbács), just west of Cluj.

Probably the richest area for music is known to the Romanians as **Câmpia Transilvanei** and to the Hungarians as **Mezőség**. This is the Transylvanian Heath, north and east of Cluj, a poor, isolated region whose music preserves a primitive feel with strong major chords in idiosyncratic harmony. Further east is the most densely populated Hungarian region, the **Székelyföld** (Székely Land), a wild, mountainous land where the music is different once again, with eccentric ornamentation and often a cimbalom in the band.

Moldavia and Maramureş

The **music of Moldavia** – with its archaic pipe and drum style – sounds wild and otherworldly, split across the divide between Transylvania and the Balkans. The music of the Csángós (Hungarians living in the Ghimeş [Gyimes] valley) often features peculiar duos of violin (or flute) and *gardon* – a sort of cello played (usually by the fiddler's wife) by hitting its strings with a stick. The fiddle playing is highly ornamented

CLASSICAL MUSIC

Classical music was lavishly funded by the communist state and still has far less elitist connotations than in the West. Main cities have a philharmonic orchestra and/or an opera house, and tickets are cheap. Additionally, the Saxon communities have maintained a Germanic tradition of singing chorales by Bach and his contemporaries.

Romanian classical music remains virtually synonymous with **George Enescu**, born near Dorohoi in 1881. His *Romanian Rhapsodies* were first performed in 1903 and remain his most popular works; his *Third Violin Sonata* is his best chamber work and also has a Romanian flavour. Later works also showed experimental features, such as the use of a musical saw in his masterpiece, the opera *Oedipe*, the most comprehensive treatment of the myth, covering Oedipus's entire life from birth to death. There is a good modern recording (1989) featuring José van Dam. Romania's greatest pianist was **Dinu Lipatti** (Enescu's godson), who died aged just 33 from leukaemia in 1950. In his lifetime he was referred to as "God's chosen instrument". His recordings (just five CDs) have never been deleted; one of them, made in Besançon just months before his death, is particularly highly regarded. **Sergiu Ceilibidache** (1912–96) studied in Berlin and conducted the Berlin Philharmonic, the Swedish Radio Symphony Orchestra, the Stuttgart Radio Orchestra and, from 1980, the Munich Philharmonic, making his US debut only in 1984. Described as "transcendentally endowed", although not very interested in music outside the mainstream Germanic repertoire, he was also a perfectionist, demanding up to eighteen rehearsals for some concerts.

The most prominent **contemporary Romanian musicians** are soprano **Angela Gheorghiu** (born in 1965) – a true diva and regular performer at the world's greatest opera houses – and violinist Alex Bălanescu, founder of the **Bălanescu Quartet**, who has worked with David Byrne, Kraftwerk, Spiritualized, Gavin Bryars and Michael Nyman amongst others.

and the rhythms complex and irregular. The extraordinary Csángó singer **Ilona Nyisztor** from Onești (in Bacău county) is one to look out for.

The music of **Maramureș** and **Oaș**, in the northwestern corner of Romania, includes magic songs and spells of incantation against sickness and the evil eye. From birth, through courtship and marriage to death, life has a musical accompaniment. The music of Maramureș, while recognizably Transylvanian, is reminiscent of Carpathian Ukraine. As often in the highlands, the music is played predominantly by Romanians, not Gypsies. With violin (*ceteră*), guitar (*zongoră*) and drum (*dobă*), it has a fairly primitive sound, lacking beguiling harmonies and with a repeated drone chord on the *zongoră* (with only four or five strings, often played vertically and back to front). Hundreds of years ago, much of the music of Europe sounded much like this. Probably in the 1930s a strange hybrid instrument appeared here and in Bihor (around Oradea), the *higheghe* or *vioară cu goarnă*, a violin with an old gramophone horn for amplification. The music of Oaș is even odder, with just a *zongoră* accompanying a high-pitched fiddle, playing the melody on two strings at once; singing is in a similarly harsh, high-pitched style.

Wallachia

Most village bands in **Wallachia** are comprised of **Gypsies**: the group is generally named **Taraf** followed by the name of their village or their lead fiddler (*primás*). These musicians (*lăutari*) are professionals who play a vital function in village life, yet their music sounds altogether different from that of their Transylvanian counterparts. The word *taraf* comes from the Arabic and suggests the more oriental flavour of this music. Songs are often preceded by an instrumental improvisation called *taksim*.

The lead instrument is the fiddle, played in a highly ornamented style. The middle parts are taken by the *ţambal* (cimbalom), which fills out the harmony and adds a rippling texture. At the bottom is the double bass, ferociously plucked rather than bowed Transylvanian style. The use of a *cobză* (lute) has given way to the *ţambal*, guitar and accordion. The staple dances are the *horă*, *sârbă* and *brâu* – all danced in a circle.

In Romanian, the word *cânta* means both "to sing" and "to play an instrument", and the *lăutari* of Wallachia usually do both. Whereas in Transylvania the bands play exclusively dance music, the musicians in southern Romania have an impressive repertoire of **epic songs and ballads**, including specific marriage songs and legendary tales like *Şarpele* (*The Snake*) or exploits of brigands. One tune you hear played by *lăutari* all over Romania, and in concerts worldwide, is *Ciocârlia* (*The Lark*).

The region's most renowned Gypsy music comes from **Clejani**, a ramshackle village southwest of Bucharest (see page 81); many of its five hundred or so Gypsies are professional musicians, much in demand throughout the area, and it's also where the Taraf de Haidouks (see page 397), as well as members of the terrific Mahala Rai Banda, hail from.

The doină

The **doină** is a free-form, semi-improvised ancient song tradition. With poetic texts of grief, bitterness, separation and longing, it might be called the Romanian blues. It is essentially private music, sung to oneself at moments of grief or reflection, although nowadays the songs are often performed by professional singers or in instrumental versions. Traditional *doinăs* can still be found in Oltenia, between the Olt and Danube rivers in the south of the country.

Flutes and pipes

The pastoral way of life is fast disappearing in Romania, and with it the traditional instrumental repertoire of the *fluier* (shepherd's flute). But there is one form – a sort of folk tone poem – that is still regularly played all over the country: the **shepherd who lost his sheep**. Referred to as early as the sixteenth century by the Hungarian poet Bálint Balassi, it begins with a sad, *doină*-like tune as a shepherd laments his lost flock. Then he sees his sheep in the distance and a merry dance tune takes over, only to return to the sad lament when he realizes it's just a group of stones. Finally the sheep are found and the whole thing ends with a lively celebratory dance.

For years, Romania's best-known musician on the international stage was **Gheorghe Zamfir**, composer of the film soundtrack for *Picnic at Hanging Rock*. He plays *nai*, or **panpipes**, which have existed in Romania since ancient times. In the eighteenth century "Wallachian" musicians were renowned abroad and the typical ensemble consisted of violin, *nai* and *cobză*. But by the end of the next century the *nai* had begun to disappear and after World War I only a handful of players were left. One of these was the legendary **Fanica Luca** (1894–1968), who taught Zamfir his traditional repertoire. Nowadays, Zamfir plays material from all over the place.

The Ceauşescu legacy

Nicolae Ceauşescu's legacy covers even folk music, which was manipulated into a sort of "fakelore" to glorify the dictator and present the rich past of the Romanian peasantry. Huge sanitized displays called **Cântarea Romaniei** (Song of Romania) were held in regional centres around the country with thousands of folk-costumed peasants bussed out to picturesque hillsides to sing and dance; this was shown on television every Sunday. The words of songs were often changed – removing anything deemed to be religious or questioning the peasants' love of their labours, and replacing it with bland patriotic sentiments or hymns to peace.

This gave folklore a pretty bad name among the educated classes, though the peasants were hardly bothered by it. They just did what they were told for Cântarea Romaniei and got on with their real music in the villages. The fact is that traditional music still flourishes throughout Romania – probably more than anywhere else in Europe – not thanks to Ceauşescu, but despite him.

Discography

Many of the following recordings can be bought from ⓦhungarotonmusic.hu, ⓦfono.hu, ⓦetnofon.hu, ⓦcrammed.be, ⓦasphalt-tango.de and ⓦcdroots.com.

TRANSYLVANIAN MUSIC

Romanian, Hungarian and Gypsy village bands, as well as *tánchaz* groups from Budapest.

Ardealul Ensemble *Gypsy Music Ffrom Transylvania* (Ethnophonie, Romania). Instrumental music led by Emil Mihaiu, perhaps the best fiddler in Transylvania.

Sándor Fodor *Hungarian Folk Music from Transylvania* (Hungaroton, Hungary). From the Kalotaszeg region's most respected Gypsy fiddler, this compelling disc of both Hungarian and Romanian music has fantastic energy and bite. One of the essential Transylvanian records.

The Mácsingó Family *Báré – Magyarpalatka* (Fonó, Hungary). One of the important musical Gypsy families from the villages of Báré and Déva in central Transylvania. This may be too raw for some tastes – the bass saws, grates and often slides onto its notes and the lead fiddle is heavily ornamented, drawing energy and emotion out of every note – but it is the real thing.

★ **Muzsikás** *Máramaros* (Hannibal/Ryko, UK). A fascinating CD from the top Hungarian *tánchaz* group joined by two veteran Gypsy musicians on fiddle and cimbalom to explore the lost Jewish repertory of Transylvania, distinguishable by the Oriental-sounding augmented intervals in the melody.

Ökrös Ensemble *Transylvanian Portraits* (Koch, US). Comprehensive guide to the various Transylvanian styles by one of the best Budapest *tánchaz* groups. Stunning fiddle-playing by Csaba Ökrös on the last track.

Palatca Band *Magyarpalatka – Hungarian Folk Music from the Transylvanian Heath* (Hungaroton, Hungary). Probably the most celebrated band of central Transylvania, led by members of the Codoba family in the village of Magyarpalatka and typically comprising two fiddles, two contras and bass. A beautiful selection of traditional dance sets – one CD from the archives, the other recent.

Szászcsávás Band *Transylvanian Folk Music* (Thermal Comfort, Hungary). Szászcsávás (Ceuaş in Romanian) is a predominantly Hungarian village in the Kis-Küküllő region with one of the area's best Gypsy bands. They have a wide dance repertoire, including Hungarian, Romanian, Saxon and Gypsy tunes.

Katalin Szvorák, Márton Balogh, Márta Sebestyén and the Hegedos Ensemble *Tündérkert (Fairyland) – Hungarian and Romanian Folk Music from Transylvania* (Hungaroton, Hungary). Released in 1988 and something of a classic, a cross section of tunes from the various regions of Transylvania.

HUNGARIAN MUSIC FROM GHIMEŞ AND MOLDAVIA

Mihály Halmágyi *Hungarian Music from Gyimes* (Hungaroton, Hungary). Halmágyi, a veteran Csángó fiddler from Ghimeş, played a violin with a resonating fifth string, producing strange and wild music. Dances, laments and a great performance of "the shepherd and his lost sheep", with running commentary.

Ilona Nyisztor *To The Fat Of The Earth, To The Sun's Little Sister* (Fonó, Hungary), *The Little Bird Has Gone Away* and *Pusztinai Nagy Hegy Alatt – Csángó Hungarian Songs from Moldavia* (both Etnofon, Hungary). Ilona Nyisztor sings Csángó songs handed down through the generations.

MARAMUREŞ

Iza *Craciun in Maramureş (Christmas in Maramureş)* (Buda/Musique du Monde, France). *Zongorá*-player Ioan Pop, with various fiddlers and drummer Ioan Petreuş, is trying to keep the traditional style intact.

Pitigoi Ensemble *Musiques de Mariage et de Fêtes Roumaines* (Arion, France). The best selection of the extraordinary music of Oaş, played by the Pitigoi brothers.

Ioan "Popicu" Pop and Ensemble *Romanian, Ukrainian and Jewish Music from Maramureş* (Ethnophonie, Romania). Exploring links between the music of Maramureş, Carpathian Ukraine and the region's Jewish heritage: the *hori* are sung individually or in groups, with or without accompaniment; the *zicali* (instrumental pieces) are performed on fiddles, guitars and drums.

SPECIFIC ARTISTS

Ion Albeşteanu *The Districts of Yesteryears* (Buda/Musique du Monde, France). Albeşteanu, who died in 1998, was an expressive violinist and singer. Here he is accompanied by a good band with beautifully textured *ţambal*, accordion and *cobză* playing.

Alexander Bălanescu *Possessed* (Mute), a fusion of classical, pop and jazz; *Luminitza* and *Angels and Insects*

(Mute), scores to the films of the same names; and *Lume Lume* (Mute), a live festival soundtrack, all serve to demonstrate Bălanescu's diverse range. *Maria T* (Mute), is a gorgeous reworking of the songs of the legendary Romanian singer Maria Tănase.

Oana Cătălina Chiţu *Divine* (Asphalt Tango, Germany). Released in 2013 to mark the centenary of Maria Tănase's

GYPSY BANDS

The extraordinary growth in the popularity of **Gypsy music** in recent years, at least outside Romania, is thanks in no small part to three bands, both of whom have gone on to achieve world acclaim: the **Taraf de Haidouks**, from the village of Clejani near Bucharest, was formed in 1989, with a fairly fluid line-up, though it usually comprises between seven and a dozen musicians playing violins, flutes, double bass and cimbalom. Their recordings are extraordinary, packed with virtuoso performances, while their live shows – they tour relentlessly throughout Europe – are fantastically entertaining. Although several of the band's founders have died in recent years, there's no shortage of ready-made replacements. **Fanfare Ciocărlia**, from the tiny village of Zece Prăjini in Moldavia, is one of the finest Gypsy brass bands in the Balkans, a twelve-piece ensemble featuring tenor and baritone horns, trumpet, tubas, clarinets, saxophones and bass drum. Completing this trio of superb Gypsy bands is **Mahala Rai Banda** from Bucharest, who combine traditional elements with Western pop and dance rhythms to blistering effect; many of their tracks have been brilliantly reworked by electronic artists, notably Shantel. The extremely fast, high-energy sound of both these bands is utterly thrilling live.

birth, Chiţu performs a dozen of the diva's songs to gorgeous effect.

Fanfare Ciocărlia *Radio Paşcani* and *Iag Bari* (Piranha, Germany). Frenetic romps, punchily recorded, with some fearsomely fast dance numbers (the pace occasionally breaks for a *doină*). *Balkan Brass Battle* sees them lock horns with those other Balkans brass heavyweights, the legendary Boban and Marko Marković Orchestra from Serbia; this was followed by *Devil's Tale*, featuring another superb collaboration, this time with Canadian guitarist Adrian Raso. Their latest release, *Onwards to Mars!*, follows the same, rumbustious tack as earlier records (these last three albums all Asphalt Tango, Germany).

Mahala Rai Banda *Ghetto Blasters* (Asphalt Tango, Germany) is an exhilarating blast of Balkan Gypsy funk, while *Balkan Reggae* is a similarly turbo-charged affair run through with a distinctive Caribbean beat.

Trio Pandelescu *Trio Pandelescu* (Auvidis/Silex, France). Virtuoso accordionist Vasile Pandelescu played for years with Gheorghe Zamfir. Recorded live with high-quality, intimate playing and delicate moments of real poetry.

Maria Tănase *Malediction d'Amour* (Oriente, Germany). A versatile talent, Tănase (1913–63) distinguished herself as an actress, an operetta singer and a music-hall star, but mainly as the finest interpreter of Romanian folk songs.

Taraf de Carancebeş *Musiciens du Banat* (Silex, France). A five-piece band of saxophone, trumpet, clarinet, accordion and bass. Stunning virtuoso playing, explaining the popularity of the Banat style.

Taraf de Haidouks *Honourable Brigands, Magic Horses and Evil Eye, Dumbala Dumbala, Of Lovers, Gamblers and Parachute Skirts* (Crammed, Belgium). Romania's most recorded Gypsy band allows you to trace the development of Gypsy music in Wallachia as new styles are absorbed without diluting the distinctive flavour of the *taraf*. *Honourable Brigands* is the best starting point, while 2001's

live set, *Band of Gypsies*, is probably their best-known recording in the West.

general compilations and Other recordings

Toni Iordache *A Virtuoso of the Cimbalom 2* (Electrecord, Romania). One of the great virtuosi of the cimbalom (dulcimer), accompanied by small folk orchestras.

Romania: Musical Travelogue (Auvidis/Silex, France). An excellent disc with music from the Banat, Maramureş and Wallachia, including good music by ethnic minorities and beautiful *cobză* playing by Dan Voinicu.

Romania: Wild Sounds from Transylvania, Wallachia & Moldavia (World Network, Germany). The best overall anthology of Romanian music, with great ensembles including the Taraf de Haidouks and the Fanfare Ciocărlia.

The Rough Guide to the Music of Romanian Gypsies A fantastic introduction to the irrepressible sounds of Gypsy music, with twenty tracks plus enhanced data and links.

The Rough Guide to Music of the Gypsies and **The Rough Guide to Music of the Balkan Gypsies** Romania is represented on both these CDs by the Taraf de Haidouks and Fanfare Ciocărlia.

Radu Simion *Pan pipe concert* (Electrecord, Romania). Simion was one of the most gifted interpreters of the *nai* (panpipe), here accompanied by various folk orchestras.

Gheorghe Zamfir *Folksongs from Romania* (Delta, US). Born in Bucharest in 1941, *nai* player Zamfir must be Romania's most recorded musician, with albums of easy-listening arrangements of anything from Vivaldi to Andrew Lloyd-Webber. Zamfir's music has little to do with the traditional music of Romania, but his arrangements of *doinas* and folk tunes have an ethereal beauty.

Various *YIKHES: Klezmer recordings from 1907–1939* (Trikont, Germany). Remastered 78s, including a coupleof 1910 tracks by Belf's Romanian Orchestra, virtually the only European Klezmer band of the period to have been recorded.

MUSIC SECTION BY SIMON BROUGHTON

Dracula and vampires

Truth, legends and fiction swirl around the figure of **Dracula** like a cloak, and perceptions of him differ sharply. In Romania he is renowned as a patriot and a champion of order in lawless times, while the outside world knows him as the vampire count of a thousand cinematic fantasies derived from Bram Stoker's novel of 1897 – a spoof-figure or a ghoul.

The disparity in images is easily explained, for while vampires feature in Romanian folklore, there is no link with the historical figure of Dracula, the Wallachian prince Vlad Basarab III, known as Vlad Țepeș – **Vlad the Impaler**. During his lifetime (c.1431–76) Vlad achieved widespread renown as a warrior against the Turks and a ruthless ruler; his reputation for cruelty spread throughout Europe via the newly invented printing presses and the word of his enemies – notably the Transylvanian Saxons. However, he was not accused of being a vampire, although some charged that he was in league with the Devil – or (almost as bad) that he had converted to Catholicism.

The historical Dracula

He was not very tall, but very stocky and strong, with a cold and terrible appearance, a strong and aquiline nose, swollen nostrils, a thin reddish face in which very long eyelashes framed large wide-open green eyes; the bushy black eyebrows made them appear threatening.

Such was the papal legate's impression of **Vlad Țepeș** – then a prisoner at the Hungarian court in Visegrád. Born in Sighișoara, he was raised at Târgoviște after his father, Vlad Dracul, became *Voivode* of Wallachia in 1436. Vlad's privileged childhood effectively ended in 1442, when he and his brother Radu were sent by their father to Anatolia, as hostages of the Turkish Sultan. Vlad Dracul was murdered in 1447 on the orders of Iancu de Hunedoara, prince of Transylvania; his sons were sent into exile in Moldavia and Transylvania to be pawns in the struggle between the Turks, Iancu and the new ruler of Wallachia. This shaped Vlad's personality irrevocably, educating him in guile and terrorism.

Seeking a vassal, Iancu helped Vlad to become **ruler of Wallachia** in 1456 but promptly died, leaving him dangerously exposed. Vlad signed a defence and trade pact with the Saxons of Brașov, but decided that it was also prudent to pay tribute to the Sultan while consolidating his power. For generations the boyars had defied and frequently deposed their rulers, including Vlad's father and his elder brother Mircea, whom they buried alive. On Easter Day in 1459, Vlad eliminated them en masse by inviting them and their families to dine; guards then seized them, impaling many forthwith, while the remainder were marched off to labour at Poienari.

His method of law enforcement was simple: practically all crimes and individuals offending him were punished by death, and Vlad's customary means of execution was **impalement**. Victims were bound while a stake was hammered up their rectum, and then raised aloft and left to die in agony. Vlad moved among his subjects in disguise, testing their honesty by leaving coins in shops and slaying all who kept them; foreigners reported the demise of theft, and Vlad symbolically placed a golden cup by a lonely fountain for anyone to drink from.

Vlad's ambitions caused feuding with the Transylvanian Saxons, beginning in 1457 when he accused them of supporting his rivals and ended the Saxon merchants' practice of trading freely throughout Wallachia. When they persisted, Vlad led his army through the Red Tower Pass to burn Saxon villages. In 1460 he annihilated the forces of his rival, Dan III, who invaded with Saxon support, and then attacked Brașov, impaling hundreds of townsfolk on a hill within sight of its defenders before marching off to ravage the Făgăraş region.

At the same time, Vlad plotted to turn **against the Turks** in alliance with Hungary and Moldavia, ruled by his cousin Stephen. Having defaulted on tribute payments for two years, and nailed the turbans of two emissaries to their heads when they refused to doff them, Vlad attacked Turkish garrisons along the Danube. A massive army led by Sultan Mehmet II marched into Wallachia in 1462, but found itself advancing through countryside denuded of inhabitants, food and water, "with the sun burning so that the armour of the ghazzis could well be used to cook kebabs". As the invaders approached the capital, Târgovişte, they found twenty thousand captives impaled on a forest of stakes 3km by 1km wide, and retreated in disorder.

Vlad's downfall has been attributed to the Saxons, who probably forged the "treason note" (in which Vlad purportedly offered to help the Sultan capture Transylvania) – the pretext for Mátyás Corvinus to arrest Vlad in 1462, after a Turkish attack had driven him over the Făgăraş mountains from Poienari. Until 1475 he was a "guest" at Visegrád, while his pliable brother Radu "The Handsome" ruled Wallachia. Vlad was released to continue the anti-Turkish struggle, spending a year in Sibiu (the townsfolk deeming it politic to be hospitable) and regaining his throne in 1476. His triumph was short-lived, however, for Radu offered the boyars a welcome alternative to "rule by the stake" and a chance to placate the Turks. In circumstances that remain unclear, Vlad was betrayed and killed. His head disappeared – supposedly sent to the Sultan as a present – while his decapitated body was reputedly buried at Snagov monastery.

The lack of an inscription on Vlad's tomb or of portraits of him in medieval church frescoes suggests that attempts were made to erase his memory, although he was remembered in the nineteenth century, and also in the Ceauşescu epoch, as a fighter for national independence.

Vampires

Horrible though his deeds were, Vlad was not accused of **vampirism** during his lifetime. However, vampires were an integral part of Eastern European folklore, known as *vámpír* in Hungarian and *strigoi* in Romanian. In essence, a vampire is an **undead corpse** that fails to decay, no matter how long in the grave. People might occasionally be born as vampires, but a vampire is usually created when a person dies and the soul is unable to enter heaven or hell, perhaps because the person has died in a "state of sin" – by suicide, for example, or holding heretical beliefs – or because the soul has been prevented from leaving the body. Hanging was dreaded, because it was believed that it "forces the soul down outward", while the Orthodox custom of shrouding mirrors in the home of the deceased was intended to prevent the soul from being "trapped" by seeing its reflection. As Catholicism and Orthodoxy competed for adherents following Turkish withdrawal, priests also claimed that the cemetery of the opposing church was unconsecrated land, raising the fear of vampires rising from the grave.

Once created, a vampire is almost immortal, and becomes a menace to the living; vampires frequently return to their former homes at night, where they can be excluded by smearing garlic around the doors and windows, or propitiated with offerings of food and drink. A newborn baby must be guarded until it is christened, lest a vampire sneak in and transform it into another vampire. Two nights of the year are especially perilous: **April 23**, St George's Day (when, as Jonathan Harker was warned in Stoker's novel, "all the evil things in the world will have full sway"), and **November 29**, St Andrew's Eve, when vampires rise with their coffins on their heads, lurk about their former homes, and then gather to fight each other with hempen whips at crossroads. Gypsies also fear *mulé* (vampires), which control the roads, trees and everything else at the exact moment of midday, when the sun casts no shadow – interestingly, the ghosts and vampires of *gadjé* (non-Gypsies) are of no account.

The greatest danger, from the seventeenth century on, was presented by **vampire epidemics**. Although novels and films claim that vampires must bite their victims and suck blood to cause contagion, in Eastern European folklore a look or touch can suffice. A classic account refers to the Serbian village of Medvegia in 1727. A soldier claimed to have been attacked by a vampire in Greece, and died upon his return home. Thereafter, many villagers swore they had seen him at night, or had dreamed about him, and ten weeks later complained of inexplicable weakness. The body was exhumed, was found to have blood in its mouth, and so had a stake driven through its heart.

This was the catalyst for an explosion of interest across Europe, until the pope and the Austrian and Prussian governments declared vampirism a fraud and made it a crime to exhume dead bodies. But peasants still dug up corpses and tore them to pieces to stop epidemics, and in 1909 a Transylvanian castle was burned down by locals who believed that a vampire emanating from it was causing the deaths of their children. As recently as 2005 six men from the village of Marotinu de Sus were jailed for ripping out the heart of a corpse they believed was "undead", burning it and drinking a solution of the ashes for protection.

Sceptics may dismiss vampires and vampirism entirely, but some of the related phenomena have rational or scientific explanations. The "return of the dead" can be explained by premature burial, which happened frequently in the past. Nor is the drinking of blood confined to legendary, supernatural creatures – numerous examples can be found in the annals of criminology and psychopathology.

Bram Stoker's Dracula

The first respectable **literary work** to arise out of the vampire craze was Goethe's *The Bride of Corinth* (1797), soon followed by Polidori's *The Vampyre*, which arose out of the same blood-curdling holiday on Lake Geneva in 1816 that produced Mary Shelley's *Frankenstein*. Other variations followed, by Kleist, E.T.A. Hoffmann, Mérimée, Gogol, Dumas, Baudelaire, Arminius Vámbéry, J.M. Rymer and Sheridan Le Fanu, whose *Carmilla* features a lesbian vampire in Styria.

These fired the imagination of **Bram Stoker** (1847–1912), an Anglo-Irish civil servant who became manager to the great actor Sir Henry Irving in 1878; in 1890 he conceived the suitably *fin-de-siècle* idea of a vampire novel set in Styria, with an antihero called "Count Wampyr"; but after detailed research the setting moved east to Transylvania, and **Count Dracula** was born. Stoker was possibly influenced by the "Jack the Ripper" murders a decade earlier in Whitechapel; he lived there for a time while writing his book. The author delved deep into folklore, history and geography, producing a masterly mix of fantasy and precise settings.

Similar books followed (not to mention Munch's painting *The Vampire*), but it was the advent of cinema and the horror **film** that ensured the fame of Dracula. The silent *Nosferatu* (1922) is perhaps the greatest vampire film, followed by Béla Lugosi's 1931 *Dracula*, while Hammer's 1958 classic *Dracula* boasted the dream coupling of Christopher Lee as the Count and Peter Cushing as Van Helsing. The BBC's *Count Dracula* (1978) is the most faithful to Stoker's novel, while Coppola's *Bram Stoker's Dracula* (1992) confuses things by including the historic Vlad Ţepeş in a prelude. There is also a fine tradition of **spoofs** such as *Love at First Bite* (1979), which opens with the communists expelling Dracula from his castle; *Blackula* (1972), an African vampire-prince in modern Los Angeles; *Count Duckula* (1988–93), the vegetarian vampire duck; and the three *Hotel Transylvania* films (2012, 2015 and 2018).

Books

The surge in interest in Eastern Europe since the end of communism, and the particularly dramatic nature of Romania's revolution and its problems since then, led to several excellent writers visiting in quick succession. In addition, there is a wealth of nineteenth-century and early twentieth-century travellers' accounts, although many are out of print; there has also been a spate of more recent, but no less fascinating, memoirs. By way of contrast, Romanian literature is still largely under-represented in translation.

MEMOIRS AND TRAVELOGUES

William Blacker *Along The Enchanted Way*. An intimate account of rural life in Maramureș and with Gypsies in a Saxon village which feelingly describes both a magical way of life and its inevitable demise in the modern world.

★ **Carmen Bugan** *Burying the Typewriter*. A genuinely powerful memoir that recalls the author's tormented childhood growing up in totalitarian Romania, before her family's subsequent defection in 1988.

Garth Cartwright *Princes Among Men – Journeys with Gypsy Musicians*. A heady musical tour of Southeastern Europe with nearly seventy pages on Romania, with terrific passages on Fanfare Ciocărlia and the Taraf de Haidouks.

Helena Drysdale *Looking for Gheorghe*. A search for a lost friend leads to unsavoury insights into life with the Securitate and finally to a hellish "mental hospital". The depiction of Romanian life is spot-on.

Tessa Dunlop *To Romania with Love*. Accomplished first book by this BBC journalist, which recalls an unlikely love affair that develops between the author and a younger man (her future husband) following an initial visit to the country in the 1990s working at an orphanage.

Emily Gerard *The Land Beyond the Forest*. One of the classic nineteenth-century accounts of Transylvania – rambling, but highly informative on folk customs, superstitions, proverbs and the like.

Jason Goodwin *On Foot to the Golden Horn*. An engaging and well-informed writer walking from Gdansk to Istanbul in 1990 – almost half the book is, in fact, set in Transylvania.

Brian Hall *Stealing from a Deep Place*. Brian Hall cycled through Hungary, Romania and Bulgaria in 1982 and produced a beautifully defined picture of the nonsense that communism had become.

Donald Hall *Romanian Furrow*. The definitive account of 1930s Romanian rural life, clearly threatened by the modern world even then.

Georgina Harding *In Another Europe*. Another cycle tour, this one in 1988. Slimmer than Brian Hall's book but concentrating far more on Romania, with a more emotional response to Ceaușescu's follies.

Eva Hoffman *Exit into History*. Not a patch on *Lost in Translation*, her account of being uprooted from Jewish Kraków to North America, but this tour of East-Central Europe in 1990 still yields seventy good pages on Romania.

★ **Patrick Leigh Fermor** *Between the Woods and the Water*. Transylvania provides the setting for the second volume in this unfolding trilogy, based on Leigh Fermor's diaries for 1933–34, when he walked from Holland to Constantinople. His precocious zest for history and cultural diversity rose to the challenge of Transylvania's striking contrasts and obscurely turbulent past; the richness of his jewelled prose is impressive.

Rory MacLean *Stalin's Nose*. With its wonderfully surreal humour, this is not exactly a factual account, but it is fundamentally serious about the effects of World War II and communism all over Eastern Europe.

Dervla Murphy *Transylvania and Beyond*. A serious, analytical book that tussles with the problems that Transylvania faced immediately post-revolution, and its ethnic tensions in particular.

Peter O'Conner *Walking Good: Travels to Music in Hungary and Romania*. An Irish fiddler in search of Gypsy music, forty years after Starkie (see below). O'Conner's quest took him to Slobozia, Cojocna and Făgăraș, staying with local people a few years before this became illegal. Entertaining.

Alan Ogden *Romania Revisited*. An anthology and bibliography of English travellers to Romania between 1602 and 1941, interwoven with the author's own journeys in 1998.

Lion Phillimore *In the Carpathians*. A fascinating account of a journey by horsecart through the Maramureș and Székelyföld just before World War I, by a proto-hippy who wants only to commune with the mountains and the trees.

Bronwen Riley *Transylvania*. Evocative account of the vanishing rural lifestyle of Transylvania and Maramureș, with superb accompanying photos.

Mike Ormsby *Never Mind the Balkans, Palincashire, Never Mind the Vampires*. This trio of books, written by an Englishman living in Transylvania, offers a marvellous insight into rural life in a fast-changing region; great insights and wit aplenty.

Walter Starkie *Raggle Taggle*. Starkie tramped through Transylvania to Bucharest, where his encounters with Gypsies and lowlife are recounted in a florid but quite amusing style.

Michael Sullivan *Patrick Leigh Fermor: Noble Encounters between Budapest and Transylvania*. In this wonderful read, the author recalls Fermor's exploits living amongst the aristocracy in the 1930s, and in doing so sheds fascinating light on the social and political upheavals of that time.

★ **Gregor von Rezzori** *Memoirs of an Anti-Semite*; *The Snows of Yesteryear*. Two evocative accounts of growing up in the largely Romanian city of Czernowitz (Cernăuţi, now in Ukraine).

HISTORY AND POLITICS

Mark Almond *The Rise and Fall of Nicolae and Elena Ceauşescu*. Very readable account by one of the best academics writing on Romania, though too kind to the sinister Silviu Brucan. Rather wayward footnotes and accents.

Dan Antal *Out of Romania*. An insider's version of the dreadful oppression under Ceauşescu and even worse disillusion after the revolution.

Dennis Deletant *Communist Terror in Romania: Gheorghiu-Dej and the Police State, 1948–65*; *Ceauşescu and the Securitate: Coercion and Dissent in Romania 1965–89*; *Romania under Communist Rule*. Fascinating coverage of many hidden aspects of communist Romania.

Tom Gallagher *Theft of a Nation: Romania since Communism*. A fine analysis of the continuing crisis of Romanian politics, including its historical roots and the IMF and EU's blindness; also *Romania After Ceauşescu*, focusing on the cynical exploitation of nationalism.

Vlad Georgescu *The Romanians: A History*. The best modern history in translation, although the importance of dissidents under Ceauşescu seems overstated.

★ **Robert Kaplan** *In Europe's Shadow*. In this superb offering from the American historian and former foreign correspondent, Kaplan recounts his enduring attachment to Romania from the time of his first visit in the early 1980s to his most recent trip in 2014; the main thread running throughout the book, however, is Romania's position in relation to both Russia and the wider continent.

Sheilah Kast & Jim Rosapepe *Dracula is Dead*. A former US ambassador to Romania and his wife give snapshots of Romania just before EU accession – rather rose-tinted, but with some revealing interviews. Updated in 2014.

Alan Ogden *Fortresses of Faith*. A history of the Saxon churches with fine black-and-white photos. He also wrote *Revelations of Byzantium*, on the painted churches of Bucovina, plus *Winds of Sorrow* and *Moons and Aurochs*, two historical tours.

Ivor Porter *Michael of Romania – the King and the Country*. A careful account of Mihai's life and of his role in history; drawing upon private papers, it captures well the melancholy of his forty years in exile.

Martyn Rady *Romania in Turmoil*. Wonderfully clear account of Ceauşescu's rise and fall.

R.W. Seton-Watson *A History of the Roumanians*. Although it largely ignores social history and eschews atmospherics, and even the author admits his despair at the welter of dynastic details, this remains the classic work in English on Romanian history before 1920.

Christine Sutherland *Enchantress: Marthe Bibesco and her World*. A brilliant snapshot of Romanian and French society and politics in the first half of the twentieth century, and of one of its most charismatic figures, Queen Marie's rival.

★ **Marcus Tanner** *The Raven King: Matthias Corvinus and the Fate of his Lost Library*. A superb, far-reaching account of the great Renaissance king of Hungary (and Transylvania), including his ambivalent relationship with Vlad the Impaler.

László Tőkés *With God, for the People*. The autobiography of the man who lit the spark of the revolution and continues to be a thorn in the establishment's side; now a member of the European Parliament.

Richard Wurmbrand *In God's Underground*. The memoirs of a Lutheran priest who spent many years incarcerated at Jilava, Piteşti and other notorious prisons.

DRACULA

Radu Florescu and Raymond McNally *In Search of Dracula*; *Dracula: A Biography*; *Dracula, Prince of Many Faces, His Life and Times*. Founts of knowledge on the Impaler but overstating his connection with Dracula.

Christopher Frayling *Vampyres*. Primarily a study of the vampire theme in literature and broader culture, but also a near-definitive review of the phenomenon itself.

Elizabeth Miller *A Dracula Handbook*. All you need to know, from the queen of Dracula studies; also *Reflections on Dracula*, and *Sense & Nonsense*, essays that entertainingly debunk many of the myths surrounding Stoker and his most famous book.

Bram Stoker *Dracula*. The Gothic horror original that launched a thousand movies. From a promising start with undertones of fetishism and menace in Dracula's Transylvanian castle, the tale degenerates into pathos before returning to Romania and ending in a not too effective chase.

FICTION

Paul Bailey *Kitty and Virgil*. A fine novel of survival in Ceauşescu's Romania, and love found and lost in Britain.

Miklós Bánffy *They Were Counted, They Were Found Wanting* and *They Were Divided*. The *Transylvanian Trilogy*, written in the 1930s, is a tale of two Transylvanian cousins that has been compared to Proust, Dostoevsky and Trollope.

Alan Brownjohn *The Long Shadows*. By a poet whose work has been intimately involved with Romania for decades, this novel is the story of Tim Harker-Jones, who travels to Romania while writing a friend's biography.

Emil Cioran *On the Heights of Despair*. A key early work (1934, reissued in 1992) by this nihilist anti-philosopher.

Mircea Eliade *Shamanism; Youth without Youth; Fantastic Tales*. The first is an interesting academic work. The latter two are fiction, which don't quite match his reputation as a magical realist in the South American tradition.

★ **Patrick McGuinness** *The Last Hundred Days*. Booker-prize nominated, this lively semiautobiographical novel tells of a young English student's involvement with an assortment of curious characters in the last, confused months leading up to the bloody overthrow of Ceauşescu.

Herta Müller *The Passport; The Land of Green Plums; Everything I Possess I Carry With Me; The Appointment*. Müller is a Schwab who left Romania in 1987 and won the Nobel Prize for Literature in 2009. *The Passport* is a tale, in a distinctive staccato style, of the quest for permission to leave for Germany; *The Land of Green Plums* deals more with repression under Ceauşescu and is more accessible. *Everything I Possess I Carry With Me* is the story of a Transylvanian-German youth deported to a labour camp in the Soviet Union, and *The Appointment* is an allegory of the struggle to remain human under communist repression. Her latest, stirring, offering, *The Fox Was Ever the Hunter*, recalls life for one young Romanian couple under the watch of the Securitate during the dying days of communism.

Liviu Rebreanu *Uprising; Ion; The Forest of the Hanged*. This trilogy comprises a picture of Romanian social life from the nineteenth century to World War I. *Uprising*, which deals with the 1907 peasant rebellion, shocked readers with its violent descriptions when it first appeared in 1933.

Elie Wiesel *Night*. Wiesel, born in Sighet in 1928, was deported to Auschwitz in 1944. After the war, he pursued an academic career in the US and was awarded the Nobel Peace Prize in 1986. This slim book opens in the Sighet ghetto, but soon moves to the death camps.

POETRY

George Bacovia *Plumb/Lead*. Along with Arghezi (none of whose work is available in translation), Bacovia is the leading prewar Romanian poet. Exquisitely melancholy.

Maria Banuş *Demon in Brackets*. Born in 1914, Banuş was a leftist activist through the 1930s and 1940s, but her intimate lyricism remains popular today.

Lucian Blaga *Complete Poetical Works*. At last, one of Romania's finest poets available in English translation.

Ion Caraion *The Error of Being*. A leading poet of the older generation, who composed in the camps of World War II.

Nina Cassian *Call Yourself Alive? Cheerleader for a Funeral*. Savagely sensual and wickedly funny work from one of Romania's best poets, who died in 2014.

Paul Celan *Selected Poems*. Romania's greatest poet and one of the best of the twentieth century. Born in Bucovina in 1920, Celan survived the camps of Transnistria and emigrated to Paris, killing himself in 1970.

Mihai Eminescu *Poems and Prose*. The national poet – it's a scandal that there isn't a paperback in English of his greatest works.

John Farleigh (ed) *When the Tunnels Meet*. Contemporary Romanian poems in versions by Irish poets, with a corresponding volume published in Romania: Dinescu, Sorescu and Blandiana interpreted by Seamus Heaney.

Ioana Ieronim *The Triumph of the Water Witch*. Prose poems about the destruction of a Saxon community by Ceauşescu, written before 1989 and only published (and shortlisted for the Weidenfeld Prize) ten years later.

Oskar Pastior *Many Glove Compartments: Selected Poems*. A Saxon, Pastior spent five years in a Soviet labour camp after World War II, after which time he was obsessed with themes of freedom and determinism.

Marin Sorescu *Let's Talk About the Weather; Selected Poems 1965–73; The Biggest Egg in the World; Censored Poems; The Bridge*. Hugely popular and respected both before 1989 and after (when he was briefly minister of culture), Sorescu died in 1996.

Adam Sorkin (trans & ed) *Transylvanian Voices; City of Dreams and Whispers*. Anthologies of contemporary poets from Cluj and Iaşi. Sorkin has also translated Magda Carneci, Ioan Flora, Saviana Stănescu and Daniela Crasnaru.

Nichita Stănescu *Bas-Relief with Heroes*. Stănescu died aged 50 in 1982, but is still very influential.

Ion Stoica *As I Came to London one Midsummer's Day; Gates of the Moment*. A poet of the older generation.

Brenda Walker (ed) *Anthology of Contemporary Romanian Poetry*. Features the work of two of Romania's best poets, Nina Cassian and Ana Blandiana. Also *Young Poets of a New Romania*.

BIOGRAPHIES

Sanda Miller *Constantin Brancusi*. This enjoyable read sheds fascinating light on the life of Romania's greatest, yet famously elusive, artist, including detailed coverage of the sculptor's childhood, his early years in Craiova, and his time living and working in Paris; there are some terrific photos too.

GUIDES

John Akeroyd *The Historic Countryside of the Saxon Villages of Southeast Transylvania*. A detailed account of the human and natural ecology of an unspoiled landscape.

Dave Gosney *Finding Birds in Romania*. This covers the Danube Delta only. Informative, but strangely it does not include a checklist of possible species.

James Roberts *Romania – a Birdwatching and Wildlife Guide; The Mountains of Romania*. Detailed guides to the fauna and habitats of Romania, and information on hiking in the Carpathians.

Romanian

Romanian is basically a **Romance language** with a grammar similar to Latin, making it easy for anyone who speaks French, Italian or (to a lesser extent) Spanish to recognize words and phrases in Romanian. Its vocabulary also contains words of Dacian, Slav, Greek and Turkish origin, with more recent additions from French, German and English. **German** may be understood – if not spoken – in the areas of Transylvania and the Banat traditionally inhabited by Saxons and Swabians.

Pronunciation is also fairly straightforward. Words are usually stressed on the syllable before last, and all letters are pronounced except for the terminal "–i".

A "**o**" sound as in done.

Ă (or **Î**) is pronounced "**uh**", midway between the O in lesson and the O in sort.

Ă "**er**" sound as in mother; the combinations AU and ĂU resemble the sounds in how and go.

C and **Ch** are hard, like "**k**" or as in country, except when C precedes E or I, when it sounds like "**ch**".

E sounds as in ten; but at the start of a word it's pronounced as in year; while the combined **EI** sounds like bay or ray.

G is hard as in gust, except in the diphthong EG (like sledge), or preceding E or I when it is soft as in gesture; GHI is hard (as in gear).

I is as in feet; except for the vowel combinations IU as in you; IA as in yap; and IE as in yes.

J is like the "**s**" in pleasure.

K only occurs in imported words like kilometre.

O is as in soft; except for OI, which is like boy, and OA as in quark.

R is always rolled.

Ş is slurred as in shop.

Ţ is a "**ts**" sound as in bits.

U sounds like book or good; but UA is pronounced as in quark.

W occurs in such foreign words as whisky and western.

ELEMENTARY HUNGARIAN

Yes Igen
No Nem
Please Kárem
Thanks Köszönöm
Hello Jó napot, servus, csokolom
Goodbye Viszontlá tósra
Cheers! Egeszegedre!
I don't understand Nem értem
Where is...? Hol van...?
When? Mikor?
Today Ma
Tomorrow Holnap
How much is it? Mennyibe kerül?

Cheap Olcsó
Expensive Drága
Good Jó
Bad Rossz
Open Nyitva
Closed Zárva
Station Palyaudvar, vasú, allomas
Hotel Szálloda
Restaurant Étterem
Bar Pince
Bread Kenyér
(No) meat (Nem) hús

ELEMENTARY GERMAN

Yes Ja
No Nein
Please Bitte
Thanks Danke
Hello Guten Tag, Grüss Gott
Goodbye Auf Wiedersehen
Cheers! Prost!
I don't understand Ich verstehe nicht
Where is...? Wo ist...?

When? Wann?
Today Heute
Tomorrow Morgen
How much is it? Wieviel kostet es?
Cheap Billig
Expensive Teuer
Good Gut
Bad Schlecht
Open Offen

Closed Geschlossen	**Bar** Kneipe
Station Bahnhof	**Bread** Brot
Hotel Gasthaus	**(No) meat** (Kein) Fleisch

WORDS AND PHRASES

BASICS AND GREETINGS

Yes Da
No Nu
And Şi
Please Vă rog
Thank you Mulţumesc
Sorry, excuse me Îmi pare rău, permiteţi-mi
Good Bun
Bad Rău
Do you speak English? Vorbiţi englezeste?
I don't understand Nu ânţeleg
Please speak slowly Vă rog să vorbiţi mai rar
Please write it down Scrieţi, vă rog
Say that again, please Vreţi să repetaţi, vă rog
I, we, you Eu, noi, dumneaţa (tu is informal)
Hello Salut
Good morning Bună dimineaţa
Good day Bună ziua (or Servus)
Good evening Bună seară
Goodnight Noapte bună
How are you? Ce mai faceţi?
What's your name? Cum vă numiţi?
Cheers! (literally good luck!) Noroc!
Good, that's fine Bun, minunat
Goodbye La revedere (or ciao, pa)
Bon voyage (literally "Good road") Drum bun
Leave me alone! Lăsaţi-ma în pace!

DIRECTIONS AND ACCOMMODATION

Where?/When? Unde?/Când?
The nearest Cel mai aproape
A (cheap) hotel Un hotel (ieftin)
Campsite Loc de campare, popas
Toilet Toaletă, WC (pronounced vay-say-oo)
Is it far? Este departe?
What bus must I take? Ce autobuz trebuie să iau?
Is there a footpath to...? Există potecă spre...?
Right, left, straight on Dreapta, stânga, dreapt ânainte
North, south, east, west Nord, sud, est, vest
Have you a room? Aveţi o cameră?
With, without Cu, fără
Twin beds Două paturi
Double bed Un pat dublu
For one person (alone) Pentru o persoană (singura)
Shower, bathroom Duş, baie
Hot Cald/fierbinte
Cold Frig/rece
How much per night? Cât costa pentru o noapte?

Is breakfast included? Micul dejun este inclus în preţ?
Have you got anything cheaper? Nu aveţi altceva mai ieftin?
Can you suggest another (a cheaper) hotel? Puteţi să-mi recomandaţi un alt hotel (un hotel mai ieftin)?

SIGNS

Arrival Sosire
Departure Plecare
Entrance Intrare
Exit Ieşire
Vacant Liber
Occupied Ocupat
No vacancies Nu mai sânt locuri
Open Deschis
Closed Închis
Admission free Intrare gratuită
Ladies' (Gents') WC WC femei (bărbaţi)
Waiting room Sală de aşteptare
Operating, cancelled (for transport services) Circulă, anulat
No smoking Fumatul oprit (Nefumatori)
No entry, danger Intrare interzisa, pericol

REQUESTS AND BUYING

I want (would like)... (Aş) vreau...
I don't want... Nu vreau...
How much? Cât costă?
A little (less) (Mai) puţin
Is there...? Există...?
Have you/do you sell...? Aveţi...?
Where can I buy...? Unde pot să cumpăr...?
Too expensive Prea scump
What do you recommend? Ce îmi recomandaţi?
Waiter, waitress Chelner, Chelneriţa
Two glasses (bottles) of beer Două pahare (sticle) de bere
Same again, please Încă un rând, vă rog
Is it any good? Merita?
Bon appétit Poftă bună
Bill, receipt Notă, chitanţă
When will it be ready? Când este gata?
At once, we're in a hurry Imediat, noi grăbim
What's the rate for the pound/dollar? Care este cursul lirei sterling/dolaruli?
Will you refund my money? Vă rog să-mi daţi banii ânapoi?

GETTING AROUND

Does this bus go to the train station? Autobuzul acesta merge la gară?
To the bus terminal La autogară
To the beach La plajă
Into the centre În centru
Does it stop at ...? Oprește la ...?
Has the last bus gone? A trecut ultimul autobuz?
I (want to) go to… (Vreau să) merg la...
Where are you going? Unde mergeţi?
Stop here (at...) Opriţi aici (la...)
Is it a good road? Drumul este bun?
It isn't far Nu este departe
Crossroads Intersecţie, răscruce
Bridge Pod
Which platform does the train to... leave from? De la ce peron pleacă trenul catre...?
When does the train leave? Le ce ora pleacă trenul?
Two seats for… (tomorrow) Două locuri pentru... (mâine)
I want to reserve a sleeper (couchette) Vreau să rezerva loc de vagon de dormit (cu cuşete)
I want to change my reservation to... Vreau să schimba rezervă pentru...
Is this the train for...? Acesta este trenul
Where do I change? de...? Unde schimb trenul?
arrival time sosire (sos.)
departure time plecare (pl.)
Is there a boat from here to...? Există curse de vapor de aici la...?
How much do you charge by the hour/for the day? Cât costa ora/ziua?

TIME AND DATES

What's the time? Aveţi ceas?
This morning Azi dimineaţă
Day Zi
Afternoon După masă
Midday Amiază
Midnight Miezul nopţii
Evening Seară
Night Noapte
Week Săptămână
Month Lună
Today Azi/astăzi
Yesterday Ieri
(Day after) tomorrow (Poi) mâine
Soon Curând
Never Niciodată
Sunday Duminică
Monday Luni
Tuesday Marţi
Wednesday Miercuri
Thursday Joi
Friday Vineri
Saturday Sâmbătă
Every day În fiecare zi
January Ianuarie
February Februarie
March Martie
April Aprilie
May Mai
June Iunie
July Iulie
August August
September Septembrie
October Octombrie
November Noiembrie
December Decembrie
New Year Anul Nou
Easter Paşte
Christmas Crăciun

NUMBERS

0 zero
1 un, una
2 doi, doua
3 trei
4 patru
5 cinci
6 şase
7 şapte
8 opt
9 nouă
10 zece
11 unsprezece
12 doisprezece
13 treisprezece
14 paisprezece
15 cincisprezece
16 şaisprezece
17 şaptsprezece
18 optsprezece
19 nouăsprezece
20 douăzece
21 douăzeci şi un(a)
30 treizeci
40 patruzeci
50 cincizeci
60 şaizeci
70 şaptzeci
80 optzeci
90 nouăzeci
100 o sută
500 cinci sute
1000 o mie

FOOD AND DRINK GLOSSARY

BASIC FOODS
brânză cheese
iaurt yoghurt
lapte milk
orez rice
oţet vinegar
ouă eggs
pâine/pîine bread
piper pepper
sandviş/tartină sandwich
sare salt
smântâna sour cream
ulei oil
unt butter
zahăr sugar

SOUPS (SUPE)
ciorbă mixed soup, with sour cream
ciorbă de cartofi potato soup
ciorbă de miel lamb broth
ciorbă de perişoare soup with meatballs
ciorbă de peşte fish soup
ciorbă ţăranească soup with meat and mixed
  vegetables
supă soup with one main component
supă de carne consommé
supă de găină chicken soup
supă de găluşti dumpling soup
supă de roşii tomato soup
supă cu tăiţei noodle soup
supă de zarzavat vegetable soup

SALADS (SALATE)
salată de cartofi potato and onion
cu ceapă salad
salată de fasole verde green bean salad
salată de icre de crap carp roe salad
salată de roşii şi castraveţi tomato and cucumber
  salad
salată de sfeclă roşie beetroot salad
salată verde green salad

MEAT AND POULTRY (CARNE ŞI PASĂRE)
berbec/oaie mutton
biftec steak
chiftele fried meatballs
crenwurst hot dog
curcan turkey
ficat liver
gâscă goose
ghiveci cu carne meat and vegetable hotpot
miel lamb

mititei spicy sausages
parizer mortadella-type sausage
patricieni sausages (skinless)
pui chicken
raţă (pe varză) duck (with sauerkraut)
rinichi kidneys
şniţel pane wiener schnitzel
şuncă ham
tocană de carne/de purcel meat/pork stew
vacă beef
varză acră cu costiţă afumată sauerkraut with smoked
  pork chops

VEGETABLES (LEGUME)
ardei (gras/iute) (green/chilli) pepper
cartofi potatoes
ceapă (verde) (spring) onion
ciuperci mushrooms
conopidă cauliflower
dovlecei courgettes/zucchini
fasole beans
ghiveci mixed fried vegetables (may be eaten cold)
lăptucă lettuce
mazăre verde peas
roşii tomatoes
sfeclă roşie beetroot
spanac spinach
usturoi garlic
varză cabbage
vinete aubergine/eggplant

FISH AND SEAFOOD (PEŞTE)
chiftele de peşte fish cakes
crap carp
icre negre caviar
midii mussels
păstrăv trout
scrumbie herring
ton tuna

FRUIT (FRUCTE)
caise apricots
căpşune strawberries
cireşe cherries
fragă wild strawberries
mere apples
pepene galben melon
prune (uscate) plums (prunes)
struguri grapes
zmeură raspberries

DESSERTS AND SWEETS (DULCIURI)

bomboane sweets (candy)
clătită (cu rom) pancake (with rum)
cozonac brioche
dulceață jam (served in a glass)
ecler éclair
gogoși, langoș doughnut
halva halva
ânghețată ice cream
măr in foietaj baked apple in pastry
mascotă chocolate fudge cake
strudel cu mere apple strudel

DRINKS (BĂUTURI)

suc de fructe fruit juice
cafea filtru filter coffee
cafea mare cu lapte large white coffee
cafea neagră sweet black coffee
cafea naturală plain black coffee
cafea turcească Turkish coffee
o ceașcă de ceai a cup of tea
bere beer
vin roșu/alb red/white wine

șampanie sparkling wine
sticlă bottle (of beer)
țuică plum brandy

COMMON TERMS

aveți... do you have a...
aș/am vrea I/we would like
cină dinner
dejun lunch
fiert boiled
friptură roast
la grătar grilled
meniu/listă menu
micul dejun breakfast
murăti pickled
notă bill
pahar a glass
piure de mashed
prăjit fried
prânz lunch
rasol poached
tare/moale hard/soft boiled
umplut stuffed

Glossary

Alimentară food store

Ardeal "forested land", the Romanian name for Transylvania

Baie bath, spa (plural Băile; not to be confused with Baia or mine)

Biserică church

Biserici de lemn wooden churches

Bivol buffalo, introduced from India by the Gypsies

Boyar or **Boier** feudal lord

Bucium alpine horn used by shepherds

Bulevardul (B-dul/Blvd) boulevard

Calea avenue

Căluş traditional Whitsun fertility rite performed by Căluşari in rural Wallachia and southwestern Transylvania

Câmpulung or **Cîmpulung** meadow or long field, for which settlements like Câmpulung Moldovenesc are named

Capră masked "goat dance" to celebrate the New Year

Casă house

Cetate fortress or citadel

CFR Romanian railways

Csángó Hungarian "Wanderers" in Moldavia

Dacians earliest established inhabitants of Romania

Drum road

Erdely The Magyar name for Transylvania

FSN Frontul Salvării Naţional, the National Salvation Front that took power during the revolution

Gadjé Rroma (Gypsy) term for non-Gypsies

Gradiniţa garden

Grind raised silt bank in the Danube Delta

Gură mouth

Horă traditional village round dance

Iconostasis literally "icon-bearer", decorated screen in an Orthodox (or Uniate) church containing tiers of icons, that separates sanctuary from nave and priest from congregation during the Eucharist

Judeţ county

Legion or Iron Guard, Romanian fascist movement, 1927–41

Lipovani ethnic group living by fishing and gardening in the Danube Delta

Litoral the coast

Magyars Hungarians, many of whom live in Romania, mainly in Transylvania

Mănăstirea monastery or convent

Maxitaxi minibus

Moară mill

Muntenia the eastern half of Wallachia, paradoxically not at all mountainous

Nai panpipes

Naos nave or central part of an Orthodox church, below the central cupola and in front of the iconostasis

Narthex entrance hall of an Orthodox church, often decorated with frescoes

Nations or **Nationes** historically, the privileged groups in Transylvania

Nedeia village fair or festival characteristic of the mountain regions

Oltenia the western half of Wallachia, flanking the River Olt

Pădure woods

PCR Partidul Communist Roman – until 1989, the Romanian Communist Party; now the Socialist Party of Labour (PSM)

Peştera cave

Piaţa square; also a market

Plaur floating reed islands, common in the Delta

Popă or **Preot** Orthodox Priest

Pronaos see Narthex

Răscoala peasant rebellion; usually refers to the great uprising of 1907

Râu river

Regat the "Old Kingdom", as Moldavia and Wallachia were known after they united in 1859

Rom or **Rroma** Gypsies

Sanctuar sanctuary or altar area of a church, behind the iconostasis

Sat village

Saxons name given to Germans who settled in Transylvania from the twelfth century

Schwaben Germans who settled in Banat in the eighteenth century; others who moved to Transylvania at this time are known as Landler

Securitate Communist security police, reborn as the Romanian Information Service (SRI)

Siebenburgen Saxon name for Transylvania (literally "seven towns")

Şoseaua (Şos.) long tree-lined avenue

Strada (Str.) street

Székely Hungarian-speaking ethnic group inhabiting parts of eastern Transylvania known as the Székelyföld

Ţara land, country (Romanian); Gypsy encampment

Târg or **Tîrg** market, fair or festival

Vătaf leader of Căluşari dancers (Romanian); tribal chieftain (Gypsy)

Vlachs or **Wallachs** foreign name for the Romanians of Wallachia, Moldavia and Transylvania before the nineteenth century

Voevod or **Voivode** Ruling prince of Transylvania or Wallachia

Small print and index

A ROUGH GUIDE TO ROUGH GUIDES

Published in 1982, the first Rough Guide – to Greece – was a student scheme that became a publishing phenomenon. Mark Ellingham, a recent graduate in English from Bristol University, had been travelling in Greece the previous summer and couldn't find the right guidebook. With a small group of friends he wrote his own guide, combining a contemporary, journalistic style with a thoroughly practical approach to travellers' needs.

The immediate success of the book spawned a series that rapidly covered dozens of destinations. And, in addition to impecunious backpackers, Rough Guides soon acquired a much broader readership that relished the guides' wit and inquisitiveness as much as their enthusiastic, critical approach and value-for-money ethos. These days, Rough Guides include recommendations from budget to luxury and cover more than 120 destinations around the globe, from Amsterdam to Zanzibar, all regularly updated by our team of roaming writers.

Browse all our latest guides, read inspirational features and book your trip at **roughguides.com**.

Rough Guide credits

Author: Norm Longley
Editors: Tom Fleming and Siobhan Warwicker
Cartography: Carte
Managing editor: Rachel Lawrence

Picture editor: Aude Vauconsant
Cover photo research: Aude Vauconsant
Senior DTP coordinator: Dan May
Head of DTP and Pre-Press: Rebeka Davies

Publishing information

Eighth Edition 2019

Distribution

UK, Ireland and Europe
Apa Publications (UK) Ltd; sales@roughguides.com
United States and Canada
Ingram Publisher Services; ips@ingramcontent.com
Australia and New Zealand
Woodslane; info@woodslane.com.au
Southeast Asia
Apa Publications (SN) Pte; sales@roughguides.com
Worldwide
Apa Publications (UK) Ltd; sales@roughguides.com
Special Sales, Content Licensing and CoPublishing
Rough Guides can be purchased in bulk quantities
at discounted prices. We can create special editions,
personalised jackets and corporate imprints tailored to
your needs. sales@roughguides.com.

roughguides.com
Printed in China by CTPS
All rights reserved
© 2019 Apa Digital (CH) AG
License edition © Apa Publications Ltd UK
All rights reserved. No part of this publication may be
reproduced, stored in or introduced into a retrieval system,
or transmitted in any form, or by any means (electronic,
mechanical, photocopying, recording or otherwise) without
the prior written permission of the copyright owner.
A catalogue record for this book is available from the
British Library
The publishers and authors have done their best to ensure
the accuracy and currency of all the information in **The
Rough Guide to Romania**, however, they can accept
no responsibility for any loss, injury, or inconvenience
sustained by any traveller as a result of information or
advice contained in the guide.

Help us update

We've gone to a lot of effort to ensure that this edition of
The Rough Guide to Romania is accurate and up-to-date.
However, things change – places get "discovered", opening
hours are notoriously fickle, restaurants and rooms raise
prices or lower standards. If you feel we've got it wrong
or left something out, we'd like to know, and if you can
remember the address, the price, the hours, the phone
number, so much the better.

Please send your comments with the subject
line **"Rough Guide Romania Update"** to mail@
uk.roughguides.com. We'll credit all contributions and
send a copy of the next edition (or any other Rough Guide
if you prefer) for the very best emails.

Acknowledgements

Norm would like to thank Tom for seeing this project through so smoothly, and for his inordinate patience. Very special
thanks to Colin Shaw, formerly of Bod in Romania but now somewhere on a narrowboat in England, and Andrei and the
team at Pan Travel in Cluj. Thanks are also due to in Bob, Sue and Di in Cisnădioara, Emanuel Enache in Sighişoara, Viola
in Micloşoara, Jonas and Ulrike at Valea Verde, Frank Marr, Razvan Marc and Tim Burford. Most importantly, thank you to
Christian, Anna, Luka and Patrick.

ABOUT THE AUTHOR

Norm has spent most of his working life in central/eastern Europe – he is also the author of
the Rough Guides to Slovenia and Budapest – but more recently has turned his hand to home
shores, contributing to the Scotland, Wales and Ireland guides. Currently writing a guidebook
to Somerset, he lives in the county and can occasionally be seen erecting marquees on The
Rec in Bath.

Photo credits
(Key: T-top; C-centre; B-bottom; L-left; R-right)

Index

Map symbols

The symbols below are used on maps throughout the book

▬▬ ▪▪	International boundary	✈	Airport	⛽	Fuel station	⌒	Arch
▬ ▬ ▬	Chapter boundary	★	Bus stop	♟	Museum	🏛	Memorial
▬▬▬	Motorway	Ⓜ	Metro station	✡	Synagogue	🕌	Mosque
▬▬▬	Pedestrianized road	⊙	Statue	♙	Monastery	🗼	Tower
▬▬	Road	@	Internet access	⊤	Fountain	🏰	Castle
⊥⊥⊥⊥	Steps	ⓘ	Information office	🔥	Lighthouse		Building
▬ ▬ ▬	Path	🅿	Parking	🌊	Waterfall		Church
▬▬▬	Railway	✚	Hospital	⌂	Cabana (mountain refuge)		Market
●▬ ▬●	Cable car/Gondola	⊠	Post office	⌒	Cave	⬭	Stadium
▬▬▬▬	Funicular	⊠	Gate	〰	Gorge		Beach
▭▭▭▭	Canal	♦	Place of interest	▲	Mountain peak		Park
▬ ▬	Ferry	∴	Ruins	⋀⋀	Mountain range	⊞	Christian cemetery
▬▬▬	Wall	⛷	Ski area	⋀	Campsite	⊡	Jewish cemetery

Listings key

■	Accommodation
●	Eating
■	Drinking/nightlife
●	Shopping